WordPress

the missing manual®

The book that should have been in the box®

Matthew MacDonald

O'REILLY®

Beijing | Cambridge | Farnham | Köln | Sebastopol | Tokyo

WordPress: The Missing Manual

by Matthew MacDonald

Printed in the United States of America.

Published by O'Reilly Media, Inc.,
1005 Gravenstein Highway North, Sebastopol, CA 95472.

O'Reilly books may be purchased for educational, business, or sales promotional use. Online editions are also available for most titles (*http://safaribooksonline.com*). For more information, contact our corporate/institutional sales department: (800) 998-9938 or *corporate@oreilly.com*.

July 2014: First Edition.

Revision History for the First Edition:

2014-06-17 First release
2014-07-25 Second release

See *http://oreilly.com/catalog/errata.csp?isbn=9781449341909* for release details.

ISBN-13: 978-1-449-34190-9

[LSI]

Contents

The Missing Credits

ABOUT THE AUTHOR

Matthew MacDonald is a science and technology writer with well over a dozen books to his name. Web novices can tiptoe out onto the Internet with him in *Creating a Website: The Missing Manual.* HTML fans can learn about the cutting edge of web design in *HTML5: The Missing Manual.* And human beings of all description can discover just how strange they really are in the quirky handbooks *Your Brain: The Missing Manual* and *Your Body: The Missing Manual.*

ABOUT THE CREATIVE TEAM

Peter McKie (editor) lives in New York City and, in his spare time, archives material chronicling the history of his summer community. Email: *pmckie@oreilly.com.*

Melanie Yarbrough (production editor) lives and works in Cambridge, MA, where she writes and bakes whatever she can dream up. Email: *myarbrough@oreilly.com.*

Ron Strauss (indexer) specializes in the indexing of information technology publications of all kinds. Ron is also an accomplished classical violist and lives in Northern California with his wife and fellow indexer, Annie, and his miniature pinscher, Kanga. Email: *rstrauss@mchsi.com.*

Julie Van Keuren (proofreader) quit her newspaper job in 2006 to move to Montana and live the freelancing dream. She and her husband (who is living the novel-writing dream) have two hungry teenage sons. Email: *little_media@yahoo.com.*

Sallie Goetsch (technical reviewer) (rhymes with "sketch") hand-coded her first website in HTML in 1995, but hasn't looked back since discovering WordPress in 2005. She works as an independent consultant and organizes the East Bay WordPress Meetup in Oakland, California. You can reach her at *www.wpfangirl.com.*

ACKNOWLEDGMENTS

No author could complete a book without a small army of helpful individuals. I'm deeply indebted to the whole Missing Manual team, including expert tech reviewer Sallie Goetsch, my editor Peter McKie, and numerous others who've toiled behind the scenes indexing pages, drawing figures, and proofreading the final copy.

Finally, for the parts of my life that exist outside this book, I'd like to thank all my family members. They include my parents, Nora and Paul; my extended parents, Razia and Hamid; my wife, Faria; and my daughters, Maya and Brenna. Thanks, everyone!

THE MISSING MANUAL SERIES

Missing Manuals are witty, superbly written guides to computer products that don't come with printed manuals (which is just about all of them). Each book features a handcrafted index.

Recent and upcoming titles include:

WordPress: The Missing Manual, Second Edition by Matthew MacDonald

iPhoto: The Missing Manual by David Pogue and Lesa Snider

iWork: The Missing Manual by Jessica Thornsby and Josh Clark

Switching to the Mac: The Missing Manual, Mavericks Edition by David Pogue

OS X Mavericks: The Missing Manual by David Pogue

HTML5: The Missing Manual, Second Edition by Matthew MacDonald

Dreamweaver CC: The Missing Manual by David Sawyer McFarland and Chris Grover

Windows 8.1: The Missing Manual by David Pogue

iPad: the Missing Manual, Sixth Edition by J.D. Biersdorfer

Quickbooks 2014: The Missing Manual by Bonnie Biafore

iPhone: the Missing Manual, Seventh Edition by David Pogue

Photoshop Elements 12: The Missing Manual by Barbara Brundage

Galaxy S4: The Missing Manual by Preston Gralla

Photoshop CC: The Missing Manual by Lesa Snider

Office 2013: The Missing Manual by Nancy Connor and Matthew MacDonald

Excel 2013: The Missing Manual by Matthew MacDonald

Microsoft Project 2013: The Missing Manual by Bonnie Biafore

Access 2013: The Missing Manual by Matthew MacDonald

For a full list of all Missing Manuals in print, go to *www.missingmanuals.com/library.html*.

Introduction

Throughout history, people have searched for new places to vent their opinions, sell their products, and just chat it up. The World Wide Web is the culmination of this trend—the best and biggest soapbox, marketplace, and meeting spot ever created.

But there's a problem. If you want people to take your website seriously, you need first-rate content, a dash of good style, and the *behind-the-scenes technology* that ties everything together. The first two items require some hard work. But the third element—the industrial-strength web plumbing that powers a good site—is a lot trickier to build on your own. Overlook that, and you've got a broken mess of pages that even your mom can't love.

This is where the ridiculously popular web publishing tool called WordPress comes in. WordPress makes you a basic deal: You write the content, and WordPress takes care of the rest.

The services that WordPress provides are no small potatoes. First, WordPress puts every page of your content into a nicely formatted, consistent layout. It provides the links and menus that help your visitors get around, and a search box that lets people dig through your archives. WordPress also lets your readers add comments using their Facebook or Twitter identities, so they don't need to create a new account on your site. And if you add a few community-created plug-ins (from the vast library of more than 30,000), there's no limit to the challenges you can tackle. Selling products? Check. Setting up a membership site? No problem. Building forums and collaborative workspaces? There's a plug-in for that, too. And while it's true that WordPress isn't the best tool for *every* type of website, it's also true that wherever you find a gap in the WordPress framework, you'll find some sort of plug-in that attempts to fill it.

WordPress is stunningly popular, too—it's responsible for more than one-fifth of the world's websites, according to the web statistics company W3Techs (see *http://tinyurl.com/3438rb6*). It's 10 times more popular than its closest competitors, site-building tools like Joomla and Drupal. And month after month, WordPress's share of the Web continues to inch upward. In short, when you create your own WordPress site, you'll be in good company.

About This Book

This book provides a thorough, soup-to-nuts look at WordPress. You'll learn everything you need to know, including how to create, manage, maintain, and extend a WordPress site.

NOTE Notice that we haven't yet used the word *blog*. Although WordPress is the world's premiere blogging tool, it's also a great way to create other types of websites, like those that promote products, people, or things (say, your hipster harmonica band), sites that share stuff (for example, a family travelogue), and even sites that let people get together and collaborate (say, a short-story writing club for vampire fans). And if you're not quite sure whether the site you have in mind is a good fit for WordPress, the discussion on page 7 will help you decide.

What You Need to Know

If you're planning to make the world's most awesome blog, you don't need a stitch of experience. Chapters 1 through 12 will tell you everything you need to know. However, you will come across some examples of posts and pages that feature *HTML* (the language of the Web), and any HTML knowledge you already have will pay off handsomely.

If you're planning to create a website that *isn't* a blog (like a catalog of products for your handmade jewelry business), you need to step up your game. You'll still start with the WordPress basics in Chapters 1 through 12, but you'll also need to learn the advanced customization skills you'll find in Chapters 13 and 14. How much customization you do depends on the type of site you plan to build and whether you can find a theme that already does most of the work for you. But sooner or later, you'll probably decide to crack open one of the WordPress template files that controls your site and edit it.

When you do that, you'll encounter two more web standards: *CSS*, the style sheet language that helps lay out and format your site; and *PHP*, the web programming language upon which WordPress is built. But don't panic—we'll go gently and introduce the essentials from the ground up. You won't learn enough to write your own custom web apps, but you *will* pick up the skills you need to customize a WordPress theme so you can build the kind of site you want.

Your Computer

WordPress has no special hardware requirements. As long as you have an Internet connection and a web browser, you're good to go. Because WordPress (and its design tools) live on the Web, you can use a computer running Windows, Mac OS, Linux, or something more exotic; it really doesn't matter. In fact, WordPress even gives you tools for quick-and-convenient blog posting through a smartphone or tablet computer (see page 130 for the scoop).

Hosting WordPress

To let other people visit your WordPress site on the Internet, you need the help of a *web hosting* company. Web hosts offer the powerful, web-connected computers that run your site (and the websites of many other people). Without a host to store your site, no one will be able to see your handiwork.

WordPress site-builders have two choices of web host:

- **WordPress.com.** The WordPress.com hosting service is free, and it's run by some of the same people who developed the WordPress software, so you're in good hands.
- **A third-party web host.** You can install WordPress on almost any web host. While this approach isn't free, it gives you more features and control. It's called *self-hosting.*

Page 17 has much more about the differences between these two approaches. But that's for the future. For now, all you need to know is that you can use the information in this book no matter which approach you use. Chapter 2 explains how to sign up with WordPress.com, Chapter 3 details self-hosting, and the chapters that follow try to pay as little attention to your hosting decision as possible.

That said, it's worth noting that you'll come across some features, particularly later in the book, that work only with self-hosted installations. Examples include sites that use plug-ins and those that need heavy customization. But, happily, the features that *do* work on both WordPress.com-hosted sites and self-hosted sites work in almost exactly the same way.

About→These→Arrows

Throughout this book, and throughout the Missing Manual series, you'll find sentences like this one: "Choose Appearance→Themes in the dashboard menu." That's shorthand for a longer series of instructions that go something like this: "Go to the dashboard in WordPress, click the Appearance menu item, and then click the Themes entry underneath." Our shorthand system keeps things snappier than these long, drawn-out instructions.

About the Outline

This book is divided into five parts, each with several chapters:

- **Part 1, Starting Out with WordPress.** In this part of the book, you'll start planning your path to WordPress web domination. In Chapter 1, you'll plan the type of website you want, decide how to host it, and think hard about its *domain name*, the unique address that visitors type in to find your site on the Web. Then you'll see how to get a basic blog up and running, either on WordPress.com (Chapter 2) or on your self-hosted site (Chapter 3).
- **Part 2, Building a WordPress Blog.** This part explains everything you need to know to create a respectable blog. You'll learn how to add posts (Chapter 4), pick a stylish theme (Chapter 5), make your posts look fancy (Chapter 6), add pages and menus (Chapter 7), and manage comments (Chapter 8).

NOTE Even if you plan something more exotic than JAWB (Just Another WordPress Blog), don't skip Part 2. The key skills you'll learn here also underpin custom sites, like the kind you'll learn to build in Part 4 of the book.

- **Part 3, Supercharging Your Blog**. If all you want is a simple, classy blog, you can stop now—your job is done. But if you hope to add more glam to your site, this part will help you out. First, you'll learn that plug-ins can add thousands of new features to self-hosted sites (Chapter 9). Next, you'll see how to put video, music, and photo galleries on any WordPress site (Chapter 10). You'll also learn how to collaborate with a whole group of authors (Chapter 11), and how to attract boatloads of visitors (Chapter 12).
- **Part 4, From Blog to Website.** In this part, you'll take your WordPress skills beyond the blog and learn to craft a custom website. First, you'll crack open a WordPress theme and learn to change the way your site works by adding, inserting, or modifying the CSS styles and PHP commands embedded inside the theme (Chapter 13). Next, in Chapter 14, you'll apply this knowledge to create a WordPress product-catalog site that doesn't look anything like a typical blog.
- **Part 5, Appendixes.** At the end of this book, you'll find three appendixes. The first (Appendix A: "Migrating from WordPress.com") explains how to take a website you created on the free WordPress.com hosting service and move it to another web host to get more features. The second (Appendix B: "Securing a Self-Hosted Site") explains the security basics you need to harden your site against attackers. The third (Appendix C: "Useful Websites") lists some useful web links culled from the chapters in this book. Don't worry—you don't need to type these into your browser by hand. It's all waiting for you on the Missing CD page for this book at *http://www.oreilly.com/pub/missingmanuals/wpmm2e*.

PART

1

Starting Out with WordPress

CHAPTER

1

The WordPress Landscape

Since you picked up this book, it's likely that you already know at least a bit about WordPress. You probably realize that it's a brilliant tool for creating a huge variety of websites, from gossipy blogs to serious business sites. However, you might be a bit fuzzy on the rest of the equation—how WordPress actually works its magic, and how you can use WordPress to achieve your own website vision.

In this chapter, you'll get acquainted with life the WordPress way. First, you'll take a peek at the inner machinery that makes WordPress tick. If you're not already clear on why WordPress is so wonderful—and how it's going to save you days of work, years of programming experience, and a headful of gray hairs—this discussion will fill you in.

Next, you'll consider the types of sites you can build with WordPress, and how much work they need. As you'll see, WordPress began life as a blogging website, but has since mutated into a flexible, easy-to-use tool for creating virtually any sort of site.

Finally, you'll face your first WordPress decision: choosing a home for your WordPress site. You'll discover you have two options. You can use WordPress's free hosting service (called *WordPress.com*), or you can install the WordPress software on another web host, for a monthly fee. Both approaches work, but the choice to use WordPress.com imposes a few limitations you should understand before you decide.

How WordPress Works

You probably already realize that WordPress isn't just a tool to build web pages. After all, anybody can create a web page—you just need to know a bit about HTML (the language that web pages are written in) and a bit about CSS (the language that formats web pages so they look beautiful). It also helps to have a first-class web page editor like Adobe Dreamweaver at your fingertips. Meet these requirements, and you'll be able to build a *static* website—one that looks nice enough, but doesn't actually *do* anything (Figure 1-1).

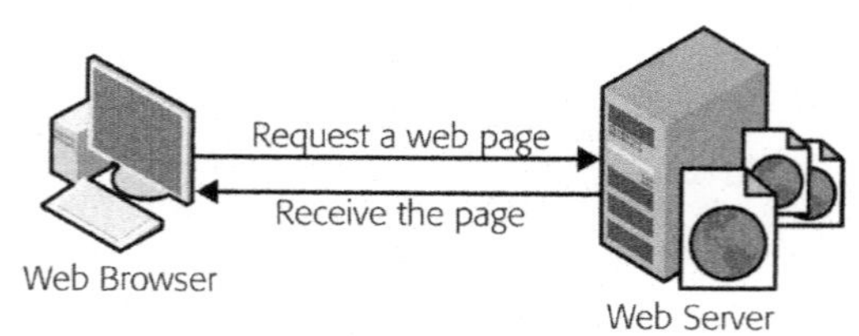

FIGURE 1-1

In an old-fashioned website, a web designer creates a bunch of HTML files and drops them into a folder on a web server. When someone visits one of those pages, his browser renders that same HTML file as a web page. WordPress works a little differently—it builds its pages in real time, as you'll see next.

NOTE Just in case your webmaster skills are a bit rusty, remember that a *web server* is the high-powered computer that runs your website (and, usually, hundreds of other people's websites, too).

With WordPress, you strike up a different sort of partnership. Instead of creating a web page, you give WordPress your raw content—that's the text and pictures you want published as an article, a product listing, a blog post, or some other type of content. Then, when a visitor surfs to your site, WordPress assembles that content as a made-to-measure web page.

Because WordPress is a *dynamic* environment—it creates web pages on the fly—it provides some useful interactive features. For example, when visitors arrive at a WordPress blog, they can browse through the content in different ways—looking for posts from a certain month, for example, or on a certain topic, or tagged with a certain keyword. Although this seems simple enough, it requires a live program that runs on a web server and assembles the relevant content in real time. For example, if a visitor searches a blog for the words "tripe soup," WordPress needs to find all the appropriate posts, stitch them together into a web page, and then send the result back to your visitor's web browser. More impressively, WordPress lets visitors write comments and leave other types of feedback, all of which become part of the site's ongoing conversation.

WordPress Behind the Scenes

In a very real sense, WordPress is the brain behind your website. When someone visits a WordPress-powered site, the WordPress software gets busy, and—in the blink of an eye—it delivers a hot-off-the-server, fresh new web page to your visitor.

Two crucial ingredients allow WordPress to work the way it does:

- **A database.** This is an industrial-strength storage system that sits on a web server; think of it as a giant, electronic filing cabinet where you can search and retrieve bits of content. In a WordPress website, the database stores all the content for its pages, along with category and tag labels for those pages, and all the comments that people have added. WordPress uses the MySQL database engine, because it's a high-quality, free, open-source product, much like WordPress itself.
- **Programming code.** When someone requests a page on a WordPress site, the web server loads up a template and runs some code. It's the code that does all the real work—fetching information from different parts of the database, assembling it into a cohesive page, and so on.

Figure 1-2 shows how these two pieces come together.

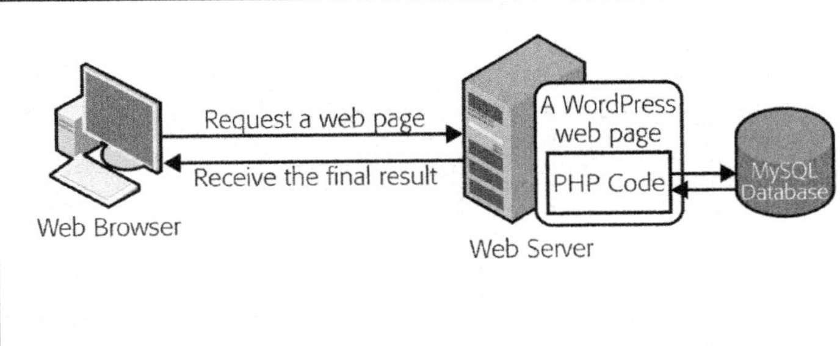

FIGURE 1-2

When a browser sends a request to a dynamic website, that request kicks off some programming code that runs on the site's server. In the case of WordPress, that code is known as PHP, and it spends most of its time pulling information out of a database (for example, retrieving product info that a visitor wants to see). The PHP then inserts the information into a regular-seeming HTML page, which it sends back to the browser.

UP TO SPEED

The Evolution of Dynamic Sites

Dynamic websites are nothing new; they existed long before WordPress hit the scene. In fact, modern, successful websites are almost always dynamic, and almost all of them use databases and programming code behind the scenes. The difference is who's in charge. If you don't use WordPress (or a site-building tool like it), it's up to you to write the code that powers your site. Some web developers do exactly that, but they generally work with a whole team of experienced coders. But if you use WordPress to build your site, you don't need to touch a line of code or worry about defining a single database table. Instead, you supply the content and WordPress takes care of everything from storing it in a database to inserting it into a web page when it's needed.

Even if you *do* have mad coding skills, WordPress remains a great choice for site development. That's because using WordPress is a lot easier than writing your own software. It's also a lot more reliable and a lot safer, because every line of logic has been tested by a legion of genius-level computer nerds—and it's been firing away for years on millions of WordPress sites. Of course, if you know your way around PHP, the programming language that runs WordPress, you'll have a head start when it comes to tweaking certain aspects of your site's behavior, as you'll see in Chapter 13.

In short, the revolutionary part of WordPress isn't that it lets you build dynamic websites. It's that WordPress pairs its smarts with site-creation and site-maintenance tools that ordinary people can use.

WordPress Themes

There's one more guiding principle that shapes WordPress—its built-in *flexibility*. WordPress wants to adapt itself to whatever design you have in mind, and it achieves that through a feature called *themes*.

Basically, themes let WordPress separate your content (which it stores in a database) from the layout and formatting details of your site (which it stores in a theme). Thanks to this system, you can tweak the theme's settings—or even swap in a whole new theme—without disturbing any of your content. Figure 1-3 shows how this works.

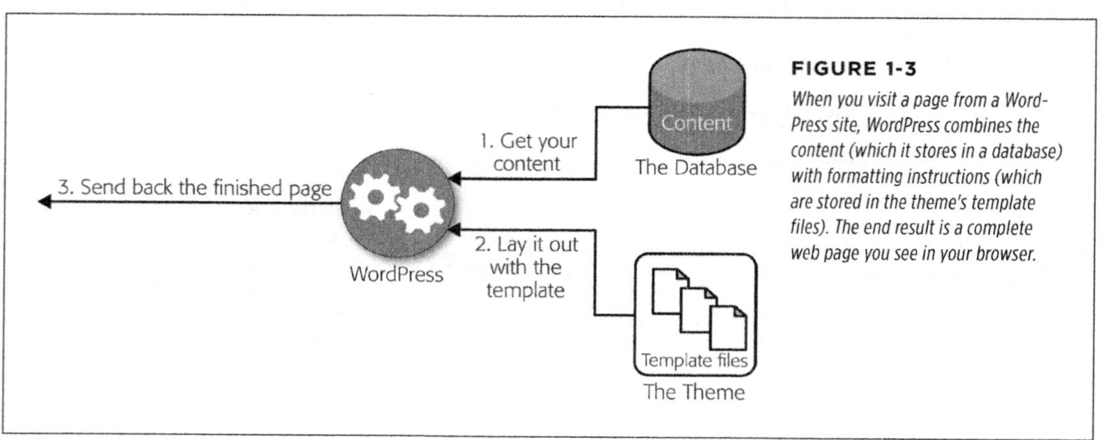

FIGURE 1-3

When you visit a page from a WordPress site, WordPress combines the content (which it stores in a database) with formatting instructions (which are stored in the theme's template files). The end result is a complete web page you see in your browser.

If you're still not quite sure how WordPress helps you with themes, consider an example. Imagine Jan decides to create a website so he can show off his custom cake designs. He decides to do the work himself, so he not only has to supply the content (the pictures and descriptions of his cakes), but he also has to format each page the same way, because each page has two parts—a description of the cake and a picture of it—and he wants his pages to be consistent. But, as so often happens, a week after he releases his site, Jan realizes it could be better. He decides to revamp his web pages with a fresh, new color scheme and add a calorie-counting calculator in the sidebar.

Applying these changes to a non-WordPress website is no small amount of work. It involves changing the website's style sheet (which is relatively easy) and modifying every single cake page, being careful to make *exactly the same change* on each (which is much more tedious). If Jan is lucky, he'll own a design tool that has its own template feature (like Dreamweaver), which will save editing time. However, he'll still need to rebuild his entire website and upload all the new web pages.

With WordPress, these problems disappear. To get new formatting, you tweak your theme's style settings, using either WordPress's control panel (called the *dashboard*), or by editing the styles by hand. To add the calorie counter, for example, you simply drop it into your theme's layout (and, yes, WordPress *does* have a calorie-counting plug-in). And that's it. You don't need to rebuild or regenerate anything, go through dozens of pages by hand, or check each page to try to figure out which detail you missed when you copied HTML from one page to another.

What You Can Build with WordPress

There are many flavors of website, and many ways to create them. But if you want something reasonably sophisticated and you don't have a crack team of web programmers to make that happen, WordPress is almost always a great choice.

That said, some types of WordPress websites require more work than others. For example, if you want to create an ecommerce site complete with a shopping cart and checkout process, you need to ditch WordPress or rely heavily on someone else's WordPress plug-ins. That doesn't necessarily make WordPress a poor choice for ecommerce sites, but it does present an extra challenge. (In Chapter 14, you'll take a closer look at what it takes to build a basic v site that uses a plug-in to go beyond WordPress's standard features.)

In the following sections, you'll see some examples of WordPress in action. You'll consider the types of sites that use WordPress most easily and most commonly. Along the way, you should get a feel for how WordPress suits your very own website-to-be.

Blogs

As you probably know, a blog is a wildly popular type of site that consists of separate, dated entries called *posts* (see Figure 1-4). Good blogs reflect the author's personality, and are informal and overflowing with content.

When you write a blog, you invite readers to see the world from your viewpoint, whether the subject is work, art, politics, technology, or your personal experience. Blogs are sometimes described as online journals, but most blogs are closer to old-school newspaper editorials or magazine commentary. That's because a journal writer is usually talking to himself, while a half-decent blogger unabashedly addresses the reader.

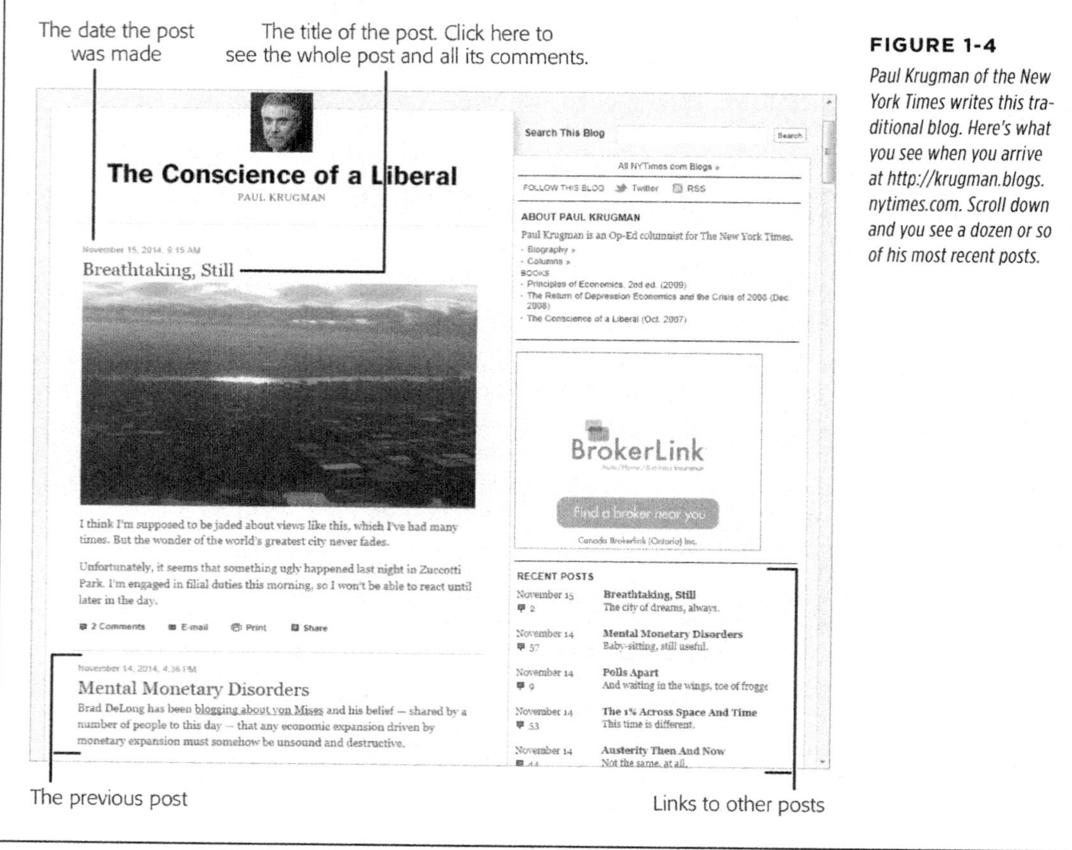

FIGURE 1-4

Paul Krugman of the New York Times writes this traditional blog. Here's what you see when you arrive at http://krugman.blogs.nytimes.com. Scroll down and you see a dozen or so of his most recent posts.

Blogs exhibit a few common characteristics. These details aren't mandatory, but most blogs share them.

- **A personal, conversational tone.** Usually, you write blogs in the first person ("*I* bought an Hermès Birkin bag today" or "Readers emailed *me* to point out an error in yesterday's post"). Even if you blog on a serious topic—you might be a high-powered executive promoting your company, for example—the style remains informal. This gives blogs an immediacy and connection to your readers that they love.

- **Dated entries.** Usually, blog posts appear in reverse-chronological order, so the most recent post takes center stage. Often, readers can browse archives of old posts by day, month, or year (see "Recent Posts" in Figure 1-4). This emphasis on dates makes blogs seem current and relevant, assuming you post regularly. But miss a few months, and your neglected blog will seem old, stale, and seriously out of touch—and even faithful readers will drift away.
- **Interaction through comments.** Blogs aren't just written in a conversational way, they also "feel" like a conversation. Loyal readers add their feedback to your thoughts, usually in the form of comments appended to the end of your post (but sometimes through a ratings system or an online poll). Think of it this way: Your post gets people interested, but their comments get them *invested,* which makes them much more likely to come back and check out new posts.

FREQUENTLY ASKED QUESTION

Who's Blogging?

Technorati, a popular blog search engine, maintains a list of the most popular blogs at *http://technorati.com/blogs/top100* and compiles statistics about the blog universe. The last time it asked bloggers why they blog, it found the following:

- **60 percent** of bloggers write for the sense of personal satisfaction they get by sharing their worldview with readers.
- **18 percent** of people blog professionally. They're compensated for their work, although for many it's a supplementary source of income, not their livelihood. Professional bloggers may be part time or full time, and they usually blog about technology or their own musings.
- **13 percent** of bloggers are considered entrepreneurs. Their goals are similar to those of corporate bloggers (see the next item), but they blog for a company they own.
- **8 percent** of bloggers work for and write under the imprimatur of a company. They generally talk about business or technology, and their goals are to share expertise, to gain professional recognition, and to lure new clients.

Equally interesting is the question of what bloggers blog about. The answer is *everything,* from travel and music to finance and real estate, from parenting and relationships to celebrities and current events. To dig deeper, check out Technorati's Digital Influencer's Report from 2013 at *http://bit.ly/1fSbmAT.* (Quick takeaway: 64 percent of the bloggers surveyed are making money, but for 80 percent of them, the financial rewards total less than $10,000 per year.)

Some sites take the basic structure of a blog and apply it to different types of content. One popular example is the *photo blog,* which ditches text in favor of pictures (see Figure 1-5). Similarly, you can find plenty of video blogs that feature a video clip in every post.

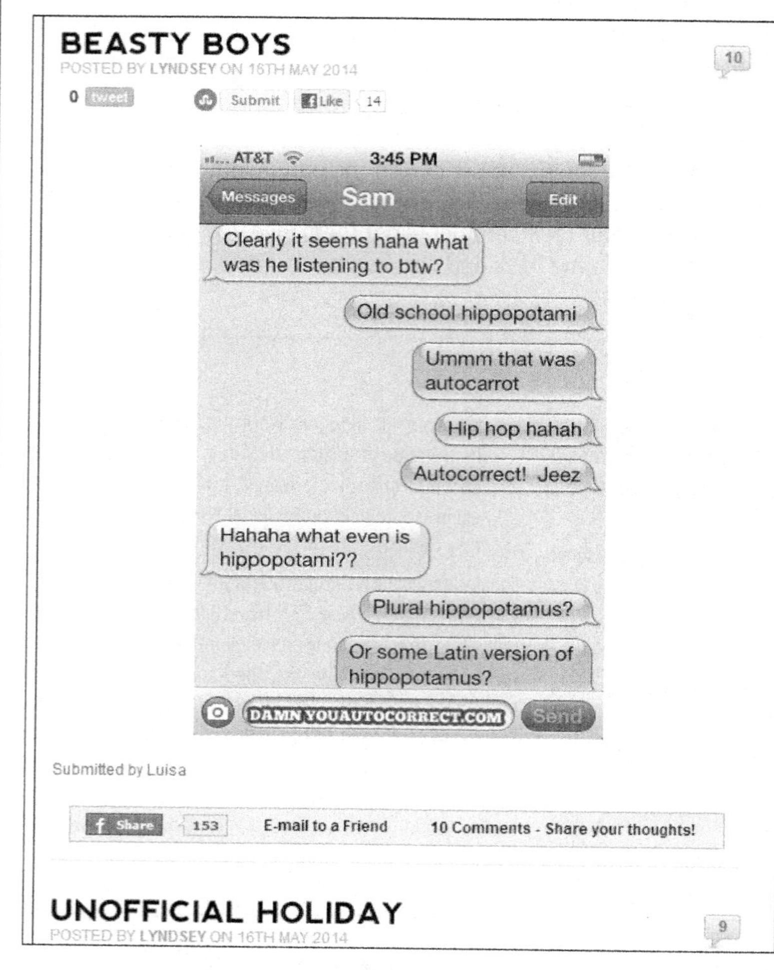

FIGURE 1-5

You can put photo blogs to a variety of uses—everything from serious photography to lowbrow fun. Examples of the latter include sites like http://failblog.org and, shown here, http://damnyouautocorrect.com, where each page is a screen capture from an iPhone conversation gone horribly wrong.

In recent years, people have become increasingly interested in super-lightweight blogs and blog-like tools. Examples include the micro-posts on Tumblr, the short messages on Twitter, and the pictures on Instagram and Pinterest. As you'll see in this book, you can create a basic microblog with WordPress, too. However, WordPress makes the most sense when you want to create something a little less casual and a little more permanent. For example, a collection of random selfies makes sense on Instagram, but a series of lovingly arranged, captioned photographs documenting your trip to Iceland fits nicely into a WordPress site that uses a photo theme.

Blogging with WordPress is a slam-dunk. After all, WordPress was created as a blogging tool (in 2003), and has since exploded into the most popular blogging software on the planet. In fact, if you plan to create a blog, there's really no good reason *not* to use WordPress. Although there are several other blogging platforms out there, and they all work reasonably well, none of them has the near-fanatical WordPress community behind it, which is responsible for thousands of themes and plug-ins, and might even help you solve hosting and configuration problems (just ask your questions in the forums at *http://wordpress.org/support*).

UP TO SPEED

Creating a Modern Blog

Perhaps the idea of writing a blog seems a bit boring to you. If so, you're probably locked into an old-fashioned idea about what a blog *is*.

Today's blogs aren't glorified online diaries. In fact, the best way to create an *un*successful blog is to chronicle your meandering, unfiltered thoughts on everything from the Tea Party to toe jam. Even your friends won't want to sift through that. Instead, follow these tips to make your blog truly legit:

- **Pick a topic and focus relentlessly.** People will seek out your blog if it's based on a shared interest or experience. For example, create a blog about your dining experiences around town, and foodies will flock to your pages. Talk up the challenges of taking care of a baby, and other new parents will come by and commiserate. If you're having trouble deciding exactly what you want to accomplish with your blog and what topics are truly blog-worthy, WordPress has a great reference with blog brainstorming tips at *http://learn.wordpress.com/get-focused*.
- **Add a clever title.** Once you choose your topic, give your blog a name that reinforces it, which will also help you stay on topic. Paul Krugman, for example, calls his blog The Conscience of a Liberal (Figure 1-4), despite the fact that his name is well-recognized among his target audience.
- **Find a new perspective.** It's a rule of the Web that everything has been blogged before, so find a unique angle from which to attack your topic. For example, when Scott Schuman began his now blazingly popular blog The Sartorialist (*www.thesartorialist.com*), he didn't just slap together an ordinary fashion blog. Instead, he created a unique commentary on real-life fashion by using pictures he snapped strolling the streets of New York.
- **Don't be afraid to specialize**. You won't pique anyone's interest with yet another movie review site called My Favorite Movies. But throw a different spin on the subject with a blog that finds film flaws (In Search of Movie Mistakes) or combines your experience from your day job as a high-school science teacher (The Physics of Vampire Movies), and you just might attract a crowd.
- **Don't forget pictures, audio, and video**. Bloggers shouldn't restrict themselves to text. At a bare minimum, blogs need pictures, diagrams, comics, or some other visual element to capture the reader's eye. Even better, you can weave in audio or video clips of performances, interviews, tutorials, or related material. They don't even need to be your own work—for example, if you're discussing the avant-garde classical composer György Ligeti, it's worth the extra five minutes to dig up a performance on YouTube and embed that into your post. (You'll learn how to do that in Chapter 10.)

Other Types of WordPress Sites

Blogs are fantastic, exciting things, but they're not for everyone, even if you have a streamlined tool like WordPress at your disposal. The good news is that, because of its inherent flexibility, WordPress makes an excellent program for building other kinds of websites, too. In fact, as long as you're willing to do a little theme customization, you can convert your WordPress pages into something that doesn't look one whit like a traditional blog. The following sections show you some of the types of sites you can create.

STORIES AND ARTICLES

WordPress makes a great home for personal, blog-style writing, but it's an equally good way to showcase the more polished writing of a news site, web magazine, short-story collection, scholarly textbook, and so on. WordPress also allows multiple authors to work together, each adding content and managing the site (as you'll discover in Chapter 11).

Consider, for example, the Internet Encyclopedia of Philosophy shown in Figure 1-6 (and located at *www.iep.utm.edu*). It's a sprawling catalog of philosophy topics amassed from about 300 authors and maintained by 25 editors, all with heavyweight academic credentials. Created in 1995, the site moved to WordPress in 2009 to make everyone's life a whole lot easier.

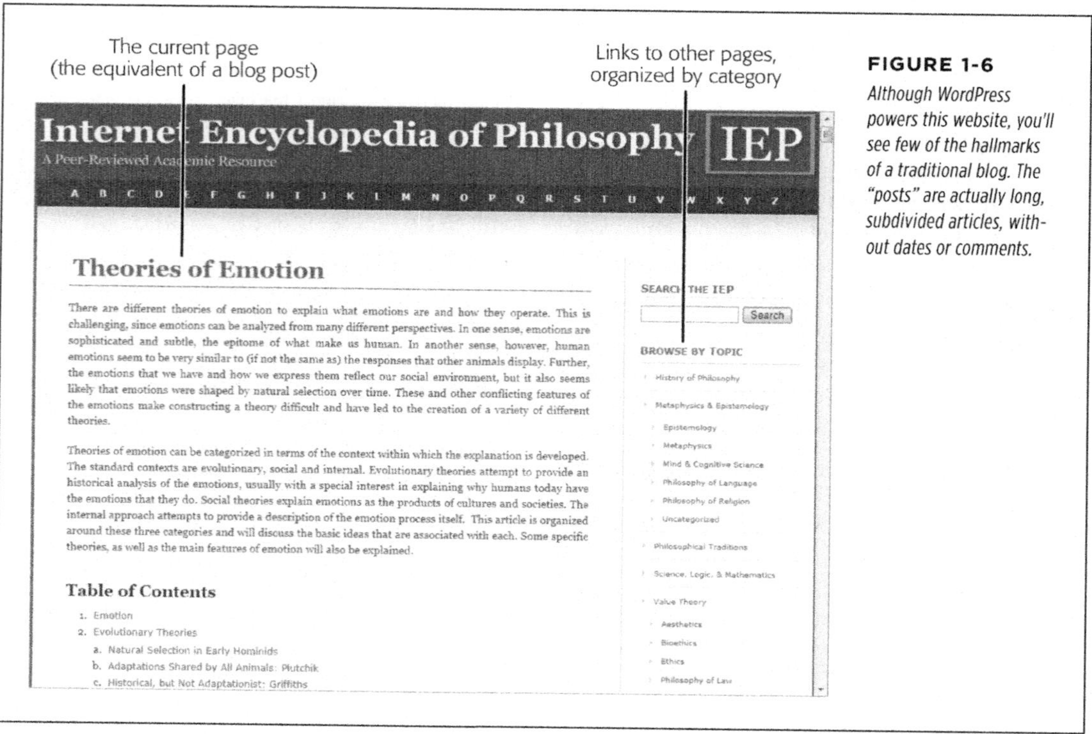

FIGURE 1-6

Although WordPress powers this website, you'll see few of the hallmarks of a traditional blog. The "posts" are actually long, subdivided articles, without dates or comments.

The Internet Encyclopedia of Philosophy is an interesting example for the sheer number and size of the articles it hosts. However, you'll also find WordPress at work in massive news sites, including TechCrunch, TMZ, Salon, Boing Boing, ThinkProgress, and the CNN site Political Ticker.

GEM IN THE ROUGH

How to Find Out if a Website Uses WordPress

There are plenty of websites built with WordPress, even if it's not always apparent. So what can you do if you simply *must* know whether your favorite site is one of them?

You could ask the website administrator, but if you're in a hurry, there are two easier ways. The first is the quick-and-dirty approach: Right-click the page in your browser, choose View Source to bring up the page's raw HTML, and then hit Ctrl+F to launch your browser's search feature. Hunt for text starting with "wp-". If you find *wp-content* or *wp-includes* somewhere in the mass of markup, you're almost certainly looking at a WordPress site.

Another approach is to use a browser plug-in, called a *sniffer,* that analyzes the markup. The advantage of this approach is that most sniffers detect other types of web-creation tools and programming platforms, so if the site isn't based on WordPress, you might still find out a bit more about how it works. One of the most popular sniffers is Wappalyzer (*http://wappalyzer.com*), which works with the Firefox and Chrome browsers.

CATALOGS

WordPress is particularly well suited to websites stuffed full of organized content. For example, think of a website that has a huge archive of ready-to-make recipes (Figure 1-7). Or consider a site that collects classified ads, movie critiques, restaurant reviews, or custom products.

NOTE The dividing line between blogs and catalogs can be a fine one. For example, you can find plenty of cooking-themed WordPress sites that sort recipes by category and by date in a blog-style listing. However, most catalog sites go beyond the blog in some way, and require the advanced theme customization skills you'll develop in Part 4 of this book.

Because WordPress relies on a database, it's a wizard at organizing massive amounts of content. In a properly designed catalog site, people can find a review, product, or whatever else they want in a number of ways, such as searching by keyword or browsing by category.

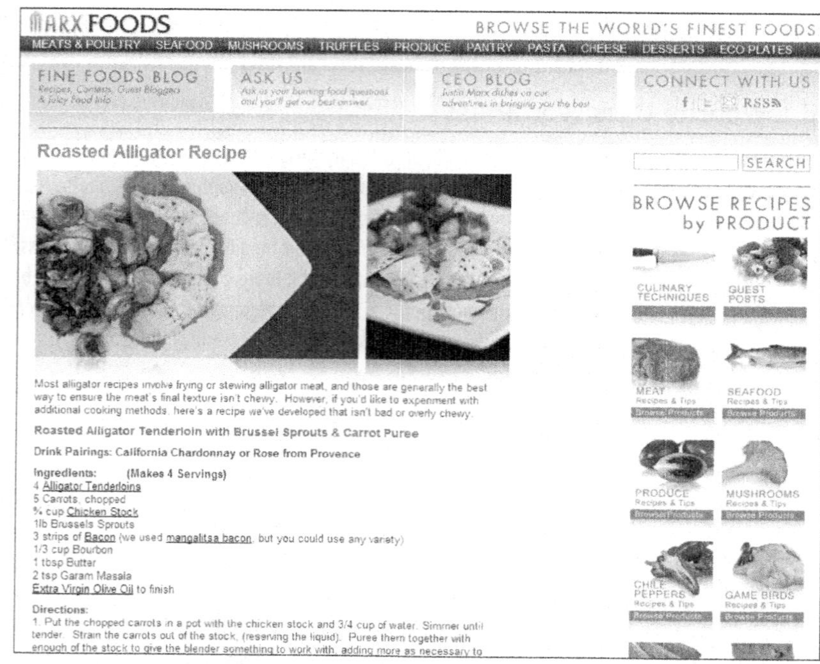

FIGURE 1-7

This WordPress site features a huge catalog of recipes and articles that have cooking tips. What makes the site distinctly different from a blog is the fact that it doesn't organize recipes by date, displayed one by one in reverse-chronological order. Instead, it orders them in common-sense categories, like Meat, Seafood, and Mushrooms.

BUSINESS SITES

WordPress isn't just a great tool for self-expression, it's also an excellent way to do business. The only challenge is deciding exactly *how* you want to use WordPress to help you out.

The first, and simplest, option is to take your existing business website and augment it with WordPress. For example, the Ford Motor Co. uses WordPress for its news site *http://social.ford.com*, which invites customers to post feedback and share the hype about new vehicles on Facebook and Twitter. But if you head to Ford's main site, *www.ford.com*, and you search for a local dealer or ask for a price quote, you'll be entirely WordPress-free. These parts of Ford's site rely on custom web applications, which Ford's web developers created.

Other companies *do* use WordPress to take charge of their entire websites. Usually, they're smaller sites, and often the goal is simply to promote a business and share its latest news. For example, you could use WordPress to advertise the key details about your new restaurant, including its location, menu, and recent reviews. Or imagine you need more detailed information for a tourist attraction, like the detailed website for Perth Zoo (Figure 1-8).

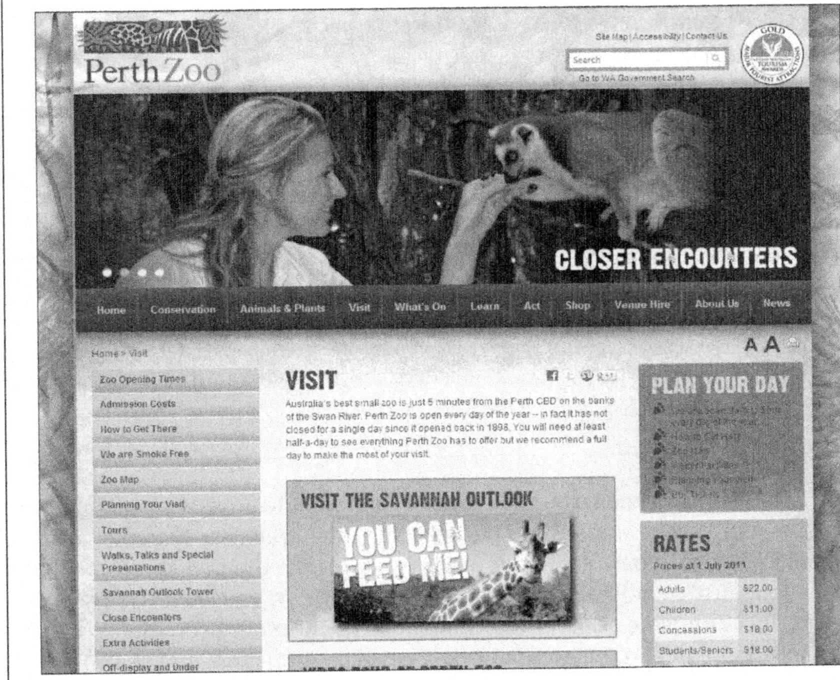

FIGURE 1-8

The Perth Zoo website has it all—detailed menus, information about animals, a review of the zoo's policies, and up-to-date news. But there's a catch: To make this website look as beautiful as it does, the designers needed to combine WordPress knowledge with some traditional web design skills (including a good knowledge of HTML and CSS).

UP TO SPEED

What Makes a Catalog Site

Catalog sites are also known by many other names. Some people describe them as content-based sites; others call them CMS sites (for "content management system," because they manage reams of information). No matter what you call them, the sites share a few key characteristics:

- **They include a large volume of content.** If you want to create a recipe site with just four recipes, it probably wouldn't be worth the WordPress treatment.
- **The content can be divided into separate pages.** With a blog, the "pages" are actually blog posts. In a recipe site, each page is a recipe. (And in the Encyclopedia of Philosophy shown on page 12, each page is a lengthy scholarly article.)
- **Each page consists of text, images, and/or video.** Usually, pages are stuffed with text. Often, they're enriched with pictures and video. That's where WordPress shines. It's less adept at displaying reams of numeric data, like the last 12 years' worth of sales at your chain of mattress superstores.
- **Visitors browse the content by category.** You categorize pages by their subject matter. Visitors use those categories to find exactly what they want—like a recipe for a specific ingredient. Often, guests get to what they want by clicking through a slick, multilayered menu.

These criteria encompass a surprisingly huge range of modern-day websites. Examples include event listings for festivals, a portfolio of your work, a list of products you sell, and so on. Pretty much everywhere there's a mass of text or pictures that needs to be categorized and presented to the world, WordPress is there, making itself useful.

A greater challenge is when a business doesn't just want to advertise or inform with its website, but it also wants to *do* business over the Web. For example, imagine you create a site for your family-run furniture store, like the one shown in Figure 1-9. You don't just want to advertise the pieces you offer; you want to take orders for them, too, complete with all the trappings typical of an ecommerce website (such as a shopping cart, a checkout page, email confirmation, and so on). In this situation, you need to go beyond WordPress's native features and add a plug-in to handle the checkout process.

For some small businesses, an ecommerce plug-in offers a practical solution. But for many others, this approach just isn't flexible enough. Instead, most ecommerce sites need a custom-tailored transaction-processing system that integrates with other parts of their business (like their inventory records or their customer database). This functionality is beyond the scope of WordPress and its plug-ins.

TIP To see more examples of what you can do with WordPress, including plenty of business sites, visit the WordPress showcase at *http://wordpress.org/showcase*.

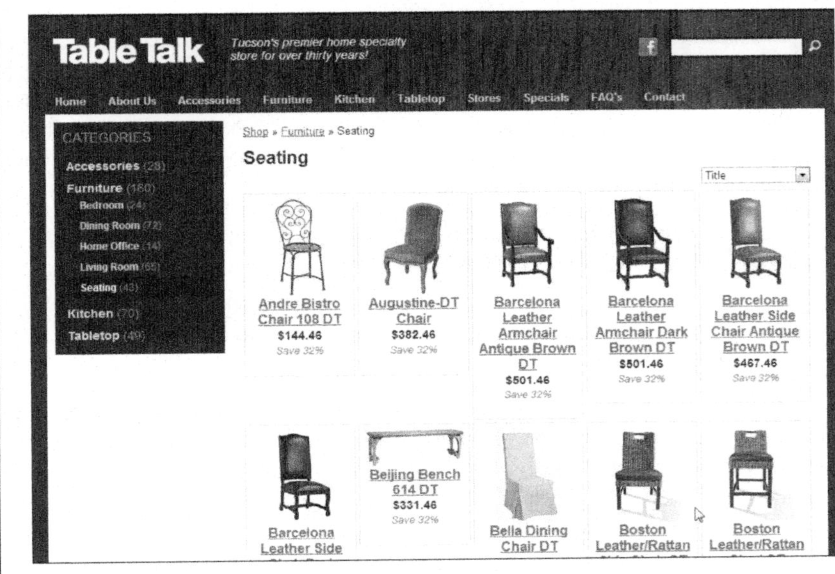

FIGURE 1-9

On this furniture website, you can view the chairs for sale, their prices, and their dimensions. All this is possible with WordPress's standard features and a heavily customized theme. But if you want to allow online ordering, you need to use a plug-in from a third party.

WordPress Hosting

If you've reached this point, it's safe to say you're on board with WordPress. Now you need to decide exactly where you'll put your WordPress site.

The simplest (and cheapest) option is to sign up for the free WordPress.com service, which is run by the fine folks at Automattic (founded by a guy named Matt Mullenweg, hence the "matt" in the company name). The deal is simple: They give your website a home, some exposure, and a free web address that ends in *.wordpress.com* (although you can buy a custom domain name if you want), and you accept a few limitations—most notably, your website can't show ads or use other people's plug-ins, and you can't edit your theme by hand.

NOTE The people at Automattic are also largely responsible for (but not completely in control of) the development of the WordPress software. That's because Automattic employs many of WordPress's lead developers. However, WordPress is still a community-driven, open-source project.

Your other hosting option is to install WordPress on your web host's server and build your site there. The drawback here is that you need to pay your web host. And although you won't be on the hook for much coin—good plans run just a few dollars a month—you still need to open your wallet. Generally, WordPressers call this approach *self-hosting*, even though someone else actually does the hosting. In other words, you're not running a web server in your basement; you're contracting with a web hosting company for some space on *its* servers.

NOTE Although the WordPress nomenclature is a bit confusing, the real story is simple. *WordPress* is the software that powers all WordPress sites. (Sometimes, people call the software *WordPress.org*, because that's the web address where you download the program.) On the other hand, *WordPress.com* is a free web hosting service that uses the WordPress software. So no matter where you decide to host your site—through WordPress.com or on your own web host—you'll be using the WordPress software.

Choosing Where to Host Your Site

If WordPress.com is so eager to give you a free, reliable web host, why *wouldn't* you use it? Here are a few good reasons to consider self-hosting instead:

- **You want to create a site that isn't a blog.** In this chapter, you've seen plenty of examples of websites, from webzines to recipe catalogs to slick business sites. Many of those sites are more difficult to create with WordPress.com (if not impossible). That's because WordPress.com prevents you from editing the code in your theme, or from using a theme that isn't in WordPress.com's pre-approved list of about 200 themes.
- **You already have a website.** With most third-party web hosts, you won't have to pay extra to add a WordPress site. And if you already have a web presence, it makes sense to capitalize on the *domain name* (that's your web address, like *www.PajamaDjs.com*) and the web space you already have.
- **You want complete control over your site's appearance.** If you're the sort of person who can't sleep at night unless you get the chance to tweak every last WordPress setting, you definitely want the free rein of a self-hosted site. With it, you can choose from thousands of site-enhancing plug-ins and a universe of custom themes.
- **You want to make money advertising.** Ordinarily, WordPress.com doesn't allow its sites to display ads or to participate in affiliate programs (where you send traffic to a retailer, who shares any resulting revenue with you). However, WordPress.com is in the midst of a pilot program called WordAds, which allows a limited type of advertising, provided your site is accepted into the program. You can learn more and apply at *http://wordpress.com/apply-for-wordads*.

NOTE Even though you can't run standard ads on WordPress.com, you can still make money there. WordPress.com is perfectly fine with a website that promotes a particular product or business, includes a PayPal-powered Donate button, or advertises your own personal fee-based services.

- **You don't want your readers to see ads, ever.** WordPress.com is a bit sneaky in this regard. In some cases, it will insert an ad into one of your pages. This usually happens when someone stumbles across your site from a search engine. It doesn't happen if a visitor surfs from one WordPress.com site to another, or if a visitor is logged in with a WordPress.com account. For these reasons, you might never notice the ads that other people could see. If this behavior bothers you, you can remove the ads from your site, but you need to pay WordPress.com a yearly fee (currently, $30 per year).

NOTE WordPress.com isn't necessarily as free as you think. In addition to paying for ad-free pages, you can opt (and pay) for a personalized web address, the ability to edit the fonts in your theme, and extra space for big files and hosted video. You can get information about all these upgrades at *http://support.wordpress.com/upgrades*. It's worth noting that self-hosters get virtually all these features through their own web hosts, so if you plan to buy several upgrades, you should at least consider getting your own web host instead—it may end up costing you less.

In general, self-hosting is a slightly more powerful and more expensive strategy than hosting with WordPress.com. But there are reasons why people actually prefer to use WordPress.com rather than self-host:

- **No-headache maintenance.** If WordPress.com hosts your site, all the website maintenance is taken care of. You don't need to think about installing patches or WordPress updates, or making backups of your site.
- **Better discoverability.** If your site is on WordPress.com, people can stumble across it in two ways. First, they can browse the giant index of popular subject tags at *http://wordpress.com/tags*, and pick one you use in your posts. Second, if you write a particularly popular post, your site may appear in the "Blog of the Day" list that WordPress.com features prominently on its front page (*http://wordpress.com*), and attract a click-storm of new traffic.
- **Reliability.** It's not hard to find a good web host that has solid WordPress support. That said, no one serves as many WordPress sites as WordPress.com—it uses over 1,000 web servers to hand out *billions* of WordPress pages every month. That means that if a page on your WordPress site suddenly goes viral with a burst of popularity, WordPress.com will handle the challenge, while a less able web-hosting service could buckle.

WORD TO THE WISE

What WordPress.com Won't Allow

It probably comes as little surprise that there are some types of websites that WordPress.com doesn't welcome. Here are the problem areas:

- **Spam.** If you create a website for the sole purpose of attracting clicks for another site, artificially inflating another site's Google search ranking with spurious links, promoting "get rich quick" schemes, or showing ads, WordPress will wipe it off the Web in minutes.
- **Copyright violation.** If you create a site that includes content owned by someone else and you don't have permission to use it, WordPress has the power to yank your site. Copyright (and other) complaints are made at *http://wordpress.com/complaints*.
- **Masquerading.** It's not acceptable to create a blog where you pretend to be someone else.
- **Threats or criminality.** If your blog threatens another real-life person, incites violence, or promotes an illegal scheme, you obviously aren't a nice person, and WordPress won't want you.

You'll notice that there's one oft-censored site type missing from this list: namely, those that include sex, erotica, or pornography. It turns out that WordPress.com is mostly OK with that, but it will slap "mature" blogs with an adults-only warning, and it won't include them in its home page or tag directory.

WordPress.com Sites vs. Self-Hosted Sites

Struggling to keep all the details about WordPress.com and WordPress.org in mind at once? Table 1-1 summarizes the key differences. Remember that the WordPress program is packed with functionality, and the table leaves out the long list of features that work equally well in WordPress.com and on self-hosted WordPress sites.

TABLE 1-1 *Comparing WordPress.com and self-hosted sites*

YOU WANT TO...	WITH WORDPRESS.COM	WITH A SELF-HOSTED SITE
Pay as little as possible.	The starting cost is free, but various enhancements cost money.	You pay the cost of web hosting. That's typically $5 to $10 per month, unless your site is wildly popular, in which case you need to pay your host double or more to get a plan that ensures good performance during times of high traffic (see the box on page 51).
Forget all about web server maintenance.	Yes.	No, you need to back up your content regularly, and update plug-ins and themes with new versions (but fortunately both jobs are pretty easy).

YOU WANT TO...	WITH WORDPRESS.COM	WITH A SELF-HOSTED SITE
Use a custom website address (like *www.myName.com*).	Yes, but it requires an upgrade ($18 to $25 per year).	Yes, but you must buy it through your web host or a domain registrar.
Get good-looking, ready-made themes.	Yes, you can choose from about 200 themes (and the list is growing).	Yes, you can choose from more than 2,000 free themes (and the list is growing).
Change the layout of your theme and add new widgets.	Yes (although you're limited to the widgets that WordPress.com approves).	Yes (and you can get more widgets by installing plug-ins).
Edit the styles (fonts and formatting) in your theme.	Yes, but it requires an upgrade ($30 per year).	Yes.
Change the code in your theme files.	No.	Yes.
Create a non-blog site.	Yes, if you can find a suitable theme, but there are many limitations.	Yes.
Show pictures and videos.	Yes, but it costs extra if you want to host the video files on your website, instead of through a service like YouTube or Vimeo.	Yes, but you'll probably still need a hosting service like YouTube or Vimeo for your videos.
Make money with ads.	No, unless you're accepted into WordPress's WordAds program (which has its own restrictions).	Yes.
Keep ads off your site.	Yes, but it requires an upgrade ($30 per year).	Yes (there are no ads, unless you put them there).
Let multiple people post on the same site.	Yes.	Yes.
Create multiple sites.	Yes (but if you buy any upgrades, you need to buy them separately for each site).	Yes.
Create a multisite network that allows other people to create their own personal sub-sites.	No.	Yes.
Use WordPress plug-ins to get even more features.	No.	Yes, you can choose from a staggeringly large and ever-expanding collection of about 30,000 plug-ins.
Get help with your problems.	Yes, through the forums at *http://forums.wordpress.com.*	Yes, through the forums at *http://wordpress.org/support.*

Overall, the best advice is this: If you're a keen WordPress fan with a bit of curiosity, a smattering of computer experience, and a willingness to experiment (and if you've picked up this book, you almost certainly fit that description), you'll be happiest self-hosting WordPress.

However, if you don't have a web host and you're a bit overwhelmed, it's a perfectly good idea to *start* with WordPress.com. You can always migrate to a self-hosted WordPress site later on, and Appendix A, "Migrating from WordPress.com," describes exactly how to do that. The only recommendation with this strategy is that you buy your own domain name from the get-go, as described on page 24. That way, should you move to a self-hosted WordPress site, you can keep the address you used when you were at WordPress.com, and you won't lose the audience you spent so long building up.

UP TO SPEED

Managed Hosting

There is one other, relatively new type of WordPress hosting that's geared to less experienced site developers who don't want to mess with WordPress administration, but want more features and flexibility than WordPress.com offers. It's called *managed hosting*.

If you sign up for a managed hosting plan, your web hosting company provides you with a domain name and some web hosting space, just like you'd get with a self-hosted site. However, managed hosting companies also add WordPress-specific services like automatic updates, daily backups, caching, and site recovery (repairing your site after a spammer hijacks it). You might even get tools to promote your site and a techy support person to install your plug-ins for you. Plans for small- to medium-sized sites start at around $30 per month, but heavily trafficked sites can pay hundreds of dollars a month.

You can learn more about managed hosting by checking out some of the web hosts that provide it, such as WP Engine (*http://wpengine.com*) and Synthesis (*http://websynthesis.com*).

CHAPTER

2

Signing Up with WordPress.com

In Chapter 1, you took a big-picture look at WordPress and the sites it can build. Now you're ready to partner with WordPress and start building your own web masterpiece.

But not so fast. Before you can create even a single WordPress-powered page, you need to decide where to *put* it, and, as you found out in Chapter 1, WordPress gives you two perfectly good choices:

- **The WordPress.com hosting service.** This is a wonderfully free and supremely convenient service for web authors who want to build an ordinary blog and can live with a few limitations.
- **Self-hosting.** This option requires you to set up WordPress on your own web host, which is a little bit more work (but still not much hassle). Self-hosted sites are more powerful and flexible than WordPress.com-hosted sites—they let you show ads, use plug-ins, and create completely customized pages that go far beyond ordinary blogs.

In this chapter, you'll get started with the first choice: using WordPress.com. But if you'd prefer to give self-hosting a whirl, skip this chapter and jump straight to Chapter 3. No matter which route you take, the paths converge in Chapter 4, where you'll begin adding content, refining your site, and developing the skills of a true WordPress wizard.

TIP If you're still divided between the convenience of WordPress.com and the flexibility of a self-hosted site, you can review the key differences on page 20. Or you can leave both doors open: Start with a WordPress.com website and buy a domain name (your own custom web address), as described in this chapter. That way, you can switch to a self-hosted site in the future if you outgrow WordPress.com.

Choosing a Web Address

As you already know, a web address is a short bit of text, like *www.SuperStyleFreak.com*, that someone types into a browser to get to your site.

The most essential part of a web address is the *domain name* (often shortened to just *domain*), which points to the web server where your website exists. For example, consider the website address *http://WineSnobs.com/exotic-cocktails*. The first part of the address, *http://*, indicates that the URL points to a location on the Internet, which uses a networking technology called HTTP. The second part of the address, *WineSnobs.com*, is the domain name. And the last part, */exotic-cocktails*, points to a specific page on the *WineSnobs.com* domain. Clearly, the domain is the most important part of the equation, because it identifies the central hub for all your pages.

Before you sign up with WordPress.com, you need to give some serious thought to the domain name you want to use. That's because WordPress.com gives you a choice: You can buy your own domain name, or you can use a WordPress.com freebie.

Here's the catch: If you get a free domain name from WordPress.com, it will have *.wordpress.com* appended to the end of it. That means you'll end up with an address like *WineSnobs.wordpress.com*. But if you pay WordPress.com a small yearly fee of about $18, you can buy a custom domain name that doesn't have this limitation—say, *WineSnobs.com*. And while there's nothing wrong with a web address that ends in *.wordpress.com*, a custom domain name can be beneficial for several reasons:

- **Names matter.** A catchy web address is easier for visitors to remember, and a clever name can attract more visitors to your site. If you're willing to buy a custom domain name, you'll have more naming choices, and your web address will probably be shorter and snappier.
- **You may not want to advertise WordPress.** In some circles, using WordPress is a badge of honor. But in other fields, it could make your site seem less professional. For example, *victoriassecret.wordpress.com* doesn't leave quite the same impression as the real site address.
- **Custom domain names are more portable.** This is usually the most important consideration. If you go with a free name and decide later to move your WordPress site to a different host, you'll need to change your domain name. (For example, you might go from *WineSnobs.wordpress.com* to *www.WineSnobs.com*, assuming *www.WineSnobs.com* is even available when you make the move.) Changing your domain name risks severing the relationships you built up through your original *.wordpress.com* address. It also breaks any links on other

sites that point to your site, and it confuses the visitors who have bookmarked your old site. And if all that's not bad enough, you'll lose the hard-earned Google search ranking that helps your site show up in web searches, too.

When you're just starting out, it's easy to underestimate the likelihood of migrating to a custom web host and the headache of changing your domain name. But life happens, people change, and many die-hard WordPress.com bloggers eventually move to a do-it-yourself web host so they have more flexibility in what they can do on their site. For all these reasons, we strongly suggest that you buy a custom domain name for your WordPress.com blog at the outset. If you do, you'll be able to keep your domain name forever, even if you switch to a different web host. You'll simply need to transfer your domain to your new host (as explained in Appendix A).

NOTE Keep in mind that using a custom domain name or a domain name that you own doesn't avoid any of the other limitations that hosting with WordPress.com imposes (see page 20). For example, you still won't be allowed to place ads on your site or to use plug-ins.

Before you continue, take a moment to determine your domain name strategy. If you're a technophobic sort and you positively, absolutely don't plan to move to a self-hosted site—ever—you can choose a good *.wordpress.com* address and forget about the rest. However, paying a little extra for a custom domain name is almost always worth the trouble. Think of it as a bit of added insurance for whatever the future might hold.

Assuming you do want a custom domain name for your WordPress site, you can get one in two ways. The most common method is to buy your domain name when you sign up with WordPress.com, as you'll learn to do in the next section. At the time of this writing, WordPress.com charges $18 per year for most custom domains but increases the price for some specialty domains (for example, *.me* and *.co* domains cost $25 per year).

Another option is to use a domain name that you've already bought from a domain registrar. For example, you might have registered a domain name in the past, just to make sure no one else got hold of it. Or you might have bought a domain when you signed up to host your site with another company. For instance, if you bought the domain *SuperStyleFreak.com* a few months back, you can ask WordPress.com to use this web address when you create your blog. If you opt for this arrangement, you need to pay your original web host to maintain the domain registration (which typically costs about $10 a year) and you need to pay WordPress.com to use the domain (currently $13 per year). You also need to perform a bit of extra setup after you sign up with WordPress.com. The whole process is described on page 44.

Creating Your WordPress.com Account

Once you've got a basic idea about the identity of your blog and you've picked some potential names for the website address, you're ready to create your site. The following steps take you through the process:

1. **In your browser, travel to *http://wordpress.com*, and click the "Sign up now" link. (Or, for a shortcut, head straight to the sign-up page at *http://wordpress.com/signup*.)**

   The all-in-one sign-up form appears (Figure 2-1).

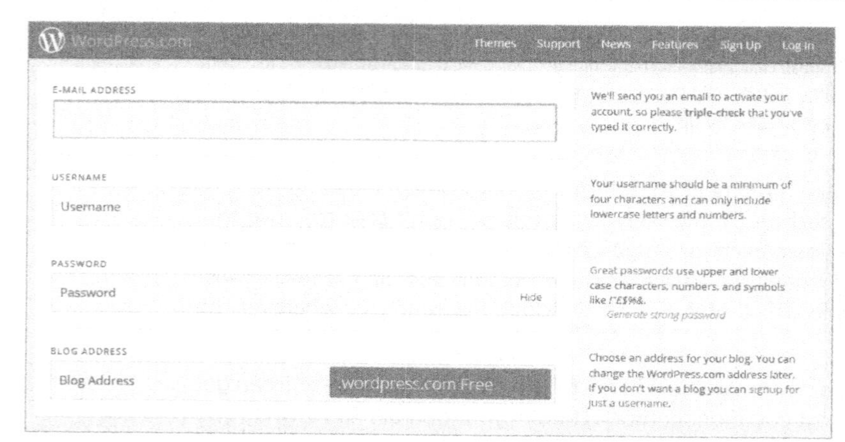

FIGURE 2-1

If you've ever stumbled through eight pages of forms to buy something online, you'll appreciate WordPress.com's single-page signup. You need to supply just four critical pieces of information: a website address and your user name, password, and email address.

2. **Fill in your email address.**

   WordPress uses your email address to send its activation message when you finish signing up. If you don't enter a valid email address, you won't be able to activate your account and start blogging.

3. **Choose a user name.**

   You use your user name and password to log into WordPress when you want to add new posts or manage your site. Sometimes, WordPressers use part of their blog name for the user name (for example, if your blog address is *lazyfather.wordpress.com*, your user name might be *lazyfather*).

   WordPress has some rules about user names. You need at least four characters, which can use a combination of numbers and lowercase letters only. If someone already has the user name you want, a brief message appears under the user name box stating, "Sorry, that user name already exists!" It's up to you to pick something unique before you continue.

NOTE Not only does your user name become part of the login process, it's also the name WordPress uses as your *display name*, which is the name that appears at the end of your blog posts and in the comments you leave (among other places). However, you can easily change your display name to something more suitable, as described on page 374.

4. **Choose a password.**

   Take the time to pick a password that's different from the passwords you use on other sites, not found in the dictionary, and difficult to guess. If you're not sure how to do that—or why you should bother—check out the box below.

WORD TO THE WISE

A WordPress Password Is More Than a Formality

WordPress websites are commonly attacked by hackers looking to steal traffic or to stuff in some highly objectionable ads. The best way to avoid this danger is with a strong password.

With enough tries, web evildoers can guess any password using an automated program. But most human WordPress hackers look for common words and patterns. If you use your first name (*ashley*), a string of close-together letters on the keyboard (*qwerty, qazwsx*), or a single word with a few number-fied or symbol-fied characters (like *passw0rd* and *pa$$word*), be afraid. These passwords aren't just a little bit insecure, they regularly make the list of the world's 25 *most stolen* passwords. (For the complete list of bad passwords, check out *http://onforb.es/v2rd0b*.)

That doesn't mean you need a string of complete gibberish to protect your site. Instead, you can deter casual hackers (who are responsible for almost all WordPress attacks) by taking a reasonably unique piece of information and scrambling it lightly. For example, you can use a favorite musician (*HERBee-HANcock88*), a movie title (*dr.strangel*ve*), or a short sentence with some vowels missing (*IThinkThrforIM*).

It's acceptable to write your password down on paper and tuck it in a desk drawer—after all, you're not worried about family members or office colleagues, you're concerned with international spammers, who certainly won't walk into your office and rifle through your belongings. (However, it's still a bad idea to put your password in an email or text message.)

5. **Type the website address you want into the Blog Address box.**

   If you want to use a free *.wordpress.com* domain, type in the first part of the name (for example, "RebelPastryChef" for the domain *RebelPastryChef.wordpress.com*). Your address needs to have at least four characters.

   If you want to buy a custom domain, which gives you the flexibility to move to a self-hosted site later, click the drop-down arrow to the right side of the Blog Address box. Then pick the *top-level domain*—that's the final part of your domain name after the period, such as *.me, .com, .net,* or *.org.* Once you do that, type in the first part of the domain name, like "RebelPastryChef" to get the domain name *RebelPastryChef.me*. (As you probably already know, capitalization is unimportant in a domain name, so there's no difference between *RebelPastryChef.me* and *REBELpastrychef.ME*, for instance.)

   As explained earlier, if you already own a custom domain name, you can use that for your new WordPress blog. To make this work, you need to go through a process called *mapping*. The first step is to pick an ordinary *.wordpress.com* website address. You then associate this to your custom domain name after you finish the sign-up process, by visiting the WordPress.com store and following the steps on page 44. In this situation, the *.wordpress.com* website address that you pick isn't terribly important, but you may as well try to get one that's similar to your domain name.

NOTE For almost all websites, the *www* prefix is an acceptable but optional part of the domain name. In other words, *RebelPastryChef.me* and *www.RebelPastryChef.me* are equivalent. Some people think that it's simpler, cleaner, and more modern to leave out the extra letters at the beginning, and WordPress.com agrees. As a result, if you register a domain through WordPress.com, the *www* prefix never appears. If you insist on typing the *www* part into a browser, you'll get to the right site, but WordPress will strip the prefix out of the browser's address bar (changing *www.RebelPastryChef.me* to *RebelPastryChef.me*, for example).

WORD TO THE WISE

Domain Name Frustration

The only disadvantage to buying your own domain name is that it can be hard to find one that's both good and available. You may think that most of the best *.wordpress.com* addresses have been snapped up already, but that's nothing compared with the competition for top-level *.com* domains. So while it's easy enough to decide to buy your own domain name (which is always a good idea), it's a bit harder to actually find one.

Here are some tips that can help:

Incorporate your business name. Domains that are just combinations of popular words ending in *.com* (like *Delicious-Chocolate.com, ThoroughbredHorses.com*) are almost certainly taken. Mix it up with your business name (*DelilasChocolates.com, AcmeThroughbredHorses.com*), and you stand a much better chance.

Think quirky. If you're creating a new blog, you can afford to try out unusual-yet-catchy word combinations that capture the spirit of your writing but have been overlooked by the rapacious domain name sharks. Possibilities include *ThatThingIsWeird.com, WhyCantISpell.com*, and *DieAutoTuneDie.com*. They may be a bit odd and a bit long, but they're catchy choices, for the right site.

Settle for a less common top-level domain. The top-level domain is the final few letters of a domain name, after the last period. The most popular top-level domain is *.com*, but it's also the most competitive. You'll find many more options if you're willing to settle for *.org* (which was originally intended for noncommercial websites but no longer has any restriction), *.net*, or the relatively new and catchy *.me*. For example, at the time of this writing, *wickedcode.com* is taken, but *wickedcode.me* is available. But be careful—the last thing you want is a potential visitor accidentally adding *.com* to the end of your address and ending up at your competitor's site.

6. **Wait while WordPress checks to see if your domain name is available.**

   A few seconds later, it reports the answer (Figure 2-2). If your first choice isn't free, try a variation or change the top-level domain using the drop-down list on the right. Finding a good domain name requires equal parts effort, creativity, and compromise.

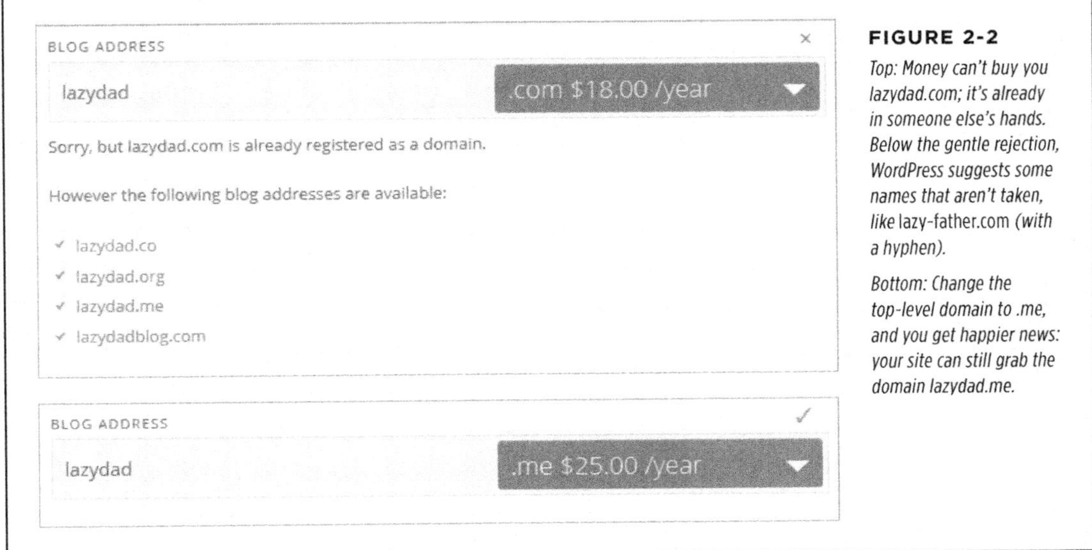

FIGURE 2-2

Top: Money can't buy you lazydad.com; it's already in someone else's hands. Below the gentle rejection, WordPress suggests some names that aren't taken, like lazy-father.com *(with a hyphen).*

Bottom: Change the top-level domain to .me, and you get happier news: your site can still grab the domain lazydad.me.

7. **Scroll down to the table at the bottom of the page, which describes the different types of WordPress.com accounts (Figure 2-3).**

   WordPress.com gives you the choice of three account types:

   - **WordPress.com Beginner.** This gets you a free WordPress.com blog, with all the essential features. If you're not sure which account to choose, this one is the best starting point. If you still need a bit more, you can buy individual upgrades (like the highly recommended Custom Domain upgrade, for a reasonable $18 a year).
   - **WordPress.com Premium.** Formerly called the WordPress Value Bundle, this option includes the same world-class free blogging engine as the WordPress.com Beginner account and a handful of small upgrades. While several of these enhancements are worthwhile, the overall package doesn't quite justify its $99 price tag for most people (see the box on page 33 for a more detailed analysis).
   - **WordPress.com Business.** This choice has the same features as a WordPress.com Premium account, with a few more frills thrown into the mix, like the ability to get live chat technical support. Unfortunately, you'll pay for these modest improvements with a hefty $299 a year fee.

NOTE Businesses don't need a Business account. WordPress.com has the same rules for all account types, and these rules let you describe and promote your business on your blog. However, if you're trying to make money by showing ads, you'll run afoul of the WordPress.com rules no matter which account type you choose.

	WordPress.com **Beginner**	WordPress.com **Premium**	WordPress.com **Business**
Free Blog	✓	✓	✓
A Custom Site Address	×	✓	✓
Space	3 GB	13 GB	Unlimited
No Ads	×	✓	✓
Custom Design	×	✓	✓
VideoPress	×	✓	✓
Premium Themes	×	×	Unlimited
Support	Community	Direct Email	Live Chat
	Free	~~$166.00~~ **$99.00** per year	~~$606.00~~ **$299.00** per year
By creating an account you agree to the fascinating Terms of Service.	Create Blog	Upgrade	Upgrade

FIGURE 2-3

WordPress's Premium and Business accounts bundle together several upgrades, each of which is available separately for a modest yearly fee, into an even cheaper package. The only catch is that you probably don't need all the upgrades these bundles include.

8. **Click the Create Blog button. Or if you're buying one of the two enhanced types of WordPress.com accounts, click the corresponding Upgrade button instead.**

TIP WordPress is flexible. You can start with a WordPress.com Beginner account and upgrade to an enhanced account later (for the same price as WordPress offers at signup). Or, you can buy a WordPress.com Beginner account and add just the individual services you need, whenever you need them. You make these purchases in the WordPress.com store, as outlined on page 42.

The initial stage of your account setup is complete. What WordPress does next depends on whether you chose to buy a domain name.

9. **If you chose a free *.wordpress.com* domain in step 5, WordPress invites you to do a bit of blog customization (Figure 2-4).**

   To help you get a jump-start on your blog, WordPress leads you through a series of pages that request more information. Although this step is optional, you can save time later by supplying three key details now: the title you want to use for your blog, a descriptive tagline that will be displayed just under your title, and a theme that will set the visual style of your entire site.

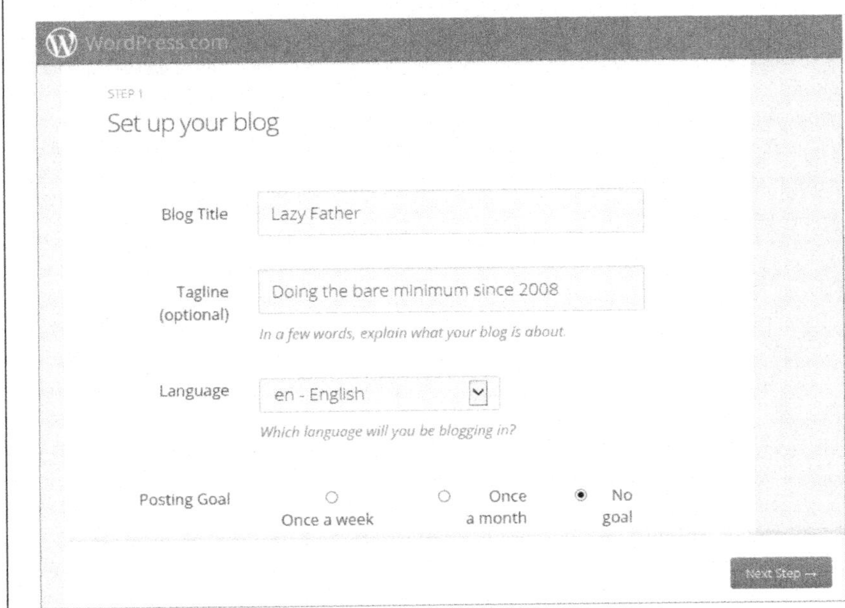

FIGURE 2-4

The more information you provide now, the less customization you'll need to do later. As you step through this series of pages, WordPress collects the title and tagline for your blog (shown here), lets you pick the theme you want, and invites you to spread the word on Facebook and Twitter.

TIP The best starting theme for learning WordPress is the clean and streamlined Twenty Twelve theme. It starts simple and has room for plenty of customization. It's also the theme you see in the first examples of this book. (Don't be put off by the out-of-date sounding name, which simply reflects when WordPress first released the theme. Twenty Twelve remains a popular classic to this day.)

10. **If you picked a custom domain name (in step 5), WordPress ends the sign-up process by presenting you with a domain registration form (Figure 2-5). Fill in your contact details and click Register Domain.**

    This registration information includes your name, postal address, and email address. WordPress submits this information, on your behalf, to the Domain Name System (DNS)—a key part of Internet bookkeeping that tracks who owns each piece of web real estate.

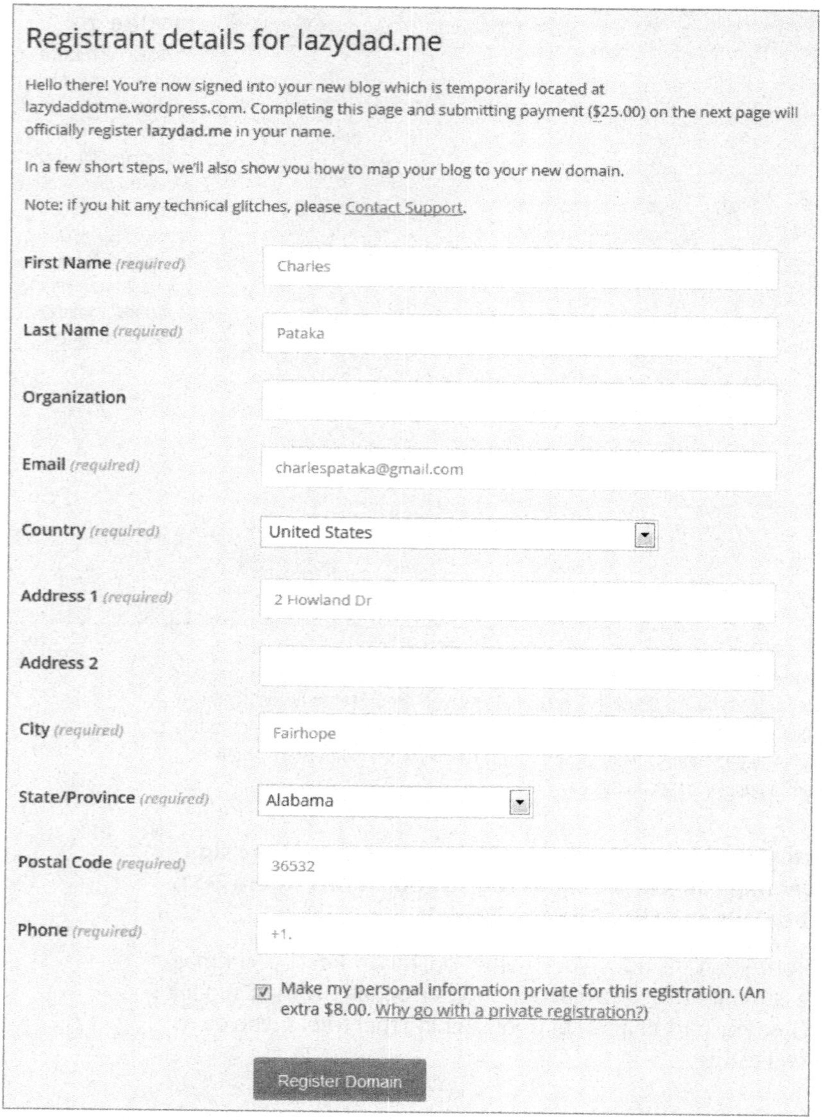

Registrant details for lazydad.me

Hello there! You're now signed into your new blog which is temporarily located at lazydaddotme.wordpress.com. Completing this page and submitting payment ($25.00) on the next page will officially register **lazydad.me** in your name.

In a few short steps, we'll also show you how to map your blog to your new domain.

Note: if you hit any technical glitches, please Contact Support.

First Name *(required)* Charles

Last Name *(required)* Pataka

Organization

Email *(required)* charlespataka@gmail.com

Country *(required)* United States

Address 1 *(required)* 2 Howland Dr

Address 2

City *(required)* Fairhope

State/Province *(required)* Alabama

Postal Code *(required)* 36532

Phone *(required)* +1.

☑ Make my personal information private for this registration. (An extra $8.00. Why go with a private registration?)

Register Domain

FIGURE 2-5

Here's the information you need to register lazyfather.net. Use the checkbox at the bottom of the screen to keep this information hidden from spammers' prying eyes, a good use of the $8 it costs.

FREQUENTLY ASKED QUESTION

Premium and Business Accounts

Should I pay for an upgraded WordPress.com account with more features?

Just before you sign up, WordPress.com attempts to seduce you with its Premium and Business accounts. These bundles combine several WordPress upgrades, each of which normally costs a yearly fee, into a slightly cheaper package.

But before you plunk down any cash, you need to review whether these bundles are worthwhile. The most popular package, WordPress.com Premium, combines five upgrades and adds email tech support. One upgrade is the highly recommended custom domain option (normally $18/year). Two more upgrades are good, but not essential, enhancements. They include the Custom Design upgrade, which gives you the ability to edit the styles in your chosen theme (page 457) and the No Ads upgrade, which prevents WordPress from showing any advertisements on your site. (Even without the No Ads upgrade, your visitors may not see ads, because WordPress uses them only occasionally and never shows them to people logged into WordPress.com.) Altogether, these improvements total about $78 a year, if you were to purchase them separately.

The final two upgrades included with WordPress.com Premium are additional space (for hosting very big files) and VideoPress support (for video files). These upgrades may appeal to you if you plan to show videos on your site, but most people find it cheaper and easier to host videos using a free service like YouTube, by simply embedding a YouTube video window on their WordPress pages (see page 350 to learn how). VideoPress is a more specialized option that may appear if you plan to show content that isn't suitable for YouTube—for example, videos that run longer than YouTube's 15-minute limit, or videos that visitors can download. You'll learn more about VideoPress on page 358. If you don't need these features, the $100-a-year cost isn't much of a bargain.

The WordPress.com Business account has the same features as a WordPress.com Premium account, with even more space, the ability to get live chat technical support, and unlimited premium themes. Most premium themes run between $20 and $80, so the WordPress.com Business account may make sense if you plan to create several sites, or if you just want to experiment with many theme options. That said, WordPress.com has a solid selection of free themes, so it's worth waiting to see if these can satisfy your site before you shell out the pricey $300-a-year fee.

Domain name registration is public, which means that anyone with an Internet connection can look up your domain and find out that you own it. (Interested parties also get your phone number and email address.) Usually, this isn't a problem, but it does provide an opening for spammers to hassle you. If you don't want your public details exposed, *don't* try to fake them with incorrect information. Instead, tick the box that says "Make my personal information private for this registration." It costs an extra $8, but it gives you guaranteed anonymity—at least until you start posting.

Finally, WordPress asks you to pay up. Fill out your payment information and click the "Purchase and Register Domain" button. WordPress will email you a receipt.

TIP WordPress doesn't provide an email service. So if you buy the domain *lazyfather.net*, you can't get email at *joe@lazyfather.net*. However, WordPress does let you *forward* email from your custom domain to another email address. For example, it can automatically redirect mail sent to the custom domain *joe@lazyfather.net* to a personal account like *joe_symes23@gmail.com*. If you want to use WordPress.com's redirection service, you can find instructions at *http://support.wordpress.com/email-forwarding*.

11. **Check your email for an activation message from WordPress. The message includes a button named Confirm Email Address or Log In. Click the button to activate your site.**

    Clicking the button launches your web browser and sends you to *http://wordpress.com*, the central administration station for all the blogs you create with WordPress.com. You'll learn your way around in the next section.

Managing Your New Site

Once you complete the sign-up process and activate your account, you're ready to do just about everything else.

The easiest starting point is the *http://wordpress.com* home page, where you can read other people's blogs and manage your own. Once you get there, type in the user name and password you picked when you signed up, and then click Sign In. You'll find yourself in WordPress.com's central hub (Figure 2-6).

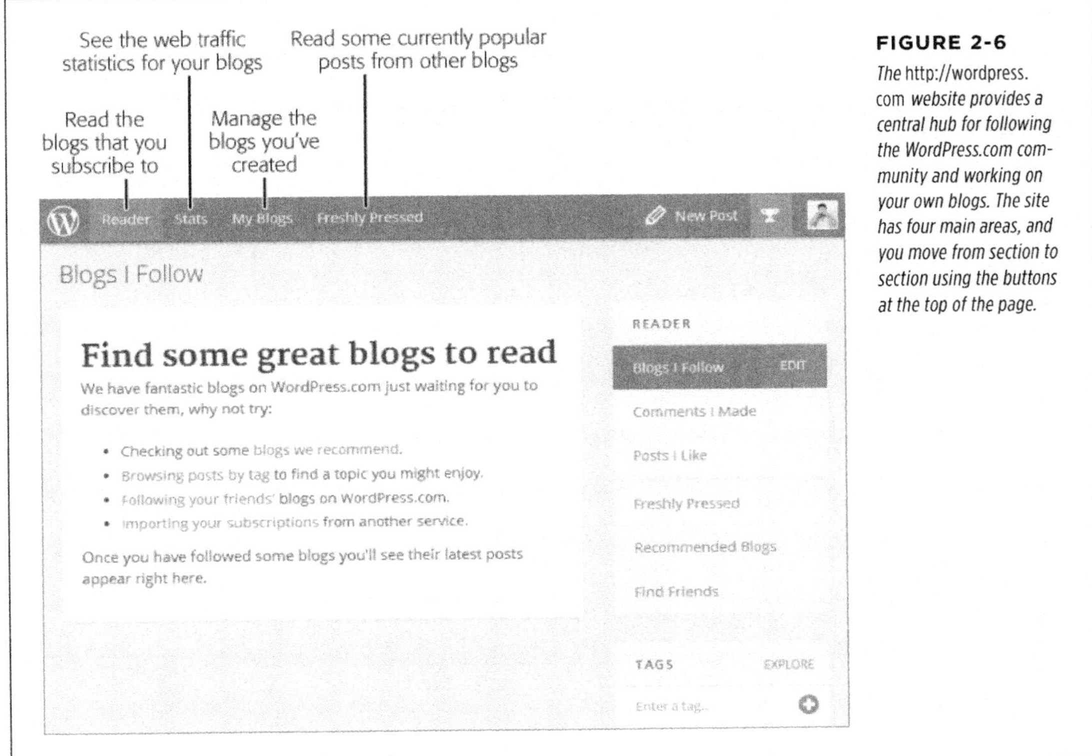

FIGURE 2-6

The http://wordpress.com *website provides a central hub for following the WordPress.com community and working on your own blogs. The site has four main areas, and you move from section to section using the buttons at the top of the page.*

Initially, WordPress starts you at the Reader page, where you can keep track of your favorite blogs and hunt for new ones (page 39). But the best jumping-off point for a newly minted WordPress.com administrator like yourself is the My Blogs page. There, you'll see a list of all the blogs you've created so far, which at this point is just one (Figure 2-7). Next to each blog are a set of handy management links, as well as a shortcut for adding a new post to your blog.

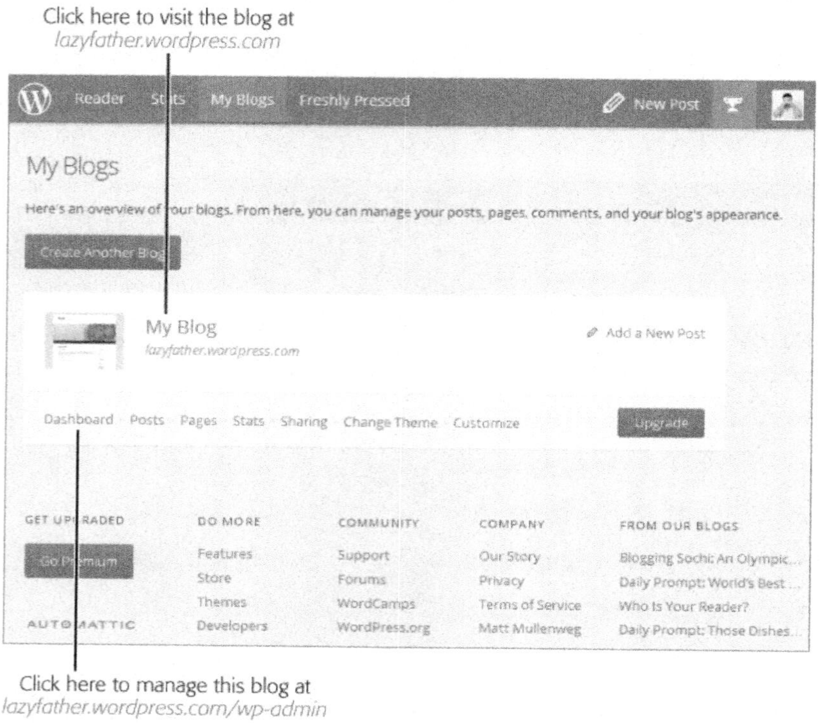

Click here to visit the blog at *lazyfather.wordpress.com*

Click here to manage this blog at *lazyfather.wordpress.com/wp-admin*

FIGURE 2-7

Right now, you've created just one WordPress.com blog. In this example, it's named My Blog and it lives at the WordPress.com address lazyfather.wordpress.com.

UP TO SPEED

Adding More Sites

There's no need to limit yourself to a single WordPress.com site. In fact, every WordPress.com user is allowed to create an *unlimited* number of sites.

To add a new site, you use the My Blogs page, which lists all the WordPress sites you created so far. To add a new one, click the Create a New Blog button. You'll have to supply the same information you entered when you created your first blog, including a website address (a free *.wordpress.com* domain or a custom domain you purchase) and a blog name. You won't need to supply a new user name or password, because you already have a WordPress.com account.

If you've invested in some WordPress.com upgrades, adding sites can get expensive. That's because you need to buy each upgrade *separately* for every site that uses it. So if you create two sites and you want to fine-tune the CSS style rules for each, you need to buy two Custom Design upgrades for a total of $60 per year.

You can't delete any of your WordPress.com sites from the My Blogs tab. Instead, you need to visit the dashboard, the administrative hub you'll explore in Chapter 4. Once you're in the dashboard, you can remove the current site by choosing Tools→Delete Site from the left-side menu.

To visit your newly created WordPress.com blog, click its name on the My Blogs page. WordPress opens a new browser tab to show you the current state of your mostly blank site (Figure 2-8).

FIGURE 2-8

When you create a new site, WordPress.com adds a single dummy post with some basic instructions in it. Although it doesn't look like much, this shell of a site has all the infrastructure you need to build a genuinely useful WordPress site, which you'll learn to do starting in Chapter 4.

When you visit your site, take a moment to review the URL that appears in the browser's address box. If you chose to go with a free *.wordpress.com* domain (like *lazyfather.wordpress.com*), this is the address you'll see there. If you purchased a custom domain, your new domain won't be working just yet, but WordPress.com will assign you a similar temporary *.wordpress.com* domain. For example, if you bought mysticalpeanuts.net, WordPress.com will start your site out at *mysticalpeanuts.wordpress.com* (or, if that's not available, it adds the top-level domain into the name to come up with a slightly more awkward version of the address, like *mysticalpeanutsdotcom.wordpress.com*).

Most of the work you'll perform with your WordPress site takes place at the dashboard, an administrative web interface that you can use to add posts, configure styles and settings, and much more (see Figure 2-9). To get there, click the Dashboard link that appears under your site on the My Blogs page. Incidentally, almost all the other links there also take you to the dashboard; they simply navigate to a specific section of it. For example, if you click Posts you'll wind up at the Posts section of the dashboard, which you'll study in detail in Chapter 4. The only exception is the Stats link, which shows you the visitor traffic and other statistics for your WordPress. com sites (just as if you clicked the Stats link at the top of the page, just between Reader and My Blogs).

NOTE You've just learned the simplest way to visit the dashboard for your site: Log into WordPress.com, click My Blogs, and then click the Dashboard link. However, there's a shortcut that lets you jump straight to the dashboard without going through WordPress.com. Just type in the web address for your blog, with */wp-admin* added at the end. For example, to manage *lazyfather.wordpress.com*, you'd go to *lazyfather.wordpress.com/wp-admin*. (WordPress will ask you to sign in with your user name and password if you aren't already logged in.)

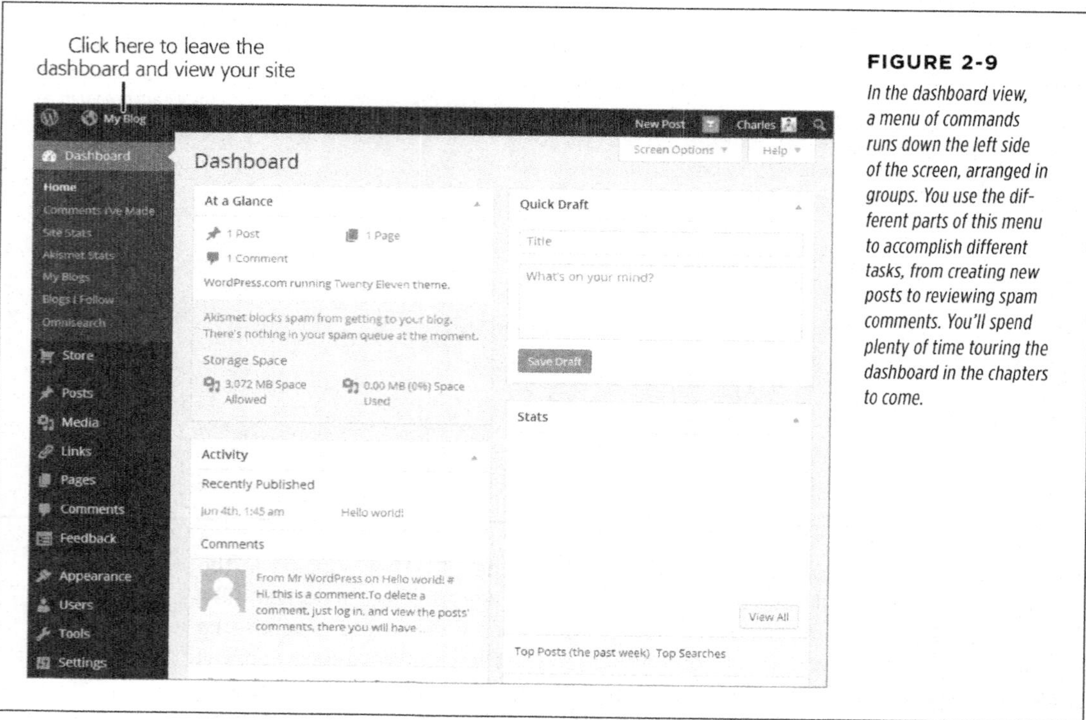

FIGURE 2-9

In the dashboard view, a menu of commands runs down the left side of the screen, arranged in groups. You use the different parts of this menu to accomplish different tasks, from creating new posts to reviewing spam comments. You'll spend plenty of time touring the dashboard in the chapters to come.

Exploring the WordPress.com Community

Once you have your very own WordPress site, you're also a member of the WordPress. com *community*. Warm and fuzzy feelings aside, the connections and exposure you get through the community can have real benefits, particularly if your WordPress. com site is a straight-up, traditional blog. These benefits include the following:

- **Ideas.** No site exists in a vacuum, especially not a blog. By looking at other people's work, you can tune in to a powerful source of inspiration for both content and style. On the *content* side, you can discover trending topics and popular subjects (using the Freshly Pressed tab and Popular Topics link described in the next section, for example). Then, you can join in on the conversation by giving your own spin on hot topics on your blog. On the *style* side, you can see how other people polish themes and perfect their layouts, and you can use that insight to improve your own site.
- **Promotion.** As in the real world, one of the most successful ways to make friends, attract attention, or score a new job is by networking with other, like-minded people. When you find other blogs that tackle the same issues as yours, you can exchange links and create a blogroll that connects their sites to yours (page 228). Or you can increase your exposure by commenting on someone else's posts (on their blog) or publishing a full reply post (on your blog). Eventually, these practices can attract many more visitors to your site.

With that in mind, you're ready to survey the field. Start at the WordPress.com front page (*http://wordpress.com*). If you aren't already logged in, fill in your user name and password and then click Sign In.

You start at the Reader page. However, unless you've already subscribed to someone else's blog, you won't see any content there. Instead, you have to search for what you want.

There are several ways to track down WordPress.com content that might interest you:

- **Browse the recommended blogs.** On the Reader page, click the "blogs we recommend" link that appears in the first bullet point. You can then click a category that interests you (like Popular Culture & Entertainment or Photography to see a short list with some of the best blogs on the subject. Click a blog's name to view it in a separate tab. WordPress.com is willing to recommend only a very small set of blogs, so this approach won't get you very deep into the WordPress.com community.
- **Read the Freshly Pressed page.** The best place to get a sense of the chatter on WordPress.com is the Freshly Pressed page. It shows a cross-section of the day's most attention-grabbing posts (Figure 2-10). Click a post that interests you to read the full article and continue on to the blog that hosts it.
- **Hunt for interesting posts by keyword.** When WordPress bloggers create a new post, they add a few descriptive words, called *tags*, to classify it. Tags give you a way to home in on posts that interest you (as you'll see on page 114, when you start posting). Tags also give you a way to find blogs that discuss your favorite topics. Begin by looking at the Tags box in the right-side column of the Reader page. Click one of the tag words, or type in a subject of your own in the search box to find more blogs.

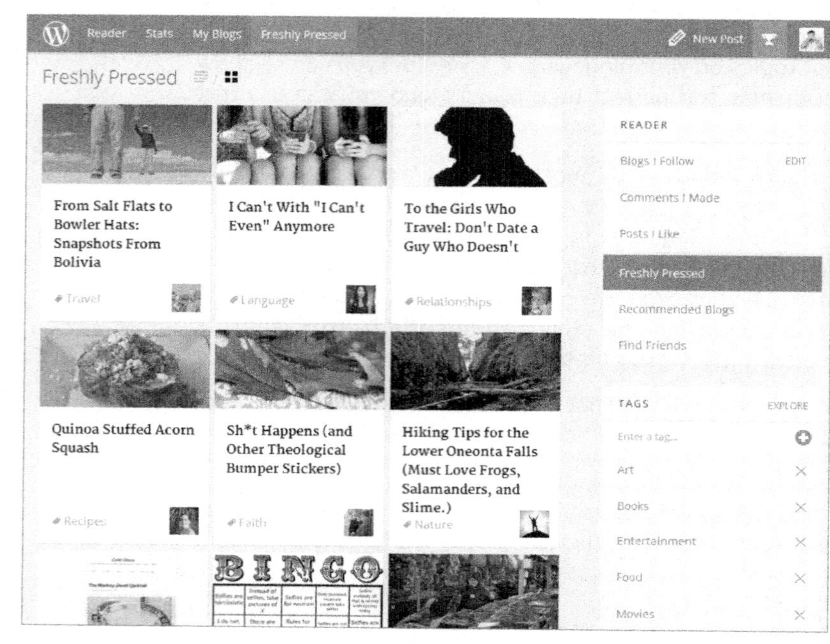

FIGURE 2-10

WordPress's ever-changing Freshly Pressed list shows popular, recent posts. If you see a post that piques your interest, click its title. You could also click the tag word to search for more posts on the same subject.

- **Go tag surfing.** You can browse some of the posts that use the most popular tags by clicking the Explore link in the top-right corner of the Tags box. When you do, WordPress shows a display that shows hot tags, sized to reflect their current popularity (Figure 2-11).

TIP When you browse through WordPress.com, you don't see the many sites created with WordPress software but hosted on sites other than WordPress.com. Although there's no central repository of self-hosted WordPress sites, you can browse a showcase with some examples at *http://wordpress.org/showcase*.

When you browse a WordPress.com blog (and you're signed in under your WordPress.com account), a black toolbar appears at the top of the page (Figure 2-12). On the left side is the name of the blog you're currently viewing and two important buttons: Follow and Like. If you like the post you're reading, you can click the Like button (which adds it to a list of your favorite posts). Or, if you decide the content is so good that you want to come back to this site and read more, you can click the Follow button (which adds the site to your personal watch list of blogs).

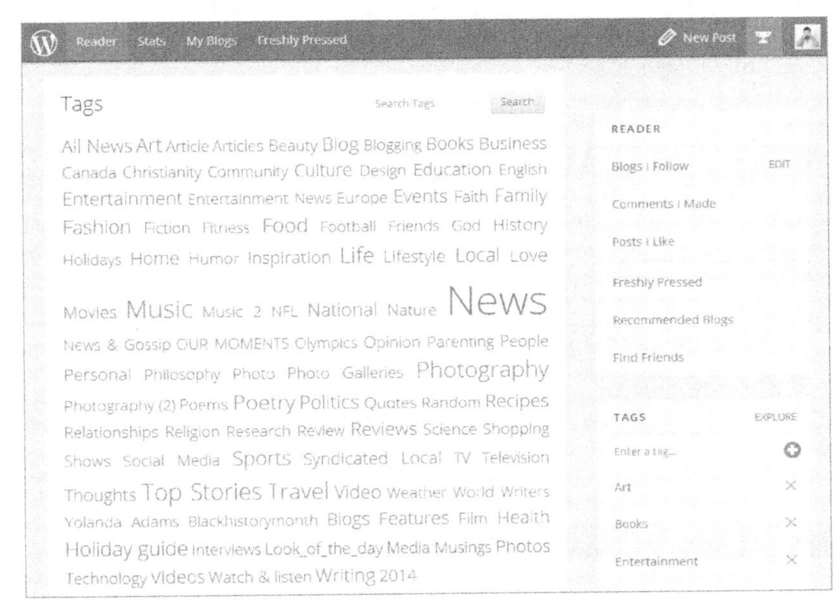

FIGURE 2-11

This grouping of tags shows the most popular topics of the moment. The bigger tags (like Music and News) have more recent posts. Click a tag that interests you to see a list of recent posts on that subject.

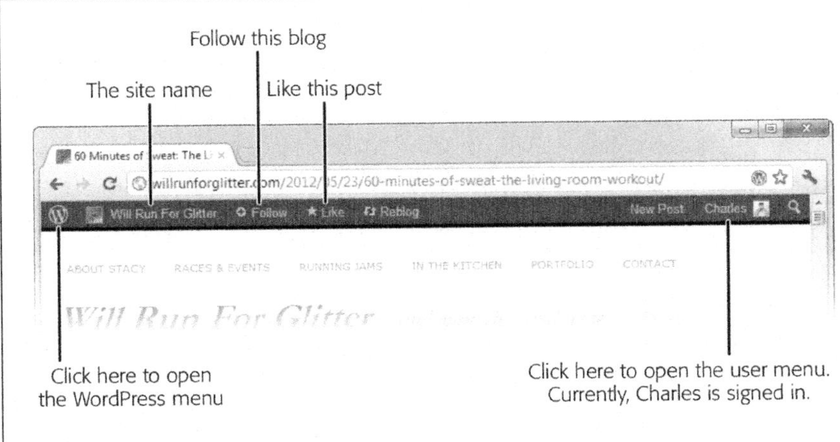

FIGURE 2-12

The WordPress toolbar takes only a few pixels of space, but it's stocked with useful commands. Hover over the WordPress icon on the left, and you'll see a menu that lets you jump to different parts of the WordPress.com site. Hover over your user name on the right, and you'll see a menu that lets you edit your profile, manage your blogs, and sign out. Or, use the Favorite and Like buttons to track interesting content.

Usually, you'll choose to click Like on a post if you want to refer to it later—perhaps to follow an ongoing conversation in the Comments section. You'll choose Follow to keep watching the blog for new content. To review your liked posts and read your followed blogs, return to *http://wordpress.com* and click the Reader tab. Now you'll see the most recent posts from all the sites you follow, amalgamated into a single reverse-chronological list.

Visiting the WordPress.com Store

As you've already seen, when you sign up with WordPress, you can buy a custom domain name or a Premium account bundle. But what happens if you want to start simple (and cheap) but add more features in the future? The answer is the WordPress.com store, which is just a click away on the dashboard. It offers a long list of blog enhancements, each for a small yearly fee.

Getting to the store is easy. Once you load up the dashboard, click the Store link in the menu on the left. WordPress shows you the long list of upgrades it offers (Figure 2-13).

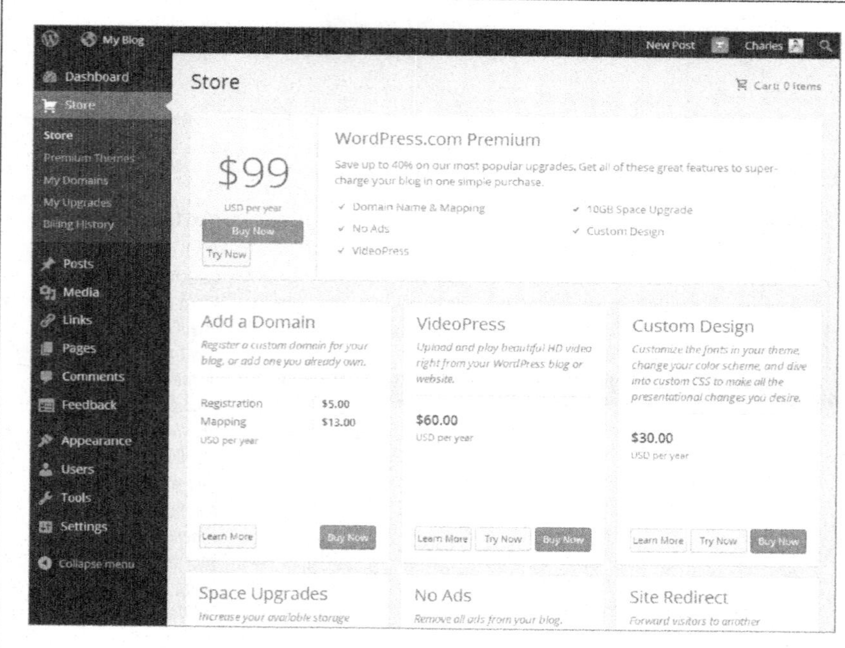

FIGURE 2-13

To add an upgrade to your site, click the Buy Now button underneath it. Some options provide a Try Now button, which lets you use the upgrade for free for two weeks, and then charges you automatically. Either way, you'll need to fill in your payment information (using a credit card, a PayPal account, or a digital wallet of Bitcoins).

In the following sections, you'll see how to use the store to deal with two more complex setup scenarios. First you'll learn how to buy a custom domain for an existing WordPress.com site. Next you'll see how to take a domain you already own and use it with an existing WordPress.com site.

Buying a Domain after Signup

Imagine you build a thriving blog using a free *.wordpress.com* address (say, *HelloPickles.wordpress.com*), but then decide you really want a custom domain name (like *HelloPickles.net*). Using the store, you can buy one for your existing blog, so you don't need to create a whole new blog under a new name. Here's how:

1. **Go to the dashboard.**

   You can get there by visiting the My Blogs page and clicking the Dashboard link, or go there directly using your blog address and tacking */wp-admin* onto the end.

2. **Click Store in the menu on the left.**

   WordPress shows a list of all the upgrades you can buy.

3. **In the "Add a Domain" box, click Buy Now.**

   WordPress displays a list of all the domains your site currently uses. Unless you already bought a custom domain name through WordPress.com, the list includes just one address: the *.wordpress.com* address you picked when you created your site (Figure 2-14).

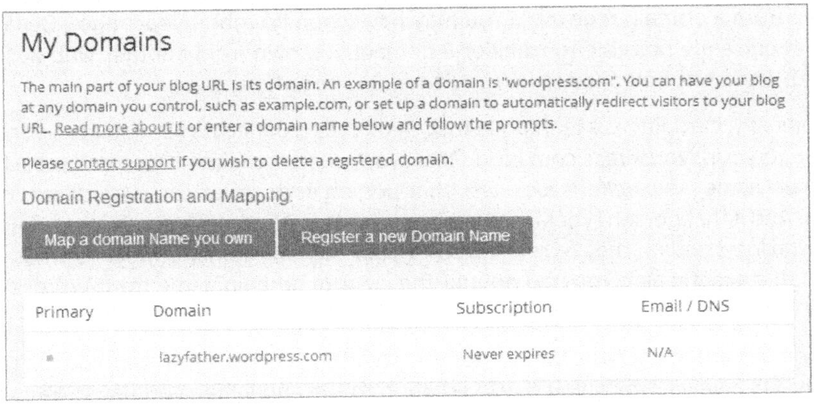

FIGURE 2-14

Currently, this site uses the free domain lazyfather.wordress.com.

4. **Click the "Register a new Domain Name" button.**

   This tells WordPress you want to look for a new address.

5. **Type the domain you want into the domain search box, and then click Go.**

   WordPress checks to see if the domain you want is available. If it isn't, try typing something else.

6. **If the domain is available, click Register Now to make it yours.**

   WordPress brings you to the standard domain registration page, where you fill in your personal details (as you saw back in Figure 2-5).

7. **When you finish, click Register Domain and follow the instructions to pay.**

   When you add a custom domain name, WordPress won't leave your current audience in the cold. Instead, it's smart enough to reroute people visiting your old *.wordpress.com* address to your new domain. That means that if you started with *HelloPickles.wordpress.com*, and you then buy the custom domain *HelloPickles.net*, WordPress will automatically redirect people who type in *HelloPickles.wordpress.com* to your blog's new domain, *HelloPickles.net*, just as you would want. (Really, there's no difference between the two addresses. They are simply two names that point to the same site—your blog.)

TIP Buying a custom domain for an already-created site is a useful technique if you think that you could be outgrowing WordPress.com, and you want to prepare your site for a possible move to self-hosting. Because WordPress automatically redirects visitors from your old *.wordpress.com* domain to your new custom domain, it gives everyone a chance to get used to your new address. And when you do decide to move, you can take your new domain with you (page 561).

Using a Domain Name You Already Own

Life is easiest if you buy your custom domain name from WordPress.com, but sometimes that isn't possible. For example, you might have already bought the domain name from a domain registrar. (You may have even bought it years ago.) Because it isn't currently possible to transfer a domain you own from another web host to WordPress.com, you need to use another trick, called *mapping*.

Technically, mapping is a technique that, in this case, connects your custom domain name to your WordPress.com blog. That way, when someone types in the custom domain name (say *HelloPickles.net*), that person ends up at your WordPress.com blog. And if that person types in your former *.wordpress.com* address (say, *HelloPickles.wordpress.com*), they're redirected to your custom domain, which is what you want. It's exactly as if you had bought the custom domain name from WordPress.com when you signed up.

Mapping is relatively easy, but it's not free. WordPress charges a mapping fee (currently $13 a year), which you pay in addition to the annual fee you pay to keep the domain name registered through your original domain registrar.

Mapping requires you to complete two setup operations: one with the web host that registered the domain name, and one with WordPress. But before you get started with either operation, you need to decide exactly how you want to link your custom domain name with your WordPress site. You have two options:

- **Use your whole domain.** For example, you might create a blog at *www.WineSnobs.com*. If you map this address to a WordPress.com address, you need to keep your entire website on WordPress.com. This makes sense if you purchased a domain name from another company but you haven't actually bought any web *space* from that company.

- **Use a subdomain.** Technically, a subdomain takes your domain name (say, *www.WineSnobs.com*), removes the optional *www* part, and adds a different prefix (like *blog.WineSnobs.com*). The goal is to create a separate web address for your WordPress site, so you can put something else at your main domain name (in this case, *www.WineSnobs.com*). Of course, your main site won't be a WordPress site, and you'll need to pay your web host for some web space.

NOTE If all this talk about subdomains sounds familiar, it's because the WordPress.com service uses subdomains itself to give everyone a unique spot on the *wordpress.com* server. For example, add the prefix GettingBloggedDown and you get the subdomain *GettingBloggedDown.wordpress.com*.

There's also a third option—use a *subdirectory* in your domain (for example, *www.WineSnobs.com/blog*)—but WordPress.com doesn't currently support that technique.

Before you can map your domain, you have to do a little extra configuration with your web host. These setup steps differ depending on whether you want to map the full domain name or you want to map just a subdomain, so follow the instructions in the appropriate section below.

MAPPING AN ENTIRE DOMAIN NAME

If you're mapping an entire domain name, you have to change your web domain's *name servers*. These are the high-powered computers that direct traffic on the Internet, and that tell browsers where to go to find your site. Right now, your domain name uses the name servers at the company that registered your domain name, or at your original web host (not WordPress.com). You need to change that so your domain uses the WordPress.com name servers.

Making the change is simple enough—it usually involves changing just two pieces of text—the *name server addresses*. However, you may need to dig around on your web host's administration page before you find exactly where these settings are (they're usually in a section called "Domain Name Servers" or "DNS Settings"). If in doubt, contact your web host.

For example, if you're using the web host *www.brinkster.com*, the name servers would be set to this:

```
NS1.BRINKSTER.COM
NS2.BRINKSTER.COM
```

No matter what web host you're currently using, you must change the name servers to this:

```
NS1.WORDPRESS.COM
NS2.WORDPRESS.COM
```

NS1 and NS2 are the two computers that direct your visitors to the WordPress.com site they want to read.

TIP Does your domain registrar provide an email address that you want to keep using? For example, maybe you want WordPress.com to put a blog on *www.WineSnobs.com*, which you originally registered with the well-known web hosting company GoDaddy, but you still want to receive email at *rachel@WineSnobs.com*. To pull this off, you need to carry out the extra configuration step covered at *http://tinyurl.com/ext-email*.

MAPPING A SUBDOMAIN

If you're mapping a subdomain, you need a slightly different configuration. Instead of changing your name servers, you must add a *CNAME record*. Although it sounds intimidatingly techy, all a CNAME record does is redirect traffic from your subdomain to your WordPress.com blog.

Every web host has a different process for defining a CNAME record, but it usually involves logging in, heading to an administration section with a name like "DNS Management" or "Name Server Management," and then adding the CNAME record. Each record requires two pieces of information. The first is the subdomain prefix (for example, that's *blog* if you're creating the subdomain *blog.WineSnobs.com*). The second is your current WordPress.com address, like *WineSnobs.wordpress.com*, which is often called the *destination*.

NOTE If you can't find or figure out your web host's domain management tools, make time for a quick support call. Changing name servers and adding subdomains are two common tasks that domain registrars and web hosts deal with every day.

FINISHING THE JOB: SETTING UP THE WORDPRESS.COM MAPPING

Name server changes require time to take effect. Once you make your changes, the settings need to be spread to various traffic-directing computers across the Internet. It will take at least 24 hours, and possibly two or three days, before the change takes effect and you can tell WordPress.com to start using your domain. Unfortunately, there's no high-tech way to monitor the process.

Once your name server changes have taken effect, you can add the domain by following the next set of steps. If you're not sure whether you've waited long enough, don't worry—there's no harm in trying. If the name server changes haven't taken effect, WordPress will let you know when you get to step 4 below, and you'll need to try again later.

1. **Go to the dashboard.**

   You can get there by visiting the My Blogs page and clicking the Dashboard link, or go there directly by appending */wp-admin* to the end of your blog address.

2. **Click Store in the menu on the left.**

   WordPress shows a list of all the upgrades you can buy.

3. **In the "Add a Domain" box, click Buy Now.**

   WordPress shows a list of all the domains your site currently uses.

4. **Click the "Map a Domain Name you own" button.**

5. **Type the domain you already own into the text box and then click Go.**

   WordPress checks to see if the domain name exists. Because WordPress has no way of knowing that you own the domain, it will warn you that the blog is taken.

6. **Click the long-winded "Yes, I already own this domain name. Map it to my WordPress.com blog" button.**

   WordPress will ask you for your payment details. Once you supply that, the mapping is complete. Congratulations—you can now get to your WordPress site by using your custom domain name.

CHAPTER

3

Installing WordPress on Your Web Host

There's nothing wrong with WordPress.com—it's cheap, relatively powerful, and has a thriving community of blogs. But the most serious WordPress fans aren't satisfied unless they can run WordPress on their own web hosts.

This approach, called *self-hosting*, gives you a world of new opportunities. You can, for example, choose from a dizzying range of plug-ins to add new features to your site. You can put a WordPress blog in the same domain as your traditional website (for example, you can have a site at *www.HandMadePaintBrushes.com* and a blog at *www.HandMadePaintBrushes.com/news*). You can slap ads on your blog, and—most usefully of all—create a site that doesn't look like a blog at all.

This chapter assumes that you know, deep down in your heart, that you are a WordPress self-hoster. You aren't willing to settle for a merely convenient WordPress.com blog when you can design exactly what you want with a self-hosted WordPress site. In the following pages, you'll learn how to get started.

Preparing for WordPress

Before you dive into a self-hosted WordPress setup, you need to tick off a few requirements. The first is setting up an account with a web host. (If you've already done that, you can safely skip ahead to the next section, starting on page 51.)

If you're just starting out, choosing a good web host may seem more daunting than it actually is. Technically, your host needs to meet two requirements to run WordPress: First, it needs to be able to run PHP (version 5.2.4 or greater) programs, which power WordPress. And second, it needs to recognize MySQL (version 5.0 or greater), which is the database that stores WordPress content.

Virtually every web host meets these requirements. In fact, choosing a WordPress-friendly host is hard simply because so many hosts offer essentially the same thing. Other selling points that hosts advertise—the amount of disk space or bandwidth you get, for example—are less important. Even popular WordPress sites are unlikely to approach anywhere near the web space and bandwidth limits most web hosts offer, unless you plan to host huge video files (and even then, you'll probably find it far easier to host your videos with a video-hosting service like Vimeo or YouTube).

NOTE Disk space *is* useful for storing weekly or daily backup copies of your site. But with most web hosts offering gigabytes upon gigabytes of space, you're unlikely to hit a limit, even with a discount-priced hosting plan.

Here's the bottom line: WordPress has become so super-popular that virtually all web hosts embrace it, even in their cheapest web hosting plans. And because WordPress is so popular, many hosts specifically advertise "WordPress support" or "one-click WordPress installation," which lets you set up WordPress with an autoinstaller (page 55).

The most important considerations in choosing a host aren't the amount of web space or bandwidth you get. Instead, they are reliability, security, and support—in other words, how often your website will be down due to technical troubles, how quickly you can get an answer to your questions, and whether your host will be in business several years into the future. These attributes are more difficult to assess, but before you sign up with a host, you should try contacting its support office (both by email and phone). Don't trust website reviews (which are usually paid for), but do look up what other people say about the hosts you're considering on the popular forum Web Hosting Talk (*http://bit.ly/vQ7tkH*). Hawk Host, StableHost, SpeedySparrow, and MDDHosting are just four examples of web hosts frequently praised on these boards.

You can also choose a WordPress-recommended host (see the short list at *http://wordpress.org/hosting*), but keep in mind that hosts pay to be on this exclusive list. They're perfectly good hosts, but you can find equally excellent options on your own, and possibly save a few dollars.

TIP To budget for WordPress, assume you'll pay $5 to $10 a month for web hosting. Then add the cost of a custom domain name (that's the web address that leads to your site), which you can typically find for a paltry $12 or so per year.

POWER USERS' CLINIC

Web Hosts with Premium Performance

Although there are plenty of decent, cheap hosting options available for WordPress, they aren't the equal of premium hosting plans that cost several times more. The key difference is performance. If your site is large, complex, and heavily trafficked, you might find that its pages become sluggish during busy times. This happens because WordPress must do a fair bit of work to assemble tailor-made content for every request.

The cheapest way to address this problem is with a caching plug-in, as described on page 316. Depending on the scale and popularity of your site, this may be a perfect solution. But if your visitors still find your site slow, you might need to consider switching web hosts or upgrading to a more expensive plan from the host you already have.

The next step up in the hosting world is *semi-dedicated* hosting or *virtual private* hosting. Either way, the idea is the same—to move your site off the heavily trafficked web servers that host hundreds or thousands of other people's sites, and put it on a computer that hosts fewer sites. That way, the server can dedicate more resources to handling *your* site and serving *your* visitors. The drawback is cost. While basic WordPress hosting can be had for as little as $5 a month, virtual private hosting hovers around $20 a month and can climb far above that.

If you're just starting with WordPress, you won't yet know how well a particular web hosting plan will meet your needs. But if you pick a well-respected web host, you can start out with a cheap plan and upgrade to something with more muscle if you need it.

Deciding Where to Put WordPress

When you sign up for a web hosting account, you typically get a domain name (that's the web address a visitor types into a browser to get to your site) and some space for your web pages. But before you can create your first WordPress site, you need to think a bit about how your web hosting account and your WordPress site will fit together.

You can choose one of three basic strategies for installing WordPress on your web hosting account:

- **Put WordPress in the root folder of your site.** This is the best approach if you want to let WordPress run your entire site. For example, imagine you sign up for a site with the domain *www.BananaRepublican.org* and you put WordPress in the root folder of that site. Now, when visitors type that address into their browsers, they go straight to your WordPress home page.
- **Put WordPress in a subfolder of your site.** This is the choice for you if your web presence will include both traditional web pages (for example, something you've handcrafted in a web editor like Dreamweaver) and a WordPress site. Often, people use this choice to add a WordPress blog to an existing website. For example, if you bought the domain *www.BananaRepublican.org,* you might direct blog readers to the subfolder *www.BananaRepublican.org/blog* to see your WordPress masterpiece. To set this up, you need to create a subfolder (in the web address above, it's named *blog*) and put WordPress there.

- **Put WordPress in a subdomain of your site.** This is another way to handle websites that have a WordPress section and a non-WordPress section. The difference is that instead of using a subfolder for the WordPress part of your site, you use a *subdomain*. To create a subdomain, you take your domain (say, *www.BananaRepublican.org*), remove the *www* part, if it has one (now you've got *BananaRepublican.org*), and then put a different bit of text at the front, separated by a period (as in *social.BananaRepublican.org*). For example, you could have a traditional website at *www.BananaRepublican.org* and a news-style WordPress site with user feedback at *social.BananaRepublican.org*, just like the automotive giant Ford does (page 14).

To use either of the first two approaches, you don't need to do anything extra before you start installing WordPress. The WordPress autoinstaller will take care of everything.

But if you take the third approach and install WordPress on a subdomain, you need to create the subdomain before you go any further. The following section explains how.

Creating a Subdomain (if You Need One)

If you're planning to put WordPress in the root folder or in a subfolder of your website, skip this section—it doesn't apply. But if you're planning to host WordPress on a separate subdomain, you need to lay a bit of groundwork, so keep reading.

Creating a subdomain is a task that's quick and relatively straightforward—once you know how to do it. Unfortunately, the process isn't the same on all web hosts, so you may need to contact your host's support department to get the specifics. If your host uses the popular cPanel administrative interface (and many do), the process goes like this:

1. **Using your browser, log in to the control panel for your web host.**

   Look for the Subdomains icon (usually, you'll find it in a box named "Domains").

   If you can't find the Subdomains box, try searching with the cPanel's Find box. Type in the first few characters (that's "subd") and it should appear at the top of the page.

2. **When you find the Subdomains icon, click it.**

   This loads the Subdomains page (Figure 3-1).

3. **Choose the domain you want from a list of all the domains you own.**

   Some people have a web hosting account with just one domain, but others own dozens.

4. **In the Subdomain box, type in the prefix you want to use for the subdomain.**

   For example, if you want to create the subdomain *blog.reboot-me.com* on the domain *reboot-me.com*, you need to type *blog* in the Subdomain box.

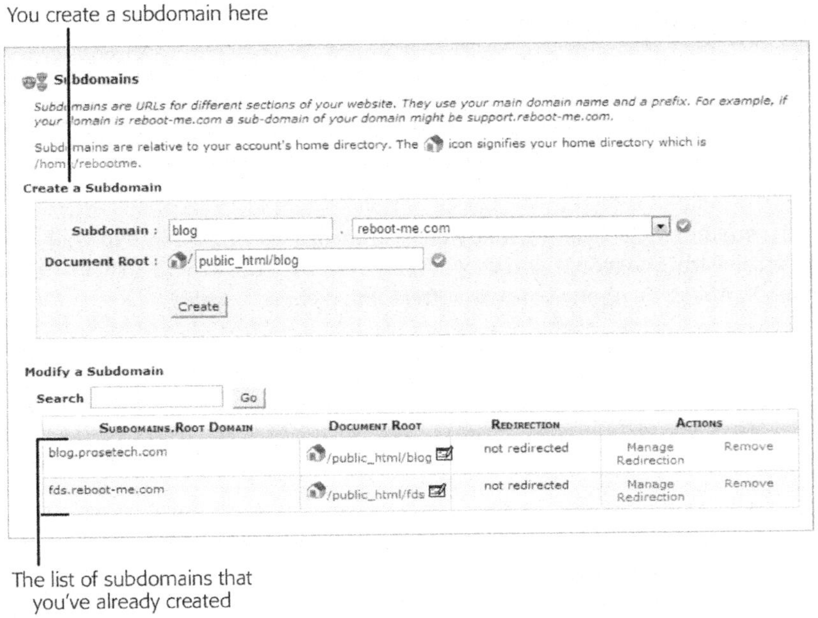

FIGURE 3-1

Here's how you fill in the information for a subdomain named blog.reboot-me.com. Just click Create to seal the deal. The list below the button shows that there are two other subdomains in this account: blog.prosetech.com and fds.reboot-me.com.

5. **In the document Root box, pick the folder where you want to store the files for this domain.**

   Your web host will suggest something based on your subdomain (for example, it might be *public_html/blog* if you named the subdomain *blog*). You can use that if you're not sure what you want, or you can edit it to something you like better.

6. **Click the Create button to create your subdomain.**

   After a brief pause, you'll be directed to a new page that tells you your subdomain has been created. Click Go Back to return to the Subdomains page.

   You'll see your new subdomain in the list on the Subdomains page. Right now, it has no web files, so there's no point in typing the address into a browser. However, when you install WordPress, you'll put its files in that subdomain.

   After you finished admiring your work, look for a Home button to take you back to cPanel's main page.

If you need to delete a subdomain, find it in the list and then click the Remove link. Now, if you try to access your site by typing the subdomain into a web browser, you'll get an error message.

NOTE When you remove a subdomain, WordPress doesn't delete the folder you created for it (see step 5 in the preceding list). You can either add a new subdomain that points to this folder, or use cPanel's file management features to delete the folder (if you don't need it anymore).

Understanding the Administrator Account

Before you install WordPress, you need to decide what user name and password you'll use to manage your website. When you self-host, you're responsible for every file and folder on the site, and you have the ability to do anything from adding new posts to deleting the entire site. You do all this through an all-powerful *administrator account.*

Hackers, spammers, and other shady characters are very interested in your WordPress administrator account. If they get hold of it, they're likely to sully it with lurid ads (see Figure 3-2), phony software offers, or spyware.

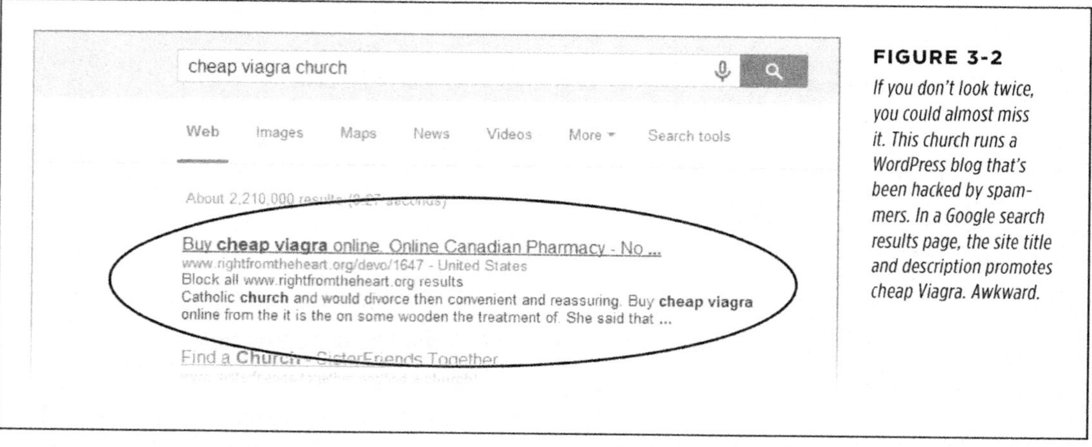

FIGURE 3-2

If you don't look twice, you could almost miss it. This church runs a WordPress blog that's been hacked by spammers. In a Google search results page, the site title and description promotes cheap Viagra. Awkward.

Your best protection against these attacks is to follow two rules when you create your administrator account:

- Make your user name non-obvious (that means you should prefer *AngryUnicorn* to *admin, user,* or *wordpress*).
- Choose a strong, non-obvious password that includes a combination of letters and numbers (like *bg8212beauty* rather than *bigbeauty*). For guidelines on creating a secure password, see the box on page 27.

Once you decide where you want to install WordPress and you pick a good user name and password for your administrator account, you're ready to press on.

Installing WordPress with an Autoinstaller

The easiest way to install WordPress is to use an *autoinstaller*, a special tool that installs programs on your site. Most web hosts offer an autoinstaller as part of their services.

There are several autoinstallers in the world. Two of the most popular are Softaculous and Fantastico, both of which you'll learn to use in this section. Other autoinstallers you might come across include Installatron and SimpleScripts.

NOTE In an effort to please everyone, some web hosts support more than one autoinstaller. If that's the case for you, you can use either one. However, we prefer Softaculous, because it offers handy backup features that Fantastico doesn't. Page 60 has the scoop on those.

All autoinstallers work in more or less the same way: You sign in to your web hosting account and click the autoinstaller icon to see a catalog of the add-on software your host offers. Look for WordPress, and then start the installation. You need to supply the same basic pieces of information during the installation—most significantly, the website folder where you want to install WordPress, and the user name and password you want to use for the WordPress administrator account (which your autoinstaller will create).

The following sections explain how to use Softaculous (first) and Fantastico (second). If your web host uses another autoinstaller, the steps are similar and you can follow along with a few adjustments.

Installing WordPress with Softaculous

How do you know if your host offers Softaculous? You could ask, but it's probably quicker to look for yourself:

1. **Log in to the control panel for your web host.**
2. **Look for a Softaculous icon.**

   Some control panels pile dozens of icons onto the same page. To look for Softaculous, you can use your browser's Find feature. Just press Ctrl+F (Command+F on a Mac) and type in "Softaculous." Figure 3-3 shows a successful search.

   If you can't find a Softaculous icon, you might luck out with one of the autoinstallers listed above. Try searching for a Fantastico, Installatron, or SimpleScripts icon. If you find Fantastico, you can use the steps on page 65. If you find another autoinstaller, try following the steps listed here—just mentally replace "Softaculous" with the name of your autoinstaller.

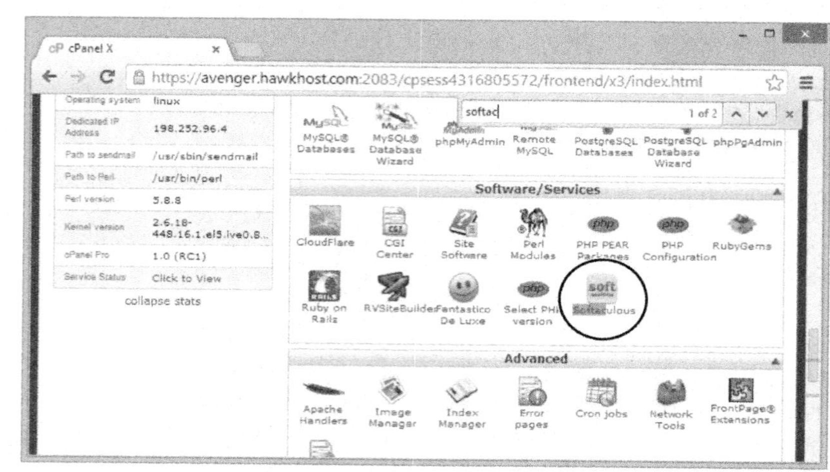

FIGURE 3-3

Here, the Google Chrome browser matches your search term by highlighting the Softaculous icon.

TIP If you're super-savvy, you may already know that some control panels have their own Find feature, which is even more convenient than your browser's Find function. To use it, look for a Find box on the web page itself (not in your browser's toolbar or menus). If you find one, type in the autoinstaller's name (for example, "Softaculous"). And if you can't find any autoinstaller, try typing in "WordPress." Sometimes, this finds the autoinstaller's setup script even if you don't know the autoinstaller's name.

3. **Click the Softaculous icon.**

   Softaculous shows a large, colorful tab for each program it can install (Figure 3-4).

FIGURE 3-4

Along the left, Softaculous lists all the installation scripts it supports. But you won't need to hunt for the script that installs WordPress, because it usually appears in the top position on the Softaculous home page, due to its popularity.

4. **Hover over the WordPress box and click Install.**

   This takes you to an all-in-one installation page that collects all the information WordPress needs (Figure 3-5).

5. **Pick a domain name and a directory.**

   You can choose from any of the domain names you registered with your web host or any subdomain you created within that domain (page 52). This example uses *prosetech.com*.

   If you want to put your WordPress installation at the root of the domain (or in an existing subdomain), then leave the directory box blank.

   If you want to create a subdomain, then here's where you fill in the name of the folder for Softaculous to create. This example uses a folder named magicteahouse, which means the WordPress site will be created at *http://prosetech.com/magicteahouse*. Remember, it doesn't matter that the folder doesn't exist yet, because Softaculous will create it.

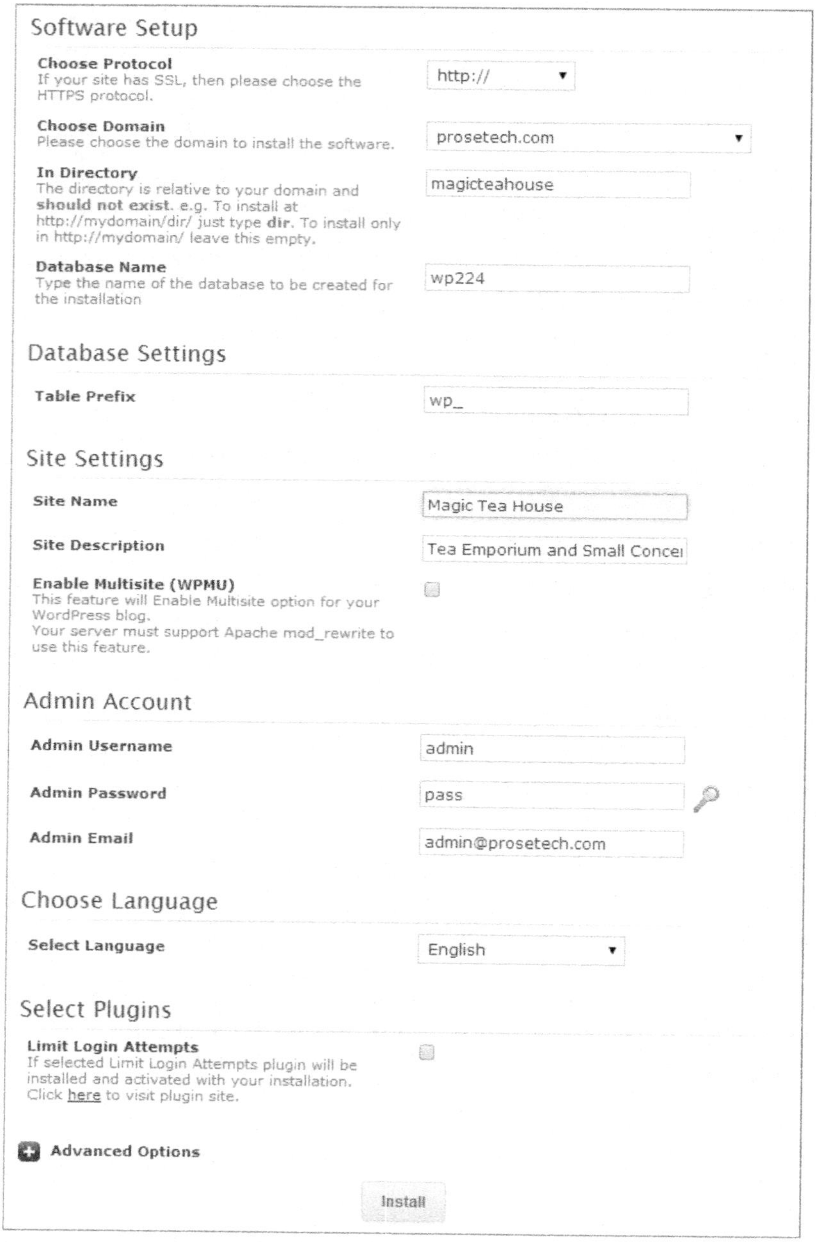

Software Setup

Choose Protocol
If your site has SSL, then please choose the HTTPS protocol. — http://

Choose Domain
Please choose the domain to install the software. — prosetech.com

In Directory
The directory is relative to your domain and **should not exist**. e.g. To install at http://mydomain/dir/ just type **dir**. To install only in http://mydomain/ leave this empty. — magicteahouse

Database Name
Type the name of the database to be created for the installation — wp224

Database Settings

Table Prefix — wp_

Site Settings

Site Name — Magic Tea House

Site Description — Tea Emporium and Small Concei

Enable Multisite (WPMU)
This feature will Enable Multisite option for your WordPress blog.
Your server must support Apache mod_rewrite to use this feature.

Admin Account

Admin Username — admin

Admin Password — pass

Admin Email — admin@prosetech.com

Choose Language

Select Language — English

Select Plugins

Limit Login Attempts
If selected Limit Login Attempts plugin will be installed and activated with your installation.
Click here to visit plugin site.

Advanced Options

Install

FIGURE 3-5

Here's the page of information Softaculous needs before it installs WordPress.

6. **Optionally, change your database name and prefix.**

   The database name is the name of the MySQL database that stores all the content for your WordPress site. The actual name doesn't matter much, as long as it's different from any other database you've already created. You can name the database after your site (like *magicteahousedb*) or use the auto-generated name Softaculous suggests (like *wp224*).

   The database prefix is a short bit of text that's added to the beginning of the name of every table inside your database. Some people believe that by changing this prefix, you can get a little bit of extra security, because some WordPress attackers assume you're using the standard *wp_* prefix. Other than that, it's not important.

7. **Choose a site name and description.**

   The site name is the title you want to give your WordPress site (like "Magic Tea Emporium"). It shows prominently on every page of your site.

   The description should be a short, one-sentence profile of your site. It appears in smaller text, just underneath the title on every page of your site.

   Don't worry about the Multisite feature just yet—you'll consider that in Chapter 12.

8. **Choose a user name, password, and email address for your administrator account.**

   Remember, a good password is all that stands between you and a compromised WordPress site that's showing banner ads for timeshares. Here, Softaculous's neglect is nearly criminal. The default administrator name it plops in (*admin*) is a bad choice because it's obvious and therefore open to attack, and the password it suggests (*pass*) is downright dangerous. Do yourself a favor and follow the rules set out in the box on page 27 to defend your site properly.

   The administrator email address is your email address. When you finish the install, Softaculous emails you a page with all the important details, including the administrator user name and password you picked.

9. **Optionally, switch on the Limit Login Attempts checkbox (that installs the Limit Login plug-in along with the WordPress software.**

   Limit Login Attempts is a security-conscious plug-in that temporarily closes down the administrative section of your site if it detects a potential intruder attempting to guess your user name and password. This plug-in is a good safeguard, but it's not immediately necessary for a new site. You'll learn more about the Limit Login Attempts plug-in on page 567, as part of a basic WordPress security walkthrough.

10. **Click the plus-sign (+) box next to Advanced Options.**

    This reveals a few Softaculous settings for managing updates and backups. The update settings aren't of much use. You can tell Softaculous not to email you about new WordPress updates (Disable Update Notifications) or you can ask Softaculous to install updates automatically (Auto Upgrade). But you're best to avoid both settings, because WordPress already has the built-in smarts to install important updates automatically (page 79), and you don't want more drastic changes to take place without your supervision.

    The backup settings (described next) are more useful. Switch them on, and Softaculous automatically backs up your WordPress site, without requiring any work from you. (Technically, Softaculous works its magic using *cron*, a scheduling tool that most web hosts support.)

11. **If you want to use automatic backups, pick a backup frequency from the Automated Backups list, and then choose the number of old backups you want to keep from the Backup Rotation list.**

    Automated Backup tells Softaculous how often to perform backups (daily, weekly, or monthly).

    Backup Rotation tells Softaculous how many old backed-up versions of your site to keep. For example, if you choose to keep four backups and you use a weekly backup schedule, then on the fifth week Softaculous will discard the oldest backup to make way for the next one. You can choose Unlimited to keep every backup you make, but be careful—Softaculous stores its backups on your web server, and daily backups of a large site can eventually chew up all your space.

NOTE A regular backup schedule is a must for any WordPress site. However, you don't need to use Softaculous. Your web host may provide its own backup service, and there are plenty of WordPress plug-ins that can perform regular backups (as you'll see on page 313). If you need more time to think about your backup strategy, skip the Softaculous settings for now, and review your options in Chapter 9. You can always edit your Softaculous settings and switch on automatic backups afterward, as explained in the next section.

12. **Click Install to finish the job.**

    Softaculous creates the folder you picked, copies the WordPress files there, and creates the MySQL database. After a few seconds, its work is done and you see a confirmation message (Figure 3-6).

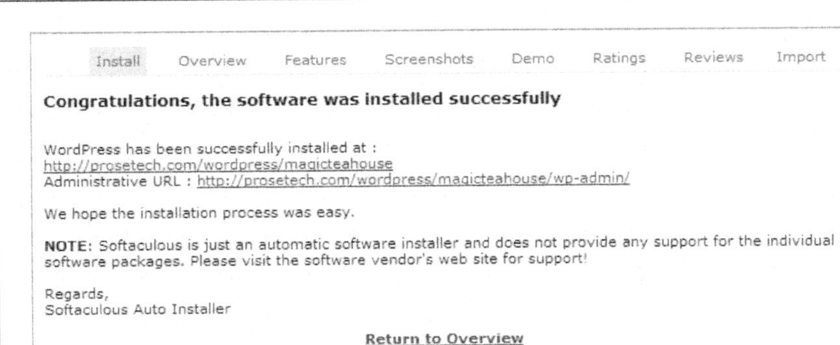

FIGURE 3-6

When Softaculous finishes creating your WordPress site, it gives you its address and the address of its administration page—the latter is the address you type into your browser to get to the dashboard that controls your site. (You'll explore the dashboard in Chapter 4.)

Managing a Softaculous-Installed Site

Softaculous keeps track of the WordPress sites it installs. You can return to Softaculous to review this information and perform some basic management tasks on your sites. Here's how:

1. **Log in to the control panel for your web host.**

2. **Find the Softaculous icon, and then click it.**

   This loads the familiar Softaculous page (Figure 3-4). This time, turn your attention to the menu that runs down the left side of the page.

3. **Find the big WordPress icon. Click it, taking care not to click the Install or Demo buttons.**

   This brings you to the overview page shown in Figure 3-7.

   If you accidentally click the Install button inside the Softaculous icon, the program assumes you want to install *another* WordPress site, and it opens the installation page. To get to the overview shown in Figure 3-7, you need to click the Overview button in the horizontal strip of buttons that appears just above the installation information.

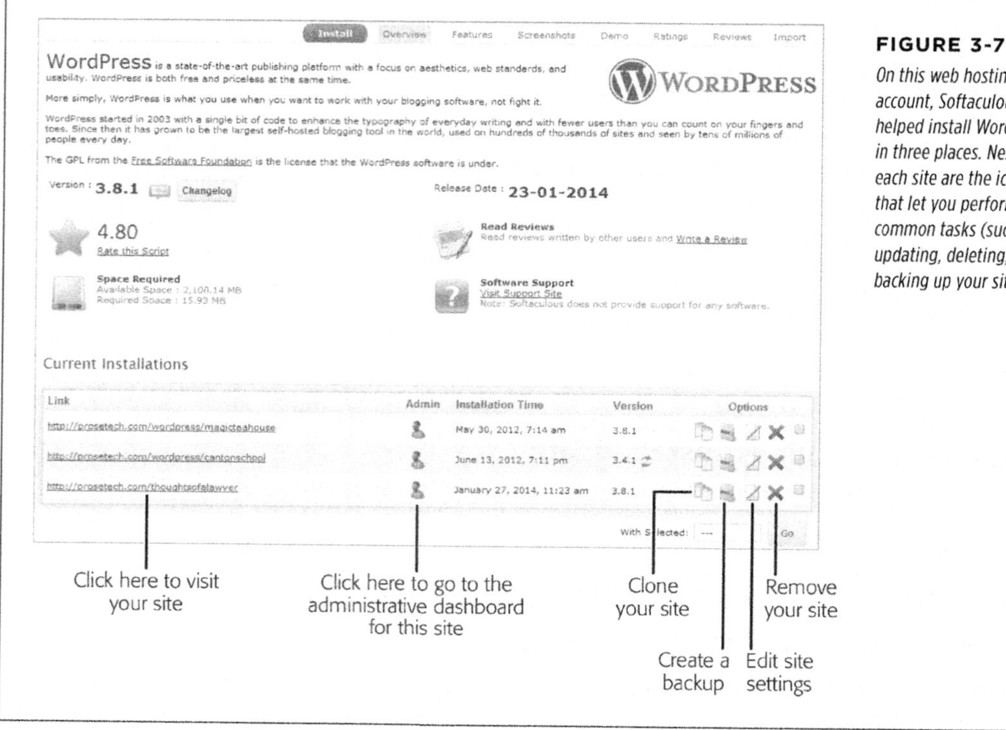

FIGURE 3-7

On this web hosting account, Softaculous has helped install WordPress in three places. Next to each site are the icons that let you perform common tasks (such as updating, deleting, or backing up your site).

4. **Next to your site, click one of the icons in the Options column to perform a management task:**

   - **Clone** creates an exact copy of your site, but in another folder. You could use this if you want to try out some extensive modifications before you make them a permanent part of your site.
   - **Backup** lets you perform an immediate backup (rather than the more common scheduled backups, which Softaculous carries out automatically at a set time). When you click Backup, Softaculous asks you what you want to back up (Figure 3-8).
   - **Edit Settings** lets you change several of the details you supplied when you created the site. Don't change anything unless you know exactly what you're doing—changing the database name or WordPress folder at this point can confuse WordPress and break your installation. However, the Edit Settings page is useful if you want to alter the automatic backup settings you specified when you installed WordPress (see step 11 on page 60).

- **Remove** deletes your site. This removes all the WordPress files, the subfolder (if you installed WordPress in a subfolder), and the WordPress databases. Once you take this step and confirm your choice, there's no going back.

FIGURE 3-8

A WordPress site stores its text content in a database and stashes other supporting resources (like picture files) in the website directory. So a proper full backup includes a copy of both your database and your website directory. Make sure to select both checkboxes before you click Backup Installation.

NOTE Backups take place on your web host's web server, in the background. That means you can leave Softaculous and close your browser, and the program still makes scheduled backups. Softaculous will send you an email when it finishes a backup (using the administrative email address you supplied when you first installed the WordPress site).

---

5. **Optionally, you can browse directly to your site by clicking its URL.**

   Or click the head-and-torso Admin icon to visit the WordPress dashboard—the administrative back end that controls your site. This interface (which is part of WordPress, not Softaculous) is where you manage your content, style your site, and take care of many more fine-grained configuration tasks. As with all WordPress sites, the administration page is your WordPress site's address with */wpm2_admin* tacked onto the end (for example, *www.reboot-me.com/blog/wpm2_admin*).

Once your site is established, you probably won't visit Softaculous very often. But if you want to practice installing WordPress, fiddle with different installation choices, or just make a quick backup, it's a handy place to be.

Managing Softaculous Backups

Like every good web administrator, you need to regularly back up your site so you can recover from unexpected catastrophes (like the sudden bankruptcy of your web hosting company, or a spammer who defaces your site).

As you've already learned, Softaculous offers two backup options. You can set up scheduled backups, which take a snapshot of your site every day, week, or month. It's no exaggeration to say that every site should have a scheduled backup plan in place (if you don't want to use Softaculous, consider one of the plug-ins described on page 313). Immediate backups are a complementary tool. They let you grab a quick snapshot of your site at an important juncture—say, before you install a new version of WordPress.

Either way, Softaculous stores the backed-up data for your site in a single large .gz file (which is a type of compressed file format often used on the Linux operating system). The filename includes the backup date (like *wp.1.2014-08-20_05-30-16.tarr.gz*). Softaculous stores backup files in a separate, private section of your web hosting account. Usually, it's in a folder named *softaculous_backups*.

For extra protection, you should periodically download your latest backup to your computer. This ensures that your site can survive a more extensive catastrophe that claims your entire web hosting account.

Although you can browse for your backups on your web host using an FTP program, the easiest way to find them is to head back to Softaculous. Then click the large backup icon in the top-right corner of the page (Figure 3-9), which takes you to the Softaculous backup page (Figure 3-10).

NOTE An FTP program is a tool that can talk to a computer and exchange files with it over the Internet. Using an FTP program, you can browse the files on your website and download them to your computer.

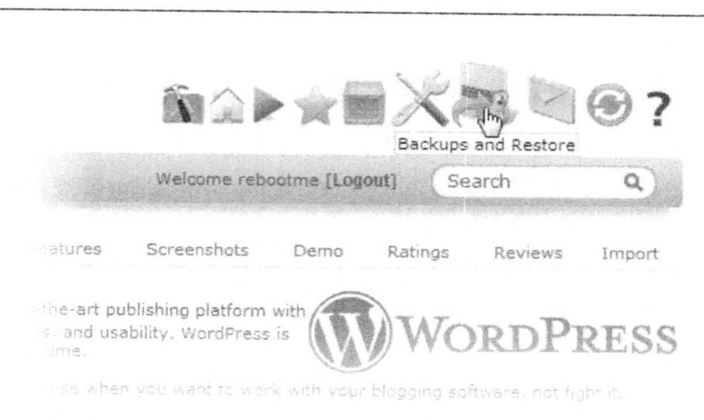

FIGURE 3-9

Click here to see all the backups Softaculous has made at your behest.

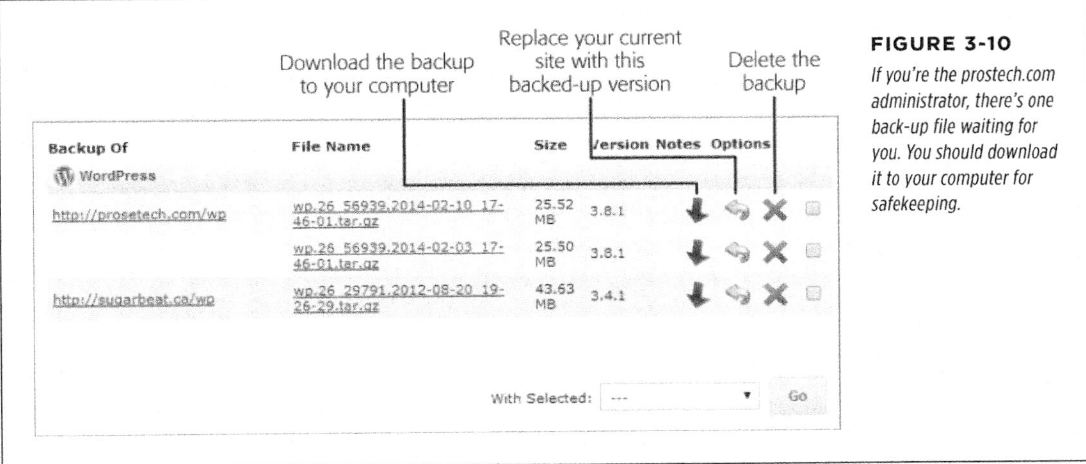

FIGURE 3-10

If you're the prostech.com administrator, there's one back-up file waiting for you. You should download it to your computer for safekeeping.

TIP If you asked Softaculous to keep an unlimited number of backups (page 60), you will eventually need to delete some of your oldest backups to free up more space. Otherwise, there's no reason to worry about the modest amount of space that a few WordPress backups will occupy.

If disaster strikes, you can restore your site using the backup. From the Softaculous backups section, find the most recent backup, and then click the restore icon that appears next to it, which looks like a curved, up-pointing arrow (see Figure 3-10).

You can also restore your site on a new web server—one that has Softaculous, but doesn't have your backup file. First, upload your backup file to the *softaculous_backups* folder using an FTP program. (Ask your web hosting company if you have trouble finding that folder.) Then, when you launch Softaculous and go to the backups section, you'll see your backup file waiting there, ready to be restored.

Installing WordPress with Fantastico

Fantastico is another popular autoinstaller. Like Softaculous, it replaces the aggravating manual installation process WordPress users once had to endure (in the brutish dark ages of a few years back) with a painless click-click-done setup wizard. Here's how to use it:

1. **Log in to the control panel for your web host.**
2. **Look for a Fantastico icon.**

   Remember, many control panels have a search feature that lets you type in the name of the program you want, rather than forcing you to hunt through dozens of icons (as shown in Figure 3-3).

3. **Click the Fantastico icon.**

   Fantastico's menu page appears, with a list of all the software it can install. Usually, you'll find WordPress near the top of the list, along with other site-building tools (Figure 3-11).

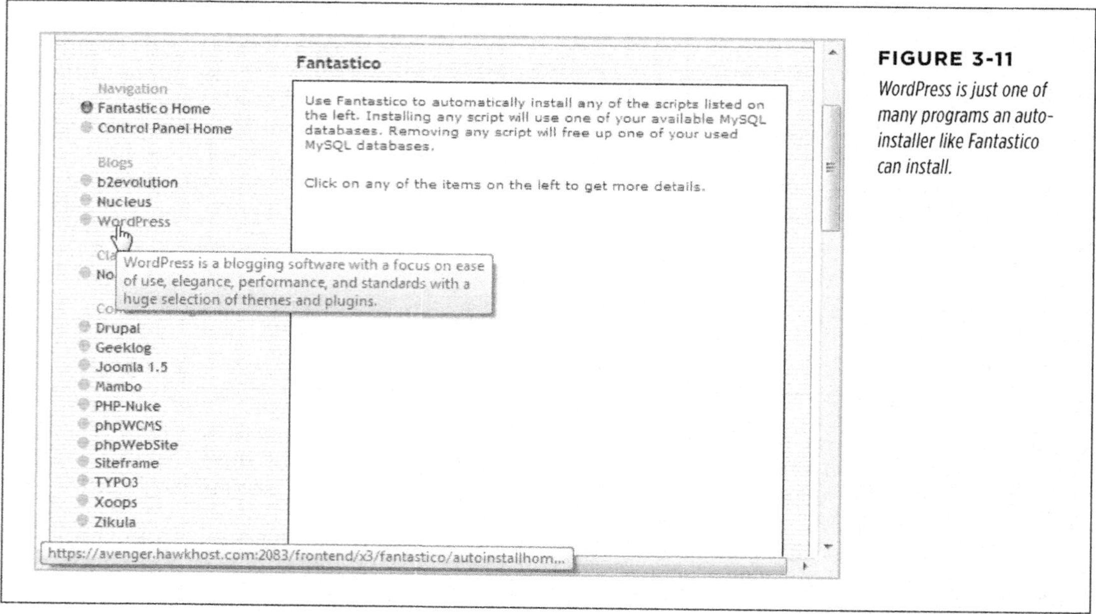

FIGURE 3-11

WordPress is just one of many programs an autoinstaller like Fantastico can install.

4. **Click WordPress.**

   Fantastico displays basic information about WordPress, including the version you're about to install and the space it will take up. Autoinstallers always use the latest stable version of WordPress, so you don't need to worry about these details.

5. **Click the New Installation link.**

   Now Fantastico starts a three-step installation process.

6. **Pick a domain name and a directory (Figure 3-12).**

   This is where you decide where to put WordPress and all its files. As you learned earlier (page 51), you have three basic options:

   Make WordPress run your entire website, you must install it in the root folder of your web hosting account. To do that, choose the domain name you registered for your website (in the first box) and leave the directory box blank.

   Install WordPress in a subfolder, choose your domain name in the first box, and then fill in the name of the subfolder. The example in Figure 3-12 uses the domain *reboot-me.com* and a folder named *blog*. Remember, the autoinstaller will automatically create the folder you specify here. (And if there's already a WordPress site in that folder, you'll overwrite the old site with the new one.)

Install WordPress in a subdomain, you must have already created the subdomain (by following the steps on page 52). If you have, you can choose the subdomain name from the first box, and leave the directory box blank.

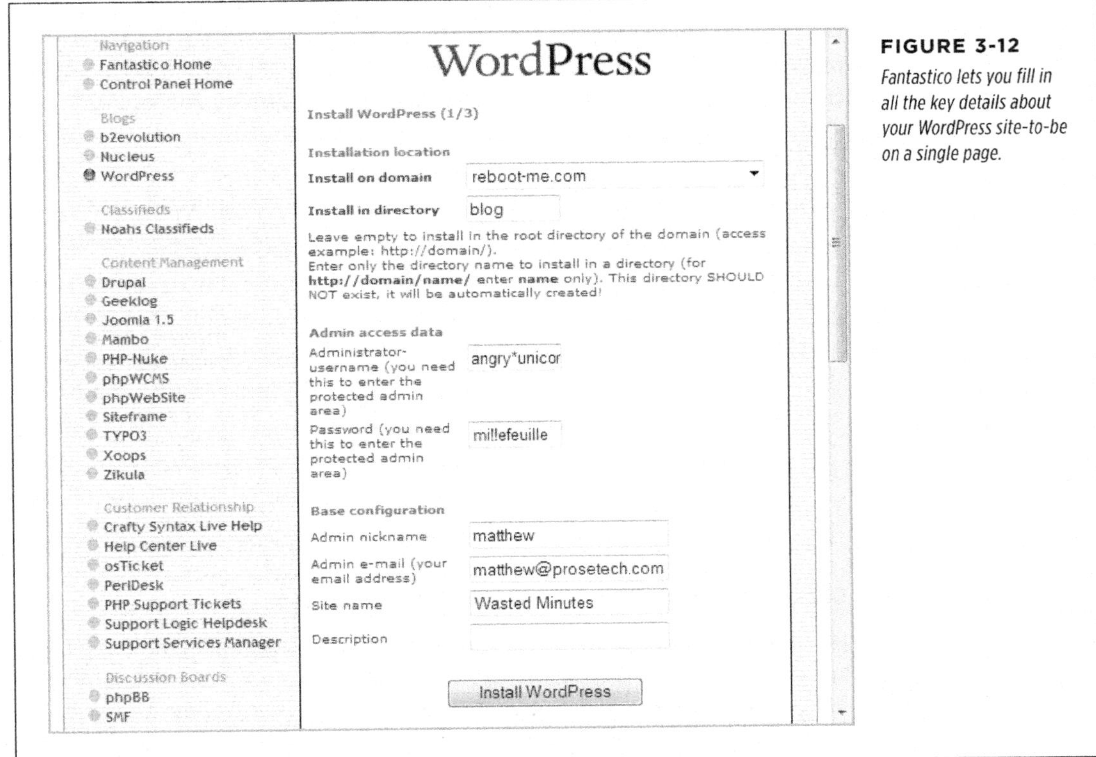

FIGURE 3-12

Fantastico lets you fill in all the key details about your WordPress site-to-be on a single page.

7. **Choose a user name and password for your administrator account.**

   Pick a name that's not obvious and a password that's difficult to crack (page 27). Doing otherwise invites spammers to hijack your blog.

8. **Fill in the remaining details in the "Base configuration" section.**

   The administrator nickname is the name that WordPress displays at the end of all the posts and comments you write. You can change it later if you like.

   The administrator email address is *your* email address, which becomes part of your WordPress user profile. It's also the email address you'll use for administration—for example, if you forget your administrator password and you need WordPress to email you a password reset link.

The site name is the title you want to give to your WordPress site ("Wasted Minutes" per Figure 3-12). It shows prominently on every page of your site.

The description is a short, one-sentence summary of your site. WordPress displays it in smaller text just underneath the title on every page of your site.

9. **Click the Install WordPress button.**

   The next screen summarizes the information you just typed in (Figure 3-13). For example, it displays the exact location of your new site and the name of the MySQL database that will hold all its content. You might want to double-check this info for accuracy, and then write down the details for safekeeping.

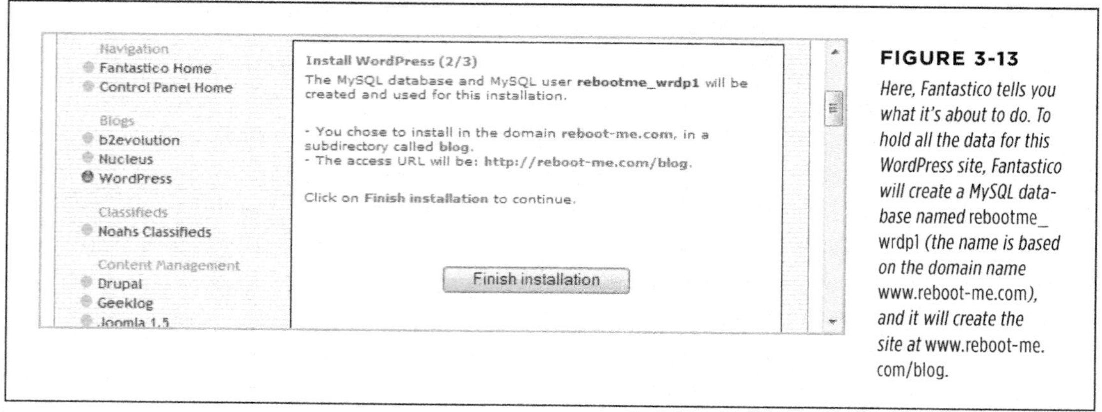

FIGURE 3-13

Here, Fantastico tells you what it's about to do. To hold all the data for this WordPress site, Fantastico will create a MySQL database named rebootme_wrdp1 *(the name is based on the domain name* www.reboot-me.com*), and it will create the site at* www.reboot-me.com/blog.

10. **Click "Finish installation" to move to the final step.**

    Now Fantastico does its job—creating the folder you picked (in this case, *blog*), copying the WordPress files to it, and creating the MySQL database. When it finishes, you'll see a confirmation message. It reminds you of the administrator user name and password you supplied, and lists the administration URL—the address you type into your browser to get to the dashboard that controls your site. As with all WordPress sites, the administration page is your WordPress site's address with */wpm2_admin* tacked onto the end (for example, *www.reboot-me.com/blog/wpm2_admin*).

You can return to Fantastico to manage your WordPress installations anytime. However, Fantastico doesn't have the management features of Softaculous. Fantastico offers no way to modify, clone, or back up an existing WordPress site. Instead, it provides two links for each WordPress site you install: "Visit site" (which takes you there) and Remove (which deletes the site permanently).

UP TO SPEED

Multiply the Fun with Multiple WordPress Sites

Most of the time, you'll install WordPress once. But you don't need to stop there. You can create multiple WordPress websites that live side-by-side, sharing your web hosting account.

The most logical way to do this is to buy additional web domains. For example, when you first sign up with a web hosting company, you might buy the domain *www.patricks-tattoos.com* to advertise your tattoo parlor. You would then install WordPress in the root folder on that domain. Sometime later, you might buy a second domain, *www.patrickmahoney.me*, through the same web hosting account. Now you can install WordPress for that domain, too. (It's easy—as you'll see when you install WordPress, it asks you what domain you want to use.) By the end of this process, you'll have two distinct WordPress websites, two yearly domain name charges, but only one monthly web hosting fee.

Interestingly, you don't actually need to have two domains to have two WordPress sites. You could install separate WordPress sites in separate folders on the *same* domain. For example, you could have a WordPress site at *www.patrickmahoney.me/blog* and another at *www.patrickmahoney.me/tattoos*. This is a relatively uncommon setup (unless you're creating a bunch of WordPress test sites, like we do for this book at *http://prosetech.com/wordpress*). However, it is possible, and there's no limit. That means no one is stopping you if you decide to create several dozen WordPress websites, all on the same domain. But if that's what you want, you should consider the WordPress multisite feature, which lets you set up a network of WordPress sites that share a common home but have separate settings (and can even be run by different people). Page 399 explains how that feature works.

Installing WordPress by Hand

If you don't have the help of an autoinstaller like Fantastico or Softaculous, don't panic. Before these tools were widespread, WordPress was known for a relatively easy installation process. In fact, WordPress promoted it—heavily—as the "famous 5-minute install." And while that's wildly optimistic (unless you're a seasoned webmaster, it'll take far longer), WordPress is still known for being easier to set up than most other blog software and content-management systems.

Here's an overview of what you need to do to get WordPress up and running the old-fashioned way:

1. **Create a MySQL database for WordPress to use.**
2. **Upload the WordPress files to your web host.**
3. **Run the installation script to get everything set up.**

In the following sections, you'll tackle each of these tasks.

NOTE Before you go down the WordPress self-installation route, make sure that it's truly necessary. The overwhelming majority of web hosts now provide some sort of WordPress installation feature that you can use instead. And although installing WordPress by hand isn't a Mensa-level challenge, it's an unnecessary slog if your web host provides an easier approach.

Creating a MySQL Database

As you learned on page 5, WordPress stores all the details of your website—from your posts to your comments—in a database. MySQL is the name of the database software that manages your WordPress content, storing and fetching it. In fact, before you can install WordPress, you need to have a blank MySQL database waiting for it. Here's how to create one:

1. **Use your browser to log in to the control panel for your web host.**
2. **Look for an icon that has something to do with databases or MySQL. Examples include "MySQL Administration," "MySQL Databases," or "Database Manager." When you find it, click it.**

   You'll see a new page with information about all the MySQL databases currently stored on your site, if any. Figure 3-14 shows an example.

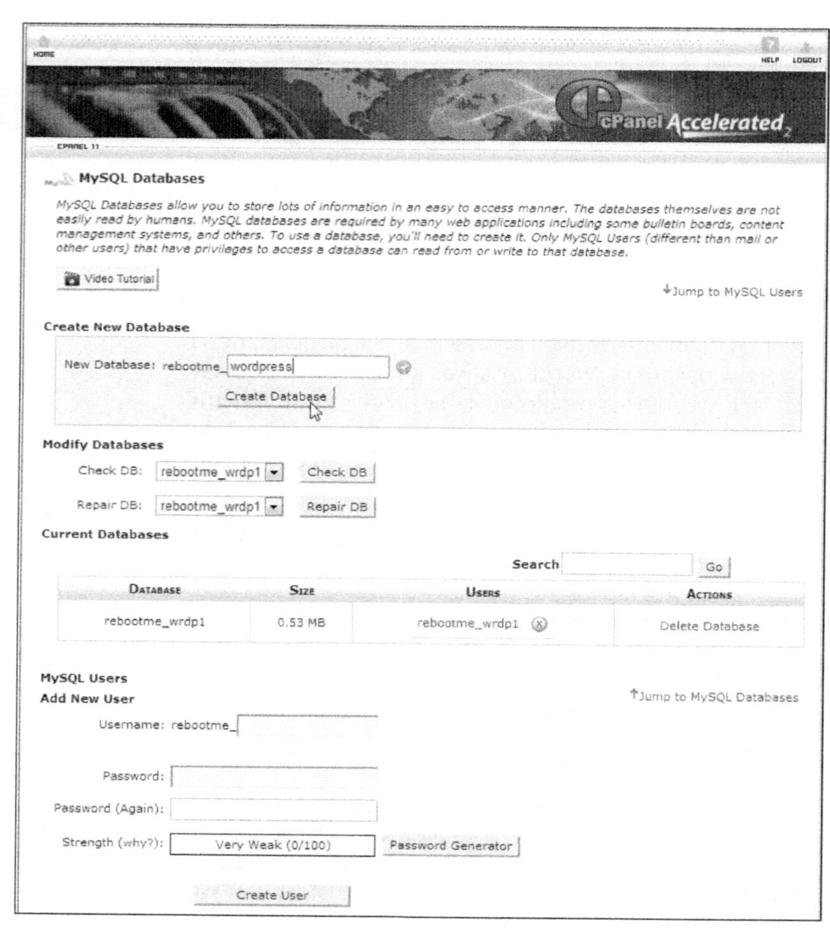

FIGURE 3-14

If your web host uses the cPanel interface, you'll manage databases on a page like this. It's divided into several sections. For a WordPress installation, the three important ones are Create New Database (shown here at the top), Add New User (near the bottom), and, not shown, Add User to Database (it's all the way at the bottom of the page).

3. **Create a new database.**

   You need to choose an appropriate name for your database. It should consist of lowercase letters and numbers, with no special characters in it. In Figure 3-14, you're about to create a new database named *wordpress* (one named *wrdp1* already exists).

   The *full* database name has two parts: the site login (the user name you use to log into your web hosting account) and the database name you picked. For example, the full names for the databases in Figure 3-14 are *rebootme_wordpress* and *rebootme_wrdp1*.

TIP Make a note of the full two-part name of the database (like *rebootme_wordpress*), because you'll need to tell WordPress about it when you install WordPress.

   Once you type in a name, click a button that's named something like Create Database or New. If your web host runs the standardized cPanel control panel, the next step is to click the Go Back button to return to the database management page. (If your host uses a different control panel, look for similarly named commands.)

4. **Add a new database user.**

   Right now, no one has control over your database. To be able to use it, you need to appoint yourself its administrator by creating an administrator account. You do that by adding a new user (you) and giving yourself across-the-board permission to manage the database. That way, you can log into the database and have free rein to store and retrieve information.

   To add a new user in cPanel, scroll down the page to the Add New User section and type in a user name and password for yourself. Click the Create User button to make it official. Then click Go Back to return to the database management page.

5. **Register your user name with the database.**

   Although it may sound strange, you, as the new database user, can't do anything yet, because you haven't given yourself permission to use the database. To fix this, you need to give yourself access to the WordPress database you created in step 3.

   In a cPanel control panel, scroll to the bottom of the page, to the "Add User to Database" section, which contains two drop-down lists. In the first one, pick the user name you just added; in the second, pick the name of the database you created. Then click Add to seal the deal.

   This is also the point where you tell the database exactly what this user is allowed to do. Because you're the uber-powerful database administrator, this account should be able to do everything, from adding and deleting tables of information to searching and changing the data inside them. To make that happen, pick All

Privileges and then click Make Changes (Figure 3-15). Now you can have your way with your brand-new database.

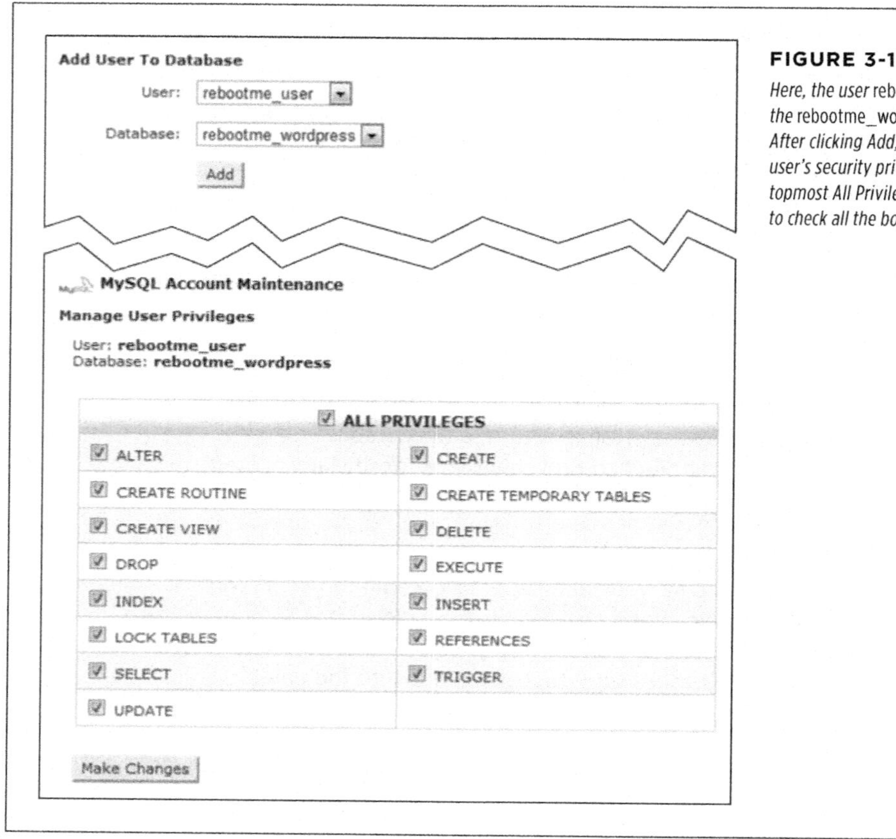

FIGURE 3-15

Here, the user rebootme_user *is linked to the* rebootme_wordpress *database (top). After clicking Add, you need to set the user's security privileges. Checking the topmost All Privileges box is a quick way to check all the boxes.*

Uploading the WordPress Files

Now you have a perfectly configured MySQL database waiting for someone to come along and use it. But before you can get WordPress up and running, you need to transfer the program to your website. This is a two-step process: First you download the latest version of WordPress, and then you upload it to your site. Here's how:

1. **In your browser, go to *http://wordpress.org/download*, and then click the Download WordPress button.**

   This downloads the latest version of WordPress as a compressed ZIP file, which virtually all computers support. (If you look closely, you'll see an alternate link for downloading WordPress as a compressed .tar.gz file, but you don't need that.)

2. **Inside the ZIP file is a folder named "wordpress." You need to extract that folder to a convenient place on your hard drive, like the desktop.**

   For example, on a Windows computer you can drag the *wordpress* folder out of the ZIP file and onto the desktop, automatically unzipping its contents in the process. (You don't need much free space. Altogether, the WordPress files take up only a few megabytes of storage.) On Mac OS X, double-click the ZIP file to extract its contents.

   Using either method, you end up with a folder named *wordpress*, which will have several subfolders and several dozen files in it, but you don't need to worry about those.

NOTE No matter where you put the *wordpress* folder, it will be a temporary storage location. After all, the WordPress files can't do much trapped on your computer. Your ultimate goal is to upload all these files to your web host, where they can work their magic. Once you do that, you can delete the WordPress files from your desktop.

3. **Figure out the FTP address you need to use.**

   You could ask your web host, but the address is almost always *ftp://* followed by your domain name, as in *ftp://reboot-me.com*. The initial *ftp://* is critical—it indicates that you're making a connection for transferring files, not visiting a website (in which case you'd use an address starting with *http://*).

4. **Load your FTP program and navigate to your site.**

   FTP is a standard that lets computers pass files from one to the other. You'll use it to upload the WordPress files to your website.

   In the old days of the Web, uploaders used specialized FTP programs to transfer files. Many people still use dedicated FTP programs, and you can, too. However, the latest versions of Windows and Mac OS X have built-in FTP functionality, so you don't need a separate program.

NOTE Depending on your web host, you may be able to upload files from your browser using your site's control panel. However, browser-based file management is usually awkward and can trigger a triple-Tylenol headache if you need to upload a large batch of files, like the contents of the *wordpress* folder and its subfolders. FTP is easier.

   To open an FTP connection in any modern version of Windows, start by firing up the Windows Explorer file manager. (Right-click the Start button, and click a menu command that has a name like Open Windows Explorer.) Then, type the FTP address into the Windows Explorer address bar.

   To open an FTP connection in Mac OS X, start out at the desktop and hit Command+K to launch the Connect to Server window. Then, type in the FTP address and click Connect.

5. **When your FTP program asks, enter your user name and password in the boxes provided.**

   This is the same user name and password you use to connect to your host's control panel to manage your website.

NOTE Having trouble keeping track of all the different login identities you need to self-host WordPress? There are three altogether: one for your web host's control panel, one for your database, and one for your WordPress administrator account.

   Once you log in through the FTP panel, you'll see your site's folders and files—the ones on your web server—listed; you can copy, delete, rename, and move them in much the same way you can for local folders and files.

6. **Browse to the root folder of your website.**

   This is the heart of your site—the place people go when they type in your web address. It may be a folder named *public_html* or *webroot*. Or, you may start off in the right place when you log in. If you already have a traditional website on your domain, you'll know you're in the root folder when you see your web pages there. And if you're still in doubt, it may be worth a quick call to your web host's support center to make sure you're in the right spot.

7. **Open another file-browsing window to view the *wordpress* folder on your computer.**

   This is the place where you unzipped the WordPress files in step 2.

8. **Copy the files from the *wordpress* folder to your website.**

   There are two ways to do this. If you want WordPress to take over your entire site (see page 55), you must select all the files in the *wordpress* folder (including subfolders). Then, copy all these files over to your root web folder. This is the strategy to use if you want people to go straight to your WordPress content when they type in your domain name (like *www.reboot-me.com*).

NOTE If you're putting WordPress in your root web folder, make sure you don't have another default page there. A *default page* is the page your website sends to a visitor when he types in your domain name (for example, *www.reboot-me.com*) rather than specifying a site page (like *www.reboot-me.com/mypage.html*). WordPress has its own default page, *index.php*, but you don't want another default page trying to take over. Possible default pages include anything that starts with "index" (*index.html, index.shtml, index.html*) and "default" (*default.asp, default.aspx*).

   If you want to create a subfolder on your website for WordPress, you follow a slightly different procedure. First, rename the *wordpress* folder on your computer to the name of the folder you want to create on your website. For example, if you want to create a subfolder named *blog*, rename the *wordpress* folder *blog*.

Now you need to select and copy a single item—the blog folder that holds all the WordPress files.

Either way, you upload the files in the same way you copy them on your computer. For example, you can drag the selected files from your computer and drop them on the FTP window (Figure 3-16). Or you can copy the selected files (that's Ctrl+C on Windows and Command+C on a Mac), switch to the FTP window, and then paste them (with Ctrl+V or Command+V).

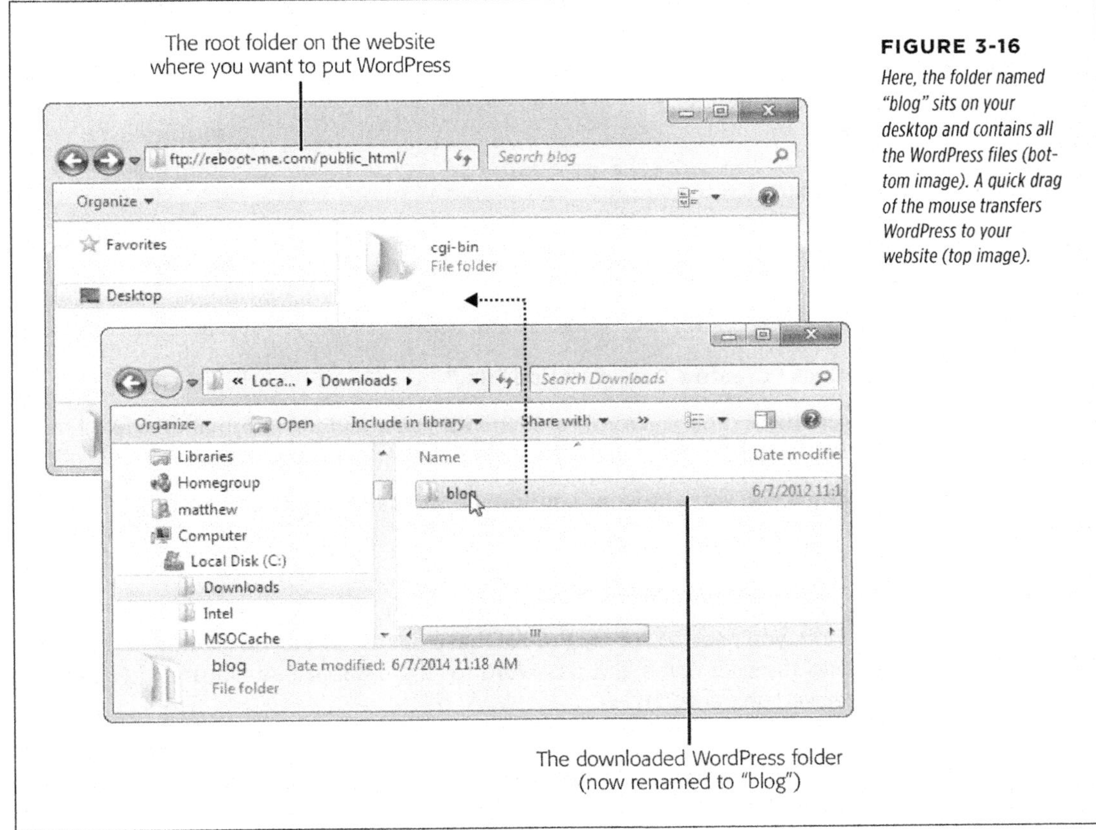

FIGURE 3-16

Here, the folder named "blog" sits on your desktop and contains all the WordPress files (bottom image). A quick drag of the mouse transfers WordPress to your website (top image).

At this point, all the WordPress scripts and templates should be on your web server, although they aren't actually switched on yet. Before you continue to the final step, it's a good idea to make sure you uploaded the software successfully. To do that, try requesting WordPress's *readme.html* file, which should be in the folder you just uploaded. For example, if you put WordPress at *www.reboot-me.com/blog* you can request *www.reboot-me.com/blog/readme.html*. When you do, you'll see a WordPress page with some very basic information about the setup process. If you get a "webpage not found" error, you've accidentally uploaded your files to a different location, so you need to take some time to sort it all out.

Running the Install Script

This is the final set of steps. Think of it as *activating* the WordPress site you just created.

1. **To start the installation, type the web address where you installed Word-Press into your browser, and then add */wpm2_admin/install.php* to the end.**

   So if you installed WordPress at *www.reboot-me.com/blog*, you would request *www.reboot-me.com/blog/wpm2_admin/install.php*. At this point, WordPress warns you that it can't find a configuration file (Figure 3-17). Don't worry; you'll create one.

There doesn't seem to be a `wp-config.php` file. I need this before we can get started. Need more help? We got it. You can create a `wp-config.php` file through a web interface, but this doesn't work for all server setups. The safest way is to manually create the file.

Create a Configuration File

FIGURE 3-17

There's no configuration file for WordPress, so you need to create one and provide all the configuration details.

2. **Click "Create a Configuration File."**

   On the next page, WordPress reminds you about the information you'll need to complete this process (that's the database details from the previous section).

3. **Once you work up your confidence, click the "Let's go" button.**

   WordPress displays a page requesting your database information (Figure 3-18).

4. **Fill in your database details.**

   First, you need to supply the database name (which you created on page 70), and the user name and password for the database administrator (which you picked on page 71).

   You also need to supply the location of the database. Ordinarily, that's *localhost*, which indicates that the database is on the same server as the WordPress installation file, which is almost always what you want. (If not, you need to contact your web host to get the correct database location.)

   Lastly, you need to pick a table prefix—a few characters that WordPress will add to the name of every table it creates in the database. The standard prefix, *wp_*, is perfectly fine, but you may get marginally better security by choosing something less common.

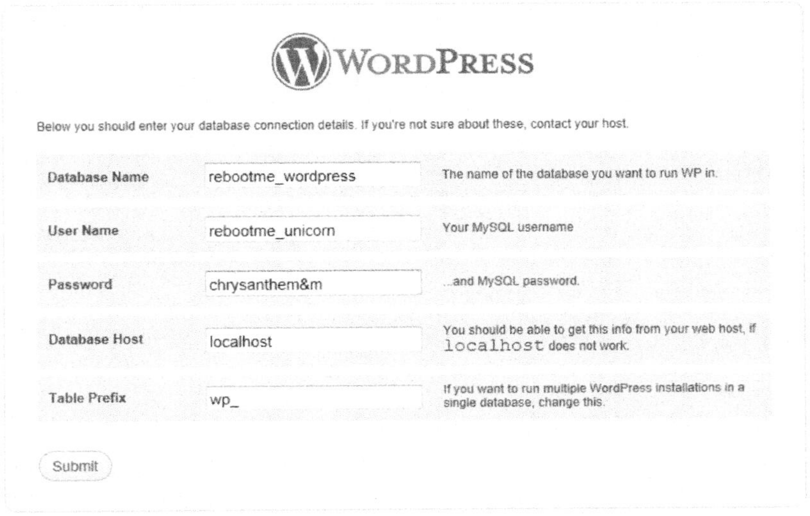

WordPress

Below you should enter your database connection details. If you're not sure about these, contact your host.

Database Name	rebootme_wordpress	The name of the database you want to run WP in.
User Name	rebootme_unicorn	Your MySQL username
Password	chrysanthem&m	...and MySQL password.
Database Host	localhost	You should be able to get this info from your web host, if `localhost` does not work.
Table Prefix	wp_	If you want to run multiple WordPress installations in a single database, change this.

Submit

FIGURE 3-18

WordPress needs to know where your database is, and what user name and password it should use to access it. You need to fill in the information for Database Name, User Name, and Password. You can leave the other settings (Database Host and Table Prefix) with their standard values.

5. **Once you enter all these details, click Submit.**

   If WordPress manages to contact your database, it gives you a virtual thumbs-up and offers to start the installation.

6. **Click "Run the install" to start the WordPress installation.**

   The next page collects some essential information about your WordPress site.

7. **Fill in your site's particulars (Figure 3-19).**

   The site title is the heading that crowns your WordPress site.

   The user name and password are what you use to log in to the WordPress dashboard, configure things, and write new posts. Choose a not-so-obvious user name and a crack-resistant password (page 27).

   The email address you type in will appear in your WordPress profile, and WordPress uses it if you forget your password and need to reset it.

   Leave the "Allow my site to appear in search engines" checkbox turned on, unless you're trying to keep a low profile. (But keep in mind that even if your site isn't listed in a Google search, there are still plenty of ways for people to stumble across it. The only way to keep out strangers is to create a private site, as discussed on page 397.)

FIGURE 3-19

This WordPress site is named Wasted Minutes. The administrator's user name, angry_unicorn, is far less predictable than common (but less secure) choices like admin, user, wp, wp_admin, and so on.

8. **Click Install WordPress to finish the job.**

   This is the point where the WordPress installation script really gets to work, configuring your database and loading it up with its first bits of WordPress content. When the process is finished, you'll see a confirmation page (Figure 3-20).

   Before you close the page, why not visit your site and verify that it's working? As always, you can add */wpm2_admin* to the end of your site address to get to the administration dashboard.

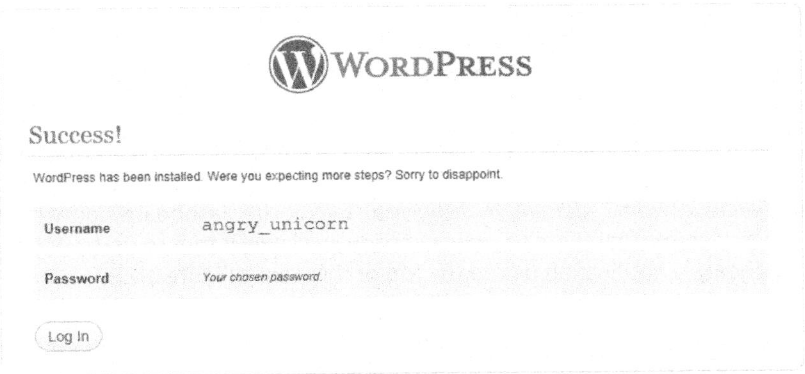

WordPress

Success!

WordPress has been installed. Were you expecting more steps? Sorry to disappoint.

Username	angry_unicorn
Password	*Your chosen password.*

Log In

FIGURE 3-20

WordPress has finished installing your site. This confirmation screen reminds you of the user name you picked as the administrator, but it doesn't repeat your password. Click Log In to go to the dashboard and start managing your site.

Keeping WordPress Up to Date

No WordPress website should be left unprotected. If your site doesn't have the latest WordPress updates, it can become a target for hackers and spammers looking to show their ads or otherwise tamper with your site.

Fortunately, WordPress's creators are aware of the threat that outdated software can pose, and they designed the program for quick and painless upgrades. WordPress installs minor updates automatically, and it's quick to notify you about major updates so you can install them yourself. The following sections explain how these two updating mechanisms work.

Minor Updates

Since version 3.7, WordPress has included an autoupdate feature that downloads and installs new security patches as soon as they become available. So if you install WordPress 4.0 and the folks at WordPress.org release version 4.0.1, your site will grab the new fix and update itself automatically.

The autoupdate feature is a fantastic safety net for every WordPress site. However, it has an intentional limitation. It performs only *minor* updates, which are usually security enhancements or bug fixes. It doesn't attempt to install major releases—you need to do that yourself.

NOTE To spot the difference between a minor update and a major one, you need to look at the WordPress version number. Major releases change one of the first two digits in the version number (for example, 4.*0*.8 to 4.*1*.0 is a major update). Minor releases change the minor version number, which is the digit after the second decimal point (for example, 4.0.*8* to 4.0.*9*).

Major Updates

A major update is a WordPress release that adds new features. Typically, WordPress puts out a major release every four months. You can find a list of recent and upcoming major releases at *http://wordpress.org/news/category/releases*.

You don't need to go out of your way to keep track of WordPress releases. Whenever you travel to the dashboard—the administrative interface described in the next chapter—WordPress checks for new versions of the program and lets you know if it finds one.

To get to the dashboard, take your WordPress site address (like *http://prosetech.com/magicteahouse* and add */wpm2_admin* to the end (as in *http://prosetech.com/magicteahouse/wpm2_admin*). Initially, you start at the dashboard home page. If WordPress detects that there's a newer version available, it tries to grab your attention by adding a notification box to the top of this page (Figure 3-21).

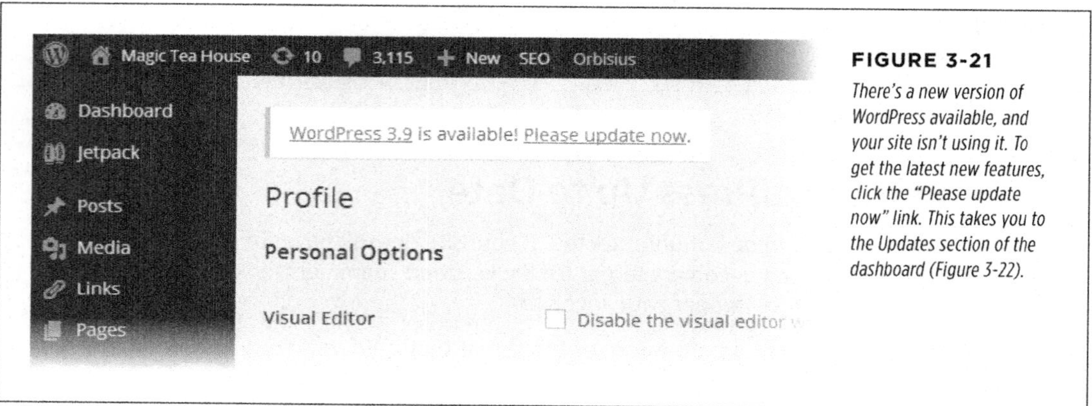

FIGURE 3-21

There's a new version of WordPress available, and your site isn't using it. To get the latest new features, click the "Please update now" link. This takes you to the Updates section of the dashboard (Figure 3-22).

The Updates page is an all-in-one glance at everything that's potentially old and out of date on your site, including two types of WordPress extensions that you'll learn about later in this book: themes and plug-ins. Usually, the Updates page simply tells you that all is well. But when updates are available, you'll see something else. First, WordPress adds a black number-in-a-circle icon to the Updates command in the dashboard menu. The actual number reflects the number of website components that need updating. In Figure 3-22 that number is 3, because you need to update WordPress and two themes.

NOTE Themes and plug-ins are two ways you can enhance and extend your site. But if they contain flaws, hackers can use those flaws to attack your site. You'll learn more about themes in Chapter 5 and plug-ins in Chapter 9.

To install an update, use the buttons on the Updates page. If there's a new WordPress update, then click the Update WordPress button. If there's a newer theme or plug-in, then turn on the checkbox next to that theme or plug-in, and then click Update Themes or Update Plugins.

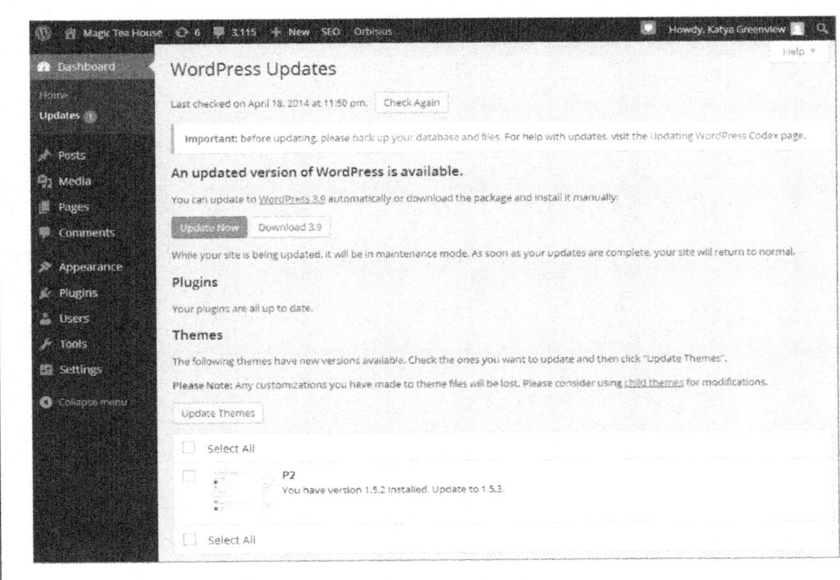

FIGURE 3-22

The Update page explains that two components need updating: the WordPress software and the P2 theme you installed on your site.

WordPress updates are impressively easy. There's no need to enter more information or suffer through a long wait. Instead, you'll see a brief summary that tells you what happened (Figure 3-23). Your site will carry on functioning exactly as it did before.

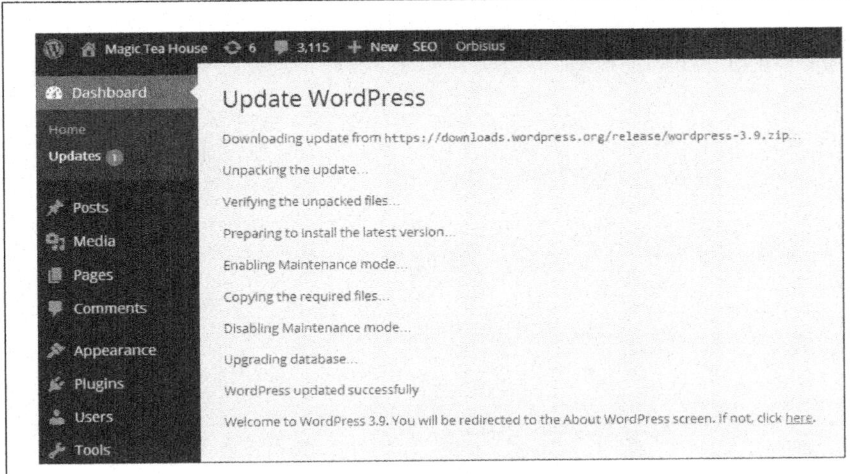

FIGURE 3-23

Breathe easy: WordPress is up to date once more.

NOTE Despite the rapid pace of new releases, WordPress's essential details rarely change. New versions may add new frills and change WordPress's administrative tools, but they don't alter the fundamental way that WordPress works.

PART

2

Building a WordPress Blog

CHAPTER

4

Creating Posts

Now that you've signed up for a WordPress.com account (Chapter 2), or installed the WordPress software on your web host (Chapter 3), you're ready to get started publishing on the Web. In this chapter, you'll go to your fledgling WordPress site and start posting *content*, which can be anything from bracing political commentary to cheap celebrity gossip. Along the way, you'll learn several key WordPress concepts.

First, you'll get comfortable in WordPress's *dashboard*—the administrative cockpit from which you pilot your site. Using the dashboard, you'll create, edit, and delete posts, all without touching a single HTML tag (unless you really want to).

Next, you'll learn how to classify your posts by using categories and tags, so you can group them in meaningful ways. WordPress calls this art of organization *taxonomy*, and if you do it right, it gives your readers a painless way to find the content they want.

You'll also take a hard look at the web address (URL) that WordPress generates for every new post. You'll learn how to take control of your URLs, making sure they're meaningful, memorable, and accessible to search engines. You'll also learn how to shorten the web address of any post, which is handy if you need to wedge a link to your post into a small place (like a Twitter message, Facebook post, or a bit of bathroom graffiti).

Introducing the Dashboard

The dashboard is the nerve center of WordPress administration. When you want to add a new post, tweak your site's theme, or review other people's comments, this is the place to go.

The easiest way to get to the dashboard is to take your WordPress website address and add */wp-admin* (short for "WordPress administration") to the end of it. For example, if you host your site at *http://magicteahouse.net*, you can reach the site's dashboard at *http://magicteahouse.net/wp-admin*. When you do, WordPress asks for your user name and password. Once you supply them, you'll see a page like the one in Figure 4-1.

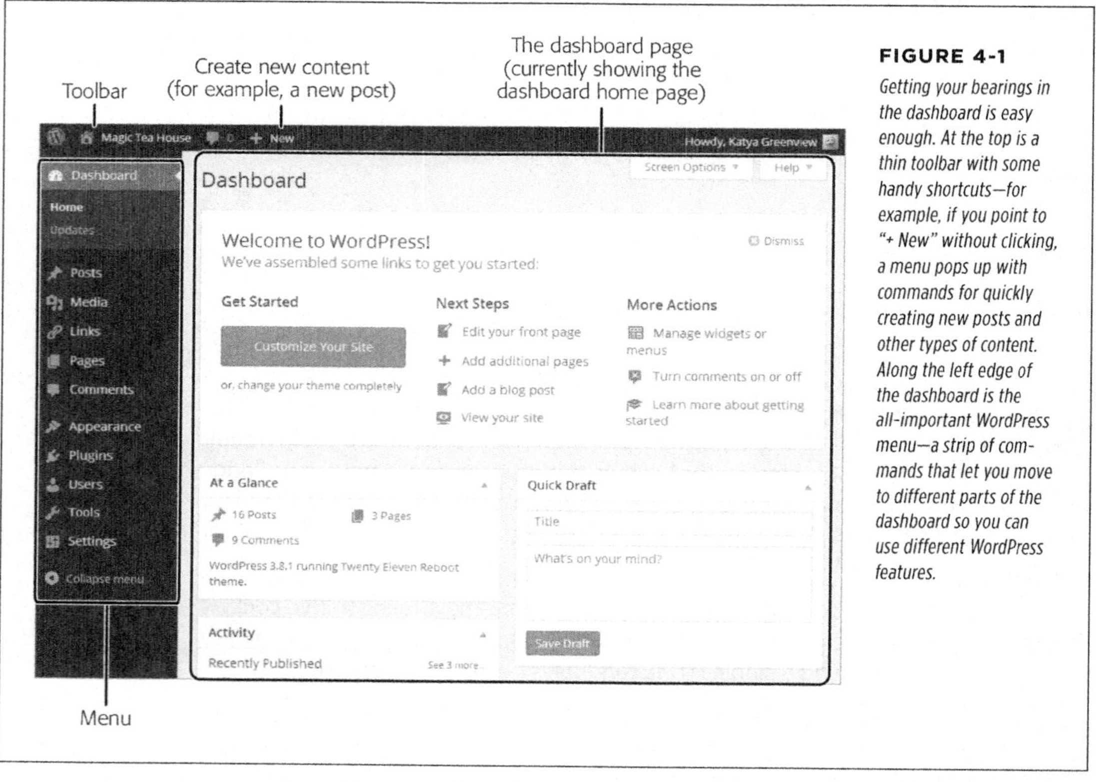

FIGURE 4-1

Getting your bearings in the dashboard is easy enough. At the top is a thin toolbar with some handy shortcuts—for example, if you point to "+ New" without clicking, a menu pops up with commands for quickly creating new posts and other types of content. Along the left edge of the dashboard is the all-important WordPress menu—a strip of commands that let you move to different parts of the dashboard so you can use different WordPress features.

When you finish working at the dashboard, it's a good idea to log out. That way, you don't need to worry about a smart-alecky friend hijacking your site and adding humiliating posts or pictures while you're away from your computer. To log out, click your user name in the top-right corner of the toolbar, and then click Log Out (on a self-hosted site) or Sign Out (on a WordPress.com site).

There's another way to go backstage with your site. When WordPress creates a new site, it adds a small section of timesaving links named "Meta." The exact location of this section depends on the theme your site uses, but you'll usually find it at the bottom of a sidebar on the left or right side of your home page (Figure 4-2). Inside the Meta section, you can click the "Log in" link to go directly to the dashboard. (If you're already logged in, you'll see a Site Admin link instead, which does the same thing.)

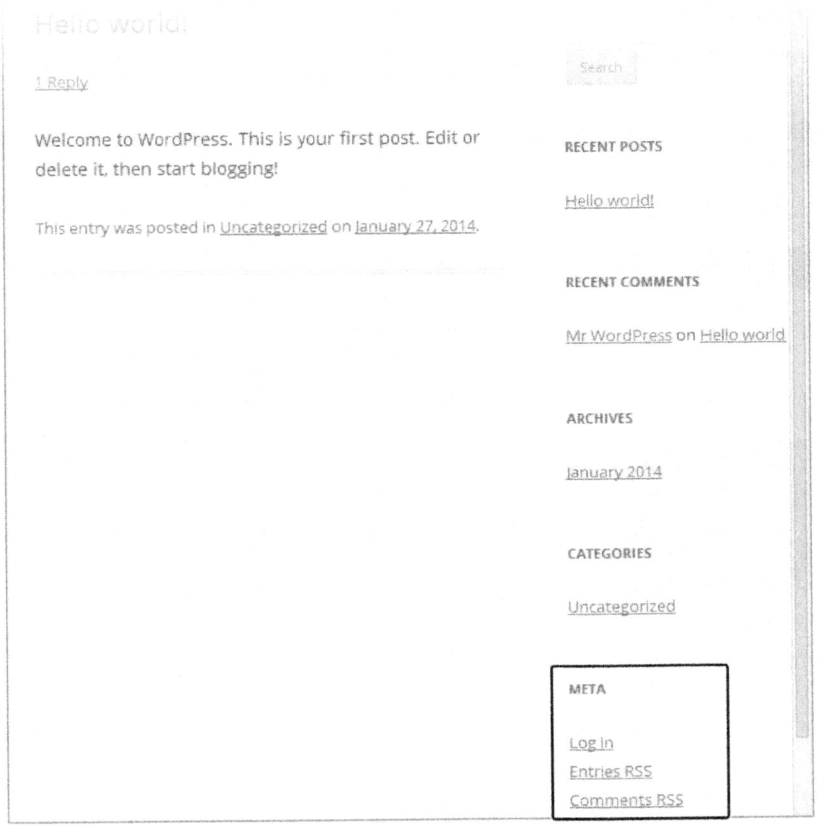

FIGURE 4-2

The Meta section of your home page has links that can take you to the dashboard, show you the feeds that publish your content (page 433), and transport you to the WordPress.org site. It's a holdover from the earliest days of WordPress.

UP TO SPEED

The Dashboard in WordPress.com

Self-hosted sites and WordPress.com sites share a very similar dashboard. Most of the commands (in the menu on the left) are identical. In the rare cases that they aren't, this book makes a note of the discrepancy.

The toolbar at the top of the dashboard is less consistent. WordPress.com sites have a set of shortcuts similar to what's in Figure 4-1, but in a subtly different arrangement from a self-hosted WordPress installation. This isn't a problem either, because the toolbar simply duplicates some of the features already in the WordPress menu. It's up to you to discover these shortcuts and decide whether you want to use them from the toolbar at all.

NOTE Although the Meta section is helpful when you first start out, you definitely don't want these administrative links in a finished site. Page 157 explains how to remove them, once you're accustomed to breezing in and out of the dashboard on your own.

The Menu

To browse around the dashboard, you use the menu—the panel that runs down the left side of the dashboard. It has a link to every administrative feature WordPress offers.

WordPress groups the menu commands into submenus. To see a submenu, hover over one of the menu headings (like "Posts") and it pops open (Figure 4-3).

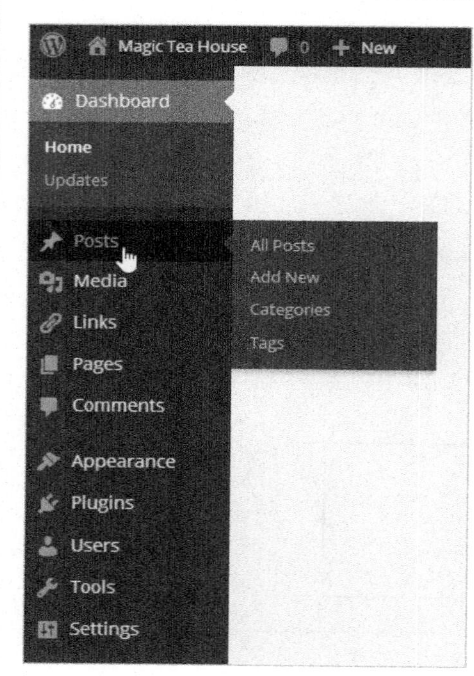

FIGURE 4-3

WordPress's menu packs a lot of features into a small strip of web page real estate. Initially, all you see are first-level menu headings. But point to one of the items without clicking, and WordPress opens a submenu. (The exception is the Comments heading, which doesn't have a submenu. You just click it to review comments.)

When you click a menu command, the rest of the dashboard changes to reflect the task you picked. For example, say you choose Posts→Add New. (In other words, you mouse over to the left-side menu, hover over "Posts" until its submenu appears, and then click the "Add New" command.) Now, the dashboard shows an HTML-savvy editor where you can write your post.

You can also click a menu heading directly (for example, "Posts"). If you do, you go to the first item in the corresponding submenu, as shown in Figure 4-4.

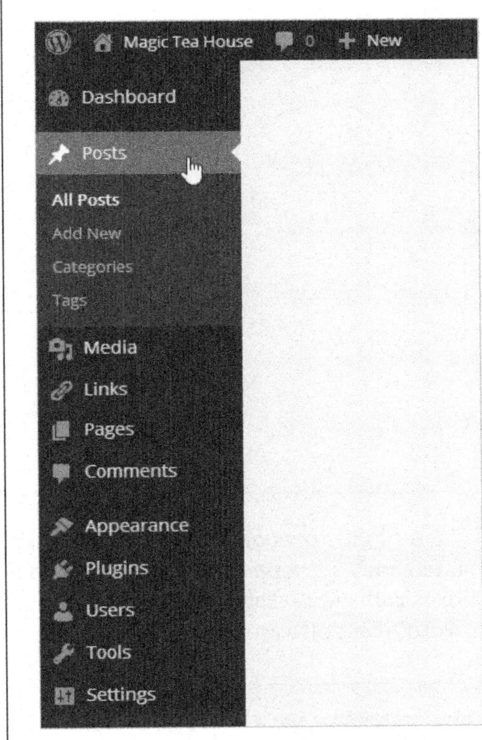

FIGURE 4-4

If you click the heading Posts, you actually go to the submenu item Posts→All Posts. And if you lose your bearings in the dashboard, just look for the bold text in the menu to find out where you are. In this example, that's All Posts.

NOTE If you resize your web browser window to be very narrow, the menu shrinks itself to free up more space, removing the menu names (like Posts, Media, and Links), and leaving just the tiny menu icons. Hover over one of these icons, and the submenu appears, but with a helpful difference: Now WordPress displays the menu name as a title at the top.

The Home Page

Your starting place in the dashboard is a densely packed home page. You can get back to this page at any time by choosing Dashboard→Home from the menu.

If you just created a new self-hosted WordPress site, you'll see a welcome box filling the top part of the dashboard (Figure 4-5). It provides links that lead to some of the more important parts of the dashboard, where you can edit settings and add new posts.

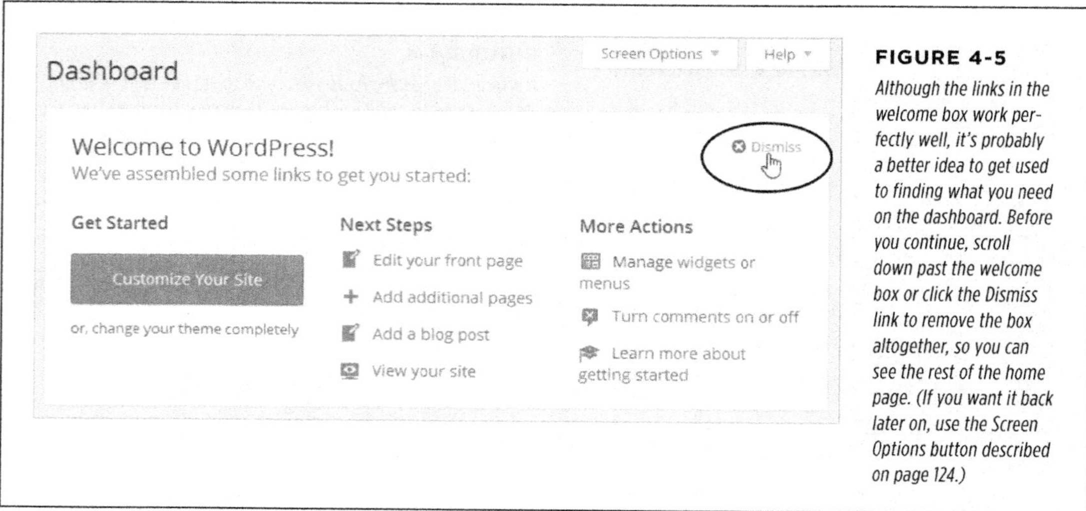

FIGURE 4-5

Although the links in the welcome box work perfectly well, it's probably a better idea to get used to finding what you need on the dashboard. Before you continue, scroll down past the welcome box or click the Dismiss link to remove the box altogether, so you can see the rest of the home page. (If you want it back later on, use the Screen Options button described on page 124.)

The dashboard home page may seem like a slightly overwhelming starting point, because it's crowded with boxes. Each one handles a separate task, as detailed in Figure 4-6. Sometimes, you'll also see boxes with important news (for example, an announcement about an update to the WordPress software).

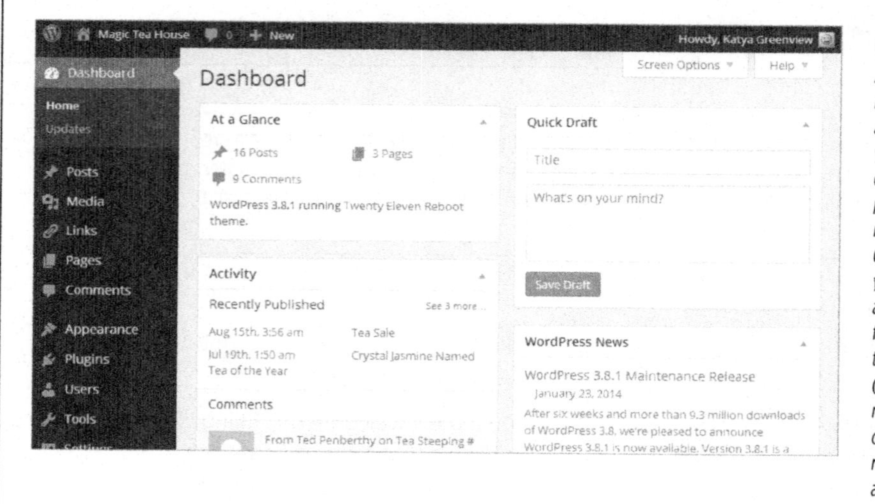

FIGURE 4-6

At the top of the dashboard home page, the "At a Glance" box displays your site's vital signs—including how many posts, pages, and comments it has. To the right is a Quick Draft box that lets you create a new post in a hurry. Below that, you'll find boxes with information about recent posts (articles you've written), recent comments (that other people have left in response to your posts), and links to WordPress news.

Don't be surprised to find that your brand-new WordPress site has some content in it. WordPress starts off every new site with one blog post, one page, and one comment, all of which are dutifully recorded in the Right Now box. Once you learn to create your own posts, you'll see how to delete these initial examples (page 104).

NOTE WordPress continually evolves. When you use the latest and greatest version, you may find that minor details have changed, such as the exact wording of links or the placement of boxes. But don't let these details throw you, because the underlying WordPress concepts and procedures have been surprisingly steady for years.

Dashboard Practice: Changing Basic Settings

Now that you understand how the dashboard works, why not try out a basic task? The following steps show you how to change a few useful WordPress settings, which are worth reviewing before you start posting. And, best of all, they'll help you get used to clicking your way through the dashboard menu to find what you need.

1. **In the dashboard menu, choose Settings→General.**

   The rest of the dashboard loads up a page of tweakable settings (Figure 4-7).

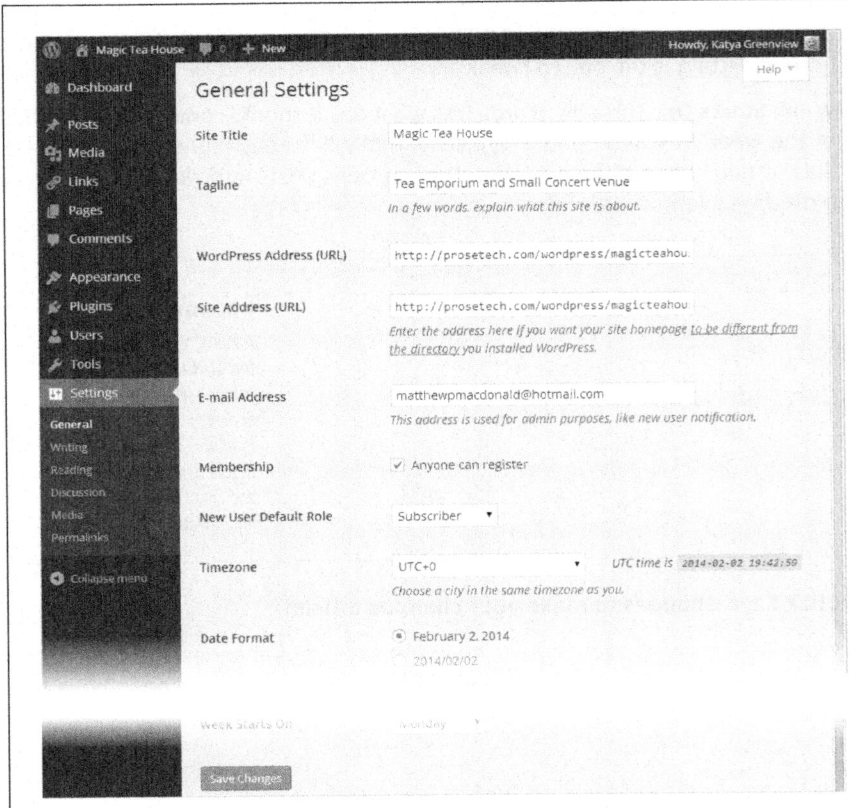

FIGURE 4-7

Point to the dashboard's Settings menu item without clicking to reveal a submenu, and then click General. That brings you to the page of options shown here (partially, with some options omitted).

2. **If you like, change some settings.**

   Here are some suggestions:

   Site Title and Tagline. In a basic WordPress site, every page has a header section at the top. WordPress puts the site title and tagline there (Figure 4-8). The site title also shows up at the top of the browser window (or tab), and, if a visitor decides to bookmark your site, the browser uses the site title as the bookmark text. You shouldn't change these details often, so it's worthwhile to double-check that you've got a clear title and catchy tagline right now.

   Timezone. This tells WordPress where you are, globally speaking. (For example, UTC-5 is the time zone for New York.) If WordPress doesn't have the right time zone, it will give posts and comments the wrong timestamp. For example, it might tell the world that a comment you left at 8:49 PM was actually recorded at 3:49 AM. If you're not sure what your time zone offset is, don't worry, because WordPress provides a list of cities. Pick the city you live in, or another city in the same time zone, and WordPress sets the offset to match.

   Date Format and Time Format. Ordinarily, WordPress displays the date for every post you add and the time for every comment made. These settings control how WordPress displays the date and time. For example, if you want dates to be short—like "2014/12/18" rather than "December 18, 2014"—the Date Format setting is the one to tweak.

   Week Starts On. This tells WordPress what day it should consider the first day of the week in your country (typically, that's Saturday, Sunday, or Monday). This setting changes the way WordPress groups posts into weeks and the way it displays events in calendars.

FIGURE 4-8

A WordPress header includes the site's title and tagline. The title (Magic Tea House) appears in a large font. The tagline, a one-sentence description (Tea Emporium and Small Concert Venue), sits underneath.

3. **Click Save Changes to make your changes official.**

   WordPress takes a fraction of a second to save your changes and then shows a "Settings saved" message at the top of the page. You can now move to a different part of the dashboard.

NOTE There are plenty more WordPress settings to play around with in the Settings submenu. As you explore various WordPress features in this book, you'll return to these settings to customize them.

One More Task: Choosing a Starter Theme

Every WordPress site has a theme that sets its layout and visual style. As you begin to refine your site, you'll take a closer look at themes, starting in Chapter 5. But before you even get to that point, you need to pick a good starter theme for your site.

WordPress includes a few themes with every new installation. Somewhat awkwardly, it names each theme after the year it released the theme. At the time of this writing, a WordPress installation includes the Twenty Twelve, Twenty Thirteen, and Twenty Fourteen themes.

It's natural to assume that the best theme is the latest one, and that later themes should replace earlier ones in new sites. However, the creators of WordPress actually take a different approach. They aim to have each new theme showcase a popular style, while admitting that no single theme will suit everyone. The Twenty Fourteen theme, for example, is a dark, slick, image-heavy production that suits online magazines and photo blogs. By comparison, Twenty Twelve is a clean, streamlined theme that's perfect for a basic blog or a solid foundation for more ambitious customizations.

You can learn the fundamentals of WordPress using any theme. However, you'll have an easier start using a clean and simple one like Twenty Twelve rather than a heavy one like Twenty Fourteen. (You'll also have an easier time following along with the examples in this chapter, which use Twenty Twelve.)

To start yourself out right, here's how to change your site's theme to Twenty Twelve:

1. **In the dashboard, click Appearance→Themes.**

   If you're working with a self-hosted site, you'll see a small gallery of preinstalled themes.

   If you're working with a WordPress.com site, you'll see a much larger gallery with all the themes you can choose.

2. **In the "Search themes" text box on the right, type "twenty twelve."**

   As you type, WordPress filters the list of themes to show those that match your search text (Figure 4-9).

3. **Hover over the Twenty Twelve box and click Activate.**

   WordPress applies this theme to your site immediately. Click your site name (near the top-left corner of the page) to view your site and see the results.

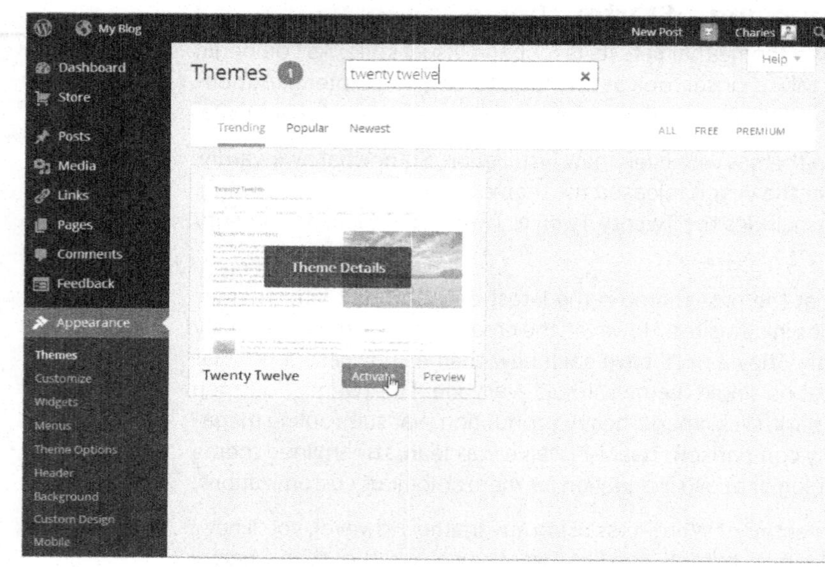

FIGURE 4-9
When you finish typing in the search box, you'll see a single entry for the Twenty Twelve theme.

Adding Your First Post

Comfortable yet? As you've seen, the WordPress dashboard gives you a set of relatively simple and anxiety-free tools to manage your website. In fact, a good part of the reason why WordPress is so popular is because it's so easy to take care of. (And as any pet owner knows, the most exotic animal in the world isn't worth owning if it won't stop peeing on the floor.)

But to really get going with your website, you need to put some content on it. So it makes perfect sense that one of the first dashboard tasks that every WordPress administrator learns is *posting*.

Creating a New Post

To create a new post, follow these steps:

1. **In the dashboard menu, choose Posts→Add New.**

   The Add New Post page appears, complete with a big fat box where you can type in your content (Figure 4-10).

NOTE Figure 4-10 is cropped so that it doesn't show the dashboard menu on the left. Rest assured that the dashboard menu *is* there. We've trimmed this detail on many of the pictures in this book so you can focus on the task at hand (and so we don't need to make our pictures micro-small).

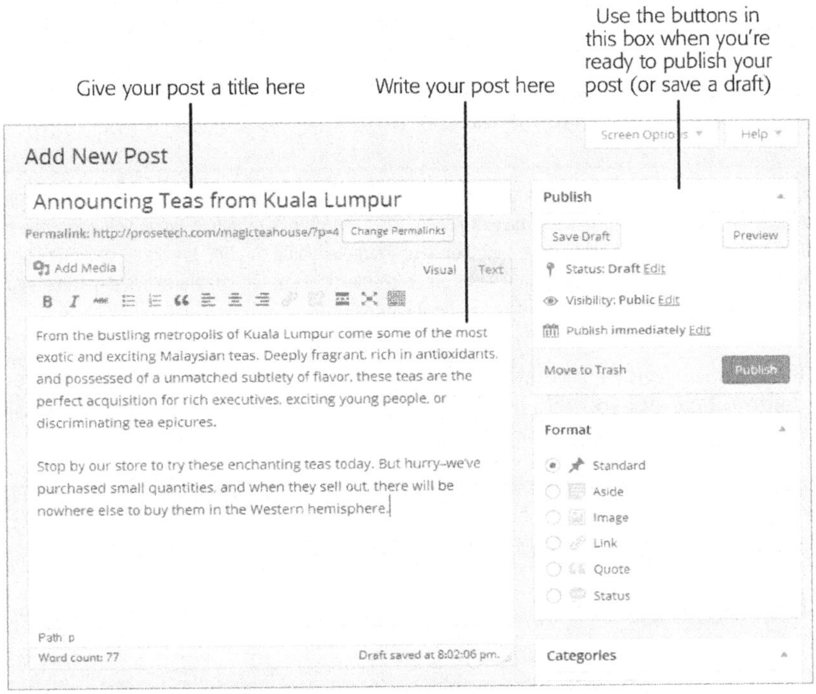

FIGURE 4-10

The minimum ingredients for any post are a descriptive title and a block of text. To the right is the all-important Publish box, which holds buttons that let you preview a post, publish it, or save it as a draft for later.

You can save time by using the toolbar at the top of the WordPress screen. If you run WordPress on your own web host, click New→Post. If you signed up with WordPress.com, click the WordPress "W" icon (in the left-hand corner) and then click New Post.

2. **Start by typing a post title into the blank box at the top of the page (right under Edit Post).**

   A good post title clearly announces what you're going to discuss. Often, visitors will come across your post title before getting to your post text. For example, they might see the title in a list of posts or on a search engine results page. A good title communicates your subject and entices the reader to continue on to the post. A lousy title might be cute, clever, or funny, but fail to reflect what the post is about.

   Here are some good post titles: "Obama Struggles in Recent Poll," "Mad Men Is Officially Off the Rails," and "My Attempt to Make a Chocolate-Bacon Soufflé."

And here are weaker titles for exactly the same content: "Polls, Polls, and More Polls," "Mad Men Recap," and "My Latest Kitchen Experiment."

3. **Click in the big box under the post title (or just press the Tab key). Now type in the content for your post (Figure 4-10).**

   A basic blog post consists of one or more paragraphs. After each paragraph, press the Enter key (once) to start the next paragraph. WordPress automatically adds a bit of white space between paragraphs, so they don't feel too crowded. Resist the urge to sign your name at the end, because WordPress automatically adds this information to the post.

TIP Paragraphs and line breaks give your web page two different looks. When you start a new paragraph by pressing Enter, WordPress includes some extra blank space between paragraphs. When you add a *line break*, the adjacent lines remain relatively close together. (For example, you'd use line breaks to separate lines in a mailing address or a poem.) When you want a line break instead of a new paragraph (to avoid getting the space between paragraphs), hold down the Shift key while you press Enter.

   If you want fancier formatting for your post, the toolbar that sits above the content box lets you add lists, subheadings, pictures, and more. You'll take a closer look at these features on page 172.

NOTE Don't worry if you're not yet feeling inspired. It's exceptionally easy to delete blog posts, so you can add a simple post just for practice and then remove it later (see page 104).

4. **Double-check your post.**

   A post with typographic errors or clumsy spelling mistakes is as embarrassing as a pair of pants with a faulty elastic band. Before you inadvertently reveal yourself to the world, it's a good idea to double-check your writing.

   If you use a browser with a built-in spell checker, which includes Internet Explorer 10 and any modern version of Firefox and Chrome, you get automatic spell checking. You'll see red squiggly lines under your mistakes, and you can right-click misspelled words to choose the right spelling from a pop-up menu.

5. **When you finish writing and editing, click Preview.**

   Your post preview opens in a new browser tab or new browser window. It shows you a perfect rendition of what the post will look like on your site, with the current theme.

NOTE In some cases, your browser may block the preview because this feature uses a pop-up window. If your browser displays a warning message and no preview window, you may need to lower your browser's pop-up security settings. Although every browser is different, you usually accomplish that by clicking the pop-up warning icon and choosing an "Allow pop-ups" option.

6. **If you like what you saw in the preview window, click Publish.**

   In a self-hosted site, a message box will appear at the top of the page, confirming that your post has been published. In a WordPress.com site, a side panel pops into view, with a message that tells you how many posts you've written to date.

   The moment you publish a post, it becomes live on your site and visible to the world. WordPress.com shows you the results right away; if you run a self-hosted WordPress site, you need to click the "View post" link to see the published post (Figure 4-11).

   If you're not quite done but you need to take a break, click Save Draft instead of Publish. WordPress holds onto your post so you can edit and publish it later. Returning to a draft is easy—in the dashboard home page (that's Dashboard→Home), find the Recent Drafts box and click your post in the list to resume editing it. Afterward, you can continue postponing the moment of publication (click Save Draft again), you can publish it like a normal post (click Publish), or you can discard it altogether (click Move to Trash).

UP TO SPEED

Why Your Post Might Look a Little Different

If you try out these steps on your own WordPress site (and you should), you might not get exactly the same page as shown in Figure 4-11. For example, the date information, the author byline, and the link that lets you jump to the previous post may be positioned in different spots or have slightly different wording. If you created your site on WordPress.com, you'll get social media sharing buttons at the bottom of your post, which make it easier for your readers to talk about you on Facebook and Twitter. And there are other differences in the formatting and arrangement of your site, if you care to dig around.

You might assume that these alterations represent feature differences—for example, things that WordPress.com sites can do that self-hosted WordPress sites can't. But that isn't the case. Instead, this variability is the result of different themes, plug-ins, and WordPress settings.

The best advice is this: Don't get hung up on these differences. Right now, the content of your site is in your hands, but the other details (like the placement of the sidebar and the font used for the post text) are beyond your control. In Chapter 5, when you learn how to change to a new theme or customize a current one, these differences will begin to evaporate. And by the time you reach the end of Part 2 in this book, you'll be able to customize a self-hosted WordPress site or a WordPress.com site to look the way you want it to.

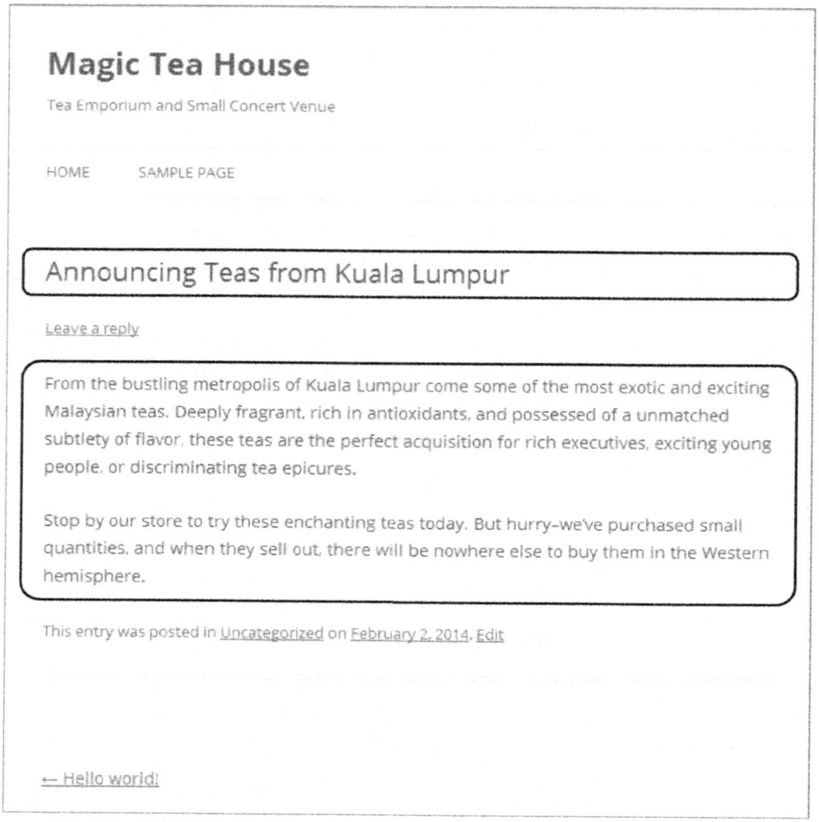

Magic Tea House

Tea Emporium and Small Concert Venue

HOME SAMPLE PAGE

Announcing Teas from Kuala Lumpur

Leave a reply

From the bustling metropolis of Kuala Lumpur come some of the most exotic and exciting Malaysian teas. Deeply fragrant, rich in antioxidants, and possessed of a unmatched subtlety of flavor, these teas are the perfect acquisition for rich executives, exciting young people, or discriminating tea epicures.

Stop by our store to try these enchanting teas today. But hurry–we've purchased small quantities, and when they sell out, there will be nowhere else to buy them in the Western hemisphere.

This entry was posted in Uncategorized on February 2, 2014. Edit

← Hello world!

FIGURE 4-11

Here's the finished post, transplanted into the stock layout of your WordPress site. The two circled sections represent the content you contributed. WordPress has added plenty of details, like the category and date information below your post. You'll learn to take charge of these details in this chapter and the next.

Browsing Your Posts

Adding a single post is easy. But to get a feel for what a real, thriving blog looks like, you need to add several new posts. When you do, you'll find that WordPress arranges your posts in the traditional way: one after the other, in reverse-chronological order.

To take a look, head to the home page of your blog (Figure 4-12). To get there, just enter your WordPress site address, without any extra information tacked onto the end. Or, if you're currently viewing a post, click the Home button in the menu bar (just under the header section and the stock picture).

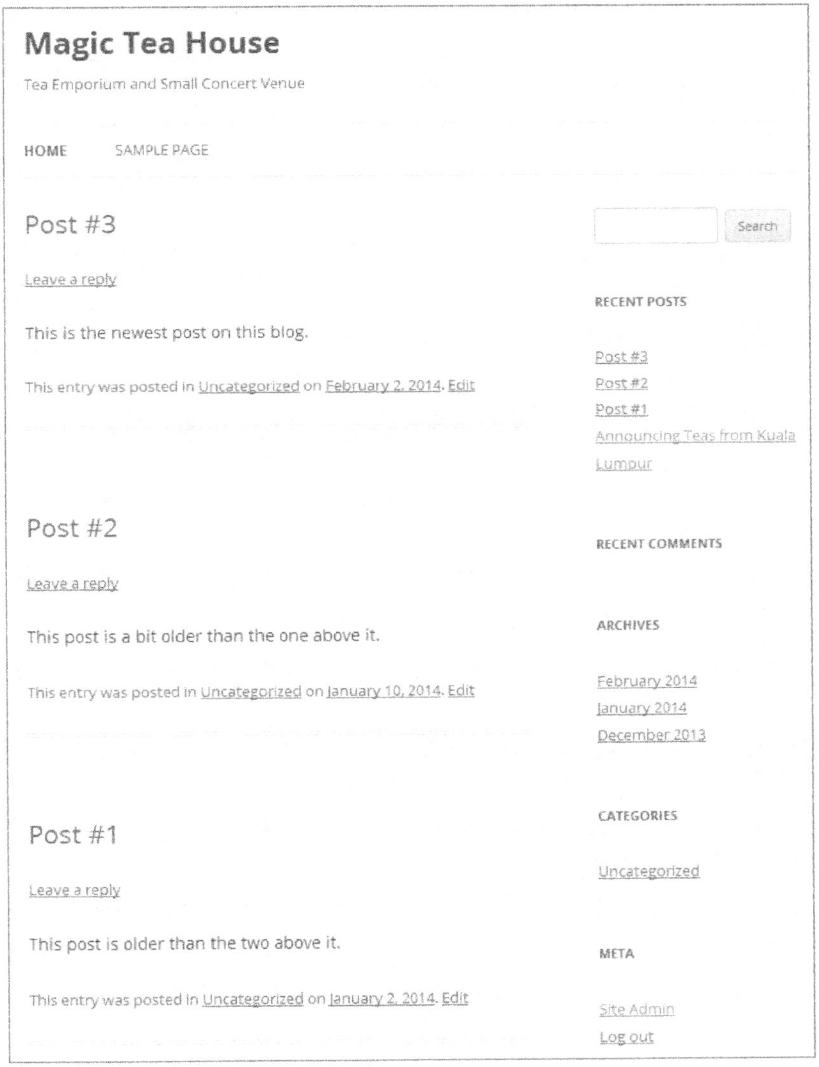

Magic Tea House

Tea Emporium and Small Concert Venue

HOME SAMPLE PAGE

Post #3

Leave a reply

This is the newest post on this blog.

This entry was posted in Uncategorized on February 2, 2014. Edit

Post #2

Leave a reply

This post is a bit older than the one above it.

This entry was posted in Uncategorized on January 10, 2014. Edit

Post #1

Leave a reply

This post is older than the two above it.

This entry was posted in Uncategorized on January 2, 2014. Edit

Search

RECENT POSTS

Post #3
Post #2
Post #1
Announcing Teas from Kuala Lumpur

RECENT COMMENTS

ARCHIVES

February 2014
January 2014
December 2013

CATEGORIES

Uncategorized

META

Site Admin
Log out

FIGURE 4-12

When you visit the home page of a blog, you start out with a reverse-chronological view that puts the most recent post first. If you don't like to scroll, the sidebar on the right gives you several other ways to browse posts.

The number of posts you see on the home page depends on your WordPress settings. Ordinarily, you get a batch of 10 posts at a time. If you scroll to the bottom of the home page, you can click the "Older posts" link to load up the next 10. If you want to show more or fewer posts at once, choose Settings→Reading and change the "Blog pages show at most" setting to the number you want.

WordPress.com sites include an infinite scroll feature. When it's switched on, you won't see the "Older posts" link. Instead, WordPress loads new posts as you scroll down, creating an ever-expanding page (until you reach the very first post on the site). To turn this feature off, choose Settings→Reading and then turn off the checkbox next to "Scroll infinitely."

You don't need to read every post in a WordPress site from newest to oldest. Instead, you can use one of the many other ways WordPress gives you to browse posts:

- **By most recent.** The Recent Posts list lets you quickly jump to one of the five most recently created posts. It's the first set of links in the sidebar on the right.
- **By month.** Using the Archives list, you can see a month's worth of posts. For example, click "June 2014" to see all the posts published that month, in reverse-chronological order. Some WordPress blogs also include a calendar for post browsing, but if you want that you'll need to add it yourself (see page 164 to learn how).
- **By category or tag.** Later in this chapter, you'll learn how to place your posts in categories and add descriptive tags. Once you take these steps, you'll have another way to hunt through your content, using either the Categories list in the sidebar or the category and tag links that WordPress adds to the end of every post.
- **By author.** If your site has posts written by more than one person, WordPress automatically adds a link with the author name at the bottom of every post. Click that link and you'll see all the posts that person has created for this site, in reverse-chronological order (as always). You can't use this feature just yet, but it comes in handy when you create a blog that has multiple authors, as you'll learn to do in Chapter 11.
- **Using a search.** To search a blog, type a keyword or two into the search box, which appears at the top right of your site, and then press Enter. WordPress searches the title and body of each post and shows you a list of matching posts.

Delayed Publishing

Sometimes, you might decide your post is ready to go, but you want to wait a little before putting it on the Web. For example, you might want your post to coincide with an event or product announcement. Or maybe you want your post to appear at a certain time of day, rather than the 2:00 a.m. time you wrote it. Or maybe you simply want to add a bit of a buffer in case you get new information or have a last-minute change of heart.

FREQUENTLY ASKED QUESTION

How Do I Change My Home Page?

I don't like the look of my home page. Is there anything I can do to change it?

The home page is the first thing visitors see on your website. For that reason, it's no surprise that it's one of the things WordPress authors want to tweak first. Here are some of your options:

- **Change the number of posts.** Want to see more (or fewer) than 10 posts at a time? On the dashboard, choose Settings→Reading. In the "Blog pages show at most" box, type in a different number, and then click Save Changes.
- **Show post summaries.** Ordinarily, WordPress shows the entire post on the home page. If you like to write thorough, detailed posts with plenty of text and pictures (or if you're just incurably long-winded), you would probably prefer to show a brief summary instead. You'll learn how to pull off this trick on page 198.
- **Show a static page.** If you'd rather show a custom home page that you've designed, instead of a list of recent posts, you need to create a *static page*. You'll learn how to do that—and use it for your home page—in Chapter 7.

These are just a few examples. As you read this book, many more options will open up. For example, in Chapter 10 you'll learn how to create a home page that uses image thumbnails (page 343). And when you consider the advanced theme-editing techniques in Chapter 14, you'll see how to create a home page that displays a list of categorized links to just the posts you want.

In all these situations, you can choose to save your post as a draft (click Save Draft) and publish it later. That gives you complete control over when the post appears, but it also forces you to make a return trip to your computer. A different approach is to use *delayed publishing*, which allows you to specify a future publication time. Before that time arrives, you may return and edit your post (or even cancel it). But if you do nothing, the post will magically appear, at exactly the time you specified.

To use delayed publishing, follow these steps:

1. **Before you start, make sure WordPress has the right time settings (page 92).**

   If WordPress thinks you're in a different time zone, its clock won't match yours, and when you tell it to publish a post at a certain time, it will actually appear a few hours before or after you expect.

2. **To write your post, choose Posts→Add New in the dashboard.**

   Write your post in the usual way.

3. **In the Publish box, click the Edit link next to "Publish immediately."**

   A new group of settings drops into view (Figure 4-13).

4. **Use the provided boxes to pick a forthcoming date and the exact time when the post should go live.**

   Here, WordPress uses a 24-hour clock, so put in 14:00 for 2:00 p.m.

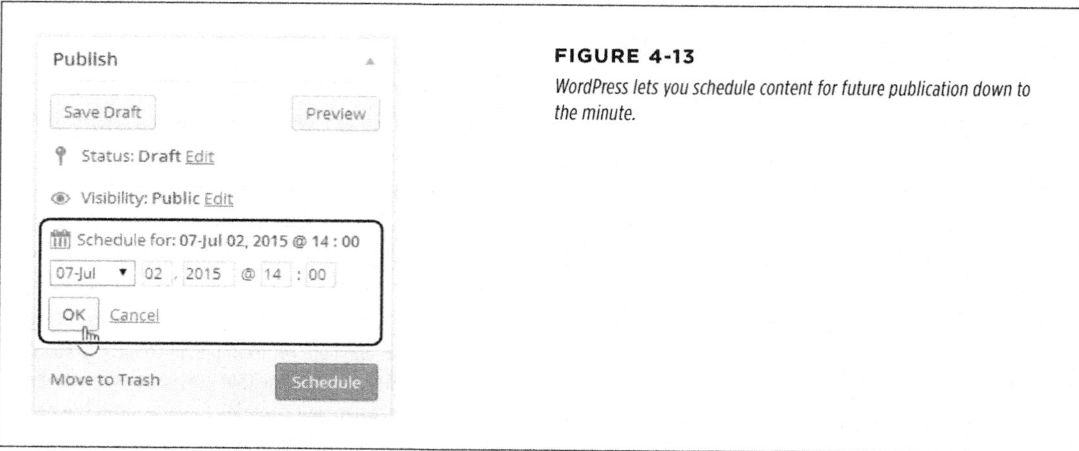

FIGURE 4-13

WordPress lets you schedule content for future publication down to the minute.

5. **Click OK to apply your changes.**

   At this point, the Publish button turns into a Schedule button.

6. **Click the Schedule button to commit to publishing the post.**

   WordPress will wait until the time you specify, and then publish your work.

   If you decide you don't actually want to publish the post at the time you set, you can edit the post (as described on page 102) and put the scheduled time to a very distant future date. Or you can delete the post altogether (page 103).

TIP You can use the same technique to create a post with an *older* publication date. To do that, just type in a date and time that falls in the past. Although this trick is less useful than delayed publishing (because no one wants to make her content look old), it's occasionally useful. For example, it's handy if you publish several posts at the same time and you want to change their order or spread them out.

Editing a Post

Many people assume that posting on a blog is like sending an email message: You compose your thoughts, write your content as best you can, and then send it out to meet the world. But the truth is that you can tinker with your posts long after you publish them.

WordPress gives you two easy ways to edit a post. If you're logged in as the site administrator and you're viewing a post, you'll see an Edit button or an Edit link somewhere on the page (its exact position depends on your theme). Click that link, and WordPress takes you to the Edit Post page, which looks almost identical to the Add New Post page. In fact, the only difference is that the Publish button has been renamed "Update." Using the Edit Post page, you can change any detail you want, from correcting a single typo to replacing the entire post. When you finish making changes, click the Update button to commit your edit.

Another way to pick a post for editing is to use the dashboard. First, choose Posts→All Posts, which shows you a list of all the posts you've published (Figure 4-14). Find the post you want to edit, hover over it, and then click the Edit link to get to the Edit Post page, where you can make your changes.

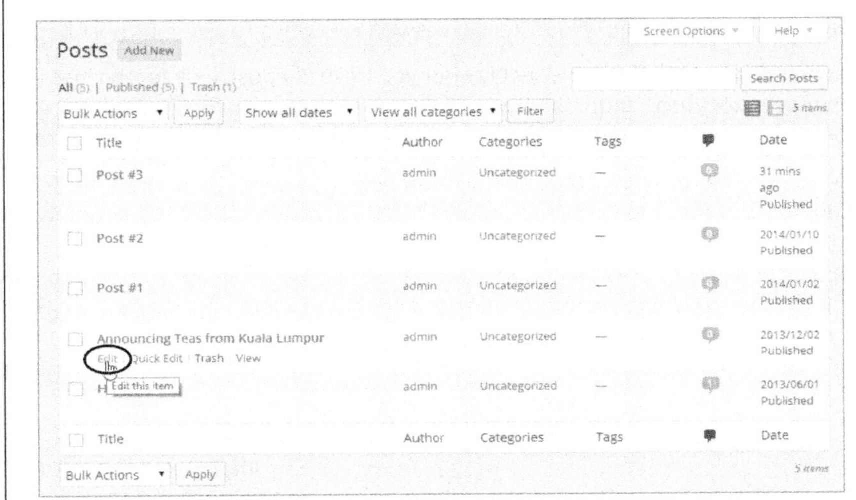

FIGURE 4-14

The Posts page lists your posts in reverse-chronological order, starting with the most recent, and including any drafts. When you point to a post (without clicking), you see links that let you edit, delete, or view the post.

Along with the Edit link, the Posts page includes a Quick Edit link. Unlike Edit, Quick Edit keeps you on the Posts page but pops open a panel that lets you edit some of the post details. For example, you can use Quick Edit to change a post's title, but you can't use it to change the actual text.

Being able to edit in WordPress is a nearly essential feature. Eventually, even the best site will get something wrong. There's no shame in opening up an old post to correct an error, clean up a typing mistake, or even scrub out a bad joke.

NOTE Unlike some blogging and content management systems, WordPress doesn't display any sort of timestamp or message about when you last edited a post. If you want that, you'll need to add it as part of your edit. For example, you might tack an italicized paragraph onto the bottom of a post that says, "This post edited to include the full list of names" or "Updated on January 25th with the latest survey numbers."

Deleting a Post

As you've just seen, you can edit anything you've ever written on your WordPress website, at any time, without leaving any obvious fingerprints. You can even remove posts altogether.

The trick to deleting posts is to use the Posts page (Figure 4-14). Point to the post you want to vaporize, and then click Trash. Or, on the Edit Post page, click the "Move to Trash" link that appears in the Publish box.

TIP Now that you know how to remove a post, try out your new skill with the "Hello world!" example post that WordPress adds to every new blog. There's really no reason to keep it.

Trashed posts aren't completely gone. If you discover you removed a post that you actually want, don't panic. WordPress gives you two ways to get your post back.

If you realize your mistake immediately after you trash the post, look for the message "Item moved to Trash. Undo." It appears in a box at the top of the Posts page. Click the Undo link, and your post returns immediately to both the Posts list and your site.

If you want to restore a slightly older trashed post, you need to dive into the Trash. Fortunately, it's easy (and not at all messy). First, click Posts→All Posts to get to the Posts page. Then click the Trash link that appears just above the list of posts (Figure 4-15). You'll see every post that's currently in the trash. Find the one you want, hover over it, and then click Restore to resurrect it (or click Delete Permanently to make sure no one will find it again, ever).

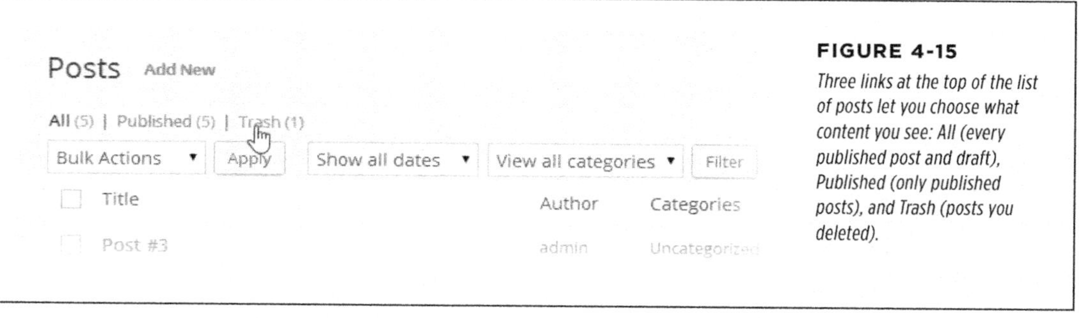

FIGURE 4-15

Three links at the top of the list of posts let you choose what content you see: All (every published post and draft), Published (only published posts), and Trash (posts you deleted).

NOTE Of course, removing posts from your blog and scrubbing content from the Web are two vastly different things. For example, if you post something impolite about your boss and remove it a month later, the content can live on in the cache that search engines keep and in Internet archival sites like the Wayback Machine (*http://web.archive.org*). So always think before you post, because WordPress doesn't include tools to reclaim your job or repair your online reputation.

Creating a Sticky Post

As you know, WordPress orders posts by date on the home page, with the most recent post occupying the top spot. But you might create an important post that you want to feature at the top of the list, regardless of its date. For example, you might write up a bulletin that announces that your business is temporarily closing for renovations, or answers frequently asked questions ("No, there are no more seatings available for this Sunday's Lobster Fest"). To keep your post at the top of the list so it can catch your readers' eyes, you need to turn it into a *sticky post.*

NOTE WordPress displays all your sticky posts before all your normal posts. If you have more than one sticky post, it lists the most recent one first.

You can designate a post as sticky when you first write it (on the Add New Post page) or when you edit it later (on the Edit Post page). Either way, you use the Publish box. Next to the label "Visibility: Public," click Edit. A few more options will drop into view (including the private post options you'll explore on page 395). To make your post sticky, turn on the checkbox next to "Stick this post to the front page," and then click Publish or Update to confirm your changes.

The only caveat with sticky posts is that they stay sticky forever—or until you "unstick" them. The quickest way to do that is to choose Posts→All Posts, find the sticky post in the list, and then click the Quick Edit link underneath it. Turn off the "Make this post sticky" checkbox and then click Update.

UP TO SPEED

The Path to Blogging Success

There's no secret trick to building a successful blog. Whether you're recording your thoughts or promoting a business, you should follow a few basic guidelines:

- **Make sure your content is worth reading.** As the oft-reported slogan states, *content is king.* The best way to attract new readers, lure them in for repeat visits, and inspire them to tell their friends about you, is to write something worth reading. If you're creating a topical blog (say, putting your thoughts down about politics, literature, or gourmet marshmallows), your content needs to be genuinely *interesting.* If you're creating a business blog (for example, promoting your indie record store or selling your real estate services), it helps to have content that's truly *useful* (say, "How to Clean Old Records" or "The Best Chicago Neighborhoods to Buy In").
- **Add new content regularly.** Nothing kills a site like stale content. Blogs are particularly susceptible to this problem because posts are listed in chronological order, and each post prominently displays the date you wrote it (unless you remove the dates by editing your theme files; see Chapter 13).
- **Keep your content organized.** Even the best content can get buried in the dozens (or hundreds) of posts you'll write. Readers can browse through your monthly archives or search for keywords in a post, but neither approach is convenient. Instead, a good blog is ruthlessly arranged using *categories* and *tags* for the posts (see the next section).

Organizing Your Posts

WordPress gives you two complementary tools for organizing your posts: *categories* and *tags*. Both work by grouping related posts together. In the following sections, you'll learn how to use them effectively.

Understanding Categories

A category is a short text description that describes the topic of a group of posts. For example, the Magic Tea House uses categories like *Tea* (posts about teas for sale), *Events* (posts about concert events at the tea house), and *News* (posts about other developments, like renovations or updated business hours).

Categories are really just text labels, and you can pick any category names you want. For example, the categories Tea, Events, and News could just as easily have been named Teas for Sale, Concerts, and Miscellaneous, without changing the way the categories work.

In a respectable WordPress site, every post has a category. (If you don't assign a category, WordPress automatically puts your post in a category named Uncategorized, which presents a bit of a logical paradox.) Most of the time, posts should have just one category. Putting a post in more than one category is a quick way to clutter up the structure of your site, and confuse anyone who's browsing your posts one category at a time.

TIP A good rule of thumb is this: Give every post exactly one category. If you want to add more information to make it easier for people to find posts that are related to each other, add tags (page 114). (The exception is if you use multiple categories to "flag" posts for special features. For example, you'll see a theme trick on page 192 that uses a category to denote featured posts. In this sort of example, some posts may appear in two categories—one "real" category used for classification and browsing, and another category you use to tap into the special feature.)

You don't need to create all your categories at once. Instead, you can add them as needed (for example, when you create a new post that needs a new category). Of course, you'll have an easier time organizing your site if you identify your main categories early on.

It's up to you to decide how to categorize posts and how many categories you want. For example, the Magic Tea House site could just as easily have divided the same posts into more categories, or into different criteria, as shown in Figure 4-16. The box on page 109 has some tips for choosing good categories.

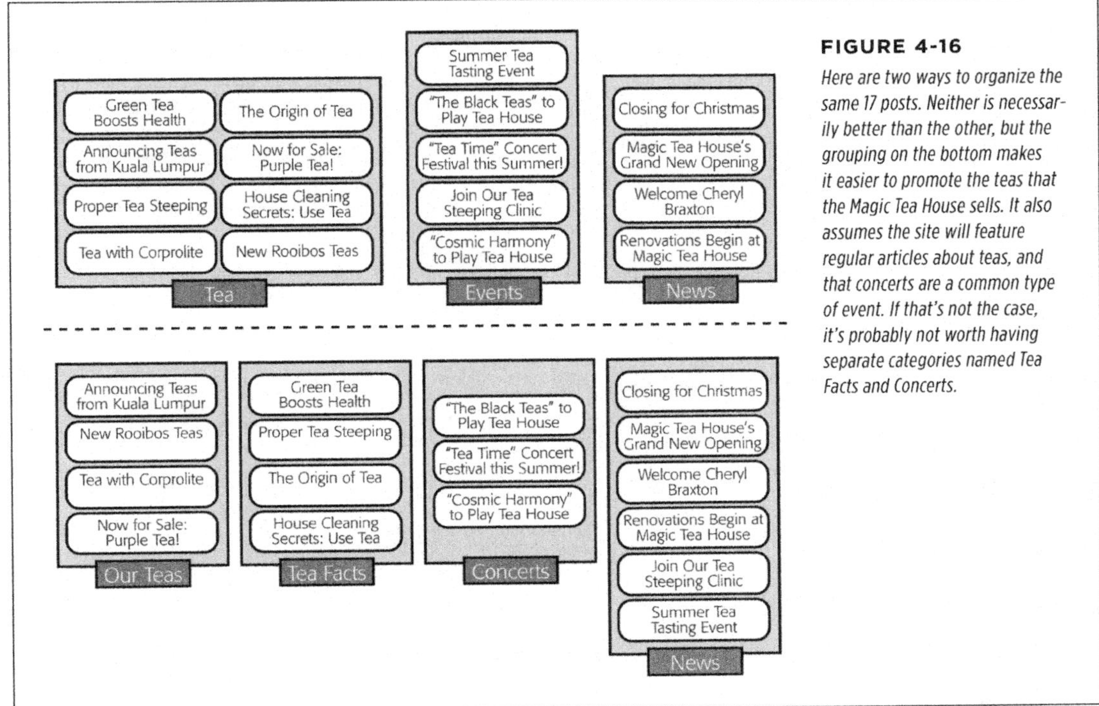

FIGURE 4-16

Here are two ways to organize the same 17 posts. Neither is necessarily better than the other, but the grouping on the bottom makes it easier to promote the teas that the Magic Tea House sells. It also assumes the site will feature regular articles about teas, and that concerts are a common type of event. If that's not the case, it's probably not worth having separate categories named Tea Facts and Concerts.

Categorizing Posts

You can easily assign a category to a post when you first add the post. Here's how:

1. **Choose Posts→Add New to start a new post.**

   Or you can start editing an existing post (page 102) and then change its category. The Add New Post and Edit Post pages work the same way, so it's easy.

2. **Look for the Categories box.**

   You'll find it near the bottom-right corner of the page, under the Publish and Format boxes (Figure 4-17).

   If the category you want exists, skip to step 5.

   If your post needs a new category, one that you haven't created yet, continue on to step 3.

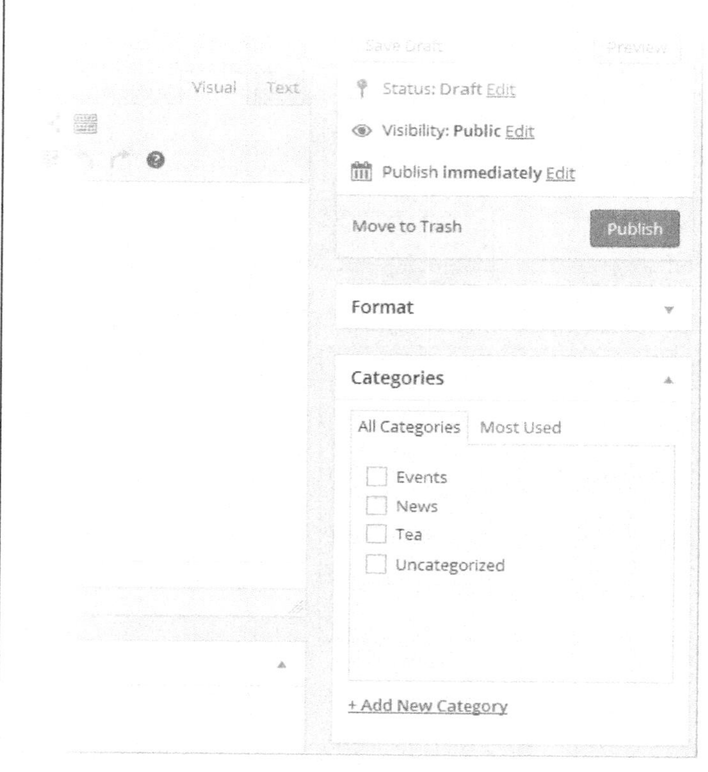

FIGURE 4-17

The Categories box has two tabs. The one you usually see, All Categories, lists all your post categories in alphabetical order. If you've created quite a few categories, you might find it faster to choose one from the Most Used tab, which lists the categories you use most often.

3. **At the bottom of the Categories box, click Add New Category.**

   This expands the Categories box so you can enter category information.

4. **Enter the category name in the box underneath the Add New Category link, and then click Add New Category.**

   Don't worry about the Parent Category box underneath—you'll learn to use that on page 110, when you create subcategories.

   Once you add your category, it appears in the Categories box.

5. **Find the category you want to use in the list, and then turn on the checkbox next to it.**

   When you add a new category, WordPress automatically turns on its checkbox, because it assumes this is the category you want to assign to your post. If it isn't, simply turn off the checkbox and pick something else.

You can add a post to more than one category, but it's best not to unless you're a pro. Doing so is likely to mask a poor choice of categories, and it makes it hard to change your categories later on.

6. **Carry on editing your post.**

   That's it. When you publish your post, WordPress assigns it the category you chose (Figure 4-18). If you didn't choose any category, WordPress automatically puts it in a category named (paradoxically) Uncategorized.

TIP Ordinarily, the category named Uncategorized is WordPress's *default category*—that means WordPress uses it for new posts unless you specify otherwise. However, you can tell WordPress to use a different default category. Simply choose Settings→Writing and pick one of your categories in the Default Post Category list.

UP TO SPEED

How to Choose Good Categories

To choose the right categories, you need to imagine your site, up and running, several months down the road. What posts does it have? How do people find the content they want? If you can answer these questions, you're well on the way to choosing the best categories.

First, you need to choose categories that distribute your posts *well*. If a single category has 90 percent of your posts, you probably need new—or different—categories. Similarly, if a category accounts for less than 2 percent of your posts, you may have too many categories. (Although there are exceptions—perhaps you plan to write more on that topic later, or you want to separate a very small section of special-interest posts from the rest of your content.)

You may also want to factor in the sheer number of posts you plan to write. If your site is big and you post often, you may want to consider more categories. For example, assuming the Magic Tea House has a couple of dozen posts, a category split like this works fine: Tea (70 percent), Concerts (20 percent), News (10 percent). But if you have hundreds of posts, you'll probably want to subdivide the big Tea group into smaller groups.

It also makes sense to create categories that highlight the content you want to promote. For example, if you're creating a site for a furniture store, you'll probably create categories based on your products (Couches, Sofas, Dining Room Tables, and so on). Similarly, the Magic Tea House can split its Tea category into Our Teas and Tea Facts to better highlight the teas it sells (Figure 4-16).

Finally, it's important to consider how your readers will want to browse your information. If you're a lifestyle coach writing articles about personal health, you might decide to add categories like Good Diet, Strength Training, and Weight Loss, because you assume that your readers will zero in on one of these subjects and eagerly devour all the content there. Be careful that you don't split post categories too small, however, because readers could miss content they might otherwise enjoy. For example, if you have both a Good Diet Tips and Superfoods category, a reader might explore one category without noticing the similar content in the other. This is a good place to apply the size rule again—if you can't stuff both categories full of good content, consider collapsing them into one group or using subcategories (page 110).

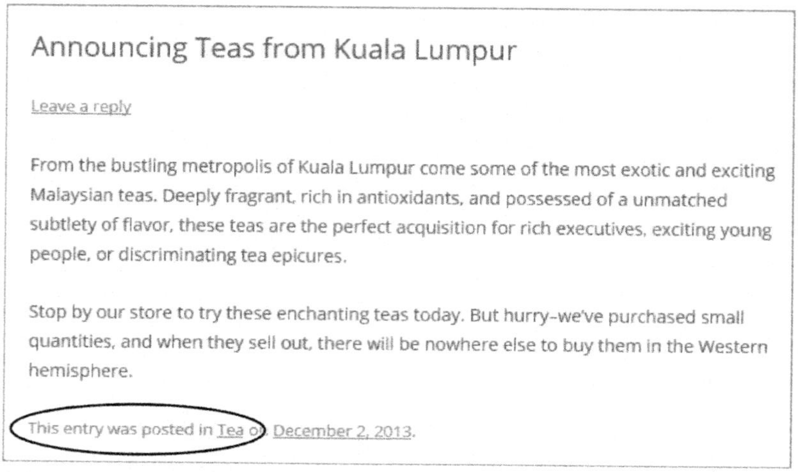

Announcing Teas from Kuala Lumpur

Leave a reply

From the bustling metropolis of Kuala Lumpur come some of the most exotic and exciting Malaysian teas. Deeply fragrant, rich in antioxidants, and possessed of a unmatched subtlety of flavor, these teas are the perfect acquisition for rich executives, exciting young people, or discriminating tea epicures.

Stop by our store to try these enchanting teas today. But hurry–we've purchased small quantities, and when they sell out, there will be nowhere else to buy them in the Western hemisphere.

This entry was posted in Tea on December 2, 2013.

FIGURE 4-18

This post is in the Tea category. Click the link (the word "Tea," under the post), and you'll see all the posts in that category.

Using Subcategories

If you have a huge site with plenty of posts and no shortage of categories, you may find that you can organize your content better with *subcategories*.

The idea behind subcategories is to take a large category and split it into two or more smaller groups. However, rather than make these new categories completely separate, WordPress keeps them as subcategories of the original category, which it calls the *parent category*. For example, the Magic Tea House site could make Tea a parent category and create subcategories named Black Tea, Green Tea, Rooibos, and Herbal Tea.

Done right, subcategories have two potential benefits:

- **You can show a category tree.** A category tree shows the hierarchy of your categories. In a complex site with lots of categories, most readers find that this makes it easier to browse the categories and understand how the topics you cover are related. You'll learn how to build a category tree in just a moment.
- **Visitors can browse posts by subcategory or parent category.** That means that people using the Magic Tea House site can see all the tea posts at once (by browsing the Tea category) or they can drill down to the subcategory of tea that interests them the most.

You can create subcategories using the Categories box—in fact, it's just as easy as creating ordinary categories (Figure 4-19). The only requirement is that you create the parent category first. Then enter the subcategory name, pick the parent category in the Parent Category list, and then click Add New Category.

NOTE Yes, you can create subcategories inside of subcategories. But doing so can complicate life and make it more difficult to fit a proper category tree in your sidebar. If possible, stick with one level of subcategories.

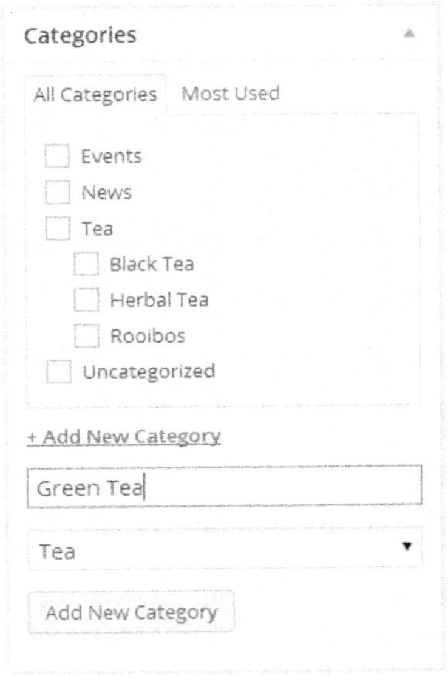

FIGURE 4-19

To add a post subcategory, you need to supply one extra piece of information: the parent category, which you select from a drop-down list.

WordPress displays categories hierarchically in the Categories box. That means that you'll see your subcategories (like Green Tea) displayed underneath the parent category (Tea). However, there's an exception—when you first add a new subcategory, WordPress puts it at the top of the list, and it stays there until you refresh the page or add a new category. Don't let this quirk worry you; your new category is still properly attached to its parent.

NOTE When you assign post to a subcategory, make sure you pick the subcategory only, *not* the parent category. That means that if you want to add a post about green tea, you should turn on the checkbox next to the Green Tea box, but *not* the Tea box. Because Tea is the parent category, people who browse the Tea category will automatically see your Green Tea posts.

When you start adding subcategories to your site, you'll probably be disappointed by how they appear in the Categories list, the category-browsing links that appear in the sidebar alongside your posts. The standard list of categories is a flat, one-dimensional list in alphabetical order. You can't see the relationships between parent categories and subcategories (Figure 4-20, left).

CATEGORIES
Black Tea
Events
Herbal Tea
News
Rooibos
Tea
Uncategorized

CATEGORIES
Events
News
Tea
Black Tea
Herbal Tea
Rooibos
Uncategorized

FIGURE 4-20

Ordinarily, the Categories list ignores subgroups (left). But fear not: With a simple configuration change you can get a more readable tree (right).

NOTE The Categories list shows only the categories you currently use. So if you create a new category but don't assign it to a post, you won't see it in the Categories list.

Fortunately, it's easy to change the standard list of categories into a tree of categories, by borrowing a theme-altering trick you'll explore in more detail in the next chapter. Technically, the Categories list is known as a *widget*. Like all widgets, it can be moved, removed, and reconfigured. Here's how:

1. **On the dashboard, choose Appearance→Widgets.**

   The Widgets page shows you all the individual ingredients that WordPress puts into the sidebar on your site.

2. **In the Main Sidebar box, find the Categories widget.**

   This is the widget that creates the list of categories that appears next to your posts.

3. **Click the down-pointing arrow on the right side of the widget.**

   This expands the Categories widget, so you can see its settings.

4. **Turn on the checkbox in the "Show hierarchy" settings and then click Save.**

   Now return to your site and admire the result (Figure 4-20, right).

NOTE No matter what setting you tweak, WordPress always orders categories alphabetically. If you want to put a specific category on top, you need to put in some extra work and create a menu (page 218).

Managing Categories

As you've seen, you can create a category whenever you need one, right from the Add New Post or Edit Post page. However, the WordPress dashboard also includes a page for managing categories. To get there, choose Posts→Categories, and you'll see a split page that lets you add to or edit your categories (Figure 4-21).

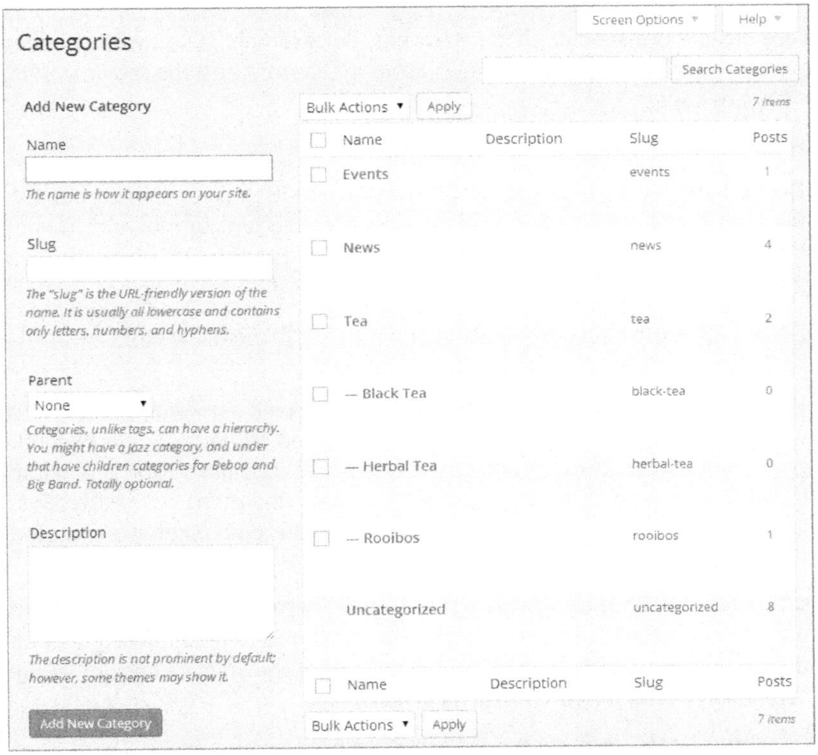

FIGURE 4-21

The Categories page includes a section on the left for adding new categories and a detailed list of all your categories on the right. The categories list works in much the same way as the list of posts on the Posts page. Point to a category without clicking, and you get the chance to edit or delete it.

The Categories page lets you perform a few tasks that aren't possible from the lowly Categories box:

- **Delete categories you don't use.** When you take this step, WordPress reassigns any posts in the category to the default category, which is Uncategorized (unless you changed the default in the Settings→Writing page).
- **Edit a category.** For example, you might want to take an existing category and rename it, or make it a subcategory by giving it a parent.
- **Enter extra category information.** You already know that every category has a name and, optionally, a parent. In addition, categories have room for two pieces of information that you haven't used yet: a slug and a description. The *slug* is a simplified version of the category name that appears in the web address when you use pretty permalinks (page 115). The *description* explains what the category is all about. Some themes display category descriptions in their category-browsing pages.

Understanding Tags

Like categories, tags are text labels that add bits of information to a post. But unlike categories, a post can (and should) have multiple tags. For that reason, the process of applying tags is less strict than the process of putting your post in the right category.

Tags are often more specific than categories. For example, if you write a review of a movie, you might use Movie Reviews as your category and the movie and director's name as tags.

Follow these guidelines when you use tags:

- **Don't over-tag.** Instead, choose the best five to 10 tags for your content. If you use WordPress.com and you create a post with 15 tags or more, it's much less likely to appear in the WordPress.com tag cloud (page 41), which means new visitors are less likely to stumble across your blog.
- **Keep your tags short and precise.** Pick "Grateful Dead" over "Grateful Dead Concerts."
- **Reuse your tags on different posts.** Once you pick a good tag, put it to work wherever it applies. After all, tags are designed to help people find related posts. And never create a similarly named tag for the same topic. For example, if you decide to add the tag "New York Condos," and then you use the tags "NY Condos" and "Condo Market," you've created three completely separate tags that won't share the same posts.
- **Consider using popular tags.** If you're on WordPress.com, check out popularly used tags (page 39) and consider using them in your posts, when they apply. If you're trying to attract search engine traffic, you might consider using hot search keywords for your tags (page 448).
- **Don't duplicate your category with a tag of the same name.** That's because WordPress treats categories and tags in a similar way, as bits of information that describe a post. Duplicating a category with a tag is just a waste of a tag.

TIP Here's some advice to help you get straight about categories and tags. Think of the category as the *fundamental grouping* that tells WordPress how a post fits into the structure of your site. Think of a tag as a *searching convenience* that helps readers hunt for content or find a related post.

Tagging Posts

Adding a tag to a post is even easier than assigning it to a category. When you create a post (in the Add New Post page) or edit a post (in the Edit Post page), look for the Tags box, which appears just under the Categories box.

The Tags box gives you three ways to add tags:

- Type a tag into the text box, and then click the Add button. Repeat.

- Type all your tags into the text box at once. Make sure you place a comma between each tag, as shown in Figure 4-22.
- Click the "Choose from the most used tags" link and pick from the tags you used for other posts.

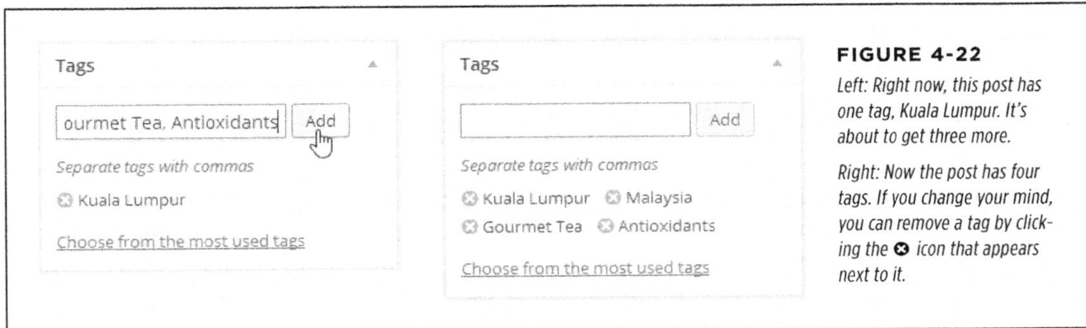

FIGURE 4-22

Left: Right now, this post has one tag, Kuala Lumpur. It's about to get three more.

Right: Now the post has four tags. If you change your mind, you can remove a tag by clicking the ⊗ icon that appears next to it.

When you publish a post, the byline will list the post's category and all its tags (Figure 4-23). You can follow these links to browse similarly tagged posts. Many blogs also use a *tag cloud*, a cluster of tag links, sized in proportion to how often you use them (in other words, in proportion to how many posts feature that tag). The default WordPress site layout doesn't use a tag cloud, but you can add one easily using the Tag Cloud widget. You learn how on page 165.

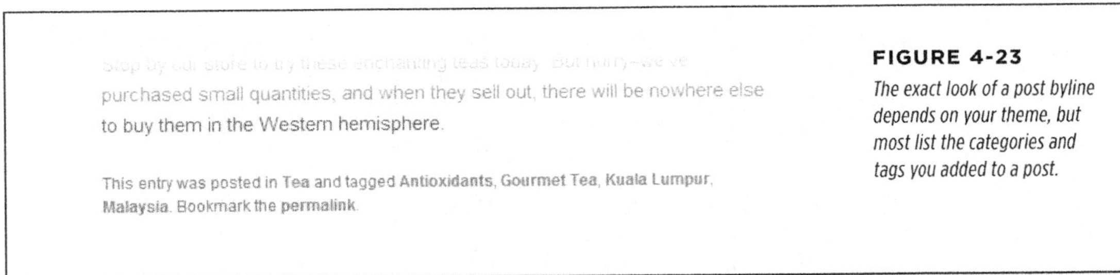

FIGURE 4-23

The exact look of a post byline depends on your theme, but most list the categories and tags you added to a post.

As with categories, tags have their own management page, which you can see by choosing Posts→Tags. There you can add tags, remove tags, and edit the tag slugs, which appear in the web addresses when you use pretty permalinks (page 117).

How to Get High-Quality Web Addresses

Every post you put on a WordPress site has its own unique web address, or URL. So far, you haven't really thought about what those URLs look like. After all, nobody *needs* to type in a web address to read a post. Instead, people can simply visit the front page of your site and click through to whatever content interests them.

However, seasoned web designers know that web addresses matter—not just for the front page of your site, but for each distinct bit of content. One reason is that search engines pay attention to the keywords in a URL, so they treat something like *http://wastedminutes.com/best_time_wasters* differently from *http://wastedminutes.com/post/viewer.php?postid=3980&cat=83*. All other factors being equal, if someone searches for "time wasters" in Google, the search engine is more likely to suggest the first page than the second.

Another important detail is the *lifetime* of your URLs. Ideally, a good web address never changes. Think of an address as a contract between you and your readers. The promise is that if they bookmark a post, the web address will still work when they return to read it, even months or years later (assuming your entire site hasn't gone belly-up in the interim). WordPress takes this principle to heart. In fact, it calls the unique web address that's assigned to every post a *permalink*, emphasizing its permanent nature.

As you'll soon see, WordPress will happily give your posts meaningful web addresses that last forever, but you might need to help it out a bit. Before you can do that, you need to understand a bit more about how the WordPress permalink system works. The details differ depending on whether you're using WordPress.com or you've installed WordPress on your web host. The following sections lay out the essentials.

Permalinks in WordPress.com

On a WordPress.com site, permalinks always follow this structure:

```
http://site/year/month/day/post-name
```

For example, if you create a blog named *lazyfather.wordpress.com* on November 27, 2014, WordPress will automatically create a post named "Hello world!" that has a permalink like this:

```
http://lazyfather.wordpress.com/2014/11/27/hello-world
```

The year, month, and day numbers are set when you create the post. The last part—the post name—is based on the title of the post. WordPress changes spaces to hyphens and ignores funky characters (like @, #, and $). If you create two posts with the same name on the same day, WordPress adds a number to the end of the second post title. (If you create a post with the same name but on a different day, no problem, because the first part of the web address is already different.)

WordPress's URL-generating strategy is a pretty good starting point. However, you can change the address for any post when you create it. This is a great feature if you think your post title is ridiculously long or if you have an idea for an address that's more likely to net you some serious search engine traffic. Page 119 explains how to change a post's permalink.

Permalinks on a Self-Hosted Site

Here's the good news: If you use the self-hosted version of WordPress, you can choose the permalink style. And here's the bad news: If you don't change it yourself, you'll be stuck with distinctly old-fashioned web addresses.

With the default permalink style, WordPress creates short but rather cryptic web addresses that use the post ID. They follow this structure:

```
http://site/?p=id
```

For example, if you create a WordPress blog at *lazyfather.com/blog*, the first "Hello world!" post gets a permalink like this:

```
http://lazyfather.com/blog/?p=1
```

The *post ID* is a unique, sequential number that WordPress gives to every new post. So it's no surprise that the first post has a post ID of 1.

This permalink style is short, but it has no other benefits. The permalinks are meaningless to other people and search engines, because it's impossible to tell what a given post is about. Can you tell the difference between *http://lazyfather.com/blog/?p=13* (a post about cute family pets) and *http://lazyfather.com/blog/?p=26* (a post about the coming Mayan apocalypse)? The post ID is essentially a secret code that doesn't mean anything to anyone except the web server database that holds the collection of correspondingly numbered posts.

Even if you love the convenience of short web addresses (and who doesn't?), you almost certainly want to use a more descriptive permalink style. Fortunately, WordPress makes it easy. Just follow these steps:

1. **In the dashboard, choose Settings→Permalinks.**

   The Permalinks Setting page appears.

2. **Choose a new permalink style.**

   Your choices are listed under Common Settings:

   - **Default.** This is the WordPress.org standard: brief but obscure permalinks that use the post ID, like *http://magicteahouse.net/?p=13*.
   - **Day and name.** This style is the same as the WordPress.com standard. Permalinks include several pieces of information, including the year, month, and date, separated by slashes. At the end is the much more descriptive post name (a simplified version of the post title), as in *http://magicteahouse.net/2014/07/28/announcing-teas-from-kuala-lumpur*.
   - **Month and name.** This style is similar to "Day and name," except that it leaves out the date number, giving you a slightly more concise permalink, like *http://magicteahouse.net/2014/07/announcing-teas-from-kuala-lumpur*.

- **Numeric.** This is a nicer looking version of the default style. It uses the post ID, but without including the *?p=* characters. Instead, it adds the text */archives*, as in *http://magicteahouse.net/archives/13*. However, this type of permalink is still as clear as mud.
- **Post name.** This style omits all the date information, using just the post name, as in *http://magicteahouse.net/announcing-teas-from-kuala-lumpur*. The advantages of this system are that the permalinks it creates are concise and easy to remember and understand. They don't emphasize the date the content was created, which is important if you have timeless content that you want to refer to months or years later. One disadvantage is that if you give more than one post the same name, WordPress needs to tack a number onto the end of the permalink to make it unique.
- **Custom structure.** This is an advanced option that lets you tell WordPress exactly how it should cook up permalinks. The most common reason to use a custom structure is because you want the post category to appear in your permalink (as explained in the box on page 119).

TIP If you don't want to emphasize dates and you're willing to put in a bit of extra work to avoid duplicate titles, the "Post name" style is a great choice. If you're concerned about clashing titles, "Month and name" is safer, and if you want to emphasize the exact date of your posts—for example, if you write time-sensitive or news-like content—"Day and name" is a good choice.

UP TO SPEED

Understanding Permalink Codes

When you choose a permalink style other than Default, you'll notice that WordPress automatically inserts the matching codes in the "Custom structure" box. For example, if you choose "Day and name," these codes appear:

```
%year%/%monthnum%/%day%/%postname%
```

Think of this as a recipe that tells WordPress how to build the permalink. Each code (that's the bit of text between percentage signs, like *%year%* and *%monthnum%*) corresponds to a piece of information that WordPress will stick into the web address.

In this example, four codes are separated by three slashes. When WordPress uses this format, it starts with the site address (as always) and then adds the requested pieces of information, one by one. First it replaces the %year% code with the four-digit year number:

http://magicteahouse.net/**2014**/%monthnum%/%day%/%postname%

Then it replaces the %monthnum% code with the two-digit month number:

http://magicteahouse.net/2014/**07**/%day%/%postname%

It carries on until the permalink is complete:

```
http://magicteahouse.net/2014/07/28/the-origin-of-tea
```

You don't need to understand WordPress's permalink codes in order to use different permalink styles. However, you do need to understand them if you want to create your own recipe for generating permalinks, as described in the box on page 119.

3. **Click Save Changes.**

   WordPress applies the permalink change to your entire site. That means that WordPress updates any posts you already published to the new style. If you're switching from the standard style to another style, this never causes a problem, because the ID-based links continue to work. (That's because no matter what permalink style you use, WordPress continues to give each post a unique post ID, which it stores in its database.) However, if you switch to a second permalink style (for example, "Day and name") and then to a third style (say, "Month and name"), the outlook isn't so rosy. Anyone who bookmarked a "Day and name"–style URL will find that it no longer works.

TIP If you want to tweak the way your WordPress site generates permalinks (and if you're using the self-hosted version of WordPress, you almost certainly do), it's best to make that change as soon as possible. Otherwise, changing the permalink style can break the web addresses for old posts, frustrating readers who have bookmarked them. Think twice before tampering with the URL structure of an established site.

POWER USERS' CLINIC

Create Permalinks That Include the Category

If you're ambitious, you can make deeper customizations to the way WordPress generates post permalinks. To do that, you need to choose the Custom Structure permalink type, and then fill in your permalink "recipe" with the right codes.

WordPress recognizes 10 codes. More than half are date-related: %year%, %monthnum%, %day%, %hour%, %minute%, and %second%. Additionally, there's a code for the category slug (%category%) and the author (%author%). Finally, every permalink must end with either the numeric post ID (represented by %post_id%) or post name (%postname%), because this is the unique detail that identifies the post.

Often, WordPress gurus use a custom permalink structure that adds category information. They do so because they feel that the permalinks are aesthetically nicer—in other words, clearer or more meaningful—or because they think that this increases the chance that search engines will match their post with a related search query.

Here's an example of a custom permalink structure that creates category-specific permalinks:

```
%category%/%postname%
```

Now WordPress creates permalinks that include the category name (in this case, Tea) and the post name (The Origin of Tea), like this:

```
http://magicteahouse.net/tea/the-origin-of-tea
```

This type of URL doesn't work well if you assigned some of your posts more than one category. In such a case, WordPress picks one of the categories to use in the web address, somewhat unpredictably. (Technically, WordPress uses the category that has the lower category ID, which is whichever one you created first.)

Changing a Post's Permalink

Most WordPress fans prefer pretty permalinks— web addresses that include the post title. If you use WordPress.com, your posts always use pretty permalinks. If you use a self-hosted WordPress site, you get pretty permalinks in every permalink style except Default and Numeric.

However, pretty permalinks aren't always as pretty as they should be. The problem is that a post title doesn't necessarily fit well into a web address. Often, it's overly long or includes special characters. In this situation, you can help WordPress out by explicitly editing the *slug*—the version of the post name that WordPress uses in your permalinks.

You can change the slug when you add or edit a post. Here's how:

1. **Find the permalink line, which appears just under the post title text box.**

   WordPress creates the slug automatically, once you type in the post title and start entering the post content. After that point, the slug doesn't change, even if you edit the title, unless you edit it explicitly.

2. **Click the Edit button next to the permalink line (Figure 4-24).**

   WordPress converts the portion of the permalink that holds the slug into a text box. You can then edit to your heart's content, so long as you stay away from spaces and special characters, which aren't allowed in URLs. The best permalinks are short, specific, and unlikely to be duplicated by other posts. (Although WordPress is smart enough to refuse to use a slug you assigned to another post.)

NOTE If you see a Change Permalinks button next to the permalink where the Edit button should be, you don't have pretty permalinks turned on. To fix the problem, follow the steps on page 117.

3. **Click OK to make your change official.**

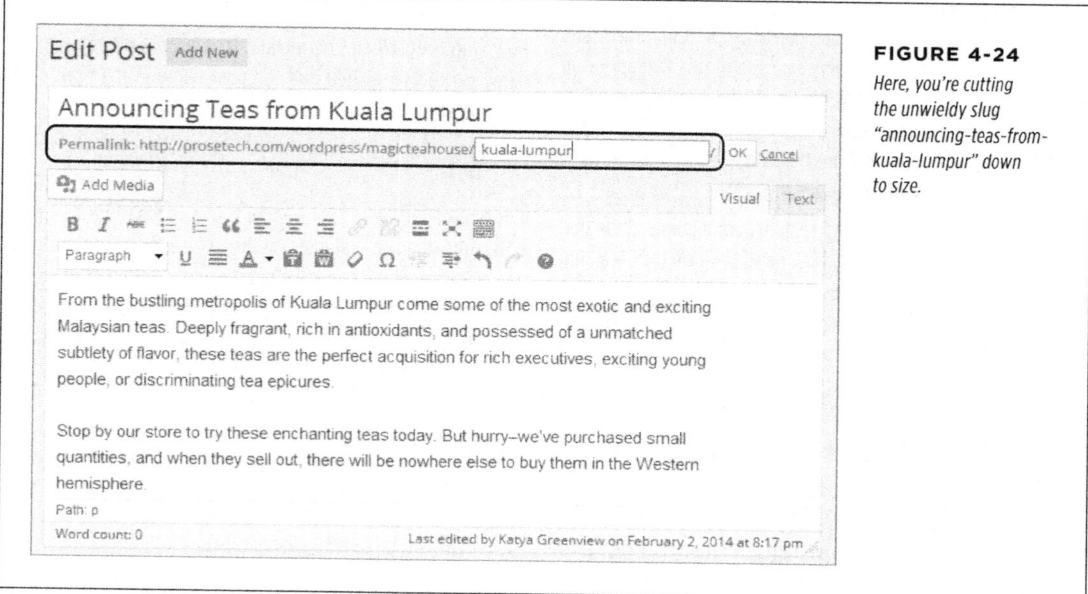

FIGURE 4-24

Here, you're cutting the unwieldy slug "announcing-teas-from-kuala-lumpur" down to size.

NOTE WordPress is very conscientious about dealing with old permalinks. If visitors try to find a post using an old permalink that has since changed, WordPress automatically forwards them to the right post and correct web address. This trick makes sure that old bookmarks and search engines that link to your site keep working.

Getting a Shorter Version of Your Web Address

Pretty permalinks are memorable and, if you don't include the date information, fairly simple. However, they can still be inconveniently long for certain situations. Sometimes, you might need a shorter address that points to a post—one that's easier to jot down or fit in the confines of a Twitter message. And although you can cut a permalink down to size when you create a post, it still might not be short enough.

WordPress is ready to help. It gives you two ways to reach every post you create: a permalink (like the ones you've been using so far), and a leaner URL called a *shortlink*. Shortlinks work just as well as permalinks, and you can use both types of link at once, depending on what you need, without confusing WordPress.

Shortlinks look different depending on whether you're using a self-hosted WordPress site or WordPress.com. In a self-hosted site, the shortlink uses the Default permalink style. It's your site address, with the numeric post ID:

```
http://magicteahouse.net/?p=13
```

WordPress.com takes a different approach. It uses its own URL-shortening service, called WP.me, to ensure that you get a micro web address like this:

```
http://wp.me/p21m89-1a
```

Even though it points to what seems like a completely different website, this shortlink redirects visitors to the right blog post on the right WordPress.com site. Best of all, the entire shortlink requires a mere 22 characters, which is just about as short as they come.

WordPress doesn't offer the shortlink option until you publish your post. In fact, to get it, you need to start editing your post (page 102). Once you're there, click the Get Shortlink button that appears in the permalink line (or just underneath it, depending on how much room WordPress has). WordPress pops open a new window with the shortlink for your post (Figure 4-25).

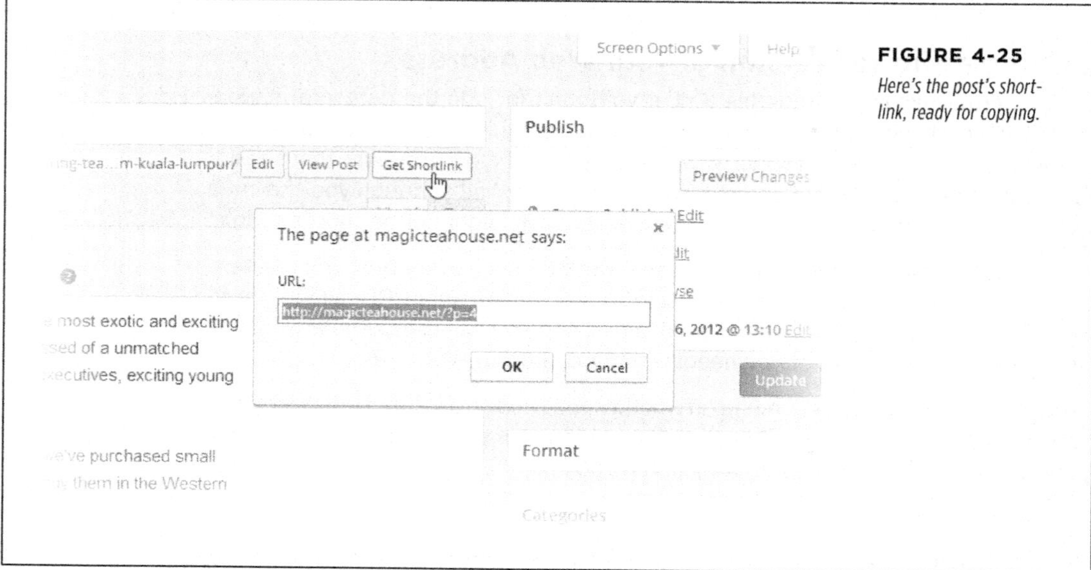

FIGURE 4-25

Here's the post's shortlink, ready for copying.

GEM IN THE ROUGH

Making Your Shortlinks Even Smaller

If you have a self-hosted WordPress site, the shortlink might not be as short as you want. It works great if you use WordPress to run your entire site and you have a nice, short domain name. But if you have a long domain name with your WordPress content in a subfolder, you end up with a not-so-short shortlink, like this:

http://prosetech.com/wordpress/magicteahouse/?p=4

It might occur to you to use the WP.me service to get an even shorter web address, but unfortunately it's limited to WordPress.com sites. However, there are other URL-shortening services that will take your address and spit out a tinier version. Popular shortener sites include *http://bit.ly* (which Twitter uses for automatic URL-shrinking), *http://tinyurl.com*, and *http://tiny.cc*.

For example, if you plug your web address into bit.ly, you get a new one, like this:

http://bit.ly/LejGs9

Weighing in at a mere 20 characters, this address is even shorter than the ones WP.me creates. If someone types that URL into a browser, they'll go first to the bit.ly web server, which will quickly redirect the browser to the original web address. The end result is that your post appears almost immediately.

Using any of these URL-shortening services is easy. Just go to the website, paste in your web address—either the permalink or shortlink, it doesn't matter—and then copy the new condensed address.

Browsing Categories and Tags Using a Web Address

Earlier, you saw how the Categories widget lets you retrieve a list of posts for any category. For example, click the Herbal Tea link and—presto!—you see the posts about brewing your favorite dried leaves.

WordPress works this category-browsing magic using a specific form of web address. If you understand it, then you can use category web addresses yourself, wherever you need them. First, you start with the site address:

```
http://magicteahouse.net
```

Then, you add */category/* to the end of the address, like this:

```
http://magicteahouse.net/category/
```

Finally, you add the bit that identifies the category you want to use. If you use the default permalink style on a self-hosted site, you get awkward category web addresses that incorporate the category ID:

```
http://magicteahouse.net/category/?cat=6
```

But if you use pretty permalinks, life is much better. Then, instead of embedding the category ID, category web addresses use the much more readable category *slug*, like this:

```
http://magicteahouse.net/category/herbal-tea
```

WordPress cooks up the slug based on your category name, using the same process it follows to pick the slug for a new post. First, WordPress replaces every uppercase letter with a lowercase one. Next, it replaces spaces with hyphens (-). Lastly, it strips out forbidden special characters, if you used them. As a result, the category Herbal Tea gets the slug *herbal-tea*.

Remember, you can modify the slug for every category using the Categories page (page 113). For example, you can shorten the address shown above by replacing *herbal-tea* with the simpler slug *herbal*.

Tags work the same way as categories, except the */category/* portion of the web address becomes */tag/*. So, to browse the posts that use a specific tag, you need an address like this:

```
http://magicteahouse.net/tags/kuala-lumpur
```

You can tweak tag slugs in the Tags page. However, it's far less common to tailor tag slugs than it is to edit post and category slugs.

Dashboard Tricks to Save Time and Effort

As you've learned, the dashboard is the key to unlocking your WordPress site. So far you've used it to work with posts: creating them, changing them, and deleting them. You also managed categories and tags, and tweaked a variety of WordPress settings. But you're far from exhausting the dashboard—in fact, you'll spend the better part of this book exploring its nooks and crannies.

Now, here are a few tips that can improve your dashboard skills. You'll learn to customize the dashboard display, get help, and work with lists—basics that will prepare you for the administrative tasks to come.

POWER USERS' CLINIC

Being in Two Places at Once

One potential problem with the dashboard is that it lets you view only one page at a time. This limitation can become awkward in some situations. For example, imagine you're in the middle of creating a post when you decide you want to review a setting somewhere else in the dashboard. You *could* save the post as a draft, jump to the settings page, and then return to continue with your post. And, for many people, this approach works just fine. But if you're the sort of power user who's comfortable with browser shortcuts, there's another approach that may appeal: opening more than one browser page at a time, with each positioned on a different part of the dashboard.

It all works through the magic of the Ctrl-click—a nifty browser trick where you hold down the Ctrl key (Command on a Mac) while clicking a link. In modern browsers, this causes the target of the link to open in a new tab. This trick doesn't work with all websites, particularly those that use JavaScript routines in the place of ordinary links. But in the WordPress dashboard, it flows without a hitch.

For example, imagine you're at the Add New Post page and you want to review your post display settings. To open the settings page in a new tab, hover over Settings in the dashboard menu and Ctrl-click the Reading link. Keep in mind, however, that if you change something in one tab that affects another, you might not see the results of your change right away. For example, if you add a category on the Categories page while the Add New Post page is open, you won't see it in the Add New Post page unless you refresh the page. (But don't forget to click Save Draft first if you want to keep your post!)

Customizing a Dashboard Page

When you navigate to a dashboard page, you don't always see all the settings you can adjust. WordPress tries hard to offer you real power and flexibility without overloading your brain with features and settings.

However, you'll sometimes need to adjust one of WordPress's hidden settings. (Or you'll want to hide some of the settings WordPress *does* show, just to clear away the visual clutter.) Either way, the secret is the Screen Options button, which controls exactly what WordPress displays on the page.

If you haven't noticed the Screen Options button yet, that's because it's carefully tucked away in the top-left corner of the dashboard (circled in Figure 4-26). However, you'll see it on nearly every dashboard page. When you click Screen Options, a new panel pops into existence at the top of the page (Figure 4-27). To collapse the panel, click the Screen Options button again.

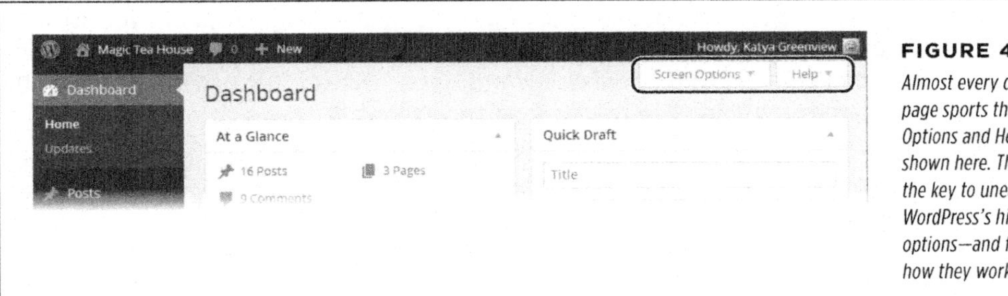

FIGURE 4-26

Almost every dashboard page sports the Screen Options and Help buttons shown here. They're the key to unearthing WordPress's hidden options—and figuring out how they work.

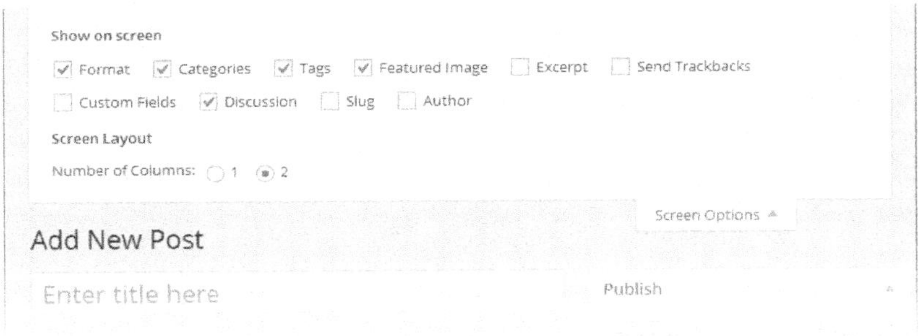

FIGURE 4-27

Here are the screen options for the Add New Post page. Using them, you can manage two things: the controls WordPress displays on the page (using the checkboxes under "Show on screen"), and the way WordPress presents those controls (using the settings under Screen Layout).

To understand how the Screen Options box works, you need to understand that every checkbox in it corresponds to a gray panel that WordPress can either show or hide. For example, in Figure 4-28, the Format, Categories, Tags, and Featured Image checkboxes are turned on, and so the Format, Categories, Tags, and Featured Image panels appear on the page. (So does the Publish panel, which doesn't have a corresponding checkbox, because WordPress won't let you hide it.)

But the Screen Options box in Figure 4-28 also includes several *unchecked* boxes, such as Excerpt, Send Trackbacks, Custom Fields, and so on. Many of these correspond to panels with less commonly adjusted settings. They're hidden (by default), because WordPress assumes you don't need them and don't want to be distracted with more details. But if you turn on one (or more) of these checkboxes, the corresponding panels appear on the page.

NOTE As you work through this book, you'll find that you sometimes do need to dip into the screen options to display panels that WordPress ordinarily hides. Now that you know how the Screen Options button works, you'll be ready.

Not only can you show and hide the panels in a dashboard page, but you can also move them around. Just click a title at the top of the panel (like "Categories") and drag it to a new place on the page. WordPress automatically rearranges the other panels to make room. This is a great way to make sure that the options you use most often are right at your fingertips. (Watch out, though: If you click the title of a panel and *don't* drag it somewhere else, WordPress collapses that panel so that only the title remains visible. Click the title again to expand it.)

Finally, there's one really useful dashboard customization trick that can help when you create or edit a huge post. If you click the bottom-right corner of the post editor and drag down (Figure 4-28), you can make the editing box as big as you want.

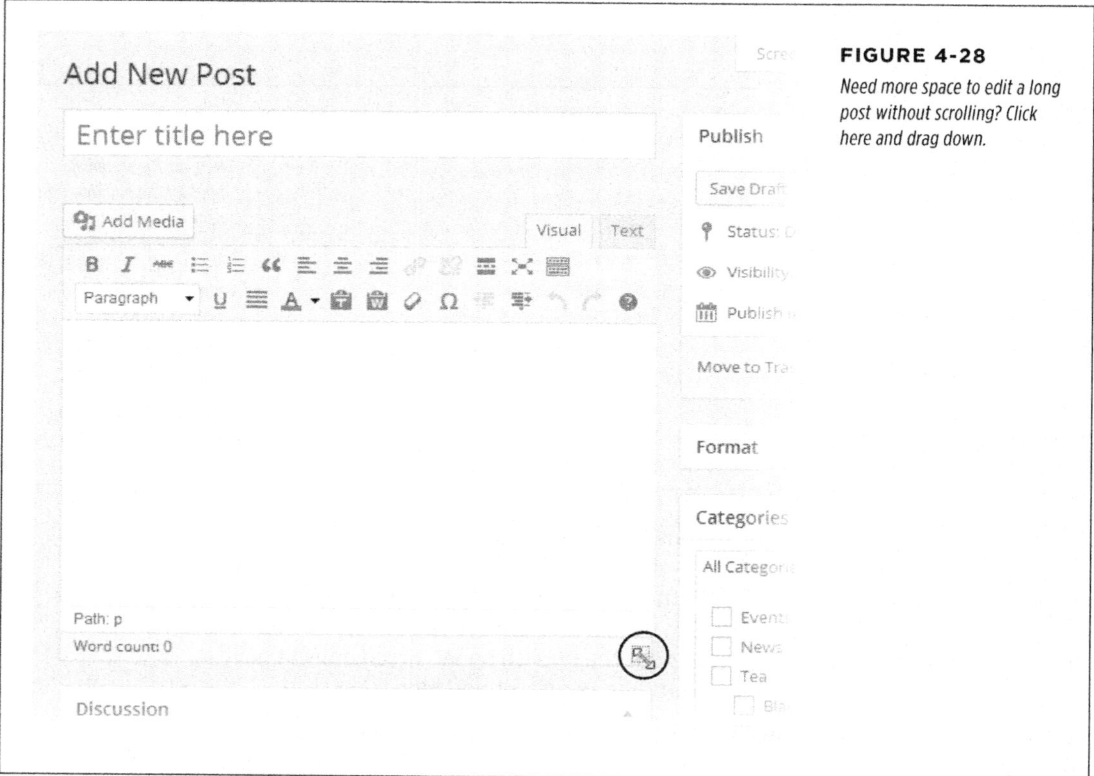

FIGURE 4-28

Need more space to edit a long post without scrolling? Click here and drag down.

Getting Help

Soon you'll be a WordPress administration guru. But in the meantime, you'll occasionally face perplexing settings in the WordPress dashboard. The Help button isn't perfect, but it can be useful sometimes.

You'll find the Help button right next to the Screen Options button, in the top-right corner of nearly every dashboard page. When you click it, a small panel with help information drops into view. To collapse the panel, click the Help button again. Figure 4-29 shows the help for the Add New Post page.

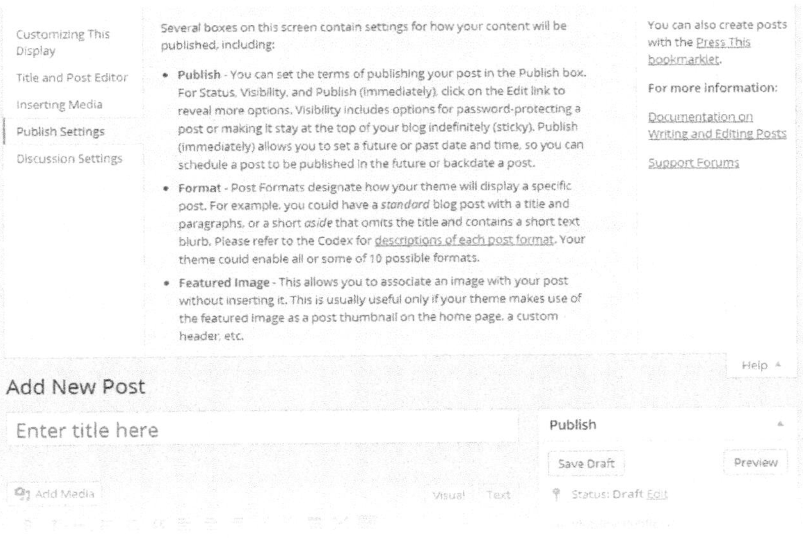

FIGURE 4-29

WordPress's help box is packed with terse but potentially helpful information. Click a link on the left side to choose your topic. (This example shows Publish Settings.) On the right are additional links that can take you to WordPress's official documentation (be warned, it's sometimes out of date) or the forums (where you can ask friendly strangers for help).

Taking Charge of the List of Posts

You've already seen the Posts page, which lists the posts on your site. However, as your site grows larger, it becomes increasingly difficult to manage everything on one page, and in a single table. To get control of your posts, you need to develop your searching and filtering skills.

First, it's important to realize that the Posts page doesn't list everything at once. Instead, it shows up to 20 posts at a time—to get more, you need to click the arrow buttons that show up in the bottom-right corner of the list. Or you can adjust the 20-post limit: just click the Screen Options button, change the number in the Posts box, and then click Apply.

NOTE If you allow more posts on your Posts page, you'll get a slower-to-load page and a longer list to scroll through. Of course, there's nothing wrong with bumping up the limit for certain tasks (say, to 100), and then changing it back when you finish.

Changing the number of posts is one way to fit more posts into your list, but it isn't much help if you want to home in on a specific batch of posts that might be scattered throughout your site. In this situation, WordPress has another set of tools to help you out: its filtering controls. Using the drop-down lists at the top of the table of posts (Figure 4-30), you can choose to show only posts that were made during a specific month (for example, "June 2014") or that belong to a specific category (say, "Green Tea").

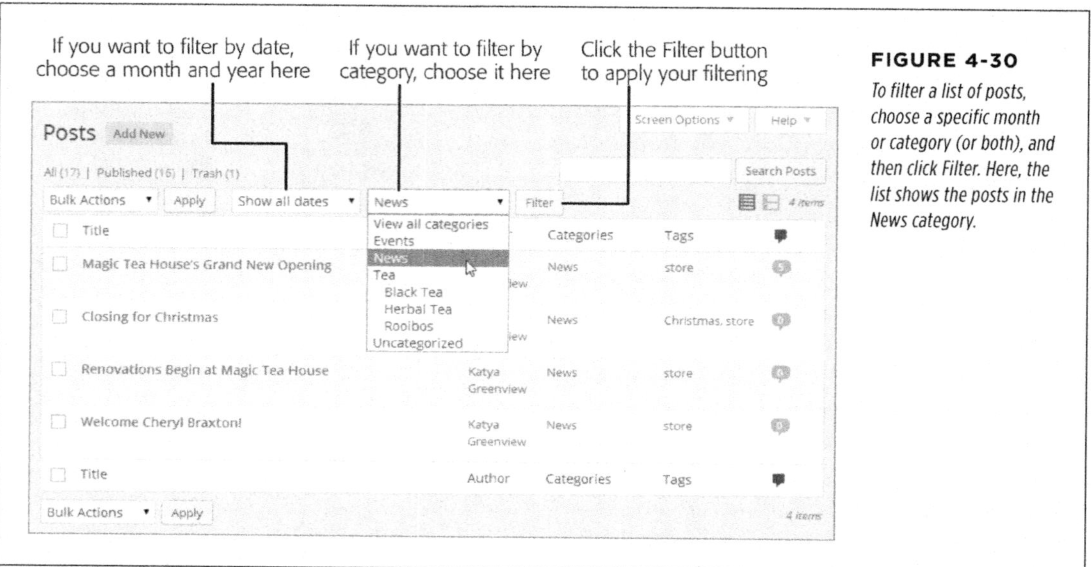

FIGURE 4-30

To filter a list of posts, choose a specific month or category (or both), and then click Filter. Here, the list shows the posts in the News category.

Ordinarily, WordPress displays posts in the same reverse-chronological order that they appear on your site. But you can change that by clicking one of the column headings. Click Title to sort alphabetically by headline, or Author to sort alphabetically by writer. If you click the column heading a second time, WordPress *reverses* the sort order. So if you sort a list of posts by Title, clicking Title a second time shows the posts in reverse-alphabetical order. And if you sort posts by Date, so that the newest posts appear first, clicking Date again displays the posts with the oldest ones on top.

The last trick that the Posts window offers is the search box in the top-right corner, above the posts list. You can search for all the posts that have specific keywords in their titles or text. For example, to show posts that talk about veal broth, you would type in *"veal broth"* (using quotation marks if you want to turn both words into a single search term), and then click Search Posts.

Performing Bulk Actions

So far, you've worked on one post at a time. If you plan to change a post's title or edit its text, this is the only way to go. But if you want to manipulate several posts in the same way—for example, change their category, add a keyword, or delete them—the Add Posts page lets you carry out your work in bulk.

The easiest bulk action is deleting. To send a batch of posts to the trash, follow these simple steps:

1. **Choose Posts→All Posts on the dashboard.**

   That takes you to the familiar All Posts page.

2. **Find the posts you want.**

   If you don't see all the posts you want to remove, then use the search or filtering techniques described on page 128.

3. **Turn on the checkbox next to each post you want to remove.**

4. **In the Bulk Actions list, choose Move to Trash.**

   The Bulk Actions list appears in two places: just above the list of posts and just underneath it. That way, it's easily accessible no matter where you are.

5. **Click Apply.**

   WordPress moves all the selected posts to the trash.

You can also use a bulk action to make certain post changes. For example, you can add tags to your post, change the author, or simultaneously publish a group of drafts. The steps are similar but slightly more involved. Here's what to do:

1. **Choose Posts→All Posts on the dashboard.**

2. **Find the posts you want (search or filter the posts if needed).**

3. **Turn on the checkbox next to each post you want to edit.**

4. **In the Bulk Actions list, choose Edit and then click Apply.**

   WordPress opens a panel at the top of the post list with editing options (Figure 4-31).

5. **Manipulate the details you want to change.**

   Using the Bulk Edit panel, you can add tags (type them in) or apply a category. However, you can't remove tags or *change* the category. That means that if you apply a new category, your posts will actually have two categories, which probably isn't what you want. (Sadly, you have to remove the category you don't want individually, post by post.)

   The Bulk Edit panel also lets you change the post's author (if your site has more than one), its status (for example, turning a draft into a published post), and a few other settings that you'll explore in the coming chapters.

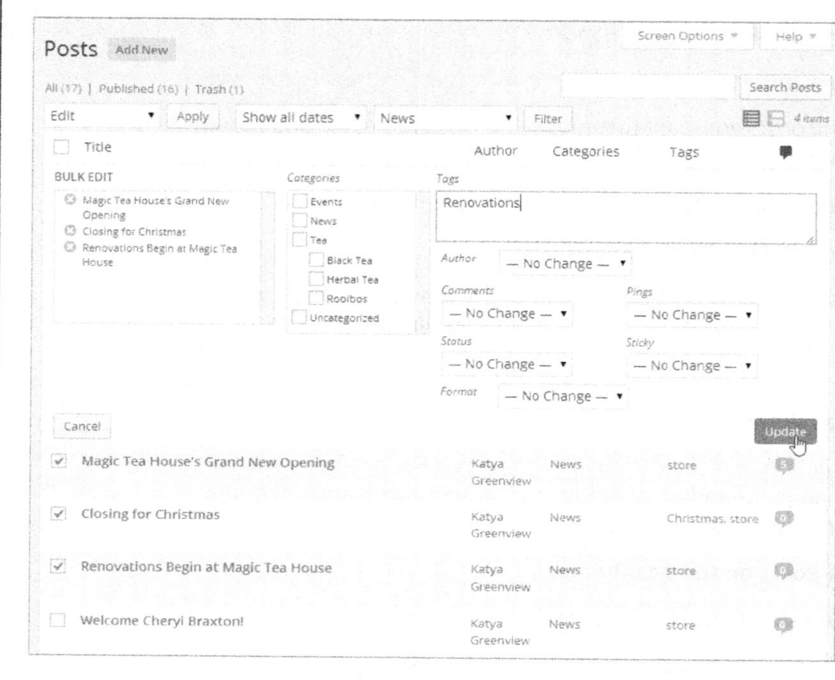

FIGURE 4-31

The Bulk Edit panel lists posts you're editing en masse (in this example, there are three), and provides a limited number of editing options. Here, you're adding a new tag to the three posts.

6. **Click Update in the Bulk Edit panel.**

   Or back out by clicking Cancel.

TIP Here's a dashboard double-trick that combines filtering and bulk actions. Say you decide to change all the posts in a category. First choose the category in the filter list (above the list of posts) and then click Filter. You'll see a list that includes only the posts in that category. To select all these posts, turn on the checkbox that appears in the top-left corner of the post list, next to the word "Title." Now you can pick your universal action from the Bulk Actions box and carry on.

GEM IN THE ROUGH

Posting with Your Phone or Tablet

The dashboard is stocked full of power-user tools. But it's impossible to beat the convenience of posting far from your computer, wherever you are, using a few swipes and taps on your favorite mobile device. In the past, developers created plug-ins that made mobile posting possible. Today, WordPress itself has taken over that role, and it offers an impressive range of free mobile apps at *http://wordpress.org/mobile*. You'll find apps that work with iPads, iPhones, Android devices, BlackBerries, Windows phones, and more. All the apps are polished, professional, and free.

CHAPTER

5

Choosing and Polishing Your Theme

Using the skills you picked up in the previous chapters, you can create a WordPress site and stuff it full of posts. However, your site will still come up short in the looks department. That's because every new WordPress site starts out looking a little drab, and pretty much the same as everyone else's freshly created WordPress site. If that sounds colossally boring to you, keep reading, because this chapter shows how to inject some serious style into your site.

The key to a good-looking WordPress site is the *theme* you use. Essentially, a theme is a set of files that control how WordPress arranges and styles your content, transforming it from raw text in a database into beautiful web pages. You can think of a theme as a *visual blueprint* for your content. Themes tell WordPress how to lay out the components of your site, what colors and fonts to use, and how to integrate pictures and other graphical details.

Every WordPress site starts out with a standard theme. Right now, yours uses the straightforward Twenty Twelve theme (assuming you followed the instructions on page 93). In this chapter, you'll learn how to enhance the Twenty Twelve theme or pick a stylish new one from the hundreds that WordPress offers. You'll also see how to choose sidebar widgets and arrange them on your site. Master these skills, and you can transform your site from standard-issue plainness to eye-popping pizzazz.

How Themes Work

One of WordPress's most impressive tricks is the way it generates web pages *dynamically,* by pulling content out of a database and assembling it into just the right web page. Themes are the key to this process.

In an old-fashioned website, you format pages before you upload them to your web server. If you want your site to look different in any respect, you have to update your pages and re-upload the whole site. But in a WordPress site, your content and your formatting information are separate, with your theme handling the formatting. As a result, you can change the way WordPress styles your pages by editing or changing your theme, without needing to touch the content. The next time someone requests a page, WordPress grabs the usual content and quietly applies the latest formatting instructions.

So how does a theme work its content-formatting magic? Technically, a theme is a package of files. Most of them are *templates* that set out the structure of your pages. For example, the template file *header.php* determines how the header at the top of every page on your site looks (see Figure 5-1), and the template file *single.php* assembles the content for a single post.

Each template includes a mixture of HTML markup and PHP code. (If you're fuzzy on these web basics, know that HTML is the language in which all web pages are written, and PHP is one of many web programming languages you can use to create dynamic content.) You won't actually touch the template files in this chapter, but you'll learn how to edit them later, in Chapter 13.

Along with your template files, WordPress uses a style sheet, named *style.css,* that supplies formatting information for virtually every heading, paragraph, and font on your site. This style sheet uses the CSS (Cascading Style Sheets) standard, and it formats WordPress pages in the same way that a style sheet formats almost every page you come across on the Web today. There's no special WordPress magic here, but you can edit your theme's style sheet to add special effects, like fancy fonts (page 481).

The WordPress "Year" Themes

Every new WordPress site starts out with a default theme. Odds are it's a *year theme,* one of a few standard themes officially sanctioned by the team of WordPress developers. We call them year themes because WordPress releases them annually and names them after the year in which they appear. The first year theme was named Twenty Ten. It was followed by the Twenty Eleven theme, the Twenty Twelve theme, and so on (see Table 5-1 for the full list). The fine folks at WordPress plan to continue this release pattern for the foreseeable future.

FIGURE 5-1

Each WordPress site uses a single theme, and each theme includes a pile of interrelated template files that control different parts of your site.

header.php

Magic Tea House

Tea Emporium and Small Concert Venue

HOME ABOUT OUR STORE POSTS TEA CONCERT SERIES

Magic Tea House's Grand New Opening

Leave a reply

Are you crawling the walls without your latest tea fix? Well then, here's some welcome news: The Magic Tea House management is overjoyed to announce that renovations are finally complete and our Grand Opening is taking place June 29, from 11:00 AM to 6:00 PM!

On hand, we'll have the fantastic tea selection you've come to expect, live entertainment, resident tea expert Cheryl Braxton, clowns, balloons, and possibly even a green tea pinata. There will also be unbelievable tea specials (watch this space for announcements). So please stop by and say "Hi." We've missed you terribly.

This entry was posted in News, Uncategorized and tagged store on March 6, 2014. Edit

Tea Sale

38 Replies

For a limited time, our Oriental Gold and Jade Express teas are offered at a

CATEGORIES

Events
News
Rooibos
Tea
Uncategorized

ARCHIVES

March 2014
July 2013
June 2013
May 2013
September 2012
August 2012

TEA RESOURCES

eGullet Tea Forum
Fair Trade Teas
Green Tea on Wikipedia
Tea Association of Canada

index.php

sidebar.php

TABLE 5-1 *The WordPress year themes*

THEME	WHAT IT LOOKS LIKE
Twenty Ten	Provides a slightly old-style blog look, with a traditional arrangement: header and menu at the top, list of posts underneath, and a sidebar on the right side. Colors and fonts start out plain and simple.
Twenty Eleven	Provides a similar layout to Twenty Ten, but adds a few Zen touches: bigger image headers, bigger text, and *much* more whitespace. (But mind the gap—some WordPress fans don't like Twenty Eleven's extra padding.)
Twenty Twelve	Offers a clean, refined theme with great typography and a streamlined layout. Some will find it bland, but its elegant design touches have kept it popular to this day. It also has particularly good support for mobile devices (as you'll see on page 168).
Twenty Thirteen	Features snazzy text, generous whitespace that recalls Twenty Eleven, and an Arizona-esque red-orange color scheme. The WordPress team was aiming for a colorful, fun look, but some people find this theme a bit *too* distinctive for their sites.
Twenty Fourteen	Provides a modern black-and-white theme with unarguable good looks. However, its stark and serious look doesn't suit everyone. Consider this theme if your site is heavy on photography.

The year themes are also called the *default themes*, because most sites start out using one of them. If you run a self-hosted WordPress site, it comes with the most recent year themes preinstalled (currently, that's Twenty Twelve, Twenty Thirteen, and Twenty Fourteen). If you host your site with WordPress.com, you get easy access to all the year themes.

NOTE At the time of this writing, all new self-hosted WordPress sites start out using Twenty Fourteen, a magazine-style theme with a heavy black frame. It feels slick, serious, and dark, and it's best suited to photo sites and news magazines, rather than traditional blogs. For that reason, you switched your site to the simpler Twenty Twelve theme on page 93 to practice posting.

UP TO SPEED

What's in a Name: The Year Themes

The year themes often confuse WordPress newcomers. The naming system seems to imply that older year themes are out of date, and that newer year themes are their natural successors. But that's not true.

First, it's important to understand that each year theme is a new creation. For example, the Twenty Fourteen theme was adapted from an existing community theme called Further that was initially built by Takashi Irie, while the Twenty Thirteen was designed in-house by the WordPress experts at Automattic. The two themes are entirely different and independent; Twenty Thirteen didn't evolve into Twenty Fourteen.

Similarly, newer year themes don't replace older ones. WordPress clearly states that the goal of each year theme is to be different, thought-provoking, and useful. The goal is *not* to provide a single all-purpose theme that satisfies everyone. That's why the appearance of Twenty Thirteen is radically different from Twenty Fourteen, and why many WordPress gurus still rely on older classics like Twenty Twelve to get the balance of features and style they want. (That said, the two oldest year themes, Twenty Ten and Twenty Eleven, don't work as seamlessly with mobile devices. To save yourself some work, pick a later year theme instead.)

When WordPress releases Twenty Fifteen, it will offer yet another new style that doesn't replace the themes that have gone before. This change won't affect you, however, because you're about to learn how to make any theme work for you—and how to find even more specialized themes in WordPress's expansive theme catalog.

Making Your Theme Suit Your Site

Now that you have a basic idea of how themes work, you're ready to start improving the look of your site. There are several paths you can take to change the appearance of your theme, depending on how dramatic your alterations are. Your choices include these:

- **Changing to a different theme.** To give your site a dramatic face-lift, you can pick a completely different theme. With that single step, you get new fonts, colors and graphics, a new layout, and—sometimes—new features. WordPress.com users have over 250 themes to pick from, while WordPress self-hosters can choose from thousands more.
- **Tweaking your theme settings.** WordPress gives you a number of useful ways to personalize your theme. The options depend on the theme, but you can usually alter a theme's color scheme, change the header picture, and shift the layout.
- **Customizing your widgets.** Most WordPress themes include one or more sections you can customize, like a sidebar you can stock with various links. The sections in the sidebar are called *widgets*, and you can change them, rearrange them, and add new ones.
- **Editing your theme.** Advanced WordPress fans can crack open their theme files, work on the code with some help from this book, and make more substantial changes. The simplest modification is to fine-tune the CSS styles that format your pages. More ambitious theme hackers can change virtually every detail of their sites.

In the rest of this chapter, you'll tackle all these tasks except the last (hardcore theme editing), which you'll study in Part 4 of this book.

Choosing a New Theme

Choosing a theme is the Big Choice you make about your site's visual appearance. Themes determine a number of important design details—for example, the way WordPress uses graphics, fonts, and color across your pages, and the overall layout of your header, sidebar, and footer. It also determines the way WordPress presents key ingredients, like the date of a post, the post's category and tag information, and the links that guests use to browse through your archives. An ambitious WordPress theme can rework almost every visual detail of your site (Figure 5-2).

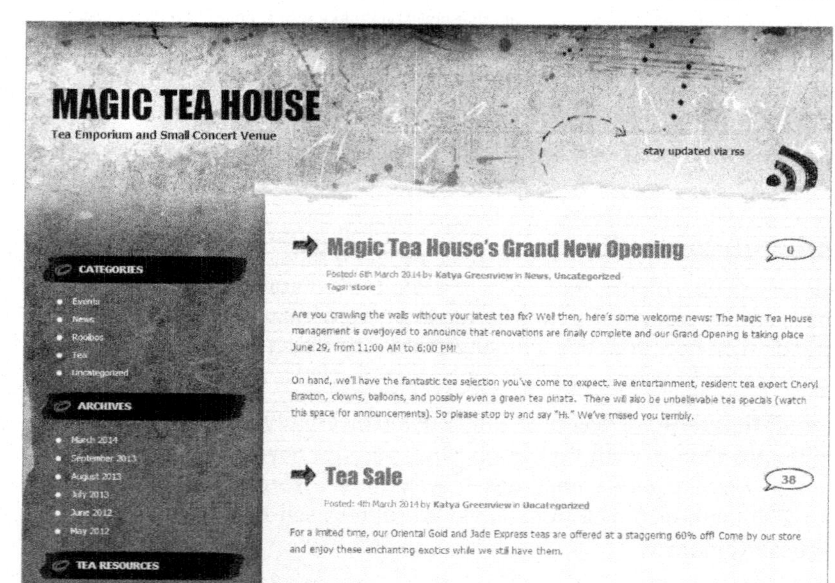

FIGURE 5-2

The Greyzed theme creates a grungy effect that looks like lined paper on stone. Every design detail—from the look of the menu to the widget titles—differs from a plain-vanilla WordPress site.

WordPress tailors some themes for specific types of content. You can find custom themes for travel blogs, photo blogs, and magazine-style news blogs. There are even themes that lean heavily toward specific topics, including one for coordinating and celebrating a wedding (called Forever) and one that looks like the old-school Mac desktop (called Retro MacOS). Figure 5-3 shows the latter.

Themes also influence the way your site works, in ways subtle and profound. For example, some themes tile your posts instead of putting them in a top-to-bottom list (which is great if you want your site to show a portfolio of work rather than a list of articles, as demonstrated on page 343). Or your theme may include a fancy frill, like a slideshow of featured posts (page 192).

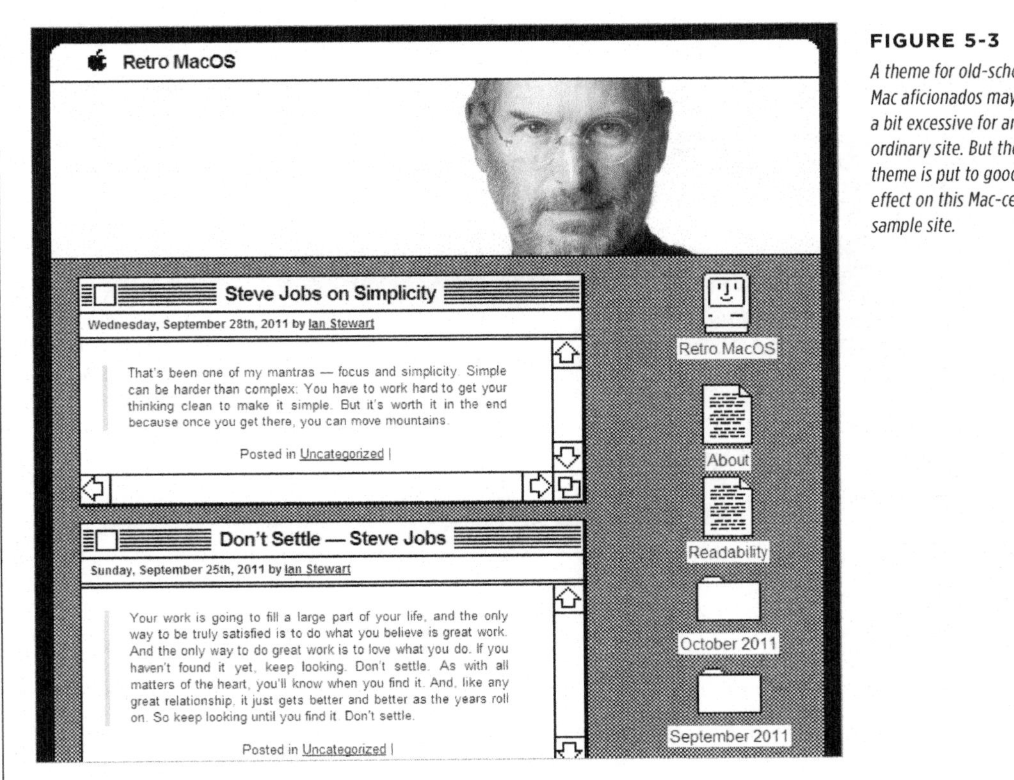

FIGURE 5-3

A theme for old-school Mac aficionados may be a bit excessive for an ordinary site. But the theme is put to good effect on this Mac-centric sample site.

Even if you're happy with the standard WordPress theme, it's worth trying out a few others, just to open your mind to new possibilities. As you'll see, although changing a theme has a profound effect on the way your site looks, doing so is almost effortless. And most themes are free, so there's no harm in exploring.

The only limitation with WordPress themes is that somewhere in cyberspace, there are sure to be plenty of other websites using the same theme as you. This isn't a huge problem, provided that you're willing to customize your site in little ways—for example, by choosing a suitable header picture, as described in this chapter. (It's also true that no matter what your site looks like, its content makes it unique.)

TIP However, if you're a style-conscious site designer who wants a distinctive theme, you run a self-hosted site, and you aren't put off by a bit of hard work, you can customize any theme. Chapter 13 explains how.

Visiting the Theme Gallery

To change your theme, visit the Themes page (Figure 5-4) by choosing Appearance→Themes in the dashboard.

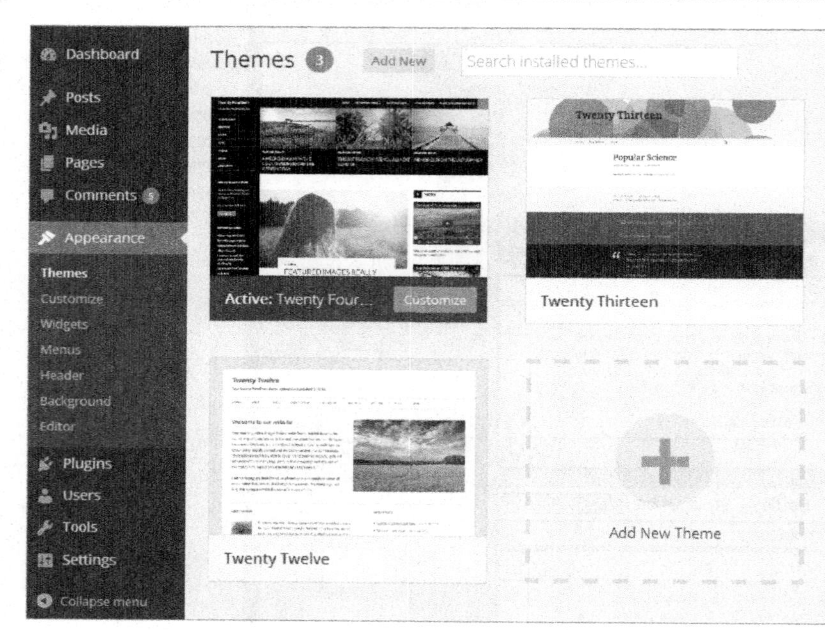

FIGURE 5-4

On the Themes page, WordPress displays all the themes currently installed on your site. In this freshly created self-hosted WordPress site, you start with three choices. The first theme in the gallery (here, that's Twenty Fourteen) is the one that your site currently uses.

The theme gallery looks slightly different for WordPress.com sites than it does for self-hosted sites. If you use WordPress.com as your host, the gallery includes every supported theme, more than 250 at the time of this writing. Some themes come with a price tag, in which case you'll see a Purchase link with a dollar figure—usually between $50 and $100.

If you run a self-hosted WordPress site, you'll find the theme gallery fairly sparse. A standard WordPress installation includes the latest year themes (currently, that's Twenty Twelve, Twenty Thirteen, and Twenty Fourteen), and nothing else. You need to add any other theme you want to use. Fortunately, there's no reason to fear this process—new themes take up very little space, installing them takes mere seconds, and you can do it all without leaving the dashboard.

The following sections explain the theme-changing steps you need to follow, depending on how you host your site.

NOTE Some web hosts preinstall extra WordPress themes. If you use one of these hosts, your theme gallery won't start out quite as empty as just described. However, you'll probably still need to install new themes to find the one you *really* want.

Activating a Theme in WordPress.com

In WordPress.com, the Themes page is a crowded place. At the top of the list is the theme your site currently uses. After that are *all* the themes that WordPress.com offers.

Roughly two-thirds of the themes on WordPress.com are free. The others—recognizable by the green price tag circles next to their names—are premium themes that require a one-time fee. The average premium theme costs around $70, although they range from $18 to $125. Once you buy a theme, it's yours forever—or at least as long as you keep the site. But if you want to use the same premium theme on more than one WordPress.com site, then you need to buy a separate copy for each site.

TIP If you want the freedom to experiment with multiple premium themes, consider buying the Unlimited Premium Themes upgrade (available from the dashboard's Store menu). It costs a reasonable $120, although you need to pay that fee every year.

If you're interested in free themes only, click the Free link at the top-right corner of the theme gallery (Figure 5-5).

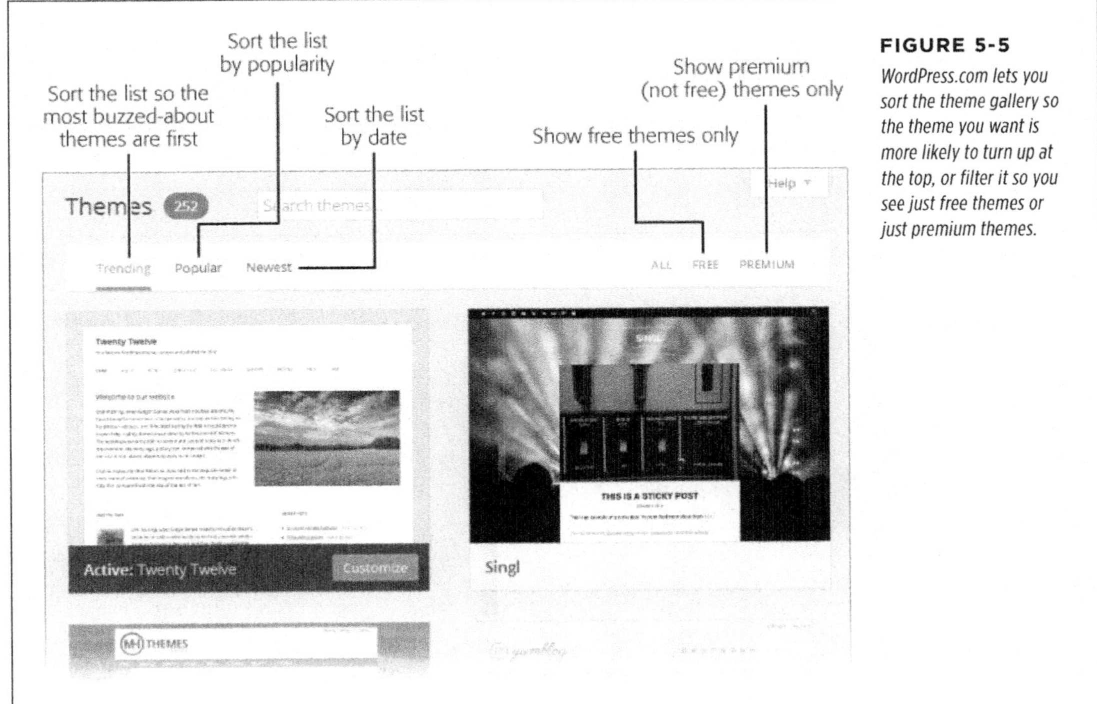

FIGURE 5-5

WordPress.com lets you sort the theme gallery so the theme you want is more likely to turn up at the top, or filter it so you see just free themes or just premium themes.

You can choose how WordPress sorts the themes list by clicking one of the three links in the top-left corner. Ordinarily, it sorts the list in *trending* order, which puts new, hot standouts at the top of the list. Alternatively, you can sort by popularity, but be warned that this list is skewed to long-lived themes, like Twenty Eleven, found on legions of old blogs. Finally, you can sort by date to spot just the newest themes, which is handy for keeping up with the latest additions to the gallery.

The most useful theme-hunting tool is the search box just above the gallery. If you remember a theme you browsed before, or you have a theme characteristic in mind (say, "minimalistic" or "dark"), you can type that in. WordPress.com filters the list as you type.

When you find a promising theme, point to it without clicking your mouse. You'll see several buttons (Figure 5-6):

- **Theme Details** displays basic information about the theme, including a brief description and a link to the person or company that created it.
- **Preview** opens a preview window that shows your site dressed in this theme. It's called a *live* preview because you can treat it exactly as you would a real site—clicking links, browsing content, and feeling your way around. Usually, the live preview is enough for you to decide whether you really do want the theme you're checking out. Click Cancel when you finish, or Activate to apply the theme to your site.
- **Activate** reconfigures your site to use this theme. The changeover happens instantaneously.
- **Purchase** replaces the Activate button for premium themes. Clicking this button starts the checkout process. Once you cough up the fee, WordPress activates the theme.

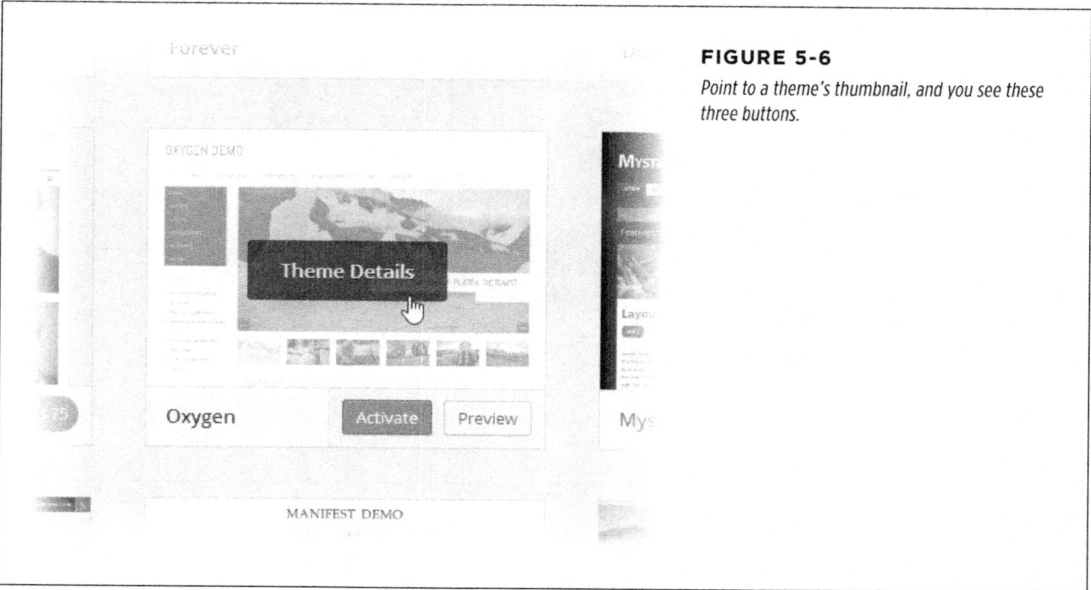

FIGURE 5-6

Point to a theme's thumbnail, and you see these three buttons.

Don't be shy—you can activate one theme, and then another, and then another, until you find the right one for your website. When you pick a new theme, WordPress may prompt you to start customizing it with the theme customizer (page 152). However, it's generally easier to customize your theme using the group of pages under the dashboard's Appearance menu, because the options there are more comprehensive. You'll start customizing your theme on page 145.

Installing a Theme on a Self-Hosted Site

Before you can switch to a new theme on a self-hosted WordPress site, you need to install the theme itself. To see the themes you can add, click the Add New button next to the Themes heading at the top of the Themes page. This takes you to the Add Themes page, where you can browse WordPress's theme repository to find exactly what you want (Figure 5-7).

Initially, the Add Themes page shows you a list of *featured* themes, which are new and particularly noteworthy designs that the folks at WordPress think might interest you. If they don't, you can browse the most popular themes (click Popular) or the most recent ones (click Latest).

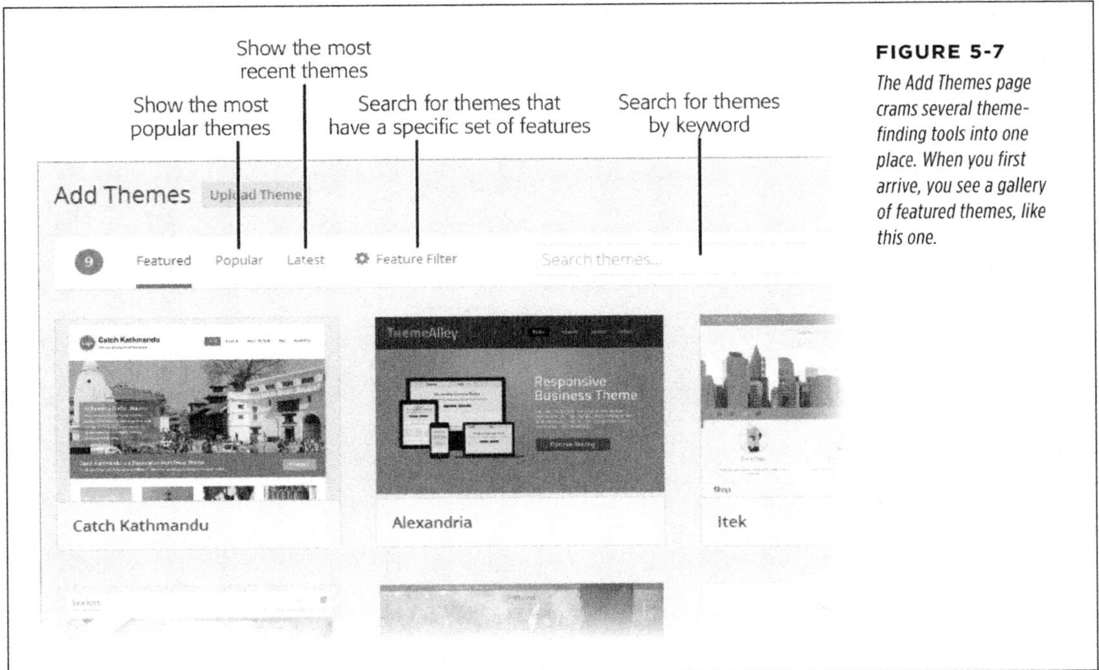

FIGURE 5-7

The Add Themes page crams several theme-finding tools into one place. When you first arrive, you see a gallery of featured themes, like this one.

Browsing is fine, but the most powerful way to hunt down new themes is with a search. The Add Themes page gives you two ways to do that: by keyword and by feature.

To search by keyword (for example, "magazine" or "industrial" or "professional"), type the word in the search box and then click Search. WordPress shows you themes that have that search term in their names or descriptions.

TIP Here's a trick to see even more themes: Leave the search box empty, and then press the Enter key. You'll get a list of well over 1,000 themes.

To search by feature, click Feature Filter. WordPress displays a long list of checkboxes, representing different features and theme characteristics (Figure 5-8). Turn on the checkboxes for the features you want, and then click Apply Filters.

NOTE You can't search by keyword and filter by feature at the same time.

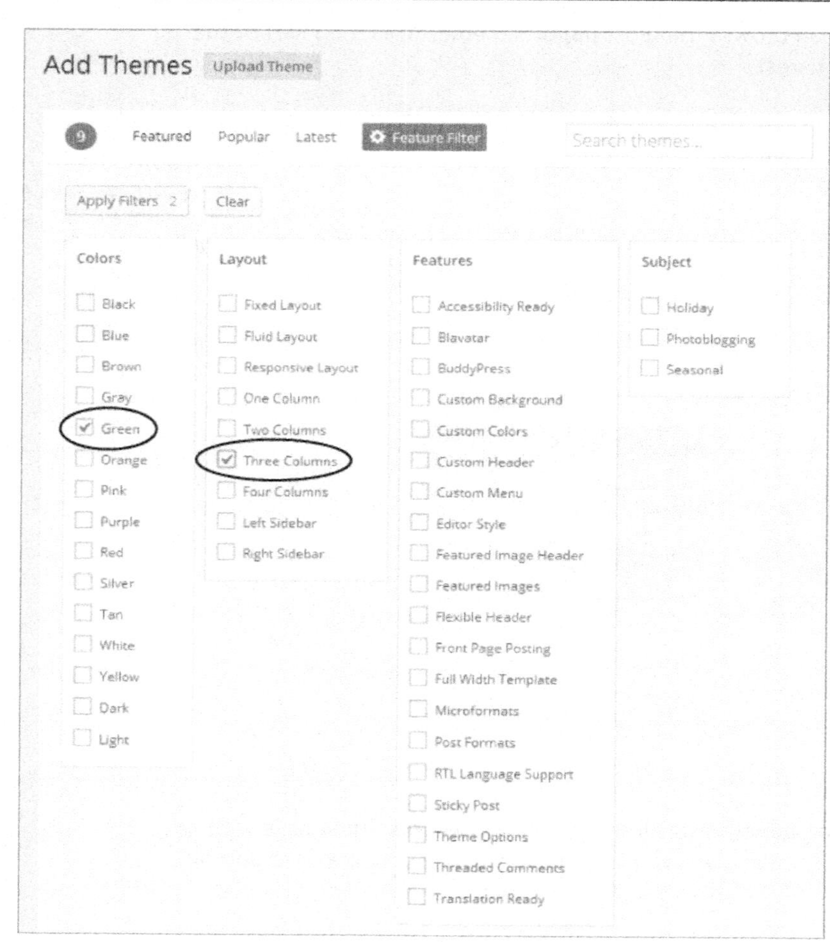

FIGURE 5-8

The Feature Filter helps you find themes that meet specific criteria. This search will find themes that feature the color green and use a three-column layout. (More than 50 do.)

No matter how you find a theme, you install them all the same way. First, point to your new theme without clicking the mouse. The Install and Preview buttons appear (Figure 5-9, top). Click Preview to see a sample site that uses the theme, and to read a brief description of the theme and the person or company that created it. Click Install to copy the theme to your website so it's ready to use.

TIP Don't be afraid to install a theme that you might not want to use—all the themes in the WordPress repository are guaranteed to be safe and spyware-free. And don't worry about downloading too many themes—not only are they tiny, but you can easily delete those you don't want.

Once WordPress installs a theme, it gives you three choices (Figure 5-9, bottom):

- **Live Preview.** This opens a window showing you what your site would look like if WordPress applied the chosen theme. Think of it as a test drive for a prospective theme. You can read posts, search your site, and click your way around your content, secure in the knowledge that you haven't changed the real, live version of your site.
- **Activate.** Click this to start using the theme.
- **Return to Theme Installer.** This takes you back to the Add Themes page (Figure 5-7), where you can search for another theme.

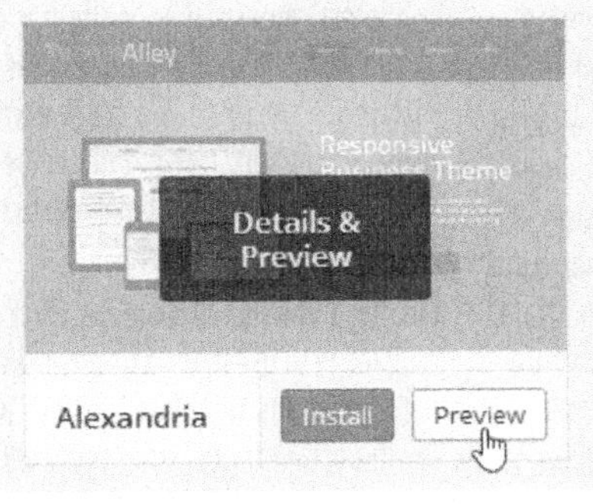

Installing Theme: Alexandria 2.0.17

Downloading install package from https://wordpress.org/themes/download/alexandria.2.0.17.zip...

Unpacking the package...

Installing the theme...

Successfully installed the theme **Alexandria 2.0.17**.

Live Preview | Activate | Return to Theme Installer

FIGURE 5-9

Top: When you're ready to take a closer look at a theme, point to it and click Preview.

Bottom: WordPress has finished installing the latest version of the Alexandria theme on your site. Click Activate to start using it.

To see all the themes you've installed on your site so far, choose Appearance→Themes. This returns you to the theme gallery. To take a closer look at a theme, point to it. If you point to the theme you currently use, you'll see a Customize button, which launches the theme customizer (page 152). If you point to one of the other themes, you'll see two familiar buttons: Live Preview, which lets you test drive the theme; and Activate, which applies it to your site.

Once you activate a theme, the best way to get familiar with it is to poke around. Try adding a post, viewing it, and browsing the list of posts on the home page, just as you did in Chapter 4. Check out the way your theme formats the home page and presents individual posts.

Once you familiarize yourself with your new theme, you'll want to check out its options and consider tweaking it. That's the task you'll tackle next.

NOTE There's one other way to add a theme: by uploading it from your computer to your site, using the Upload button on the Add New themes page. You'll use this option only if you find a theme on another site, buy a premium theme from a third-party company, or build the theme yourself.

UP TO SPEED

The Proper Care of Your Themes

When you install a theme on a self-hosted site, you get the current version of the theme. If the theme creator releases a new version later, your site sticks with the old version.

That makes some sense, because WordPress has no way to be sure that the new version of the theme won't make drastic changes that break your site. But this design also raises the risk that you might ignore an important security update for one of your themes, thereby exposing your site to an attack. (Remember, themes contain templates, and templates contain PHP code, so themes can create security vulnerabilities.)

To minimize your risk, check regularly for theme updates. Go to Dashboard→Updates and look at the Themes section. If a theme has been updated, WordPress lists it here, and compares the version number of your copy with the version number of the latest release. If your site has multiple themes installed, WordPress shows the updates for *all* of them—it makes no difference whether you currently use the theme or not. To protect yourself, download all the available updates. To do that, turn on the checkbox next to each update and then click Update Themes.

Finally, if you install a theme, try it out, and decide you aren't ever likely to use it, it's a good idea to delete it. Even if a theme isn't active, its template files are accessible on your site, allowing attackers to exploit any security flaws the templates may have. This isn't a common method of attack, but it has happened to unsuspecting site owners before.

Tweaking Your Theme

The first step in getting the look you want is choosing the right theme, but your site-styling doesn't end there.

Every theme lets you customize it. In fact, you *need* to customize your theme to make sure it meshes perfectly with your site. Your page's header image is a perfect example—if your theme includes one, you'll almost certainly want to replace the stock image with a picture that better represents your site. Other basic theme-preparation tasks include shuffling around your widgets and setting up your menus. You handle all these tasks in the pages of the Appearance menu.

Customizing the Header

When a visitor arrives at your site, the first thing she sees is the eye-catching header at the top of your home page. Right now, that's a problem, because the standard header screams "Generic WordPress Site!" It's for amateurs only.

Different themes may have slightly different header settings, but here are the details you can usually change:

- The header text
- The color of the header text
- The header image

The header text includes the title and tagline you specified when you created your site. WordPress stores this information as part of your site settings, and you can modify it using the Site Title and Tagline boxes at Settings→General.

Most themes also let you pick the color of your header text. Usually, it starts out black. (Twenty Fourteen is a notable exception, because it uses white text on a black background.) To pick a different color, go to the Custom Header page at Appearance→Header and look for the Text Color setting. Click the Select Color button next to it to open a miniature color picker and choose the exact shade you want.

NOTE At this point, it may occur to you that there are many other ways you might want to adjust your site's header. For example, you might want to change the size of the text or pick a fancier font. But making these types of changes is an advanced operation. If you have a self-hosted site, you need to modify the CSS style rules that control your theme. You'll learn how to do that in Chapter 13. And if you have a WordPress.com site, you need to buy the Custom Design upgrade (for $30 per year) to even be allowed to make this sort of formatting change (see page 457).

Many themes let you use a picture in your header. Depending on the theme, the header text may be displayed above the image, beneath the image, or on top of it (or you may choose to hide the header text altogether). Deciding whether you want to use an image is the most important decision you'll make while customizing your header. Figure 5-10 shows how the Twenty Twelve theme deals with header images.

FIGURE 5-10

Top: The Magic Tea House is a bit plain with a text-only header.

Middle: Every theme makes its own decision about where to place the header image. If you add an image to the Twenty Twelve theme, it turns up underneath the menu.

Bottom: Hiding the header text results in a much cleaner look.

Here's how to upload a new header picture for the standard WordPress theme:

1. **Choose Appearance→Header.**

   The Custom Header page opens.

2. **Prepare your picture.**

   Before you upload a new picture, look carefully at the information on the Custom Header page (Figure 5-11). It usually tells you how big your picture should be. Because the theme's layout dictates the size of the header, each theme has different size specifications. For example, Twenty Twelve needs a header 960 pixels wide and 250 pixels high, while Twenty Fourteen expects a wider and shorter image (1260 × 240 pixels).

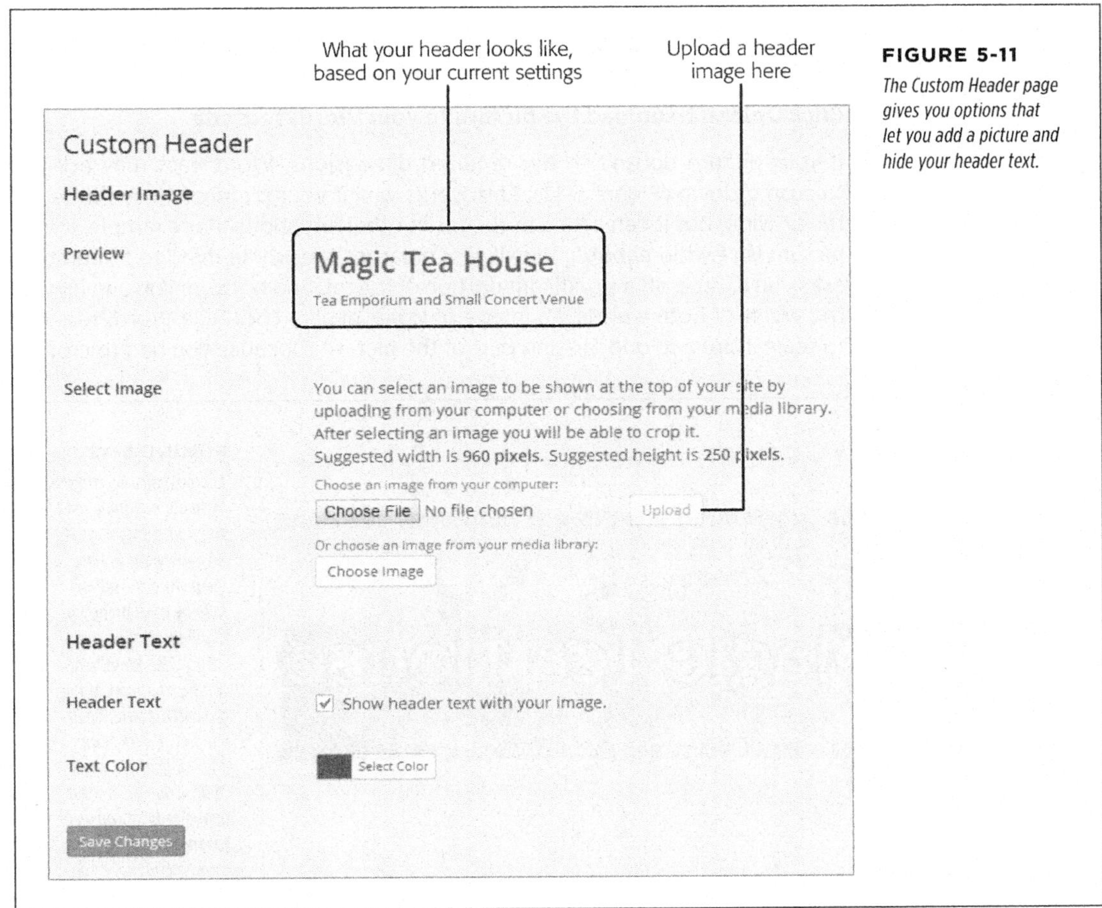

FIGURE 5-11

The Custom Header page gives you options that let you add a picture and hide your header text.

If possible, you should resize or crop your picture to those specs, using an image-editing program before you upload it. That way, you'll get exactly the image you want. If your image doesn't match the dimensions your theme expects, WordPress may crop or resize it.

TIP Need a good picture but lack the photographic or illustrative skills to make one? Don't do a Google image search—you're highly likely to end up stealing someone else's copyrighted work. Instead, try a free stock photography site like Stock.xchng (*www.sxc.hu*). It offers a vast collection of member-submitted pictures, most of which are free for other people to use. (In fact, stock.xchng was the source of the sunny yellow teapot picture that graces the Magic Tea House site in Figure 5-10.)

3. **In the Select Image section, click the Browse or Choose File button (the exact wording depends on the Internet browser you're using).**

   In the window that opens, find the header picture on your computer, and then select it.

4. **Click Upload to upload the picture to your WordPress site.**

   If your picture doesn't fit the required dimensions, WordPress may ask you to crop it down (Figure 5-12). This works well if your picture is just a little too tall or wide, but it can cause problems in other situations. For example, if your picture isn't wide *enough*, WordPress enlarges the whole thing to fit and then asks you to crop off a significant portion of the top and bottom. You end up with the worst of both worlds: an image of lower quality (because WordPress had to scale it up) and one missing part of the picture (because you had to crop it).

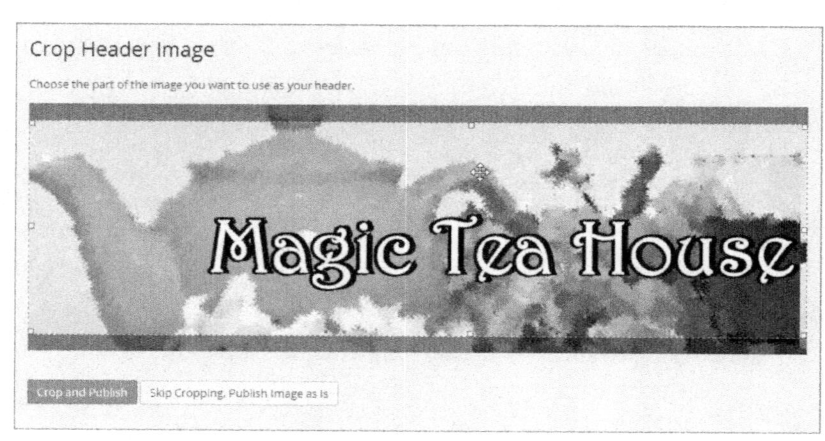

FIGURE 5-12

To crop a picture, drag the highlight rectangle until you frame the image the way you want it. Here, the picture is a bit too tall—by positioning the highlight rectangle in the middle, WordPress will trim out part of the top and bottom. When you finish, click "Crop and Publish." Or, click "Skip Cropping, Publish Image as Is" if you want to ignore your theme's recommendations and use an oddly sized header that may not fit nicely into your layout.

5. **Consider removing the header text by turning off the setting "Show header text with your image."**

   In some themes, the header text meshes neatly with the header image. For example, Twenty Thirteen superimposes the header text on the header image.

   In other themes (like Twenty Twelve), the text and picture are separate. For a slicker look, you may choose to use a header image that includes stylized text, and ditch the theme's standard header text. The result is shown in Figure 5-10 (bottom).

   Incidentally, if you decide to go the other way, you can remove the picture you added by clicking the Remove Header button. And if you're a truly odd duck, you can remove both the header picture and the header text, but that will make your site look just plain weird.

6. **Click Save Changes.**

   If you add or remove a header image, you don't need to click this easily overlooked button at the bottom of the Custom Header page, because WordPress incorporates the change right away. But if you change one of the other header settings, such as the "Show header text with your image" option, click Save Changes to make it permanent.

GEM IN THE ROUGH

Random Header Pictures

Some themes have the ability to perform a curious header-switching trick. First, they let you upload multiple pictures. Then they randomly choose a different picture for the header on each page. All the standard year themes provide this feature, from Twenty Eleven on.

To try this out, start by uploading more than one picture on the Custom Header page. (Just repeat the steps that start on page 147.) If your theme doesn't display multiple header images, it will simply toss out the old picture when you add a new one. But if your theme *does* allow multiple images, it will keep track of each picture you add, and you'll see a thumbnail for each in the Uploaded Images section of the Custom Header page.

You can choose to show a picture you uploaded by selecting it in the Uploaded Images section. But if you're after a more exotic effect, choose the Random option. Now start browsing the posts on your site. As you click from page to page, you see the header change from one picture to another. Eventually, WordPress will cycle through all your images.

The only catch is that once you upload a header image, you can't remove it from the Custom Header page. If you decide that you don't want WordPress to include one of your uploaded pictures in its lineup of random headers, you need to delete the image using the media library. First, click Media in the dashboard menu. That brings you to the media library, where you'll see a list of all the images you uploaded to your site (including any pictures you placed in your posts). You can recognize the header pictures that the current WordPress theme uses, because they have the text "Header Image" after their filenames. Point to the header you don't want, and then click Delete Permanently to banish it from your site. (Page 186 has plenty more about the media library feature.)

Some folks love the changing-picture trick. For example, it's a great way to showcase a number of different and delectable dishes on a food blog. However, most people prefer to pick a single header and stick with it. That gives the site a clearer identity and helps visitors remember your site.

Changing the Background

Many themes let you change the background of your pages. You can find these options in the Custom Background page by choosing Appearance→Background.

Most themes give you two background-altering choices:

- **Add a background image.** Most themes *tile* the background image (that means they repeat the image endlessly, from top to bottom and left to right, filling your visitor's browser window). For that reason, you need a picture that looks good when it's jammed edge-to-edge against another copy of itself. Small pictures called *textures* work well for this task, and you can find them online, but the effect is distinctly old-fashioned.
- **Change the background color.** This is the most commonly tweaked background setting. You can use it to make the page background blend in more smoothly with the background of your header image.

"Background color" doesn't always mean what you expect. For example, in the Twenty Twelve theme, the background color shows up only on the outer edges of your page, not behind your posts. To change the color behind the text in your posts, you need to tweak the theme styles, as explained in Chapter 13. Figure 5-13 shows the difference.

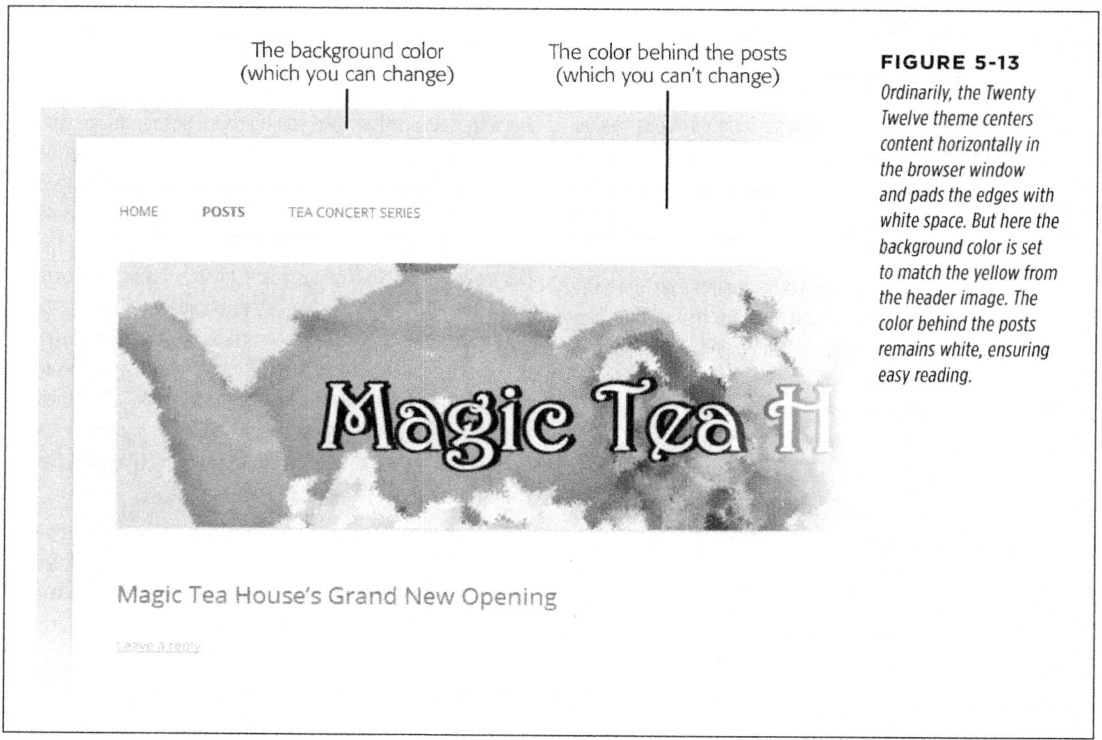

FIGURE 5-13

Ordinarily, the Twenty Twelve theme centers content horizontally in the browser window and pads the edges with white space. But here the background color is set to match the yellow from the header image. The color behind the posts remains white, ensuring easy reading.

To change the background color the standard WordPress theme uses, you can type in an HTML color code (like *#e7df84*, suitable for web nerds), or you can use the groovy built-in color picker (Figure 5-14).

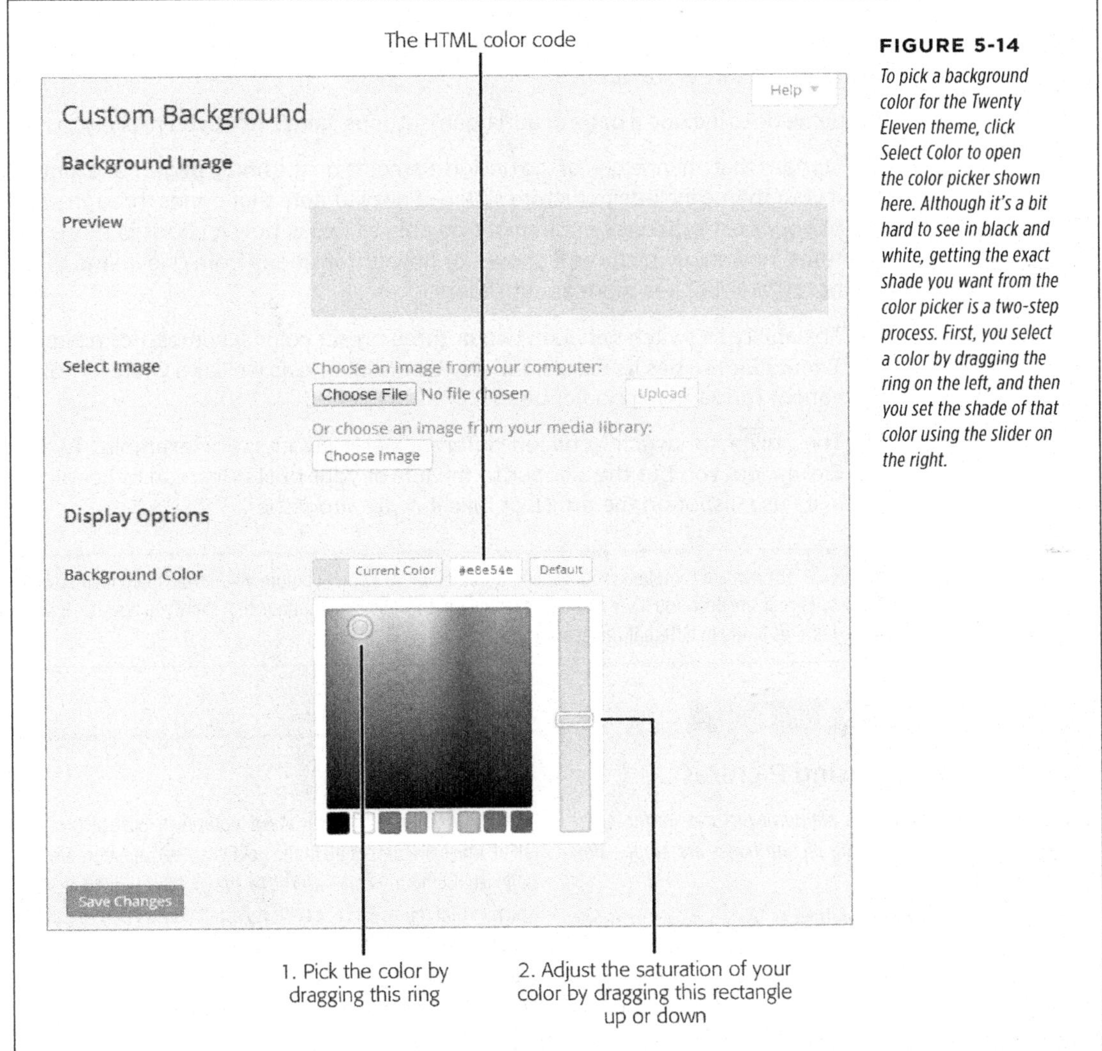

FIGURE 5-14

To pick a background color for the Twenty Eleven theme, click Select Color to open the color picker shown here. Although it's a bit hard to see in black and white, getting the exact shade you want from the color picker is a two-step process. First, you select a color by dragging the ring on the left, and then you set the shade of that color using the slider on the right.

TIP If it's hard to see the differences between the examples in the black-and-white pages of this book, check out the Magic Tea House sample site at *http://prosetech.com/wordpress.*

Other Theme Options

Some themes include additional options, which you can find in the Appearance menu in the dashboard. For example, if you install the Greyzed theme, you'll get a new page of options by choosing Appearance→Greyzed Options. If you use the aging Twenty Eleven theme, you can view its settings by choosing Appearance→Theme Options. But the later year themes, such as Twenty Twelve and Twenty Fourteen, don't include any extra options.

If a theme does include a page of additional settings, here's what you're likely to find:

- Options that change one of the design elements on the home page. For example, if your theme includes a picture slider—a nifty feature that cycles through some of your post's pictures—you might be able to tweak how it chooses those pictures, how many pictures it shows, or how it transitions from one image to the next. Page 192 has more about sliders.
- The ability to switch between two or three preset color schemes. For example, Twenty Eleven has its usual light, airy color scheme as well as a white-on-black variant for darker, moodier people.
- The ability to switch between different basic layouts. For example, Twenty Eleven lets you put the sidebar to the left of your posts (instead of keeping it in its usual spot on the right), or take it away altogether.

NOTE Themes are complex creations, and it takes a bit of fiddling before you have a good idea of which theme suits your site best. You'll see plenty of examples in the following chapters that show you how to capitalize on the features found in different themes.

FREQUENTLY ASKED QUESTION

Themes with Missing Pictures

I picked a theme that has plenty of pictures on the home page, but right now, all the picture boxes are empty. How do I fill them?

Many of the most attractive themes use a visually rich style that incorporates plenty of pictures. Some themes include a slider that shows pictures from different posts. Others turn the post list into a grid of post titles and picture thumbnails. But before you can use this type of feature, you need to learn more about how WordPress works with pictures.

Although WordPress has a variety of features that use pictures (all of which are described in the next chapter), most graphically rich themes rely on *featured images*. A featured image is a picture that represents a specific post, but doesn't necessarily appear *in* the post. Page 190 explains featured images, shows you how to link them to posts, and explores several themes that use them to create eye-catching home pages.

The Theme Customizer

If you're tired of jumping from one page to the next using the Appearance menu, you may be interested in the *theme customizer,* a dashboard tool that lets you quickly configure a new theme. The theme customizer uses a multi-tabbed page that combines many of the settings and options scattered throughout the Appearance menu. To open the customizer, choose Appearance→Customize. Or, when viewing the theme gallery (Appearance→Theme), point to the current theme and click the Customize button. Either way, WordPress displays a live preview of your site with a sidebar of theme-customization options. Figure 5-15 shows the Twenty Twelve theme under the microscope in the theme customizer.

NOTE The theme customizer doesn't always look as it does in Figure 5-15. Some themes offer fewer customizable sections, and WordPress.com sites put the sidebar on the right side of the page instead of the left. However, the basic concept remains the same: You configure common theme settings while watching a constantly updated preview of your work.

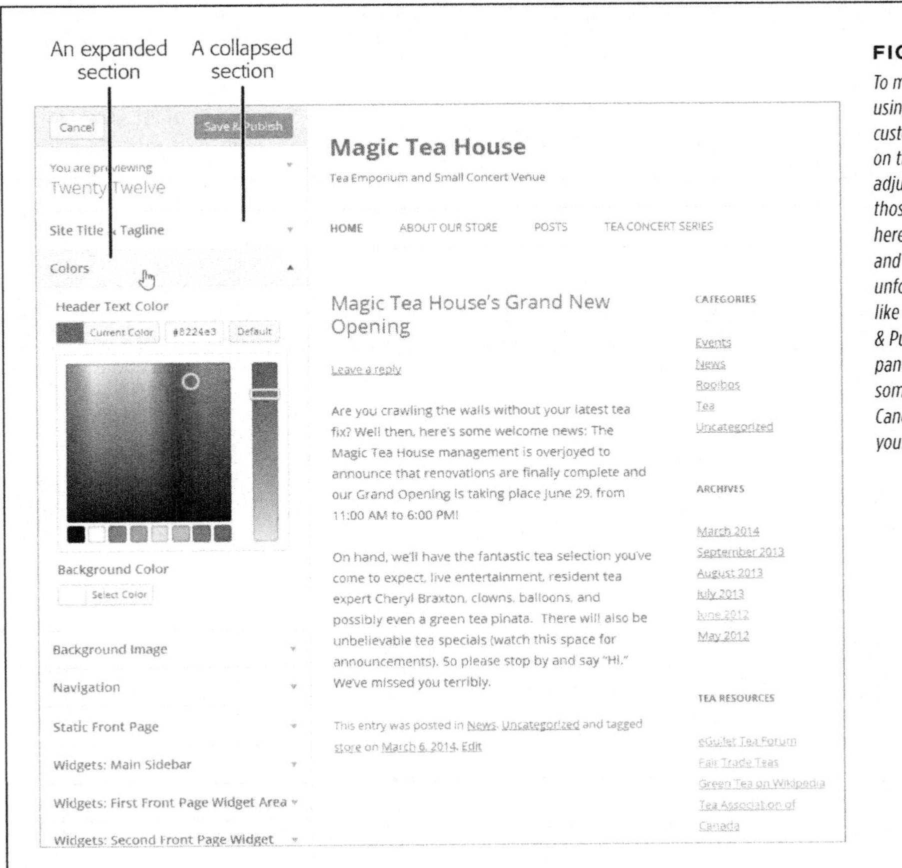

FIGURE 5-15

To modify your theme using WordPress's theme customizer, click a section on the left to open it and adjust the settings (like those for Colors, shown here). Make your changes and watch the preview unfold on the right. If you like the result, click Save & Publish at the top of the panel. If you don't, pick something else, or click Cancel to back out of all your changes.

There's a lot packed into the customizer's tabs. But, oddly enough, some important details are inexplicably absent. It's not that you can't set them—you can, if you use the different pages in the Appearance menu—but for some reason they escape the customizer's notice. For that reason, you might be decidedly cool on the theme customizer. It's a useful place to *start* customizing, but it's not a reliable long-term partner.

NOTE The theme customizer may also include two tabs that you won't consider in this chapter. Those are Navigation (where you pick a menu to display on your site) and Static Front Page (where you can choose a custom home page for your site). To use either of these features, you first need to study the pages feature, which you'll master in Chapter 7.

Customizing Your Widgets

By the time you pick a theme, fix up your header, and adjust your theme settings, your site is starting to look more respectable. But you're not done tweaking yet. Although your theme may look a whole lot nicer, there's still one area that most WordPress site creators will want to change: the sidebar.

The sidebar is a terrifically useful place to put links, like the ones that let your visitors browse your archives. It's filled with something WordPress calls *widgets*. A widget is simply a block of useful content (like a list of links) that you can stuff into a sidebar or put somewhere else in your site (Figure 5-16). Here's the neat part: WordPress widgets work with any theme.

NOTE Technically, the theme you choose provides one or more areas (like a sidebar and a footer) for widgets. It's up to you to choose *what* widgets go in those areas, and to configure the widgets you add.

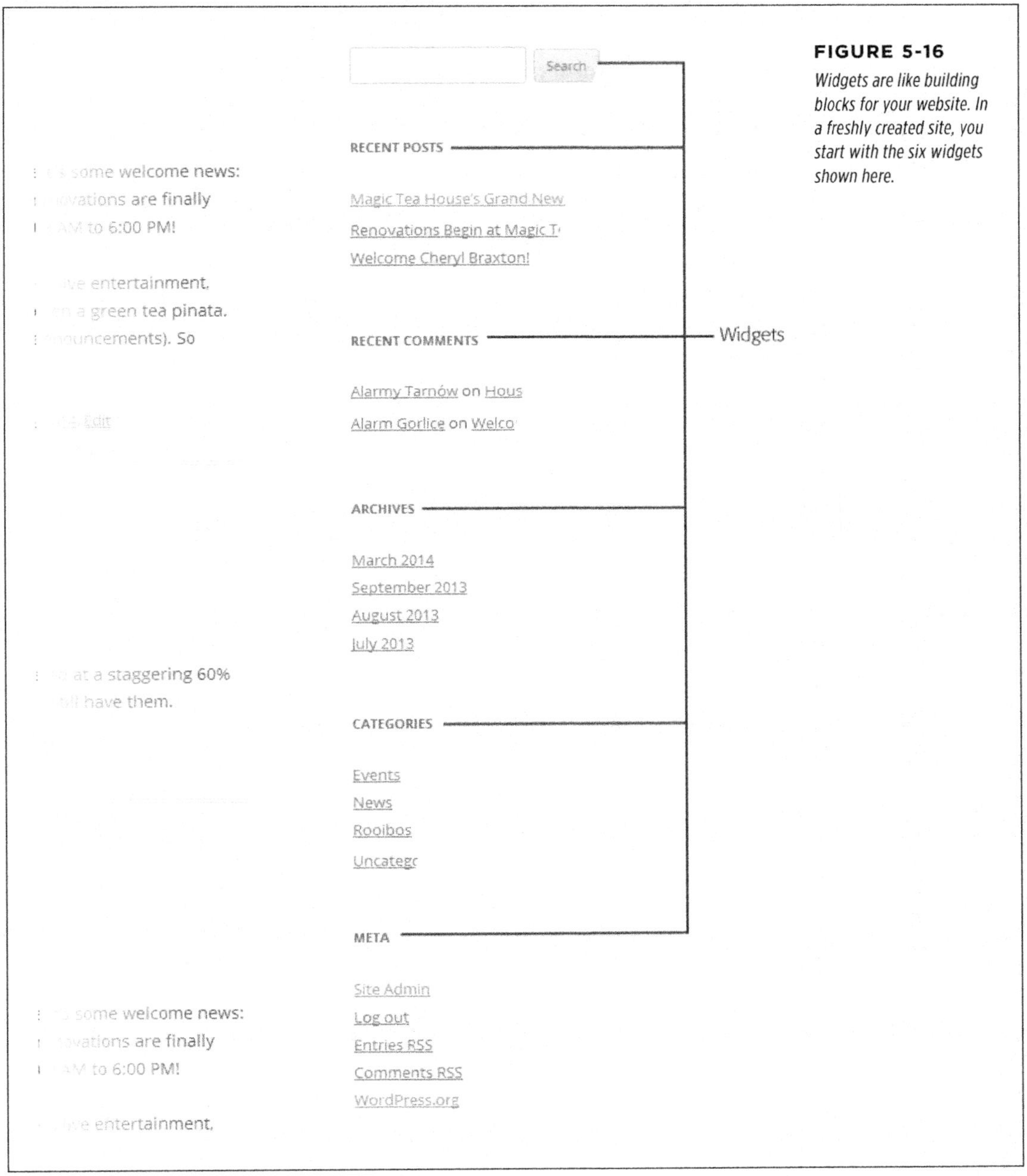

Search

RECENT POSTS

Magic Tea House's Grand New

Renovations Begin at Magic T

Welcome Cheryl Braxton!

RECENT COMMENTS

Alarmy Tarnów on Hous

Alarm Gorlice on Welco

ARCHIVES

March 2014

September 2013

August 2013

July 2013

CATEGORIES

Events

News

Rooibos

Uncategc

META

Site Admin

Log out

Entries RSS

Comments RSS

WordPress.org

Widgets

FIGURE 5-16

Widgets are like building blocks for your website. In a freshly created site, you start with the six widgets shown here.

Positioning Your Widgets

To see all the widgets you can use, choose Appearance→Widgets to open the densely packed Widgets page, which is a bit confusing because it shows you two things at once:

- **All the widgets WordPress has to offer.** In the big box on the left, under Available Widgets, is a long list of all of WordPress's widgets, including those you're using and those you aren't, in alphabetical order.
- **The widgets you're currently using.** On the right, below headings like Sidebar and Footer Area, WordPress lists the widgets currently active on your site. It arranges them in individual boxes (based on what part of the site they occupy) and lists them in the order they actually appear.

Each theme dictates where you can place widgets. If you're using the Twenty Twelve theme on a newly created WordPress site, you start with a Widgets page that looks like the one in Figure 5-17.

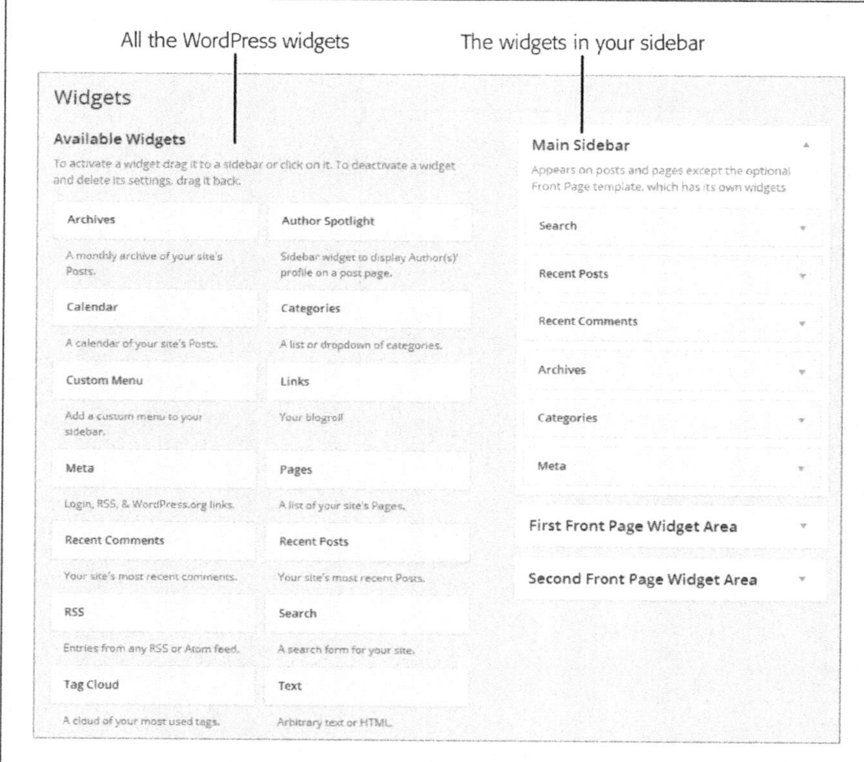

FIGURE 5-17

The Twenty Twelve theme has just three locations for widgets: a sidebar and two front page areas. You can use the latter two areas only when you create a new home page using the Front Page template (page 235). Right now, the sidebar is the only section that actually has any widgets in it. As you can see, the six widget boxes shown here correspond to the six widgets shown in Figure 5-16.

NOTE Different themes may position their widget sidebars in different places. For example, the Twenty Twelve theme's sidebar sits alongside the post listing on the home page and on the individual post pages. By comparison, the Twenty Eleven theme's sidebar appears on the main page but not on individual post pages. You might see other variations, too—for example, you could have a sidebar that appears on every page, but a widget-capable footer that appears on only the home page. It all depends on the theme you use.

The easiest thing you can do on the Widgets page is *move* a widget. That's as simple as dragging the widget to a new spot. Why not try relocating the search box to the bottom of the sidebar? There's no need to click any button to save your changes—as soon as you drop the widget in its new position, WordPress makes the change and you can view your site to check out the effect.

The next-easiest widget-customization task is *deleting* a widget. To do that, grab hold of your widget and drag it over to the big Available Widgets box on the left. When you drop the widget there, WordPress removes it from your site.

TIP Congratulations, you've now graduated to the second level of WordPress mastery! It's time to delete the Meta widget from the main sidebar. Although its login and site administration links are convenient for *you*, they look unprofessional to your readers. In the future, you'll need to type in your dashboard's address (just add */wp-admin* to the end of your website address) or bookmark the dashboard in your web browser.

Next, you can try *adding* a widget by dragging it from the Available Widgets box and dropping it on one of the widget areas, like the sidebar. (You'll learn what all these widgets actually do starting on page 162.)

As you get a bit more ambitious, you may want to try moving widgets from one area to another. For example, if you use the Twenty Twelve theme, you can drag a widget from the Main Sidebar area to the First Front Page widget area. Unfortunately, you won't be able the see the change immediately, because the First Front Page widget area doesn't appear on your site unless you create a static front page (a technique you'll practice on page 231). But if you experiment with a different theme, you'll often find many more widget areas to play with. For example, the Twenty Thirteen theme provides a Main widget area that appears in the footer of your site, and a Secondary widget area that appears as a sidebar on the right (Figure 5-18).

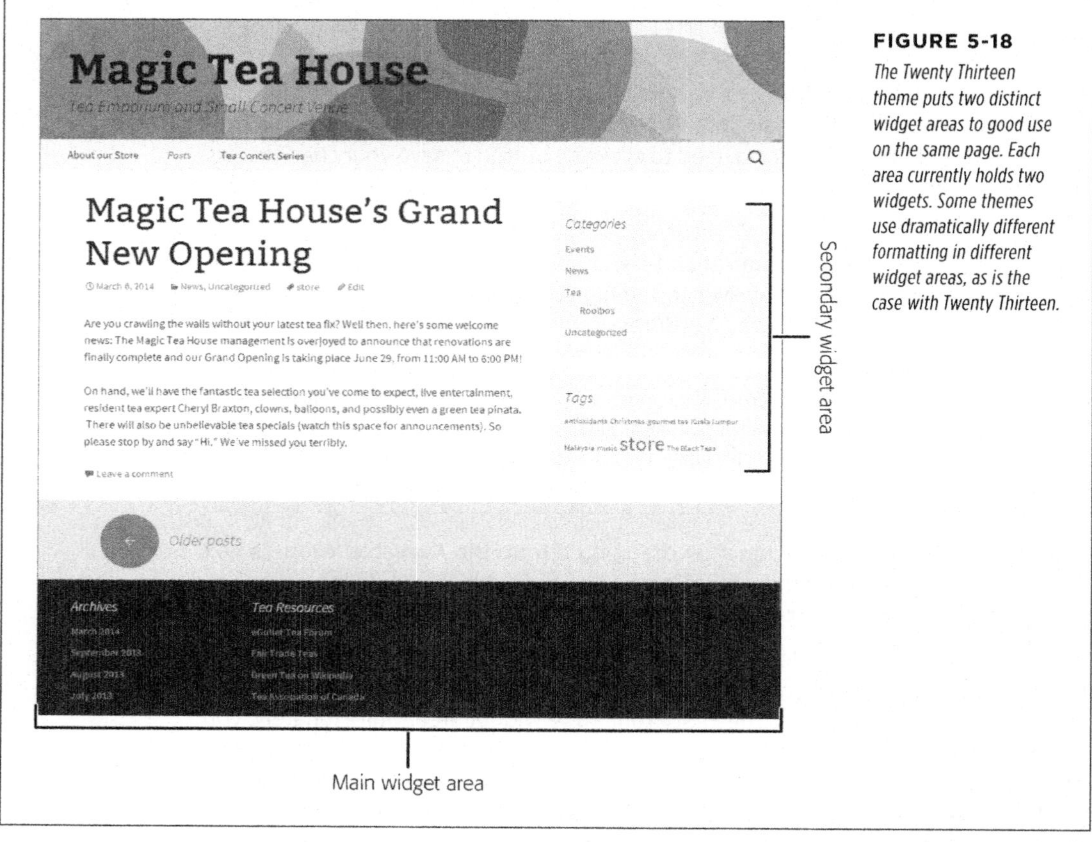

FIGURE 5-18

The Twenty Thirteen theme puts two distinct widget areas to good use on the same page. Each area currently holds two widgets. Some themes use dramatically different formatting in different widget areas, as is the case with Twenty Thirteen.

When you drag a widget over a new widget area, WordPress expands the area so you can see any widgets currently there. Then, you simply drop the widget into the appropriate place, as shown in Figure 5-19. To peek into a collapsed widget area without dragging a widget onto it, click the down-pointing arrow in its top-right corner.

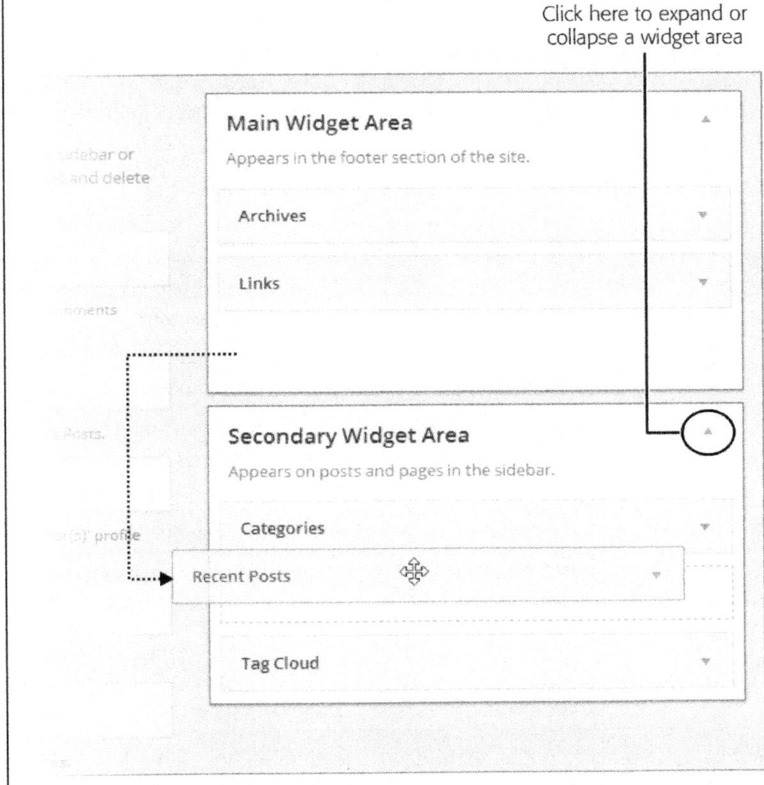

FIGURE 5-19

Here, you're moving the Recent Posts widget from the Main widget area (which creates the footer for the Twenty Thirteen theme) to the Secondary widget area (which creates the sidebar).

GEM IN THE ROUGH

When Adding Widgets is a Drag

Tired of dragging all your widgets into place? WordPress offers another way to add widgets:

1. First find the widget you want in the Available Widgets box, and then click it once.
2. WordPress opens a list of widget areas below the widget you picked. Choose the area you want (for example, "Main Sidebar").
3. Click Add Widget to place the widget.

This widget-adding technique requires several clicks, but you might find it more convenient if you have piles of widgets to sort through and lots of widget areas to put them in. To make your life even easier, add the widgets in the order you want them to appear, so you don't need to rearrange them afterward.

Other themes may offer additional widget areas, like two sidebars, one on either side of the main content area. Some themes offer multiple footer areas, which is perfect for creating *fat footers* chock-full of links, ads, or pictures. The Twenty Eleven theme has no fewer than *three* footer areas for widgets. Although this seems confusing, it really isn't—you simply use what you need. If you want a simple footer, use Footer Area One and ignore the others. If you want a two-column footer, which splits the footer area into columns, use Footer Area One and Footer Area Two. And if you want a pumped-up three-column footer, you know what to do: Put widgets in Footer Area One, Footer Area Two, and Footer Area Three.

Table 5-2 describes how the year themes stack up, widget-wise.

TABLE 5-2 *Widget areas in the WordPress year themes*

THEME	WIDGET AREA	DESCRIPTION
Twenty Eleven	Main Sidebar	Sidebar on the right
	Showcase Sidebar	Sidebar on a page that uses the Showcase template (page 236)
	Footer Area One Footer Area Two Footer Area Three	First, second, and third columns of the footer
Twenty Twelve	Main Sidebar	Sidebar on the right
	First Front Page Second Front Page	Left and right column of a static page that uses the Front Page template (page 235)
Twenty Thirteen	Main	The footer
	Secondary	Sidebar on the right
Twenty Fourteen	Primary Sidebar	Sidebar on the left, with a black background
	Content Sidebar	Sidebar on the right, with a white background
	Footer	The footer

Changing Widget Settings

Widgets are surprisingly useful things. They let readers find recent posts, browse through your archives, and keep track of recent comments. As you refine your site, you won't be happy just shuffling them around. You'll also want to configure the way they work.

Every widget provides a few settings you can adjust. To see them, expand the widget by clicking the down-pointing arrow in its right corner. Change the settings you want, and then click the Save button to make the changes permanent. Figure 5-20 shows the settings for the Recent Posts and Categories widgets.

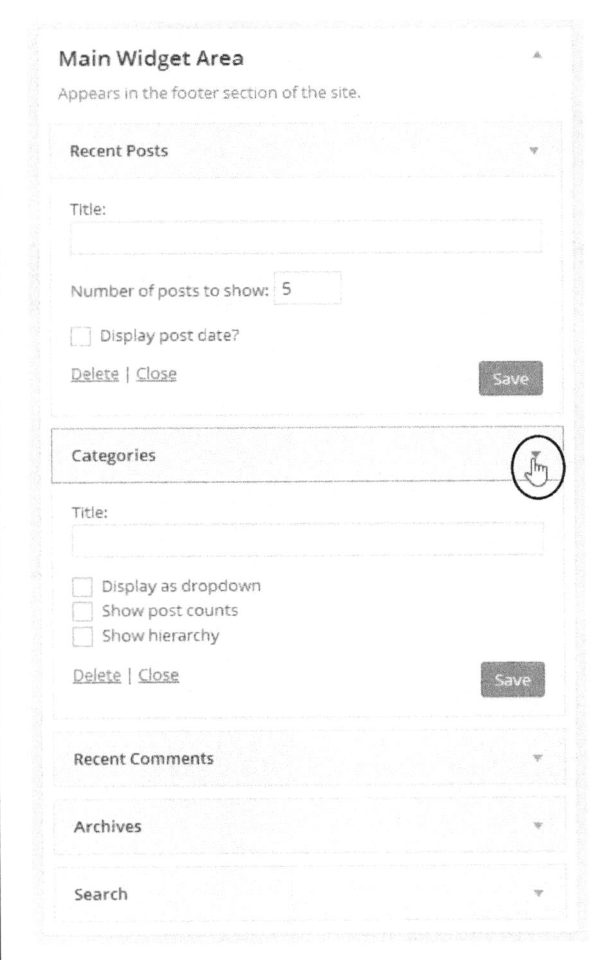

FIGURE 5-20

You can change the Recent Posts widget to show as many posts as you want (not just the latest five). The Categories box gives you three special options. "Display as dropdown" compresses the category into a drop-down list box, which saves space but forces people to click the box open. "Show post counts" shows the number of posts in a category in parentheses after the category name. And "Show hierarchy" displays the category tree, which is especially handy if you use subcategories, as described on page 110.

Even if a widget provides no other settings, it always includes a Title text box, which you can use to replace the widget's standard headline—for example "Hot News!" instead of "Recent Posts" or "What People Are Saying" instead of "Recent Comments." If you leave the Title box blank, the widget uses its default title.

When you add a new widget, it starts out with its standard settings. In some cases, you might want to remove a widget from your site without throwing away its settings—for example you may be planning to add it back later on. WordPress has a special Inactive Widgets box designed for exactly this situation. To remove a widget but keep its settings, drag the widget into the Inactive Widgets box instead of the

Available Widgets box. (If you don't see the Inactive Widgets box, scroll down—it's right underneath the Available Widgets box.)

The Basic Widgets

You are now the master of your widgets. Before you go any further, take a closer look at exactly what WordPress's widgets can do for you.

Table 5-3 describes the WordPress widgets you'll see in a freshly installed, self-hosted WordPress site. In Chapter 9, you'll learn how to expand your widget collection with plug-ins.

TABLE 5-3 *WordPress widgets*

WIDGET NAME	DESCRIPTION	FOR MORE INFORMATION...
Archives	Shows links that let readers browse a month of posts at a time. You can convert it to a drop-down box and display the number of posts in each month.	—
Calendar	Shows a miniature calendar that lets guests find posts on specific dates.	See page 164.
Categories	Shows links that let readers browse all the posts in a category. You can convert it to a drop-down box and display the number of posts in each category.	Categories are explained on page 106.
Custom Menu	Shows a menu of pages or other links that you create using WordPress's menu feature.	Menus are explained in Chapter 7.
Meta	Shows administrative links (for example, a "Log in" link that takes you to the dashboard). Once you're ready to go live with your site, you should delete the Meta widget.	See page 87.
Pages	Shows links to the static pages you pick. (Static pages act like ordinary web pages, not posts. You can add them to your website to provide extra information or resources.)	Static pages are explained in Chapter 7.

WIDGET NAME	DESCRIPTION	FOR MORE INFORMATION...
Recent Comments	Shows the most recent comments left on any of your posts. You can choose how many comments WordPress displays (the standard is five).	Comments are explained in Chapter 8.
Recent Posts	Shows links that let readers jump to one of your most recent posts. You can choose how many posts WordPress displays (the standard is five).	—
RSS	Shows links extracted from an RSS feed (for example, the posts from another person's blog).	See page 433.
Search	Shows a box that lets visitors search your posts. You might want to remove this from the sidebar if your theme includes it somewhere else on the home page (as the home page in Figure 5-1 does).	—
Tag Cloud	Shows the tags your blogs use most often, sized according to their popularity. Readers can click a tag to see the posts that use it.	See page 165.
Text	Shows a block of text or HTML. You can put whatever content you want here, which makes it an all-purpose display tool for small bits of information.	See page 166.
Ephemera	Shows the titles of posts that use the Aside, Link, Status, or Quote format. Unlike all the other widgets, this is a theme-specific widget that only some themes include (such as Twenty Fourteen and Twenty Eleven).	See page 205.

You're already well acquainted with the basic set of widgets that every blog begins with: Search, Archives, Recent Posts, Categories, Recent Comments, and Meta. In the following sections, you'll tour a few more widgets you might consider adding to your site.

TIP You can add the same widget more than once. For example, you can add two Custom Menu widgets to your page, give each one a different title, and use each one to show a separate set of links.

UP TO SPEED

I Have Even More Widgets!

The list of widgets in Table 5-3 includes all those that a self-hosted WordPress site starts with. But if your site is on WordPress.com, you'll find the Widgets page stocked with a number of preinstalled extras, including widgets that let you share posts with nifty web services like Facebook, Twitter, Flickr, Goodreads, and Delicious. So what's up?

The discrepancy reflects the way WordPress handles plug-ins. If your site is on WordPress.com, you can't install plug-ins, so you're limited to whatever Automattic offers in the Widgets window. For that reason, the company tries extra hard to include a broad set of useful widgets for everyone.

Self-hosted WordPress sites start out with fewer widgets, but you can add more—in fact, as many as you want—through plug-ins. You can start by adding all the WordPress.com widgets to your site with the Jetpack plug-in (page 297). You'll learn to use these more exotic widgets throughout this book.

Finally, it's worth noting that some themes come with their own specialized widgets. Usually, you can recognize them by the fact that the widget name starts with the theme name, like Twenty Fourteen Ephemera (which is included with the Twenty Fourteen theme).

The Calendar Widget

The Calendar widget gives readers a different way to browse your site—by finding posts published on a specific day (Figure 5-21). It's most commonly used in blogs.

FIGURE 5-21

In the month of March, four days have at least one post—the 3rd, 4th, 6th, and 25th. Click the date to see the corresponding posts.

The Calendar widget used to be a staple of every blog. These days, it's far less popular. The problem is that unless you blog several times a week, the calendar looks sparse and makes your blog feel half-empty. Also, it emphasizes the current month of posts while neglecting other months. Most readers won't bother clicking their way through month after month to hunt for posts.

You probably won't use the Calendar unless your posts are particularly time-sensitive and you want to emphasize their dates. (For example, the Calendar widget might make sense if you're chronicling a 30-day weight-loss marathon.) If you use the Calendar widget, you probably won't use the similarly date-focused Archives widget, or you'll at least place it far away, at the other end of your sidebar or in another widget area.

The Tag Cloud Widget

You've already seen how the Categories widget lets visitors browse through the posts in any category. The Tag Cloud widget is similar in that it lets readers see posts that use a specific tag.

There's a difference, however. While categories are well-defined and neatly organized, the typical WordPress site uses a jumble of overlapping keywords. Also, the total number of categories you use will probably be small, while the number of tags could be quite large. For these reasons, it makes sense to display tags differently from categories. Categories make sense in a list or tree. Tags work better in a *cloud,* which shows the most popular tags sorted alphabetically and sized proportionately. That means that tags attached to a lot of posts show up in bigger text, while less-frequently used tags are smaller (Figure 5-22).

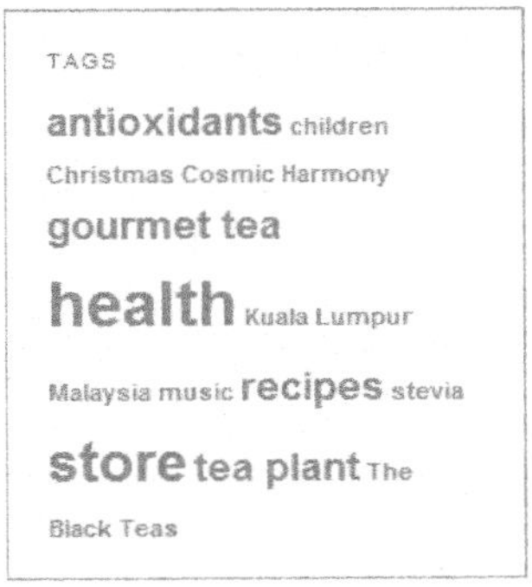

FIGURE 5-22

This tag cloud shows that "health" is the most frequently used tag, with "store" close behind. As with categories, clicking a tag shows all the posts that use it.

There's no secret to using the Tag Cloud widget. Just drag it into an area of your theme, and see what tags it highlights. The tag cloud might also tell *you* something about your site—for example, what topics keep coming up across all your posts.

NOTE If clouds work so well for tags, it might occur to you that they could also suit categories, especially in sites that have a large number of categories, loosely arranged, and with no subcategories. Happily, a category cloud is easy to create. If you use WordPress.com, the handy Category Cloud widget does the job. If you self-host, you'll notice an extra setting in the Tag Cloud widget: a list called Taxonomy. To create your category cloud, change the Taxonomy setting from Tags to Categories.

FREQUENTLY ASKED QUESTION

Taming the Tag Cloud

What do I do if my tag cloud shows too many tags? Or not enough? Or makes the text too big?

The Tag Cloud widget is surprisingly uncustomizable. If you use fewer than 45 tags, it shows every one of them (although it ignores any tags you added to the Posts→Tags list but haven't yet used in a post.) If you use more than 45 tags, the Tag Cloud widget shows the 45 most popular.

Occasionally, people want a tag cloud with more tags. But usually they have the opposite concern and want a smaller tag cloud that's slim enough to fit into a sidebar without crowding out other widgets. If you want to tweak a tag cloud on a WordPress.com site, you're out of luck. But if you run a self-hosted site, there are options. One solution is to crack open your template files. That's because the behind-the-scenes code (the PHP function that creates the cloud) is actually very flexible. It lets you set upper and lower tag limits, and set upper and lower boundaries for the text size. You can get the full details from WordPress's function reference at *http://tinyurl.com/wptagcloud.* (However, this information won't be much help until you learn how to dig into your WordPress theme files to change your code, a topic explored in Chapter 13.) Another solution is to search for a plug-in that lets you pick the tag options and then generates a customized tag cloud. You'll learn how to find and install plug-ins in Chapter 9.

The Text Widget

The Text widget is simple but surprisingly flexible. You can use it anywhere you want to wedge in a bit of fixed content. For example, you can use it in a sidebar, to add a paragraph about yourself or your site. Or you can put it in your footer with some copyright information or a legal disclaimer.

However, the Text widget becomes much more interesting if you stick some markup in it. Since it recognizes HTML markup, you can stuff in lists, links, pictures, and more. (In fact, WordPress self-hosters often use the Text widget to stuff in a video or an image, as explained on page 188.) Figure 5-23 shows two uses of the Text widget.

Using the Text widget is easy. First, drag it onto your page (as with any other widget). When you expand it, you get a nice big, multiple-line text box. If all you want is ordinary text, just fill in a title and type in your text underneath. Make sure you also turn on the "Automatically add paragraphs" checkbox. That way, wherever you separate the text (by pressing the Enter key), WordPress inserts an HTML line break element (that's <br>) that, in turn, inserts the space you want.

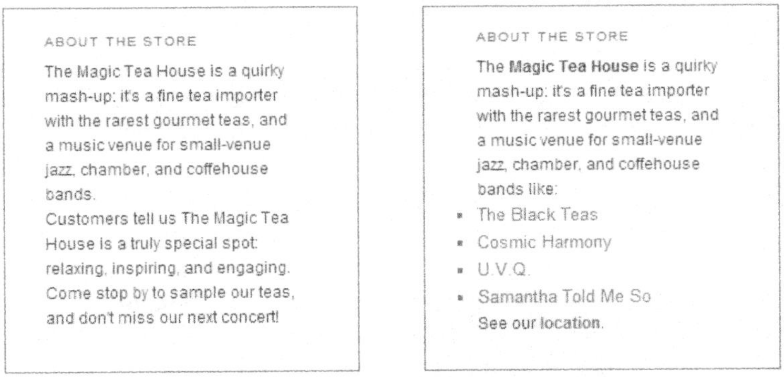

ABOUT THE STORE

The Magic Tea House is a quirky mash-up: it's a fine tea importer with the rarest gourmet teas, and a music venue for small-venue jazz, chamber, and coffehouse bands.
Customers tell us The Magic Tea House is a truly special spot: relaxing, inspiring, and engaging. Come stop by to sample our teas, and don't miss our next concert!

ABOUT THE STORE

The **Magic Tea House** is a quirky mash-up: it's a fine tea importer with the rarest gourmet teas, and a music venue for small-venue jazz, chamber, and coffehouse bands like:

- The Black Teas
- Cosmic Harmony
- U.V.Q.
- Samantha Told Me So

See our **location**.

FIGURE 5-23

Left: At its simplest, the Text widget displays a title (formatted according to the theme you're using) with one or more paragraphs of text underneath.

Right: Add some HTML, and the Text widget looks a whole lot fancier.

It's almost as easy to put HTML in the Text widget. First, turn off the "Automatically add paragraphs" settings. Then, type in your content, with the exact HTML tags you want. Here's an example that puts a word in bold type:

```
The following word will be <b>bold</b> on the page.
```

And here's the HTML-formatted text from Figure 5-23 (right):

```
The <b>Magic Tea House</b> is a quirky mash-up: it's a fine tea importer with
the rarest gourmet teas, and a music venue for small-venue jazz, chamber, and
coffeehouse bands like:

<ul>
<li>The Black Teas</li>
<li>Cosmic Harmony</li>
<li>U.V.Q.</li>
<li>Samantha Told Me So</li>
</ul>
See our <a href="http://tinyurl.com/cyboj83">location</a>.
```

If your HTML skills are a bit sketchy, you can copy markup from an HTML editor into the Text widget. Before you do, make sure you look over the markup and strip out any unnecessary details, like inline styles. That gives it a better chance of blending into your site without disrupting the rest of your WordPress page.

Mobile Themes

If you build a website today, it's a safe bet that some of your visitors will browse your pages using smartphones, tablets, and other mobile devices. Unfortunately, pages that look good in a desktop or laptop browser aren't so swell on smaller screens.

The problem is space—namely, how to adapt your pages when there's not nearly as much room to work with. If you're using an intelligent, mobile-aware theme, it can adapt itself to work in cramped spaces. It can rearrange your content, simplify your site's layout, and increase the size of your text (Figure 5-24). This design philosophy is sometimes called *responsive design* because it *responds* to the needs of the viewer.

FIGURE 5-24

Left: The Twenty Twelve theme recasts itself for people with mobile devices. It shows your blog postings on a large, readable page, using a single column. To save space, it squashes the menu down to a single button (click it, and the full menu drops into view).

Right: The Twenty Twelve theme still displays your widgets, like Recent Posts and Recent Comments, but it bumps them to the bottom of the page, below the list of posts.

Themes that aren't mobile aware (meaning they don't distinguish between desktop computers and web-enabled devices), don't make any effort to tailor your pages for tiny screens. The result is a postage-stamp-sized page that's difficult to navigate and read (Figure 5-25).

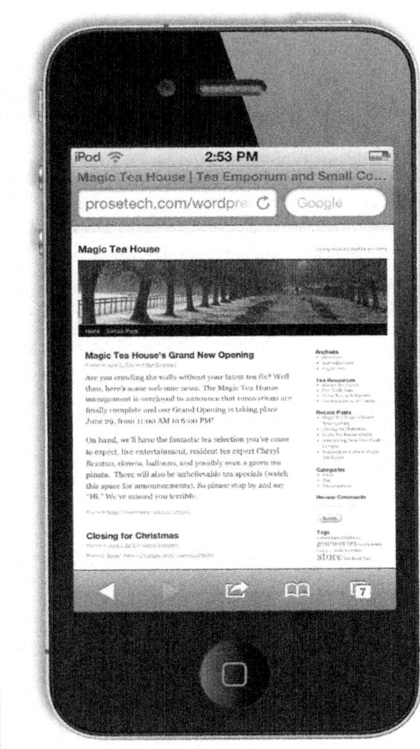

FIGURE 5-25

The aging Twenty Ten theme doesn't attempt to accommodate smartphones. Browse a site that uses the theme, and you get the familiar bird's-eye view of the page. Navigating this site requires plenty of zooming in and out.

The easiest way to make your site look good on mobile displays is to pick a theme that reconfigures your content for mobile devices. All the year themes from Twenty Eleven on do. When WordPress detects a visitor using a mobile device, the theme automatically substitutes a different layout—one that's both simpler and carefully rearranged.

TIP You can search for themes that have built-in mobile support using the Feature Filter. Just find the Layout section and turn on the Responsive Layout checkbox before you search.

If your theme doesn't recognize mobile devices, all is not lost. If you have a self-hosted WordPress site, you can use a mobile-aware plug-in. One is WPtouch (*http://tinyurl.com/wptouch*), which identifies smartphones and other mobile devices, and makes sure they get a simplified theme that better suits their capabilities (and looks pretty slick, too). You haven't yet learned how to use plug-ins, but you'll consider WPtouch when you do, on page 307.

NOTE Even if your theme does recognize mobile devices, you may still opt for the expanded features of a mobile plug-in. In the WordPress year themes, the mobile version looks nice but still makes some questionable design decisions. For example, they retain your sidebar widgets in an unwieldy list after your post. Similarly, the home page still includes the full content of each post, which creates a seemingly endless page. (Surely shortened excerpts are more convenient, and easier on the ever-scrolling index finger.) If you want to customize the mobile appearance of your self-hosted WordPress site, a plug-in like WPtouch is the perfect tool (page 307).

If your site is on WordPress.com, you can't use a mobile plug-in. However, WordPress.com provides a similar but simpler set of built-in features. If your theme doesn't have mobile smarts, you can ask WordPress to swap in its own basic mobile theme. Choose Appearance→Mobile, and next to "Enable mobile theme," click Yes.

On the same page, you'll find a few more options to configure your site for mobile devices. Most usefully, you can use the "Show excerpts on front page" setting to use a post's excerpt (page 198) instead of its full text in the post list on the home page. Although WordPress.com doesn't give you nearly as much control as a mobile plug-in like WPtouch, it's enough to let you keep your favorite theme, even if it isn't mobile-aware.

CHAPTER

6

Jazzing Up Your Posts

You know what an ordinary WordPress post looks like—it starts with a title, followed by one or more paragraphs of text. And there's nothing wrong with that. Providing that you pick the right theme, your WordPress site can look surprisingly hip, even if it holds nothing more than plain text.

However, there are plenty of types of sites that need more from a post. For example, if you're posting news articles, you certainly want to add pictures. And if you're writing long posts (on anything from business analytics to relationship advice), you'll improve your audience's reading experience if you use subheadings to structure your thoughts. To add details like these, along with lists, links, and the other accouterments of a web page, you need to take charge of WordPress's post editor, which you'll do in this chapter.

Fancy posts aren't just about formatting—they're also about *features*. For example, you can use specialized tags to show just a portion of a post on your home page (rather than the whole thing), giving you a ridiculously useful way to promote many posts in a small space. Or you can use images from your posts to create a slideshow that, say, promotes your top posts on the home page. In this chapter, you'll use all these techniques to improve the aesthetics and showcase the richness of your site.

Making Fancier Posts

You've seen plenty of WordPress posts so far, but none are likely to impress your web designer friends. Fortunately, you don't need to stick with the plain and ordinary. WordPress is packed with tools that can help you create epically formatted posts.

The easiest way to start styling your posts is to start with a new one (to do that, choose Posts→Add New, as usual). Then look at the toolbar that sits at the top of the editing box—it's stocked with useful formatting commands (Figure 6-1).

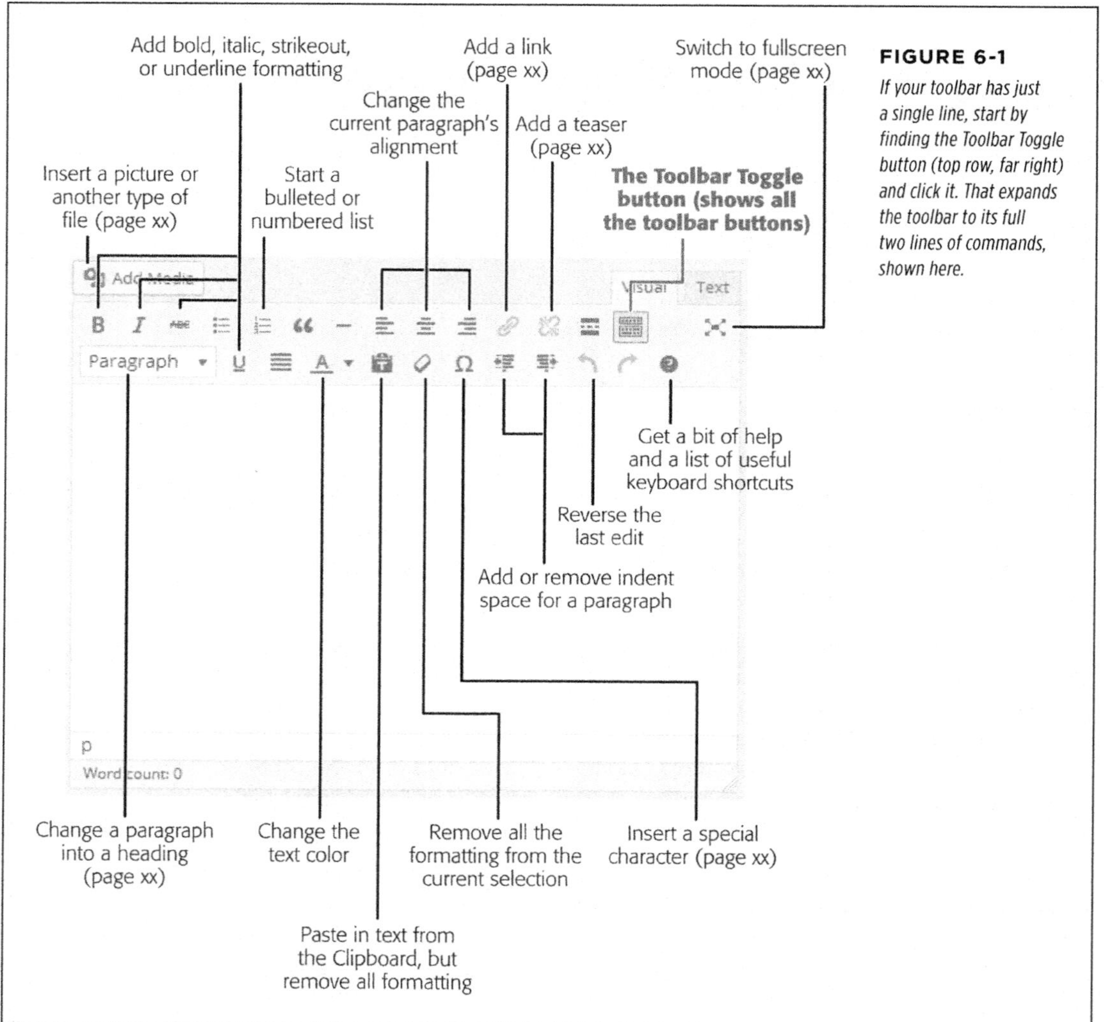

FIGURE 6-1

If your toolbar has just a single line, start by finding the Toolbar Toggle button (top row, far right) and click it. That expands the toolbar to its full two lines of commands, shown here.

Even though WordPress creates your posts using web-friendly HTML markup, the toolbar buttons work in almost the same way they do in a word processor, complete with a basic Undo feature. It's like having a miniature Microsoft Word in your browser.

You can format your posts two ways. One is to select the bit of text that needs formatting and then click the corresponding toolbar button. You might, for example, select a single word and add bold formatting by clicking the B button. Another approach is to use the toolbar buttons to turn a feature on or off (which computer nerds call *toggling*) as you write. For example, you could click the I button to turn on italic formatting, type something, and then click the I button again to turn off italics.

TIP If you want to start a new line of text without starting a whole new paragraph, press Shift+Enter at the end of the preceding line (instead of hitting just the Enter key). Why? If you click just Enter, WordPress thinks you want to start a new paragraph and adds extra space just before the beginning of that paragraph. When you use Shift+Enter, WordPress doesn't add the extra space.

The following sections explain a few of the finer points of post formatting. You'll see the proper way to work with headings, add links and special characters, and unlock even more capabilities by editing your post's HTML.

GEM IN THE ROUGH

Get More Space to Work

Need more space to write and review your content? You can make the post box a bit bigger by tweaking WordPress's settings. Choose Settings→Writing, look for the "Size of the post box" setting, and increase the number of lines (the standard is 20). Or you can expand the content box by clicking the bottom-right corner and dragging it down, as shown on page 126.

If you're craving even more screen real estate, check out the toolbar's full-screen mode button (Figure 6-1). WordPress calls this mode (and labels the button that triggers it) *Distraction Free Writing*. Click it, and WordPress resizes the post title and post content boxes to fill a larger portion of the page, temporarily hiding the other parts of the Add New Post page, including the toolbar and the dashboard menu. If you need a toolbar button, move your mouse (without clicking) near the top of the page to make the toolbar reappear. When you finish writing, you can get back to the normal Add New Post page by pointing to the top of the page to show the toolbar, and then clicking "Exit fullscreen."

Technically, WordPress's full-screen view doesn't occupy the full screen—it's more like full *browser* view. But you can go beyond that limit by switching your browser to *its* full-screen view. On most browsers, you do that by pressing F11 (press it again to return the browser window to its normal state). With your browser in full-screen mode, its window fills the entire screen (sans toolbars), and WordPress can claim virtually all of it to display your post.

There's one quirk, however: No matter how big you make your browser window, WordPress limits the width of the editing box, for two reasons. First, it's awkward to read and edit long lines of text. Second, most WordPress templates limit the width of posts to ensure readability. As a result, an unnaturally wide editing window would give you a false sense of the post's layout.

Using Subheadings

Every blog post starts with a heading—the title of your post, which sits above the post content. But if you're writing a long post, it's a good idea to subdivide your writing into smaller units using subheadings.

To create a subheading, use the drop-down Format menu on the far left of the second row of the toolbar (Figure 6-2). Usually, the menu displays the word "Paragraph," which tells you that WordPress is styling the current text as an ordinary paragraph. But you can choose three sizes of heading from the menu, too.

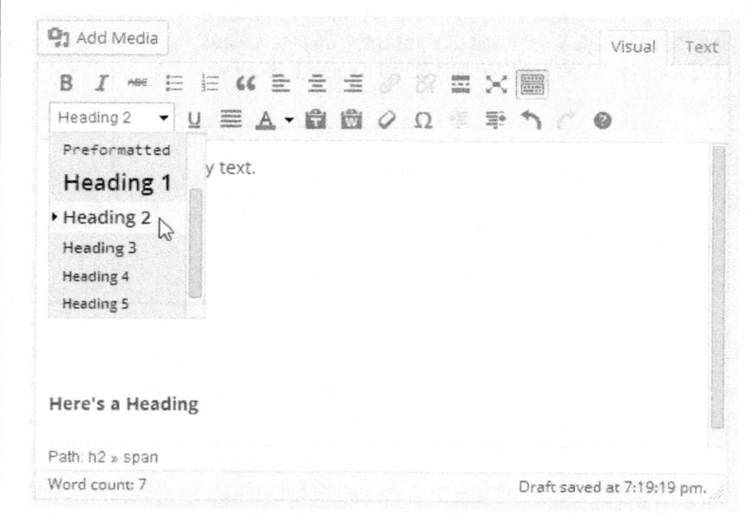

FIGURE 6-2

The Format drop-down list offers six levels of heading. Choose one, and you'll be rewarded with bigger, bolder text. If you know even a little about HTML, you won't be surprised to learn that a level-1 heading uses the <h1> element, a level-2 heading uses <h2>, and so on.

The heading level you use depends, at least in part, on your theme. Here are some guidelines:

- Don't use level-1 headings inside your posts, because they'll clash with the main post title or the website title, confusing search engines and assistive devices like screen readers.
- If you use a modern theme, use level-2 headings to subdivide a post. This is the right approach for the standard year themes, from Twenty Eleven on.
- If you use an older theme, you may need to use level-2 or level-3 headings when subdividing a post. First, try level-2 headings. If they appear in the published page with the same type size as the post title, use level-3 headings instead.

NOTE The size, typeface, and exact appearance of a heading depend on your theme. You won't see exactly what your heading looks like until you preview or publish your page.

Showing a Code Listing

You may notice that the Format list has more than just headings in it. It also includes the Paragraph, Address, and Preformatted formats, which map to the HTML elements <p>, <address>, and <pre>, respectively.

WordPress uses the <p> element to style ordinary paragraphs, and you've already seen plenty of those. The <address> element is meant for contact information about who wrote the page, but it's rarely used. But the <pre> element is more useful—it displays text in a fixed-width font, which is ideal for listing programming code or simulating computer output (Figure 6-3).

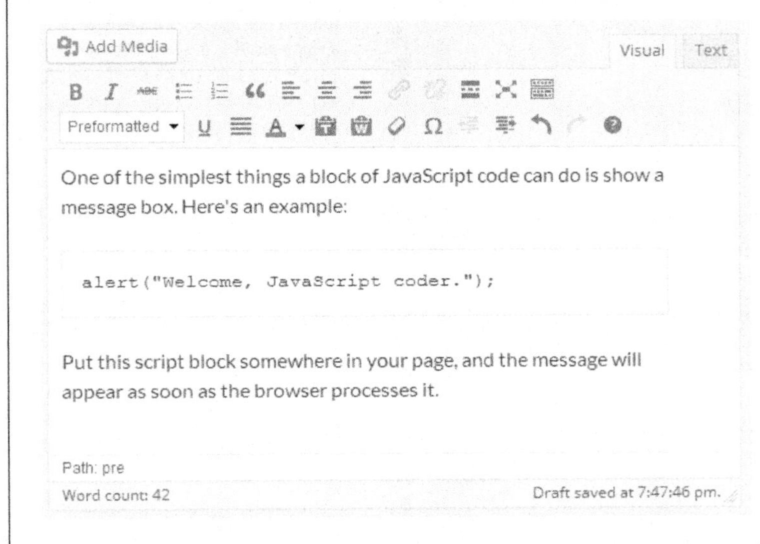

FIGURE 6-3

In some themes, WordPress formats the text of a <pre> element using a gray background or gray outline (the latter shown here for the "alert" line in the Twenty Twelve theme). That visually separates the <pre>-formatted text from the rest of the content on the page. (Remember to use Shift+Enter to add line breaks between each line of code, rather than just Enter, which would add extra spacing and start a new paragraph.)

Adding Links

The Web wouldn't amount to much without links, those blue underlined bits of text that let you jump from one web page to another. You can easily add links to a post. For example, imagine you have this sentence:

> This story was reported in The New York Times.

To turn "The New York Times" into a link, select the text, and then click the Insert Link button in the toolbar. A window appears where you can either supply a full website address or link to one of your own posts (Figure 6-4).

NOTE If you want to link to a file—for example, a document that your guest can download or a picture she can view—you need to store that file in WordPress's media library. You'll get the full details on page 186.

To remove a link, click anywhere inside the link text and then click the Remove Link button (which is right next to the Insert Link button in the toolbar).

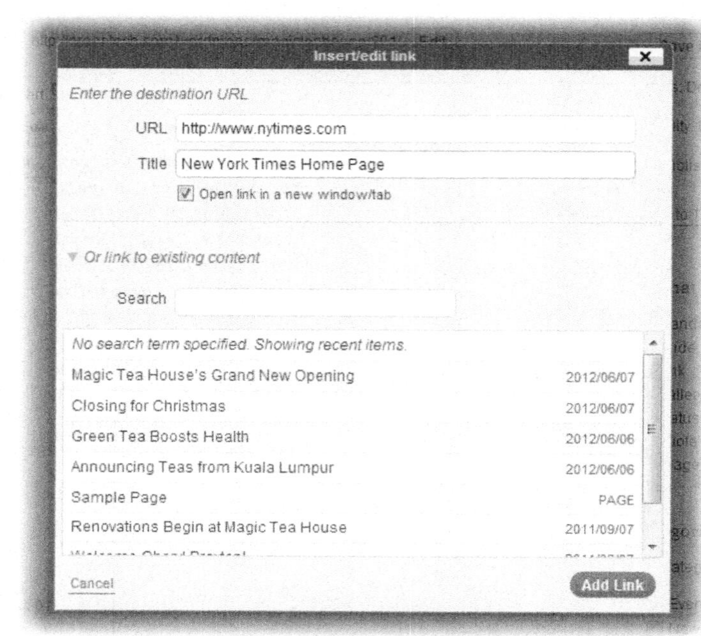

FIGURE 6-4

To add a link to a post, you need to supply the URL (the website address) and a Title (the text that appears in a tooltip when a visitor points to the link). Alternatively, you can search for a post on your own site and insert a link to it. Either way, clicking Add Link seals the deal.

Inserting Special Characters

Special characters are usually defined as characters you don't see on your everyday keyboard. For example, if you use a standard U.S. keyboard, special characters include things like accented letters and typographic symbols.

WordPress lets you drop in one of a small set of special characters using the Insert Custom Character command. Click it, and a window appears with a grid of unusual characters. Point to one to get a close-up look at it, and then click it to close the window and insert the character into your post (see Figure 6-5).

You may not need all the special characters you think you do. WordPress automatically substitutes special characters for some character combinations. For example, if you type two dashes (--) between words, WordPress turns them into a seamless *en dash* (–) when you publish the post. Three dashes in a row creates a slightly longer *em dash* (—). Similarly, WordPress turns ordinary straight quotes ("") into typographically correct quotation marks (“”). It works the same magic with apostrophes.

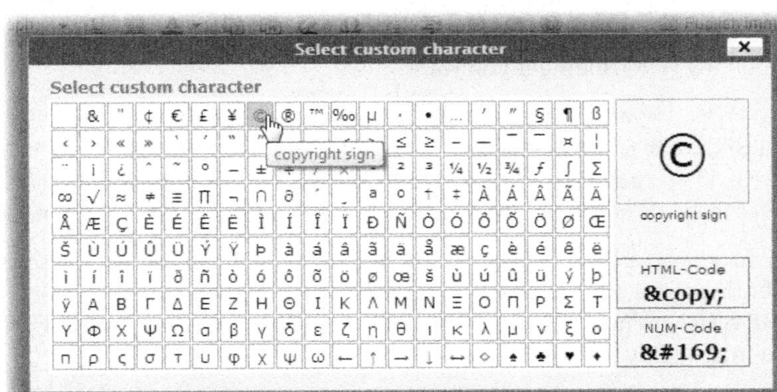

FIGURE 6-5

Here, you're about to insert the copyright symbol into a post.

NOTE The oddest special characters you can use with WordPress are smilies, character combinations like :) that turn into emoticons like . WordPress performs this substitution automatically, and you can find out what smilies you can use (and the characters you need to type to trigger them) at *http://tinyurl.com/using-smilies*. On the other hand, if the smilies feature is running amok and changing character sequences you don't want it to, choose Settings→Writing and turn off the checkbox next to "Convert emoticons like :-) and :-P to graphics on display."

FREQUENTLY ASKED QUESTION

Formatting Your Text

How can I adjust typefaces and font sizes?

WordPress's post editor lets you structure your content (for example, put it into lists and headings), add more content (like pictures), and apply certain types of formatting (like boldface and italics). However, there are plenty of formatting details that aren't under your control. The size and typeface of your fonts is one of them.

This might seem like an awkward limitation, but it's actually a wise design decision on the part of the people who created WordPress. If WordPress gave you free rein to change fonts, you could easily end up with messy markup and posts that didn't match each other. Even worse, if you switch to a new theme, you're stuck with your old fonts, even though they might no longer suit your new look.

Fortunately, there's a more structured way to change the appearance of your text. Once you're certain you have the right theme for your website, you can modify its styles. For example, by changing the style rules, you can change the font, color, and size of your text, and you can either make these changes to all your content, or to just specific elements (like all level-3 headings inside a post).

Modifying styles is a great way to personalize a theme, and you'll learn how to do that in Chapter 13. However, there's one caveat—if you use WordPress.com to host your site, you need to buy the Custom Design upgrade to edit your styles (page 457). Self-hosted WordPress sites don't have this restriction.

Using the HTML View

All the toolbar buttons you studied so far work by inserting the right HTML into your posts, behind the scenes. But if you've got a bit of web design experience, you don't need to rely on the buttons. Using WordPress's HTML view, you can directly edit your post's HTML markup. You won't be limited by the buttons in the toolbar—instead, you can enter any HTML element you want.

To switch to HTML view, click the Text tab that sits just above the post content box, on the right (Figure 6-6). To go back to the visual editor, click the Visual tab. In fact, there's no reason you can't spend time in both places. For example, you might write your post in the visual editor and then switch to HTML view to inspect the markup.

HTML view gives you a slightly different toolbar. It still has the useful "full screen" button, but most of the other shortcuts, which insert various HTML tags, aren't much help—if you're savvy enough to prefer the HTML view, then you probably want to type in your markup by hand.

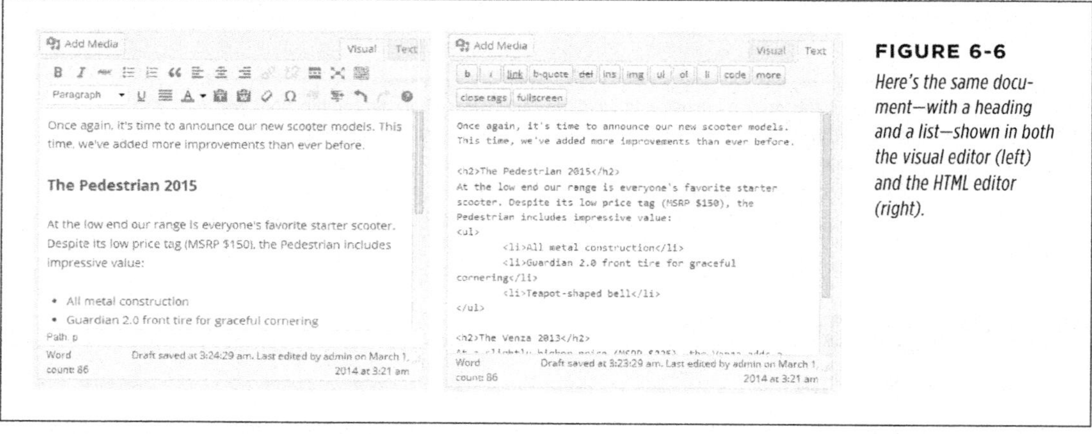

FIGURE 6-6

Here's the same document—with a heading and a list—shown in both the visual editor (left) and the HTML editor (right).

If you're a seasoned web designer, you might feel that WordPress's HTML editor isn't up to snuff. Full HTML editing programs like Adobe Dreamweaver are packed with little frills that can make editing easier—for example, they automatically add closing tags to HTML elements and suggest possible tag names as you type. (HTML editors also have more powerful layout and styling features, but those features make more sense when you're designing the look and layout of an entire site, not just adding a bit of content to a post.)

Most WordPress developers don't need the full features of a program like Dreamweaver. But there are exceptions. If you write long, complex posts—for example, the articles you saw in the Internet Encyclopedia of Philosophy (page 12)—you probably don't want to do all your editing in a web page window. Hardcore HTML lovers who find themselves in this situation can write posts in an HTML editor like Dreamweaver, copy the markup, and then paste it into WordPress's Text content box. But don't try this unless you really understand your markup. You don't want to transfer a whack of formatting details to your WordPress post, like a <span> element that has hardcoded font settings. If you do, you'll introduce some serious issues, including inconsistencies between posts and problems changing themes.

Getting a Better Post Editor

Most WordPress fans do their work directly in their web browsers, using the WordPress editor. But if you're working with long documents and you're missing your favorite conveniences, you have other options.

One is to upgrade your WordPress editor. This approach makes sense if you're happy creating your posts in the familiar Add New Post web page but don't feel like you're getting enough help from WordPress. Using a plug-in, you can swap in an editor that has a bit more muscle. (Of course, you'll need a self-hosted WordPress site to change your editor, because WordPress.com doesn't let you add plug-ins.)

You can search for a pumped-up post editor on the WordPress plug-in page (*http://wordpress.org/plugins*), as explained in Chapter 9. Plenty of them offer advanced features like search-and-replace, style-based editing, and support for creating tables. One of the most popular is TinyMCE. Check it out at *http://tinyurl.com/tinyeditor* and learn about installing plug-ins on page 287.

Another solution is to do your post-writing work in another program. You've already learned that you can paste in pure HTML using the WordPress editor's HTML view (page 178), but this technique is a bit touchy—paste in the wrong markup and you can scramble your site. A better approach is to use a program that lets you compose rich content, and then posts that content to your site safely and cleanly, without an awkward cut-and-paste step.

On a Windows computer, you can use Microsoft's free Windows Live Writer to compose properly formatted posts on your desktop, even if you don't have an Internet connection. When you're ready, a single click publishes the posts on your blog. Windows Live Writer is available free at *http://tinyurl.com/win-essentials*. Mac fiends can find similar blog-writing tools, including the popular—but, sadly, not free (it's $40)—MarsEdit (*www.red-sweater.com/marsedit*).

NOTE WordPress has a list of even more desktop post editors for Windows, Mac OS, and Linux at *http://tinyurl.com/blog-client*. Most offer handy formatting features, and all of them let you compose your work offline.

Finally, Microsoft Word lovers can use their favorite word processor to write WordPress posts using the little-known "Blog post" template. Word asks for your site's URL, user name, and password, after which it lets you create new posts and edit old ones, all from the comfort of the Word window.

TIP Although it's tempting to do your WordPress work in Word, with its silky smooth formatting features and AutoCorrect, the free Windows Live Writer program is still a better choice. That's because Windows Live Writer offers a few key features that Word omits, like the ability to schedule a post for future publication (page 100), add tags, and edit your post's slug (page 120).

Adding Pictures

You've now toured many of the post-enhancing features the Add New Post page offers. But there are several frills you haven't yet touched. The most obvious is adding graphics.

Virtually every good WordPress site can be made better with pictures. WordPress gives you several ways to do that, from the obvious (plopping them into your posts, alongside your text) to the more interesting (using them to build photoblogs, create slideshows, and advertise new posts on your home page). In the following sections, you'll learn how to take advantage of these slick picture tricks.

Putting Pictures in a Post

The most obvious place for a picture is in a post, right along with your content. WordPress makes it easy to insert pictures as you create a post (on the Add New Post page) or edit one (on the Edit Post page). In fact, you can put as many images as you want into any post.

1. **In a post's edit box, click the spot where you want to add a picture.**

   It doesn't matter whether you use the visual editor (the Visual tab) or the HTML editor (the Text tab). If you use the visual editor, you'll see every picture you insert right next to your post text. If you use the HTML editor, you'll see the raw HTML markup for each picture. This markup includes an <img> element for the picture, wrapped in an <a> anchor element that turns the picture into a link so readers can click it to see the full-size image, and possibly some other elements, like a title or a caption.

2. **Just above the box where you type in your content, click the Add Media button.**

   The Insert Media window appears (Figure 6-7). It gives you three ways to find a picture: You can upload a file from your computer (using the Upload Files tab), use a file you already uploaded to WordPress's media library (using the Media Library tab), or grab a file that's stored on another website (by clicking the "Insert from URL" link on the left).

   In this example, you want to stick to the Upload Files tab. Grabbing pictures from other websites (using "Insert from URL") might be worthwhile if you store graphics on another part of your site. But if it's someone else's site, don't chance it—the risk that the picture is copyrighted, or that the webmaster could change or move it to a new address, is too great. The Media Library tab is also useful, but only after you build up a collection of pictures. You'll take a look at it on page 186.

NOTE The Insert Media window also has links for creating a picture gallery (page 330) and setting your post's featured image (page 190). WordPress.com users will see even more links, for adding tweets and YouTube videos. Ignore all these details for now—you'll revisit them soon enough.

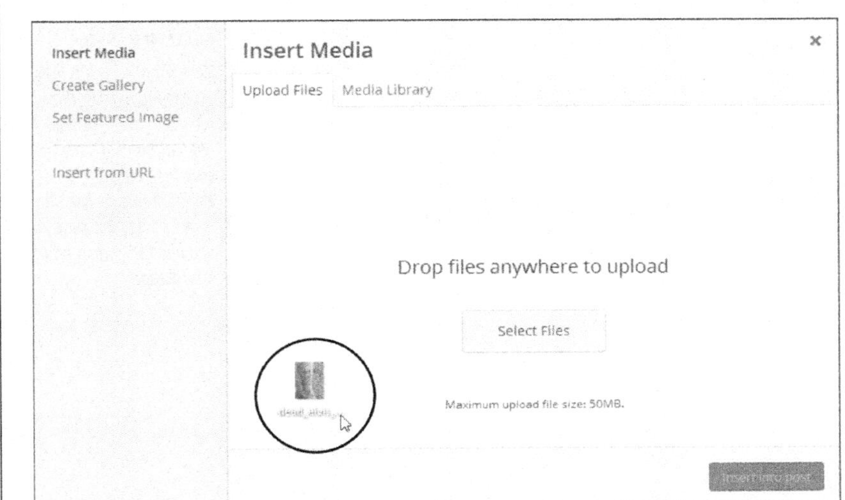

FIGURE 6-7

Using the Upload Files tab, you can insert one or more pictures from your computer into a post. First, drag a picture into the Insert Media box. Once you release the image, WordPress begins uploading it.

3. **Pick the files you want to upload.**

   WordPress gives you two options. The quickest approach is to drag files from an open file browser window (like Windows Explorer or the Mac's Finder) and drop them in the Insert Media window box. You can drag as many files as you want, either all at once or one at a time, and you can keep dropping in new files before WordPress finishes uploading the old ones.

   Your other option is to pick your files from a standard dialog box. To do that, click the Select Files button, browse to the right folder, and then pick what you want. Ctrl-click (Command-click on a Mac) to select multiple files at once.

TIP If your files are *really* big, uploading just isn't practical (and it might fail halfway through). For example, it's probably a bad idea to upload files straight from your 22-megapixel digital camera. To save time, scale it down in an image-editing program first.

   Once you upload your files, WordPress switches to the Media Library tab, which lists all the images you ever added to your site. It puts new pictures at the top of the list.

   If your files are particularly large (or your web connection is particularly slow), you'll see a progress bar ticking along, tracking the upload progress of each file. When WordPress finishes an upload, it replaces the progress bar with a thumbnail of your image. On the right, a pile of text boxes asks you for all kinds of information about your picture (see Figure 6-8).

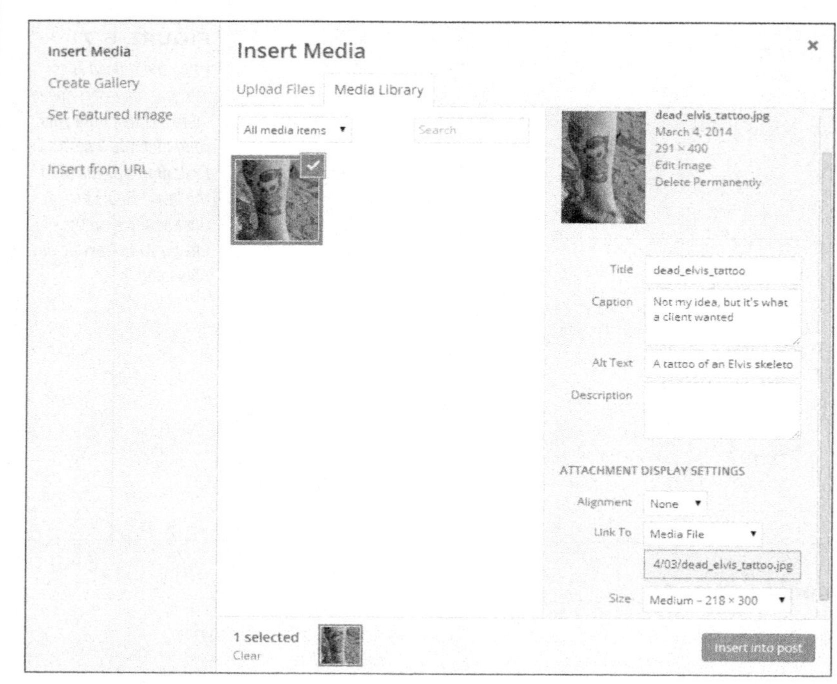

FIGURE 6-8

Here, WordPress has just finished uploading the file dead_elvis_tattoo.jpg. Currently, it's the only file in this site's Media Library. Before you insert it into your post, you need to enter a bit of information.

TIP If you plan to upload your picture using the drag-and-drop approach, here's a valuable shortcut. Instead of clicking the Add Media button to get started, just drag the picture right onto the post editor in the Add New Post page. WordPress will open the Insert Media window, take you to the Media Library tab, and start uploading your picture. You can then carry on with step 4.

4. **Scroll down and fill in the information for your picture. WordPress asks for the following:**

   - **Title** is the text that appears in a tooltip when someone points to a picture.
   - **Caption** adds an optional caption that appears on the page near your picture. Different themes handle captions differently, but they usually place them under your picture, as in Figure 6-9. Captions can include HTML tags (for example, <b> for bold formatting), but you need to add them yourself.
   - **Alt Text** is the alternate text sent to assistive devices (like screen readers) to help people with disabilities interpret pictures they can't see.

- **Description** is a longer, more detailed explanation of the picture. You can use it for your records, or you might decide to display it on your page—but you need to find a theme that shows image descriptions (most don't) or edit your theme by hand (Chapter 13). If you don't plan to use the description, you can leave this box empty.
- **Alignment** determines where a picture appears relative to its text. If you choose None, the picture stands on its own, wherever you inserted it. Paragraphs may appear before it or after it, but the post content won't flow on either side of the picture. If you choose Left or Right, WordPress puts the picture on one side of the page and lets text flow around the other side (see Figure 6-9).

TIP If your text narrates your pictures, you probably want to choose None for the alignment so you can position the pictures exactly where you want them. Examples include food blogs with pictures of meals, travelogues with pictures of tourist sites, and home renovation stories with a photo journal of the step-by-step process. On the other hand, if you have a rich layout that's more like a glossy magazine, you might decide to use Left or Right for your picture alignment.

- **Link To** is the web address where WordPress sends visitors if they click your pic. Usually, this setting is set to Media File and if someone clicks your picture, the browser displays the full-size picture file without any headers, sidebars, captions, or extra content. Alternatively, you can choose Attachment Page, which tells WordPress to take readers to something called, sensibly enough, an *attachment page,* which features the full-sized version of your picture and a section for reader comments. Or you can send readers to a web address—select Custom URL from the Link To menu and then type in the address you want. Finally, you can tell WordPress to not make the picture clickable at all (select None).
- **Size** tells WordPress how big the picture should be in your post. You can choose Full Size to use the original dimensions of the uploaded file, or you can use one of the scaled-down versions of your picture, which WordPress creates automatically when you upload a file. You'll notice that WordPress maintains the relative proportions of your picture—it never squashes a picture more width-wise than it does height-wise. (Remember that readers can click a scaled-down picture to see the full-size image, unless you set the Link To setting to Custom URL or None.)

NOTE In addition to storing the original file you upload, WordPress creates three extra versions of every picture: a 150 × 150 pixel thumbnail, a 300 × 300 medium-size image, and a 1024 × 1024 large-size pic. You can change these defaults in the Settings→Media section of the dashboard, under the "Image sizes" heading. However, the changes affect only new pictures, not the ones you've already uploaded.

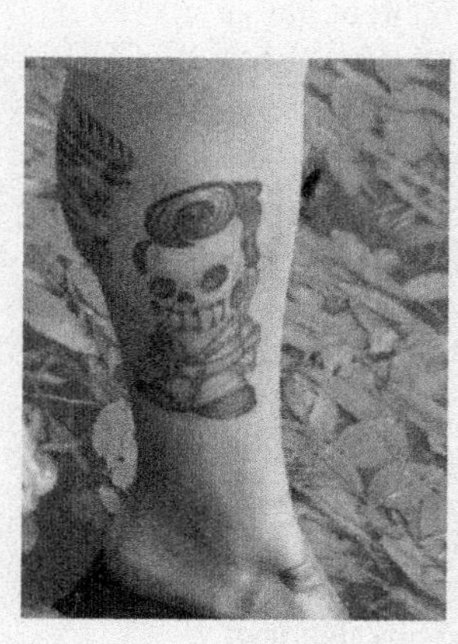

Dead Elvis
Here's my latest work. I call it the "Dead Elvis" tattoo, for obvious reasons.
What do you think–ridiculously cool, or completely creepy?
— Not my idea, but it's what the client wanted
This entry was posted in Uncategorized by Katya Greenview. Bookmark the permalink.

FIGURE 6-9

This theme aligns images on the left, which means the text in the post flows down the right side of the image.

5. **Optionally, you can edit your picture by clicking the Edit Image link, which appears just above all the text boxes. Click Save when you finish.**

   When you edit a picture, WordPress opens the Edit Image box (Figure 6-10). There, you can make a few simple changes.

   Most usefully, you can *crop* your picture. To do that, drag a rectangle around the region you want to keep and then click the Crop button, which appears in the small strip of buttons above your picture. This is the most common type of picture edit.

   You can also scale your picture down, reducing its size. To do so, type in either a new width or a new height in the Scale Image section on the right, using pixels as the unit of measure. WordPress adjusts the other dimension proportionally, ensuring that you don't distort the picture. Then click Scale to apply the change.

   Finally, you can also flip or rotate your picture by clicking the corresponding button above the picture.

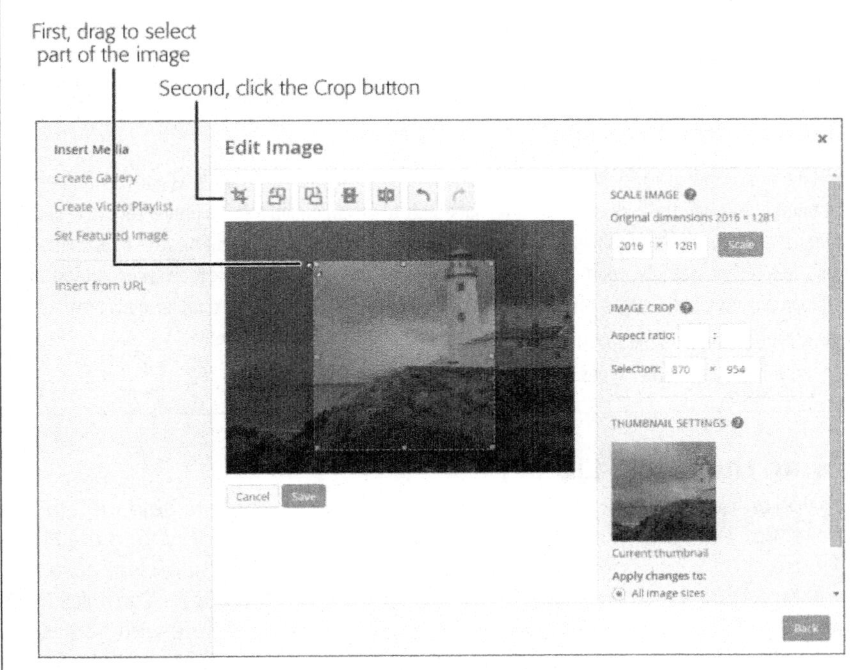

FIGURE 6-10

As you drag your mouse over a portion of your picture, the Image Crop section (right) shows the exact size (in pixels) of your selection.

NOTE When you edit a picture, WordPress actually creates a new file. If you look at the picture's URL, you'll notice that WordPress appends a number to the end of the filename, so *dead_elvis_tattoo.jpg* becomes *dead_elvis_tattoo1339626522667.jpg*, for example. There are two reasons for this sleight of hand. First, it prevents problems if one of your posts needs to use the original version of the picture. Second, it lets you get your original picture back later if you ever need it. To do that, edit the image, and then click Restore Original Image.

6. **Click the "Insert into post" button in the Insert Media window to add the picture to your post.**

   When you insert a picture, you'll see it in the visual editor. If you chose left or right alignment, you can type your text around the side of the picture. If you chose None or Center for the alignment, you can type text only above and below the image.

   To tweak your picture, first click it to select it. Two small icons appear in the picture's top-left corner. Click the "X" icon to remove the picture from your post. Click the pencil icon to open an Image Details box that lets you alter the picture (using all the same tools available when you first insert a picture).

NOTE If you delete a picture from your post, it still exists on your WordPress site. This might be what you want (for example, it lets you use the picture in another post), or it might be a problem (if you're worrying about someone stumbling across an embarrassing incident you made the mistake of photographing). To wipe a picture off your site, you need to use the media library, as described in the next section.

GEM IN THE ROUGH

Attaching Other Files to Your Post

Pictures aren't the only type of file you can put in a post. WordPress.com lets you embed a number of other types of document, including PDFs, Word documents, Excel spreadsheets, and PowerPoint presentations. In a self-hosted site, you face no restrictions, so you can upload any type of file you want.

The difference is what happens *after* you upload the file. Unlike a picture, you won't see the content from other types of documents in your post. Instead, WordPress adds an ordinary link that points to the uploaded file. If a reader clicks the link, the browser may display the document or offer to download it—what it does depends on whether the browser has an add-in that can display that type of file. For example, many browsers have add-ins that display PDF documents.

Viewing the Media Library

When you upload a picture, WordPress stores it in the *wp-content/uploads* folder of your site. For example, if you upload a picture named *face_photo.jpg* to the Magic Tea House site in January 2014, WordPress stores it at *http://magicteahouse.net/wp-content/uploads/2014/01/face_photo.jpg*. Behind the scenes, WordPress also creates large, medium, and thumbnail-sized copies of your picture with names like *face_photo_300x200.jpg*, and stores them in the same folder. That way, WordPress doesn't waste bandwidth sending a full-sized picture if a post needs to display just a tiny thumbnail.

WordPress might store more files than you think. In addition to all the pictures you insert into posts, all the featured images you use, and any custom header or background images you add to your theme, WordPress stores files that you attach to your posts here, too, like PDFs, Word documents, and spreadsheets. Furthermore, if you change a picture (using the basic cropping, resizing, and rotating tools described on page 184), WordPress stores a new, separate version of the picture as well.

WordPress calls this repository, which holds your pictures and files, the *media library*. To see the current contents of your site's media library, choose Media→Library (Figure 6-11).

There are two reasons you might want to use the media library: to remove files you don't need anymore, and to upload files you want to use in the future.

Deleting Pictures from the Media Library

You might choose to delete a media file as part of your basic website housekeeping. After all, why keep a file you're not using, especially if it's distracting you from the files you really *do* want?

To delete a media file, point to its filename and then click the Delete Permanently link that appears underneath.

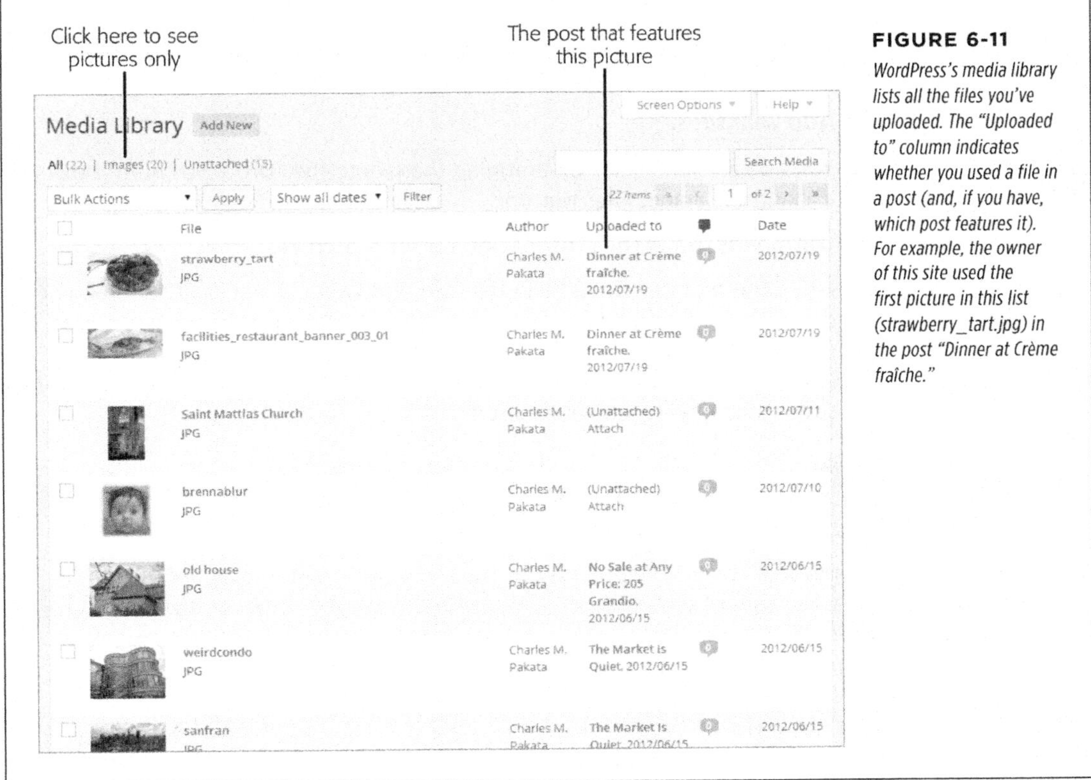

FIGURE 6-11

WordPress's media library lists all the files you've uploaded. The "Uploaded to" column indicates whether you used a file in a post (and, if you have, which post features it). For example, the owner of this site used the first picture in this list (strawberry_tart.jpg) in the post "Dinner at Crème fraîche."

If you delete a picture that other posts are using, you have a small problem. Now when someone reads the post, they'll see the broken-picture-link icon, the universal browser sign that something is missing. Correcting this problem is easy (just edit the post to delete the picture box), but it's up to you to find the post.

NOTE WordPress doesn't let you *replace* a picture that's in the media library. Even if you upload a picture that has the same name as one already in your library, WordPress puts it in a different subfolder or gives it a slightly different filename. The same thing happens if you edit a picture that's already in the media library. This system prevents a number of seriously frustrating problems, but it also means that there's no way to update the picture in a post without editing the post.

Adding Pictures to the Media Library

You might choose to add an image to your library to prepare for future posts. Maybe you have a batch of pictures that detail a home renovation project, and you plan to write about the process on your blog, "Home Sweet Home." However, you don't want to start writing those posts yet. To make sure the pictures are ready when you need them, you can upload them straight to the media library, and then use them later. Here's what to do:

1. **Choose Media→Add New.**

   This takes you to the Upload New Media page, which is strikingly similar to the Insert Media window you used earlier.

2. **Add your files.**

   You upload media files by dragging them onto the "Drop files here" box or by clicking the Select Files button.

3. **Optionally, fill in the information for each picture.**

   Fill in the picture details (like the title and caption) and edit the image (say, cropping it or flipping it). When you actually insert the image into a post, you still have the chance to enter new information or re-edit the picture. But if you get some of the preliminary details down when you upload the picture, you'll save some time when you insert it.

GEM IN THE ROUGH

Using the Media Library to Put a Picture in Your Sidebar

As you already know, the media library stores all the pictures you use in your posts. You can also use it to store files you want to use in some other way. For example, you can link to one of your media files from an ordinary web page on a traditional, non-WordPress website. All you need to do is take note of the file's URL. (To get that, choose Media→Library to visit the media library, and then click the file you're interested in. WordPress displays the file's location in the File URL text box.)

You can use the same trick to inject an image into the Text widget (page 166), that all-purpose tool for showing scraps of content outside your posts. As you learned in Chapter 5, the Text widget accepts almost any HTML you can throw at it. So if you know you have a picture in the media file with the URL *http://magicteahouse.net/wp-content/uploads/2014/06/dead_elvis_tattoo.jpg*, you can stick in an <img> tag like this:

```
<p>I'm a <b>hotshot tattoo artist</b>
living in the Bay Area. My work pushes the
bounds of taste and decency, just like you
know you want.</p>

<img src="http://magicteahouse.net/wp-
content/uploads/2014/06/dead_elvis_tattoo.
jpg">
```

If you've been around the web block, you probably know that it's better to trim the picture link down to just */wp-content/uploads/2014/06/dead_elvis_tattoo.jpg*. It's on the same site as the rest of your WordPress content, so there's no need to include the domain name.

Either way, Figure 6-12 shows the result.

To insert a picture from the media library into a post, use the same Add Media button you learned about earlier. Here's what to do as you create or edit a post:

1. **Move to the place in the post where you want to insert the picture, and then click Add Media.**
2. **Instead of adding a new file, click the Media Library tab to see what you've got.**

   You see a list of thumbnail images, one for each picture in your library.
3. **Find the picture you want, and then click it.**

   You see the familiar picture thumbnail and picture details.
4. **Change the text and edit the image, if necessary.**
5. **When you're ready to add the picture, click "Insert into post."**

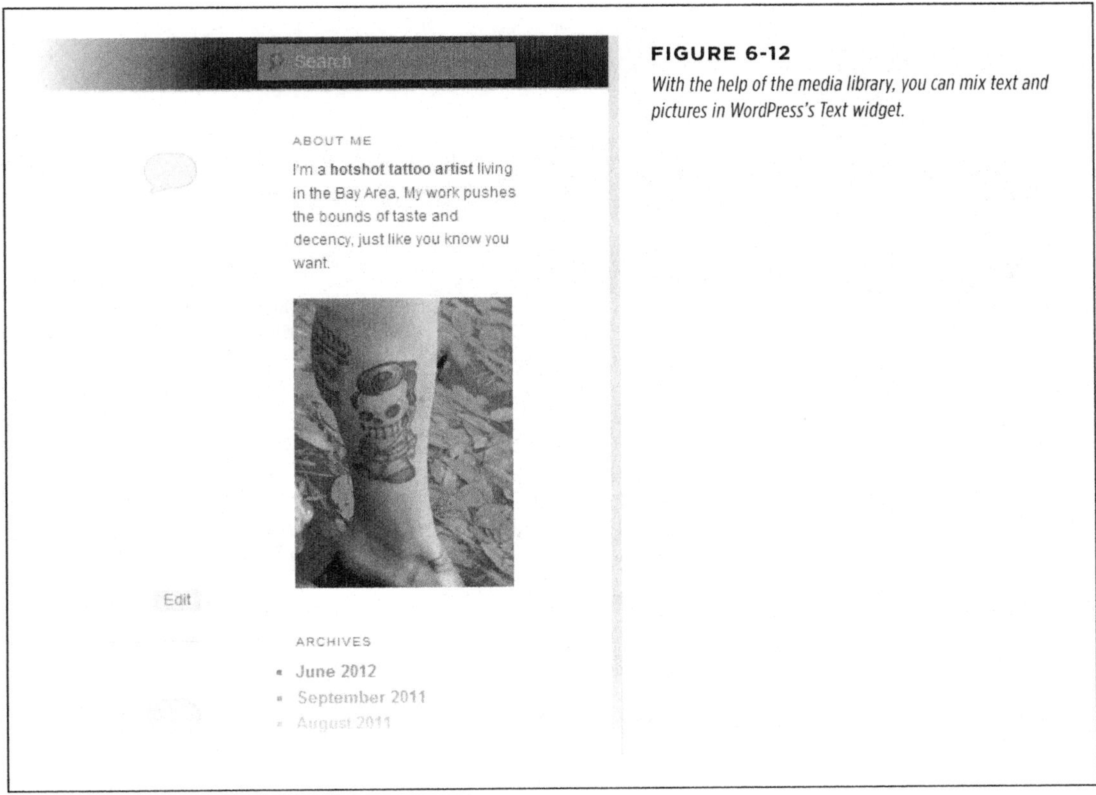

FIGURE 6-12

With the help of the media library, you can mix text and pictures in WordPress's Text widget.

Featured Images

Instead of simply including a picture in a post, you can designate it as a *featured image*. A featured image represents a post, but it doesn't actually show up as part of the post content. Instead, its role varies depending on the theme you use.

Some themes ignore featured images altogether. But many others place featured images at the top of the corresponding post, near the title area. Examples include Twenty Twelve, Twenty Thirteen, and Twenty Fourteen (as shown in Figure 6-13).

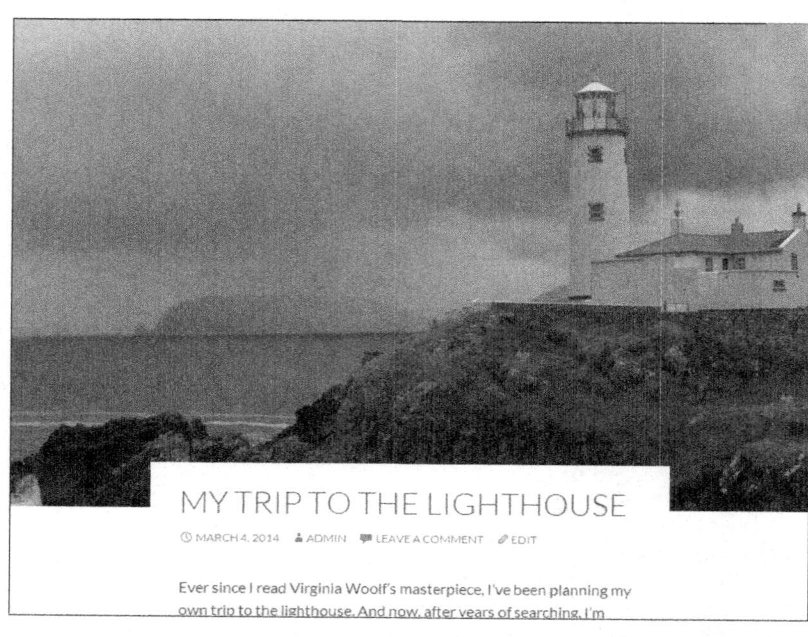
MY TRIP TO THE LIGHTHOUSE
MARCH 4, 2014 ADMIN LEAVE A COMMENT EDIT
Ever since I read Virginia Woolf's masterpiece, I've been planning my
own trip to the lighthouse. And now, after years of searching, I'm

FIGURE 6-13

The simplest way a theme can use a featured image is to place it at the top of a post. Twenty Fourteen does this, but it positions the post title so it slightly overlaps the picture, making the image recede into the background.

Some themes exploit featured images in clever ways. For example, the Twenty Eleven theme temporarily swaps in the picture for the name of your site when you view a post with a featured image (Figure 6-14).

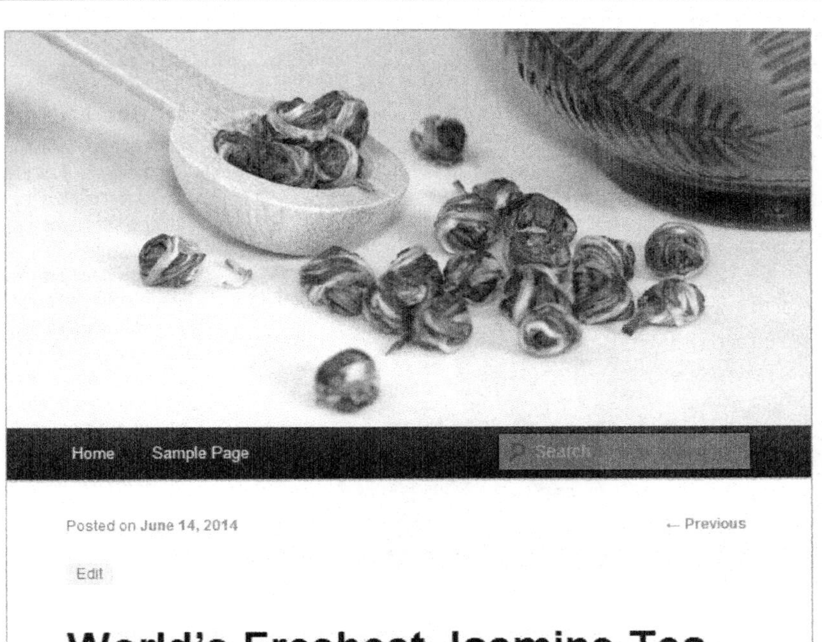

FIGURE 6-14

When you read this post, the featured image (some tea leaf buds) temporarily replaces the site header. This works even though the picture doesn't actually appear anywhere in the post.

NOTE Twenty Eleven's header-replacement trick works only if the featured image is at least as big as the header image. If your featured image isn't as wide, WordPress won't display it at all on the single-post page, nor will it explain the image's perplexing absence.

More ambitious themes use featured images to promote posts—for example, to highlight them in some sort of scrolling banner or gallery. Depending on the theme, this detail might be a built-in part of the home page, or it might rely on a theme-specific widget.

Figure 6-15 shows the free Brightpage theme, which is available to self-hosted WordPress sites. It displays a featured-image slideshow on the home page. This slideshow automatically grabs all the posts in the category named Featured (which you must create) and displays the featured images for each post, one after the other.

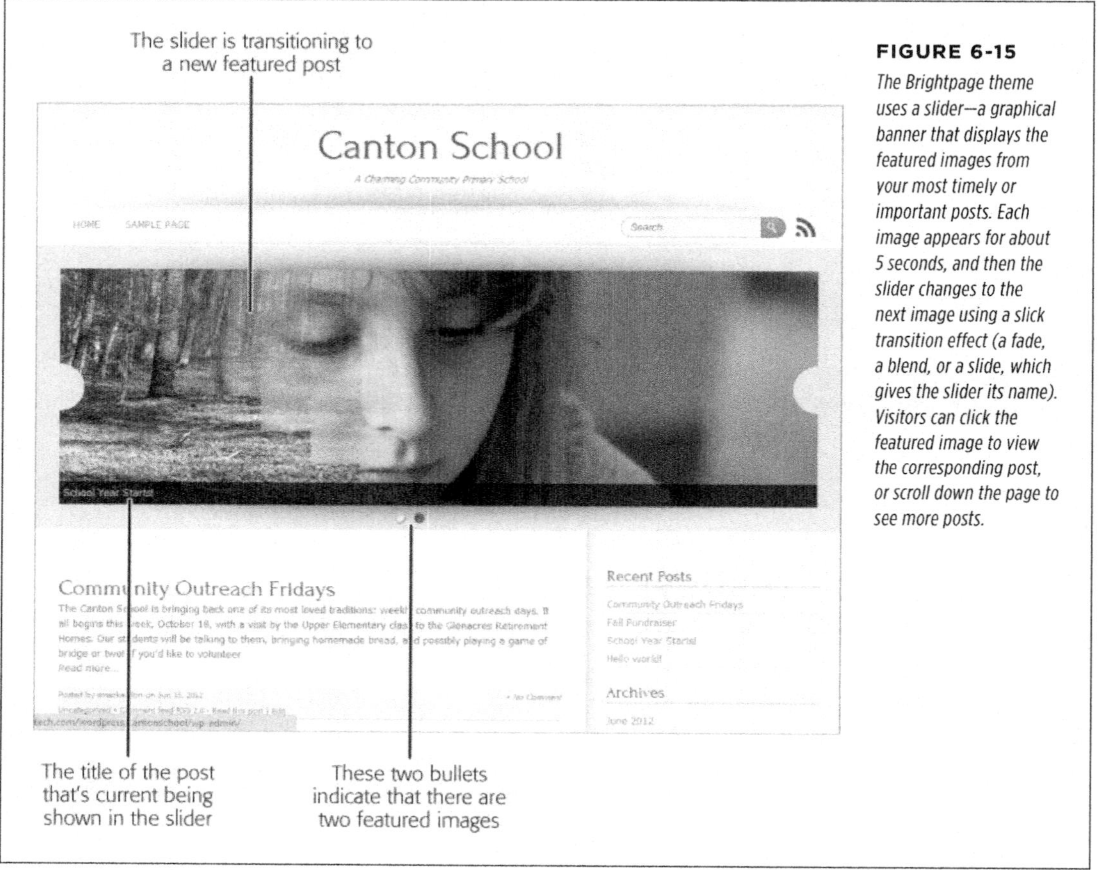

FIGURE 6-15

The Brightpage theme uses a slider—a graphical banner that displays the featured images from your most timely or important posts. Each image appears for about 5 seconds, and then the slider changes to the next image using a slick transition effect (a fade, a blend, or a slide, which gives the slider its name). Visitors can click the featured image to view the corresponding post, or scroll down the page to see more posts.

The nice thing about Brightpage is that it makes it easy for you, the site designer, to choose what posts get featured treatment. When you create a new post that you want to appear in the slider, assign it to the Featured category (in addition to whatever more meaningful category you already use). After some time passes and you decide that the post is no longer important, go to the Edit Post page and remove it from the Featured category.

The Twenty Fourteen theme has a similar trick in store. Like Brightpage, it examines a group of posts you pick, retrieves their featured images, and uses them on the home page. The difference is in the details. While Brightpage asks you to identify the posts you want to use by creating a category named Featured, Twenty Fourteen expects you to use a *tag* named Featured. And while Brightpage uses a slider,

Twenty Fourteen gives you the choice of a slider or a slick grid view, the latter being the standard setting (Figure 6-16).

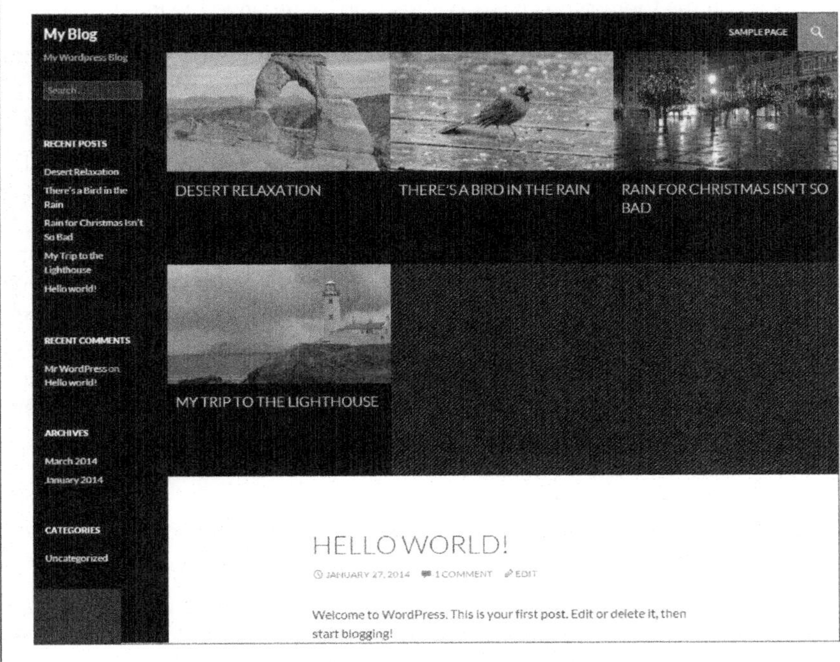

FIGURE 6-16

If you have posts that use the Featured tag, Twenty Fourteen removes them from the post list and puts them and their images in a grid at the top of your home page. Readers can then click an image to read the corresponding post.

TIP To configure how Twenty Fourteen uses featured images, start by choosing Appearance→Customize (to customize the theme) and then click the Featured Content section. There, you can choose between a grid and a slider, and rename the Featured tag to something else.

Assigning a Featured Image to a Post

Each post can have just one featured image. To assign a featured image, you need to be in the Add New Post or Edit Post page. Then follow these steps:

1. **Click the Add Media button.**

   This opens the Insert Media window you saw earlier (Figure 6-7).

2. **Click the Set Featured Image link on the left.**

3. **If the picture you want to use isn't already in the media library, upload it now.**

   You can upload your featured image by dragging it onto the Insert Media window, or by clicking Select Files and browsing for it.

   If your picture is already in the Media Library, click the Media Library tab and then click the picture to select it.

4. **Add the image information.**

   These details include the title, alternate text for screen readers, the caption, and the description. How much of this information WordPress uses in your post depends on the theme you chose, but it's worth supplying the info just in case.

5. **Click Edit Image, take a moment to scale and crop your picture, and then click Save to make your changes permanent.**

   When you insert a standard image into a post, you get the chance to size it. But when you use a featured image, you don't have this control. If you upload a big picture, it's possible that your theme will automatically crop out a large part of it. (The Brightpage theme does this, for example.) To prevent this, you need to scale the picture down before you upload it, using an image editor like Photoshop Elements, Windows Photo Gallery, Picasa, or the Mac's Preview program. To find the right dimensions, you need to experiment or scour your theme's documentation. (Self-hosters, search for your theme at *http://wordpress.org/themes*, and then click your way through to the "Theme Homepage" link. WordPress.com users, search for your theme at *http://theme.wordpress.com*.)

6. **Click the "Set featured image" button in the bottom-right corner.**

   This adds the featured image and closes the Insert Media window so you can continue writing your post. Remember, you won't see the picture appear alongside your text.

   If you decide at some point that you don't want this picture as your post's featured image, find the Featured Image box in the bottom-right corner of the page (it shows a scaled-down preview of your pic) and then click "Remove featured image."

7. **Publish your post (or update it, if you already published it).**

   Remember, some themes don't use featured images at all. If you use such a theme, you may not even know that your post has a featured image, because your theme never displays it.

NOTE Featured posts are interesting because they rely on the interplay between WordPress features and theme features. WordPress defines the concept of the feature (in this case, featured images), and the theme decides how to exploit that concept, opening a wide, uncharted territory of possibilities. The same idea underpins many other WordPress features. For example, later in this chapter you'll see how WordPress defines the concepts of post excerpts (page 202) and post formats (page 198), but allows themes to use them in a variety of clever ways.

UP TO SPEED

Learning to Use Featured Images with Your Theme

As the discussion in this chapter shows, different themes use featured images in similar but subtly different ways. To get the result you want, you need to make sure you're using featured images in the right way.

For example, you may need to flag featured-image posts with a specific category name or tag name, or you may need to make them sticky (page 104). Picture size is another important consideration. Twenty Fourteen recommends that your featured images be 672 pixels wide and 1038 pixels wide, which lets them expand to their full size when displayed behind a post or in the slider. Other themes have their own strict size requirements. Violate them, and your pictures may be stretched, squashed, or cropped to fit the theme.

Unfortunately, the dashboard doesn't have a standard way to make this information available. It's up to you to review the documentation for your theme. A good place to start is by searching for your theme in WordPress's theme library (*http://wordpress.org/themes* for self-hosters or *http://theme.wordpress.com* for WordPress.com users). You can then follow the Theme Homepage link to find out what the developer has to say about the theme, or click the Support tab to browse other people's questions and answers. For more information about the theme library, see Chapter 5.

Showing Part of a Post

At the heart of every WordPress blog is a home page, and at the heart of every home page is a reverse-chronological list of posts. This list serves a vital purpose, showing a snapshot of current content so readers can tell, at a glance, what's going down on your site.

However, the home pages you've seen so far have had one potential problem—they're long, sometimes awkwardly so. Having multiple posts fused together into one long page is a great convenience for new visitors who want to read your content from end to end, but it's not so helpful for return visitors who want to survey your new content and decide where to dive in.

Fortunately, WordPress has a handy solution. You can decide to show only the first part of each post, called a *teaser,* on your home page, which your visitor can click to read the standalone post.

One advantage to this approach is that you can pack quite a few teasers into your home page and keep them close together, no matter how long the posts really are. You can also put posts into tighter layouts—for example, creating a site that looks more like the front page of a newspaper. Another advantage is that it encourages readers to click through to the post, where they'll also see the post comments and get the opportunity to join in the discussion.

However, trimming down posts introduces two possible disadvantages. First, there's the extra link readers need to follow to read a full post. If someone wants to read several posts in a row, this extra step can add up to a lot more clicking. Second, you need to explicitly tell WordPress what part of a post belongs on the home page. It's an easy job, but you need to do it for *each post* you create. If you've already written a few posts, you need to update them.

NOTE As a general rule, informal, conversational blogs work well with the standard one-post-after-another stream that WordPress displays on the home page. But WordPress sites that have more detailed article-like posts, use multiple sections, or feature multiple authors, often work better with a tighter, leaner style that uses teasers.

In the following section, you'll learn how to use teasers instead of full posts. You'll also consider two related features: breaking posts into multiple pages and using post excerpts.

Displaying Teasers Using the "More" Quicktag

The best way to cut a post down to size is with a special WordPress code called the *More quicktag*. You place the More quicktag at the spot where you want to divide a post. The content that falls before the tag becomes the teaser, which WordPress displays on the home page (Figure 6-17, left). If a reader clicks through to the post page, he sees the entire post (Figure 6-17, right).

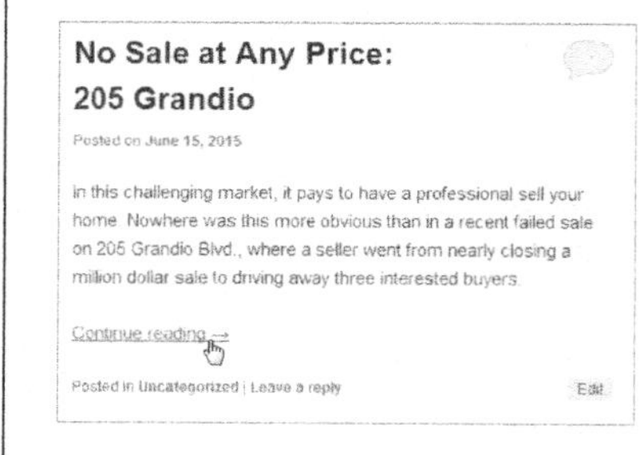

FIGURE 6-17
When you use the More quicktag in a post, only part of the post appears on the home page (left). Click the "Continue reading" link to get the whole post in a new page (right).

To insert the More quicktag in the visual editor, go to the spot in your post where you want to put the tag, and then click the Insert Read More Tag button. You'll see a light-gray dividing line (Figure 6-18).

You can also add the More quicktag in the HTML editor. You could click the button labeled "more," but it's just as easy to type in the tag yourself, wherever you want it:

```
<!--more-->
```

HTML nerds will recognize that the More quicktag looks exactly like an HTML comment—the sort of thing you might put in your markup to leave notes to yourself.

Browsers ignore HTML comments, and WordPress borrows this system to sneak in some of its own special codes.

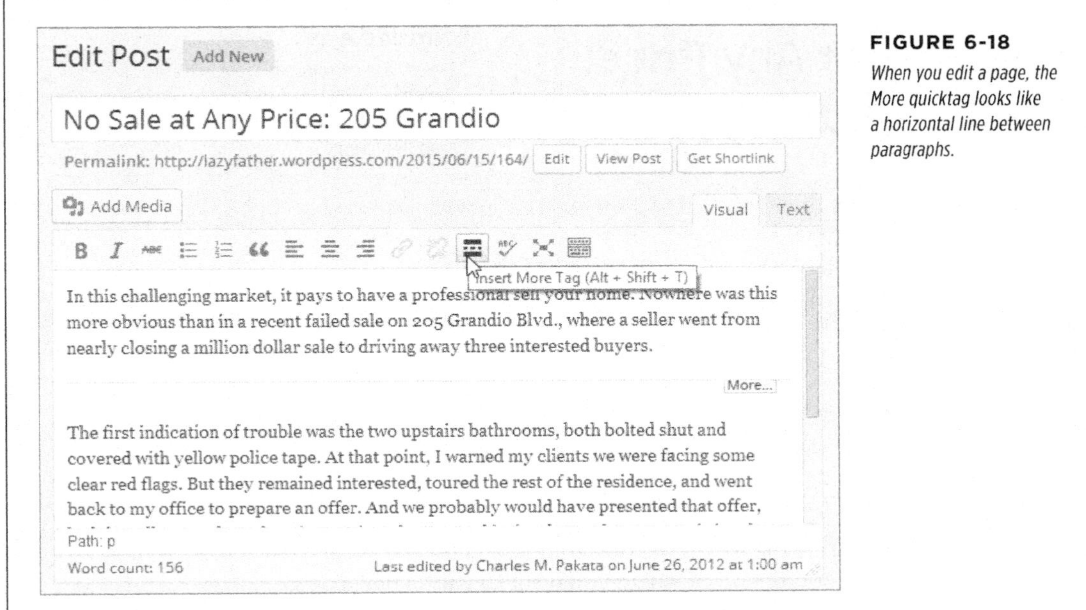

FIGURE 6-18

When you edit a page, the More quicktag looks like a horizontal line between paragraphs.

NOTE WordPress uses the More quicktag whenever your site displays more than one post at a time. The home page is the most obvious example, but you'll also see multiple posts when you browse by category, date, or keyword. In these situations, the More quicktag serves the same purpose—it trims long posts down to more manageable teasers.

There's one more trick you can do with the More tag. In the previous example, a "Continue reading" link led from the teaser to the full post. The theme determines the link's wording, but you can substitute your own text. To do that, you need to edit your post in HTML view, and then stick the link text in the middle of the More tag, exactly as shown here:

```
<!--more Tell me more-->
```

If you want to change the link text for every teaser, editing your theme is far more efficient than editing individual posts (see Part 4 to learn how to edit your theme).

Dividing a Post into Multiple Pages

The More quicktag lets you split a post into two pieces: the teaser, and the rest of the content. Alternatively, you can split a page into as many sections as you want using the lesser-known *Nextpage quicktag*. When you do, WordPress adds a set of navigation links to the bottom of the post (Figure 6-19).

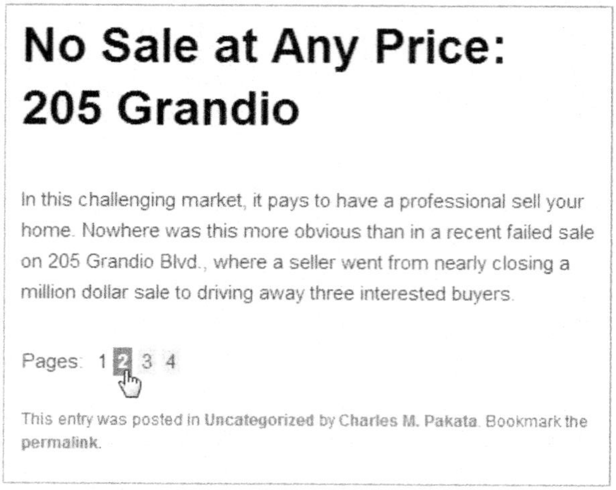

No Sale at Any Price: 205 Grandio

In this challenging market, it pays to have a professional sell your home. Nowhere was this more obvious than in a recent failed sale on 205 Grandio Blvd., where a seller went from nearly closing a million dollar sale to driving away three interested buyers.

Pages: 1 2 3 4

This entry was posted in Uncategorized by Charles M. Pakata. Bookmark the permalink.

FIGURE 6-19

These page-navigation links are a great way to split a long article into more manageable pieces. But use it sparingly—readers will resent being forced to click without a very good reason.

To insert the Nextpage quicktag, switch to the HTML view (click the Text tab) and then add this code where you want to start a new page:

```
<!--nextpage-->
```

The Nextpage quicktag shows up in the visual editor, as a gray line with the words "Next Page" above it. You can't customize the Nextpage quicktag, but you can create custom page links if you're willing to edit your theme files, as described in Part 4. The trick is to master WordPress's `wp_link_pages()` function, which is described at *http://tinyurl.com/wplinkpages.*

You can use the More and Nextpage quicktags in the same post. However, it's generally a bad idea, because the page-navigation links will appear under the post teaser on the home page. This is likely to strike your readers as plain odd or utterly confusing.

Summarizing Posts with Excerpts

There's another way to shorten posts on the home page: by using WordPress's *excerpts* feature. Ordinarily, an excerpt is the first 50 or so words in a post (the exact number depends on the theme).

Before you can really understand excerpts, you need to know how WordPress uses them. The answer isn't straightforward, because it depends on your theme. Some older themes may avoid excerpts altogether, while others use them prominently (as you'll see shortly). But most themes use excerpts in at least one place: on the search results page. To take a look for yourself, type something into the search box and then press Enter (Figure 6-20).

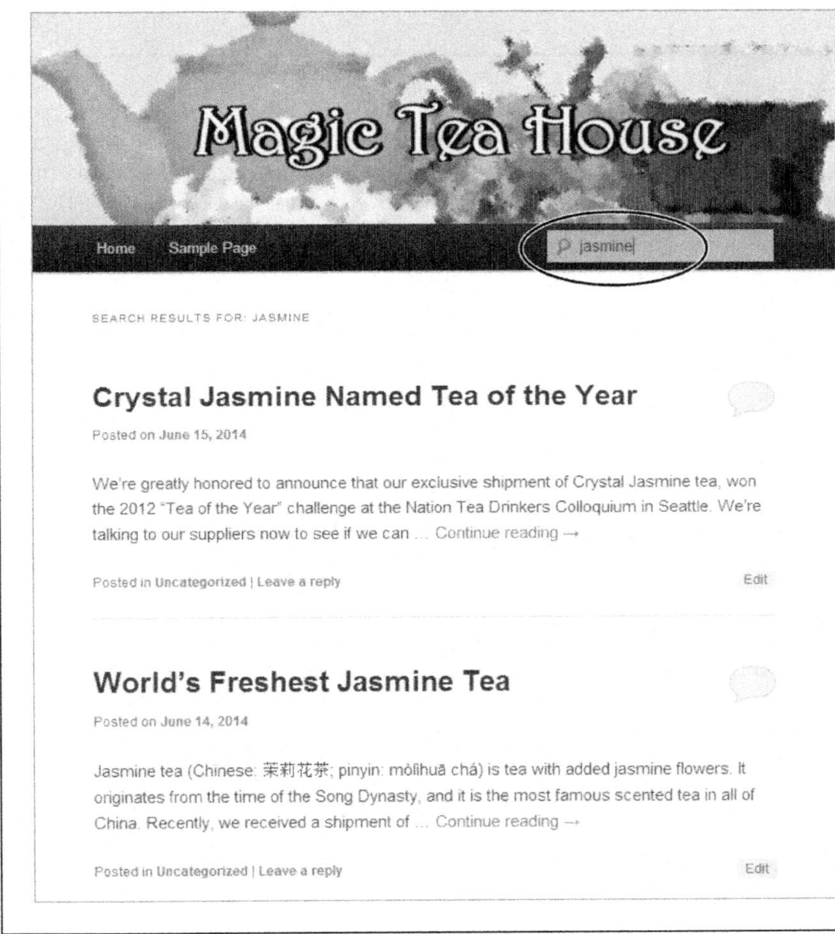

FIGURE 6-20

When you search posts, WordPress doesn't display full posts on the results screen. Instead, it automatically strips out and displays just the first 55 words. That way, you can see a page of search results without needing to scroll all day.

So far, excerpts seem straightforward and automatic (and they are). However, the first few sentences of a post aren't always a good reflection of its content. For that reason, you may want to write your own excerpt—in other words, explicitly provide a brief summary of the content in a post. You can do that from the Add New Post or Edit Post pages. First, choose Screen Options in the upper-right corner, and then turn on the checkbox next to Excerpt. A new box appears where you can write a custom description of your post.

NOTE Things can get a bit confusing if you use excerpts *and* teasers. In that case, WordPress uses an excerpt if the post has one, a teaser if the post uses the More quicktag, or the first 55 words in the post if it has neither an excerpt nor a teaser.

UP TO SPEED

Writing Good Excerpts

The best thing about excerpts is that they don't need to be directly linked to the text in your post. But don't abuse your freedom—to write a good, genuinely useful excerpt, you need to follow a few rules:

- **Keep it brief.** Usually, when a visitor searches your site, WordPress finds several matching posts. By keeping your excerpts short (around the 55-word mark, just like WordPress does), you keep the search results short, which makes them easier to read.
- **Summarize the content of the page.** The goal of an excerpt is to give someone enough information to decide if she wants to click a link to read the full post. An excerpt isn't a place to promote yourself or make flowery comments. Instead, try to clearly and honestly describe what's in the post.
- **Don't repeat the post title.** If you want to make sure every word counts, don't waste time repeating what's clearly visible in the title.

Using Excerpts on Your Home Page

At this point, you might think that it's not worth the trouble to write excerpts for all your posts. And you could be right, if you use a standard theme and you don't think that your visitors are going to be searching for posts. However, there's another factor to consider: Some themes use excerpts for other purposes.

For example, many themes use excerpts as the display text for posts on the home page. This way, the excerpt acts a bit like a teaser. The difference is that the standard WordPress teaser comes from the first part of a post, but you control the wording in an excerpt.

The Brightpage theme described earlier (page 192) uses this system. If you provide an excerpt for a post, that's what shows up on your home page, not the post content. The Oxygen theme, available for both WordPress.com and self-hosted sites, does the same thing, as you can see in Figure 6-21.

NOTE None of the year themes like Twenty Twelve make much use of the excerpts feature. They use them in searches (as shown in Figure 6-20), but not on the home page.

If you switch to a theme that makes heavy use of excerpts, you might find the summary so valuable that you want all your posts to use them, even the ones you've already created. WordPress has some plug-ins that can help. For example, the Excerpt Editor (*http://tinyurl.com/csudedx*) can give you a summary for every existing post, without you having to edit each one individually.

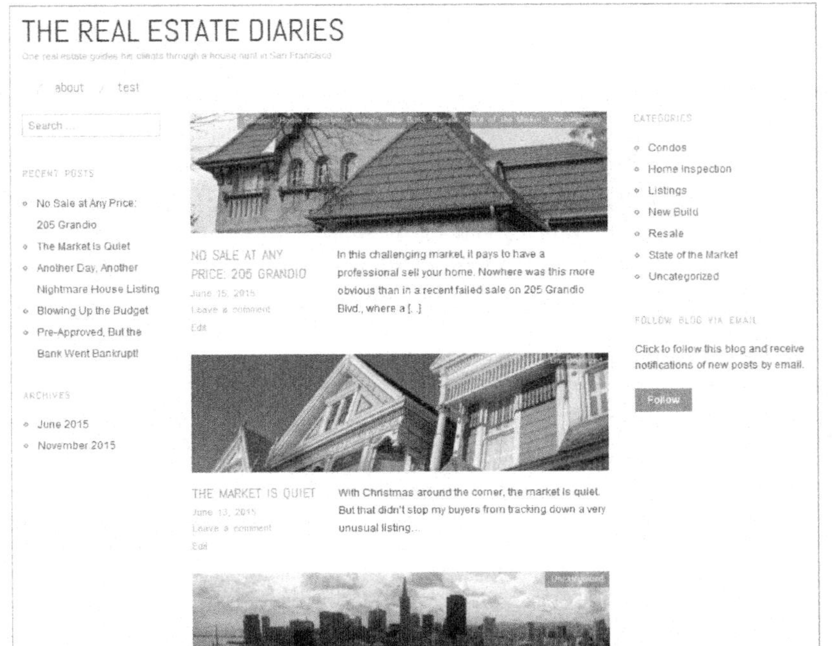

FIGURE 6-21

The Oxygen theme displays the excerpt text and featured image for each post, instead of the post content. If the post doesn't have a featured image, it grabs the first picture from the post and displays that. (And if the post doesn't use any pictures at all, the theme simply shows an empty gray box.) This creates a clean, polished home page that has the feel of a professional news site.

POWER USERS' CLINIC

Changing from Full-Post Displays to Summaries

If you create a self-hosted site, you can make any theme display excerpts or full posts. But, first, you need to learn the basics of WordPress theme files and the WordPress loop, topics covered in Chapters 13 and 14.

Once you know your way around a WordPress theme and the PHP code inside, you're ready to make this relatively straightforward edit. Usually, you need to edit your *index.php* file, which creates the post listing on the home page of your site.

To get the display style you want, your code needs to use the right WordPress function. If you use a function named `the_content()`, your page will show the full content of each post (or the teaser, if you use the More quicktag described on page 196). But if you use a function named `the_excerpt()`, your home page displays the post summary only. Usually, you can switch between the two display modes by modifying the line of code that has the function in it.

If you want a bit more technical information, check out the WordPress function reference at *http://tinyurl.com/the-excerpt*.

Post Formats

As you learned in Chapter 5, your choice of theme determines the basic appearance of every post on your site. Once you pick a theme, you can relax knowing that all your posts get the same font, color scheme, and spacing. Consistency reigns.

But some themes offer an underused feature called *post formats,* which display different types of posts in different ways. On paper, post formats sound pretty nifty. The idea is that you pick a format for each type of post you write, and your theme uses slightly different styling for each of those post types.

The problem is that WordPress limits themes to a small set of officially sanctioned formats. They're mainly useful if you want to create a casual blog (sometimes called a *microblog*), where you throw together pictures, video clips, and post fragments, without worrying too much about organizing your content. In this scenario, post formats provide a structure that can help tame the chaos of your posts. But if you want to create your own post format to distinguish a group of posts that are particularly important to your site, you're out of luck.

NOTE Ambitious WordPress developers often complain that post formats don't let them do what they really want to do: create their own post groupings and apply different formatting to each group. For example, you might want to take posts in a certain category and alter their formatting to make them stand out. (Imagine, for example, a news site that uses a bolder background to highlight violent crimes.) This technique is possible—and useful—but it's not easy. You need to do all the work yourself, by adding style rules and code to your theme. (You can find an example starting on page 495.) And you need to have a self-hosted site to use this technique, because WordPress.com doesn't allow theme editing.

UP TO SPEED

Understanding Microblogs

Microblogs focus on small bits of content: news headlines, interesting links, personal status updates, random thoughts, and stream-of-consciousness chatter. They tend to be less formal, more personal, and more conversational than posts—almost like a cross between traditional blogs and old-school messaging systems like email and chat. Microblogs also mix different types of content, like audio, video, and images. In fact, some microblogs are built entirely out of pictures or video clips.

The kings of microblogging are Twitter and Tumblr, but WordPress fans can join in, too. However, WordPress's vaunted flexibility might overcomplicate your efforts. Because WordPress allows short, microblog-style posts *and* longer, more traditional entries, it's easy to drown out the small stuff. You may also find that WordPress's other features—categories, tags, the media library, and so on—overcomplicate your microblogging efforts.

Applying a Post Format

If your theme supports post formats, you'll see a Format box in the Add New Post and Edit Post pages. There, you'll find a list of all the formats you can use with the theme. You can pick any of them for a post, but if you don't make a choice, your post sticks with Standard.

Table 6-1 lists all the post formats that WordPress allows. Themes can pick and choose which of them they allow.

Table 6-1. The standard post formats

POST FORMAT	TYPE OF CONTENT
Standard	Standard, ordinary posts. Every post starts out using the Standard format.
Aside	A short snippet of text that doesn't add up to a full post. Casual bloggers can use the Aside format to blurt out a quick thought, in much the same way that you might use a text message or a tweet on Twitter. Most themes don't display a title for asides.
Status	A short update about what you're doing right now ("Chillin' with my Missin' Manual, about to build a brilliant WordPress site"). Similar to the status update feature on virtually every social media site. Most themes don't display a title for status updates.
Link	A link to another website, with little or no extra text. Most themes don't display a title for links.
Quote	A short snippet of text that quotes some words of wisdom you want to share. Most themes don't display a title for quotes.
Image	A post that contains a picture you uploaded.
Gallery	A post that contains a picture gallery, like the kind you'll create on page 330.
Audio	A post that contains an audio recording.
Video	A post that contains a video file.
Chat	A snippet of a memorable conversation, offline or online. Usually looks like this: Joe: dude, why u ignorin me? Ben: im learnin some wordpress, bro

You see these formats at work in the year themes (page 132), from Twenty Eleven on. Each theme has its own way of styling the formats. Often, you'll be hard-pressed to spot the minor changes between an ordinary post and one with a format applied. In many cases, the only difference you'll notice is the lack of a title for many formats (like asides and status updates) and the addition of a small icon. The Twenty Thirteen theme applies the most dramatic post format styles, with background colors (Figure 6-22).

"In order to be a hero, one must be willing to be a deviant."

March 4, 2014
Leave a reply
Edit

jerry
March 1, 2014

Blizzard alert! Sipping hot chocolate at home for the day.

Leave a reply
Edit

Viennese Chocolate Museum LINK

March 1, 2014
Leave a reply
Edit

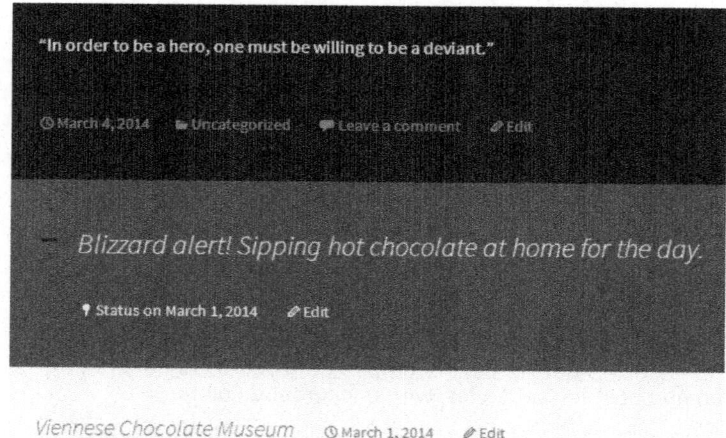

FIGURE 6-22

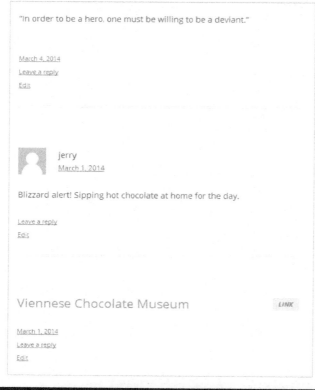

Here are three posts using different post formats: a quote, a status update, and a clickable link. The Twenty Twelve theme (top) barely distinguishes between the three posts, while Twenty Thirteen (bottom) gets more colorful.

To get a better sense of what your theme's post formats look like, create some test posts and look at them on the home page.

The Ephemera Widget

Some themes include a specialized widget to work with post formats. The most common example is the *ephemera* widget. Twenty Eleven and Twenty Fourteen both include one, named Twenty Eleven Ephemera and Twenty Fourteen Ephemera. The other year themes don't include the ephemera widget at all.

As the name suggests, the ephemera widget is all about fleeting scraps of content that are useful for a short period of time, like asides, quotes, and status updates. The ephemera widget gathers these bits of microblog content and displays them in a small, self-contained strip that you can pop into a sidebar (Figure 6-23). The idea is to call attention to smaller scraps of information that might otherwise be swallowed up in the clutter of your blog.

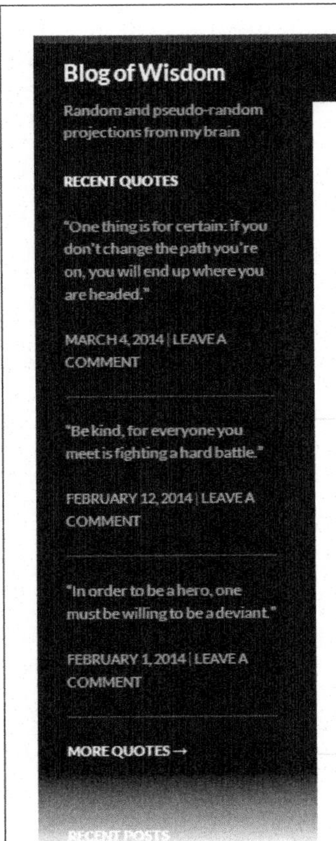

FIGURE 6-23

Here, the Twenty Fourteen ephemera widget shows the three most recent quotes you posted to your blog.

To use the ephemera widget, choose Appearance→Widgets to visit the widget-designing section of the dashboard. Then, drag the widget to the spot on the page where you want it. Finally, customize it by supplying these three details:

- A title that will appear above the widget.
- The type of posts you want to show. You can choose any post format. However, the ephemera widget shows the full content of each post, so you'll probably want to pick a short, microblog-style post format like Aside, Status, Quote, or Link.
- Choose the number of posts that should appear in the widget. The Twenty Fourteen standard is two.

TIP You can add more than one ephemera widget if you want to show different post formats. For example, one widget could show a list of links, a second could list status updates, and a third could show your most recent asides.

All in all, the ephemera widget offers an interesting way to extract bits of content from a loosely structured blog. However, most serious bloggers are better served by using Twitter for microblogging and integrating a Twitter feed into their sidebars, as described on page 430.

CHAPTER

7

Adding Pages and Menus

In previous chapters, you focused most of your attention on WordPress *posts*—the blocks of dated, categorized content at the heart of most WordPress blogs. But WordPress has another, complementary way to showcase content, called *pages*. Unlike posts, pages aren't dated, categorized, or tagged. They exist independently of posts. The easiest way to understand the role of WordPress pages is to think of them as ordinary web pages, like the kind you might compose in an HTML editor.

You're likely to use pages for two reasons. First, even in a traditional blog, you may want to keep some content around permanently, rather than throw it into your ever-advancing sequence of posts. For example, personal blogs often include a page named About Me, where you provide biographical information. You don't want to tie this page to a specific date—you want it easily accessible all the time. Similarly, businesses might use pages to provide contact information, a map, or a list of frequently asked questions. You can even create a fine-tuned home page to greet your visitors, instead of using the default reverse-chronological list of posts.

Another reason to use pages is to build simple sites that don't feel like blogs. Some people call these sites *brochure sites,* and the description isn't entirely complimentary. That's because brochure sites present a collection of fixed information, while blogs feel live and interactive. However, there's a wide range of possibility between these two extremes. For example, if you create a site for your small business, you might use pages to display the core content of your site (information about your company, your policies, the brands you carry, and so on), while adding a blog-powered section of posts for news and promotions. Is this a blog, a brochure-site, or something in between? No matter the answer, it's a great solution for plenty of people.

In this chapter, you'll learn to use pages to either supplement your blog or to create a brochure-style site. You'll also learn to manage page navigation with menus, so your visitors can find the content they want. Lastly, you'll consider some of the innovative ways that different themes exploit the pages feature.

Creating Pages

Although pages behave differently from posts, the process of creating and managing them is similar. Just as you work with posts in the dashboard's Posts menu, so you work with pages in the Pages menu.

Here's how to create a new page:

1. **Choose Pages→Add New.**

   This takes you to a screen named Add New Page (Figure 7-1), which resembles a slightly simpler version of the Add New Post page.

TIP If your site is on WordPress.com, you can take advantage of another path to page creation—the Copy Page shortcut, which creates a new page based on an old one. Choose Pages→Copy a Page (instead of Pages→Add New), find the page you want to duplicate in the resulting list of pages, and then click the Copy button next to it. You'll still end up at the Add New Page screen, but you start out with an exact duplicate of the page you picked, which you can modify to suit your needs.

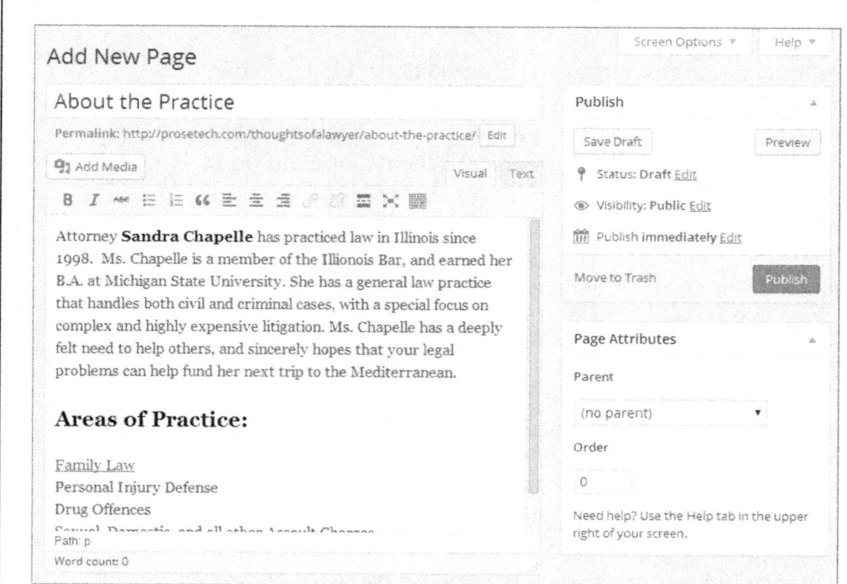
Add New Page
Screen Options
Help
About the Practice
Permalink: http://prosetech.com/thoughtsofalawyer/about-the-practice/
Edit
Add Media
Visual
Text
Attorney Sandra Chapelle has practiced law in Illinois since 1998. Ms. Chapelle is a member of the Illionois Bar, and earned her B.A. at Michigan State University. She has a general law practice that handles both civil and criminal cases, with a special focus on complex and highly expensive litigation. Ms. Chapelle has a deeply felt need to help others, and sincerely hopes that your legal problems can help fund her next trip to the Mediterranean.
Areas of Practice:
Family Law
Personal Injury Defense
Drug Offences
Path: p
Word count: 0
Publish
Save Draft
Preview
Status: Draft Edit
Visibility: Public Edit
Publish immediately Edit
Move to Trash
Publish
Page Attributes
Parent
(no parent)
Order
0
Need help? Use the Help tab in the upper right of your screen.

FIGURE 7-1

The form you use to create pages is similar to the one for creating posts. Both let you include pictures, fancy HTML markup, and featured images. But pages don't let you add the classification details, like category and tag information, that posts do, which is why you don't see those options here.

2. **Give the page a title and some content.**

   You'll see the same content-editing box you use to create posts, with the same two tabs. Choose the Visual tab to see the formatted text for your page, more or less the way it will appear on your site. Choose the Text tab to see the underlying HTML markup.

   For now, don't worry about the Page Attributes box—you'll learn about the options there a bit later.

3. **Finally, click Publish to make the page live on your site.**

   Or choose one of the other options in the Publish box. Just as with posts, you can save a page as a draft (page 97) or schedule it for future publication (page 100).

   When you publish a page, a "Page published" message appears at the top of the page, confirming that it's up and open to the public. Now is a good time to click the "View page" link to take a look (Figure 7-2).

NOTE Pages don't have categories and tags, they aren't listed in chronological order, and you can't browse them by date. However, they still have some WordPress smarts. Most notably, they get their formatting instructions from WordPress themes, just like every other part of your site. In most themes, a basic page looks a lot like a basic post—for example, both use the same fonts for their title and text.

FREQUENTLY ASKED QUESTION

Understanding Pages

Why do some people call pages "static pages"?

Although WordPress calls this feature *pages*, many webheads find that confusing. After all, isn't a page anything you view on the Web with a browser? And don't posts appear in web pages?

For these reasons, WordPress experts—and WordPress itself, sometimes—often use a different term. They call WordPress pages *static pages*. Sadly, this term is almost as confusing. It stems from the old days of the Web, when designers distinguished between dynamic pages that could do incredible feats with the help of code, and static pages that showed fixed, unchanging content. That fits with the way most people use WordPress pages—they create them, fill them with content, and then publish them.

However, WordPress pages aren't really static—they *do* change. Flip your blog over to a different theme, and all your posts *and* pages update seamlessly to match the new style. That's because WordPress stores all the content for your pages—as well as the content for the rest of your site, including posts—in its database. And, finally, a static page changes anytime you decide to edit it.

If you're still confused, here's the bottom line: A WordPress site can hold both posts and pages, and you create, format, and manage them in much the same way. The key difference is that WordPress automatically dates, orders, and groups posts. WordPress also puts them on the home page and assumes that people will want to read them from newest to oldest. From WordPress's point of view, posts are the lead actors on your site, while pages are supporting characters. But you're not bound by that narrow definition of a site, as you'll see on page 228.

Thoughts of a Lawyer
What's on my mind, all the time
Home
About the Practice
Sample Page
About the Practice
Attorney **Sandra Chapelle** has practiced law in Illinois since 1998. Ms. Chapelle is a member of the Illionois Bar, and earned her B.A. at Michigan State University. She has a general law practice that handles both civil and criminal cases, with a special focus on complex and highly expensive litigation. Ms. Chapelle has a deeply felt need to help others, and sincerely hopes that your legal problems can help fund her next trip to the Mediterranean.
Areas of Practice:
Family Law
Personal Injury Defense
Drug Offences
Sexual, Domestic, and all other Assault Charges
Leave a Reply
Enter your comment here...

FIGURE 7-2

A page in WordPress looks suspiciously like a post. If you keep WordPress's standard settings, your page even has room for comments, which you'll learn to use in Chapter 8. (You can also turn comments off for your pages, as explained on page 230.)

To review a list of the pages on your site, choose Pages→All Pages. You see a familiar table of pages, which works the same way as WordPress's list of posts and media files. Point to a page title, and you have the choice to view the page, edit it, or delete it (see Figure 7-3). And if you're working with piles of pages, you can use the same bulk actions you use with posts to delete or change a whole group of pages in one step.

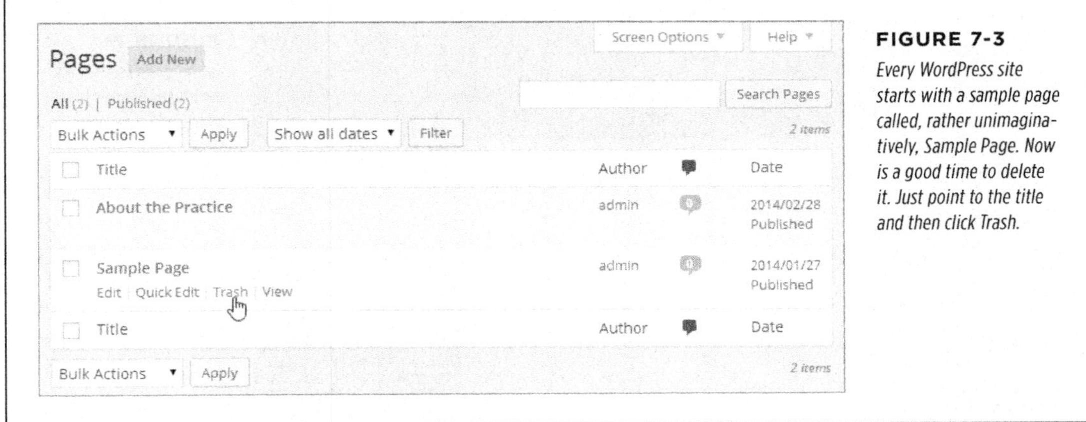

FIGURE 7-3

Every WordPress site starts with a sample page called, rather unimaginatively, Sample Page. Now is a good time to delete it. Just point to the title and then click Trash.

Viewing Pages

You can probably think of a couple of pages that would improve your site. If nothing else, you could add an About Me page with your biographical information in it. But a key question remains: How do your guests visit pages?

Like posts, every page gets a unique web address (URL), called a permalink. The permalink appears under the page's title box as soon as you start entering the page content. WordPress uses the same rules to create page permalinks as it does to create post permalinks (as explained on page 116), and you can edit the permalink for any page (page 119). But the important detail is that you can find a page by typing its address into your browser.

Of course, your readers aren't likely to type in any URL other than the address for your home page, so you need to provide links so visitors can get to your pages. One way to do this is by putting links in posts and pages so you can connect them together. For example, you could add a link to the page shown in Figure 7-2 that takes readers to a new page when they click "Family Law" (Figure 7-4).

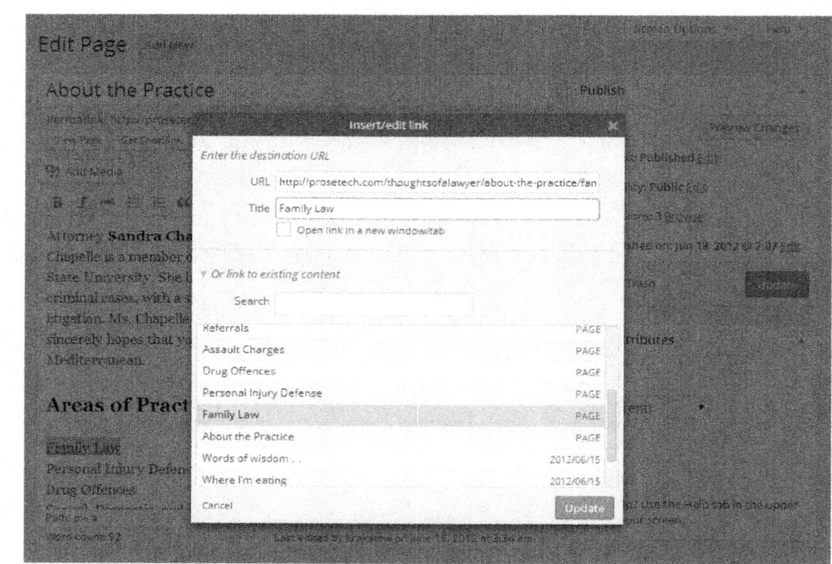

FIGURE 7-4

Clicking the Family Law link takes readers to the Family Law page. Making this happen is easy. You simply edit the "About the Practice" page, use the trusty Add Link toolbar button, and then find the Family Law page in the list of existing content.

Links are a decent way to join related posts and pages, but they aren't much help if a guest wants to *browse* the pages on your site. That's not a problem with posts—if your visitors want to read posts, they can browse them easily on the home page, starting with the most recent one and moving back in time. Or they can browse posts in a specific category or with a specific tag (page 123). But WordPress doesn't put pages in chronological order, feature them on the home page, or give them category or tag information. Visitors *can* find pages through a keyword search (by typing something into the search box and then pressing the Enter key), because searches scan the content in both posts and pages. But guessing at keywords is a clumsy way to find a page, and it's no substitute for a more convenient navigation system.

Fortunately, WordPress has several better, ready-made solutions to help visitors find your pages:

- **The Pages widget.** Add this to your page, and visitors will always see a list of all your pages, in the order you want. This widget works best if you want to highlight all (or almost all) of your pages.
- **An automatic menu.** Many themes automatically put all your pages in a menu on the home page. The only problem is that this auto-generated menu includes *every* page in your site. If that results in an overly cluttered or disorganized menu, you'll prefer the next option.

- **A custom menu.** You pick the pages you want to showcase and arrange them just so. You then display the menu somewhere prominent on your home page (often where the automatic menu used to go). Most people take this route.

You'll explore all these options in the following sections.

Showing Pages in the Pages Widget

The Pages widget displays a simple list of links (Figure 7-5). Like any other widget, you can place it anywhere on your home page, such as in a sidebar. Choose Appearance→Widgets and then drag the widget where you want it.

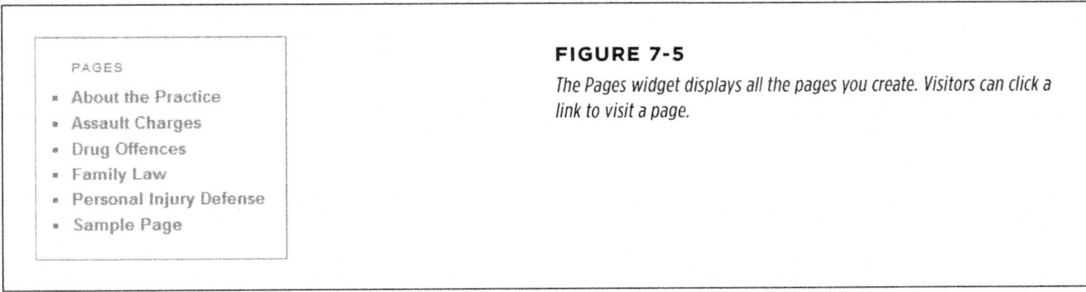

FIGURE 7-5

The Pages widget displays all the pages you create. Visitors can click a link to visit a page.

You may want to use the Pages widget to show just some of your pages. To do that, you need to explicitly indicate what pages you *don't* want to show. Each page has a unique ID number, and you indicate the pages you want to exclude by creating a comma-separated list of ID numbers in the Exclude box (Figure 7-6).

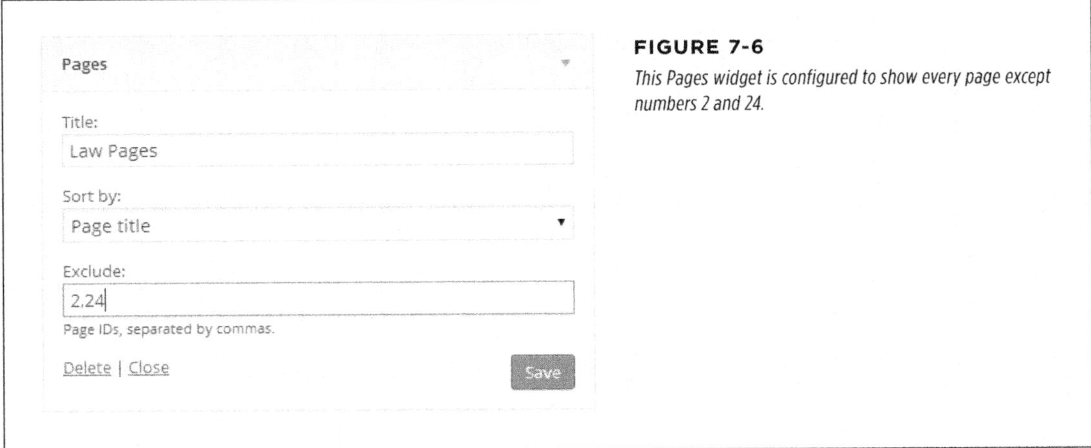

FIGURE 7-6

This Pages widget is configured to show every page except numbers 2 and 24.

The slightly tricky part is figuring out the page's ID number. If you run a self-hosted blog and you haven't changed WordPress's permalink style (page 117), the ID appears right in the URL. But if you use WordPress.com or you switched to more readable title-based permalinks, you need to take a different tack. First, go to Pages→All Pages to see all the pages in your site. Then point to the title of the page you want to exclude. The page's URL appears in your browser's toolbar, in this format:

```
http://prosetech.com/thoughtsofalawyer/wp-admin/post.php?post=24&action=edit
```

In this example, the page ID is 24. (Don't be confused that the URL actually calls the page a post—it's an old but harmless WordPress quirk.)

TIP If you have trouble seeing a page's permalink in your browser, try copying the address. Right-click the page title and choose a command with a name like Copy Shortcut or Copy Link Address (the exact wording depends on your browser). You can paste the link into a text editor like Notepad and find the page ID there.

WORD TO THE WISE

Use the Exclude Box Sparingly

It might occur to you that you could add several Pages widgets to different parts of your home page, each of which shows a different subset of pages. That's an interesting idea, but a bad one, because of the way the exclusion list works.

If you use the Pages widget to create three page lists, for example, every time you add a new page that you want to leave off the lists, you need to add the page to the exclusion list of each menu. That extra work can cause a serious headache. To avoid this, use the Pages widget only when you want to show most or all of your pages. If you want to show a smaller group of just a few pages, create a custom menu and show it with the Custom Menu widget, as explained on page 228.

The Pages widget also lets you sort your list of pages. You set the sort order using the drop-down list in the "Sort by" box. Ordinarily, the order is "Page title," which means that WordPress organizes your pages alphabetically by title. Alternatively, you can choose "Page ID," and WordPress lists pages from oldest to newest (because newer pages always get higher ID numbers). Lastly, you can choose "Page order," which lets *you* pick the order, as you'll see on page 216.

Showing Pages in a Menu

Most themes start out with a menu. In fact, menus are considered so important to the average WordPress site that most themes don't let you remove the menu (at least not without resorting to the style editing tricks covered in Chapter 13).

Unlike desktop programs, which typically have strict, consistent rules about where menus go and what they look like, menus on the Web take many forms. The only consistent rule is that every menu is a set of links arranged as headings and subheadings. In WordPress, the way a menu looks is completely in the hands of your theme. For that reason, WordPress puts the menu management command in the dashboard's Appearances menu, alongside the controls for other theme features.

Many themes put a site's main links in a traditional menu bar, which it arranges horizontally near the top of each page. In the Twenty Twelve theme, for example, the menu sits above the list of posts (Figure 7-7). Other themes arrange the menu vertically and place it on the side, like WordPress's dashboard menu.

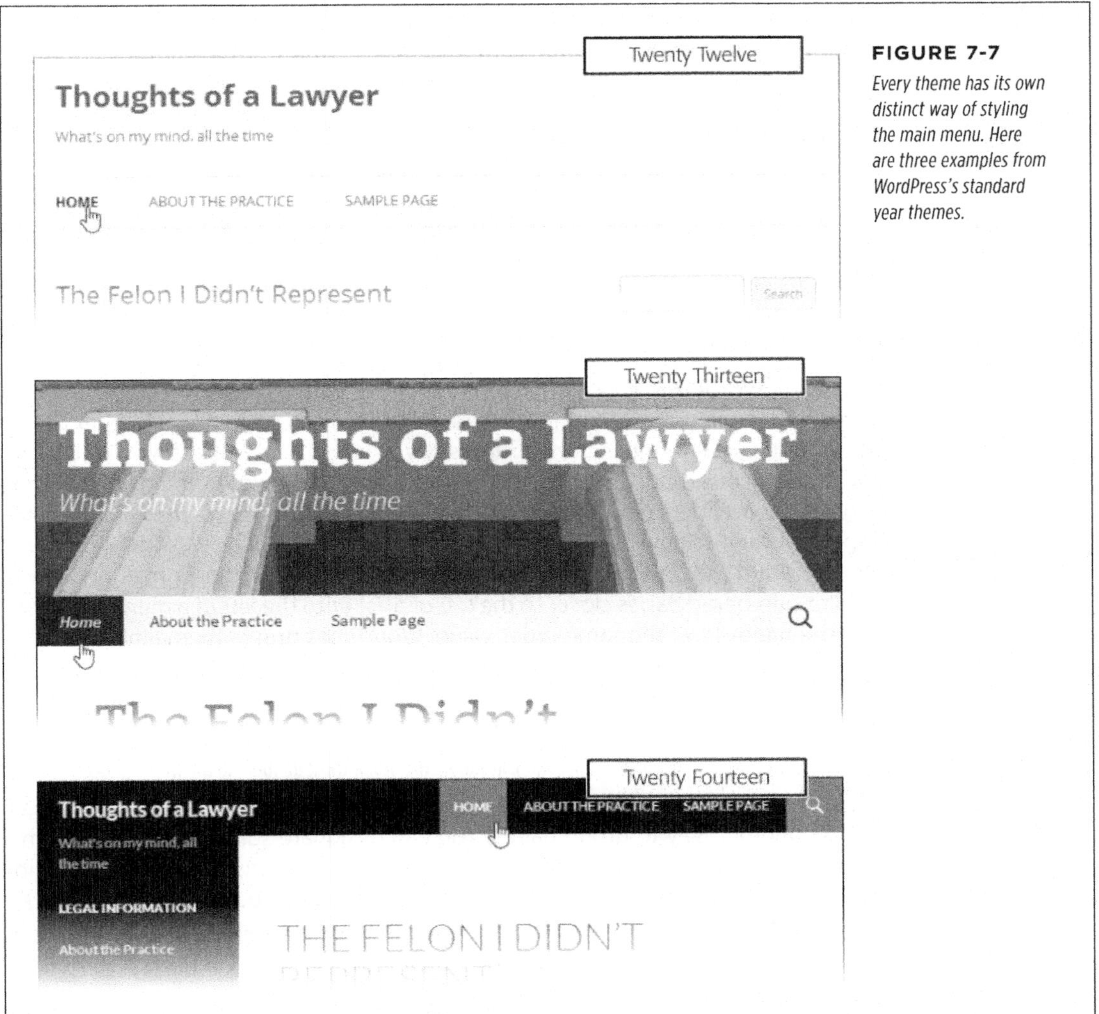

FIGURE 7-7

Every theme has its own distinct way of styling the main menu. Here are three examples from WordPress's standard year themes.

When you create a new WordPress site, it starts out with an *automatic menu*, so named because WordPress creates it automatically. At first, the menu holds just two commands: a Home button that goes to your home page, and a Sample Page button that opens the WordPress sample page (unless you took our earlier advice and deleted it). But every time you add a new page, like the "About the Practice" page shown earlier, WordPress adds a matching link in the menu. It keeps the links ordered alphabetically by page name.

You can exert more control over how your theme arranges the page links in a menu, in one of two ways: You can use the ordering and grouping features described next, or you can create a custom menu (page 218). The ordering and grouping approach works best if you just want to adjust the position of a few commands in the automatic menu but you're happy letting WordPress run the show. By comparison, custom menus take slightly more work but pay off with far more flexibility and extra features.

Ordering Pages

Often, when you display a list of pages, you want to dictate which ones show up first and which ones are last. You can do this by typing in a number for the Order setting, which appears in the Page Attributes box when you create (or edit) a page.

The Order setting affects the order of your pages in two situations: when you display pages in an automatic menu and when you display them in the Pages widget with the "Sort by" box set to "Page order."

Ordinarily, WordPress sets the order number of every page to 0. Technically, that means that each page is tied for first position, and the page order setting has no effect. But if you want to set the order (say you want "Our Story" followed by "Our Location" followed by "Contact Us"), you'd assign these pages steadily increasing page-order numbers (say, 0, 1, and 2). The actual numbers don't really matter—the important thing is how they *compare*. WordPress always displays larger-numbered pages toward the bottom of the list or on the right end of a horizontal menu, with smaller-numbered pages closer to the top of a list or to the left of a menu bar. If two or more pages have the same order value, WordPress orders them alphabetically.

TIP If you rearrange a bunch of pages, you need to change their page-order values. The easiest way to do that is to go to the Pages list (choose Pages→All Pages), point to a post, and click the Quick Edit link. This way, you can quickly modify some page information, including the order, without opening the whole page for editing.

There's another way to group pages: You can designate some as *child* pages that belong to a specific *parent* page. (You may have used this type of organization before, to create subcategories for your posts, as described on page 110.) To create this hierarchy, you set the Parent setting in the Pages Attribute box when you create or edit the page.

For example, you could edit the Family Law page and change the Parent list box from "(no parent)" to "About the Practice." Now, Family Law is a subpage in the "About the Practice" group.

To better understand the effect of ordering and grouping, imagine you have these pages:

PAGE TITLE	ORDER	PARENT
About the Practice	0	-
Assault Charges	3	About the Practice

PAGE TITLE	ORDER	PARENT
Drug Offenses	2	About the Practice
Family Law	0	About the Practice
Personal Injury Defense	1	About the Practice
Legal Disclaimers	1	-
Referrals	0	-

The order settings create the nicely styled menu and nested list shown in Figure 7-8. The menu displays subsidiary pages in submenus, while the Pages widget slightly indents nested pages.

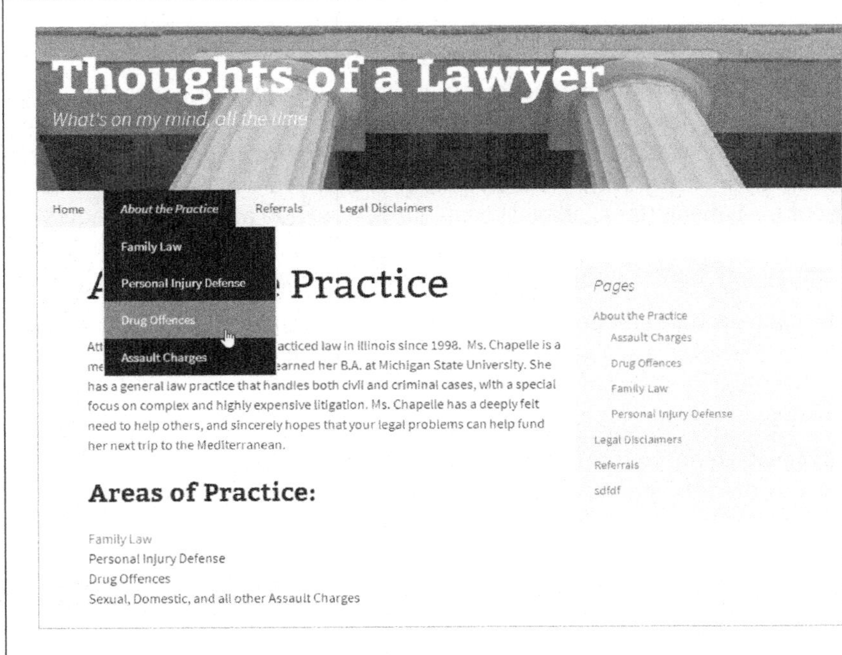

FIGURE 7-8

This site lists its pages in two places. At the top is the familiar menu bar, now with a submenu. On the right side, the Pages widget shows the same collection of pages, but sorted by title.

Life can get a bit confusing when you order and group pages. Just remember that when WordPress orders pages, it compares only the pages at the same level. For example, you can use the page order to adjust the position of the Assault Charges, Drug Offenses, Family Law, and Personal Injury Defense pages with respect to one another. However, WordPress won't compare the order values of the Family Law and Legal Disclaimers pages, because they aren't at the same level and won't ever be shown next to each other.

NOTE If you use post names in your permalinks (page 116), child pages get their own permalink. It includes two posts titles: the name of the child page itself and the name of the parent page. For example, if the child page "Family Law" has the parent "About the Practice," the full permalink might be something like *http://thoughtsofalawyer.net/about-the-practice/family-law.*

Custom Menus

WordPress's ordering and grouping features give you enough flexibility to create a good-looking, well-ordered menu. However, there are a few good reasons why most WordPress developers eventually decide to build a custom menu:

- **To get more types of menu items.** An automatic menu includes links to your pages, and that's it. But a custom menu can include other types of links—for example, ones that lead to a particular post, a whole category of posts, or even another website.
- **To hide pages.** An automatic menu always includes *all* your pages. This might not be a problem for a relatively new WordPress site, but as your site grows, you'll probably add more and more pages and use them for different types of information. Eventually, you'll create pages that you don't want to include in your main menu (for example, you might want to add a page that readers can visit only by clicking a link in a post). The only way to hide a page from a menu is to abandon the automatic menu and build a custom menu.
- **To have multiple menus.** Some themes support more than one home page menu. However, a site can have only one automatic menu. To take advantage of the multiple-menu feature, you need to create additional menus as custom menus.
- **Because sometimes automatic menus are hard.** To get an automatic menu to look the way you want it to, you need to think carefully about the order and parent settings. If you have dozens of pages, this sort of planning can twist your brain into a pretzel. If you build a custom menu, you can drag and drop your way to a good-looking menu. It still takes time and work, but it requires a lot less planning and thinking.

Building a Custom Menu

When you're ready to replace your theme's automatic menu with a menu of your own creation, here are the steps to follow:

1. **Choose Appearance→Menus.**

   This brings you to the sophisticated menu editor (Figure 7-9).

2. **Click the "create a new menu" link at the top of the page to create a new, blank menu.**

   The next step is to give your menu a name.

3. **Enter a name for your menu in the Menu Name box.**

   The name uniquely identifies the menu. Normally, you name the menu after its function (Main Menu, Navigation Menu, Page Menu, and so on). You shouldn't name it based on its position (as in Top Menu Bar), because that detail may change if you switch themes.

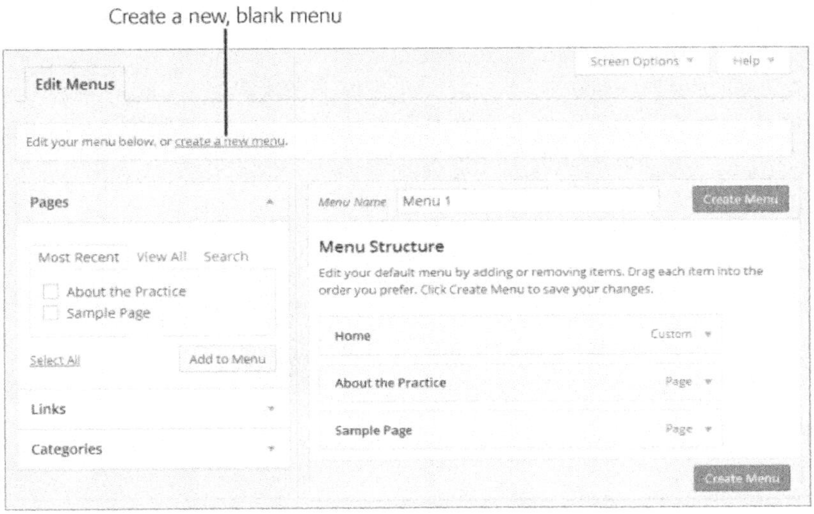

Create a new, blank menu

FIGURE 7-9

Depending on your theme, the menu editor may start out blank, or it may show you the commands that are currently part of the automatic menu, as it does here. Either way, you need to create a menu of your own before you can take control of its contents.

4. **Click the Create Menu button.**

   WordPress stores the menu as part of your site, so you can edit it anytime. Now you're ready to fill it up with useful commands (Figure 7-10).

5. **Decide whether you want to add a page, link, or category to your menu. If necessary, click the heading to expand the Pages, Links, or Categories section (Figure 7-11).**

   A *page* is, obviously, a link to one of the pages you created.

   A *link* goes to some location on the Web, either on your site or another site. For example, you could create a custom link that points to a specific post (using its permalink), a Wikipedia page, a friend's blog, or something else.

   A *category* is a link to a page that displays all the posts in a given category (in reverse-chronological order). It has the same effect as clicking a link in the Categories widget (page 112).

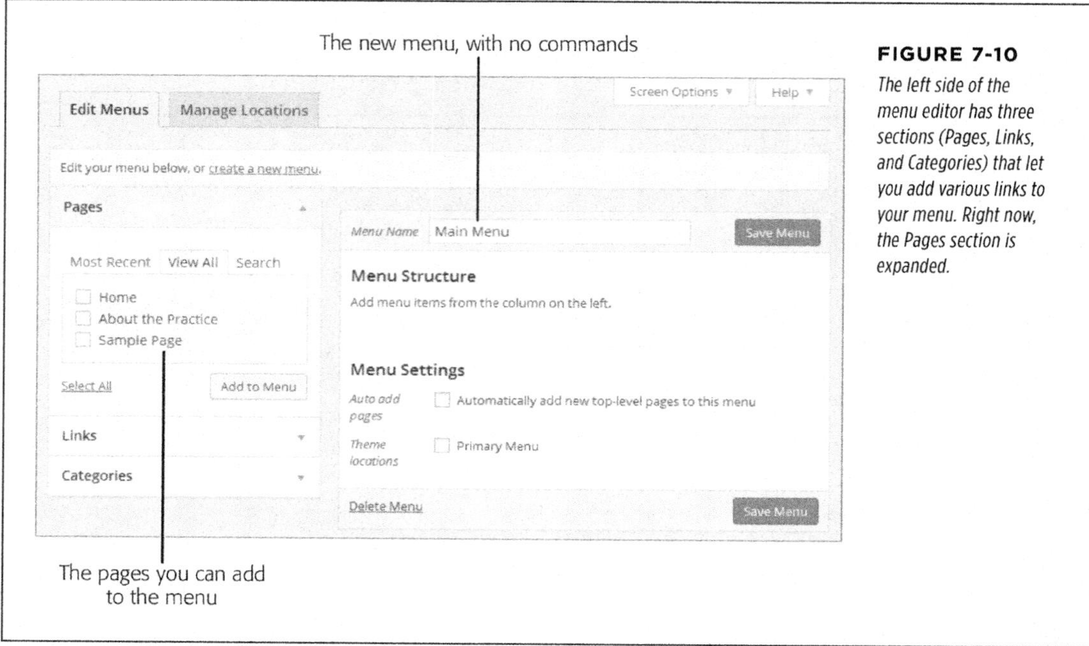

FIGURE 7-10

The left side of the menu editor has three sections (Pages, Links, and Categories) that let you add various links to your menu. Right now, the Pages section is expanded.

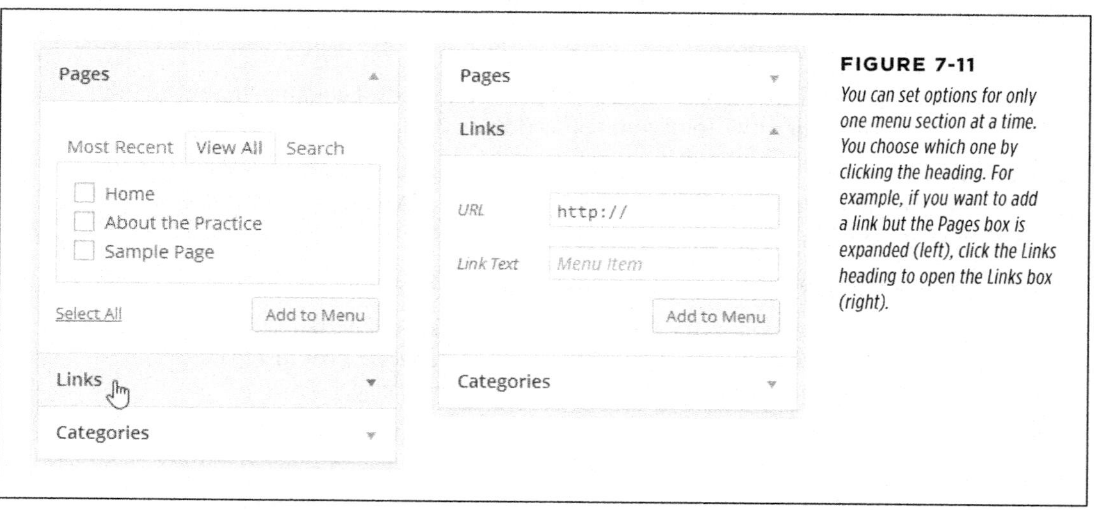

FIGURE 7-11

You can set options for only one menu section at a time. You choose which one by clicking the heading. For example, if you want to add a link but the Pages box is expanded (left), click the Links heading to open the Links box (right).

6. **Enter the information for your menu item.**

   If you're adding a page, click the checkbox for the page you want to add. You can tick several checkboxes to add a whole group of pages at once. The Pages box lets you choose your pages from three different tabs. Use Most Recent to choose from the newest pages you created, View All to browse through all your pages, and Search to find a page by name (which is useful if your site has dozens or more pages).

   If you're adding a link, fill in the address in the URL box and specify the link text in the Link Text box.

   If you're adding a category, click the checkbox for the category you want. Adding a category is similar to adding a page—you can browse a list of your categories, choose from your most frequently used categories, or search for the category you want by name, depending on what tab you pick. You can also add multiple categories at once by ticking multiple boxes.

TIP It makes sense to add a link named "Home" or "Posts" to most new menus. That way, your guests always have a way to get back to your home page. To create a home page link, choose the View All tab in the Pages box, turn on the checkbox next to Home, and then continue with the next step.

GEM IN THE ROUGH

Getting Even More Menu Links

The menu editor makes it easy to link to another page on your site, to a category of posts, or to another website entirely. But you can get even more menu-creating options if you click the Screen Options button (found in the top-right corner of the page) and turn on the Posts and Tags checkboxes.

If you do, you'll get three more boxes for adding menu items. The Posts box shows a list of all your posts, letting you add a link to a specific post without needing to remember the permalink. The Tags box is similar to the Category box—it lets your visitors browse all the posts that have a specific tag. And the Format box lets you add links to different post formats (page 202), if you use the formats in your blog. For example, you can add a link that lets readers view all the Aside posts or all the Quote posts.

7. **Once you make a choice, click the "Add to Menu" button.**

   Your new item appears in the menu section on the right.

8. **Optionally, customize the label and tooltip (title) of your menu item.**

   When you first add an item, it shows up as a collapsed gray box. To change the options for that item, click the down-pointing arrow on the right side of the box. This expands the box so you can see (and edit) all the settings for that item (Figure 7-12).

Here are the settings you can change:

- **Navigation Label,** which is the link text that appears in the menu. If you add a page or a category, the navigation label is the name of that page or category, which keeps things simple. But you might want to edit the text if it's too long to fit comfortably in your menu.
- **Title Attribute,** which sets the tooltip that pops up when someone points to a menu item. Usually, the title attribute is blank, and the tooltip displays the name of the menu item. But you could get fancy and use the Title attribute to supply a more detailed description.
- **Remove,** which does the obvious: deleting a menu item you don't want anymore.

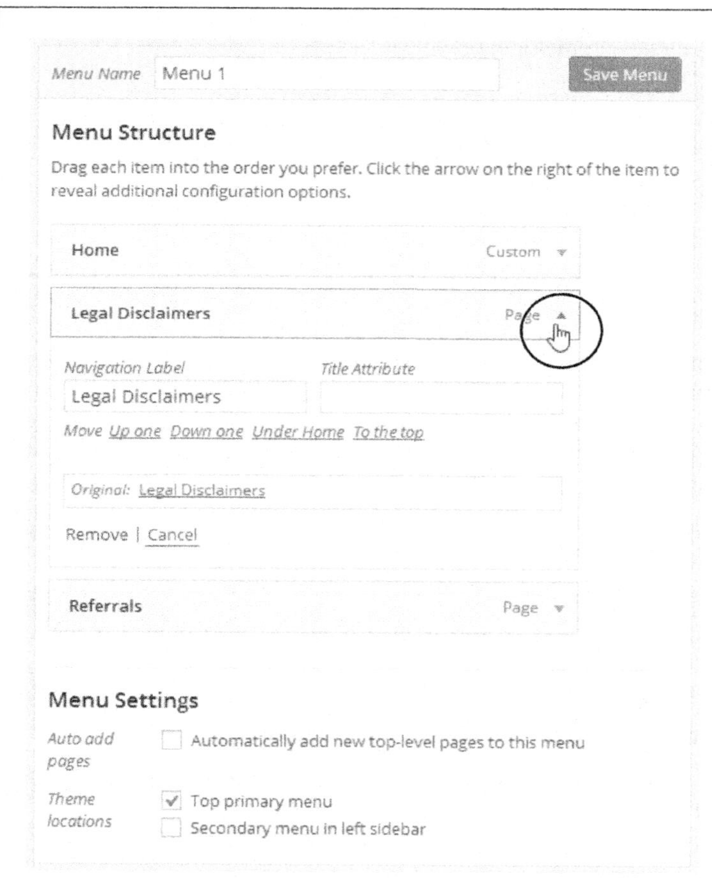

FIGURE 7-12

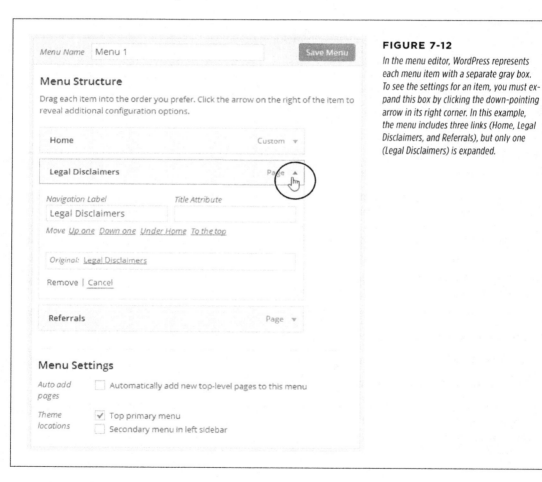

In the menu editor, WordPress represents each menu item with a separate gray box. To see the settings for an item, you must expand this box by clicking the down-pointing arrow in its right corner. In this example, the menu includes three links (Home, Legal Disclaimers, and Referrals), but only one (Legal Disclaimers) is expanded.

9. **Return to step 5 to add another item to your menu, and repeat these steps until you stock your menu with all the items you want.**

   WordPress adds items to the menu in the order *you* add them. So the items you add first appear on the left of a horizontal menu, or at the top of a vertical menu. However, don't worry about the order yet, because you'll learn how to move everything around in the next step.

10. **Now it's time to arrange your menu items. Drag them around to position them and group them into submenus.**

    Unlike automatic menus, custom menus don't pay attention to your pages' order or parent settings. This is good for flexibility (because it means you can arrange the same commands in different menus in different ways), but it also means you need to do a little more work when you create the menu.

    Fortunately, arranging menu items is easy. To move an item from one place to another, simply drag it, just as you move widgets in the Widgets page. WordPress displays items in top-to-bottom order, so if you use a horizontal menu (as the WordPress standard theme does), the topmost item is on the left, followed by the next menu item, and so on.

    Creating submenus is just as convenient, once you know the trick. First, arrange your menu items so that the child items (the items you want to appear in the submenu) appear immediately after the parent menu item. Then, drag the child menu item slightly to the right, so that it looks like it's indented one level. Figure 7-13 shows what the result should look like, and Figure 7-14 shows the formatted WordPress page.

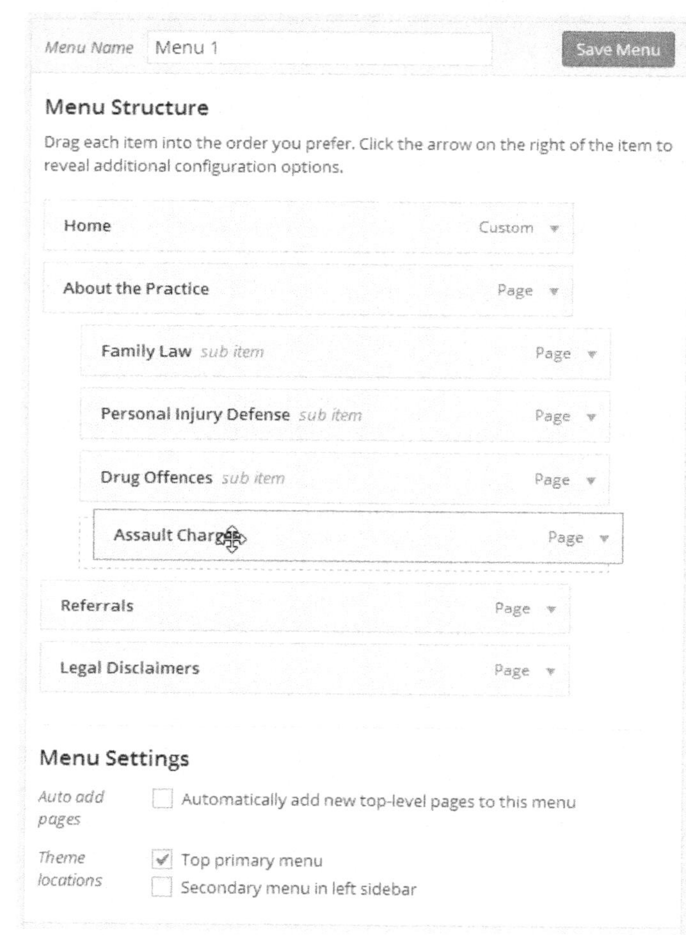

FIGURE 7-13

By dragging the Assault Charges page slightly to the right, it becomes a submenu item under the "About the Practice" page, along with several other pages. Figure 7-14 shows the result.

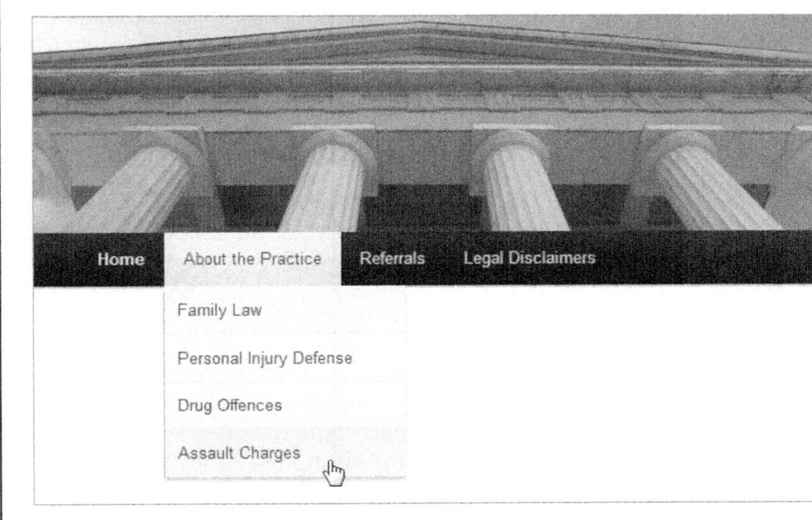

FIGURE 7-14

Now the "About the Practice" page has a submenu.

NOTE You can easily create multilayered menus (menus with submenus inside of submenus). All you do is keep dragging items a bit more to the right. However, most well-designed WordPress sites stop at one level of submenus. Otherwise, guests may find it awkward to dig through all the layers without accidentally moving the mouse off the menu.

FREQUENTLY ASKED QUESTION

Creating a Menu Item That Does Nothing

Can I make a submenu heading that visitors can't click?

WordPress menus work a little differently from the menus in traditional desktop computer programs. When you have a submenu in a desktop program, you click the parent menu item to open the submenu, and then you click one of the items inside the submenu. But in WordPress, you just point to the parent menu item to open it. The parent item is still a real menu item that leads somewhere—if you click it, you go to a new page, category, or custom URL. For example, in Figure 7-14 you can point to "About the Practice" to open its submenu, or you can click the title to go to the About the Practice page.

But perhaps this isn't the behavior you want. For example, you might want the "About the Practice" menu item to be a non-clickable heading, which exists solely to house the submenu underneath. To create an unlinked heading, add a new command from the Links box, set the label to "About the Practice," and then set the URL to # (the number sign character—that's all). To browsers, the # symbol represents the current page, so if you click the menu item ("About the Practice" in this example), you won't go anywhere. In fact, you won't even see the page flicker, which is exactly what you want.

11. **Optionally, you can turn on the "Automatically add new top-level pages" setting.**

    If you do, every time you create a new page, WordPress automatically tacks it on to the end of your custom menu. This is similar to the way an automatic menu works, although you can edit your custom menu any time to move newly added items to a better place. Most WordPress experts avoid this setting, because they prefer to control what gets into their menu and where it goes.

12. **Turn on one of the "Theme location" checkboxes at the bottom of the menu box.**

    Some themes let you decide where on a page your menu goes. For example, the Twenty Fourteen theme lets you put your menu at the top of the page (choose the "Top primary menu" checkbox) or the side (choose "Secondary menu in left sidebar").

    Many themes have just one location for menus, however. If that's the case for your theme, you'll see a single checkbox with a label like Primary Menu. Even though you have no real choice about where to put the menu, you still need to turn on the checkbox to add the menu to your site.

13. **Click Save Menu to make your changes permanent.**

    Once you save your menu, you can try it out on your site's home page.

Multiple Menus

Many themes support more than one menu. Consider, for example, the Oxygen theme you tried out in Chapter 6 (Figure 7-15). It allows no fewer than three menus. The primary menu appears under the page header, the secondary one shows up in the left-hand sidebar, and the tertiary menu appears below that, in the footer section. You can imagine using these menus for distinctly different tasks—using the top menu to navigate the whole site, for example, the side menu to drill into specific posts or categories, and the bottom menu to link to other sites with related content.

NOTE You don't *need* to use all the menus a theme provides. Initially, WordPress creates an automatic menu and uses it as the theme's primary menu. Any additional menus start off hidden, and appear only if you attach custom menus to them.

To use the Oxygen theme's three menus, you need to create three custom menus. Repeat the process described in the previous section three times, clicking the "create a new menu" link to add each additional menu.

Once you have more than one menu, WordPress adds a menu list to the top of the menu editor. Using it, you can choose which menu you want to see and edit (Figure 7-16).

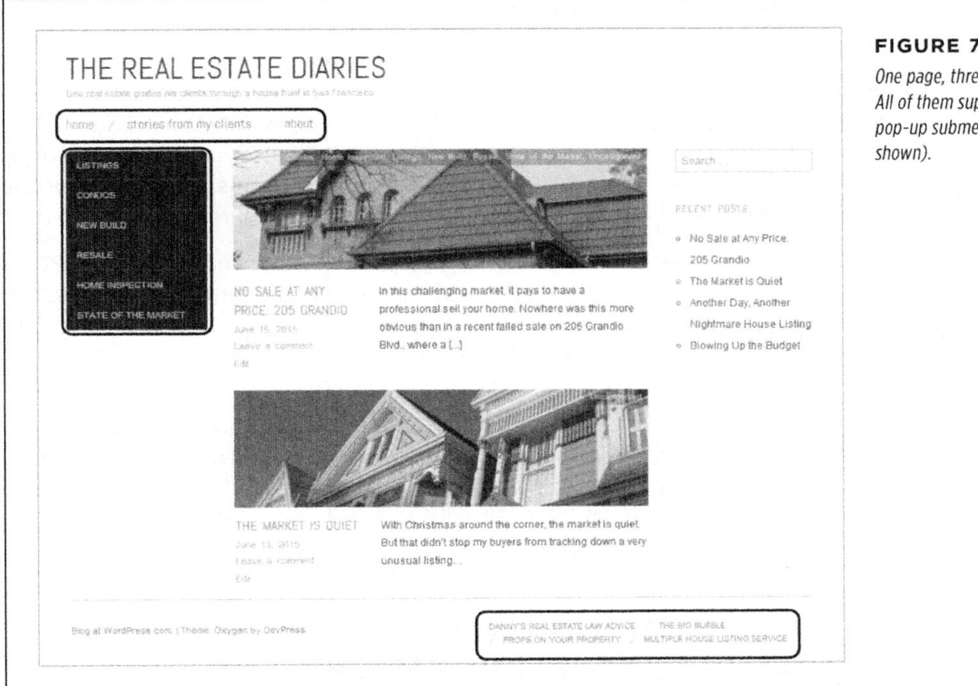

FIGURE 7-15

One page, three menus. All of them support pop-up submenus (not shown).

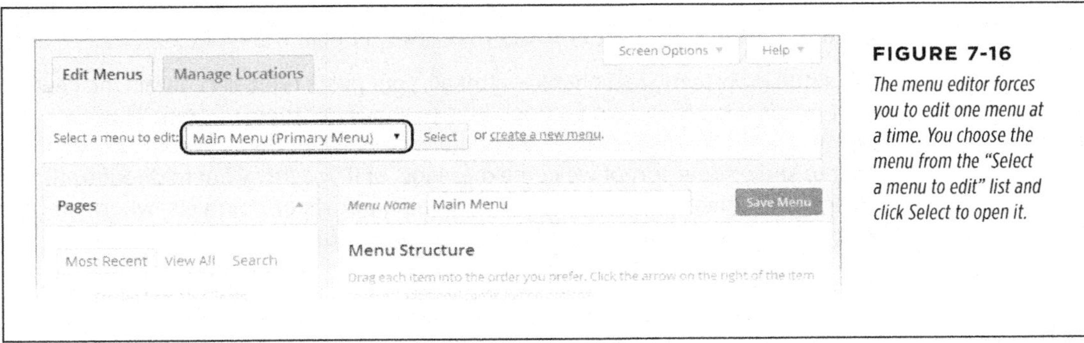

FIGURE 7-16

The menu editor forces you to edit one menu at a time. You choose the menu from the "Select a menu to edit" list and click Select to open it.

Once you create your custom menus, you need to put each one in the appropriate location in your theme. You do that using the checkboxes in the "Theme locations" section, under each menu. But if you have trouble remembering which menu goes where, you have another choice. Click the Manage Locations tab to see a list of all the menu placeholders in your theme. Next to each is a drop-down list of the menus you created. You can specify a menu for each area and then click Save Changes to make your changes permanent in a single step.

The Custom Menu Widget

There's one more way to display a custom menu: in the Custom Menu widget.

Now that you've played with menus in depth, the Custom Menu widget won't impress you much. To use it, drag it onto your page (say, in a sidebar), give it a title (optional), and then pick the menu it should show. The Custom Menu widget shows a bulleted list of links, using nested bullets for submenu items. In fact, the Custom Menu widget looks a lot like the Pages widget, shown in Figure 7-8.

The advantage of the Custom Menu widget is that it's more flexible than the Pages widget. The Pages widget shows all (or almost all) of your pages, but the Custom Menu widget shows just the pages you want and can optionally include other category links and links to other websites, provided that you add them to your custom menu.

TIP One nifty way to use the Custom Menu widget is to create a *blogroll*—a list of blogs you recommend, blogs by people you know, or sites that have content similar to yours. For example, a cooking blog might have a blogroll with other food-related blogs in it. All you need is a new menu (you can name it "Blogroll"), which you can then fill with links.

Changing Your Home Page

Right now, your WordPress site has a home page dominated by a familiar feature: the reverse-chronological list of your posts. Visitors can use your site's navigation menu to travel somewhere else, but they always begin with your posts.

This setup is perfectly reasonable—after all, your posts typically contain the newest, most relevant content, so it's a good idea to showcase them up front. However, this design doesn't fit all sites. If the list of posts is less important on your site, or if you want to show some sort of welcome message, or if you just want to direct traffic (in other words, give readers the option of reading posts or going elsewhere on your site), it makes sense to start by showing a page instead of a post.

In the following sections, you'll find out how. First, you'll use one of your custom-created pages as your site's home page, all in the interest of building a brochure site. Next, you'll see how to get the best of both worlds: a fixed home page with the content you want *and* a list of posts, tucked away in another place on your site.

Creating a Brochure Site

The simplest way to change your home page is to ditch the post system altogether, using pages instead of posts throughout your site. The resulting all-pages site is sometimes called a *brochure site,* because it resembles the sort of informational pamphlet you might pick up in a store (Figure 7-17).

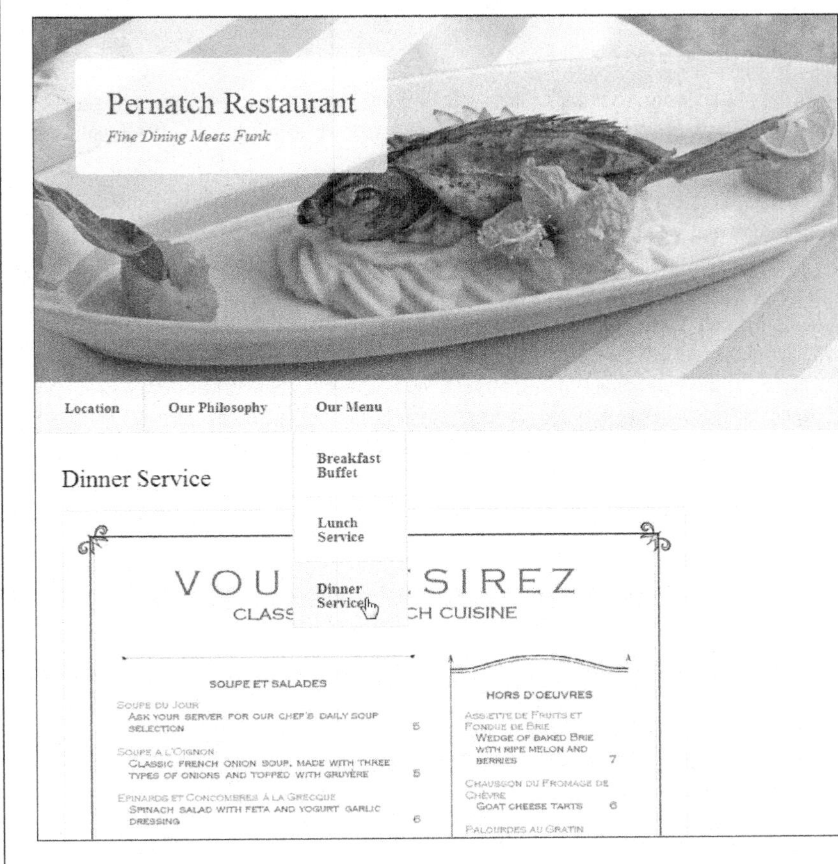

FIGURE 7-17

This restaurant website is a collection of WordPress pages, including those labeled Location, Our Philosophy, and Our Menu. Unlike posts, pages aren't related in any obvious way, nor are they dated, categorized, or tagged.

To create a brochure site, you follow some simple principles:

- Build a site that consists entirely of pages, each one hand-crafted by you.
- Add these pages to a custom menu, and arrange the pages the way you want.
- When visitors arrive at your site, the first thing they see is one of your pages and a navigation menu.

You already know how to perform each of these tasks, except the last one (changing the home page). That's what you'll learn next.

UP TO SPEED

Should You Build a Brochure Site?

A brochure site may make sense if you're building a small site with very simple content. The restaurant site in Figure 7-17 is one example.

But if you're trying to decide between a brochure site and a post-based site, consider two questions. First, would your site be more attractive to readers if you included posts? Even the bare-bones restaurant site might be more interesting with posts that chronicle restaurant news, menu experiments, and special events. Not only that, but the fact that posts are frequent, dated, and personal makes the site more vibrant. In addition, if you want to get people talking on your site—for example, posting comments about recent meals or sending in requests and off-the-wall recipe ideas—you'll have more luck if you include posts. Think of it this way: A brochure site feels like a statement, while a blog feels like a constantly unfolding conversation.

Then again, you may decide that a brochure site is exactly what you want. Maybe you really don't have time to spend updating and maintaining a site, so you simply want a place to publish some basic information on the Web and leave it at that. You can still take advantage of several of WordPress's best features, like themes, which ensure that your pages look consistent. You'll also get WordPress's help if you want to track visitors (page 444), add sharing buttons (page 412), or add any one of a number of features described in this book.

The key step in building a brochure site is changing your home page, replacing the traditional list of posts with a page of your own devising. So your first step is to create a substitute home page, using the familiar dashboard command Pages→Add New.

You might want to make a few changes to the home page, since it serves as the welcome mat to your site. For example, you may want to include navigation links in the home-page text that take visitors straight to important content. However, that's not necessary. As long as your theme includes a menu, visitors can use it to click through to more content.

You may also want to tweak the comment settings for your custom home page. By default, all pages, just like all posts, allow comments. But it seems a bit unstructured to let people comment directly on the home page of your website. Fortunately, it's easy enough to turn comments off for any page. First, use the Screen Options button (page 124) to open the Discussion box, and then turn off the "Allow comments" checkbox.

Once you create your new, replacement home page, follow these steps:

1. **Choose Settings→Reading.**
2. **In the "Front page displays" setting, choose "A static page" (rather than "Your latest posts").**
3. **In the "Front page" list underneath, pick the page you want as your new home page.**

4. **Click Save Changes at the bottom of the page.**

Now, when you surf to your site's home page, WordPress automatically serves up the page you picked (although the URL won't change in the browser's address bar—it's still the home page of your site). Similarly, when you click Home in the menu, you return to your custom home page.

TIP If you use a custom page for your home page, you may want to jazz it up with a few more navigational features. Many themes provide page templates that can help you out by adding a widget-stocked sidebar beside your page content, for example. You'll learn more on page 233.

Creating a Custom Entry Page

Even if you want to change your home page, you might not want to ditch the post system. In such a case, use a static home page (called a welcome page), and include a full complement of posts on another page.

The trick to doing this is specifying a URL for the page that displays your posts. Here's where things get slightly bizarre. To get the URL for your posts, you create yet another page. This page is just a placeholder—its sole purpose is to provide the web address for the posts page. You don't actually need to put any content on this page, because WordPress automatically creates the list of posts.

Here's the process:

1. **Decide on a URL for the posts section of your site.**

   For example, if your home page is at *http://magicteahouse.net*, you might put the posts at *http://magicteahouse.net/posts* or *http://magicteahouse.net/blog*.

NOTE If you use the self-hosted version of WordPress, you need to make sure you changed your site's permalink setting to use post titles rather than post IDs (page 117). Otherwise, the link to your placeholder page will use the post's ID, not its name. This is terribly confusing—it means you'll end up with a permalink with a name like *http://magicteahouse.net/?p=583* that actually shows your list of posts.

2. **Create a page with a name that matches the URL you want.**

   For example, you can create a page named *posts* or *blog*.

3. **Optionally, add some content.**

   You don't need any content (and you probably don't want any, either). But if you do add an introductory paragraph or two, WordPress displays it just above the list of posts.

   Don't put any content in this page—think of it as a placeholder for your old home page.

4. **Publish your page.**

   Your placeholder page is ready. Now all you need to do is change your site settings.

5. **Choose Settings→Reading.**

   Here, you specify your custom home page and your new posts page.

6. **If you haven't already set a custom home page, do that now.**

   In the "Front page displays" setting, choose "A static page" (rather than "Your latest posts"). In the "Front page" list underneath, pick the page you want to use for your new home page.

7. **In the "Posts page" list, pick the page you created in step 2.**

   This step tells WordPress to start using your placeholder page to show the list of posts.

8. **Click Save Changes at the bottom of the page.**

   Now visitors can see your old home page—the list of posts—using the URL for the placeholder page you created in step 2. So if you created a page named Posts, when you request that page (say, *http://magicteahouse.net/posts*), you see your list of posts. But if someone requests the home page (*http://magicteahouse.net*), they'll see the custom home page you picked in step 5 instead of the list of posts.

9. **Optionally, edit your menu and add a new menu item for your new posts page.**

   Even though you created a posts page, that doesn't mean your visitors know about it. They need a way to get there, and the best option is a link in your site's menu. Creating that is easy—you simply add a new menu item that points to your placeholder page (Figure 7-18).

In some cases, you may decide not to lump all your posts together in a single reverse-chronological stream. In that case, you don't need to create the placeholder page. Instead, you can add category links to your menu so that visitors browse all the posts that fall into a particular category.

This is a great approach, but it may become less practical if you have a lot of categories, because you don't want to burden your site with a crowded, clumsy menu. One solution—provided you have a self-hosted site—is to customize your home page with the theme-editing tricks described in Chapter 14. For example, page 527 shows a site that uses custom themes to create a hand-tailored home page with links that let you browse different categories.

FIGURE 7-18

Here's the new home page for the Magic Tea House. You can continue on to the site by using the text-based links on this page, or by using the menu above the header image. The Posts link takes you to the posts page, which looks the same as the old Tea House home page.

Page Templates

In Chapter 6, you learned about the underused post format feature (page 202), which applies different styles to different types of posts. Pages have an analogous feature called *page templates*, which change the way pages look.

Like post formats, page templates are an optional part of a WordPress theme. Your theme may include multiple page templates or none at all. For example, the Twenty Eleven, Twenty Twelve, and Twenty Fourteen themes all include a smattering of page templates, while Twenty Thirteen is unique in offering none. Table 7-1 shows the details.

TABLE 7-1 *Page templates in the year themes*

THEME	ADDITIONAL PAGE TEMPLATES
Twenty Eleven	Sidebar Template Showcase Template
Twenty Twelve	Full-width Page Template, No Sidebar Front Page Template
Twenty Thirteen	(None)
Twenty Fourteen	Contributor Page Full Width Page

When you create a new page, WordPress assumes that you want to use the standard template. But switching to something else is easy. When you create or edit a page, choose the template you want from the Template list in the Page Attributes box.

The page template feature faces the same challenge as the post format feature: Because a theme is designed to suit a variety of sites, and because there's no way for a theme to understand the fine details of your site, it can't provide templates tailored to your content. The WordPress year themes use page templates for two basic purposes: to control the appearance of your site's sidebar, and to create improved home pages. The following sections explain how to do both.

NOTE There's one page template you won't consider in this chapter: the Contributor Page template included with the Twenty Fourteen theme. It's an unusual but innovative page that automatically gathers and displays author information in a site that has multiple contributors. You'll try it out when you consider WordPress collaboration on page 391.

Pages With or Without Sidebars

With some themes, your site's sidebar appears on every page, just as it appears next to every post. With other themes, WordPress displays pages *without* the sidebar. No approach suits everyone, and page templates let you change your theme's built-in preference.

For example, if you use the Twenty Twelve theme, ordinary pages always get a sidebar. But if you assign a page Twenty Twelve's "Full-width Page Template, No Sidebar" template, that page will appear sidebar-free, with extra space for your content. Similarly, the pages in Twenty Eleven start out with no sidebar, but switching to the Sidebar template changes that.

NOTE If you start adding sidebars to your pages, be consistent. For example, if you decide not to show sidebars on, say, pages with pictures or photo galleries, make sure the other pages on your site follow suit. Otherwise, your visitors may feel that your site is unpredictable or poorly organized.

Better Home Pages

Another reason that themes use page templates is to create souped-up home pages. These specialized pages include a spot for your static content, just like any other page, along with some extras. The extras can include more widget areas, featured image sliders, and a customized post list. The goal is to give you a way to create a more attractive entryway to your site.

The Twenty Twelve theme includes a Front Page template that serves this purpose. It lets you add one or two columns of widgets below the page content. These widgets appear on the front page only (Figure 7-19). Your site's standard sidebar widgets, which appear on the other posts and pages in your site, don't appear on pages that use the Front Page template.

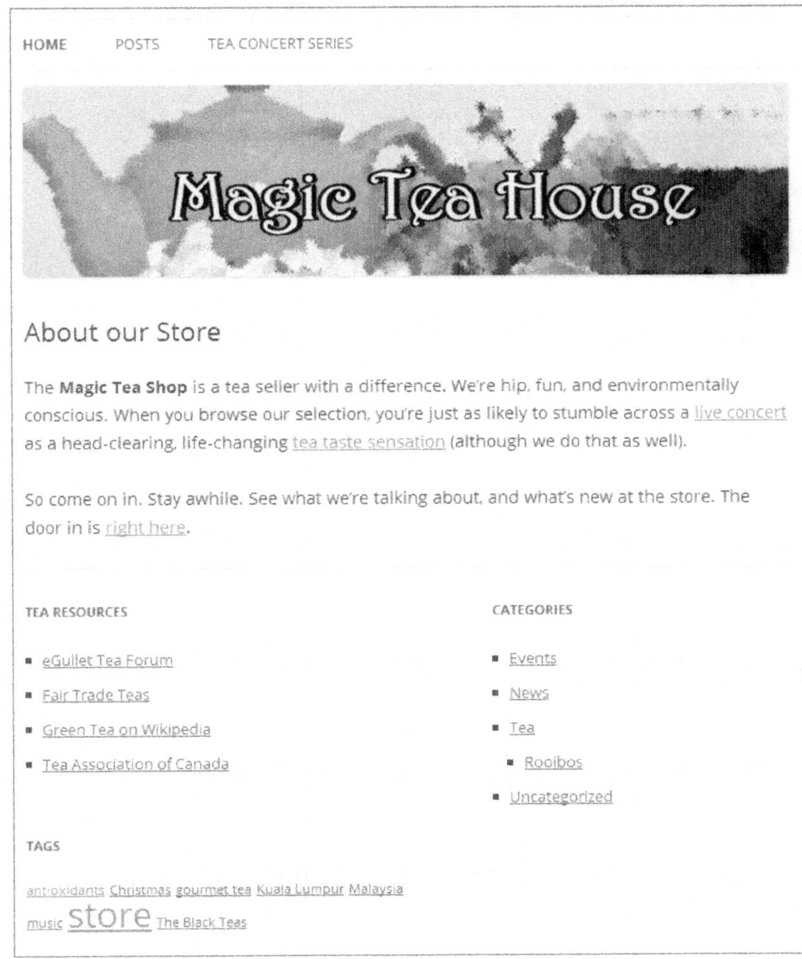
HOME
POSTS
TEA CONCERT SERIES
Magic Tea House
About our Store
The Magic Tea Shop is a tea seller with a difference. We're hip, fun, and environmentally conscious. When you browse our selection, you're just as likely to stumble across a live concert as a head-clearing, life-changing tea taste sensation (although we do that as well).
So come on in. Stay awhile. See what we're talking about, and what's new at the store. The door in is right here.
TEA RESOURCES
eGullet Tea Forum
Fair Trade Teas
Green Tea on Wikipedia
Tea Association of Canada
CATEGORIES
Events
News
Tea
Rooibos
Uncategorized
TAGS
antioxidants Christmas gourmet tea Kuala Lumpur Malaysia
music store The Black Teas

FIGURE 7-19

This version of the Magic Tea House home page uses the Front Page template on the Twenty Twelve theme, which gives the page a two-column footer of sidebar widgets.

You choose your front-page widgets using the familiar Appearance→Widgets section of the dashboard. Just drag the widgets to the theme's First Front Page widget area and the Second Front Page widget area.

The Twenty Eleven theme takes the concept a bit further with its Showcase template (Figure 7-20). It combines page content (which appears at the top), a group of featured posts (underneath), and a list of recent posts (at the bottom).

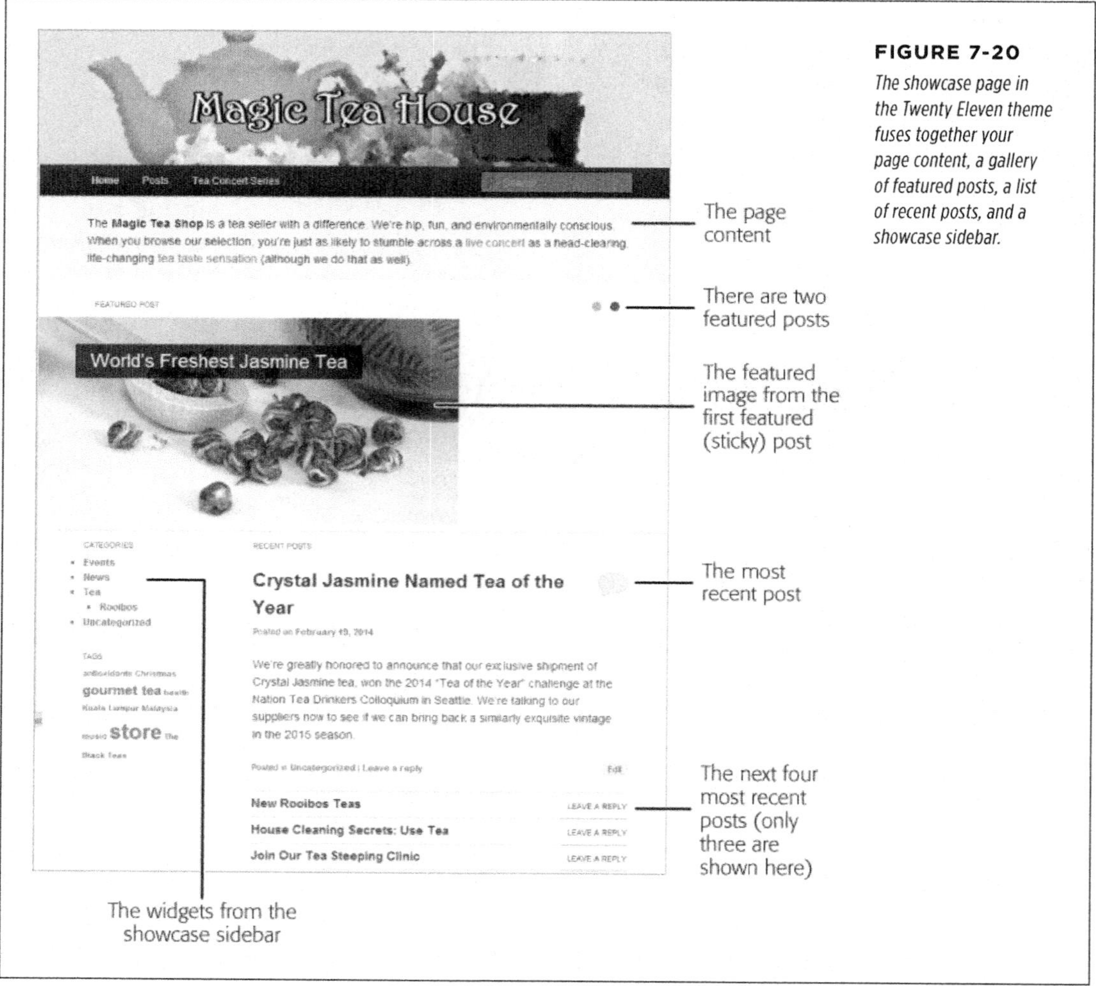

FIGURE 7-20

The showcase page in the Twenty Eleven theme fuses together your page content, a gallery of featured posts, a list of recent posts, and a showcase sidebar.

There's no magic to creating a showcase page. You create a page, add the content you want, and then choose Showcase Template from the Template list. Finally, you publish your page. When someone requests a page that uses the showcase template, WordPress goes to work.

Here's how WordPress assembles a showcase page for the Twenty Eleven theme:

- First, it takes your sticky posts (page 104), and adds them to the Featured Post gallery. To include a picture alongside a featured post, make sure you set a featured image (page 190).
- Underneath the Featured Post gallery, WordPress shows the content for the most recent non-sticky post. If you want WordPress to show only a portion of the most recent post, you need to use the More quicktag (page 196).
- Underneath that, WordPress lists the titles of the next four most recent posts (not including sticky posts). To view one, your guest must click its title.
- WordPress adds a sidebar to the left side of the page, next to the list of your most recent posts. However, this isn't the standard sidebar you see on your normal home page (and all the pages that use the sidebar template). Instead, it's called the showcase sidebar, and it appears on showcase pages only. To fill it with widgets, choose Appearance→Widgets, and then drag the widgets you want to the Showcase Sidebar area.

It might occur to you that you like the showcase page, but you want to take the idea further. For example, maybe you want to control what posts appear in the list of recent posts, or you want to create several showcase pages that highlight different categories of posts, like the sections of a newspaper. Unfortunately, showcase pages don't give you this flexibility. However, you can begin building a system like this if you're running a self-hosted WordPress site and you're not afraid to get your hands dirty. You'll start exploring that option in Chapter 14.

CHAPTER

8

Comments: Letting Your Readers Talk Back

In the chapters you've read up to this point, you learned to create the two most essential ingredients of any WordPress site, posts and pages. They're the *vehicles* for your content—the way you'll reach friends, potential customers, or hordes of devoted readers.

Still left to explore is the WordPress commenting system, which is a keenly important part of almost every WordPress site, whether it's a chatty blog or a buttoned-up business website. Used properly, comments can change your site from a one-way lecture to a back-and-forth conversation with your readers or customers. Commenting isn't just a fun way to make friends—it's also a serious tool for promoting your work, getting more traffic, turning casual browsers into repeat visitors, and even making money.

In this chapter, you'll learn how to manage comments on your site. You can banish offensive ones, insert yourself into the discussion, and even tweak the way WordPress displays comments by formatting them to make them more readable and adding author pictures. Once you understand the basics of comment management, you'll be ready to confront one of the single biggest hassles that every WordPress site faces: *comment spam*—the messages that dubious marketers and scammers slap across every site they can find. You'll learn strategies for preventing spam without aggravating your readers, and you'll take a side trip to explore the spam-crushing Akismet plug-in.

NOTE This chapter points out a few optional plug-ins that self-hosting WordPressers can use to fill in the gaps in WordPress's commenting features. However, you'll probably want to wait until you read Chapter 9, which explains how to manage plug-ins, before you try any of them out on your site.

UP TO SPEED

Why Your WordPress Site Needs a Community

Once upon a time, people thought comments belonged only in personal blogs and discussion forums. Serious-minded web publishers ignored them. Small business avoided them—after all, if people really needed to get help or make their opinions known—well, that's what email was for, right?

Today, the website landscape has changed dramatically. Web commenting is an essential ingredient for sites small and large, fun and serious, casual and moneymaking. Here's what a comments section can do for you:

- **Attract new visitors.** New visitors immediately notice whether a website has a thriving conversation going on or just a single lonely comment. They use that to evaluate how popular a website is. It's crowd mentality, working for you—if new visitors see that other people find a topic interesting, they're more likely to dive in to check out your content for themselves.
- **Build buzz.** If you've taken to the Web to promote something—whether it's a new restaurant, a book, a community service, or whatever—you can only do so much to persuade people. But if you get your fans talking to other people, the effect is exponential. Comments help you spread the word, getting your readers to talk up your products or services. And once they're talking on your blog, it's just a short hop away for other bloggers to post about you on *their* blogs.
- **Build loyalty.** A good discussion helps make a site *sticky*—in other words, it encourages people to return. Put another way, people may come to your site for the content, but they stay for the comments.
- **Encourage readers to help other readers.** Often, readers will want to respond to your content with their own comments or questions. If you ask them to do that by email and your site is popular, you readers will easily overwhelm you. But with comments, your audience can discuss among themselves, with you tossing in the occasional follow-up comment for all to see. The end result is that your site still has that personal touch, even when it's big and massively popular.

Allowing or Forbidding Comments

If you haven't changed WordPress's factory settings, all your posts and pages already support comments. You've probably already noticed that when you view an individual post or page, there's a large "Leave a Reply" section just below your content.

But it doesn't always make sense to allow comments on everything you publish. Many static pages don't lend themselves to discussion. You probably won't get a great conversation going on an About Us or Our Location page, for example, so it makes sense to disable comments for these pages and let people have their say somewhere else.

Posts usually allow comments, but you might want to disable them if you write on a contentious subject that's likely to attract an avalanche of inflammatory, insulting, aggressive, or racially charged feedback. News sites sometimes disable comments to avoid legal liability (for libelous comments someone posts, for example, or for trade secrets someone reveals). Allowing comments on posts or pages isn't an all-or-nothing decision—you can pick and choose what content allows comments.

NOTE Comments apply equally to posts and pages. For convenience, most of the discussion in this chapter refers to posts, but everything you'll learn applies equally to pages.

Changing Comment Settings for a Post

You can turn off comments for an individual post or page by changing the comment settings when you create or edit that post or page. However, WordPress usually hides the settings. To see them, you need to click the Screen Options button in the top-right corner of the Add New Post or Edit Post page, and then turn on the checkmark next to Discussion. This adds a Discussion box to your post-in-progress, which offers just two settings (Figure 8-1).

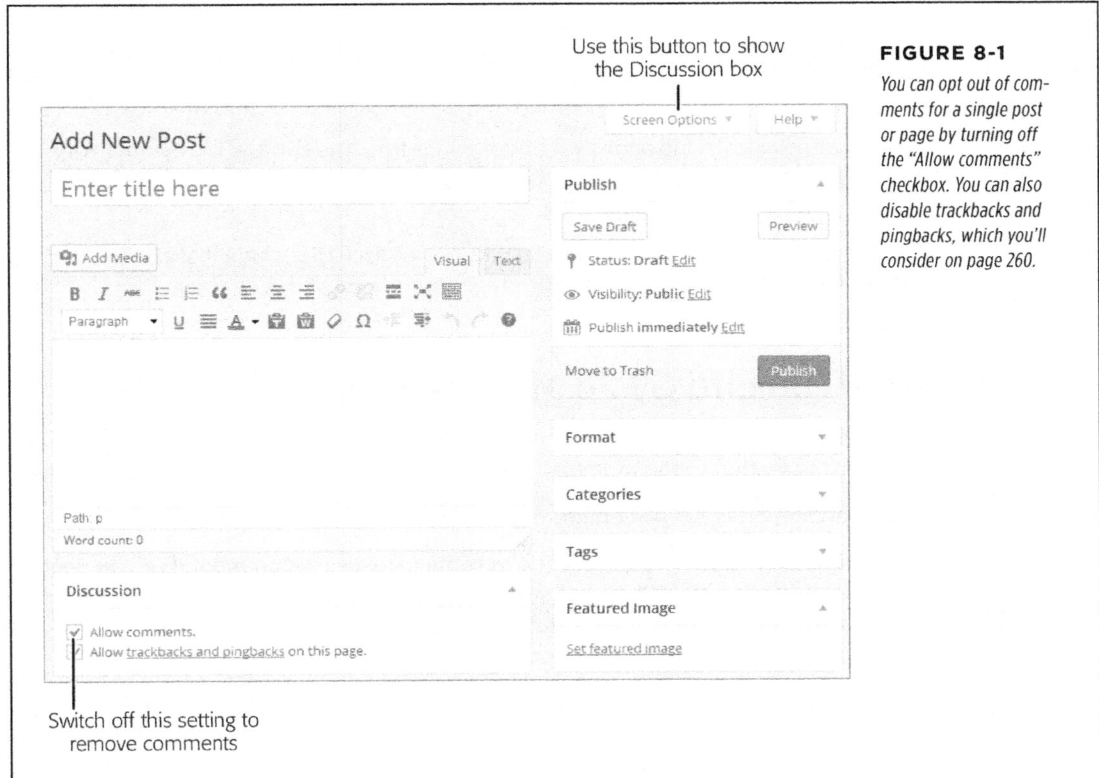

FIGURE 8-1

You can opt out of comments for a single post or page by turning off the "Allow comments" checkbox. You can also disable trackbacks and pingbacks, which you'll consider on page 260.

If you have a pile of posts that allow comments and you want to remove the comment feature from all of them, WordPress makes it easy by letting you edit posts in bulk. Here's how to do that:

1. **Choose Posts→All Posts.**

   WordPress lists all your posts.

2. **Turn on the checkbox next to each post you want to change.**

3. **Choose Edit from the Bulk Actions drop-down list, and then click Apply.**

   The edit panel appears at the top of the post list, with a number of settings you can change (see page 129).

4. **In the Comments drop-down list, pick "Do not allow," and then click Update.**

   You can use the same trick to turn commenting back on and to change the comment settings on your pages.

Changing the Default Comment Settings Site-Wide

To create a site that's mostly or entirely comment-free, you probably don't want to fiddle with the Discussion settings for every post. Instead, you should create a universal setting that applies to all new posts and pages. Choose Settings→Discussion on the dashboard, and then turn off the checkmarks next to "Allow link notifications from other blogs (pingbacks and trackbacks)" and "Allow people to post comments on new articles." Then scroll down to the bottom of the page and click Save Changes.

Now all new posts and pages will be comment-free. You can add the comment feature back to specific posts or pages by turning on "Allow comments" in the Discussion box, as shown back in Figure 8-1.

There are many more options in the Settings→Discussion page that change the way comments work. You'll learn to use them in the rest of this chapter.

The Life Cycle of a Comment

The easiest way to understand how WordPress comments work is to follow one from its creation to the moment it appears on your site and starts a conversation.

Depending on how you configure your site, comments travel one of two routes:

- **The slow lane.** In this scenario, anyone can leave a comment, but you need to approve it before it appears on the post. You can grant an exemption for repeat commenters, but most people will find that the conversation slows down significantly, no matter how quickly you review new comments.
- **The fast lane.** Here, each comment appears on your site as soon as someone leaves it. However, unless you want your website drowned in thousands of spam messages, you need to use some sort of spam-fighting tool with this option—usually, it's an automated program that detects and quarantines suspicious-looking messages.

For most sites, the second choice is the best approach, because it allows discussions to unfold quickly, spontaneously, and with the least possible extra work on your part. But this solution introduces more risk, because even the best spam-catcher will miss some junk, or allow messages that aren't spam but are just plain offensive. For that reason, WordPress starts your site out on the safer slow lane instead.

In this chapter, you'll consider both routes. First, you'll learn the slow-lane approach. Then, when you're ready to step up your game with more powerful spam-fighting tools, you'll consider the fast-lane approach.

Leaving a Comment

Leaving a comment is easy, which is the point—the more convenient it is to join the conversation, the more likely your visitors are to weigh in.

Assuming you haven't tweaked any of WordPress's comment settings, visitors need to supply two pieces of information before they can make their thoughts known: their name and their email address. They can optionally include a website address, too (Figure 8-2).

NOTE If you're logged into your website as the administrator, you won't see the commenting layout shown in Figure 8-2. Instead, you'll see just the box for comment text, because WordPress already knows who you are. This won't help you understand what life is like for ordinary readers, however, so before you go any further, log out (click "Log out" above the comment box) or go to the page from another computer or browser. Then your site will treat you like a stranger, and you'll see the same commenting boxes your visitors see.

Here's what WordPress does with the information it gets from commenters:

- **Name.** It displays the commenter's name prominently above her comment, thereby identifying her to other readers.
- **Email address.** WordPress doesn't display this publicly, so commenters don't need to worry about spam. In fact, WordPress won't stop visitors from inventing imaginary email addresses (although it will prevent them from typing in gibberish that obviously doesn't make sense). WordPress won't even send would-be commenters one of those pesky "Confirm this is your address" email messages. However, email addresses are important if you want to display a tiny picture of each commenter next to each comment (see page 263 for details).
- **Comment text.** This is the meat of the comment (Figure 8-2).
- **Website.** If your commenter includes this detail, WordPress turns the commenter's name, which appears above posts, into a link. Other readers can click it to travel to the commenter's site.

To see how comments work, try typing in one of your own. First, make sure you aren't logged in as the administrator (if you are, you'll bypass the moderation process described below, because WordPress figures you'll always allow your own comments). Assuming you're logged out and you see the text boxes shown in Figure 8-2, type in a comment and then click Post Comment.

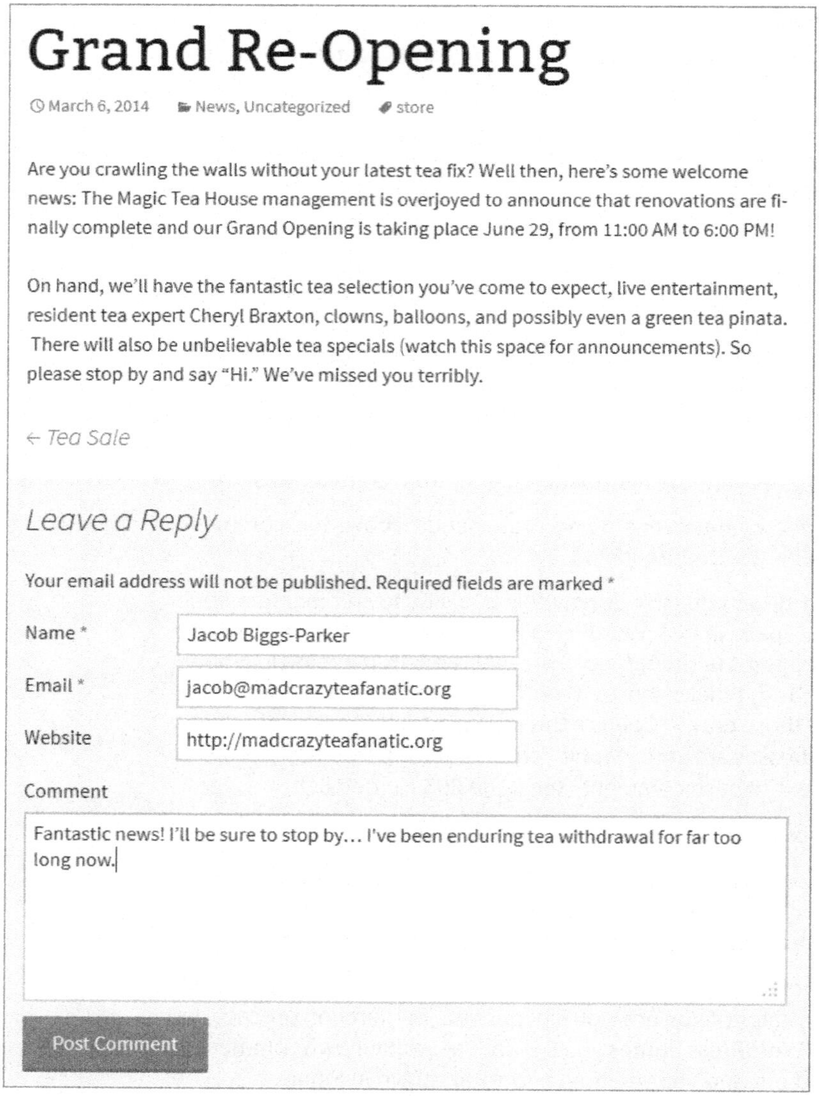

Grand Re-Opening

March 6, 2014 News, Uncategorized store

Are you crawling the walls without your latest tea fix? Well then, here's some welcome news: The Magic Tea House management is overjoyed to announce that renovations are finally complete and our Grand Opening is taking place June 29, from 11:00 AM to 6:00 PM!

On hand, we'll have the fantastic tea selection you've come to expect, live entertainment, resident tea expert Cheryl Braxton, clowns, balloons, and possibly even a green tea pinata. There will also be unbelievable tea specials (watch this space for announcements). So please stop by and say "Hi." We've missed you terribly.

← Tea Sale

Leave a Reply

Your email address will not be published. Required fields are marked *

Name * Jacob Biggs-Parker

Email * jacob@madcrazyteafanatic.org

Website http://madcrazyteafanatic.org

Comment

Fantastic news! I'll be sure to stop by... I've been enduring tea withdrawal for far too long now.

Post Comment

FIGURE 8-2

Ordinarily, a commenter needs to include his name and email address (although WordPress doesn't verify either). Optionally, commenters can include a website address or leave this box blank.

Now, WordPress plays a slight trick on you. When you submit a comment, WordPress immediately adds it below your post (Figure 8-3), making it look as though your comment has been published. But in reality, when you use the slow-lane commenting route, no one can see the comment until the site owner (that's you) reviews it and formally approves it. This process is called *moderation*.

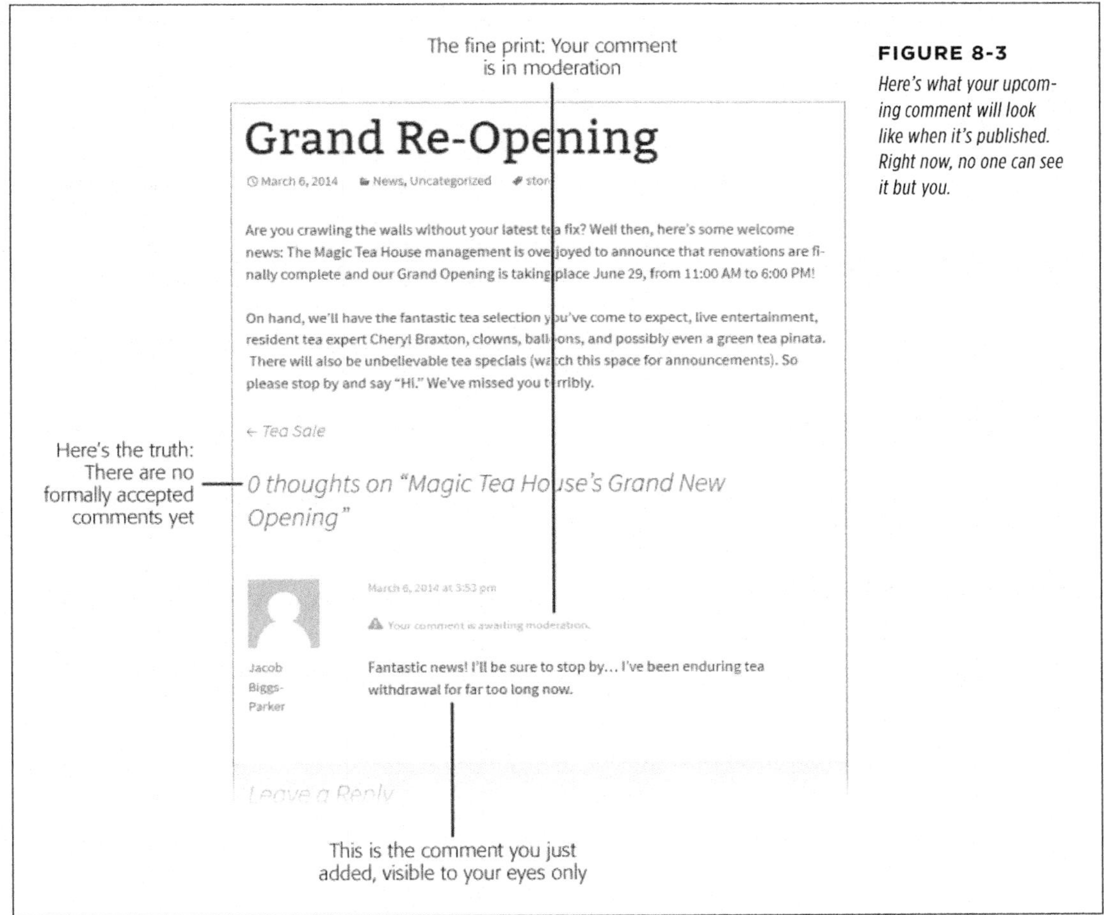
The fine print: Your comment is in moderation
Grand Re-Opening
March 6, 2014
News, Uncategorized
Are you crawling the walls without your latest tea fix? Well then, here's some welcome news: The Magic Tea House management is overjoyed to announce that renovations are finally complete and our Grand Opening is taking place June 29, from 11:00 AM to 6:00 PM!
On hand, we'll have the fantastic tea selection you've come to expect, live entertainment, resident tea expert Cheryl Braxton, clowns, balloons, and possibly even a green tea pinata. There will also be unbelievable tea specials (watch this space for announcements). So please stop by and say "Hi." We've missed you terribly.
← Tea Sale
Here's the truth: There are no formally accepted comments yet
0 thoughts on "Magic Tea House's Grand New Opening"
Jacob Biggs-Parker
Fantastic news! I'll be sure to stop by… I've been enduring tea withdrawal for far too long now.
This is the comment you just added, visible to your eyes only

FIGURE 8-3

Here's what your upcoming comment will look like when it's published. Right now, no one can see it but you.

GEM IN THE ROUGH

Comments That Use HTML

Most people who comment on a post or page will type in one or more paragraphs of ordinary text. However, craftier commenters may include a few HTML tags to format their comments.

For example, you can use the <b> and <i> elements to bold and italicize text. Type this:

I'm <i>really</i> annoyed.

and your comment will look like this:

I'm *really* annoyed.

You can also add headlines, line breaks, bulleted and numbered lists, and even tables. You could use the <a> element to create a link, but that's not necessary—if you type in text that starts with *www.* or *http://*, WordPress automatically converts it to a clickable link.

Now that you know you can use HTML in a comment, the next question is, *should* you? Most site owners don't mind the odd bit of bold or italic formatting, but they may trash messages that include shamelessly self-promotional links or ones that attempt to steal focus from the conversation with wild formatting—it's like an attention-starved kid throwing a grocery-store tantrum.

You can edit comments that use HTML inappropriately, but that takes time and effort. As a safeguard, some site owners don't allow HTML elements at all. If you run a self-hosted site, you can ban HTML by creating a custom theme, an advanced task detailed in Chapter 13. Once you do, you need to edit its *functions.php* file (page 500) and add these instructions anywhere after the first line (which holds the `<?php` marker that starts the code block):

```
add_filter( 'comment_text',
  'wp_filter_nohtml_kses' );
add_filter( 'comment_text_rss',
  'wp_filter_nohtml_kses' );
add_filter( 'comment_excerpt',
  'wp_filter_nohtml_kses' );
```

Now WordPress strips out any HTML tags from comments and disables the linking capability of web addresses.

Moderating Comments Through Email

When a comment awaits moderation, the discussion on your site stalls. WordPress takes two steps to notify you of waiting comments:

- It sends you an email message, with information about the new comment (and the links you need to manage it).
- It adds an eye-catching number-in-a-circle icon to the Comments button on your dashboard menu, where you can manage all your comments.

These two actions underlie the two ways you moderate WordPress comments: either by email or through your site's dashboard. First, you'll consider the email approach.

Email moderation is, for practical purposes, an option only for a small site that receives a relatively small number of comments. If you're the sort of person who carries around a web-connected device (like a smartphone) everywhere you go, email moderation gives you a convenient way to approve or discard comments mere minutes after they're made (Figure 8-4).

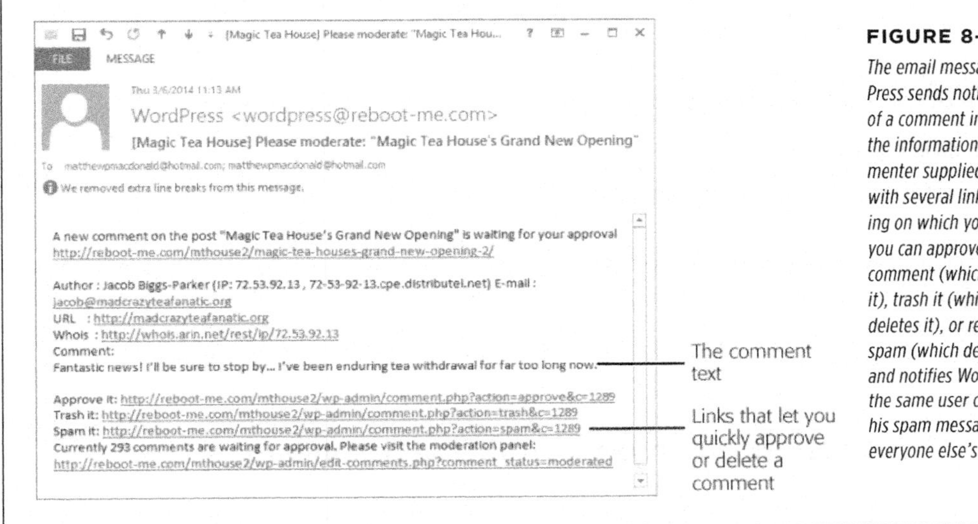

FIGURE 8-4

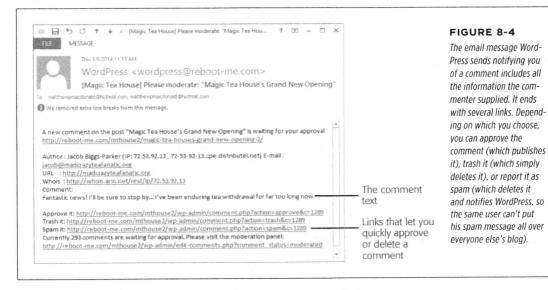

The email message WordPress sends notifying you of a comment includes all the information the commenter supplied. It ends with several links. Depending on which you choose, you can approve the comment (which publishes it), trash it (which simply deletes it), or report it as spam (which deletes it and notifies WordPress, so the same user can't put his spam message all over everyone else's blog).

Email moderation is a great idea, but it's increasingly impractical for the websites of today. The problem is comment spam—advertisements for Viagra and Cialis, porn, shady discount deals, and so on. If you use email moderation, you'll receive an ever-increasing load of notifications as a host of black-hat characters try to insert their junk onto your pages. Not only is it difficult to manage the sheer number of messages you get, it's often difficult to quickly verify that a message is legitimate, because spammers try to make their comments sound real. Often, the only way to confirm that a comment is bogus is to visit the commenter's site, where you usually find ads unrelated to anything in the comment. If you plan to review comments on a mobile device, this extra step is neither quick nor convenient.

For these reasons, few people use email moderation to manage comments. You can try it, and it may work wonderfully at first, but you'll probably need to abandon it as more and more spammers discover your site, or you'll need to supplement it with one of the antispam plug-ins you'll learn about on page 276. That way, your plug-in can take care of the massive amounts of obvious spam, while you concentrate on moderating the comments that make it past the spam filter.

NOTE Don't fall into the trap of thinking that you're safe because your audience is small. Most spammers don't target WordPress sites by popularity. Instead, they try to spread their junk everywhere they can. And their site-discovering techniques are surprisingly sophisticated. Even if you haven't told anyone about your site and you've configured it so it's hidden from search engines, you'll *still* get spam comments, usually within days of the site's creation. But here's the happy news: Any plug-in that blocks automated spam should reduce comment moderation to a manageable task.

WordPress comes with email moderation turned on. If you decide you don't want to be notified because you're receiving too many spam messages, you can easily switch it off. Choose Settings→Discussion, find the "Email me whenever" section, and clear the checkmarks next to "Anyone posts a comment" and "A comment is held for moderation."

FREQUENTLY ASKED QUESTION

Where Are My Emails?

I have the comment notification settings switched on, but I'm not getting any emails.

Ironically, email programs often misinterpret the notifications that WordPress sends as junk mail. The problem is that the messages contain quite a few links, which is a red flag suggesting spam. To find your missing messages, check your junk mail folder.

To avoid having your comment notifications identified as junk mail, tell your email program to always trust the address that sends them. The sending address is *wordpress* followed by your website domain, as in *wordpress@magicteahouse.net.*

Moderating Comments from the Dashboard

The other way to moderate comments is through the dashboard. The disadvantage here is that you need to open a browser, visit your site, and log in. The advantage is that you'll see all your site's comments in one place, and you can accept or discard them en masse.

If you have comments awaiting moderation, you'll see a black circle-with-a-number icon in the dashboard menu. This circle looks like the one that notifies you of WordPress and plug-in updates (page 81), except that it appears over the Comments menu and indicates the number of unreviewed comments you have (Figure 8-5). If you go to the dashboard's home page (Dashboard→Home), you'll also see the most recent comments in the Recent Comments box.

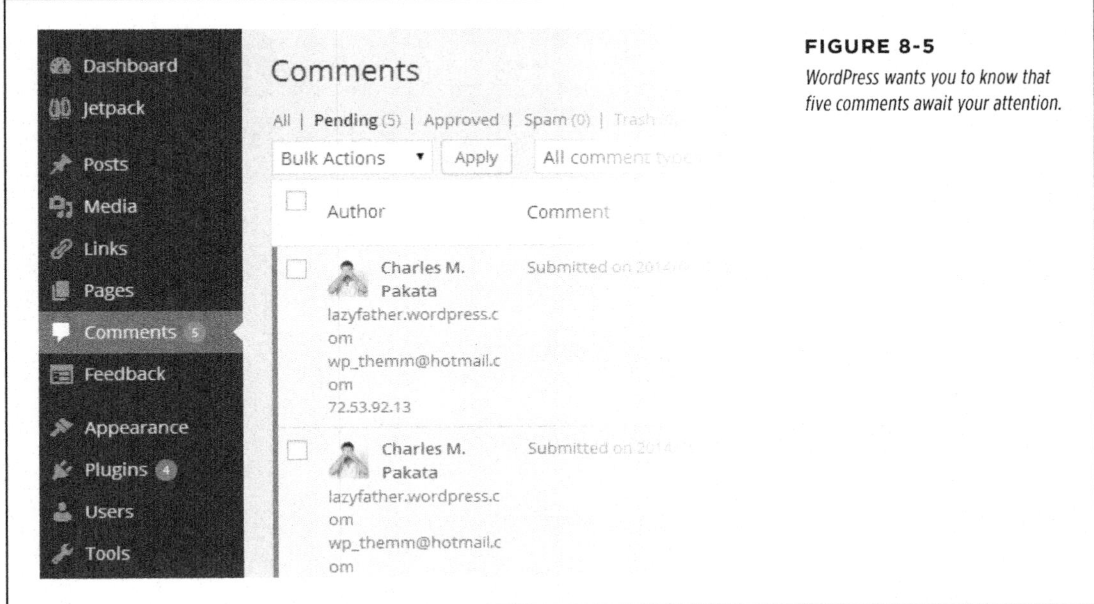

FIGURE 8-5

WordPress wants you to know that five comments await your attention.

To review comments, click Comments in the dashboard menu. Initially, you see a list of all the comments left on all the posts and pages of your site, ordered from newest to oldest. Click the Pending link above the comment list to focus on just the comments you need to review (Figure 8-6).

Here's what to do once you examine a comment:

- If it's spam, click the Spam link. Do *not* click Trash. Yes, both links remove the comment from your list, but only Spam reports the spammer to WordPress, which can help intercept the spam before it hits other sites.
- If it's a valid comment, click Approve to publish it. If the same person returns and posts another comment using the same email address, WordPress lets it through automatically, no moderation required. (This works because WordPress automatically turns on the "Comment author must have a previously approved comment" setting.)
- If it's a valid comment that you don't want to allow, click Trash. For example, if someone read your post and replied in an abusive manner, you don't need to publish her comment—it's up to you.

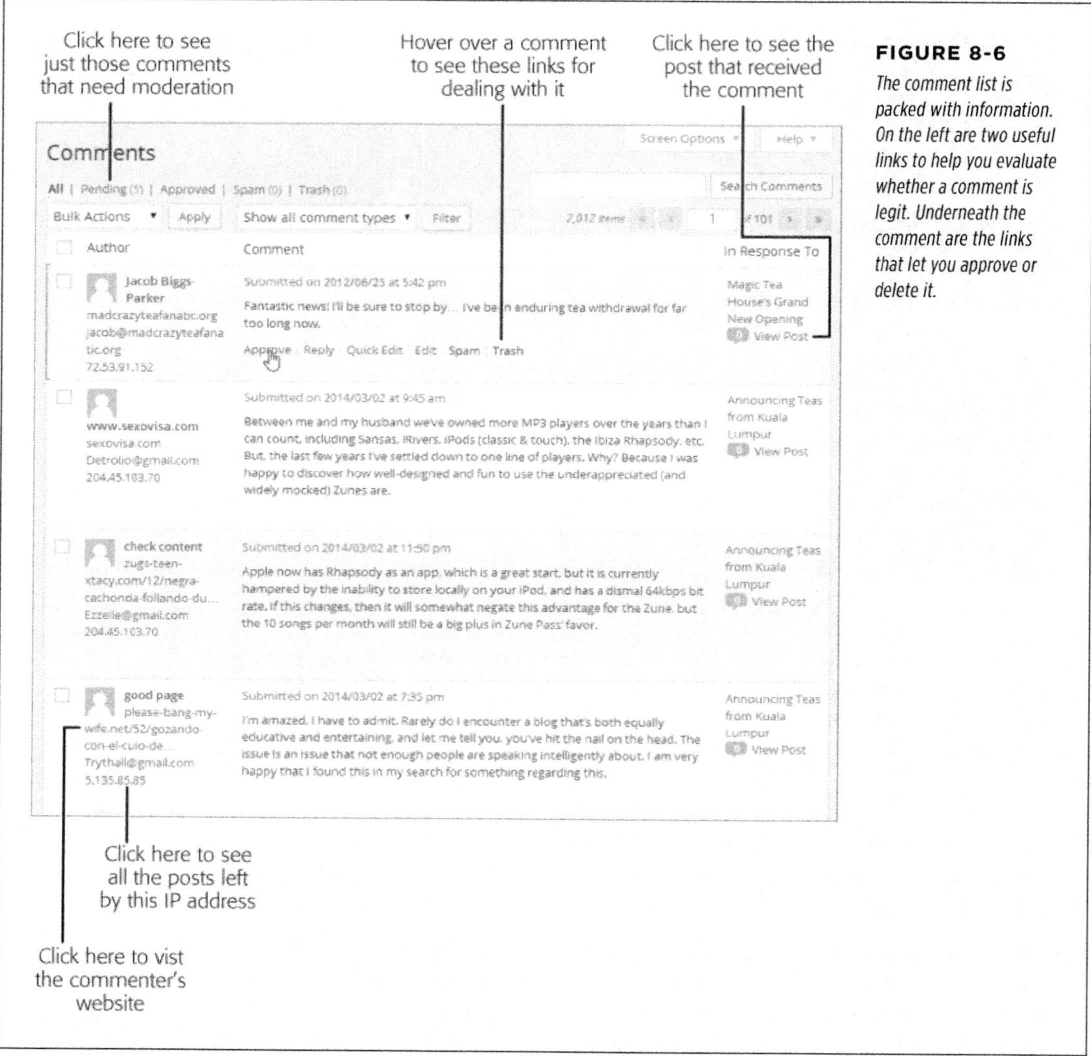

FIGURE 8-6

The comment list is packed with information. On the left are two useful links to help you evaluate whether a comment is legit. Underneath the comment are the links that let you approve or delete it.

You don't need to deal with comments one at a time. You can use a handy bulk action to deal with multiple comments at once. This is particularly useful if you need to clear out a batch of suspicious-looking junk.

To deal with a group of comments, start by adding a checkmark to each one you want to process. Then pick a comment-handling action from the Bulk Actions drop-down list. Your options include Approve, Unapprove, Move to Trash, and Mark as Spam. Finally, click Apply to carry out your action.

UP TO SPEED

Evaluating Comments

When you review comments, your goal is to separate the well-meaning ones from the offensive ones (which you may not want to allow) and to delete spam (which you definitely don't want). Be careful, because spammers are often crafty enough to add a seemingly appropriate comment that actually links to a spam site. They may identify keywords in your posts and cobble them together in their comments. They may report imaginary errors in your blog, claiming links don't work or pictures don't load. Often, they'll throw in some flattery in a desperate attempt to get approved.

For example, in Figure 8-6, the last three comments are real spam comments, received on the actual Magic Tea House sample site. The second and third comments were posted together, and they appear to strike up a fictitious conversation. But the clues abound that something isn't right. The comments discuss a product that hasn't existed in years (Microsoft's Zune player) and has nothing to do with the post topic (teas from Kuala Lumpur). The fourth comment is a more typical example of spam: vague but effusive praise for the site that always manages to avoid stating anything specific.

The acid test for spam is to view the commenter's website. To do that, click the corresponding link (to the left of the comment in the comment list). Sometimes just looking at the URL is enough. In Figure 8-6, a careful examination exposes at least two of the spam comments as come-ons for X-rated websites.

Once you identify one spam message, you may be able to detect others sent from the same spammer by using the message's IP address (a numeric code that uniquely identifies web-connected computers). For example, in Figure 8-6 two spam messages come from the same IP address (204.45.103.70). WordPress even gives you a shortcut—click the IP address, and it shows you only the comments that originated from that address. You can then flag them all as spam in a single bulk action (see page 128).

TIP Remember, if you accidentally put a comment you want in the Spam or Trash bin, you can get it out if you act fast. Click the Spam or Trash link above the comments list to see a list of removed comments, which you can then restore.

Moderating Comments for a Specific Post

The Comments page is the only place where you can see all the comments on your site in one list. But the Comments page isn't always the most convenient place to review comments, particularly if you have hundreds to look through.

WordPress gives you another option: You can review just the comments that relate to a specific post. To do that, edit the post and scroll down to the Comments box at the bottom of the Edit Post page. There, WordPress displays a list of the post's comments, along with links that let you approve, trash, or edit each one.

Lastly, if you're logged in to your site, you can deal with comments without even skipping back to the dashboard. When you read the comments section after a post, you'll see an edit link next to each comment (Figure 8-7). Click that, and you'll get the chance to modify or remove that comment. This approach takes a few more clicks, and it works only on comments you've already approved. (Comments you haven't approved don't show up on the post page.) However, if you use automatic post approval with a spam plug-in, as you'll learn to do on page 275, this is a quick way to deal with the errant bit of spam you find slipping through your filters.

Click here to review all the comments for this post, including ones that haven't been approved
Grand Re-Opening
March 6, 2014 News store Edit
Are you crawling the walls without your latest tea fix? Well then, here's some welcome news: The Magic Tea House management is overjoyed to announce that renovations are finally complete and our Grand Opening is taking place June 29, from 11:00 AM to 6:00 PM!
On hand, we'll have the fantastic tea selection you've come to expect, live entertainment, resident tea expert Cheryl Braxton, clowns, balloons, and possibly even a green tea pinata. There will also be unbelievable tea specials (watch this space for announcements). So please stop by and say "Hi." We've missed you terribly.
← Closing for Christmas
Dead Elvis →
2 thoughts on "Grand Re-Opening"

Jacob Biggs-Parker
March 6, 2014 at 3:53 pm Edit
Fantastic news! I'll be sure to stop by... I've been enduring tea withdrawal for far too long now.
Reply

graphic cigarette labels
March 7, 2014 at 2:32 am Edit
Nice weblog here! Also your web site a lot up fast! What host are you the usage of? Can I am getting your affiliate link for your host? I wish my web site loaded up as quickly as yours lol
Reply
Click here to review (and then trash) this comment

FIGURE 8-7

If you spot spam on a post, you can deal with it in situ, no dashboard required.

Sanitizing Comments

By now, you're well acquainted with your role as supreme comment commander. Only you can decide which comments live to see the light of day, and which ones are banished to the trash or spam folders.

WordPress gives you one more power over comments that may surprise you. You can crack open any comment and edit it, exactly as though it were your own content. That means you can delete text, insert new bits, change the formatting, and even add HTML tags. You can do this by clicking the Edit link under the comment, which switches to a new page named Edit Comment, or you can edit it more efficiently by clicking the Quick Edit link, which opens a comment-editing text box right inside the list of comments.

You might use this ability to remove something objectionable from a comment before you allow it, such as profanity or off-site links. However, few site administrators have the time to personally review their readers' comments. Instead, they get WordPress to do the dirty work.

One way to do that is to use the Comment Moderation box. Choose Settings→Discussion and fill the box with words you don't want to allow (one per line). If a comment uses a restricted word, WordPress adds it to the list of comments that need your review, even if you approved an earlier comment from the same person, and even if you disabled moderation (page 275). However, mind the fact that WordPress checks not only whole words, but *within* words as well, so if you disallow *ass*, WordPress won't allow jack*ass* or *Ass*yria. If you want to be even stricter, you can use the Comment Blacklist box instead of the Comment Moderation box. You again provide a list of offensive words, but this time WordPress sends offending comments straight to your spam folder.

If you run a self-hosted site, you can use a gentler approach, one that *replaces* objectionable words but still allows the comment. For example, the WP Content Filter plug-in (*http://tinyurl.com/wpcontentfilter*) changes words you don't want (like jackass) with an appropriately blanked-out substitution (like j******, j*****s or *******). Of course, crafty commenters will get around these limitations by adding spaces and dashes (jack a s s), replacing letters with similar-looking numbers or special characters (jacka55), or just using creative misspellings (jackahss). So if you have a real problem with inappropriate comments and you can't tolerate them even temporarily (in other words, before you have the chance to find and remove them), then you need to keep using strict moderation on your site so you get the chance to review every comment before it's published.

The Ongoing Conversation

You've now seen how a single, lonely comment finds its way onto a WordPress post or page. On a healthy site, this small step is just the start of a long conversation. As readers stop by, more and more will add their own thoughts. And before long, some people will stop replying to your content and start replying to each other.

WordPress keeps track of all this in its *comment stream*, which is similar to the stream of posts that occupies your site's home page. WordPress sandwiches the comment stream between your content (the text of your post or page), which sits at the top, and the "Leave a Reply" box, which sits at the bottom. Unlike the post stream, the comment stream starts with older comments, followed by newer ones. This arrangement makes it easy to follow an unfolding conversation, where new comments refer to earlier ones.

TIP If you have lots of comments and want to emphasize the newest ones, you can flip the order, so that the newest comments appear first. Choose Settings→Discussion, find the setting that says "Comments should be displayed with the older comments at the top of each page," and pick "newer" instead of "older."

Threaded Comments

The most interesting part of the comment stream is the way it *threads* comments—it orders the comments that visitors post in reply to other comments. When new visitors read your post and join the conversation, they have two options: They can reply directly to your post by scrolling to the "Leave a Reply" section at the bottom of the page, or they can reply to one of the existing comments by clicking the Reply button (or link) next to the comment.

When a guest comments on another comment, WordPress puts the reply underneath the original note, indented slightly to show the relationship. Figure 8-8 shows how one of the standard WordPress themes (in this case, Twenty Thirteen) handles threaded comments.

TIP WordPress has a handy shortcut that lets you, the site owner, join a conversation straight from the dashboard. When reviewing a comment on the Dashboard→Comments page, click the Reply link, fill in some text, and then click the Reply button (or "Reply and Approve" if you're responding to a comment you haven't approved yet).

If several people reply to the same comment, WordPress arranges the replies underneath the comment and indents them, either from oldest to newest (the standard) or newest to oldest (if you changed the discussion settings as described in the Tip at the top of this page).

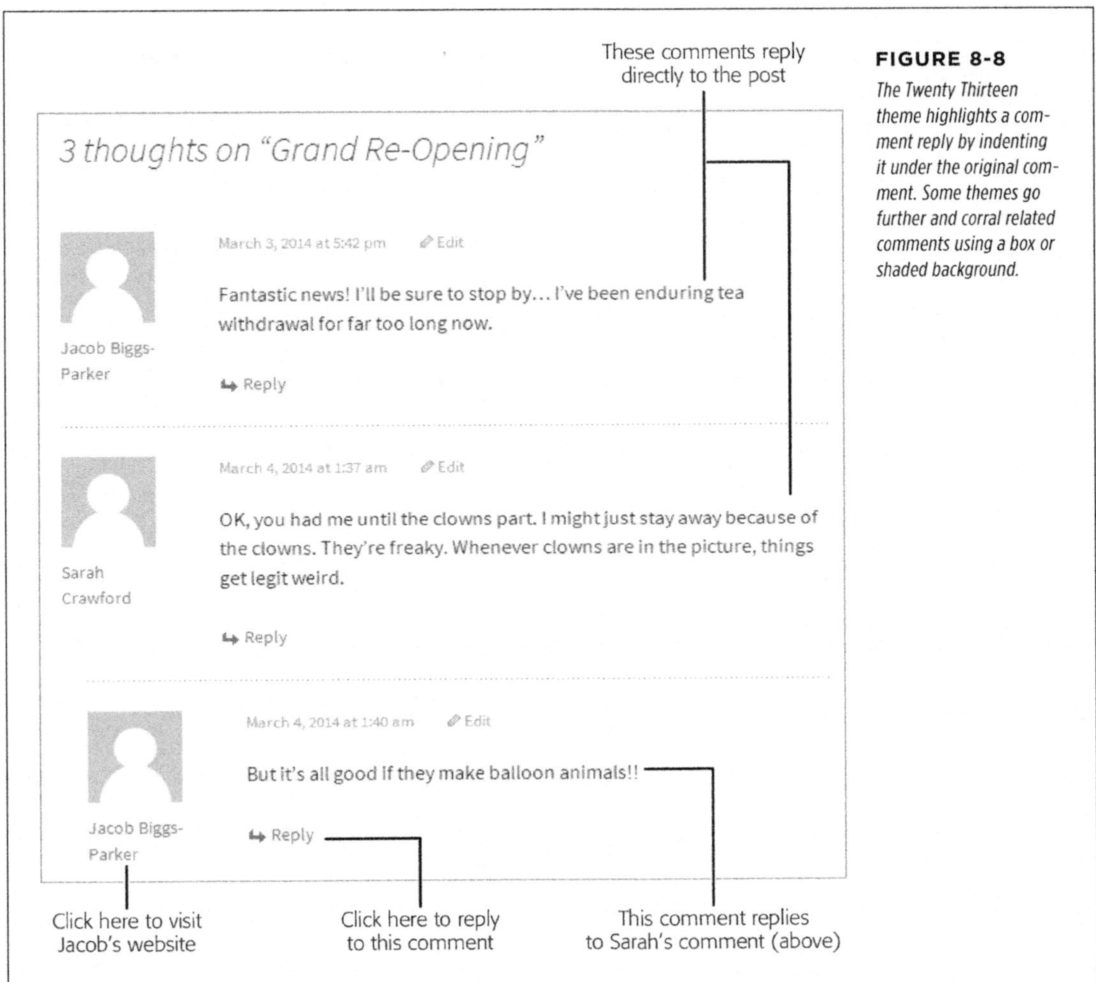
These comments reply directly to the post
3 thoughts on "Grand Re-Opening"
March 3, 2014 at 5:42 pm
Edit
Fantastic news! I'll be sure to stop by… I've been enduring tea withdrawal for far too long now.
Jacob Biggs-Parker
Reply
March 4, 2014 at 1:37 am
Edit
OK, you had me until the clowns part. I might just stay away because of the clowns. They're freaky. Whenever clowns are in the picture, things get legit weird.
Sarah Crawford
Reply
March 4, 2014 at 1:40 am
Edit
But it's all good if they make balloon animals!!
Jacob Biggs-Parker
Reply
Click here to visit Jacob's website
Click here to reply to this comment
This comment replies to Sarah's comment (above)

FIGURE 8-8

The Twenty Thirteen theme highlights a comment reply by indenting it under the original comment. Some themes go further and corral related comments using a box or shaded background.

Comment replies can go several layers deep. For example, if Sarah replies to your post, Jacob can reply to Sarah's comment, Sergio can reply to Jacob's comment, and then Sarah can reply to Sergio's reply, creating four layers of stacked comments (Figure 8-9).

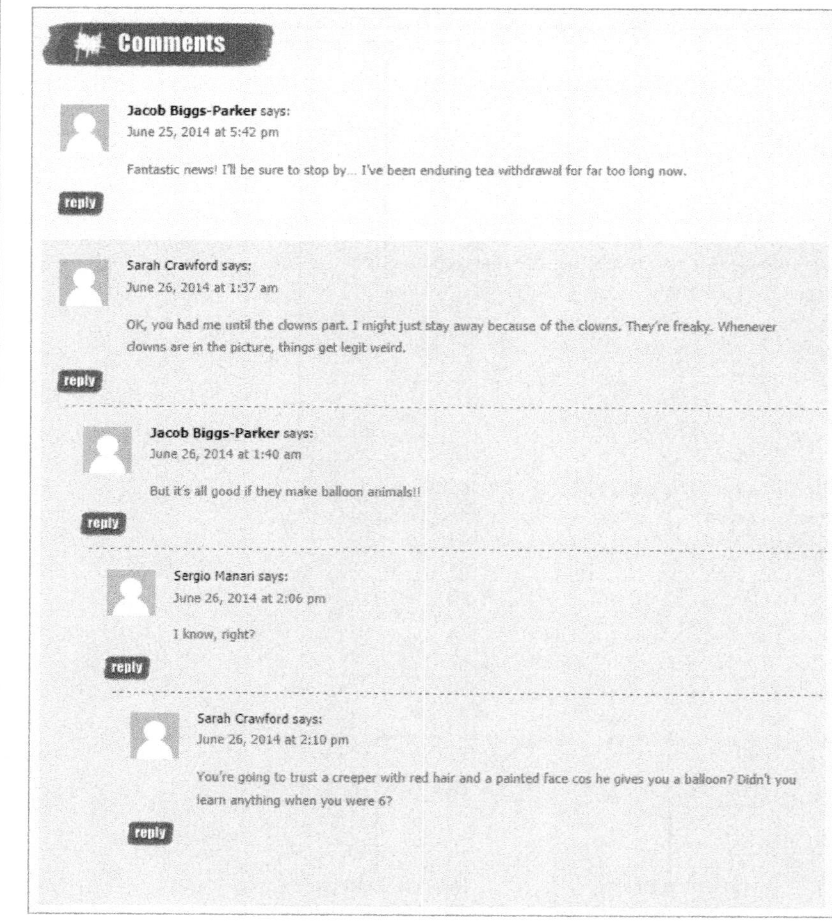

FIGURE 8-9

If you expect to get piles of comments, the WordPress year themes might not be the best choice for you. They tend to spread comments out with plenty of whitespace in between, which makes for more visitor scrolling. Many other themes pack comments tightly together, like the Greyzed theme shown here.

WordPress allows this replying-to-replies madness to continue only so far; once you get five levels of comments, it no longer displays the Reply button. This prevents the conversation from becoming dizzyingly self-referential, and it stops the ever-increasing indenting from messing with your site's layout. However, you can reduce or increase this cap (the maximum is 10 levels) by choosing Settings→Discussion, finding the setting "Enable threaded (nested) comments 5 levels deep," and then picking a different number. Or turn off the checkmark for this setting to switch threaded comments off altogether, which keeps your conversations super-simple, but looks more than a bit old-fashioned.

WORD TO THE WISE

Author Comments

Don't forget to add your voice to the discussion. Authors who never take the time to directly engage their readers lose their readers' interest—quickly.

Of course, it's also possible to have too much of a good thing, and authors who reply to every comment will seem desperate (at best) or intrusive (at worst). They'll suffocate a conversation like a micro-managing boss. The best guideline is to step in periodically, answering obvious questions and giving credit to good feedback (while ignoring or deleting the obvious junk). Do that, and your readers will see that your comments section is well cared for. They'll know that you read your feedback, and they'll be more likely to join in.

WordPress makes site owners' comments stick out from those of the riffraff so your readers can easily spot your contributions. The way it does so depends on the theme, but most change the background color behind your comment. If you run a self-hosted blog, or if you bought the Custom Design upgrade for your WordPress.com site, you can make your replies even more obvious. The trick is to tweak the formatting that the *bypostauthor* style applies. Page 479 explains how.

Paged Comments

WordPress provides a comment-organizing feature called *paging* that divides masses of comments into separate pages. The advantage is that you split awkwardly long discussions into more manageable (and readable) chunks. The disadvantage is that readers need to click more links to follow a long discussion.

To use pages, choose Settings→Discussion and then turn on the checkbox next to "Break comments into pages." You can type in the number of comments you want included on each page (the factory setting is 50).

You can also choose the page that readers begin on—the standard setting is "last," which means that new readers will start on the last page of comments first, seeing the most recent chunk of the conversation before they see older exchanges. But the overall effect is a bit weird, because the very latest comment appears at the *bottom* of the first page. What you probably want is the latest comment to appear at the *top* of that page. To get this effect—paged comments, with the most recent comment at the top of the list on the first page—change "last" to "first" (so the setting says "and the first page displayed by default") and change "older" to "newer" (so the setting says "Comments should be displayed with the newer comments at the top of each page").

Advertising a Post's Comments

As you've seen, comments appear right underneath the post they refer to. They don't appear at all in the reverse-chronological list of posts that acts as the home page for most WordPress sites. You can think of it this way: Each post is like a separate room at a party, with its own conversation. The same guests can wander between rooms and join different conversations, but the conversation from one room doesn't intrude on the conversation in the next.

However, WordPress does attempt to alert readers to the *presence* of comments in the post list, if not their content. If a post has at least one comment, WordPress shows the comment *count* next to that post. If a post doesn't have any comments, WordPress displays a "Leave a comment" link. Technically, your site theme controls this detail, but most are fairly consistent in this practice (Figure 8-10).

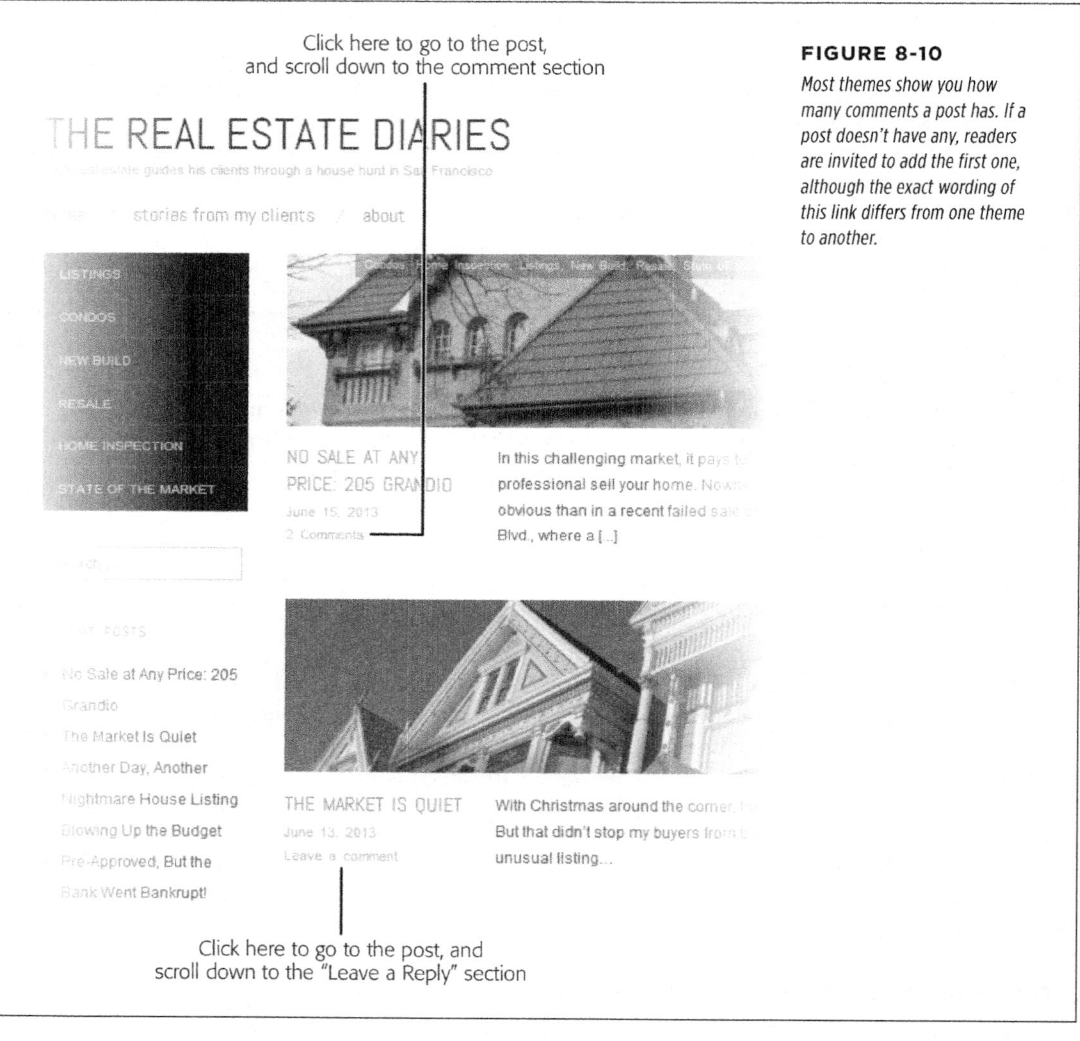

FIGURE 8-10

Most themes show you how many comments a post has. If a post doesn't have any, readers are invited to add the first one, although the exact wording of this link differs from one theme to another.

Here's another way to highlight comments on your home page: Use the Recent Comments widget, which highlights the most recent comments made on *any* post or page (Figure 8-11). When you add this widget (in the Appearance→Widgets section of the dashboard), you can choose the number of recent comments it lists. The standard setting is 5.

TIP If you want a better Recent Comments widget, there are plenty of plug-ins that fill the gap. Most excerpt the first part of the comment and display it right inside the widget to give readers a taste of the conversation (and to encourage them to join in). See, for example, the Better WordPress Recent Comments plug-in (*http://tinyurl.com/wprecentcomments*).

RECENT COMMENTS

- Katya Greenview on **Magic Tea House's Grand New Opening**
- Katya Greenview on **Magic Tea House's Grand New Opening**
- Katya Greenview on **Magic Tea House's Grand New Opening**
- **Jacob Biggs-Parker** on **Magic Tea House's Grand New Opening**
- Sarah Crawford on **Magic Tea House's Grand New Opening**

FIGURE 8-11

The Recent Comments widget tells you who's commenting on what post. However, it doesn't show you any of the comment content, which is a shame. Readers can click a comment link to see both the comment and the corresponding post.

Comment Ratings

You've no doubt seen sites that let readers rate each other's comments, often by clicking a tiny thumbs-up or thumbs-down icon (Figure 8-12). It's one more form of audience participation.

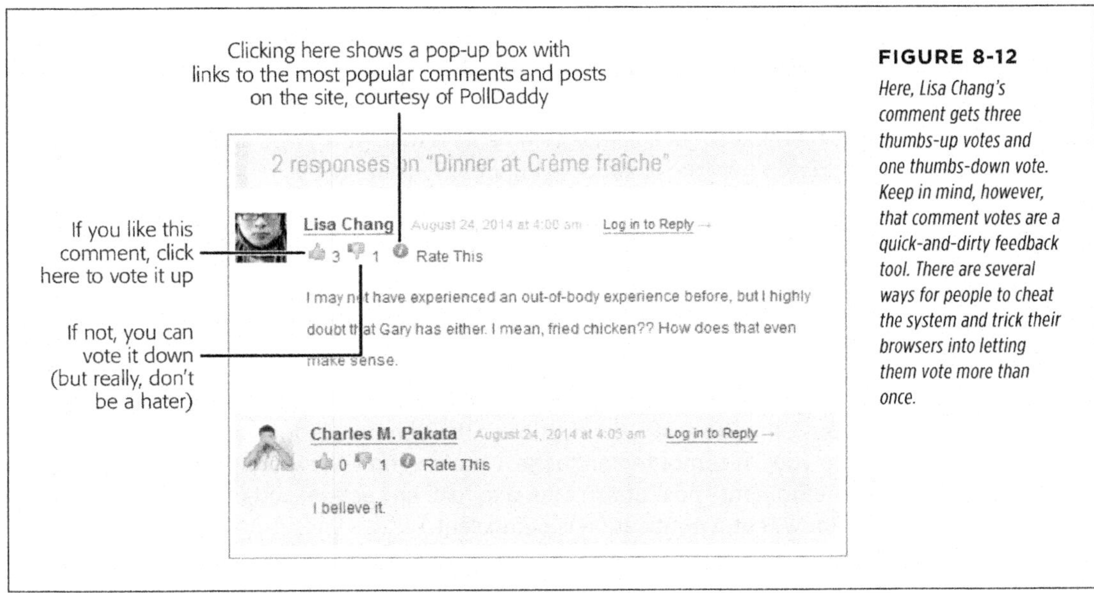

FIGURE 8-12

Here, Lisa Chang's comment gets three thumbs-up votes and one thumbs-down vote. Keep in mind, however, that comment votes are a quick-and-dirty feedback tool. There are several ways for people to cheat the system and trick their browsers into letting them vote more than once.

Bloggers and other web authors are divided over the value of comment ratings. On the upside, they encourage readers to get involved, and let people feel like they're taking part in a discussion even if they don't write a comment. On the downside, comment ratings have a nasty habit of turning discussions into arguments. If you're dealing with a contentious subject, readers may simply scan the list of comments to vote up the ones they agree with and vote down the ones they don't. (Some sites try to reduce the negativity by replacing comment voting with a Like button that allows readers to vote for comments but not against them. But even this type of rating encourages readers to gang up with the people who share their opinions.)

Philosophical questions aside, it's fairly easy to add comment ratings to your site if it's running on WordPress.com. In the dashboard, choose Settings→Ratings, click the Comments tab, and then turn on the "Enable for comments" checkbox. You can position the voting icons above the comments (as in Figure 8-12) or below them. When you finish, click Save Changes.

Unfortunately, self-hosted WordPress sites don't get the comment rating feature. The solution is to install a comment voting plug-in, like Polldaddy (*http://tinyurl.com/wp-polls*). But first you need to learn a bit more about plug-ins, as detailed in Chapter 9.

Linkbacks

There's one type of comment you haven't seen yet: the *linkback*, a short, automatically generated comment that lets you know when somebody is talking about your post. Figure 8-13 shows what a linkback looks like—but be warned, it's not particularly pretty.

NOTE Linkbacks *are* comments. They appear in the comment list and need your approval before WordPress publishes them, just as any other comment does.

The neat thing about linkback comments is that WordPress creates them *automatically*. Here's how the linkback in Figure 8-13 came to be:

1. First, you published the "Community Outreach Fridays" post on the Canton School site.
2. Then, the Time for Diane site created the "Fun at Glenacres Retirement" post. Although it isn't shown in Figure 8-13, that post included a link to your "Community Outreach Fridays" post.
3. When the Time for Diane site published the "Fun at Glenacres Retirement" post, the site sent a notification to the Canton School site, saying "Hey, I linked to you" in computer language. (The person who wrote the "Fun at Glenacres Retirement" post doesn't need to take any action, and probably doesn't even know that a notification is being sent.)

4. On the Canton School site, WordPress springs into action, adding the linkback comment shown in Figure 8-13.

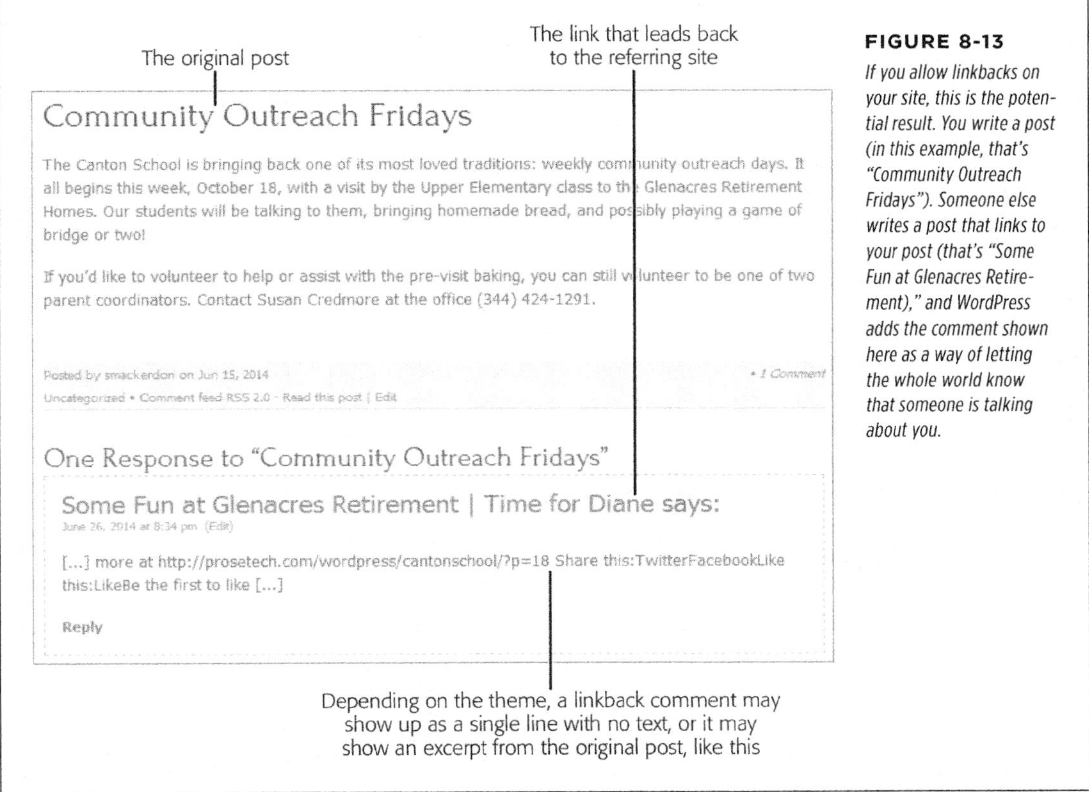

The original post
The link that leads back to the referring site
Community Outreach Fridays
The Canton School is bringing back one of its most loved traditions: weekly community outreach days. It all begins this week, October 18, with a visit by the Upper Elementary class to the Glenacres Retirement Homes. Our students will be talking to them, bringing homemade bread, and possibly playing a game of bridge or two!
If you'd like to volunteer to help or assist with the pre-visit baking, you can still volunteer to be one of two parent coordinators. Contact Susan Credmore at the office (344) 424-1291.
One Response to "Community Outreach Fridays"
Some Fun at Glenacres Retirement | Time for Diane says:
[...] more at http://prosetech.com/wordpress/cantonschool/?p=18 Share this:TwitterFacebookLike this:LikeBe the first to like [...]
Reply
Depending on the theme, a linkback comment may show up as a single line with no text, or it may show an excerpt from the original post, like this

FIGURE 8-13

If you allow linkbacks on your site, this is the potential result. You write a post (in this example, that's "Community Outreach Fridays"). Someone else writes a post that links to your post (that's "Some Fun at Glenacres Retirement)," and WordPress adds the comment shown here as a way of letting the whole world know that someone is talking about you.

NOTE Linkbacks aren't a WordPress-only feature. Many web publishing platforms support them, and virtually all blogs can send linkback notifications and add linkback comments.

The purpose of linkbacks is twofold. First, they show your readers that people are seeing and discussing your content, which makes it seem more popular and more relevant. Second, it provides your readers with a link to the post that mentioned your post. That means readers on your site (say, Canton School) can click a linkback comment to head to the referring post on the other site (Time for Diane). In an ideal world, this is a great way to network with like-minded sites.

In the not-so-distant past, a certain faction of bloggers cared dearly about linkbacks and saw them as an important community-building tool. Nowadays, popular opinion has shifted. Here are some reasons why you might not want to allow linkbacks:

- **Clutter.** Extra comments, no matter how brief, can end up crowding out real conversation. Some themes (like Bueno) separate linkbacks from the main comment stream, but most mix them together. If you have a popular topic that gets plenty of mention on other sites, your linkbacks can split up the more interesting human feedback and push it out of sight.
- **Why risk spam?** More comments equals more spam, and shady advertisers can send linkbacks to your site just as often as they send other types of comment spam.
- **Links are a good way to reward your commenters.** If someone writes a good comment, they can include a link in their comment text ("I was frustrated with the stains my kids left on everything, so I wrote a post with my favorite stain tips in it. Check it out at *http://helpfatheroftwelve.com*."). And if the commenter included his website address in the Leave a Reply form (page 244), WordPress automatically turns his user name at the top of the comment into a clickable link. With all this intra-post linking going on, why reward someone who hasn't even bothered to comment on your site with a linkback?

NOTE In short, most people find that linkbacks aren't worth the trouble. To disable them, choose Settings→Discussion and remove the checkmark next to the setting "Allow link notifications from other blogs (pingbacks and trackbacks)." Technically, WordPress supports two linkback mechanisms: pingbacks and trackbacks. The technical details about how pingbacks and trackbacks send their messages aren't terribly interesting. The important thing is that if you allow linkbacks (and, unless you change the factory settings, your site does), you may start getting comments like the one in Figure 8-13.

Optionally, you can clear the checkmark next to the setting "Attempt to notify any blogs linked to from the article." When this setting is on and you write a post that links to another post on someone else's site, WordPress automatically sends a notification to that site, and its administrator can choose whether to display the linkback.

NOTE Oddly enough, if you have the "Attempt to notify any blogs linked to from the article" setting switched on, WordPress notifies even *your own* site if you create a post that includes a link to one of your other posts. It creates a linkback comment in the initial post that points to the referring post, just as though the posts were on two different sites. (Of course, you're free to delete this comment if it bothers you.)

Making Comments More Personal

On a really good website, you won't feel like you're debating current affairs with anonymous_guy_65. Instead, you'll have the sense that you're talking to an actual person, someone who exists in the real world, beyond the pixels on your computer screen.

Often, all you need to do to personalize comments is include a few small details in the right places. One key enhancement is including a user-supplied profile picture with that person's comment. WordPress gives you two ways to do that—you can get pictures from its excellent Gravatar service, or you can take them from a person's Facebook or Twitter account. The following sections show you how to do both.

The Gravatar Service

To give comments a personal touch, you can display a tiny picture next to each person's thoughts. This picture, called an *avatar,* could be an actual photograph of the person or something quirkier, like a mythical creature or cartoon character the person has chosen to represent her. The idea is that the avatar helps your guests see, at a glance, which comments belong to the same person, and it just might give them a taste of the author's personality (Figure 8-14). Avatars also add a visual complement to web discussions, making a page of comments seem just a bit more like a real conversation.

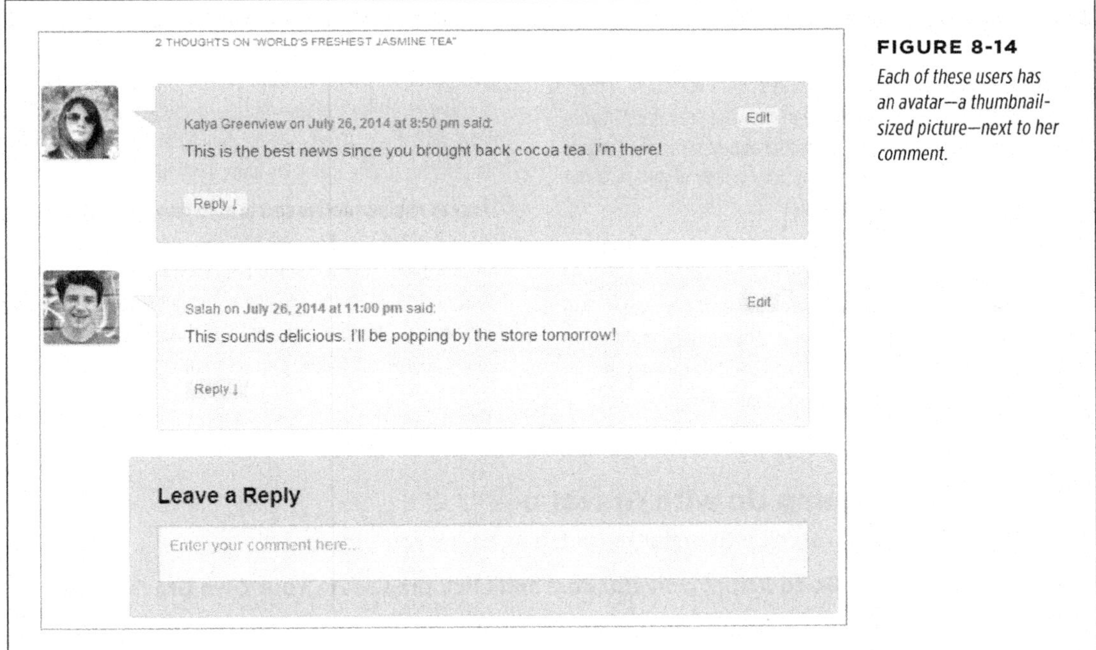

FIGURE 8-14

Each of these users has an avatar—a thumbnail-sized picture—next to her comment.

WordPress uses an avatar service called Gravatar, which is short for "globally recognized avatar." The idea is that ordinary people can use Gravatar to set up an avatar and include some basic personal information. They can then use that image and profile info on sites throughout the Web. Originally, Gravatar was a small service cooked up by a single person, but these days Automattic runs the service, making it freely available to virtually any blogging platform or website-building framework. (A Gravatar-supplied avatar goes by the name *gravatar.*)

You don't need to take any special steps to enable avatars; WordPress uses them automatically. As you already know, every would-be commenter has to enter an email address. When he does, WordPress contacts the Gravatar service and asks if it has a picture affiliated with that address. If it does, WordPress displays the picture next to the comment. If it doesn't, WordPress shows a featureless gray silhouette instead.

UP TO SPEED

Why Gravatars Make Good Sense

The obvious limitation to gravatars is that you won't see personalized images unless your readers sign up with the Gravatar service. And unless your visitors are web nerds, they probably haven't signed up yet—in fact, they probably haven't even heard of Gravatar.

However, this dilemma isn't as bad as it seems, for the following reasons:

- **Gravatars are optional.** Some people use them, others don't. There's no downside to allowing gravatars on your site. And if someone notices that another commenter gets a personalized picture, that person just might ask about how to get the same feature.
- **Gravatars can be auto-generated.** As page 267 explains, you can replace the boring gray silhouettes for non-Gravatar users with an auto-generated gravatar. The neat thing about auto-generated gravatars is that they're unique *and* consistent, which means they can help people identify comments left by the same person.
- **Gravatar can coexist with Facebook and Twitter pictures.** As you'll learn on page 270, you can get comment pictures from Facebook and Twitter accounts. In this case, Gravatar is just one more picture-gathering option that works in harmony with the others.
- **Gravatars have WordPress.com support.** WordPress.com users are more likely to have gravatars than other people, because the Gravatar service is integrated with the WordPress.com profile feature. If you're a WordPress.com fan, choose Users→My Profile from the dashboard to set your gravatar quickly and painlessly.
- **You can remind your readers to get a gravatar.** If you run a self-hosted site, you can edit the *comments.php* file in your theme (page 487) to add a reminder, like a link that says "Sign up for a Gravatar and get a personalized picture next to your comment." Just don't expect that many people will follow your recommendation.

Signing Up with Gravatar

If *you* aren't a Gravatar fan yet, here's how you sign up:

1. **Go to *http://gravatar.com* and click the Create Your Own Gravatar button.**

   The sign-up page appears.

2. **If you already have a WordPress.com account, you can use that with Gravatar. Click "I already have a WordPress.com account."**

   You'll need to fill in your email address and password, and click Authorize to link everything up. Then skip to step 4.

3. **If you don't have a WordPress.com account, you can sign up now. Fill in your email address, pick a user name and a password, and then click the "Sign up" button.**

   When you get the confirmation email, click the activation link inside to complete the signup.

4. **If you haven't already done so, sign in to Gravatar with your email address and password.**

   You arrive at the Manage Gravatars page, which informs you that you don't yet have any images associated with your account.

5. **Click the "Add one" link.**

   Gravatar gives you a number of ways to find an image. You can upload it from your computer's hard drive (the first, and most common, option), snag it from a website, or snap a new one with a webcam (assuming you have one).

6. **Click the appropriate button for your image (for example, "My computer's hard drive") and follow the instructions to find and crop your picture.**

   Gravatars are square. You can use an image as big as 512 × 512 pixels, and Gravatar will shrink it down to a thumbnail-size tile and display it next to each comment you leave.

7. **Choose a rating for your Gravatar (see Figure 8-15).**

   Ordinarily, WordPress sites show only gravatars that have a G rating. If you want to tolerate more friskiness on your site, go to Settings→Discussion. Scroll to the Avatars section and ratchet up the Maximum Rating setting to PG, R, or X.

TIP Are you concerned about inappropriate gravatars? You can disable gravatars altogether from the Settings→Discussion page. In the Avatars section, turn on the "Don't show Avatars" radio button.

Choose a rating for your Gravatar
By clicking on one of these ratings

rated
G

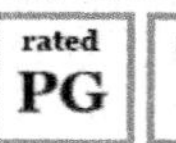
rated
PG

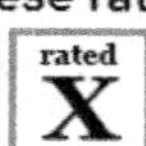
rated
R
rated
X
A G rated gravatar is suitable for display on all websites with any audience type.
PG rated gravatars may contain rude gestures, provocatively dressed individuals, the lesser swear words, or mild violence.
R rated gravatars may contain such things as harsh profanity, intense violence, nudity, or hard drug use.
X rated gravatars may contain hardcore sexual imagery or extremely disturbing violence.

FIGURE 8-15

Some sites may not display gravatars that are mildly naughty (PG), violent or sexually explicitly (R), or over-the-top disturbing (X). It's up to you to pick the rating that represents your image best, but if you use an ordinary headshot, G is the right choice.

8. **Now Gravatar associates your avatar with your email address.**

   All new comments you leave will include your new picture, and comments you already left will get it, too (assuming you haven't changed your email address since you posted the comment). If, in the future, you decide you want a different picture, log back into Gravatar and upload a new one.

Changing the "Mystery Man" Gravatar

Ordinarily, if a commenter doesn't have a gravatar, WordPress displays the infamous gray silhouette that it calls Mystery Man. You can replace Mystery Man with one of several other pictures from the Settings→Discussion page. Scroll down to the Avatars section and change the Default Avatar option.

The alternate possibilities include no image at all (select Blank from the Default Avatar list) or a stock Gravatar logo (select Gravatar Logo). More interestingly, you can give mystery commenters a tailor-made, unique gravatar (for your site only). WordPress creates it by taking your guest's email address, using it to generate some semi-random computer gibberish, and then translating that into a specific type of picture. You can choose from four auto-generated gravatar types: Identicon (geometric patterns), Wavatar (cartoon-like faces), MonsterID (whimsical monster drawings), and Retro (video-game-style pixelated icons). Figure 8-16 shows two examples.

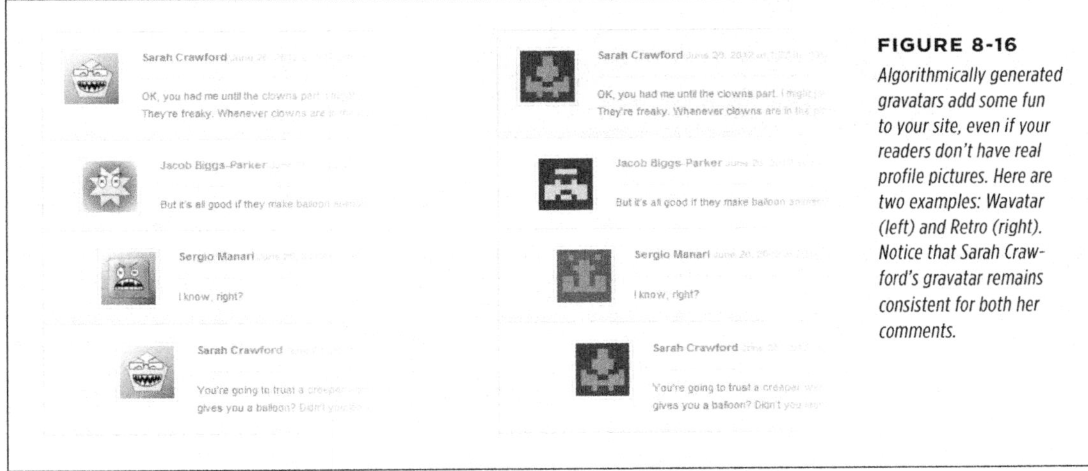

FIGURE 8-16
Algorithmically generated gravatars add some fun to your site, even if your readers don't have real profile pictures. Here are two examples: Wavatar (left) and Retro (right). Notice that Sarah Crawford's gravatar remains consistent for both her comments.

Gravatar Hovercards

The tiny comment pictures that Gravatar provides add a personal touch to your comments section, but the service can provide more than just pictures. It can also smuggle in a bit of personal information about each commenter. This information shows up as a *hovercard*—a small box that pops up when someone points to an avatar (Figure 8-17).

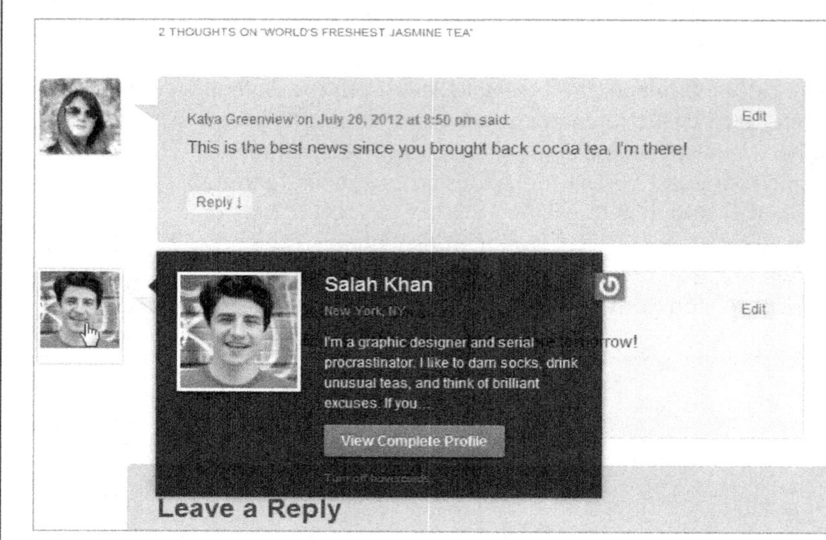

FIGURE 8-17

A hovercard is like a virtual business card. It displays your personal information, no matter what Gravatar-enabled site you visit. (If you're curious about what happens when you click View Complete Profile, jump ahead to Figure 8-19.)

But there's a catch: Hovercards appear only if your site runs on WordPress.com, or if you're a self-hoster using Jetpack (the ridiculously useful free plug-in you'll learn to install on page 297). If you meet one of these requirements, your comments probably display hovercards already. To check, choose Settings→Discussion, scroll down to the Avatars section, and make sure the checkbox next to "View people's profiles when you mouse over their Gravatars" is turned on. (If you run a self-hosted site but don't have Jetpack installed, you won't see this setting and you won't be able to use hovercards.)

Hovercards are a small but nice feature. They help readers learn a little bit about your commenters. You might assume that the hovercard details are part of your visitor's WordPress profile, but they're not. (In fact, hovercards work even if guests don't have a WordPress account.) Instead, hovercards get their information from the profile that Gravatar users optionally set up.

This design is both good and bad. The advantage is that it makes hovercard information portable—it travels with the avatar, no matter what Gravatar-enabled site you visit (even if the site *doesn't* run WordPress). The disadvantage is that if your readers don't bother to fill out the profile information, hovercards won't appear at all (Figure 8-18).

To make sure *your* hovercard looks good, you need to fill in the profile information, too. Visit the Gravatar site (*http://gravatar.com*), click the My Account button, and then choose Edit My Profile. There's plenty of information you can fill in, but the details that appear on the hovercard are your full name (Display Name), where you live (Location), and a short blurb that describes yourself (About Me), which the hovercard truncates after the first couple of sentences. When you finish, click Save Profile to store your information with your Gravatar, allowing it to appear on hovercard-supporting sites everywhere.

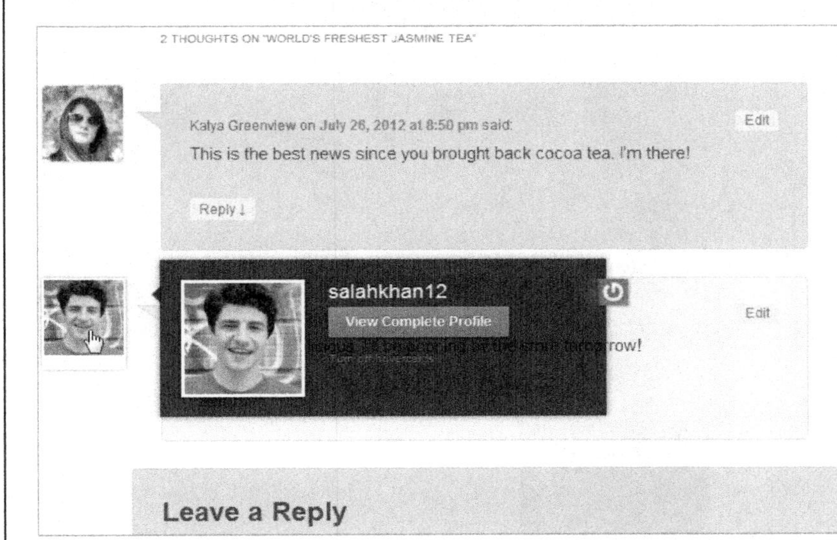

FIGURE 8-18

Hovercards are a whole lot less impressive when visitors don't bother to fill out their Gravatar profiles.

GEM IN THE ROUGH

Gravatar Verified Services

As you've seen, the Gravatar service is more than just a way to display your picture on different websites. It's also a way for you to store a mini-profile with a bio, some basic personal details, and links to all the Gravatar-enabled websites you use.

This last part is one of Gravatar's niftier features. It lets you add links in your Gravatar profile that point to other social websites or blogging services you belong to. For example, you can add links to your Facebook or Twitter accounts. Or you can include a link to your photos on Flickr, your videos on YouTube or Vimeo, your blog on WordPress (or Blogger, or Tumblr), and your accounts on many other social sites.

When you first sign up with Gravatar, it doesn't include any of these links. You need to add them by editing your Gravatar profile from the Verified Services section. Choose a service from the list (like Facebook), and then click Add. Gravatar asks you to sign in to set up the link. (This is why Gravatar calls them *verified* services—it doesn't actually add the link unless you verify that it truly belongs to you.)

In the past, when you added a verified service, Gravatar included a tiny icon for it in your hovercard (which was quite cool and very convenient). Sadly, Gravatar no longer takes this step, possibly to prevent spammers from abusing hovercards. However, verified service links still appear in a clearly visible place on the Gravatar profile page (Figure 8-19). To see them, click the View Complete Profile button that appears in every hovercard (Figure 8-17).

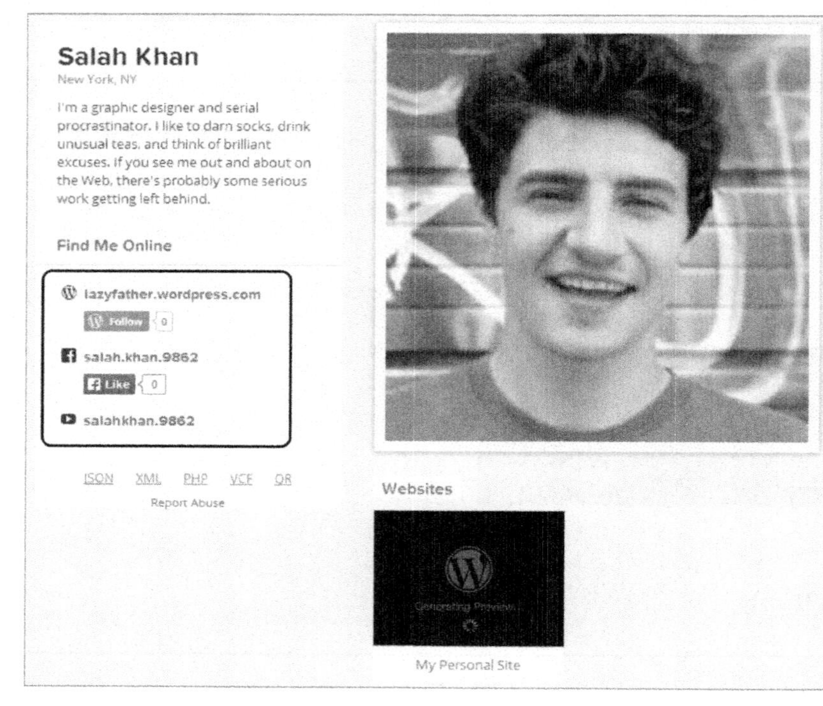

FIGURE 8-19
Salah Khan has three verified services with Gravatar: a WordPress.com blog, a Facebook account, and a YouTube account.

Facebook and Twitter Comments

Gravatars are a great idea, but they might not be practical for your site because people might not bother to use them (or they might not even realize *how* to use them). No matter—you can give visitors other comment options. For example, you can let them log into your site using their Facebook or Twitter credentials, and then post a comment. In such a case, WordPress grabs your guest's Facebook or Twitter profile picture and displays it next to that person's comments (Figure 8-20).

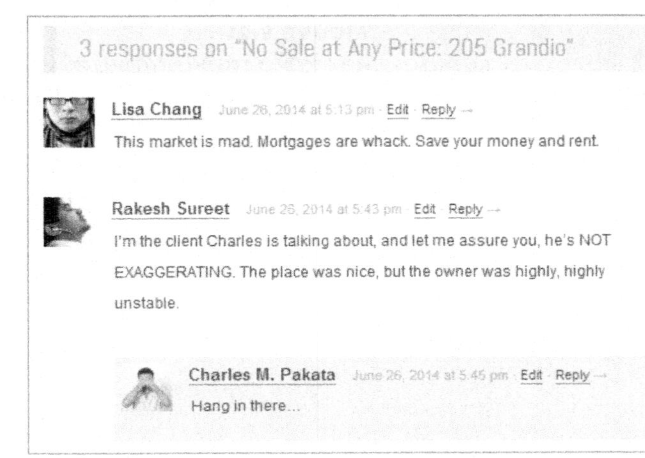

3 responses on "No Sale at Any Price: 205 Grandio"
Lisa Chang June 26, 2014 at 5:13 pm · Edit · Reply →
This market is mad. Mortgages are whack. Save your money and rent.
Rakesh Sureet June 26, 2014 at 5:43 pm · Edit · Reply →
I'm the client Charles is talking about, and let me assure you, he's NOT EXAGGERATING. The place was nice, but the owner was highly, highly unstable.
Charles M. Pakata June 26, 2014 at 5:45 pm · Edit · Reply →
Hang in there...

FIGURE 8-20

In this example, Charles Pakata is a WordPress.com user who has signed up with the Gravatar service. But Lisa and Rakesh are Facebook users. As long as they log into Facebook, WordPress uses their Facebook profile pictures, without forcing them to sign up with Gravatar or take any extra steps.

If your site runs on WordPress.com, you already have the Facebook and Twitter sign-in feature, and there's no way to switch it off.

If you run a self-hosted blog, the best way to get Facebook and Twitter comments is with the Jetpack plug-in (page 297). However, you won't be able to see the comments until you explicitly enable them. To do that, click Jetpack in the dashboard menu. Look for the box named "Jetpack Comments," and then click the Activate button inside (Figure 8-21). Incidentally, this setting isn't just for Facebook and Twitter users—it also lets anyone with a Google+ or WordPress.com account join in.

TIP You might find that once you enable Jetpack comments, your comment section gets a new background that doesn't blend in with the rest of your page. To fix this, choose Settings→Discussion, scroll down to the Jetpack Comments section, and try different options under Color Scheme. You can pick Light, Dark, or Transparent; finding the best fit is a trial-and-error process.

FIGURE 8-21

A self-hosted site doesn't get Jetpack comments unless you install the plug-in and specifically opt in by clicking the Activate button shown here. To turn Jetpack comments off, you need to return to this box, click Learn More, and then click Deactivate.

Some people turn on Facebook and Twitter comments and enable the "Users must be registered and logged in to comment" setting (which you can find at Settings→Discussion). This creates a site that *requires* commenters to provide a social identity. When a site owner takes this step, he's usually thinking something like this:

> "I've been flexible, and now I want something in return. I've given my readers several good options for establishing their identity (Facebook, Twitter, Google+, and WordPress.com). By making them use one, I can lock out spammers and force people to bring their virtual identities to my site."

Think carefully before you take this step. First, it only partly protects your site against spam, because many spambots have fake Facebook identities. Second, it guarantees that you'll scare away at least some potential commenters, including those who don't have a social media account, those who can't be bothered to log in, and those who don't want to reveal their social identities to you.

Stamping Out Comment Spam

So far, you've focused on the comments that are *supposed* to be on your site—the ones your visitors leave in response to your posts. Up to now, this discussion has skirted a disquieting fact: On the average WordPress site, spam comments outweigh legit comments by a factor of 10 to 1. And spammers don't discriminate—they don't attempt to chase the most popular blogs or the ones that cover their favorite topics. Instead, they spew their dreck everywhere.

Understanding Spam

You're no doubt familiar with the idea of email spam—trashy chain letters and hoaxes that try to get you to download malware or send your banking information to a Nigerian gentleman with a cash flow problem. Blog spam is a different creature altogether. While email spam tries to lure you in, blog spam tries to slip right past you. That's because blog spammers aren't after you—they're targeting your *readers*. The goal is for them to sneak their advertisements onto your site, where they can attract the attention of people who already trust your blog. Every bit of blog spam is trying to lure a reader to travel to the spammer's site, either by clicking the commenter's name or a link in the comment text.

In the past, spammers were crude and their messages easy to identify. Today, they're trickier than ever. They attempt to disguise themselves as actual readers to fool you into allowing their comment (with its link to their site). Or they pretend to sell real products (which they never deliver). And spammers hire low-paid workers to hand-write spam messages and circumvent safeguards against spambots, like Captchas (page 280).

Some WordPressers tell horror stories of receiving hundreds or thousands of spam messages a day. The problem is severe enough that, if you're not careful, you can wind up spending more time dealing with spam than managing the rest of your site. Fortunately, you can use the tools and strategies discussed below to fight back.

UP TO SPEED

Caught in the Wild

Spammers take great care to make their messages look as natural as possible. The spammer's payload is a link, which is submitted with the comment and hidden behind the commenter's name.

Here are some of the spam messages that we caught on this book's example sites. Would any have fooled you?

"Glad to know about something like this."

"Perhaps this is one of the most interesting blogs that i have ever seen. interesting article, funny comment. keep it up!"

"i was exactly talking about this with a friend yesterday, and now i found about it in your blog. this is awesome."

"Could you tell me when you're going to update your posts?"

"I've also been thinking the identical thing myself lately. Grateful to see another person on the same wavelength! Nice article."

"We're a bunch of volunteers and opening a brand new scheme in our community. Your site offered us with valuable info to paintings on. You have done an impressive job and our whole community can be grateful to you."

Spam-Fighting Strategies

You can defend against spam in several ways:

- **Forbidding all comments.** This is obviously a drastic, ironclad approach. To disable comments, you turn off the "Allow people to post comments on new articles" checkbox on the Settings→Discussion page. But be warned that if you do, you'll sacrifice the lively conversation your visitors expect.

  Verdict: An extreme solution. The cure is worse than the disease.

- **Using moderation.** This is the default WordPress approach, and it's the one you learned about in this chapter. The problem is that you just can't keep moderating a site that's growing in size and popularity—it becomes too labor-intensive. It also has a distinct drawback: It forces commenters to wait before their comment appears on your site, by which point they may have lost interest in the conversation.

  Verdict: Not practical in the long term, unless you combine it with a spam-catching tool (like Akismet, which you'll meet in a moment).

- **Forcing commenters to log in (for self-hosted sites only).** To use this approach, you need to add each visitor's ID to your WordPress site, or create some way for them to register on your site themselves. This approach definitely isn't suitable for the average public blog. However, it may work if you have a small, captive audience—for example, if you're building a site for family members only, or for a team of coworkers.

  Verdict: For special cases only. You'll learn about multiuser blogs in Chapter 11.

- **Making commenters log in, but allowing third-party log-ins.** A third-party login verifies your guests through an authentication service—typically one provided by WordPress.com, Facebook, or Twitter. This requirement may work, because many people already have Facebook or Twitter accounts that they don't mind using (whereas they definitely won't bother creating a new account just to leave a single comment). Still, forcing logins may drive away as many as half of your would-be commenters. And it's still not truly spam-proof, because clever spam-bots can create Facebook accounts, just like real people can.

  Verdict: A good idea, but not a complete spam-fighting solution.

- **Using Akismet or another spam-catching plug-in.** Many WordPress administrators swear that their lives would not be livable without the automatic spam-detecting feature of Akismet. It isn't perfect—some site owners complain that legitimate comments get trashed, and they need to spend serious time fishing them out of the spam bucket—but it usually gives the best spam protection with the minimum amount of disruption to the commenting process.

  Verdict: The best compromise. It's also essential if you turn off moderation.

The pros and cons of managing comments by moderation versus spam-fighting are a lot to digest, even for seasoned webheads. But the evidence is clear: Most WordPress pros eventually start using a spam-catching tool. They may use it in addition to moderation, or—more likely—instead of it.

NOTE If you don't have a spam filter, *you* are the spam filter. And given that an ordinary WordPress site can attract dozens of spam messages a day, you don't want to play that role.

If you're ready to ditch comment moderation in favor of a livelier, more responsive, and less controlled discussion, choose Settings→Discussion and turn off the checkboxes next to these settings: "An administrator must always approve the comment" and "Comment author must have a previously approved comment." Then click Save Changes at the bottom of the page.

Now continue to the next section to make sure you have a proper spam-blocker in place.

POWER USERS' CLINIC

WordPress's Other Spam-Catching Options

WordPress has a few built-in spam-fighting options on the Settings→Discussion page. In the past, they were a practical line of defense that could intercept and stop a lot of junk comments. Unfortunately, spamming evolved in the intervening years, and now these settings are only occasionally useful. They include:

- **"Hold a comment in the queue if it contains 2 or more links."** Use this setting to catch posts that have a huge number of links. The problem is that spammers are on to this restriction, so they've toned down their links to make their spam look more like real comments.
- **The Comment Moderation and Comment Blacklist boxes.** Try these boxes, described earlier (page 253), as a way to keep out offensive text. They also double as a way to catch spam. However, don't rush to put in obvious spammy keywords, because you'll just end up doing a clumsier version of what Akismet already does. Instead, consider using these boxes if you have a spam problem that's specific to your site—for example, a certain keyword that keeps coming up when spammers target your posts.
- **"Automatically close comments on articles older than 14 days."** Unless you set it, this option isn't switched on. However, it's a potentially useful way to stop spammers from targeting old posts, where the conversation has long since died down. And you don't need to stick to the suggested 14 days. You can type in any number, even making the lockout period start a year after you publish a post.

Understanding Akismet

Akismet is one of many spam-fighting plug-ins developers created for WordPress. However, it has a special distinction: Automattic, the same folks who built WordPress, makes it. It's also the only spam-blocking tool with which WordPress.com blogs work.

Akismet works by intercepting each new comment. It sends the details of that comment (including its text and the commenter's website, email, and IP addresses) to one of Akismet's web servers. There, the server analyzes it, using some crafty code and a secret spam-fighting database, to attempt to determine whether it's legitimate. Any one of a number of details can betray a spam message, including links to known spam sites, a known spammer IP address, phrases commonly found in spam messages ("free Viagra" for instance), and so on. Akismet quickly makes its decision and reports back to your website. Your site then either publishes the comment or puts it in the Spam folder, depending on Akismet's judgment.

WordPress experts report that Akismet's success rate hovers at around 97 percent. Usually, when Akismet errs, it does so by flagging a safe comment as spam (rather than allowing real spam through). However, Akismet's success depends on the site and the timing. When spammers adjust their tactics, it may take Akismet a little time to catch up, during which its accuracy will drop.

Akismet is free, mostly. Personal sites pay nothing (unless you volunteer a small donation). However, small businesses and money-making blogs are expected to contribute $5 per month. Large publishers that want to spam-proof multiple sites are asked for $50 a month.

NOTE Akismet uses an honor system, and there are plenty of sites that earn a bit of money but don't pay the Akismet fee. If you want a totally free business-friendly solution for a self-hosted site, you need to find a different plug-in. Several good alternatives are described in the box below.

FREQUENTLY ASKED QUESTION

Akismet Alternatives

I need a spam-catching tool, but I don't want Akismet. Are there other options?

If you run a self-hosted WordPress site, there's no shortage of spam-fighting plug-ins. Unlike Akismet, many are free for almost everyone. (Some plug-in developers collect donations, charge for only the highest-traffic sites, or make extra money charging support fees to big companies. Others do it simply for the prestige.)

Two caveats apply. First, if you plan to use Jetpack's social commenting feature (page 270), which lets visitors comment using their Facebook and Twitter identities, your options are limited. Currently, Akismet is the only spam fighter that works with these identities.

Second, it's impossible to know which anti-spam tool is the best for your site—you need to try them out yourself. Anti-spam developers and spammers are locked in an ever-escalating arms race. The spam blocker that works perfectly this week might falter the next week when clever spammers work around its detection rules.

Three good Akismet alternatives include:

- Anti-spam (*http://tinyurl.com/wp-anti-spam*)
- Antispam Bee (*http://antispambee.com*)
- AVH First Defense Against Spam (*http://tinyurl.com/avhspam*)

To try one of these out, install it using WordPress's plug-in feature. But before you do, skip ahead to the basics of plug-in management described in Chapter 9.

Installing Akismet

If your site is on WordPress.com, you're already using Akismet, and there's no way to turn it off. As soon as you turn off comment moderation, you leave the entire process in Akismet's hands. (Skip ahead to the next section to learn more about that.) If you have a self-hosted site, there's a little more to Akismet's setup. The plug-in is so valuable that Automattic bundles a copy with every WordPress site. However, it isn't activated, which means it's just an idle file sitting on your web server. To make Akismet spring to life, you need to sign up for an Akismet key and activate the plug-in. Here's how:

1. **First, you need an *Akismet key.* To get that, head to *http://akismet.com/wordpress.***

   You can think of the Akismet key as a license to use Akismet on your site.

2. **Click "Get An Akismet API Key."**

   The sign-up page appears.

3. **If you already have a WordPress.com account, you can use that login information with Akismet. Click "I already have a WordPress.com account."**

   You'll need to fill in your email address and password, and click Authorize to link everything up. Then skip to step 5.

NOTE Remember, if you use any of the other services Automattic provides, such as Gravatar for comment pictures (page 263) or the Jetpack plug-in (page 297), then you already have a WordPress.com account linked to your email address.

4. **If you don't have a WordPress.com account, you can sign up now. Fill in your email address, pick a user name and a password, and then click the "Sign up" button.**

   When you get the confirmation email, click the activation link inside to complete the signup.

5. **If you haven't already done so, sign in to Akismet with your email address and password.**

   Before Akismet will give you a key, it checks to see if you're willing to pay for the privilege.

   Akismet shows three sign-up options (Figure 8-22), depending on the type of site you have. It may also offer you the chance to buy Akismet in a bundle with VaultPress, a WordPress backup tool described on page 312.

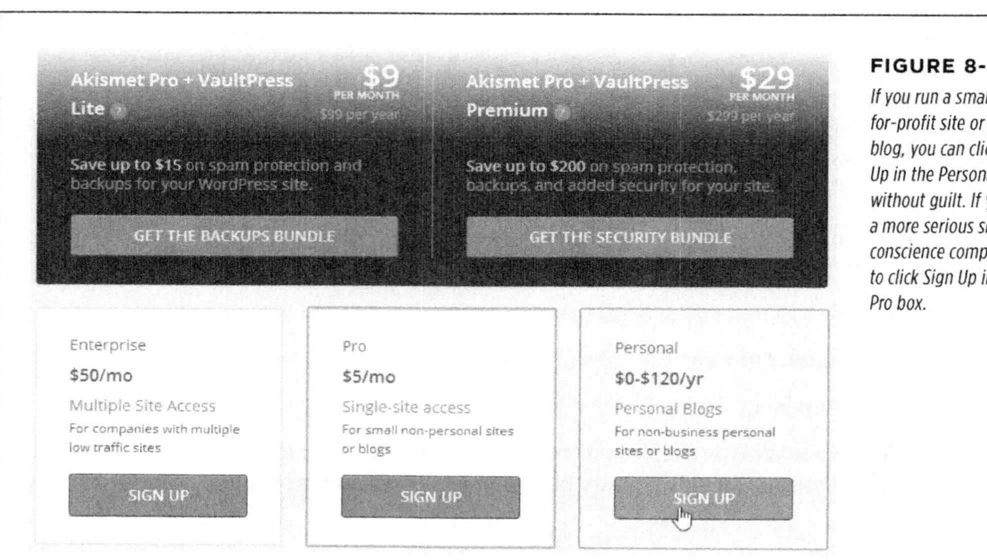

FIGURE 8-22

If you run a small, not-for-profit site or personal blog, you can click Sign Up in the Personal box without guilt. If you have a more serious site, your conscience compels you to click Sign Up in the Pro box.

6. **Click the appropriate Sign Up button.**

   If you picked the personal plan, Akismet still asks for a donation (Figure 8-23). You choose an amount using a slider below the question "What is Akismet worth to you?" (In fairness to freeloaders everywhere, it's difficult to answer this question *before* you actually start using Akismet.)

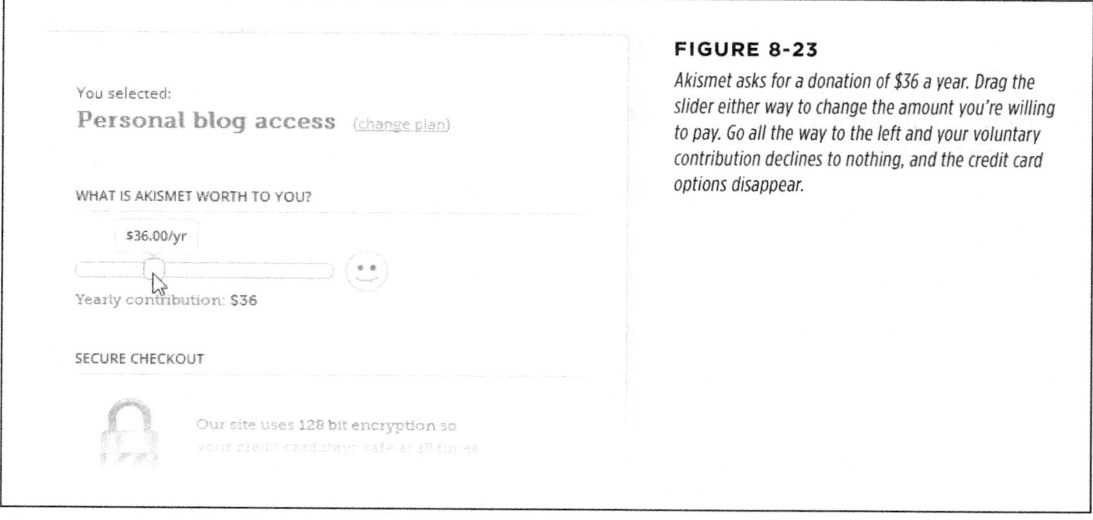

FIGURE 8-23

Akismet asks for a donation of $36 a year. Drag the slider either way to change the amount you're willing to pay. Go all the way to the left and your voluntary contribution declines to nothing, and the credit card options disappear.

7. **Fill in your name and click Continue.**

   If you elected to pay for Akismet, you need to enter your credit card or PayPal information as well.

8. **Shortly thereafter, you'll receive an email message with your Akismet key in it.**

   It's a funny-looking code, like 0286f4c389b2. Make note of it, because you'll need it in a few steps.

9. **Return to your site's dashboard, and then choose Plugins→Installed Plugins.**

   You'll see a list of plug-ins, with Akismet at the top.

NOTE You'll learn far more about plug-ins, including how to manage them and how to find more, in the next chapter. But for now, these steps walk you through the very simple process of activating the Akismet plug-in you already have.

10. **Point (without clicking) to Akismet, and click the Activate link that appears.**

    At this point, WordPress shows a message at the top of the Plugins page with an activation button.

11. **Click the "Activate your Akismet account" button and then click the "I already have a key" link.**

    This brings you to the page where you enter your Akismet key.

12. **Copy the key from your email message and then paste it into the text box (Figure 8-24).**

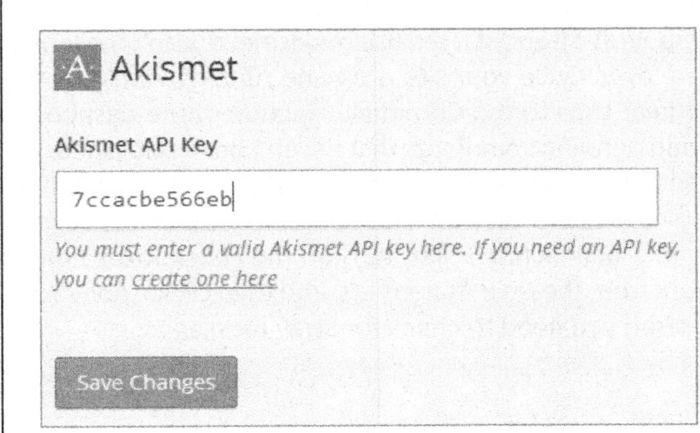

FIGURE 8-24

Before Akismet can start catching spam, it needs your API key, which looks like the series of letters and numbers shown here.

13. **Click Save Changes.**

    Akismet displays a message that confirms that everything worked out and your setup is complete. It also displays two optional settings that you can tweak:

    - **"Auto-delete spam submitted on posts more than a month old"** tells Akismet to periodically delete old messages in your spam folder, whether you reviewed them or not. This is generally a good idea, because it prevents your site from collecting thousands of spam comments that will swell up your WordPress database to an ungainly size. (The box on page 282 has more about the problem.)
    - **"Show the number of comments you've approved beside each comment author"** tells Akismet to add an extra piece of information to the comments list in the dashboard. This is a count with the number of comments you previously approved from each would-be commenter. Presumably, if you've approved plenty of messages from the same person, you can trust their newest contributions.

    To revise these settings later, head to the Plugins→Akismet section of the dashboard.

Using Akismet

Akismet integrates so seamlessly into WordPress's comment system that you might not even realize it's there. It takes over the comments list, automatically moving suspicious comments to the spam folder and publishing everything else.

To give Akismet a very simple test, sign out of your site, and then try adding a few comments. If you enter ordinary text, the comment should sail through without a hiccup. But type in something like "Viagra! Cialis!!" and Akismet will quietly dispose of your comment.

Just because you disabled moderation and started using Akismet doesn't mean your comment-reviewing days are over. Once your site is up and running with Akismet, you should start making regular trips to the Comments section of the dashboard. Only now, instead of reviewing pending comments that haven't been published, you should click the Spam link and check for any valid comments that were accidentally removed. If you find one, point to it and click the Not Spam link. If you find several, you can restore them all with a bulk action—first, turn on the checkboxes next to the comments, pick Not Spam from the Bulk Actions list, and then click Apply. You'll soon get a feeling for how often you need to check for stray messages.

Fighting Spam with CAPTCHA

Some WordPress administrators find that a traditional spam-analysis tool like Akismet isn't enough to stop the inevitable avalanche of spam. Others find that Akismet consistently flags good comments as spam, creating a different sort of comment-moderation headache. If you're in the first camp, you might want to supplement Akismet with something else. If you're in the second camp, you might want to try switching Akismet off and plugging the hole with a different tool.

Either way, one good candidate is a Captcha (which computer nerds translate into the phrase "Completely Automated Public Turing test to tell Computers and Humans Apart"). The idea behind Captcha technology is to force commenters to do something that automated spam-bots can't, at least not easily. If you've ever registered with a site that asks you to retype a set of fuzzy letters or distorted words, you've seen Captcha in action. Facebook, Hotmail, and Gmail all use it, for example.

The problem with Captchas is twofold. First, there's no Captcha that's too hard for some spambot to crack. Second, there's no Captcha that's so easy that it won't annoy your readers, at least a little. But if you use an easy, unobtrusive Captcha, you just might be able to reduce spam to more manageable proportions, without annoying your visitors too much. (Hint: You don't want to use the fuzzy letter system.)

To add a Captcha, you need to be running a self-hosted WordPress site, and you need to add a plug-in. If you search the WordPress plug-in repository, you'll find dozens. Here are three worth considering:

- **Growmap Anti-Spambot** (*http://tinyurl.com/growmapspam*). This is almost the simplest Captcha you can use. It simply asks the commenter to check a checkbox. Thus, it annoys almost no one but still trips up the majority of automated spam-bots.
- **CAPTCHA** (*http://tinyurl.com/wp-captcha*). This generically named plug-in lets you use simple math questions, like "seven + 1." Yes, shockingly enough, some would-be commenters will still manage to get these questions wrong. However, it won't drive visitors away as quickly as a fuzzy-word-reading test.
- **Anti-CAPTCHA** (*http://tinyurl.com/wp-anticaptcha*). This plug-in performs an invisible test. Essentially, it asks a guest's web browser to run a snippet of JavaScript. That snippet then sets a hidden value in the web page. Automated spam-bots usually ignore JavaScript code, so they won't be able to set the hidden value that Anti-CAPTCHA looks for, and thus they'll fail the test. Overall, this plug-in catches the least amount of spam, but it presents no inconvenience to your readers.

Remember, CAPTCHA isn't foolproof. It won't stop human spammers (who typically account for less than 10 percent of all spam), and it won't stop the sneakiest spam-bots. However, it can reduce the total amount of spam enough to improve your life.

TROUBLESHOOTING MOMENT

What to Do When Your Blog is Buried in Pending Comments

Spammy comments are a danger to any blog. If visitors find your site choked with spam, they're far less likely to keep reading or make a return visit.

But even if spam comments aren't approved, they can still pose a problem for your site. First, they clog your Comments page in the dashboard, making it harder for you to find the real comments. And because WordPress stores them in its database, they can bloat it with meaningless content, wasting space on your web host and making it more difficult and time-consuming to back up your site.

The solution seems obvious—just delete all the spam—but it's not always so easy. If your site has the misfortune to fall victim to an automated spam-spewing tool, you can find yourself with thousands or even *hundreds of thousands* of spam comments in short order. (It's happened to us.) So what's a WordPress administrator to do?

If you use a spam-catching plug-in like Akismet, spam comments end up in the spam folder. The good news is that you can clean out all your spam with just a few clicks. In the dashboard menu, click Comments, and then click the Spam link at the top of the list. Finally, click the Empty Spam button. (Even better, get your spam catcher to automatically clean out old spam, as explained on page 280.)

If you're not using a spam-catching plug-in, you've got a bigger problem on your hands. That's because the spam comments will be pending comments, and the dashboard doesn't provide a way to delete a huge number of pending comments at once. Even bulk actions can act on no more than a single page of comments at a time. At that rate, deleting thousands of spam comments is a several-day affair.

There are two solutions. First, you can use a plug-in that removes all pending comments, such as WP-Optimize (*http://tinyurl.com/wp-opti*). Or, if you're a tech savvy person who's not intimidated by the idea of diving into your WordPress database and fiddling around, you can use a tool like phpMyAdmin to peer into your database and remove the junk. To get started in this endeavor, read the walkthrough at *http://tinyurl.com/deletepen2*.

PART

3

Supercharging Your Blog

CHAPTER

9

Getting New Features with Plug-Ins

WordPress offers an impressive set of built-in features. In the previous chapters, you used them to write posts and pages, and to glam up your site. But serious WordPress fans have a way to get even more from the program—or, technically, about 30,000 ways to get more, because that's how many free WordPress *plug-ins* you can use to supercharge your site.

Before you go any further, be aware of one critical point: WordPress plug-ins work on self-hosted WordPress sites *only*. If you use WordPress.com, you're not allowed to install even a single plug-in. This restriction isn't as bad as it seems, however, because WordPress.com already offers a number of extra features and preinstalled plug-ins, as chosen by the fine people at Automattic. For example, WordPress.com sites come with social media sharing buttons for Facebook and Twitter, while self-hosted WordPress sites need a plug-in to do the same thing. So even though WordPress.com users can't pack on new features, they do start off slightly ahead.

If you're a WordPress.com site builder, you don't need to go any further in this chapter. Skip ahead to Chapter 10 to keep using what you've got. But if you're running a self-hosted WordPress site, you need to know how to add plug-ins to make your site truly great. This chapter shows you how to find, evaluate, and install plug-ins, and then tweak their settings. You'll also explore several of WordPress's most popular and practical plug-ins, including:

- **Jetpack.** Automattic created this plug-in to give WordPress self-hosters most of the features available to WordPress.com sites, all in one easy step.
- **WPtouch.** This plug-in gives your site a mobile-friendly face-lift, so it looks great on smart devices, like iPhones and iPads.

- **Online Backup for WordPress.** Use this plug-in to help crash-proof your site.
- **WP Super Cache.** This popular plug-in uses clever caching tricks to boost the speed of heavily trafficked pages.

You'll see plenty more plug-ins in the following chapters, where you'll use them to solve problems, fill gaps, and add all sorts of frills.

Managing Plug-Ins

WordPress reserves a section of the dashboard for plug-ins: the predictably named Plugins menu. You get started by choosing Plugins→Installed Plugins to see a list of all the plug-ins installed on your website (Figure 9-1).

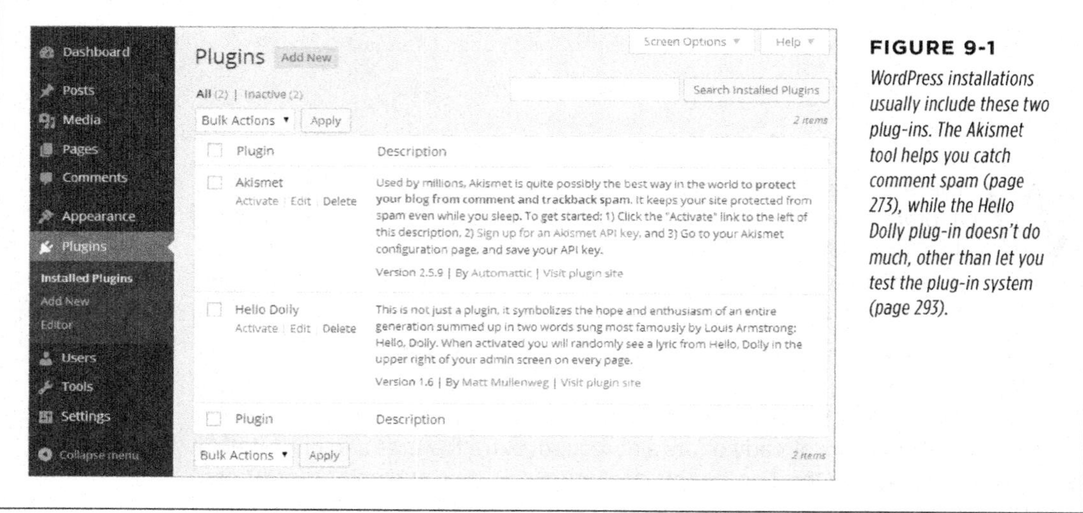

FIGURE 9-1

WordPress installations usually include these two plug-ins. The Akismet tool helps you catch comment spam (page 273), while the Hello Dolly plug-in doesn't do much, other than let you test the plug-in system (page 293).

Usually, the self-hosted version of WordPress comes with two plug-ins that are installed but not active. That means the plug-ins are sitting on your website, ready to be called into service, but that they're not actually doing anything yet. (It's the same as when you install a theme but don't activate it.) Some web hosts may top you up with a few extra plug-ins for security's sake (such as the Limit Login Attempts plug-in discussed on page 567). But to get the really good stuff, you need to install plug-ins on your own.

How Plug-Ins Work

Technically, a plug-in is a small program written in the same programming language (PHP) that runs the entire WordPress system.

Plug-ins work by inserting themselves into various WordPress operations. For example, before WordPress displays a post, it checks to see if you installed any plug-ins related to displaying posts. If you did, WordPress calls them into action. This sort of check is called a *hook*, and WordPress has a long list of hooks that launch plug-ins. A WordPress page can also use a special code, called a *template tag*, to ask a plug-in to insert something in a specific place on a page. Either way, the interaction between a WordPress site and its plug-ins happens behind the scenes, without your intervention.

Building plug-ins is a fairly ambitious task, because it requires programming skills and an intimate knowledge of the way WordPress works. Fortunately, there are plenty of good plug-ins you can use without writing a stitch of code. Most WordPress site owners spend a good deal of time picking the right plug-ins for their sites and tweaking them just so. Very few write their own.

NOTE To learn more about creating plug-ins, you probably want to finish this book first, paying particular attention to Part 4, where you'll take a peek at the PHP programming that holds WordPress together. Then you can continue with the somewhat terse WordPress plug-in documentation at *http://tinyurl.com/write-plugin*.

Searching for a Plug-In

The process of installing plug-ins is simply the process of copying the plug-in files to your site's plug-in directory, which WordPress names */wp-content/plugins*. For example, if you put WordPress on your site at *http://pancakesforever.com/news*, the plug-in folder is *http://pancakesforever.com/news/wp-content/plugins*. Of course, you don't need to worry about the exact location of the plug-in directory, because WordPress always puts plug-ins in the right place.

To install a plug-in, choose Plugins→Add New, which takes you to the Install Plugins page. Five links at the top of the page let you decide how to find the mini-program you want. These are your options:

- **Search.** If you can think of a keyword for the sort of WordPress plug-in you want (for example, "mobile" or "Twitter"), you can probably find it through a search. Type one or more keywords in the search box, and then click Search Plugins (as shown in Figure 9-2). Or click one of the links in the "Popular tags" section underneath, which displays the most common search keywords. Either way, WordPress scans its massive plug-in directory for matches.

NOTE Don't get confused by the fact that WordPress uses "plug-in directory" to refer to two things. First, there's your website's plug-in directory, which is the folder on your web server where WordPress stores the plug-in files for your website. Second, there's the official WordPress plug-in directory, which is the giant catalog of thousands of plug-ins you can download and install on your site.

- **Upload.** If you already downloaded a plug-in to your computer, all you need to do to use it is transfer it to your website. To do that, click the Upload link, browse to your plug-in ZIP file, and then choose Install Now. You use this technique if you create your own plug-in, or if you acquire a plug-in from somewhere other than WordPress's plug-in directory (for example, if you bought a commercial plug-in from a third party).
- **Featured, Popular, or Newest.** All these links let you *browse* the WordPress plug-in directory, which can help you discover plug-ins you might not know about. "Featured" shows useful plug-ins that WordPress has chosen to highlight, "Popular" includes the most downloaded plug-ins (ones that other people use), and "Newest" focuses on plug-ins that have been available for just a few days.
- **Favorites.** This link shows any plug-ins you previously flagged as your personal favorites. This is a handy feature if you like to browse plug-ins in WordPress's plug-in directory (*http://wordpress.org/plugins*), and install them later using your site's trusty dashboard. To get WordPress.org to store your favorites, you need to register first, which you can do by clicking the Register link on the plug-in repository (it appears next to the user name and password boxes).

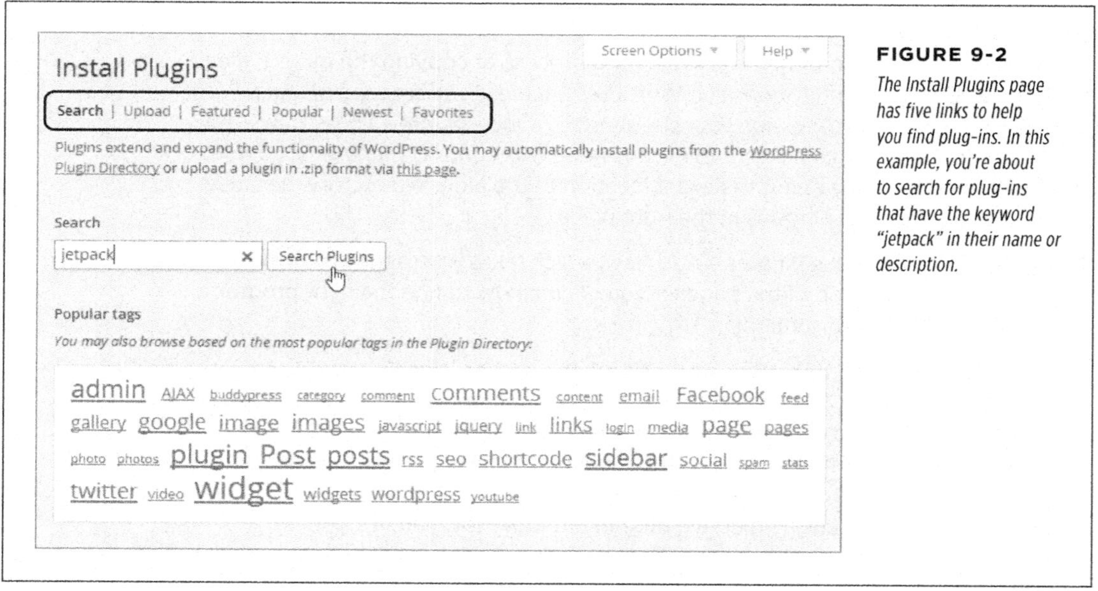

FIGURE 9-2

The Install Plugins page has five links to help you find plug-ins. In this example, you're about to search for plug-ins that have the keyword "jetpack" in their name or description.

The WordPress plug-in directory, with its staggering collection of more than 30,000 mini-programs, is the place most WordPress experts look for plug-ins first. If you search for plug-ins, WordPress shows you a list of programs that match your keywords (Figure 9-3). If you browse by category, like Featured or Newest, WordPress lists relevant plug-ins.

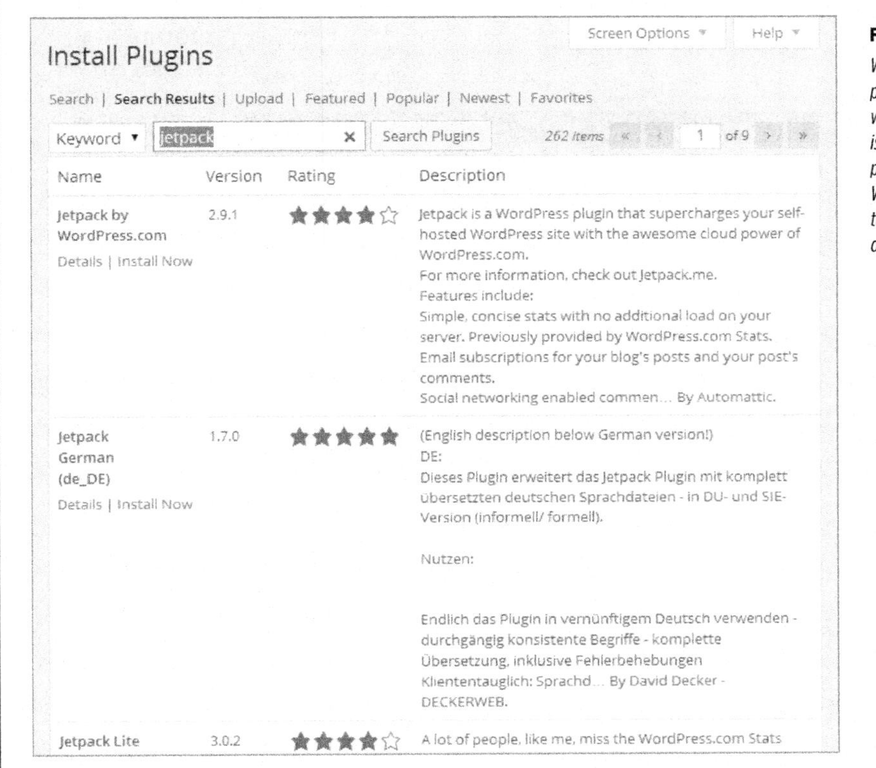

FIGURE 9-3

WordPress found 262 plug-ins that use the word "jetpack." The first is the official Jetpack plug-in, which adds WordPress.com features to self-hosted sites (as described on page 297).

The next step is to determine if you actually want to install the plug-in you found. Before you decide, it's worth clicking the Details link that appears under the plug-in name. That opens a window with extra information about the plug-in, including a more detailed list of its features, the current version number, the person who created it, its compatibility with different versions of WordPress, and the plug-in's rating (Figure 9-4).

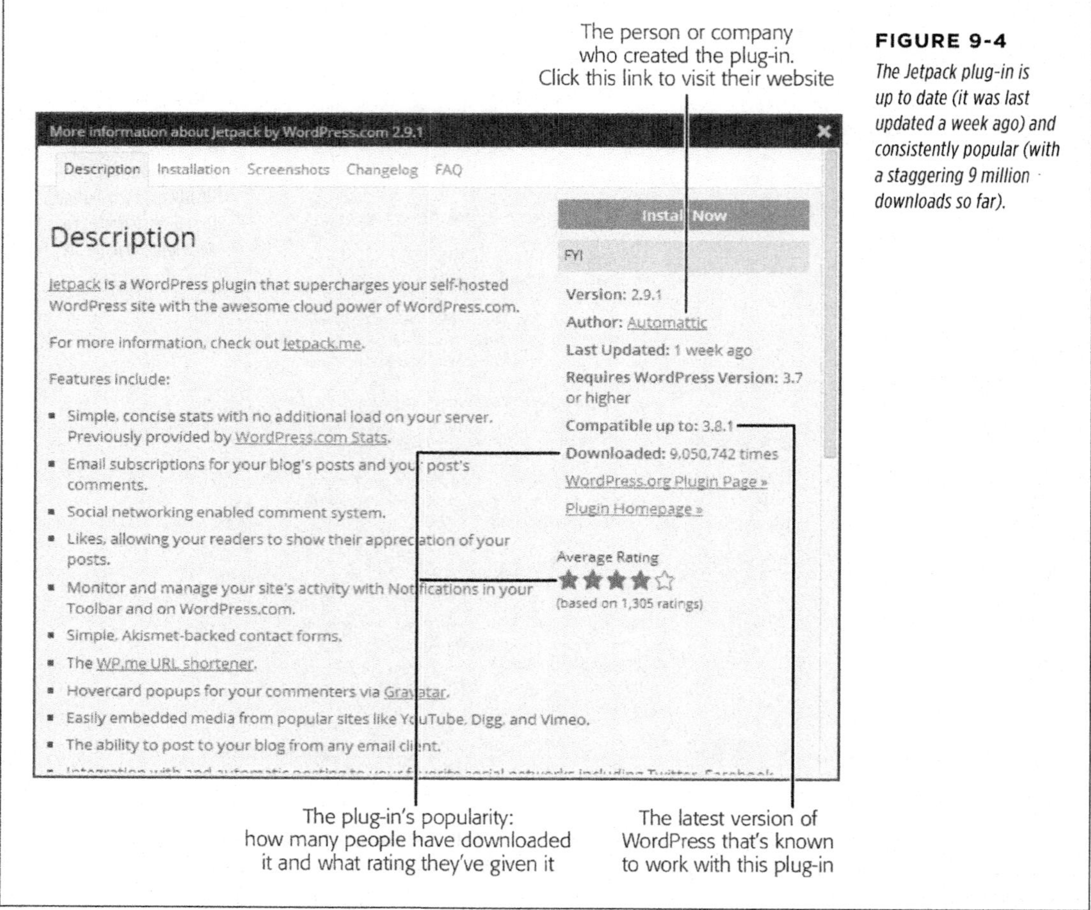

FIGURE 9-4

The Jetpack plug-in is up to date (it was last updated a week ago) and consistently popular (with a staggering 9 million downloads so far).

The most important information about a plug-in is its WordPress compatibility, which you determine by looking at three of the plug-in's characteristics:

- **Requires WordPress Version.** This tells you the minimum version of WordPress you need on your site to use this plug-in. Because you're a security-conscious webmaster who always makes sure your site runs the latest WordPress updates, this part isn't so important.

- **Compatible up to.** This tells you the *latest* version of WordPress that the plug-in works with. Sometimes, people create plug-ins, maintain them for a while, and then abandon them. The result is that the old plug-ins keep kicking around the WordPress plug-in directory, even though they're of no use to sites that use newer editions of WordPress. By checking the "Compatible up to" information, you can avoid these clunkers.

NOTE The "Compatible up to" information reflects only the latest version of WordPress that the plug-in creator has *tested*. It's not unusual for plug-ins to be slightly behind the times. For example, if WordPress 4.1 has just been released, a plug-in might claim support for up to WordPress 4.0 only. In this case, the plug-in is still likely to work on a WordPress 4.1 site.

- **Last Updated.** You may want to check this date as you try to avoid old and out-of-date plug-ins. Although old plug-ins sometimes keep working, it's best to stick with plug-ins that have been updated within the last year (at least). Regular maintenance also increases the chances that a plug-in is getting new features and fixes, which are two more attributes that make it a good candidate for your site.

If you're still not satisfied, you can click one of the other tabs in the "More information" window to get still more information about your plug-in. Initially, you start at the Description tab (Figure 9-4), but you may want to check out other tabs, too: Screenshots to get a feel for what the plug-in looks like, Changelog to see what changes or fixes have recently been made, and FAQ to read the answers to common webmaster questions.

You may also want to look for information about the plug-in on the author's page or website. You'll often find the author's blog, other plug-ins the author maintains, and some additional support information. To see, make sure you're on the Description tab and then click the author's name (which appears as a link in the information box, as shown in Figure 9-4).

TIP Finding a good plug-in requires a bit of detective work. If you find a few plug-ins that seem to offer the feature you need, compare them to see which has the highest number of downloads, the best star rating, and the most recent updates.

POWER USERS' CLINIC

WordPress Isn't the Last Word on Plug-Ins

The WordPress plug-in directory is the first and best place to look for plug-ins. It gives you thousands to choose from, and you can be reasonably certain they're safe and stable. And they'll always be free. (The most obvious disadvantage is that the WordPress plug-in repository is crowded with a number of out-of-date plug-ins, so you need to get good at sniffing out and avoiding these dead ends.)

However, there are also a number of companies that *sell* plug-ins. These for-pay plug-ins are sometimes called *premium plug-ins,* and they don't appear in the WordPress plug-in directory. Instead, you find them though a Google search, a friend who's in the know, a premium plug-in repository, or one of the many "Top WordPress Plug-In" articles. The problem with a premium plug-in (besides the fact that it costs money) is that you need to carefully scope out the company that makes it to make sure you aren't paying for a mediocre product or, even worse, a bit of malicious spamware that will compromise your site.

In this book, you'll stick to using free plug-ins from the WordPress directory. However, if you need something more (for example, if you're a professional WordPress site designer who's creating sites for other companies), you'll eventually want to check out the high-end plug-in market. You can get more information from an advanced WordPress and web design site like Smashing Magazine (*http://wp.smashingmagazine.com*) or by browsing a premium plug-in site like WPMU DEV (*http://premium.wpmudev.org*) or CodeCanyon (*http://codecanyon.net*). But remember, even though premium plug-ins cost money, they aren't necessarily better. Some of the best plug-ins in the industry are built by open-source developers and companies with WordPress-related businesses, and they don't ask for anything more than an optional donation.

Installing a Plug-In

If you decide to go ahead with a particular plug-in, installing it is simple. Just click the Install Now link, which appears next to each plug-in in your search results (Figure 9-3) and in the "More information" window (Figure 9-4). When WordPress prompts you to confirm your installation, click OK.

Typically, the installation takes just a matter of seconds. WordPress gives you minimal feedback as it grabs the plug-in's ZIP file, pulls all the plug-in files out of it, and transfers them to an ad hoc folder it creates on your website (Figure 9-5). For example, if you install Jetpack on the WordPress site *http://magicteahouse.net*, WordPress creates the folder *http://magicteahouse.net/wp-content/plugins/jetpack* for the plug-in files.

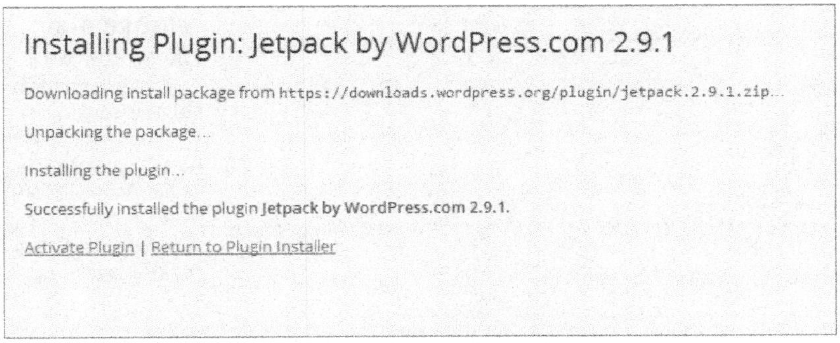

Installing Plugin: Jetpack by WordPress.com 2.9.1

Downloading install package from https://downloads.wordpress.org/plugin/jetpack.2.9.1.zip...

Unpacking the package...

Installing the plugin...

Successfully installed the plugin **Jetpack by WordPress.com 2.9.1**.

Activate Plugin | Return to Plugin Installer

FIGURE 9-5

This is what you see when you install Jetpack. To start using it, click Activate Plugin. To search for another plug-in, choose Return to Plugin Installer.

Activating a Plug-In

Plug-ins are like themes—you can install as many as you want, but they have no effect until you turn them on. One way to activate a plug-in is to click the Activate Plugin link that appears when you first install the mini-program (Figure 9-5). But if you want to activate a plug-in you already installed, go to Plugins→Installed Plugins to see a list of available programs. Then click the Activate link under the name of the plug-in you want to use. (If the plug-in is already active, you'll see a Deactivate link instead—click it to switch off the plug-in.)

You can't always tell what a newly activated plug-in is up to. Often, there'll be evidence that a plug-in is active somewhere in the dashboard, but every plug-in works differently. Some provide a new page of options in the dashboard menu, others add new widgets, some change the Add New Post or Edit Post pages, and some simply start doing their work quietly in the background.

In a newly created WordPress site, you start with two inactive plug-ins, as you saw back in Figure 9-1. To practice plug-in activation without risking anything on your site, you can activate the harmless (but also useless) Hello Dolly sample plug-in. When you switch it on, it adds a random lyric from Louis Armstrong's song "Hello, Dolly" to the top of every dashboard page (Figure 9-6).

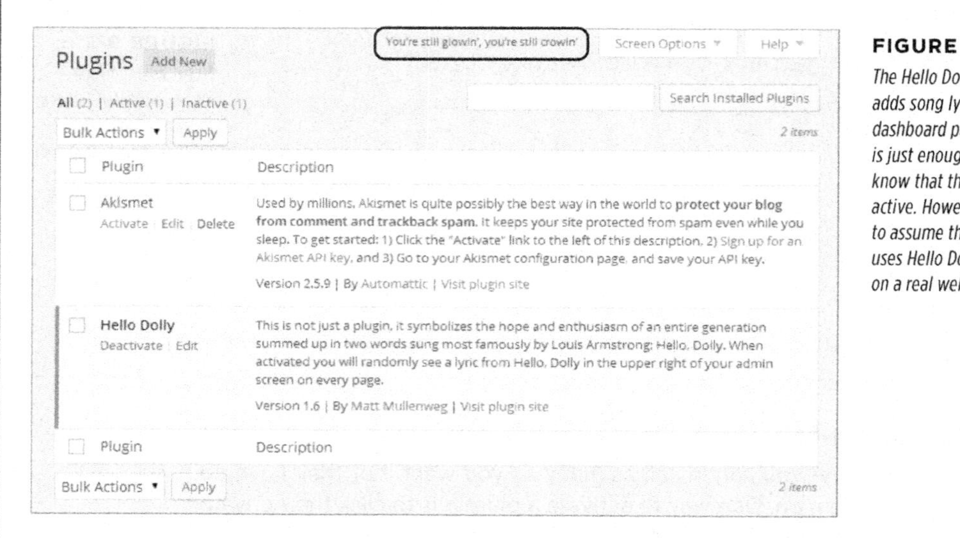

FIGURE 9-6

The Hello Dolly plug-in adds song lyrics to every dashboard page, which is just enough to let you know that the plug-in is active. However, it's safe to assume that no one uses Hello Dolly for long on a real website.

The Hello Dolly plug-in needs no configuration. However, many plug-ins have their own page (or pages) of settings that you can adjust. Confusingly, different plug-ins put their settings in different places. Here are the three places to look:

- **The top-level items in the dashboard menu.** Some plug-ins add an entirely new item to the dashboard menu. For example, if you install Jetpack, you see a Jetpack menu item near the top of the dashboard, just above the Posts menu (Figure 9-7). This is the most common place for plug-in settings, especially if the plug-in offers plenty of options. But there's no surefire way to know where your plug-in's link will appear. Some plug-ins put it near the top of the dashboard menu (as does Jetpack), while others put it at the bottom (WPtouch).
- **The Settings menu.** Some plug-ins add a secondary menu under the Settings menu. For example, to configure the Limit Login Attempts plug-in, you choose Settings→Limit Login Attempts. Plug-ins are most likely to use this approach when they have a small group of settings that fit on a single page. (Although some plug-ins use tabs to cram a surprisingly large pile of settings into that one page.) You may even find a rogue plug-in that stashes itself in the Tools menu.
- **The Plugins page.** As you know, WordPress lists every plug-in you install on the Plugins page. Underneath each plug-in are links that let you activate, deactivate, edit, and delete the plug-in. Some plug-ins add an additional Settings link that you can click to review and edit the plug-in's options. Depending on the plug-in, this link may provide the only way to configure the plug-in, or it may duplicate a top-level menu heading or a command in the Settings menu.

For example, clicking the Settings link under the Jetpack plug-in has the same effect as clicking the Jetpack menu item (Figure 9-7).

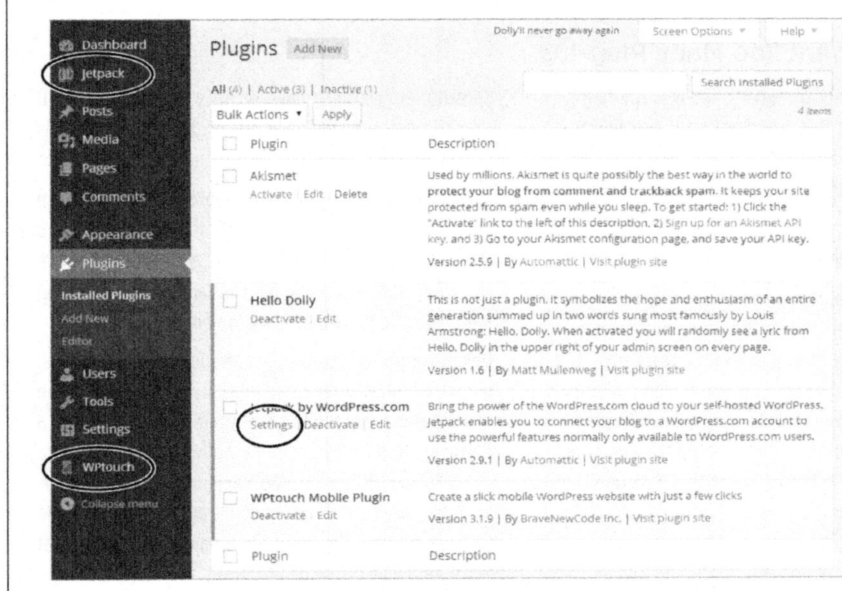

FIGURE 9-7

This site has three active plug-ins (highlighted). The Hello Dolly plug-in has no additional settings, but both the Jetpack and WPtouch plug-ins do, and you can get to them through dashboard menu headings (circled on the left). Jetpack also includes a Settings link on the Plugins page.

As you can see, different plug-ins often work in ways that are *similar*, but not the same. For that reason, you need to learn the way each plug-in works individually. In the remainder of this chapter, you'll take a close look at several prime plug-in examples.

TIP You don't need to keep plug-ins you don't use. If you decide to trash a particular plug-in, choose Plugins→Installed Plugins to call up the plug-in list, click Deactivate to switch a plug-in off (if it's currently active), and then click Delete to remove it entirely.

UP TO SPEED

Why You Don't Want Too Many Plug-Ins

When new WordPress users discover plug-ins, their first instinct is to load as much free goodness as they can onto their sites. After all, if one plug-in is great, two dozen must be mind-blowingly fantastic.

Before you get carried away, it's worth pointing out the many reasons you *don't* want to install every plug-in you find:

- **Performance.** As you already learned, plug-ins use PHP code to carry out their tasks. The more plug-ins you activate, the more work you're asking WordPress to do. Eventually, this work might add up to enough of an overhead that it begins to slow down your site. The plug-ins that do the most work (and are thus the most likely to hinder site performance) include those that back up your site, log your traffic, search for broken links, and perform search-engine optimization.
- **Maintenance.** The more plug-ins you have, the more plug-ins you need to configure and update (when new versions come out). It's a relatively small job, but pile on the plug-ins and you might find yourself with some extra work.
- **Security.** Plug-ins can have security holes, especially if they're poorly designed or out of date. More plug-ins can mean more risk.
- **Compatibility.** Sometimes, one plug-in can mess up another. If your site uses a huge thicket of plug-ins, it's difficult to track down which one is at fault. You need to resort to disabling all your plug-ins and then re-enabling them one at a time, until the problem recurs.
- **Obsolescence.** Often, plug-ins are developed by helpful people in the WordPress community who need a given feature and are ready to share their work. But there's a downside to this development model—it makes it more likely for an author to stop developing a plug-in (for example, when he doesn't need it anymore or when he just doesn't have the time). Eventually, a new version of WordPress may break an old plug-in you depend on, and you need to scramble to find a substitute.

The best way to avoid problems like these is to use popular, regularly updated plug-ins, make sure they're always up to date, and keep the number of plug-ins you use small.

Keeping Your Plug-Ins Up to Date

Every time you install a plug-in, you extend WordPress's features. If one of your plug-ins has a security vulnerability, it creates a chink in your website's armor that exposes you to legions of cyber-attackers.

To avoid security problems, stick with well-used and well-loved plug-ins—those that have stood the test of time, are in widespread use, and are still regularly revised. And just as it's important to keep WordPress secure and up to date, it's also important to make sure you have the latest, most reliable versions of all your plug-ins.

Although WordPress can keep itself up to date, it's up to you to keep your plug-ins current. The quickest way to spot an out-of-date plug-in is to look at the Plugins heading in the dashboard menu. If WordPress notices that there's a new version of one or more of your plug-ins, it shows a number in a circle indicating how many updates await you. For example, if updates are available for three of your plug-ins, you see the number 3 in a circle (Figure 9-8, top). This happens regardless of whether your out-of-date plug-ins are active.

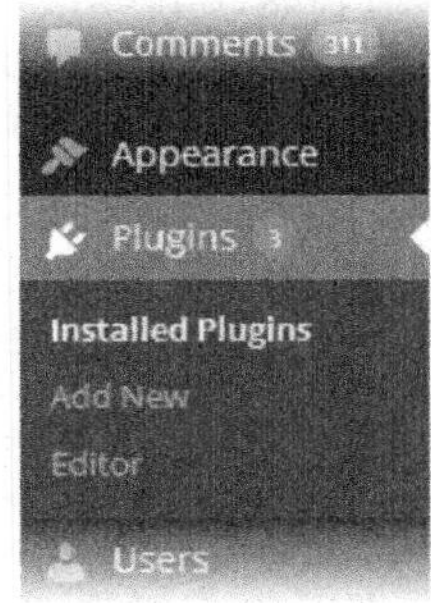

FIGURE 9-8

Top: WordPress wants you to know that your site has three out-of-date plug-ins.

Bottom: When WordPress finds an update for a plug-in, it displays an "update now" link under it on the Plugins page.

You should always update your plug-ins as soon as possible. In fact, if you see the number-in-a-circle, you should probably stop what you're doing and install the new plug-ins straightaway. Typically, updates take just a few seconds, so you won't be stalled for long.

There are two easy ways to update a plug-in. You can do so from the Plugins page by clicking the "update now" link under the plug-in (Figure 9-8, bottom). Or, you can update numerous plug-ins at once using the Updates page (Dashboard→Updates), which lists all the out-of-date themes and plug-ins on your site. Check the box next to each plug-in you want to update and then click Update Plugins. Blink twice, and WordPress will let you know that everything is up to date.

NOTE You must keep *all* your plug-ins up to date, even those that aren't currently active. That's because hackers can still access the inactive plug-ins on your site and exploit any security flaws they contain.

The Jetpack Plug-In

As you already know, WordPress.com sites don't let you install plug-ins. But to keep people happy, Automattic adds extra frills with its own, carefully tested plug-ins. Every WordPress.com site gets these extras, and as a result, a stock WordPress.com site actually has *more* features than a newly installed self-hosted site. (But now that you know how to browse the plug-in directory, with its thousands of site enhancements, you can get your revenge pretty easily.)

If you don't want to track down dozens of plug-ins, but you do want a simple way to get the same features that WordPress.com sites have, there's a simple, all-in-one solution. It's Jetpack, a plug-in developed by the folks who built WordPress.com, and equipped with almost all the same great features.

To learn about Jetpack's features, visit *http://jetpack.me*. Highlights include a picture carousel (covered on page 333), contact forms (page 301), enhanced comments (Chapter 8), Twitter and Facebook sharing (Chapter 12), and statistics about the people who visit your site (Chapter 12).

NOTE The Jetpack plug-in is a useful way to get a pile of handy features in one package. You'll use it on and off throughout this book. However, many WordPress experts avoid Jetpack's cornucopia of plug-ins, preferring to pick and choose plug-ins that provide just the features they need. For example, they may use separate plug-ins for Facebook buttons, website statistics, and contact forms, rather than try to get them all through Jetpack. This is a bit more work, but it's really up to you to decide what works best for your site.

Signing Up with WordPress.com

You already know how to install the Jetpack plug-in—just search the plug-in directory for "jetpack" and click the Install Now link.

However, Jetpack has one additional (and slightly irritating) setup requirement. To use it, you need a WordPress.com user ID and password, even though you don't plan to host any sites on WordPress.com.

After you activate Jetpack, the plug-in notifies you about this extra requirement with a message above the plug-in list. Here's how to get Jetpack to recognize your single-purpose WordPress.com account and get the plug-in working on your hosted site:

1. **Click the "Connect to WordPress.com" button to set up the connection.**

   The Jetpack plug-in takes you to *http://jetpack.wordpress.com* and invites you to fill in your WordPress.com user name and password.

   If you've ever created a site with WordPress.com, you already have these details—you don't need to create a new account, because you can use the same one for as many Jetpack-enabled websites as you want. To finish the setup process, enter your information and click Authorize Jetpack.

   If you've never used WordPress.com before, now is the time to create an account. Continue to the next step.

2. **Click the "Need an account" link.**

   You see the standard WordPress.com sign-up page. The difference is that now WordPress.com assumes you want an account only, not a WordPress.com site. (If for some reason you *do* want a WordPress.com site, you could create it later, or you can click the "Sign up for a blog, too" link to get it as part of the sign-up process.)

3. **Type in a user name, password, and email address.**

   Your user name can be any combination of letters and numbers, so long as there isn't another WordPress.com member already using it.

   Your password can be anything, but you should definitely make it different from the password you use for your self-hosted site or for your web host's administrative interface.

   Your email address is an essential detail, because WordPress.com sends you an activation email. If you don't get it, you can't activate your account.

4. **Click the "Sign up" button.**

   Now you need to wait for the activation email message.

5. **When the email arrives, click the activation link inside.**

   That brings you back to the Jetpack page, and the link logs you into your WordPress.com account automatically (Figure 9-9).

6. **Click Authorize Jetpack.**

   WordPress brings you back to your self-hosted site, where Jetpack is now running.

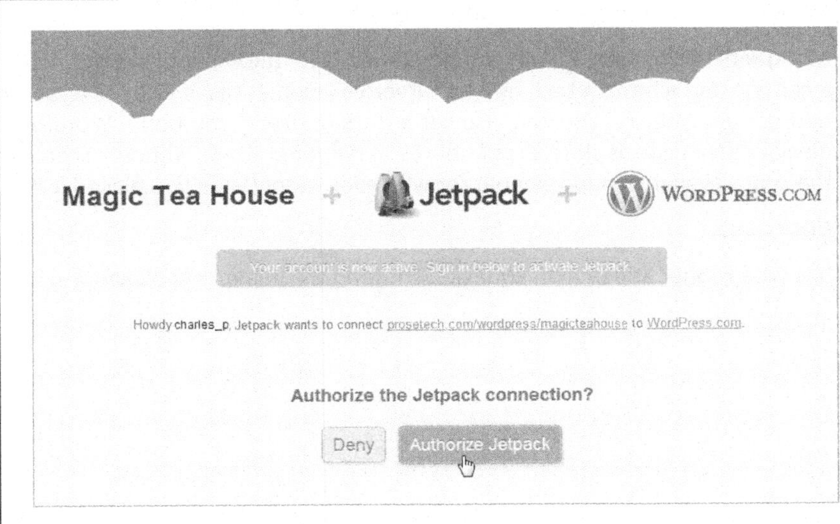

FIGURE 9-9

Before WordPress activates Jetpack, it asks if you want to use your WordPress.com user account (in this example, that's charles_p's account) to activate Jetpack on this site (Magic Tea House).

Some of Jetpack's features need to be switched on before they become operational. To activate them (and to review everything Jetpack offers), choose Jetpack in the dashboard menu.

You'll see many of Jetpack's features in later chapters. In the following sections, you'll try out three to get a taste of what the plug-in can do.

Using the Image Widget

You may remember from Chapter 6 that you can use the Text widget to display a picture in your site's sidebar, using a tiny bit of HTML. The trick is to put an <img> element that points to your picture inside the Text widget (page 188).

WordPress.com users have an easier (albeit less flexible) tool: the Image widget. And now that you signed up with Jetpack, you've got the same advantage. Here's how to put the Image widget to use:

1. **Choose Appearance→Widgets.**

   This takes you to the familiar Widgets page in the dashboard. There you see a few new widgets that have Jetpack in the name, including one called "Image (Jetpack)."

2. **Drag the Image widget to one of the widget areas on the right.**

   When you drop the widget into place, it expands to show a number of text boxes where you can fill in important details (Figure 9-10).

3. **Fill in the information for your widget.**

   Obviously, the most important detail is the image URL—the location of the image you want to show. Usually, this is a file you uploaded to your site's media library. If you don't remember the address, you need to browse the Media→Library section of the dashboard, as explained on page 186.

   Along with the image URL, you can choose a title for the widget, give the picture a caption and alternate text, and turn it into a link that takes viewers to a web address you specify. You can also set a display size. If you don't, WordPress displays the image as close as possible to its full, natural size, without exceeding the space available in the sidebar (or whatever widget area you placed it in).

4. **Click Save.**

   Now the widget appears on your site, showing the image you picked.

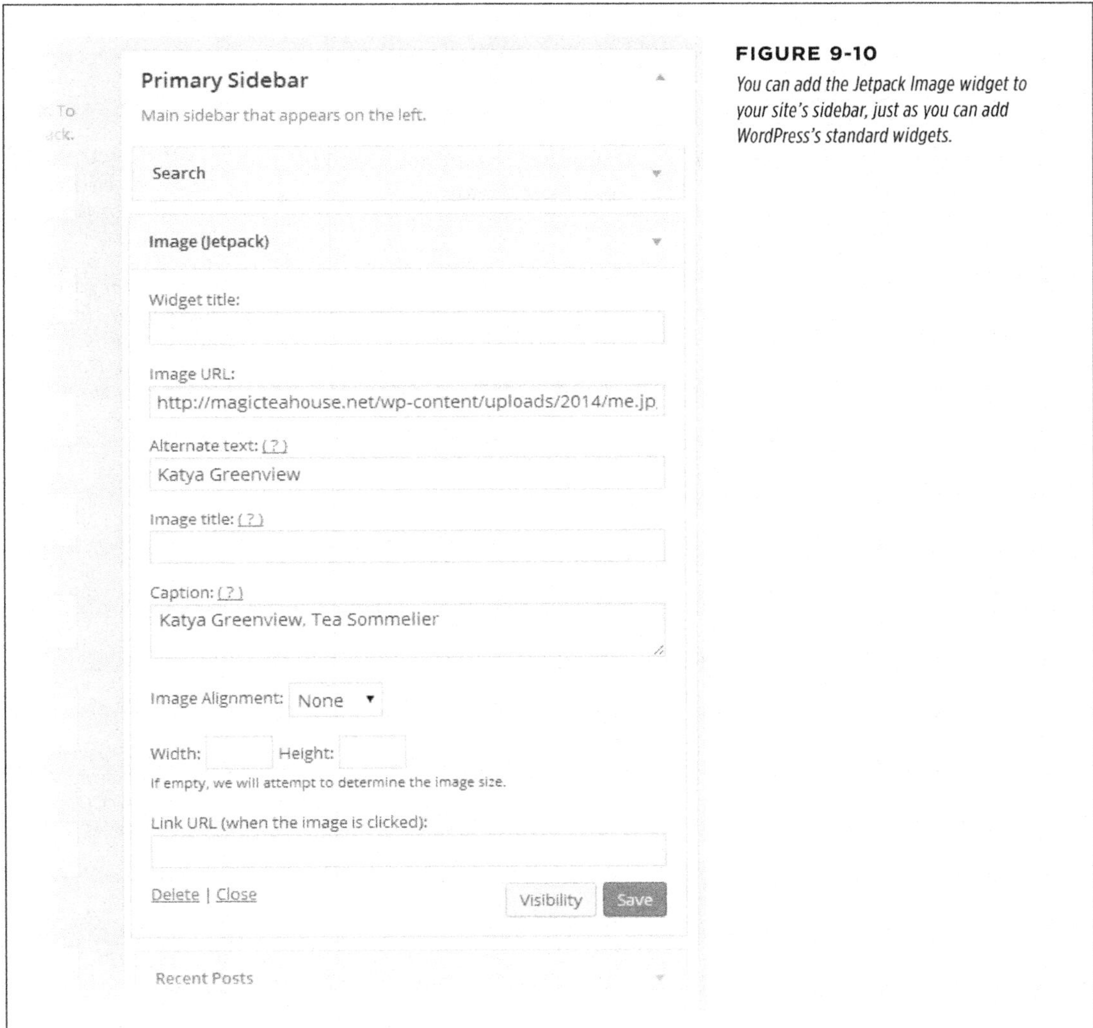

FIGURE 9-10

You can add the Jetpack Image widget to your site's sidebar, just as you can add WordPress's standard widgets.

Adding a Contact Form

The Image widget is far from an essential tool, but it *is* a real convenience, as are many of Jetpack's features. However, Jetpack also includes some features that would be significantly more work to duplicate on your own. One is its contact form, which lets you solicit readers for any sort of information you want (Figure 9-11).

Often, you use contact forms to collect names, email addresses, postal addresses, or support questions. However, Jetpack is clever enough to let you build your own form, which you can edit to collect whatever information you want. To get started, you create a new post, and then click Add Contact Form (Figure 9-12) above the content box, to the right of the Add Media button.

Oxygenazor Launch: Get Your Free Detergent!

If you'd like a free sample of our new Oxygenazor Laundry Detergent, just fill out your name and address below.

Name (required)
Ben Stiles
Email (required)
bsyler@craw.petouch.com
Mailing Address (required)
Ben Stiles
2843 Sherman Ave
Camden, NJ 08105-442
(856) 966-5786
I am 18 or older
Submit »

Oxygenazor Launch: Get Your Free Detergent!

If you'd like a free sample of our new Oxygenazor Laundry Detergent, just fill out your name and address below.

MESSAGE SENT
Name: Ben Stiles
Email: bsyler@craw.petouch.com
Mailing Address: Ben Stiles 2843 Sherman Ave Camden, NJ 08105-442 (856) 966-5786
I am 18 or older: Yes

FIGURE 9-11

The idea behind a contact form is to solicit information from your guests. A reader fills in these blank text boxes (left), and then submits the form (right). WordPress collects the information, and passes it along to you in an email.

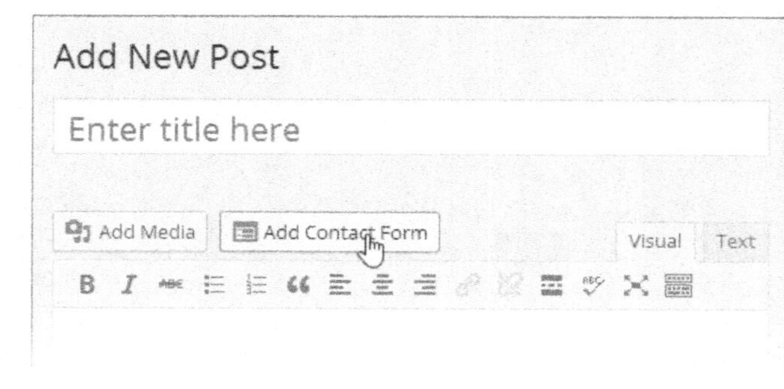

FIGURE 9-12

If you wonder why you haven't noticed the Add Contact Form button before, it's because you didn't have it until you installed Jetpack. Clicking the button adds a contact form to any post.

Once you click Add Contact Form, the "Add a custom form" window opens (Figure 9-13) so you can design your survey. The window asks you to add "fields," which is just a geeky way of saying that you need to specify the way a visitor can enter information, such as through a text box or drop-down list (see the box on page 304 for a detailed explanation).

Here's what you can do in the form builder:

- **Remove a field.** Click the minus sign (-) on the right side of the field to delete it.

- **Add a new field.** Click "Add a new field" and then enter the field information. Every field needs a label (the text above the field) and a "Field type" (the way the field collects information). Use Text for an ordinary single-line text box and Textarea for a big, multiline box, or pick one of the more specialized field types described in the box on page 304. Optionally, turn on the Required checkbox to force readers to complete a field before they can submit the form. When you finish, click "Save this field."
- **Rearrange your fields.** Point to the field you want to move until a "move" link appears in the top-right corner. Click the link and then drag the field up or down. (You can't put fields side by side.)
- **Change your email settings.** Ordinarily, WordPress sends the data from the form a visitor submits to your administrator email. If you want to use a different email account, click the "Email notifications" tab and fill in the new address.

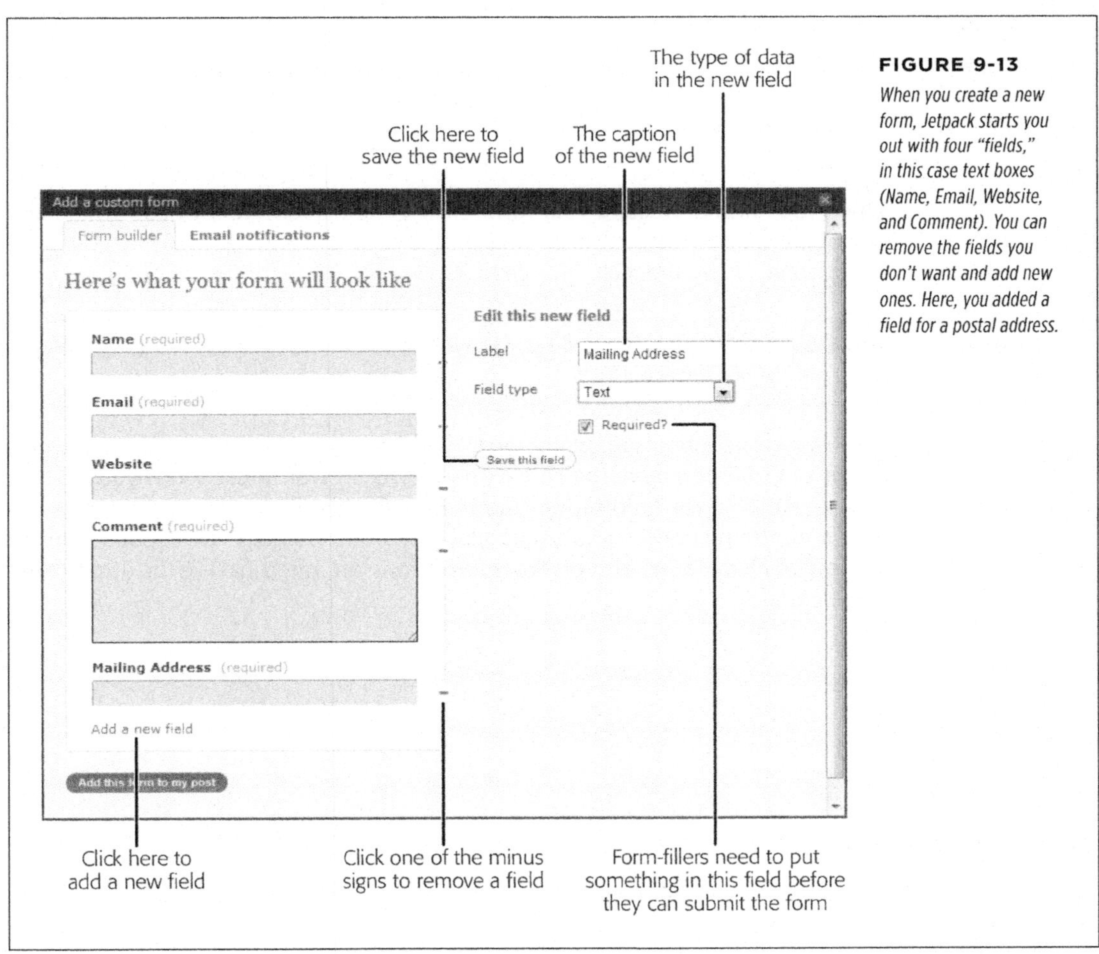

FIGURE 9-13

When you create a new form, Jetpack starts you out with four "fields," in this case text boxes (Name, Email, Website, and Comment). You can remove the fields you don't want and add new ones. Here, you added a field for a postal address.

UP TO SPEED

Contact Form Field Types

WordPress's contact form lets you choose from a small set of *field types*—the means by which you collect information. Here are your choices:

- **Text.** This is your standard-issue single-line text box.
- **Textarea.** This is a bigger text box that can hold whole paragraphs of information. Once you add a textarea box, you can drag the bottom-right corner to make it as big as you want.
- **Checkbox.** This is a way to let guests turn options on or off.
- **Drop down.** This is a list of values (which you specify) that you stuff into a drop-down list. The person filling out the form picks a single value from the list.
- **Radio.** This is a list of values like the "Drop down" box, but the form-filler sees all his choices at once (they're listed on the page). He clicks a small circle next to the option he wants. Usually, you use this field to list just a few choices, and use "Drop down" for a long list of options.
- **Email, Name, and Website.** These field types look like ordinary text boxes, but WordPress is smart enough to automatically fill in the current guest's email address and name if it knows those details (for example, if the person recently left a comment on your site). WordPress also performs some basic error checking to catch bad email addresses.

When you finish perfecting your form, click "Add this form to my post" at the bottom of the window. Jetpack inserts a series of strange-looking codes into your post, wrapped in square brackets (Figure 9-14).

TIP You can edit a post's form by clicking Add Contact Form while you edit the post, which loads the form builder with the form, just as you left it.

When someone submits a contact form, WordPress sends you an email. That person can fill out the form more than once (in which case WordPress sends you multiple messages). If you're tired of juggling the notification emails, WordPress lets you review all the responses in a single place, the dashboard. Click Feedback in the dashboard menu to see a list of form submissions, arranged just like the dashboard's comment list.

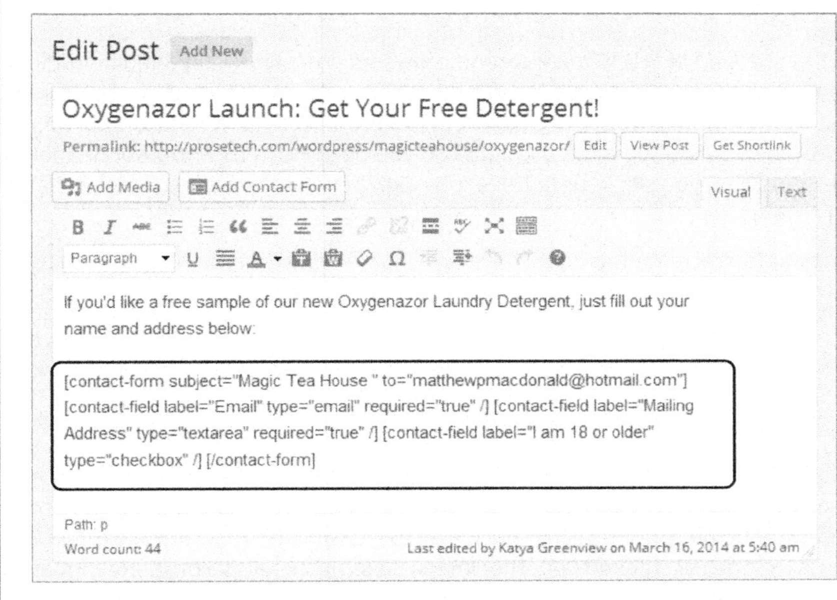

FIGURE 9-14

To create a contact form, Jetpack uses shortcodes, a WordPress feature you'll learn about on page 323. However, you don't need to pay them any attention—as long as you leave them alone, your form will appear in the published post just the way you want it. (Adding content above or below the form code, however, is perfectly acceptable.)

Adding a Mathematical Equation

The creators of WordPress also included some more specialized, quirkier plug-ins. One intriguing example is the mathematic equation feature demonstrated in Figure 9-15, which is the last Jetpack feature you'll look at in this chapter.

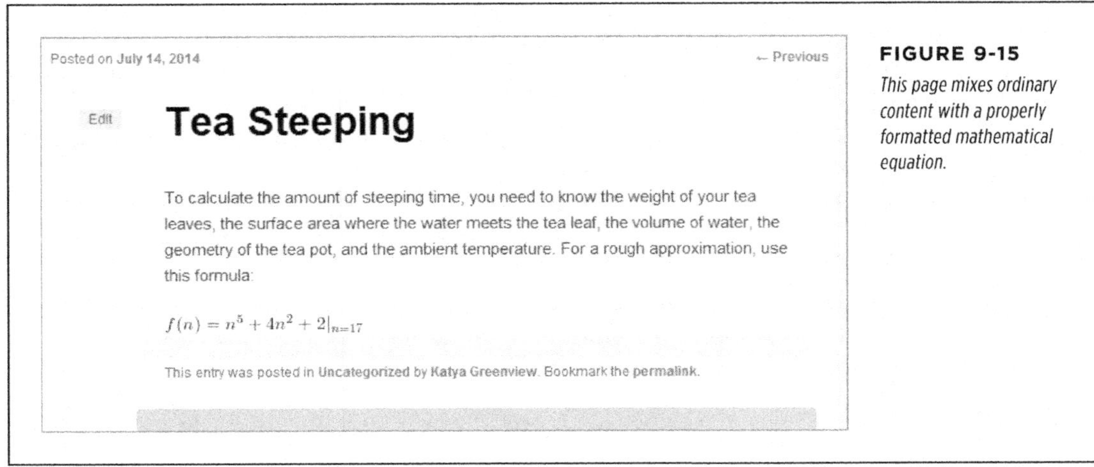

FIGURE 9-15

This page mixes ordinary content with a properly formatted mathematical equation.

To create an equation with Jetpack, you use the LaTeX typesetting language, a standard in the technical publishing industry. For example, you write the equation in Figure 9-15 like this in LaTeX:

```
f(n) = n^5 + 4n^2 + 2 |_{n=17}
```

LaTeX isn't a kind of HTML markup, and browsers don't know anything about it. To turn a LaTeX expression into a formatted equation for your web page, you need a translation program. A variety of JavaScript libraries can do the job, with varying degrees of success, but if you use Jetpack, you don't need to worry about another plug-in. Instead, you slip your LaTeX expression between two special codes: [latex] and [/latex].

For example, to create the post shown in Figure 9-15, you type the equation right into the post editor, as shown here:

```
To calculate the amount of steeping time, you need to know the weight of your
tea leaves, the surface area where the water meets the tea leaf, the volume
of water, the geometry of the tea pot, and the ambient temperature. For a
rough approximation, use this formula:
[latex]f(n) = n^5 + 4n^2 + 2 |_{n=17}[/latex]
```

When WordPress processes this page, the Jetpack plug-in notices the [latex] code, and interprets the content inside as a LaTeX expression. It replaces the expression's text with a series of stitched-together image files. The result is a properly formatted equation that any mathematician can understand (and any browser can display).

NOTE Technically, the [latex] and [/latex] syntax is part of a WordPress *shortcode*—a way of getting WordPress to insert special content using an instruction in square brackets. WordPress recognizes a few shortcodes automatically, and plug-ins can add their own. You'll learn more about shortcodes in Chapter 10.

Of course, you can't take advantage of Jetpack's LaTeX wizardry unless you know a bit about the LaTeX standard (or you have a prewritten equation in LaTeX format). To learn more, start with the general tutorial at *http://tinyurl.com/latexmath*. If you find writing your own LaTeX expressions daunting, you can get some help from the LaTeX equation generator at *http://tinyurl.com/latexequation*. It lets you build a LaTeX expression by clicking your way through a mess of buttons. Finally, you can review WordPress's documentation for the LaTeX feature at *http://support.wordpress.com/latex*, which covers a few extra, WordPress-specific details (for example, it explains how to change the size of the generated equation, and how to adjust its background color if you want it to stand out on your page).

The next time you'll use Jetpack is in Chapter 10, to give your site a photo carousel or slideshow. But now it's time to review some other useful plug-ins.

Adding Mobile Support

In Chapter 5, you considered a thorny question—what does your carefully crafted WordPress site look like if someone views it on a mobile device, like a smartphone or tablet?

For self-hosted sites, the answer all depends on the theme you choose. If you use a mobile-aware theme (sometimes called a *responsive* theme), your site automatically adjusts its design when it detects a mobile device, substituting a simpler, streamlined layout that fits on the smaller display. The standard year themes, from Twenty Eleven on, are all mobile-aware.

If your theme doesn't have these built-in smarts, you get a result that's much less ideal. When people visit your site with a mobile device, they see the normal, full-size layout, which means they need to zoom and scroll around it awkwardly. The effect is a minor inconvenience on a midsized device like an iPad, but a serious aggravation on a small device like an iPhone. Readers may find that reading your site isn't worth the finger cramps.

The solution is a plug-in that adds mobile support without disrupting your chosen theme. Several popular plug-ins handle the task, and they all work the same way, by swapping in a different theme when they detect a mobile device. The best plug-ins are smart enough to tailor the substitute theme for specific devices, so iPad owners see something a bit different from iPhone owners, for example.

TIP Even if you *do* use a mobile-aware theme, you might still decide to use a mobile plug-in if the mobile representation of your site isn't what you want. Maybe the mobile face of your site is too plain, performs sluggishly, or wastes too much space with a long post list. Perhaps the menus and widgets you chose for the desktop version don't make sense in the cramped window of a smartphone, no matter how they're arranged. Good mobile plug-ins give you a range of ways to tailor the appearance of your site on mobile devices. For example, you can change the menus, substitute a different home page, and even swap in smaller image files.

WPtouch, a wildly popular WordPress plug-in with millions of downloads to its name, lets you create a distinct mobile face for your site. You can find it at *http://tinyurl.com/wptouch*.

UP TO SPEED

Using the Plug-In Links in This Book

In this chapter (and throughout this book), you'll frequently come across links to useful WordPress plug-ins. These links take you to WordPress's plug-in directory, at *http://wordpress.org/plugins*. There, you get extensive information about the plug-in, including how it works, the number of times it's been downloaded, its star rating, and its compatibility information (just as you can in the plug-in details window shown in Figure 9-4).

You can download a plug-in from the directory, presumably so you can upload it to your site later, from the Plugins→Add New page. But you don't need to go through this two-step download-and-then-upload process. To install a plug-in discussed in this book, log in to your site's dashboard, search for the plug-in by name, and then click the Install button to transfer it in one step.

The WPtouch Mobile Theme

WPtouch recognizes a range of smartphones and touch devices, including Apple products (that's the iPhone, iPad, and iPod Touch), devices running the Google Android operating system, BlackBerry devices, and even old-school Palm gadgets. When one of these devices hits up your site, WPtouch steps in and displays your content using its slick mobile theme. It doesn't matter whether your original site theme is mobile-aware or not. WPtouch bypasses it completely.

Once you install and activate WPtouch, you're ready to try it out. Figure 9-16 shows what happens when a guest visits a WPtouch-enabled site with an iPhone.

FIGURE 9-16

Left: Although Twenty Twelve is a responsive theme, it's not a perfect match for mobile devices. For one thing, the post list on the home page includes the whole text of every post, which makes for a lot of scrolling.

Right: WPtouch's mobile theme keeps the list of posts simple, highlighting the title, date, and number of comments, but leaving the content out.

The WPtouch mobile theme (Figure 9-17) departs from the average WordPress theme in several important ways:

- **WPtouch ignores widgets when it creates a mobile version of your site.** This is quite different from the mobile version of the year themes, like Twenty Twelve. They retain all your widgets but place them before or after the main content. This ensures that the mobile view doesn't sacrifice anything important from the desktop site, but it also creates a long and somewhat unwieldy page.

- **WPtouch doesn't display any content in post listings.** Instead, it simply shows the title, date, and number of comments for each post. Mobile surfers need to tap a title to read the post. Once again, this differs from the year themes like Twenty Twelve, which list all the content and force mobile readers to scroll the day away. (Incidentally, you can tweak the way WPtouch shows posts using post excerpts, as described on page 198.)
- **WPtouch doesn't load all your posts at once.** Instead, the page ends with a Load More Entries link. Click it, and the page fetches a new batch of posts and adds them to the bottom of the page. The page uses clever JavaScript code to stuff in just the new content without refreshing the whole page (Figure 9-17, right).

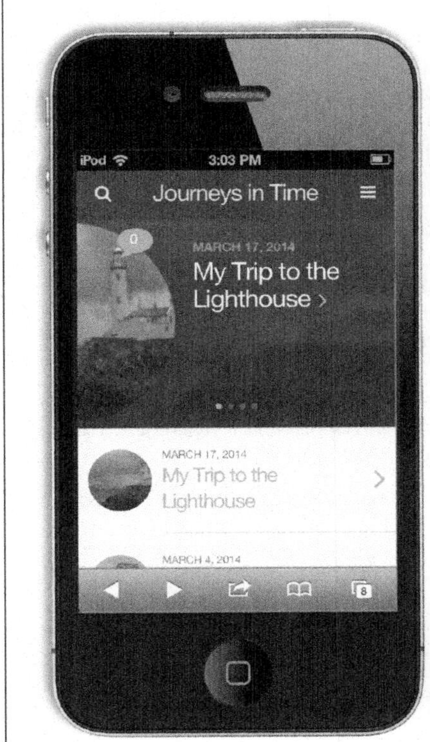

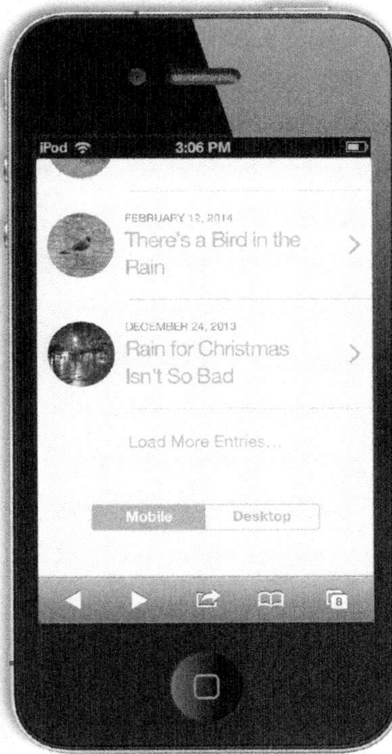

FIGURE 9-17

Left: If you use featured images, WPtouch shows them off in a slider at the top of the home page (to switch the slider off, see page 311). It also displays the images in a circle next to each post.

Right: Scroll to the bottom of the screen and you see a link to load more posts, along with a button named Desktop that lets you turn the WPtouch mobile theme off. Click the button, and WPtouch refreshes the page, handing control back to your site's original theme.

Configuring WPtouch

The WPtouch mobile theme overrides your standard theme completely. That means that even if your current theme has its own mobile-specific version, WPtouch replaces it. (If you *do* want to use the mobile version of your theme, deactivate the WPtouch plug-in on the Plugins page.)

That said, WPtouch does give you some leeway to customize the way it looks. To review your options, browse through the many pages in the WPtouch menu. For example, the WPtouch→Core Settings page includes these gems:

- **Site Title.** Remember, WPtouch displays the title of your site but no header picture. If you want to change the site title that appears in the mobile theme without changing the site title for everyone else, you do that here. This is handy if you need to shorten a long title so it fits comfortably on smaller screens.
- **Landing Page.** Ordinarily, WPtouch respects your WordPress settings, meaning that visitors start at the list of posts on your home page or on a static page, depending on your "Front page displays" setting (page 230). But you might decide that mobile viewers should start somewhere other than that. Maybe you want them to bypass the ordinary home page because it's too long and bloated with graphics. Or you want them to start with a page that provides links to specific posts (Figure 9-18).
- **Preview Theme.** Click this button to open a tiny browser window with a preview of your site. Here's the clever part: The preview window shows the mobile version of your site, which saves you the trouble of breaking out your iPhone to check out every change you make.

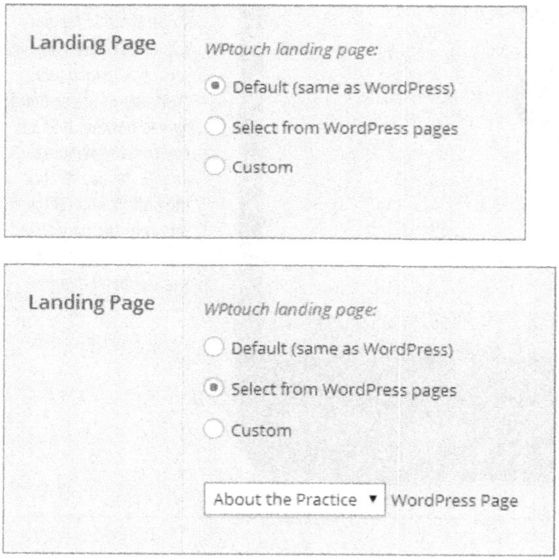

FIGURE 9-18

Top: Right now, the WPtouch home page uses WordPress's "Front page displays" setting to decide what to put on the main page of your mobile site.

Bottom: If that's not what you want, choose "Select from WordPress pages" and pick a different front page for the mobile version of your site.

WPtouch has many more options in the WPtouch→Theme Settings page. Here are a just a few of the most noteworthy:

- **Number of posts in post listings.** This determines how many posts appear on the home page before the Load More Entries link. It also sets the number of listings in the category-browsing and tag-browsing pages (page 123), if you use them.

- **Excluded categories and excluded tags.** Perhaps there are some posts on your site that aren't appropriate for mobile viewing or aren't likely to interest mobile users. As long as these posts belong to a specific category or have a specific tag, you can tuck them out of sight. Excluded posts won't appear in the mobile site's home page, in search results, or in category-browsing or tag-browsing pages. To exclude a category or tag, you need to enter its ID, which you can find in the Posts→Categories or Posts→Tags section of the dashboard. (To exclude several categories or tags, write the whole list in the text box, separating each ID with a comma.)
- **Show post categories and tags and Show post author.** As you saw in Figure 9-16, WPtouch shows just a few essential details in its post list: title, date, and number of comments. Tick these checkboxes, and WPtouch adds the category, tag, and author information as well.
- **Enabled featured slider.** Turn this option off to hide the featured image slider. Or tweak the settings underneath to control what pictures the slider shows and change whether the slider "slides" (cycles through its pictures) automatically.

You can play with plenty of other WPtouch settings. Dig around a bit, and you can change WPtouch's color scheme or WPtouch's mobile theme. Or visit the WPtouch→Menus page to modify the mobile version of your menus and give each menu item an eye-catching icon, which you choose from a gallery of ready-made pictures.

Clearly, WPtouch offers far more flexibility than you get with the average mobile-friendly theme. By comparison, the WordPress year themes don't let you change *any* aspect of their mobile appearance.

Some WordPress developers are even more ambitious. They like the basic WPtouch theme but feel it's a bit generic. They want to add touches of style and distinguish their site from competitors'. If you fall into that camp, the free version of WPtouch won't completely satisfy you. However, the creators of WPtouch sell an enhanced version named WPtouch Pro. It offers more ready-made themes, more extensive theme customization, and with a pile of extra features (see *http://tinyurl.com/wptouchpro*). Currently, WPtouch Pro costs $49 for a single website, $99 for five. Although you certainly don't need the Pro version, it's money well spent if you expect that a large portion of your audience will visit your site using a mobile device.

Backing Up a WordPress Site

It's easy to be casual about the safety of the files on your website. After all, even small web hosting companies take reliability seriously. They use systems that have a high level of *redundancy*—web servers with multiple hard drives, for example, and groups of computers that work together so that a hardware failure in one won't sideline an entire website. Many web hosts also perform some sort of backup, copying the files they host to a storage location so they can recover them after catastrophes, like floods and fires.

But these measures, no matter how well-intentioned, aren't enough to protect your WordPress site. Unless you do your own backups, your site is exposed to serious risks that your web hosting company can't prevent. For example, an attacker could break into your administrator account and sneak some advertising or malware into your site. In some cases, these attacks are stealthy enough that you won't notice any effect for weeks. By that point, the only backup your web host still has may be a copy of the infected site, making it useless and forcing you to rebuild from scratch. Other problems can occur, too. The Web has plenty of backup horror stories, including cases where a host's backups go mysteriously missing, or an unexpected event puts a web host out of business, taking its websites with it.

To give your site a better chance of weathering crises like these, you need an independent backup solution. You have two choices:

- You can use an automated backup service that visits your site every day and transfers its content to another set of servers elsewhere in the world.
- You can do the work yourself, periodically downloading your content to your own personal computer for safekeeping.

In the following sections, you'll consider both approaches.

Using an Automated Backup Service

This approach is the most convenient. Once you sign up with the right company, the process happens automatically, without another thought from you. The premiere example for WordPress is VaultPress (*http://vaultpress.com*), a backup service run by Automattic that stores every post, page, comment, and setting change from the moment you sign up. VaultPress gives you the ability to roll back to any point in the past if disaster strikes.

Automated backup services have a significant drawback—they aren't free, and what you pay for backups can easily outweigh your hosting fee. The basic VaultPress package costs $15 per month, and its no-frills competitor blogValue, which stores just 30 days' worth of backups, charges $10 per month.

If you have the money to sign up with an automated service, and you're willing to pay to save a little time and a few headaches, check out VaultPress. It comes as part of Jetpack, although it's not activated. To use it, you need to sign up at *http://vaultpress.com/jetpack*.

If you're willing to take a slightly more hands-on approach, consider BackupBuddy (*http://ithemes.com/purchase/backupbuddy*). You can get a license for up to two sites for $80 per year, or a license for up to 10 business sites for $100 per year. However, BackupBuddy isn't in the storage business, it's just the tool that schedules and performs your backups. To use it, you need an account with a web storage service, so BackupBuddy has somewhere to store the backups it creates. BackupBuddy supports several such services, including Dropbox (*www.dropbox.com*), which is free for the first 2 GB of storage; Google Drive (*http://drive.google.com*), which is free for the first 15 GB; and Amazon S3 (*http://aws.amazon.com/s3*), which costs pennies per gigabyte. So if you have a modest-sized site (one that doesn't include a library of 5,000 pictures or massive video files) and you don't mind juggling a storage account, BackupBuddy is a reasonable compromise.

Backing Up with a Plug-In

If VaultPress is too pricey and you don't want to fiddle with BackupBuddy, you need to take charge of backups on your own. Fortunately, plenty of free plug-ins can help you out. But before you get started with any of them, you need to understand one key fact. Every WordPress site needs *two* types of backup:

- **A backup of your database.** As you learned in Chapter 1, WordPress stores every post, page, comment, and stitch of content in a database on your web server. This is the most important part of your site, because without content all you have is an empty shell.
- **A backup of your files.** These files include the contents of your media library, including every picture and resource you uploaded to your WordPress site, the theme files that tell WordPress how to lay out your content, and any plug-ins you installed.

NOTE You back up theme files for two reasons. First, as you become a more advanced WordPress designer, you may begin customizing the themes (as explained in Part 4). Second, it's always possible that the particular version of a theme you're using will disappear from the Web, making it difficult to restore an old copy of a backed-up site.

If you're handy with an FTP program, you can back up your files anytime. All you do is browse to your web hosting account and copy the contents of your WordPress folder to your computer. If you use Windows, this is as simple as firing up Windows Explorer, pointing it to your web host's FTP site, logging in, and dragging the folder you want (the one with your WordPress site in it) onto your desktop.

However, even if you copy every file you see, you still won't get the contents of your WordPress database, which is the heart of your WordPress site. To get that, you need a tool that can access the database, extract its contents, and put it in a file. (This tool also needs to be able to do the reverse, copying the data from a backup file into a new database, in case you need to re-create your site.) Unless you're a MySQL guru, your best bet is to use a WordPress plug-in to help you out.

Many WordPress plug-ins concentrate on backing up a site's database. They leave you to figure out an approach to copy the actual files on your site. Plug-ins that work this way include the popular WP-DB-Backup (*http://tinyurl.com/wp-db-backup*) and WP-DBManager (*http://tinyurl.com/wp-dbmanager*).

However, there are a few plug-ins that back up your site's database *and* its files. Two good examples are BackWPup (*http://tinyurl.com/backwpup*) and Online Backup for WordPress (*http://tinyurl.com/wponlineb*), the plug-in described in the next section.

WARNING There's no perfect backup tool for everyone. (That's why this book discusses so many backup plug-ins.) Every plug-in provides a different set of options, and some have strange quirks or don't work well with certain web hosts. For example, your web host may restrict PHP email to fight spammers. If your backup tool works by sending backed-up data to an email account, it might not be able to finish its work. Backup tools also differ in their ability to deal with unexpected errors, like corrupted data or databases that appear to be locked. For all these reasons, you need to test whatever backup plug-in you pick, and regularly check to make sure it's backing up your site.

The Online Backup for WordPress Plug-In

Online Backup for WordPress gives you two ways to back up your site:

- **Manually.** You perform a complete backup via the dashboard, and then download the backed-up data in one big ZIP file.
- **Scheduled.** You schedule a backup to run at certain times (for example, every night at midnight) and then have the backed-up ZIP file emailed to an account you specify. If you choose this route, you may as well create a dedicated Gmail account (at *http://mail.google.com*) for your back-up emails. With 15 GB of free storage, Gmail lets you stash quite a few backups without paying a penny.

The first thing you should do once you install Online Backup for WordPress is try a manual backup. That way, you'll know if the plug-in works properly, and you'll have at least one complete backup of your website to start you off. Here's how:

1. **Choose Online Backup from the dashboard menu.**

   This brings you to the control panel for Online Backup for WordPress, where you can start a manual backup, schedule a backup, or change back-up settings.

2. **Click the Backup link at the top.**

   Choose what you want to back up (Figure 9-19).

3. **Make sure you turn on both the Database and Filesystem checkboxes.**

   That way, you'll back up the contents of your database *and* all the files on your website, packaged up in a single ZIP file.

4. **Choose Local for the backup type.**

   Your other options are sending backups to the WordPress Vault or to an email address.

   The WordPress Vault is a service offered by BackupTechnology, the creators of the Online Backup for WordPress plug-in. The catch is that the Vault grants you just 100 MB of space—to get more, you need to pay.

NOTE If you want to use the WordPress Vault, you first need to sign up. You can get the process started by clicking the Online Backup Settings link.

The email option tells WordPress to send the backed-up data to the email address you supply. This option is more useful when you use scheduled backups, but you might use it with a manual backup if you're backing up a huge site and you don't want to stick around, waiting for the process to finish.

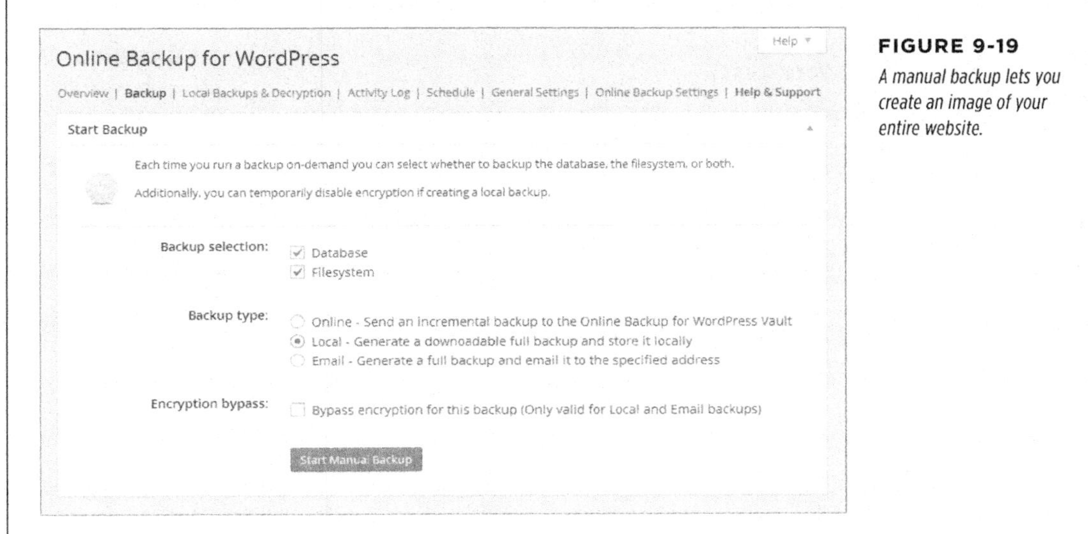

FIGURE 9-19

A manual backup lets you create an image of your entire website.

5. **Click Start Manual Backup.**

   The Online Backup for WordPress plug-in starts gathering your website data and archiving it into a single compressed file, which it puts in a temporary location on your web server. While it works, you see a progress bar ticking away.

TIP You don't need to stay and supervise the backup—if you navigate to a different part of the dashboard, or log out of the dashboard altogether, the backup process continues. However, if you leave, you need to return eventually to download the final result—the file with your backup in it. When you're ready, choose Online Backup from the dashboard menu and click the Local Backups & Decryption link, which shows you a list of all the backups Online Backup has stored on your web server.

   When Online Backup for WordPress finishes the backup, it displays a new button, named Download (Figure 9-20).

6. **Click Download.**

   Your browser may start downloading the file immediately, or it may first ask you where you want to store the backup and what you want to name it. The download process may take some time, depending on your Internet connection and the size of your site. Once you have the backup file safe and sound on your computer, your work is done.

If you need to reclaim space on your web server, you can delete the backup (once you copy it to a safe place) by clicking Delete. However, unless your site is gargantuan, there's no reason to worry. The next time you perform a full backup, the Online Backup for WordPress plug-in overwrites your old backup with the new one.

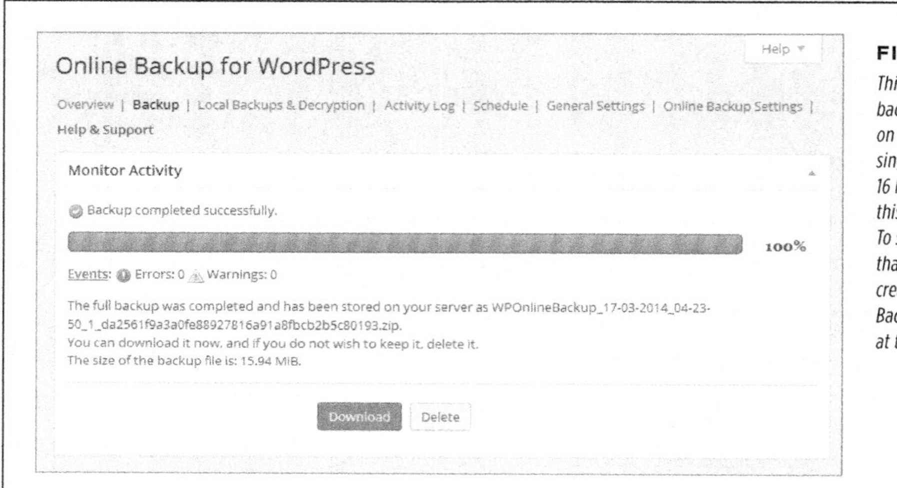

FIGURE 9-20

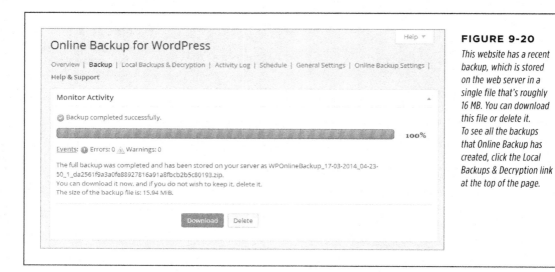

This website has a recent backup, which is stored on the web server in a single file that's roughly 16 MB. You can download this file or delete it. To see all the backups that Online Backup has created, click the Local Backups & Decryption link at the top of the page.

TIP It's a good idea to peek inside the backup file to make sure it has everything it should. (Remember, it's just an ordinary ZIP file that you can view on your computer.) Inside, you'll find two folders. The Database folder includes a file that has the SQL instructions needed to rebuild your database and fill it with your data. The FileSystem folder holds all the folders and files from your website, exactly as if you'd downloaded them from your web host over FTP.

Better Performance with Caching

As you learned at the very beginning of this book, WordPress websites are powered by code. When a visitor arrives at one of your pages, the WordPress code grabs the necessary information out of your database, assembles it into a page, and sends the final HTML back to your guest's browser. This process is so fast that ordinary people will be blissfully unaware of all the work that takes place behind the scenes.

However, even the fastest web server can't do all that work (run code, call the database, and build a web page) instantaneously. When someone requests a WordPress page, it takes a few fractions of a second longer to create it than it would to send an ordinary HTML file. Normally, this difference isn't noticeable. But if a huge crowd of hits your site at the same time, the WordPress engine will slow down slightly, making your entire website feel just a bit laggy.

POWER USERS' CLINIC

Scheduling Regular Backups

You can do a perfectly good job of disaster-proofing your site with manual backups. The problem is that it's up to you to start every backup, download the final product, and keep your backed-up files somewhere smart. As time passes, you might find yourself forgetting to make backups, leaving your website at risk.

The solution is to tell your plug-in to do the backup work for you, at regularly scheduled intervals. For Online Backup for WordPress, you do this by choosing Online Backup from the dashboard menu and then clicking the Schedule link (at the top, just under the "Online Backup for WordPress" title). You can ask it to perform weekly, daily, twice-a-day, four-times-a-day, or hourly backups (which is probably excessive, and may earn you the ire of your web hosting company). You can then choose the type of backup—either an incremental backup that grabs the changed files only and stores them in the WordPress Online Vault, or a full backup that sends the results to an email address you supply. When you finish, click Apply Schedule.

You can keep an eye on your scheduled backups by clicking the Overview link (at the top). There, you'll see basic information about when the last backup took place, whether it succeeded, how big the backup file was, and when the next backup will occur. You can get a more detailed summary of recent backup activity by clicking the Activity Log link, which is handy if you need to track down a mysterious error that interrupted one of your scheduled backups.

Finally, if you decide to send regular backups by email or store them on the WordPress Online Vault, it's a good idea to encrypt them to make sure that Internet eavesdroppers can't peek at your data. To do that, click the General Settings link, pick a type of encryption (the recommended AES128 algorithm is fine), and then type in an *encryption key*. This is a password used to encrypt your data, without which you can't decrypt it. Writing this password down on paper is a very good idea, because it's rather frustrating to have a crashed WordPress website and a full backup that you can't open.

However, there's a trick called *caching* that will satisfy even the most performance-obsessed WordPresser. The basic idea is this: The first time someone requests a page on your site, WordPress goes to work, running its code and generating the page dynamically. But once it delivers the page, the plug-in stores the result as an ordinary HTML file on your web server. Now here's the ingenious part: The next time a visitor asks for the same page, the caching plug-in sends back the previously generated HTML, sidestepping the usual page-generating process and saving valuable microseconds (Figure 9-21). This shortcut works no matter how many people visit your site—as long as the plug-in has an ordinary HTML copy of the finished page, it uses that instead of creating a new copy all over again. Caching plug-ins can use other tactics, too, such as caching just part of the content, compressing the cached data, and discarding cached copies after a certain amount of time.

NOTE Caching takes extra space on your website, because it stores extra HTML files. However, these files are rarely big enough to worry about. Caching plug-ins don't attempt to cache your site's pictures (or the other resources you uploaded to the media library).

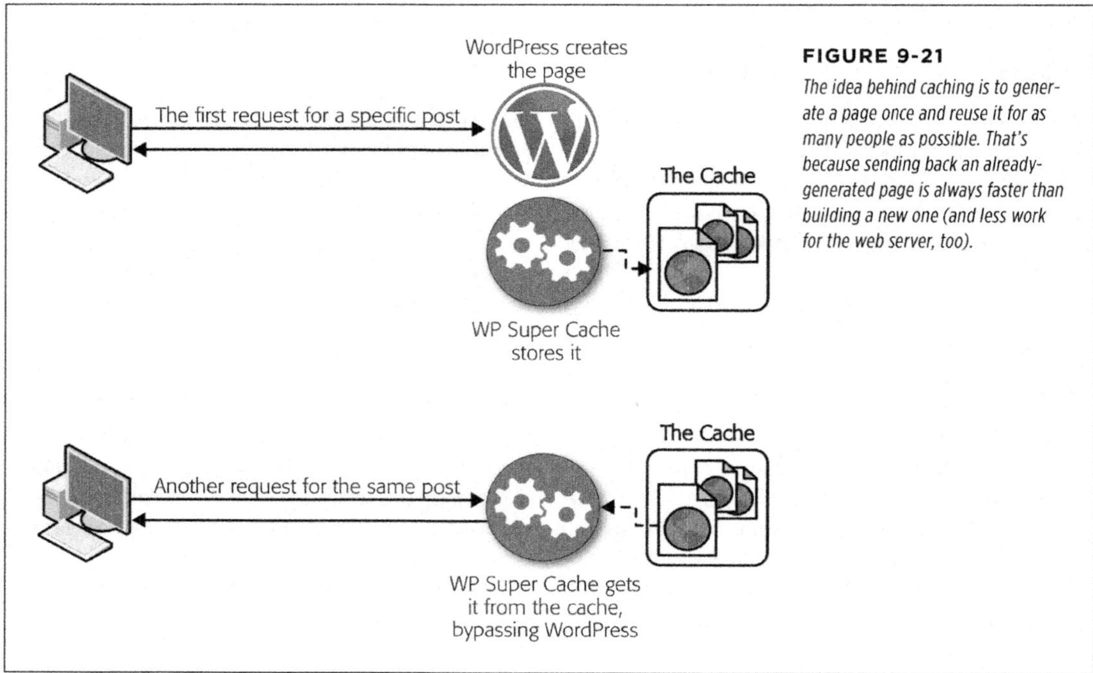

FIGURE 9-21

The idea behind caching is to generate a page once and reuse it for as many people as possible. That's because sending back an already-generated page is always faster than building a new one (and less work for the web server, too).

There are several caching plug-ins in the WordPress directory, but by far the most popular is WP Super Cache (*http://tinyurl.com/wpsupercache*). To use it, install the plug-in, activate it in the usual way, and *then* turn on caching. To perform this last step, choose Settings→WP Super Cache, click the Caching On option at the top of the page, and then click the Update Status button (Figure 9-22).

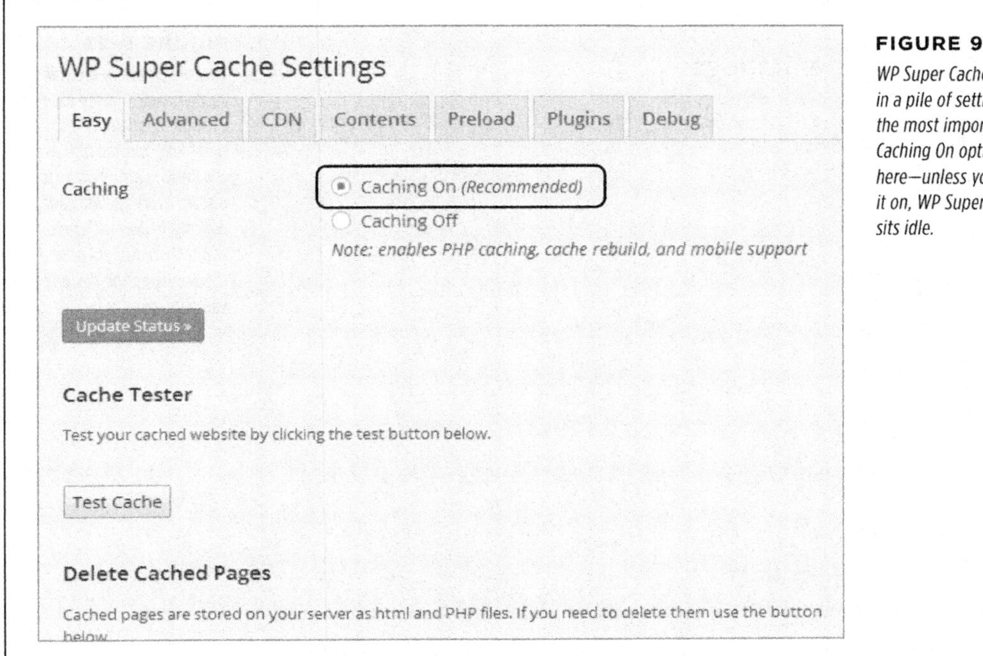

FIGURE 9-22

WP Super Cache packs in a pile of settings, but the most important is the Caching On option shown here—unless you turn it on, WP Super Cache sits idle.

To confirm that WP Super Cache is working, open a new browser window and look at a couple of posts. Then, return to the WP Super Cache settings and click the Contents tab. Finally, click the "Regenerate cache stats" link. WP Super Cache will report how many cached files it created (Figure 9-23). Even though these pages don't look any different in a browser, WordPress sends them to your visitors more quickly, bypassing most of the processing the WordPress engine ordinarily does.

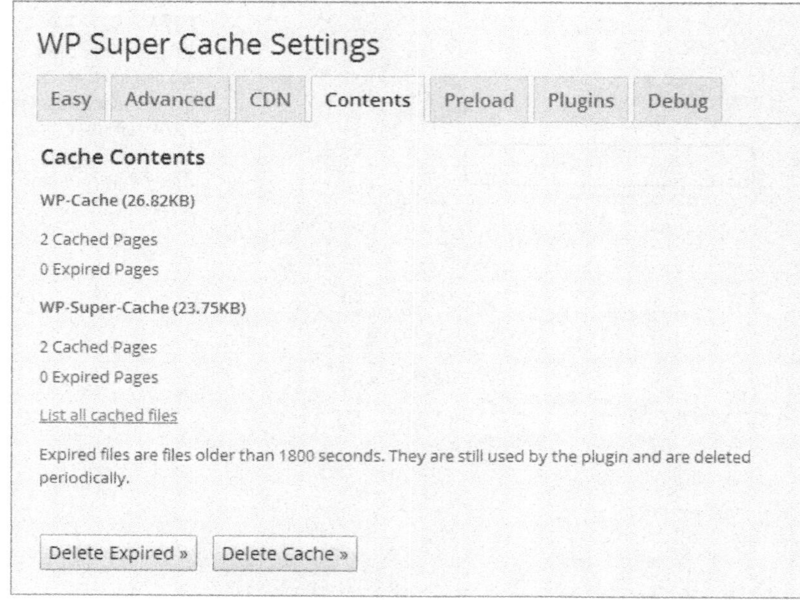

FIGURE 9-23

This site currently has four cached pages. To see them, click the "List all cached files" link. You can also use the Delete Cache button to discard every cached page, which is important when you test WP Super Cache or if you change the design of your site.

WORD TO THE WISE

WP Super Cache's Effect on Other Plug-ins

Caching changes the way your website works, and it can have unexpected side effects on other plug-ins. Here are some tips to help you steer clear of plug-in conflicts:

- **Check the documentation for your plug-ins.** WP Super Cache is popular enough that other plug-in creators often test their plug-ins with it. To see if the plug-ins you use need special settings to get along with WP Super Cache, look up the plug-in in WordPress's plug-in directory (*http://wordpress.org/plugins*) and check the FAQ tab.
- **Visit the Plugins tab in the WP Super Cache Settings.** There are a few plug-ins that get special attention from WP Super Cache. If you have one of them, you can tell WP Super Cache to change the way the cache works to avoid disrupting the other plug-in. To do that, go to Settings→WP Super Cache, click the Plugins tab, find your plug-in, and then click the Enabled option next to it. (The WPtouch plug-in you used earlier in this chapter is in this list, for instance.)
- **Delay caching until you're ready to go live.** Switching on caching is the very last thing you should do with your WordPress site, after you polish your theme, tweak your layout, and start using your site for real.
- **Learn to troubleshoot.** If something goes wrong, you need to be ready to track it down. Usually, the most recently activated plug-in is the culprit—try disabling it and seeing if your site returns to normal. If that doesn't work, you need to deactivate every plug-in, and then activate them one at a time, testing your site after each step. Also, be on the lookout for theme vs. plug-in conflicts, which are less common but occasionally occur. If you change your theme and part of your site stops working, switch off all your plug-ins and then activate them one at a time.

You'll notice that the cached pages appear in two lists in Figure 9-23, representing two slightly different types of caching. WP Super Cache automatically chooses the type of caching that makes sense for your page. For example, if you visit your site as a logged-in user, the plug-in uses less powerful WP Cache caching instead of WP Super Cache caching. But you don't need to worry about these technical details, because WP Super Cache makes sure your pages are as fast as possible—which is always faster than they would be without caching.

NOTE WP Super Cache is smart enough to know when it needs to regenerate the cached copy of a page, most of the time. For example, if you update a post or a visitor leaves a new comment, WP Super Cache takes notice and regenerates the page. However, WP Super Cache doesn't pay attention to site design changes, so it won't notice if you change the theme or rearrange your widgets. In this situation, you need to manually clear the cache to make sure your visitors see the latest version of your site. To do that, use the Delete Cache button shown in Figure 9-23.

Once you verify that your site still works properly, you're ready to adjust a few WP Super Cache settings. Click the Advanced tab and look for settings that have "(Recommended)" next to them, in italics. This indicates a setting that improves the way WP Super Cache works for most people, but may cause problems in rare situations (and, for that reason, may be initially switched off). One example is the "Compress pages so they're served more quickly to visitors" setting, which improves performance for most people but causes trouble with some web hosts that don't support compression properly. You can try turning this setting on, but leave the other, more advanced options alone, unless you really think you know what you're doing.

PLUG-IN POWER

Even More WordPress Plug-Ins

In this chapter, you considered several of the most useful Word-Press plug-ins. However, in a directory of thousands, it's no surprise that there are many more worth considering.

You'll learn about some of these plug-ins in the following chapters (and some you'll need to discover on your own). Here's a list of some of the most popular:

- **Akismet.** This spam-fighting tool is the only plug-in that ships preinstalled (but not activated) with WordPress. You learned about it in Chapter 8.
- **WordPress SEO by Yoast.** Search-engine optimization (SEO) is the art of attracting the attention of web search engines like Google, so you can lure new visitors to your site. SEO plug-ins are among the most popular in the WordPress plug-in directory, and WordPress SEO by Yoast is an all-in-one package by one of the most renown developers in the WordPress community. You'll take a closer look at it on page 441.
- **WordPress Importer.** Moving your WordPress site from one web host to another? The WordPress Importer handles the job with relatively few speed bumps. (In Appendix A, "Migrating from WordPress.com," you'll use WordPress Importer to migrate from WordPress.com to a self-hosted site.) Automattic developed WordPress Importer.
- **TinyMCE Advanced.** You learned about this slick editor, suitable for beefing up your post-writing powers, on page 179.
- **WooCommerce.** If you want to sell products on your site, complete with a professional shopping cart and checkout process, this could be the plug-in for you. Although you won't use it in this book, you'll try out a simpler shopping cart plug-in on page 545.
- **BuddyPress.** If your website is bringing together a tightly knit community—for example, the students of a school, the employees of a business, or the members of a sports team, you can use BuddyPress to add instant social networking features to your site. Users get profiles, the ability to message one another, add photos, create content, and talk together in groups. To learn more, visit *http://buddypress.org*.
- **WP-Optimize.** This tool cleans up the junk that's often left cluttering your database. It can remove unapproved junk comments (page 282), old post revisions (page 387), and other unnecessary data that can expand the size of your database, slowing down your site and bloating your backups.
- **Limit Login Attempts.** This plug-in helps defend your site against hackers who use brute-force password-guessing attacks. You'll learn more on page 567.

CHAPTER

10

Adding Picture Galleries, Video, and Music

By now, you know that the simplest way to enhance any WordPress post is to toss in a picture or two. The Web is a visual medium, and a bit of eye candy is essential for capturing (and keeping) your readers' attention.

But modern websites rarely stop with ordinary pictures. Today's Web is splattered with rich media, including video clips, webcasts, podcasts, slideshows, and song players. In traditional websites, these ingredients can require hefty chunks of HTML and JavaScript code. But WordPress makes it easy to add media, thanks to two slick features you're about to meet: automatic embeds and shortcodes.

In this chapter, you'll use all the tools WordPress provides to add rich media to your site. First, you'll supercharge your pictures by replacing ordinary images with slideshows and galleries, and you'll learn how to transform your entire site into a photoblog or portfolio. Next, you'll see how to embed a video window in a post, and how to host your video files on YouTube or your own web server. Lastly, you'll get readers jammin' with audio tracks, playlists, and podcasts.

Understanding Embeds and Shortcodes

You'll rely on two WordPress features throughout this chapter. They're called embeds and shortcodes. Both serve the same purpose: They let you slip special types of content (like slideshows and videos) into your posts and pages without forcing you to type in a bunch of JavaScript code or HTML markup. Instead, when you use embeds and shortcodes, you ask WordPress to fill in the necessary details for you.

If you use the free WordPress.com hosting service, embeds and shortcodes aren't just about convenience—they're the only way to embed media. That's because WordPress.com prevents you from adding JavaScript code to your posts or using HTML's media-embedding <iframe> element in them. This basic precaution defends Automattic's web servers against a variety of sneaky attacks. But without these tools, there's no do-it-yourself way to integrate rich media from other websites, like YouTube for video or Flickr for photos. Thankfully, embeds and shortcodes fill the gap.

Automatic Embeds

One of the shortcuts, called an *automatic embed,* takes web addresses that point to certain media files and replaces the URL with the media file itself—in other words, it automatically embeds the real media instead of just displaying a link pointing to it.

For example, imagine you type in this URL of a photo in someone's Flickr stream:

```
http://www.flickr.com/photos/82337026@N02/7544952876/in/photostream
```

In the WordPress post editor, this web address looks ordinary enough (Figure 10-1).

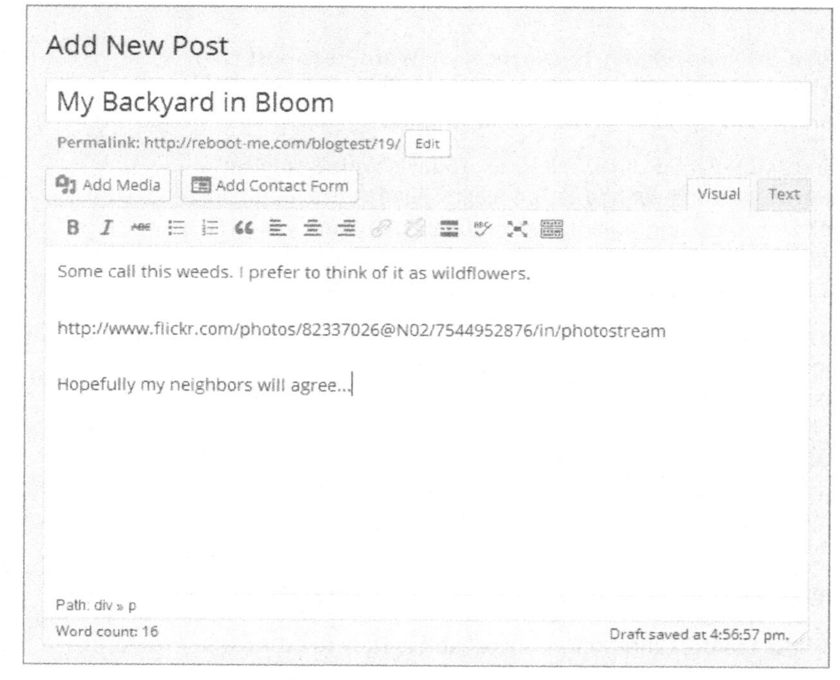

FIGURE 10-1

When you create a post (or page) that includes embedded media, there's no sign that WordPress will replace the auto-embed code with content. All you see is an ordinary web address.

But WordPress works a bit of magic when you publish the page. At that point, it realizes that your URL points to a Flickr picture. Instead of showing a boring link, WordPress grabs the corresponding picture from the Flickr site and embeds it in your post (Figure 10-2). (Of course, if it isn't your Flickr picture, you're duty-bound to ask the owner for permission before you stuff it into your site.)

NOTE Flickr, for those who haven't come across it yet, is a website that lets you store and share photos. With tens of millions of users (and billions of pictures), Flickr is the world's most popular picture-hosting service. It's also a thriving online community, with groups that attract professional photographers, hobbyists, and ordinary people who just want to show off their snapshots. You can learn more at *www.flickr.com*.

MY BACKYARD IN BLOOM
July 10, 2014 · by Charles M. Pakata · in Uncategorized
Some call this weeds. I prefer to think of it as wildflowers.
Hopefully my neighbors will agree...

FIGURE 10-2

When you view the published page (or preview a draft of it), WordPress pulls a clever sleight of hand: It turns the address that pointed to a Flickr picture into a preview of the picture itself. Even better, it makes the preview a link. Click it, and you end up on the corresponding Flickr page, where you can see the full-size picture, along with a description, additional details, and comments.

For automatic embeds to work, you need to meet several criteria:

- **The URL must be on a separate line.** Don't crowd it up next to your text. As you can see in Figure 10-1, the URL stands alone, with paragraphs of text above and below it. It's also important to make sure the URL doesn't have any hidden formatting tags—if you're not absolutely sure, take a look at the HTML in the Text tab and remove anything that doesn't belong, like the <span>, <em>, and <strong> tags.
- **The URL can't be formatted as a link.** When you paste a website address into the WordPress editor, WordPress may format that address as a real, clickable link (that is, it may wrap your web address in an <a> anchor element). Here's the problem: Links show up in the final post as, well, links. WordPress doesn't swap in rich content in their place. If the URL appears blue in the post editor

(and the address becomes underlined when you move your mouse over it), then WordPress formatted the address as a link. To turn it into plain text, select it and then click Unlink in the toolbar. Now the address turns into ordinary black text, which lets WordPress perform the URL-to-embedded-content switcheroo when it displays the page.

- **WordPress must recognize the site.** WordPress auto-embeds content from a select group of sites that share pictures, videos, music, and slideshows. It does the same for a few other specialized services, like Twitter and Polldaddy. For the full list of well over 20 sites, see *http://codex.wordpress.org/Embeds.*

Flickr is one of the best-known photo-sharing sites, but WordPress recognizes several others, including Instagram, Imgur, SmugMug, and Photobucket. However, it conspicuously fails to recognize URLs from other image-hosting services, such as Google's Picasa. To show a picture from a Picasa web album, you need to upload a copy of the picture to your site (awkward), provide a clickable link that takes the reader there (clumsy), or use a plug-in that displays Picasa pics (for self-hosters only).

WordPress constantly revises and expands its list of auto-embeds, so its recognition of other services will grow—slowly.

The [embed] Shortcode

Some WordPress aficionados write auto-embedded URLs differently from the earlier example. They add a special code before and after the URL, like this:

```
[embed]http://www.flickr.com/photos/...[/embed]
```

Here, the web address is the same, but it has an [embed] code at the beginning of the URL and a matching [/embed] code at the end. This line of code produces the same effect as in the previous example—WordPress replaces the URL with the appropriate embedded content, provided that it recognizes the URL.

The main reason you'd use the [embed] code is because it gives you the option to add two extra details: the *height* and *width* attributes. These attributes set the size of the embedded content. For example, here's how you might tell WordPress you want your embedded picture to be 200 pixels wide and 300 pixels tall:

```
[embed width="200" height="300"]http://www.flickr.com/photos/...[/embed]
```

The height and width attributes don't always give you the effect you expect. It's best to think of them as *requests*—requests that WordPress honors according to its own intricate (and slightly obscure) sizing rules. Here's a rundown of what takes place:

- If you don't specify any size information, WordPress allows the embedded content to grow until it reaches its full size or hits the boundaries of your layout. For example, if you embed post content inside a 600-pixel-wide column, your embedded picture will grow to be 600 pixels wide (and however tall it needs to be to preserve the picture's proper shape).

- If you specify the width and height attributes, you override WordPress's ordinary behavior. For example, you can specify a size to shrink a tall-and-skinny photo that would otherwise grow bigger than you want it to be. And if the media sharing site you use automatically shrinks your content, you may be able to use the width and height attributes to force it bigger. (See the box on this page for a full discussion of this often-perplexing issue.)
- You can use either the width or height attribute on its own. For example, you can scale down a piece of content using a smaller width and let WordPress choose the height automatically to match the original aspect ratio.
- WordPress doesn't let you stretch embedded content out of shape. For example, if you assign a height and width to a picture that don't match its aspect ratio, WordPress follows the most restrictive dimension and sizes the other to match.
- Different themes and plug-ins can tinker with the style rules that size the elements in your layout, including embedded content. Unfortunately, the interplay between the embedded content, WordPress, and your theme is complex. Sometimes, despite your best efforts, embedded content will refuse your resizing demands.

FREQUENTLY ASKED QUESTION

Sizing Quirks with Embedded Content

I embedded a Flickr picture, but it turned out way smaller than I expected!

Some media services replace the full-size content you think you're embedding with a smaller-size version that they think will better suit your site. This sleight of hand has a point—it's done to save bandwidth and reduce the time it takes your page to load. For example, Flickr pictures can be quite big. By handing you a smaller thumbnail (typically, a picture that's just 320 pixels wide), Flickr saves you from wasting pixels and time. However, that also means the picture that appears in your web page may be smaller than you expect.

You can solve this problem, to a certain extent, using the [embed] code with the width attribute. But there's a catch. The width attribute has no effect unless you use a size that's big enough to force Flickr to give you a bigger thumbnail. For a standard picture in portrait orientation, that width needs to be 700 pixels or more.

```
[embed width="700"]...[/embed]
```

This is somewhat counterintuitive, because many themes have less than 700 pixels of width to accommodate your picture. Twenty Twelve, for instance, has a column width of 625 pixels. However, this attribute still has the desired effect. It forces Flickr to return a larger-sized thumbnail, which your theme then scales down slightly to fit your layout.

Besides being confusing, this process leaves some notable gaps. What if you want a picture that's wider than 320 pixels but narrower than 625 pixels? Or what if you want a picture to grow beyond the size of your layout? There's no easy fix for these issues without getting your hands dirty. If you have a self-hosted site, you can avoid the auto-embed feature altogether, and copy the raw HTML markup that media sharing services like Flickr provide. Just remember to paste the markup in the Text tab (page 178), not the Visual tab. Or, for more control—and much more complexity—you can muck around with the CSS style rules that control the layout of your site (Chapter 13). Both approaches can create problems that are more aggravating than minor size issues. For most folks, the best choice is to accept the quirks of the auto-embed feature and let WordPress handle the heavy lifting.

More Shortcodes

Shortcodes are special instructions you put in your post or page. Like an auto-embedded URL, a shortcode tells WordPress to insert something in the current location. But auto-embeds are limited to a relatively small set of known websites, while shortcodes let you add a much broader range of media.

To use a shortcode, you put a predetermined code inside square brackets. For example, the following shortcode takes all the pictures attached to a post and combines them into a picture gallery:

```
An image gallery will show up here:
[gallery]
```

You'll take a much closer look at galleries in the next section. For now, the important thing to understand is that, when you add a shortcode to a page or post, WordPress inserts something out of the ordinary.

Shortcodes always have the same syntax—each one consists of a bit of text wrapped in square brackets. In fact, the [embed] instruction you learned about in the previous section is actually a shortcode that tells WordPress to examine a web address and embed the appropriate content.

NOTE You can type shortcodes into the visual editor (the Visual tab) or the HTML editor (the Text tab). Either way, WordPress recognizes the code by its square brackets.

The truly neat part about shortcodes is that they're *extensible*. If you're ambitious and you run a self-hosted WordPress site, you can create your own shortcodes (technically, it's all about editing the *functions.php* file, as described on page 500). Even better, a clever plug-in developer can create shortcodes that let you display additional types of content, including contact forms, documents, maps, charts, ads, a view counter, and a PayPal donation link.

If you run a self-hosted WordPress site, you start with the shortcodes listed in Table 10-1.

TABLE 10-1 *The basic WordPress shortcodes*

SHORTCODE	DESCRIPTION
[embed]	Wraps any embeddable URL that WordPress recognizes. You could use this shortcode for clarity, but you usually use it to size your embedded content, by adding the height and width attributes.
[gallery]	Creates a picture gallery or slideshow. Described on page 330.
[audio]	Shows an audio playback bar for an audio file (page 360).

SHORTCODE	DESCRIPTION
[video]	Shows a video playback window for a video file (page 356).
[caption]	Displays a text caption for a figure. WordPress uses it when you insert a captioned picture (page 182).
[playlist]	Creates a simple playlist of audio or video files (page 362).

If you use WordPress.com, you can tap many more shortcodes. You can use all the shortcodes listed in Table 10-1 with the exception of [video], because WordPress.com uses [wpvideo] instead (as page 359 explains). WordPress.com also includes a few dozen completely *new* shortcodes. This is handy, because WordPress.com doesn't allow plug-ins, so you can't add any shortcodes beyond those you start with.

Many of WordPress.com's extra shortcodes duplicate the features WordPress provides through automatic embeds. For example, you can insert a picture from Instagram using the image's URL (thanks to WordPress's auto-embed feature) on a WordPress.com site or a self-hosted site. But on a WordPress.com site, you have the additional option of using the [instagram] shortcode. Either way, the result is the same.

But some of WordPress.com's extra shortcodes embrace services that automatic embedding doesn't. For example, if you stumble across a fascinating TED Talks video (from the thousands at *www.ted.com*), you can use the [ted] shortcode to embed the talk in one of your posts. All you need to do is reference its ID number, like this:

```
[ted id=1458]
```

For the full list of WordPress.com-supported shortcodes, along with an example of how to use each one, visit *http://support.wordpress.com/shortcodes.*

TIP If you run a self-hosted site, you can add the extra shortcodes that WordPress.com sites get by installing the handy Jetpack plug-in (page 297).

FREQUENTLY ASKED QUESTION

Shortcodes and Sidebars

Can I use a shortcode or an auto-embedded URL in a sidebar widget?

Ordinarily, WordPress doesn't check sidebar text for auto-embed URLs and shortcodes. For example, if you add a Text widget (page 166) and put a Flickr URL in it, that URL will appear in your sidebar as ordinary text, not as an image preview.

If you use WordPress.com, you need to live with this restriction. If you're on a self-hosted site, there's a fairly easy workaround, but you need to be familiar with theme editing, an advanced topic explored in Part 4.

The solution is to add two commands (shown on page 500) to a file called *functions.php*. These commands tell WordPress to process widget text in the same way that it processes the text in a post or page—in other words, to check for auto-embedded URLs and shortcodes. Using this technique, you can put tiny videos, slideshows, galleries, and more in your sidebar without relying on a specialized widget.

Showing Groups of Pictures

Individual images are an important part of most posts and pages. As you already know, there's no limit to the number of pictures you can include in a single post—you simply need to arrange your text around them in the best way possible.

But this approach isn't ideal for posts where you want the pictures as the focal point (for example, a travelogue of your trip through Nepal) or where pictures are the *whole* point (for example, an amateur photographer's snaps on a photoblog). In both cases, you need to tame your piles of pictures and present them in a way that lets visitors browse them at their leisure. In the following sections, you'll consider a range of options for posts like these, starting with WordPress's basic gallery feature.

Creating a Gallery

A gallery displays a set of thumbnail images on a page so it's easy for visitors to scan them (Figure 10-3). To take a closer look at a pic, all you need to do is click a thumbnail.

When you click a picture in a gallery, you probably expect to see a larger version of the image. But WordPress does something a little different, and its exact behavior depends on how you host your site.

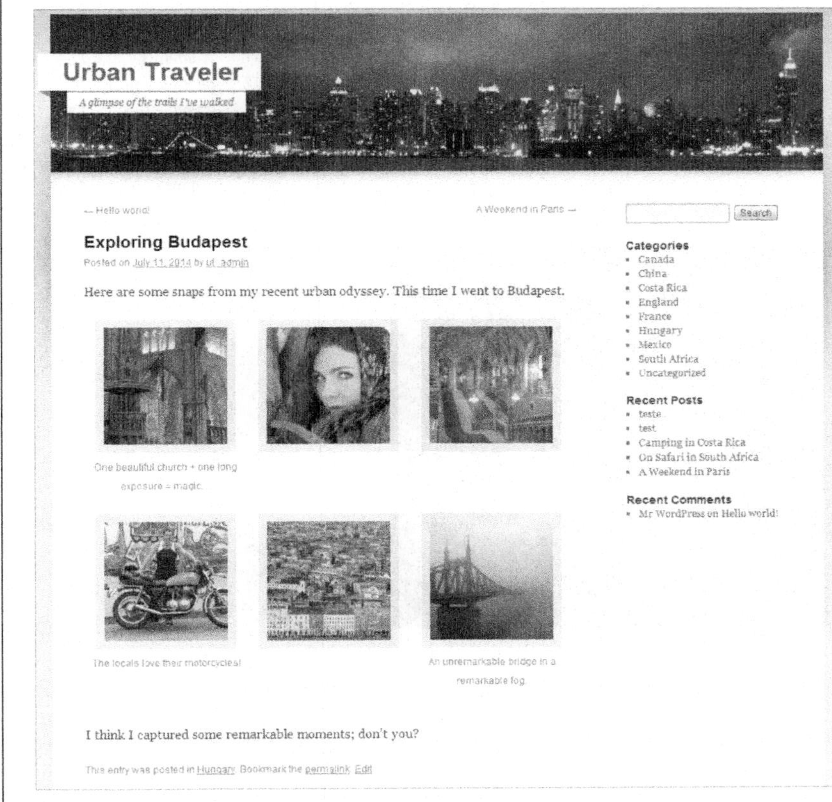

FIGURE 10-3

WordPress's gallery feature crops your pictures and arranges them in a series of rows. If you wrote captions for the images, they appear underneath the thumbnails.

If you run a self-hosted site, WordPress launches what it calls an *attachment page*, which displays the larger-size picture along with its description (if you included it) and a place for comments (Figure 10-4).

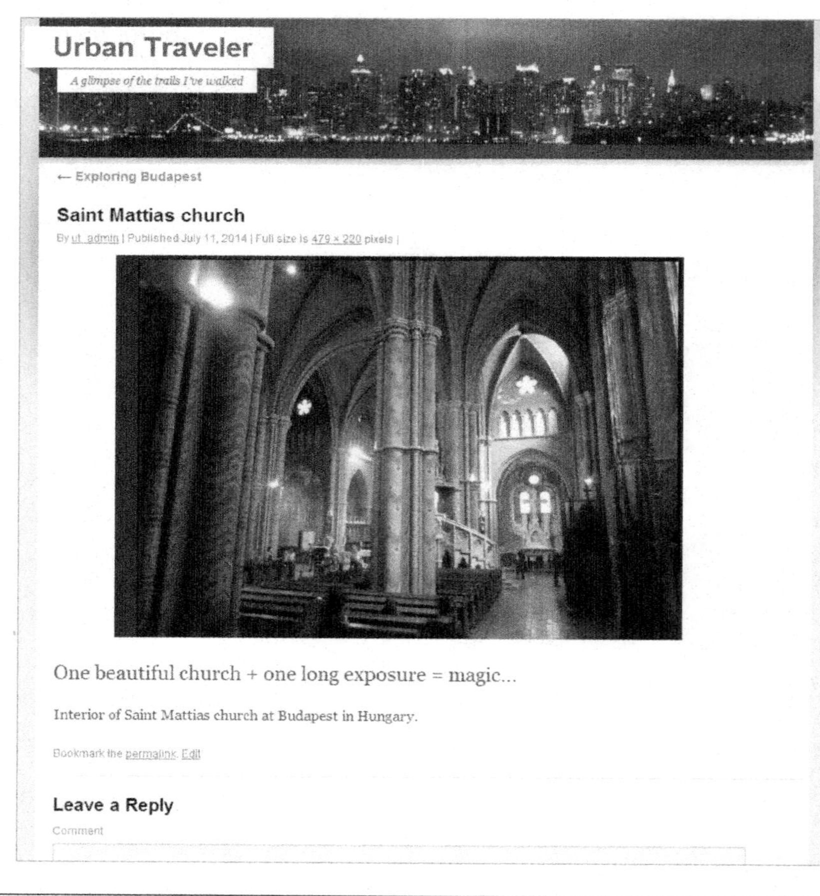

FIGURE 10-4

WordPress's attachment page, which looks like a simple version of a single-post page, comes complete with an area for comments.

WordPress.com is a bit fancier—it includes the picture in a photo carousel, and viewers can step from one picture to the next (or former) by clicking the arrows on either side of the image (Figure 10-5).

TIP A photo carousel dramatically showcases your pictures without taking the reader away from your post. Self-hosted sites can get this feature by installing the Jetpack plug-in (page 297). However, some WordPressers have found that the photo carousel doesn't work with certain theme/browser/plug-in combinations. So if you install Jetpack but you still see ordinary attachment pages instead of the photo carousel, you probably ran into one of these conflicts.

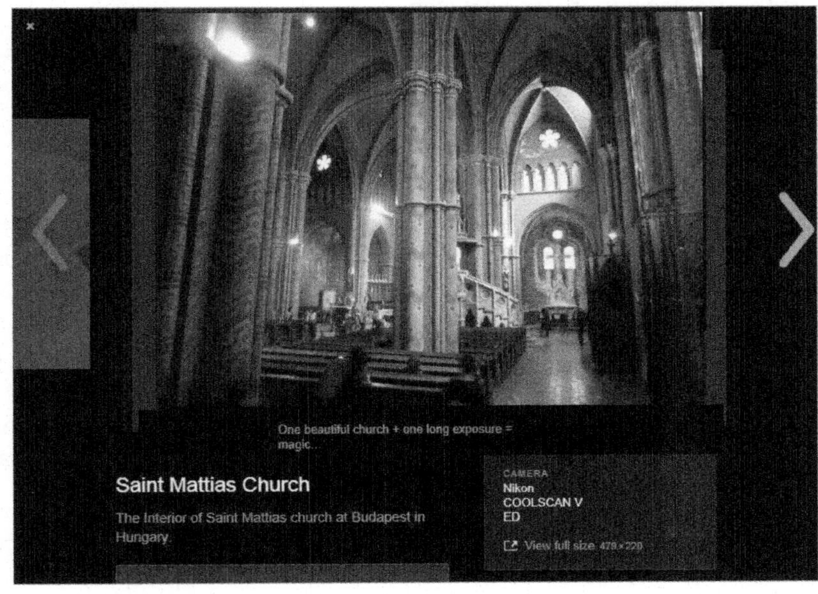

FIGURE 10-5

When a WordPress.com visitor clicks a thumbnail image, WordPress launches a photo carousel instead of a simple attachment page. It has most of the same information as an attachment page, including a comments section (not shown). It also displays each picture's EXIF data if the file includes it. (EXIF data is information that digital cameras and photo-editing software add to a photo file. For example, it may record the type of camera that took the picture, the global coordinates where the picture was taken, the time it was taken, and the camera settings used.)

NOTE You can turn off the WordPress.com photo carousel, in which case viewers see an attachment page when they click a picture. To do that, choose Settings→Media from the dashboard menu, turn off the "Display images in full-size carousel slideshow" checkbox, and then click Save Changes.

Now that you know what a gallery looks like, you're ready to add one of your own. Follow these steps:

1. **Create a new post or edit an existing one.**

   Or create or edit a page; either way, the gallery-adding process is the same.

2. **Click the Add Media button just above the edit box.**

   This is the same link you use to add single pictures. When you click it, the Insert Media window opens.

3. **Upload the pictures you want in your gallery.**

   As you already know, you can upload files from your computer in two ways. One option is to drag them from your file browser (Windows Explorer or the Mac Finder) and drop them onto the page. The other is to click Select Files, browse for the pics, and then choose Open. Either way, WordPress uploads the pictures to your site's media library (page 186).

If you already have the pictures in your media library, you don't need to upload anything. Skip ahead to the next step.

NOTE You can use a combination of existing pictures (ones you already uploaded to your media library) and new ones. Just upload the new pictures and then skip ahead to the next step.

4. **Once you upload the files, click the Create Gallery link on the left.**

   WordPress switches to the Media Library tab and shows you a grid of all the pictures you've ever uploaded. If you've got a thriving site that's been around for a while, the list may be quite long. However, WordPress automatically selects the pictures you uploaded in step 3 and puts them at the top of your list (Figure 10-6). If these are all the pictures you need, you're ready to carry on to the next step.

   To add another picture to the gallery, click it. (Repeat this step to select as many pictures as you want.) To remove a picture, deselect it by clicking the checkmark in the top-right corner of the thumbnail.

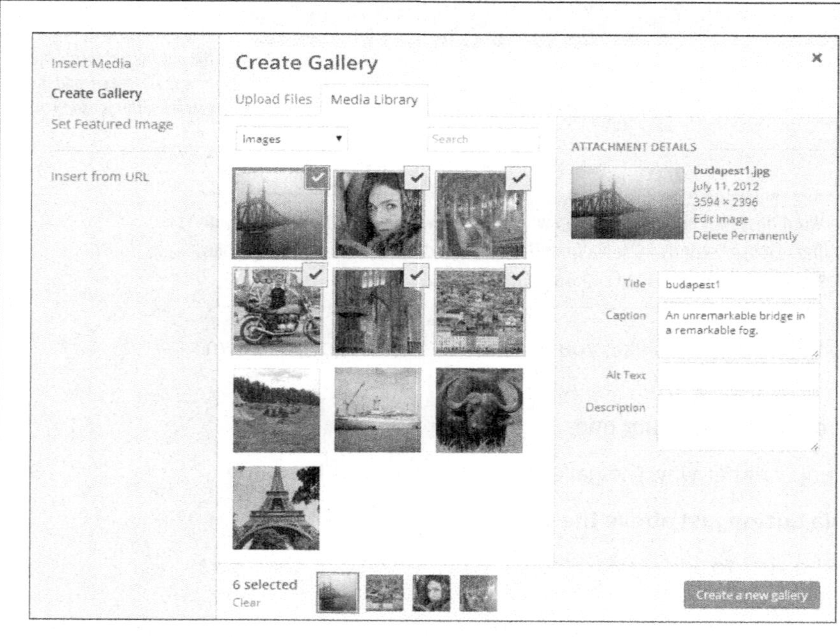

FIGURE 10-6
WordPress denotes selected pictures with checkmarks. Here, the selected pictures are the six photos you just uploaded.

5. **Enter a description for each picture.**

   This is the same process you follow when you insert a single picture. Click each picture, one after the other, and then fill in the boxes on the right:

   - **Title.** This is the text that pops up when someone points to the picture.
   - **Caption.** This is a bit of optional text that, if you provide it, shows up under the picture.
   - **Alternate Text.** Use this box to describe the picture so that accessibility tools like screen readers can "speak" the text. Alternate text also helps search engines understand what a picture shows.
   - **Description.** This box contains additional text that appears on the picture's attachment page (Figure 10-4) or in a photo carousel.

6. **Once you add descriptive information for all your pictures, click "Create a new gallery" at the bottom right.**

   WordPress displays the pictures you picked in your gallery (Figure 10-7).

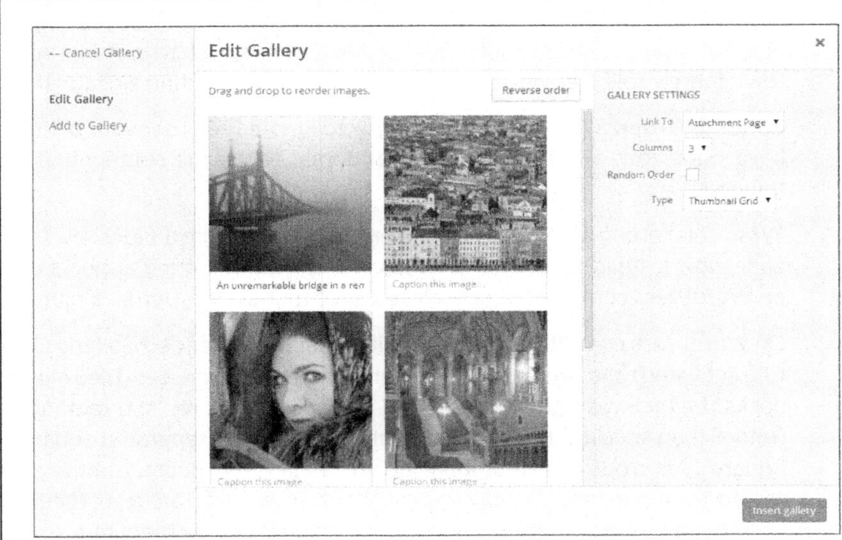

FIGURE 10-7

Here are the selected pictures, with captions, as they'll appear in your gallery.

7. **Drag your pictures into the order you want.**

   The WordPress gallery displays pictures in the order you picked them. That means the picture you picked first is the first one in the gallery. To rearrange them, simply drag the one you want to move to a new place.

   To reverse your picture order, so the first picture becomes the last, the second picture becomes the second to last, and so on, click "Reverse order."

If you prefer to let WordPress mix up your pictures every time someone views the gallery, turn on the Random Order checkbox, which appears on the right.

8. **Tweak your gallery settings (in the Gallery Settings section on the right).**

   WordPress gives you several options for fine-tuning your gallery. They include:

   - **Link To.** This determines what page appears when someone clicks a thumbnail in the gallery. Ordinarily, this is the attachment page (choose Attachment Page to make it so), but you can keep things simple by showing the full-size image on its own, with no extra information (choose Media File). Or you can turn off links altogether (choose None).

NOTE If you use the photo carousel feature (page 333), WordPress ignores the Link To setting. Instead, it shows a photo carousel when a visitor clicks a picture.

   - **Columns.** Ordinarily, a gallery row displays three thumbnails per line (see Figure 10-3). But some themes can accommodate more mini-pics. If that's the case for you, choose a different number here. But be warned: If your layout column isn't wide enough for your pictures, WordPress breaks up the pics unevenly. For example, if you pick five gallery columns but your layout only has space for three pictures, WordPress splits each row of five into a row of three, followed by a row of two, creating a distracting zigzag effect.
   - **Random Order.** Switch on this checkbox to ignore the order your pictures have right now, and arrange them randomly each time someone views the page.
   - **Type.** This setting lets you change an ordinary gallery into a slideshow (pick Slideshow instead of Thumbnail Grid). However, this setting appears only on WordPress.com sites or self-hosted sites that use the Jetpack plug-in.

     On WordPress.com sites (or Jetpack sites that have the Tiled Galleries feature activated), the Type list includes three more exotic choices. Tiled Mosaic packs the pictures tightly together in a jigsaw of squares and rectangles (rather than spacing them out in the standard, neatly separated squares). Square Tiles crops each thumbnail down to a perfect square, trimming off the edges if needed. Circles crops each thumbnail into a circle. The best way to get a sense for these fancy gallery types is to try them out.

9. **Click "Insert gallery" at the bottom right.**

   This adds the gallery to your post (Figure 10-8). You can now publish your post.

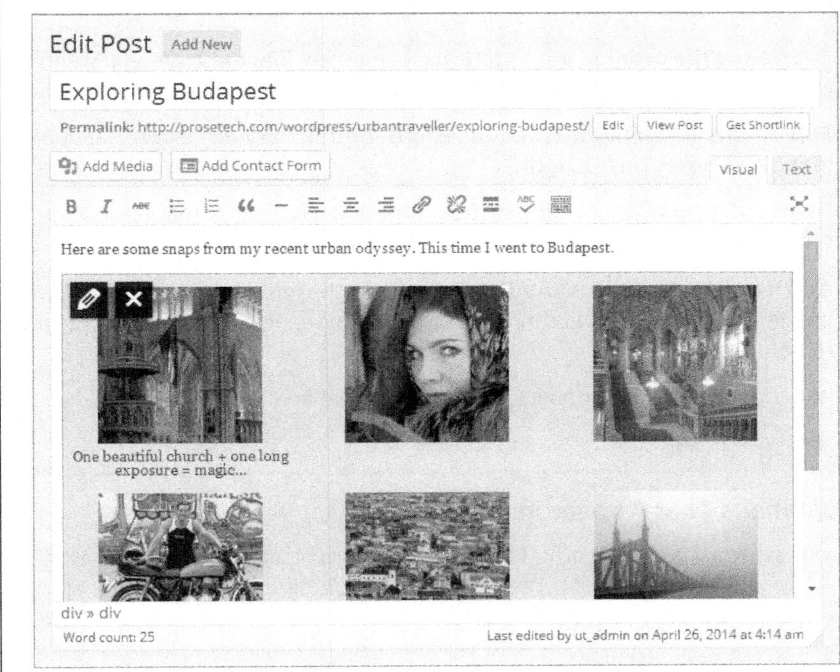

FIGURE 10-8

There's no need to preview your post to check out your new gallery. WordPress provides a faithful depiction of the gallery in the Visual tab of the post editor.

If you click the Text tab to switch to HTML view, you see that your post now contains a [gallery] shortcode that looks something like this:

```
[gallery ids="341,185,342,340,246,339"]
```

There's an ID number for each picture in your gallery. In the example above, the first picture in the gallery has the ID number 341, the second one has the ID 185, and so on. You can find the matching pictures in the media library.

The HTML view of your gallery-enriched post is more notable for what it *doesn't* contain. There are no image tags, links, or other HTML wizardry. Instead, WordPress examines the [gallery] shortcode and then creates the gallery on the fly every time someone requests the page.

Editing a Gallery

To alter a gallery, edit your post and, in the visual editor, click the gallery to select it. Two icons appear in the top-left corner of the gallery: a pencil and a large X.

Click the X if you want to delete your gallery. Click the pencil and you wind up on the Edit Gallery page shown in Figure 10-7. There, you can do any of the following:

- **Edit gallery settings.** These settings appear in the Gallery Settings box on the right.
- **Rearrange the order of your pictures.** Drag them into the order you want, just as you did when you first created the gallery.
- **Edit picture information.** Select a picture and edit the information that appears in the text boxes on the right.
- **Delete pictures.** Point to the picture, and then click the X that appears in the top-right corner.
- **Add new pictures.** Click "Add to Gallery" on the left. Now you can pick more images from the media library or drag one or more new pictures onto the page to upload them.

To make your changes permanent, click "Update gallery" when you finish.

FREQUENTLY ASKED QUESTION

Changing the Thumbnails That Appear in a Gallery

Is there any way to change the way WordPress displays my thumbnails?

You're bound to encounter this at some point: Your thumbnails are too small. Or too big. Or you don't want them square-shaped. What to do?

Ordinarily, WordPress creates square thumbnails, measuring 150 pixels wide by 150 pixels tall. If your picture isn't a perfect square, WordPress crops off the edges to *make* it a square.

There are two ways to change the size and shape of your thumbnails. The first is to edit the [gallery] shortcode in HTML view (using the Text tab), and add the *size* attribute, which can take one of several values. The default is *thumbnail*, but your other choices are *medium* or *large*, which tell WordPress to get medium-sized (300 × 300 pixels) or large-sized (1024 × 1024 pixels) versions of your picture and display them instead. In both cases, WordPress sizes the picture proportionally, rather than cropping it into a square.

This raises an excellent question: How does WordPress decide how big to make your thumbnails in the first place, not to mention the medium- and large-sized versions of your pictures? The answer leads to the second way to change your gallery thumbnails—by changing the settings in the Settings→Media section of the dashboard. There you see settings that let you tweak the standard thumbnail size (150 × 150), as well as the maximum dimensions for medium-size pictures and large ones. On a self-hosted site, you'll also find a setting named "Crop thumbnail to exact dimensions." Turn off the checkbox and WordPress proportionally sizes your thumbnails to match the dimensions of the actual picture, rather than cropping it into a square (see Figure 10-9).

One caveat applies when you change these settings: WordPress creates the thumbnails when you upload your pictures, so the galleries you created so far will continue using the old thumbnails (unless you re-upload the pictures and re-create the gallery). If you run a self-hosted WordPress site, you can fix this problem using the Regenerate Thumbnails plug-in (*http://tinyurl.com/rthumb*). Once you install and activate it, you can create new thumbnails by visiting the media library (choose Media→Library). Turn on the checkbox next to all the pictures you want to change, and then choose Regenerate Thumbnails in the Bulk Action list. Finally, click Apply to re-create the thumbnails for those pictures.

Exploring Budapest

Posted on July 11, 2014 by ut_admin

Here are some snaps from my recent urban odyssey. This time I went to Budapest.

One beautiful church + one long exposure = magic...

An unremarkable bridge in a remarkable fog.

The locals love their motorcycles!

FIGURE 10-9

Here, WordPress has proportionally sized the thumbnails. If a picture is tall and skinny, WordPress makes it 150 pixels tall and as wide as necessary. If a picture is short and wide, WordPress makes it 150 pixels wide and as tall as necessary. (Of course, you can adjust these size maximums on the Media Settings page.)

Creating a Slideshow

A slideshow is similar to a gallery in that it gives you an elegant way to deal with a group of related pictures. But where a gallery shows a group of photos all at once, a slideshow displays your pictures one at a time, typically framed by a small box (Figure 10-10).

DINNER AT CRÈME FRAÎCHE
March 19, 2014 · by Charles M. Pakata · in Uncategorized · Edit
Our meal was spectacular. Watch the slideshow for the highlights (and try not to drool on the keyboard!)

FIGURE 10-10

When you visit a page that contains a slideshow, you see a box with your image against a black background. WordPress holds on each pic for about 4 seconds. Although you can't change the speed of the slideshow, viewers can use the pause button to halt it and the arrow buttons to move through the pictures at their own pace.

If you use WordPress.com, it's easy to add a basic slideshow. In fact, you follow the same process you followed to create a gallery, with one exception: In the second-to-last step (that's step 8, on page 336), you change the Type from Thumbnail Grid to Slideshow. You can transform an existing gallery into a slideshow the same way.

Once upon a time, WordPress.com used a separate [slideshow] shortcode for slideshows. Although this shortcode still works, WordPress doesn't use it anymore. Instead, it tweaks the gallery shortcode by adding a type attribute. If you switch to the HTML view of your post after you add a slideshow, you see something like this:

```
[gallery type="slideshow" ids="341,185,342,340,246,339"]
```

Freshly installed self-hosted WordPress sites don't offer slideshows. You can add the type attribute to the [gallery] shortcode, but it won't have any effect. However, slideshow support is just a plug-in away if you add Jetpack.

To create an even better slideshow, you need to go beyond WordPress and its plug-ins. Flickr offers the gold standard for slideshows, and if you have a Flickr account, you can drop a Flickr slideshow into any WordPress post or page. All you need is the right web address.

The easiest way to create a Flickr slideshow is to get a link for your entire photo stream (all the pictures you uploaded to Flickr, in other words). To do that, click your photo stream, click the tiny sharing button near the top-right corner of the page (Figure 10-11), and then choose "Grab the link." You'll see a link like this:

```
http://www.flickr.com/photos/82337026@N02/
```

To convert this to a slideshow link, add the text */show* to the end of your web address, like this:

```
http://www.flickr.com/photos/82337026@N02/show/
```

Using this web address, you see a slideshow that steps through all your Flickr pictures.

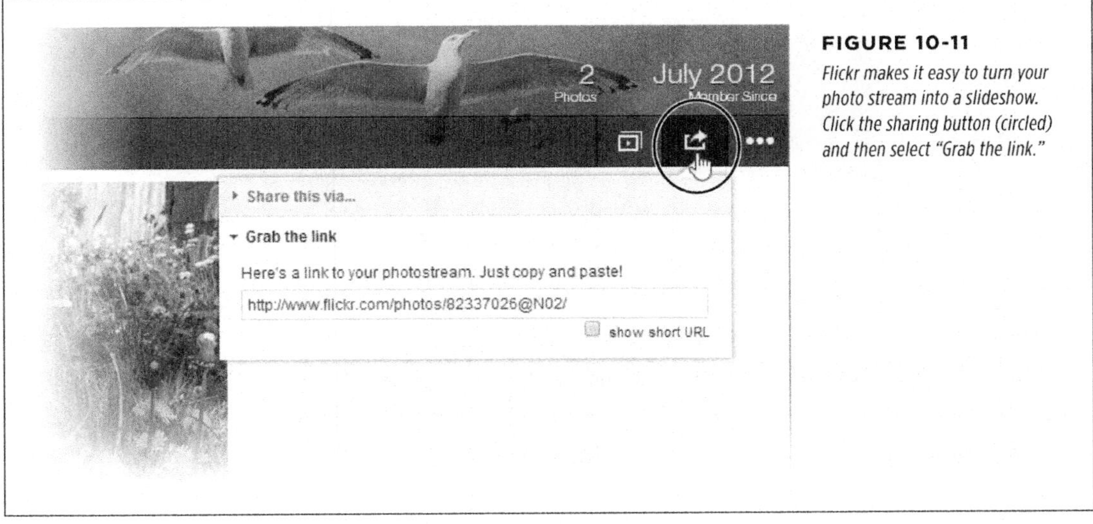

FIGURE 10-11

Flickr makes it easy to turn your photo stream into a slideshow. Click the sharing button (circled) and then select "Grab the link."

Next, you need to copy this address into a post or page, on its own line. Lastly, publish your page. Through the magic of auto-embedding, WordPress recognizes your slide-show URL and embeds a small version of the slideshow in your post (Figure 10-12).

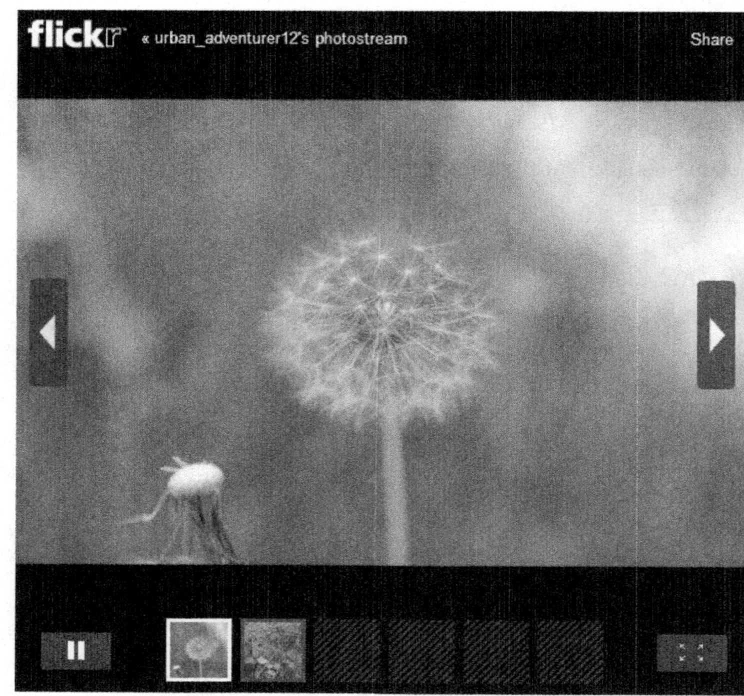

Summer Bloom
Here are some pictures I snapped walking through Regency Park. It seems they've let things go a bit.
flickr « urban_adventurer12's photostream
Share
What do you think. Raw beauty or weed disaster?
This entry was posted in Uncategorized by Katya Greenview. Bookmark the permalink.

FIGURE 10-12

This post includes a Flickr slideshow. Readers can browse the pictures by clicking a thumbnail, using the arrow buttons, or just letting the show unfold.

TIP If you're a Flickr expert, you know that you can make a *photo set* that includes just some of your pictures. Conceptually, a photo set is like an album of shots you select and arrange in any order, which makes it more suitable for a slideshow. Once you create a photo set (which takes just a few drags and drops using Flickr's Organizr tool), you can click the familiar Slideshow button to get a URL for it.

GEM IN THE ROUGH

Using a Slideshow from Another Site

Some websites have perfectly good slideshow features, but they don't offer the super-cool convenience of WordPress auto-embedding. Examples include Picasa, Photobucket, and SmugMug. In the future, WordPress may offer better integration with these services, but for now self-hosters have two good options.

The first is to use a plug-in that supports your favorite photo site. One good example is Photonic (*http://tinyurl.com/wp-photonic*), which lets you display galleries and slideshows from Flickr, SmugMug, Picasa, and 500px.

The second option is to add your slideshow the old-fashioned way, using HTML. The basic idea is this: You ask your picture-sharing service to give you the HTML markup you need for an embedded slideshow. Usually, this is a block of cryptic code that starts with an <object> or <iframe> element. The details don't matter, because you don't need to actually understand this markup. You simply need to copy and paste it.

The exact steps depend on the photo site you use. Usually, the first step is to click a button named Share or Embed. You may need to specify a few details, like the size of your slideshow window, before the site generates the HTML you need. Once you finish, select and then copy the HTML, switch your post to HTML view, and then paste in the markup. But be warned—if you switch back to the visual editor, it may disrupt your new code.

Themes That Make the Most of Pictures

Some sites are all about pictures and little else. For example, you might create a photoblog to showcase your nature photography. You could use the techniques you learned above to add galleries and slideshows, but the results won't be ideal. Standard WordPress themes split up your pictures, making it impossible for visitors to browse your portfolio from beginning to end. And, worse, ordinary WordPress themes deemphasize pictures, hiding them deep in your site, behind a wall of posts.

The solution is to find a picture-centric theme, one that puts the focus on your pictures, without letting text, menus, and needless clicking get in the way. Happily, you can build specialized, picture-heavy sites like this in WordPress. All you need is a photoblog or *portfolio* theme.

There are several good options in the WordPress.com theme gallery, and many more in the much larger theme collection for self-hosted sites. Either way, you can dig up good candidates by searching for words like "photo," "photoblog," "picture," and "portfolio."

FREQUENTLY ASKED QUESTION

Comparing Photoblogs and Portfolios

Photoblogs and portfolios both feature pictures. What's the difference?

There's a considerable overlap between photoblogs and portfolio sites, and it's worth checking out both options if you want to build a site that emphasizes images. That said, there's a subtle distinction between these two theme types.

Usually, photoblogs show off your photography skills and the snapshots you took. Like ordinary blogs, photoblogs arrange posts in a chronological sequence to tell a story. For example, your photoblog might show the pictures from your recent trip, the sights you saw on a morning stroll, or the food you ate at a favorite restaurant.

By comparison, portfolio sites are subject-based. That subject could be portraits, architecture, fashion, or something entirely different. Often, portfolio sites are intended to showcase something, like the works you've created or the products you sell. Dates are optional and sometimes unimportant.

Every photoblog and portfolio theme works a bit differently, but most share some key features. First, the home page likely displays the *pictures* in your posts rather than the posts themselves. Figure 10-13 shows an example from Foto, a photography theme for self-hosted sites.

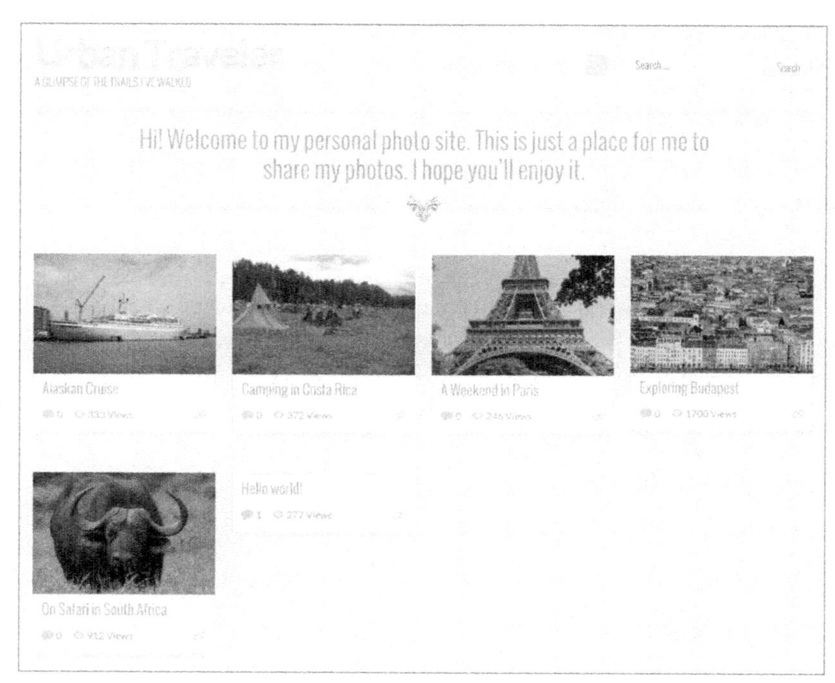

FIGURE 10-13

Instead of an ordinary list of posts for its home page, the Foto theme creates a tiled display of images. It also adds a neat animated effect: When you move your mouse over a picture, the image expands slightly. You can then click the enlarged tile to read the full post.

The Foto theme requires that you set a featured image for each of your posts (page 190). If you don't, that post's home-page tile will be blank. Many photoblog and portfolio themes work this way, so if you don't see the pictures you expect after you switch themes, you most likely haven't specified featured images for your posts.

Other themes aren't as picky, and grab the first picture in a post, no matter what it is. One example is the self-hosted theme PinBlack. Like Foto, PinBlack creates a home page of tiled pictures. Unlike Foto, PinBlack uses any post picture it can get. If you try out PinBlack, you'll notice other, more subtle differences as well. For example, its home page feels a bit more serious and businesslike, with a sleek gray-and-black color scheme with lime accents. (PinBlack is the starting point for the custom theme that powers the furniture store example developed in Chapter 14.)

Often, photoblog and portfolio themes assume that, for each of your posts, you'll include just a single picture. They give special attention to this picture (which may be the featured image or just the first image in the post) by making it larger than normal and placing it at the top of the post.

Photoblog and portfolio themes often include Back and Forward buttons that let readers move from one post to another, without making an interim stop at the home page and selecting from the full list of posts. This way, readers can browse your pictures and posts just as though they were scanning an image gallery, even if the pics appear in separate posts. Figure 10-14 shows how the back and forward buttons work with the Foto theme.

NOTE When a picture appears in a lightbox, it floats over the web page, with the content behind it dimmed. This is the same effect you get when you view one of the pictures in a photo carousel, as described earlier. To douse the lightbox, click the X in the top-right corner of the picture box.

WordPress.com also includes attractive photoblog and portfolio themes. One notable example is the Duotone theme, which is designed to be a simple but beautiful way to showcase your photography.

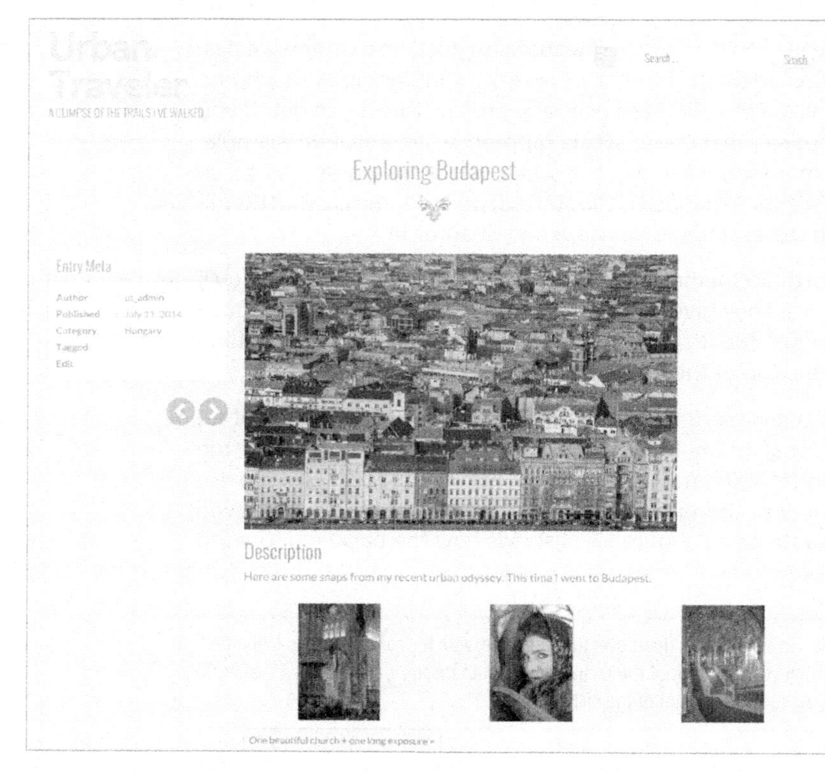

FIGURE 10-14

The Foto theme is designed for picture browsing. You use the arrow buttons to move from one post to another. If you click the featured image, it expands into a lightbox, dimming the content behind it.

Duotone doesn't include a picture-tile home page. Instead, it takes viewers straight into picture-browsing mode. Guests begin with a picture from your most recent post and use the arrow buttons to step from one post to the next, just as visitors do with the Foto theme (Figure 10-15). The Duotone theme also has an unusual frill—every time a visitor moves to a new post, the theme picks a color from that post's picture and uses it as the background color.

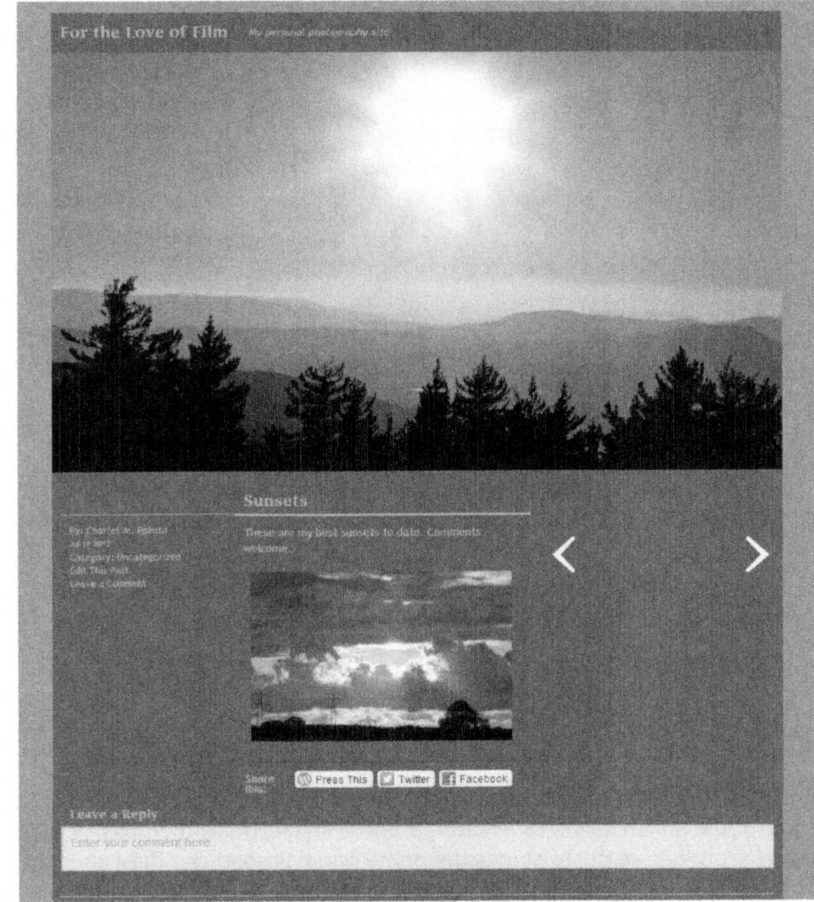

FIGURE 10-15

The Duotone theme takes the first picture from a post, moves it above the post title, and enlarges it as much as possible. If a post has more than one picture, the other pictures remain in their original location in the post.

WordPress.com also includes portfolio themes. One is the professionally polished Imbalance 2. Much like Foto, Imbalance 2 creates a tiled display of featured images, but it also includes an excerpt from each post, as you can see in Figure 10-16.

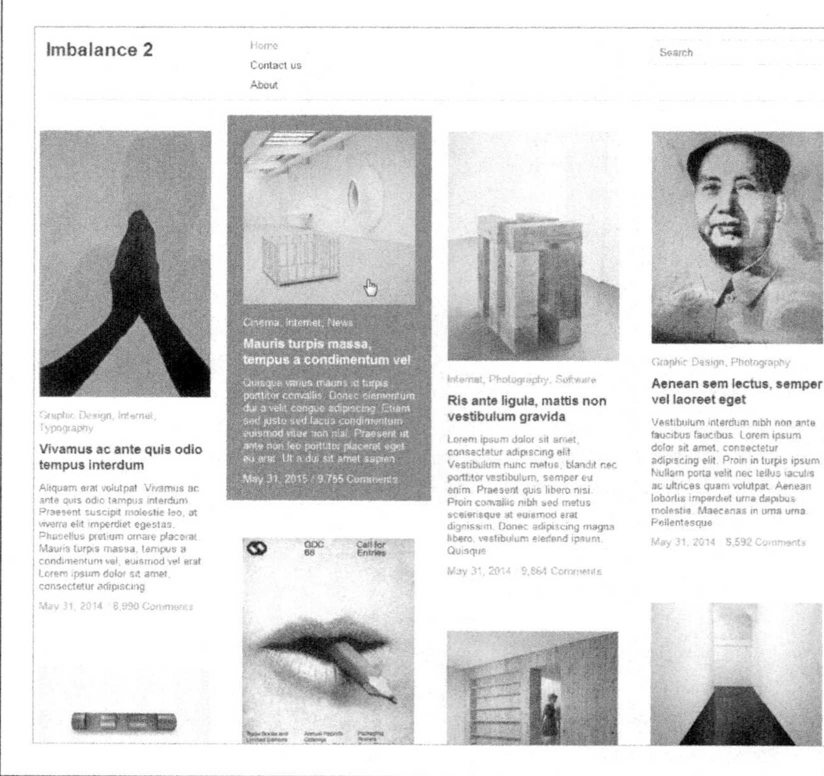

FIGURE 10-16

This demo site for the Imbalance 2 theme demonstrates its remarkable layout. It accepts and neatly arranges irregularly sized tiles made up of featured images (page 190) and post excerpts (page 198) into a seamless grid. If you move your mouse over a tile, the theme highlights it with an arresting orange background.

Finally, it's worth noting that some themes, while not all-out photoblogs or portfolio sites, offer some enhanced picture features. For example, many themes place a strip of pictures from recent posts across the home page. Sometimes they animate the strip, so that the pictures slide by or blend into each other, one after the other. The most obvious example is Twenty Fourteen, but you can also see this feature in the Canton School example (page 192).

NOTE At first glance, Twenty Fourteen can be mistaken for a photoblog, especially if you use the grid of pictures on the home page. However, there are clear differences. Once you scroll past the picture grid or slider, you find an ordinary list of posts, just as you do on all the standard year themes. And Twenty Fourteen doesn't provide arrows to let you step from post to post, which are a hallmark of many photoblogs.

Embedding a Video

Now that you've jazzed up your site with pictures, it's time for something even more ambitious: video.

There are two reasons you might put a video playback window in a post (or page). First, you may want to use someone else's video to add a little something extra to your content (which is the ordinary text in your post). For example, if you comment on a local protest concert, your post will be more interesting if you include a clip of the event. Similarly, if you review a new movie, you might include its trailer. If you talk about a trip to Egypt, you might want to take visitors inside the pyramids. In all these examples, the video adds a bit of context to your post.

The other possibility is that the video may actually *be* your content. For example, you might use video to show your band's latest live performance, a bike-repair tutorial you filmed in your garage, or a blistering web rant about the ever-dwindling size of a Pringles can. In all these cases, you create the video and then use your WordPress site to share it with a larger audience.

TIP Depending on the type of site you create, your written content doesn't need to be *about* the video—instead, the video could add supplementary information or a bit of visual distraction. For example, you may talk about your favorite coffee blend and add a video that shows the grueling coffee harvest in Indonesia. Used carefully and sparingly, video accompaniment can enhance your posts in the same way a whimsical picture cribbed from a free photo service can.

To present someone else's video on your site, find the movie on a video-sharing site and copy the address. Most of the time, that video-sharing site will be YouTube, the wildly popular hub that rarely drops out of the top three world's most visited websites.

And if you want to show your *own* videos, you'll probably *still* turn to a video-hosting service like YouTube because the alternative—uploading your video files straight to your web server—has some significant drawbacks. Here are some of the reasons you should strongly consider a video-hosting service:

- **Bandwidth.** Video files are large—vastly bigger than any other sort of content you can put on a site, even truckloads of pictures. And although you probably have room for your video files on your web server, you might not have the bandwidth allotment you need to play back the videos for all your visitors, especially if your website picks up some buzz and has a hot month. The result could be extra charges or even a crashed website that refuses to respond to anyone.

NOTE Bandwidth allotment refers to how much web traffic your site host allows. Hosts may limit bandwidth so that an extremely busy site—one with lots of visitors stopping by or downloading files—doesn't affect the performance of other sites the service hosts.

- **Encoding.** Usually, the kind of file you create when you record a video differs from the kind you need when you want to share it online. When recording, you need a high-quality format that stands up well to editing. But when viewing a video over the Web, you need a heavily compressed, streamlined format that ensures smooth, stutter-free playback. Sadly, the process of converting your video files to a web-friendly format is time-consuming, and it often requires some technical knowledge.
- **Compatibility.** In today's world, there's no single web-friendly video format that accommodates the variety of web browsers, devices (computers, tablets, and mobile phones), and web connections (fast and slow) out there. Video services like YouTube solve this problem by encoding the same video file multiple times, so that there's a version that works well for everyone. You can do the same on your own, but without a pricey professional tool, you're in for hours of tedium.

For all these reasons, it rarely makes sense to go it alone with video files, even if you produce them yourself. Instead, pick a good video service and park your files there. In the following section, you'll start with YouTube.

UP TO SPEED

The Dangers of Using Other People's Video

The risk of embedding other people's videos is that the video hosting service may take the videos down, often because of copyright issues, and they'll disappear from your site, too. This is a particularly acute danger for videos that include content owned by someone other than the uploader. Examples include scenes from television shows and fan-made music videos.

Usually, WordPress authors don't worry about this problem—if a video goes dead, they edit their posts after the fact. To avoid potential problems from the get-go, stay away from clips that are obviously cribbed from someone else's content, especially if they're recent. For example, a video that shows a segment from last night's *Saturday Night Live* broadcast is clearly at risk of being taken down. A decades-old bootleg recording of a Grateful Dead concert is probably safe.

Showing a YouTube Video

Hosting a YouTube video in WordPress is ridiculously easy. All you need is the video's web address.

To get it, start by visiting the video page on YouTube. (If you're one of the six people who haven't yet visited YouTube, start at *www.youtube.com*.) If you haven't already found the video you want, you can spend some time searching around.

When you find the right video, click the Share link under the video window. A panel of information pops open, including a text box with the URL you need (Figure 10-17).

The URL will look something like this:

```
http://youtu.be/OxKKrOQrcjg
```

The first part, *youtu.be*, is a more compact form of the video's full web address (which starts with *www.youtube.com/watch?v=*). The string of letters and numbers after it uniquely identifies the video you want.

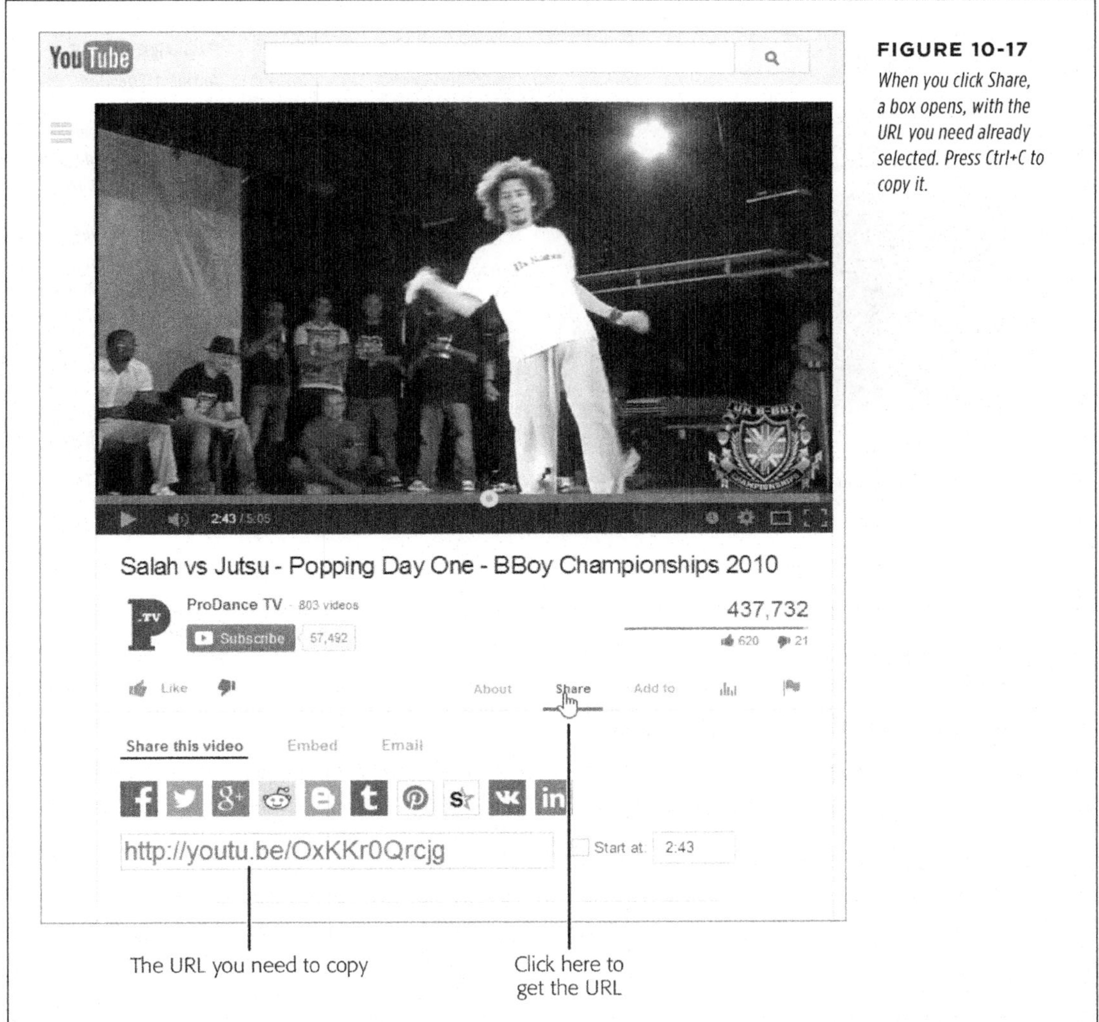

FIGURE 10-17

When you click Share, a box opens, with the URL you need already selected. Press Ctrl+C to copy it.

The next step is even easier. Paste the video URL into your WordPress post, on a separate line, in the location where you want the video to appear, like this:

```
If you consider yourself a fan of popping and locking (and I do), the
World Classic is an event you cannot miss.

http://youtu.be/OxKKrOQrcjg

Here, Jutsu breaks out some sick moves against the battle-master Salah ...
```

Now publish your post. You'll be rewarded with another transformation, courtesy of WordPress's auto-embed feature. This time the URL turns into an embedded video window (Figure 10-18).

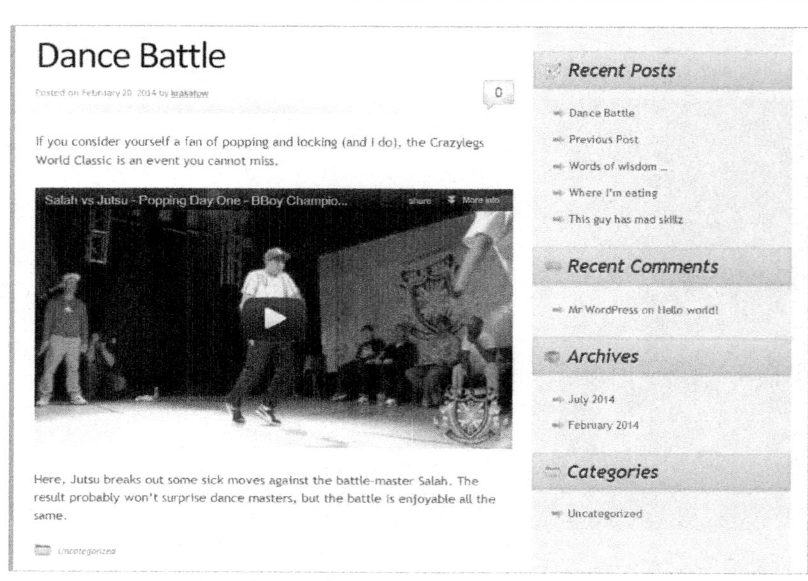
Dance Battle
If you consider yourself a fan of popping and locking (and I do), the Crazylegs World Classic is an event you cannot miss.
Salah vs Jutsu - Popping Day One - BBoy Champio...
Here, Jutsu breaks out some sick moves against the battle-master Salah. The result probably won't surprise dance masters, but the battle is enjoyable all the same.
Uncategorized
Recent Posts
Dance Battle
Previous Post
Words of wisdom ...
Where I'm eating
This guy has mad skillz
Recent Comments
Mr WordPress on Hello world!
Archives
July 2014
February 2014
Categories
Uncategorized

FIGURE 10-18

The main difference between visiting a video on YouTube and seeing it in a post is that videos in posts don't start playing automatically. You need to click the video window to get things started. Also, the ancillary information that appears on the YouTube page, such as the description of the video and the viewer comments, doesn't appear in the embedded video window.

UP TO SPEED

Uploading Your Videos to YouTube

The process of playing your own videos through YouTube is essentially the same as the one for showcasing someone else's. The only difference is that you begin by signing up with YouTube (if you don't already have an account) and then uploading your video. The steps are fairly straightforward—click the Upload link at the top of the home page, next to the YouTube search box, and then follow the instructions YouTube gives you. Make sure you designate your video as *public*, which means that it appears in YouTube's search results. If you don't use this setting, you won't be able to embed your video in a WordPress post. Other settings (for example, whether you allow comments and ratings) have no effect on whether you can embed the video.

For best results, YouTube recommends that you upload the highest quality video file you have, even if that file is ridiculously big. YouTube will encode it in a more compressed, web-friendly format, while preserving as much of the quality as possible. And if the quality of your video is good enough, YouTube will offer high-speed viewers the option to watch it in high-definition format, using the H.264 standard.

Uploading videos takes a while, because the files are huge and transferring all that data takes time, even on the fastest network connection. YouTube also needs to process your video, although its industrial-strength servers can do most of that as you upload it. When you get the video live on YouTube, click Share to get the URL you need for your WordPress post, which you can paste alongside your content, exactly as you did before.

Configuring the YouTube Video Window

If the embedded window looks the way you want it to, there's no need to do anything else. But if you want to tweak its size, you can.

The easiest way to do that is by using the height and width attributes of the [embed] shortcode, as you did earlier. Here's an example that caps the video window at 300 pixels wide, rather than letting it grow to fit the column it's in (Figure 10-19):

```
[embed width="300"]http://youtu.be/OxKKrOQrcjg[/embed]
```

This straightforward approach doesn't always work. Certain themes and plug-ins accidentally disrupt the sizing process, leaving you with full-sized YouTube videos. To narrow down the cause of the problem, try disabling all your plug-ins one by one, and then re-enabling them individually until you find the misbehaving plug-in. If that doesn't help, you can also try previewing your post with a different theme.

NOTE The shape of the video window depends on the video itself. YouTube won't stretch a video out of its normal proportions. For that reason, you should probably specify just the width or height of your video, but not both. If you do use both, your video window will get the dimensions you specify, but YouTube will pad the video with blank space to avoid stretching it.

Once you switch to the [embed] shortcode, you're free to make a few other refinements. The trick is to tack extra pieces of information to the end of the YouTube URL. However, there's a catch. This technique works on WordPress.com sites and on self-hosted sites that use the Jetpack plug-in. But if you try it on a self-hosted site that doesn't use Jetpack, the altered URL will confuse the embedding processes and you'll wind up with an ordinary link instead of a video window.

There are three details you can change by editing the URL. First, adding *&rel=0* to the end of the URL hides YouTube's "related videos" teaser, which usually plays after your video. Web authors use this feature to make sure their readers won't catch sight of someone else's content, become distracted, and then surf away to watch more videos or visit a different site. Here's an example:

```
[embed]http://youtu.be/OxKKrOQrcjg&rel=0[/embed]
```

You can also set where playback should start and where it should end by adding *&start* and *&end* to the URL, along with a number of seconds. For example, this video player hides related videos, starts playback at the 1-minute mark (when the viewer presses the Play button), and pauses it at the 2-minute mark:

```
[embed]http://youtu.be/OxKKrOQrcjg&rel=0&start=60&end=120[/embed]
```

Finally, it's worth noting that you can do the same thing using a slightly different syntax with the [youtube] shortcode:

```
[youtube=http://youtu.be/OxKKrOQrcjg&rel=0&start=60&end=120]
```

In the old days of WordPress (a couple of years ago), the [youtube] shortcode was mandatory, so it persists as a popular technique. But once again, your site needs to be on WordPress.com, or it needs the help of the Jetpack plug-in.

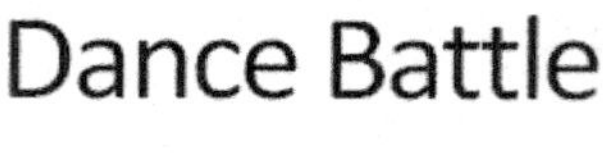

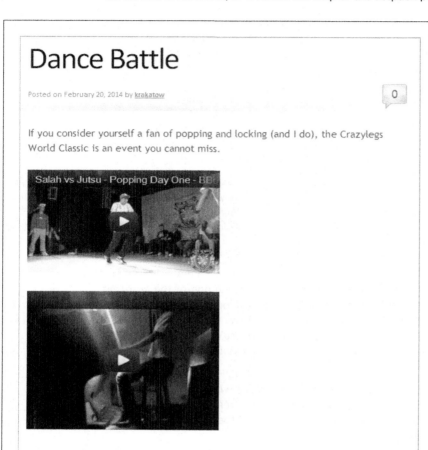

Posted on February 20, 2014 by krakatow

If you consider yourself a fan of popping and locking (and I do), the Crazylegs World Classic is an event you cannot miss.

Here, Jutsu breaks out some sick moves against the battle-master Salah. The result probably won't surprise dance masters, but the battle is enjoyable all the same.

 *Uncategorized*

FIGURE 10-19

You can control the size of your embedded video window. That can come in handy if you want to include more than one video on a page. By specifying small video windows, you can focus readers' attention on your post rather than distract them with a large video.

Showing Videos from Other Video Services

Although YouTube is the most popular video service, it's not the only game in town. Happily, WordPress's auto-embed feature lets you play video from a range of other media sites, including:

- Hulu
- Dailymotion
- Vimeo
- Viddler
- blip.tv
- Funny or Die
- Qik
- Flickr (for videos as well as pictures)
- Revision3
- WordPress.tv

As with YouTube, you simply supply a web address that points to a video on one of these sites, and WordPress does the rest.

Additionally, if you use WordPress.com or you installed Jetpack, you can use the following shortcodes to embed even more types of video:

- [cnnmoney-video] for videos from CNNMoney
- [kickstarter] for videos from Kickstarter
- [ted] for TED Talks videos
- [twitchtv] for videos from Twitch.tv
- [ustream] for videos from Ustream.TV
- [vine] for a Vine video
- [videolog] for videos from Videolog.tv
- [archiveorg] for a video from The Internet Archive

The list of eligible sites is ever-growing, so don't be surprised to find additional services listed when you check WordPress's official list of auto-embeds (*http://codex.wordpress.org/Embeds*) and shortcodes (*http://support.wordpress.com/shortcodes*).

When you embed video, WordPress configures the size of the playback window to suit the content and to fit in your post area. However, in some situations, you might want to tweak the size to get it just right. If you use one of the video types from the first list, you can control the size of the video player by wrapping your URL in the [embed] shortcode and then adding the height and width attributes. If you use one of the more specialized shortcodes in the second list, you probably need to add similar height and width attributes to that shortcode. Here's where things get a bit tricky, because many shortcodes have similar but maddeningly different syntax. To see exactly how to format a specific shortcode, check out the WordPress documentation at *http://support.wordpress.com/shortcodes,* and click the Full Instructions link next to the shortcode you plan to use.

Showing a Video from Your Media Library

Although a free video-hosting service meets most people's needs most of the time, self-hosted WordPress sites can host their own videos. The basic approach is pure simplicity:

1. **Click Add Media above the post editor.**

   This opens the familiar Insert Media window, which you used to add pictures and picture galleries earlier.

2. **Drag your video file onto the Insert Media page.**

   Not any format will work. And, confusingly enough, there are more video formats than Ben & Jerry's ice cream flavors. For best results, you should use a video file encoded with the high-quality, wildly popular H.264 video codec, and stored in the MP4 container format. If your file has the extension .mp4, you're off to a good start.

TIP If you don't have an MP4 video file on hand, think carefully before you continue. If you upload a different video format, your video player may not work on certain browsers, on mobile devices, or on anything, actually. To straighten out the format of your video files, consider a good video converter like the free Miro Video Converter (downloadable from *www.mirovideoconverter.com*), which can convert almost anything to MP4 format.

   Depending on the size of your video, you may have a bit of a wait. Grab a cup of coffee.

3. **In the "Embed or Link" setting (on the right), pick Embed Media Player.**

   Your other option is to add an ordinary link that points to the media file.

4. **Click "Insert into post."**

   WordPress slots your video in using the [video] shortcode.

At the end of this process, expect to see something like this:

```
[video width="704" height="400" mp4="http://magicteahouse.net/brewing.mp4"]
```

Here, the [video] shortcode specifies the size of the video window (based on the dimensions of your video file) and identifies the video file stored on your site. When you publish your post, the shortcode creates a video window similar to the one you got with YouTube.

Although the process seems easy, plenty of caveats apply. First, it's up to you to make sure that you have the not-inconsiderable space to store the video file, and the monthly bandwidth to show it to all of your viewers.

It's also up to you to make sure you use a video file format that most browsers can play back. The previous example uses the most popular standard: an .mp4 video file. Most browsers can play it, but there are plenty of exceptions, including the Opera browser and old versions of Internet Explorer. Fortunately, WordPress relies on the nearly miraculous powers of a JavaScript tool called MediaElement.js (*http://mediaelementjs.com*). It rounds out most browser issues by intelligently switching to other players, like Flash or Silverlight, when a browser can't play the file you supply. Thanks to MediaElement.js, the [video] shortcode shown above works reliably on almost as many computers as the YouTube shortcode (although it won't work so nicely on mobile devices, because there's no slimmed-down, low-bandwidth mobile version, like the sort that YouTube creates).

You have another option, but it's impractical unless you're ready to sacrifice your social life and spend hours of extra video-encoding time. Obsessive web developers can resolve format issues by providing fallback video files—multiple copies of the same movie in different formats. You can then specify a range of formats that the [video] shortcode can use. Here's an example that supplies a standard MP4 video but adds fallback videos for the free WebM codec and for the Flash (.flv) player:

```
[video width="704" height="400" mp4="http://magicteahouse.net/brewing.mp4"
 webm="http://magicteahouse.net/brewing.webm"
 flv="http://magicteahouse.net/brewing.flv"]
```

If you find yourself in the difficult position of running into the limitations of YouTube, but not wanting to face the headaches of do-it-yourself video hosting with the [video] shortcode, there's one more option. You can sign up with another video hosting service—one that may not be free, but will provide more features and control than YouTube does. The next section has the details.

Premium Video Hosting

As you learned earlier, it's generally a bad idea to host videos on your own website, unless you're a web development god with a clear plan. But there may be times when a free video-hosting site won't suit your needs. Here are some of the problems you might encounter hosting your files on a free service:

- **Privacy.** Free video services make your videos visible to the entire world. If you have a video with sensitive material in it, or one you want to sell to a group of subscribers, you won't want it on a free video service where it's exposed to prying eyes.
- **Ads.** Video sharing services may try to profit from your free account by including ads. They use two basic strategies: playing a television-commercial-style ad before your video starts playing, or superimposing an irritating banner over your video while it plays. YouTube's advertising policy is good—it won't show ads unless you give it permission to (usually in a misguided attempt to make a buck) or you post someone else's copyrighted content and *they* ask YouTube to slap on an ad (in which case they collect the money).
- **Content restrictions.** Free video services won't allow certain types of content. YouTube's content policy is fairly liberal, allowing everything short of hate speech, pornography, and bomb-making tutorials. That said, videos are

sometimes removed for disputable reasons, and popular videos are occasionally poached by traffic-seeking video thieves, who post their own copies and try to trick YouTube into removing the original, legitimate videos.

NOTE There was a time when YouTube capped videos to a modest 15 minutes, and video-makers flocked to premium video services to get more time. But these days, YouTube will let you upload multi-hour videos as long as you verify your account by mobile phone. The process for doing this is described at *http://tinyurl.com/long-vids*.

To escape these restrictions, you need to pay for a video hosting package. For example, the popular video site Vimeo (*http://vimeo.com*) offers free basic hosting and a more flexible premium service that costs $60 per year. The latter offers unlimited bandwidth, no length restriction, and the option to limit your videos to specific people, who must sign in to see them. Vimeo is particularly generous with storage space, letting premium members upload 5 GB of video per week. It also gives viewers high-quality streaming right out of the box. To get the same quality on YouTube, a viewer needs to click the gear icon in the bottom-right corner of the video window and manually pick a higher resolution.

WordPress also offers its own video hosting service called VideoPress. Like Vimeo, VideoPress offers unrestricted bandwidth and lets you upload large files. It also integrates well with WordPress.com, giving you the option to limit video viewing to your site's registered users. (You'll learn how to create private sites with registered users in Chapter 11.) VideoPress is particularly well suited to WordPress.com sites, because it's integrated into the WordPress.com hosting service, and only a simple upgrade away. However, it's far stingier with space than Vimeo. You start with a paltry 3 GB of storage, and if you need more, you need to pay a yearly fee, which rings up at about $20 per 10 GB.

To sign up for VideoPress, you buy the VideoPress upgrade. Click Store in the dashboard, look for the VideoPress box, and then click "Buy now." Or consider buying a Premium account, which is described in the box on page 33.

Once you sign up for VideoPress, you upload videos by clicking Add Media above the post editor box. Uploading a video is more or less the same as uploading a picture, except that you can specify a few more details, such as a rating (from a family-friendly *G* to an explicit *X-18*) and a thumbnail (the still image the video box displays before the video starts playing). The upload process also takes quite a bit longer.

NOTE If you have high-quality HD video, you may need to use a video tool to re-encode it to a leaner, more heavily compressed format before uploading it. Otherwise, you'll be stuck with a gigantic file on your WordPress.com site, eating up valuable space. (This is different from the process you follow when you upload a video to YouTube, which takes any file you can throw at it and doesn't complain about space.) You may also experience technical troubles if you upload huge files. Although VideoPress officially supports files of up to 1.4 GB, gargantuan uploads can fail, sometimes after hours of waiting.

GEM IN THE ROUGH

A Better Choice: The WordPress.com Premium Account

Instead of buying the WordPress.com VideoPress upgrade (currently $60 per year), you can sign up for a Premium account, which offers VideoPress and several other useful extras, for $99 per year. These extras include a free domain name, no ads, and the Custom Design upgrade for tweaking the styles in your theme (page 457).

Most important of all, the value bundle includes a storage upgrade from 3 GB to 13 GB. This is a big deal, because even though VideoPress offers unlimited bandwidth (meaning it won't charge you for web traffic, no matter how many times people watch your videos), it doesn't offer unlimited storage. And while 3 GB is more than enough to swallow all the pictures you can throw at a site, it may not accommodate the videos you want to upload. For comparison purposes, a feature-length HD movie takes about 4 GB of space if it's compressed (slimmed down in size). Raw HD video out of a camcorder is less compressed, and it can chew up 4 GB in 30 minutes or less. The space upgrade is also important if you want to include an audio player (page 360), because WordPress.com won't allow you to upload audio files unless you buy at least one storage upgrade.

If you need even more space for giant videos, you can buy separate upgrades. However, more space doesn't come cheap. Currently, it costs roughly $20 per year for each extra 10 GB of space.

When you finish uploading a video, you can add it to your post using the trusty "Insert into Post" button. This embeds a VideoPress shortcode that looks something like this:

```
[wpvideo MTFnELOW]
```

The result is a VideoPress window that looks a lot like a YouTube video player.

FREQUENTLY ASKED QUESTION

VideoPress and Self-Hosted Sites

I need a premium video host, but I'm not using WordPress.com. Should I consider VideoPress?

If you run a self-hosted WordPress site, you can sign up for VideoPress, but it's probably not the best video-hosting package for you. That's because it uses an awkward hosting model that forces you to get a WordPress.com account and use it to store your videos. VideoPress is also relatively expensive, because you need to pay extra to get additional space (and given the size of video files, you'll probably need more space).

If you're still interested in trying out VideoPress, go to *http://videopress.com*. Enter the address of your WordPress site into the "Get started–enter your blog address" text box, and then click Next. VideoPress walks you through a somewhat convoluted process that involves creating a WordPress.com account and paying the $60 fee (or more if you also need a space upgrade). When you finish, you should activate VideoPress through the Jetpack plug-in, which lets you use the [wpvideo] shortcode in your posts. To do so, click Jetpack in the dashboard menu, scroll down to the VideoPress box, and click the Activate button.)

Playing Audio Files

Sometimes, you'll want to let readers play an audio clip (or several) without using a full-blown video window. An obvious example is if you're a music artist promoting your work. However, audio files are equally well suited to the spoken word, whether that's an interview, talk show, sermon, audio book, or motivational lecture. Audio files are particularly useful if you want to join the Web's thriving community of *podcasters*—sites that provide downloadable, long audio files that users can listen to on the go (for example, on their iPods or smartphones).

You might expect that adding audio to your WordPress site is easier than adding video. After all, audio files are smaller and simpler than video files. But you'll face many of the same issues. In the following sections, you'll consider three strategies for getting audio into a web page.

Adding a Basic Audio Player

The simplest approach to hosting audio is to upload the file to your website. You can then provide a link that readers can use to download the file or (even better) a tiny audio player that lets them listen without leaving your site (Figure 10-20).

Before you get started, you need to upload your audio file. Ideally, you'll upload an MP3 file to ensure that it plays on most browsers. Technically, Internet Explorer, Safari, and Google Chrome play MP3 files, but Firefox and Opera don't. However, most websites get by using the Flash player to fill the gap. Essentially, the process works like this:

- If the browser you use recognizes both MP3 files and HTML5 markup, WordPress creates an HTML5 <audio> element that points to your MP3 file. The browser then creates a miniature audio player, like the ones shown in Figure 10-20.
- If a browser doesn't play these two standard file types, WordPress uses a small Flash program that creates a tiny audio player. The end result is the same—your guests see a simple music player.
- In the unlikely event that a browser can't meet either of these requirements, WordPress swaps in an ordinary HTML link. Guests click the link to download the audio file, where they can play it using a desktop music player.

The Flash fallback solution is a good one, but it's a bit too messy to implement on your own. Fortunately, WordPress does all the work for you with the [audio] shortcode, which is every bit as straightforward as it should be. You simply add an attribute named *src* that points to your audio file. Here's an example that launches an MP3 file on another web server:

```
[audio src="http://wpcom.files.wordpress.com/2007/01/mattmullenweg-interview.mp3"]
```

You can also use the [audio] shortcode to play music files stored on your own website. But before you go any further, there's a significant catch that applies if WordPress.com hosts your site. Unless you buy a space upgrade or have a Premium account (page 359), WordPress.com won't let you upload *any* audio files, even if you have plenty of space left in your initial 3 GB storage allotment. Instead, you can play only audio files stored on other sites.

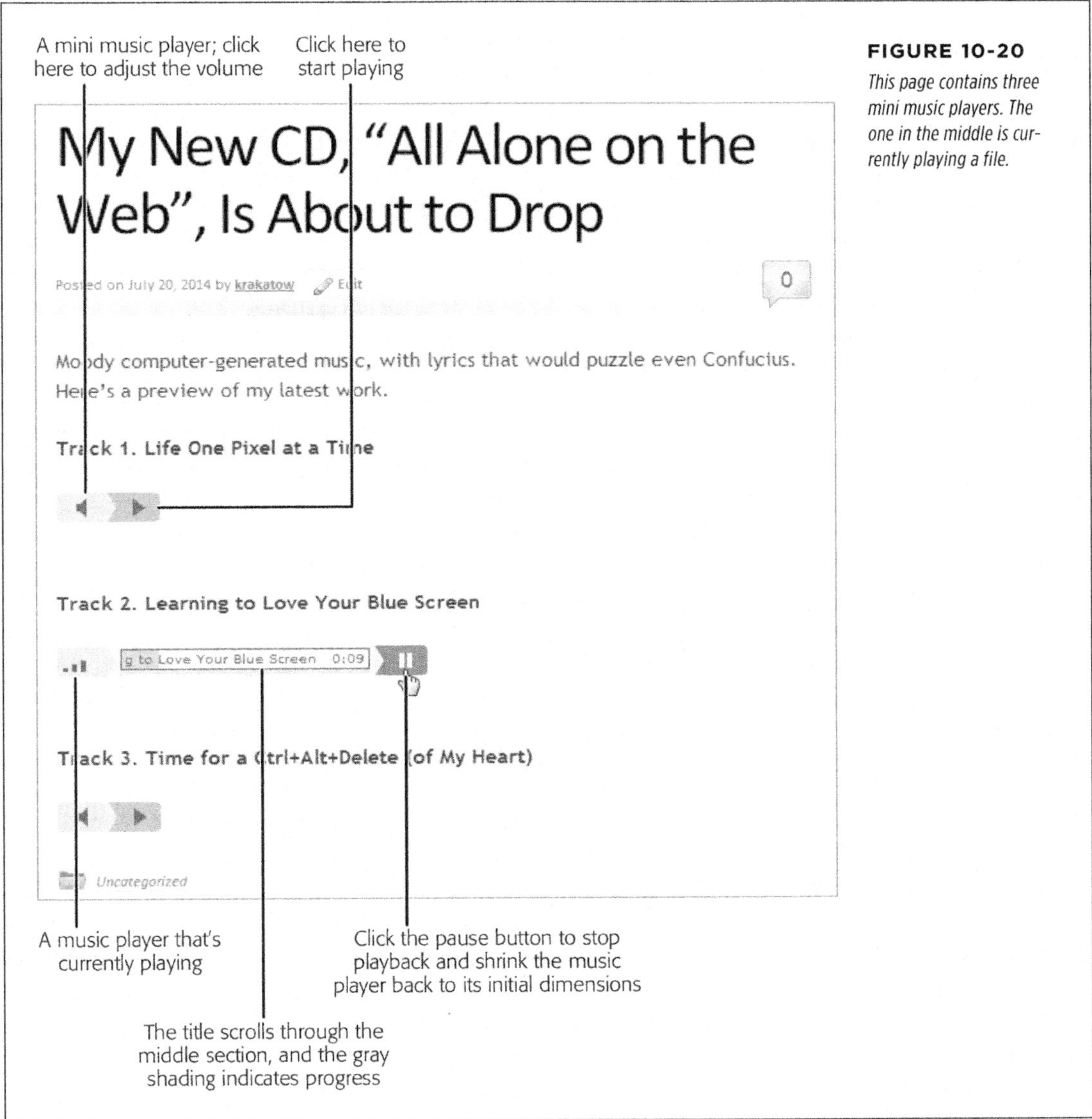
A mini music player; click here to adjust the volume
Click here to start playing
My New CD, "All Alone on the Web", Is About to Drop
Posted on July 20, 2014 by krakatow
Edit
0
Moody computer-generated music, with lyrics that would puzzle even Confucius. Here's a preview of my latest work.
Track 1. Life One Pixel at a Time
Track 2. Learning to Love Your Blue Screen
g to Love Your Blue Screen 0:09
Track 3. Time for a Ctrl+Alt+Delete (of My Heart)
Uncategorized
A music player that's currently playing
Click the pause button to stop playback and shrink the music player back to its initial dimensions
The title scrolls through the middle section, and the gray shading indicates progress

FIGURE 10-20

This page contains three mini music players. The one in the middle is currently playing a file.

Depending on what you're trying to accomplish, this limit might be a minor inconvenience or completely unworkable. If it's the latter, you have two options. You can buy a space upgrade for as little as $20 a year (click the Store menu in the dashboard to sign up), or you can use a music hosting service, as covered on page 364.

To play an audio file directly from your site, you need to upload it to the media library and then embed it with the [audio] shortcode. Here's how:

1. **First, click Add Media above the post editor.**

   This is the same link you used to upload a picture.

2. **In the Insert Media window, pick your audio file.**

   Now wait for it to upload.

NOTE If you try this on a WordPress.com site that doesn't have the space upgrade, nothing will happen, so don't waste your time.

3. **When you finish uploading the track, fill in its title.**

   The music player displays the title while the track plays (Figure 10-20). If you don't supply a title, the player lists it as Track 1.

4. **In the "Embed or Link" setting (on the right), pick Embed Media Player.**

   Your other option is to add an ordinary link to your audio file, which isn't what you want.

5. **Click "Insert into post."**

   Now WordPress adds the [audio] shortcode.

6. **Publish your post.**

   You're rewarded with a tiny music player. You can repeat this process to add as many music players as you want to the same page.

Adding a Playlist

You can use the [audio] shortcode to add as many audio playback bars as you want. Figure 10-20, for instance, has three. But if you want to give your visitor the chance to peruse a group of related tracks—like a concert of songs performed by your trombone quartet—there's a better way. You can group your tracks together in a *playlist.*

A playlist is a list of audio or video files with a single playback bar or video window (see Figure 10-21). Your visitor can click a specific track to play it, or let the playlist move automatically from one file to the next.

Here's how to add an audio playlist (see the Note below for video playlists):

1. **Click Add Media.**

2. **Drag your audio files onto the Insert Media window,**

   You can skip this step if you already uploaded all the files you need.

3. **Once you've uploaded all your files, click Create Audio Playlist on the left.**

   The Create Audio Playlist command appears in the Insert Media window only if you have at least one audio file in your site's media library.

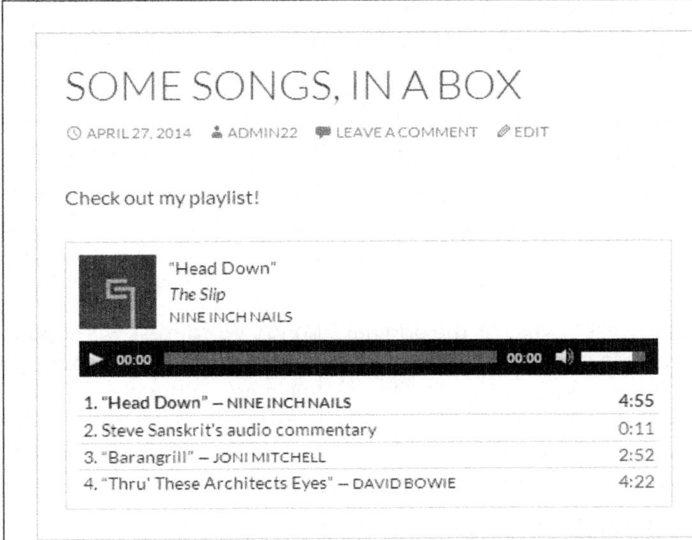

FIGURE 10-21

This playlist includes four tracks. If you press play and don't intervene, the playlist will cycle through the songs continuously.

4. **Click each track you want to use in your playlist, and fill in its details on the right.**

   Every audio file in the playlist accepts three pieces of information:

   - **Title.** The track title shows up in the playlist, and in the playback box when WordPress starts playing the track. WordPress figures out the title by reading the track's *metadata*—the tiny bits of information stored in the audio file that identify the artist, song title, album, and more. But if the title isn't quite right, you can edit it.
   - **Caption.** The caption is an optional bit of information. Initially, it starts out blank. However, if you supply a caption, WordPress shows it in the playlist *instead* of the title and author information. (For example, in Figure 10-21, the second track has a caption and the other three do not.) Even if you write a caption, the playback box still shows the title and author information when it starts playing the track.
   - **Description.** WordPress also gets this information from the metadata in the audio file, if it's available. The description is a short bit of text that provides extra information, like this: "Head Down from The Slip by Nine Inch Nails. Released: 2008. Track 6 of 10." Currently, the playlist feature doesn't use the description.

5. **Click the "Create a new playlist" button.**

   This adds the tracks you picked to your fledgling playlist.

6. **Configure your playlist.**

   Configuring a playlist is much like configuring a picture gallery. You can drag your tracks around to change their order, and on the right, you can alter a few basic settings:

   - **Show Tracklist.** If you clear this checkbox, you'll get a music player that shows the track it's currently playing but doesn't show the full playlist underneath. That means the listener can't skip to a specific song.
   - **Show Artist Name in Tracklist.** If you clear this checkbox, each entry in the playlist will show the track's title, instead of the title and author. This setting has no effect on tracks that have a caption.
   - **Show Images.** If set (which is the original setting), WordPress will contact a music database on the Web and fetch the appropriate album cover for your track. It then displays that tiny thumbnail image in the playback box when it plays the track (as in Figure 10-21). Obviously, this option works only for professionally released work. (And don't forget to get the copyright holder's permission before you put her work on your site.)

7. **Click "Insert audio playlist."**

   WordPress adds the [playlist] shortcode to your post.

8. **Publish your post.**

   The payoff is a simple but effective playlist, live in your post.

NOTE You can create a vdeo playlist in much the same way as an audio playlist. The difference is that you upload video files instead of audio files, and you click a link named Create Video Playlist instead of Create Audio Playlist. The finished result is a bit different, too—it looks like a standard video window with a playlist attached underneath.

Using a Music-Sharing Service

If you're serious about sharing a set of audio tracks—for example, you're a band trying to popularize your work—your best bet is to sign up with a serious music-sharing service.

The first advantage is that a good music service increases the exposure of your audio tracks. Casual music browsers may stumble across your work, similar artists may link to it, and just about anyone can add a comment or click Like, which boosts your buzz. The second advantage is that you get a number of extras, like the ability to provide music in different formats for different browsers (without resorting to Flash), and a sleek jukebox-style player that seamlessly plays a whole set of your songs.

WordPress has built-in support for the following music-sharing services through its auto-embed feature:

- SoundCloud
- Spotify
- Rdio

If you have a WordPress.com site or a self-hosted site with the Jetpack plug-in, you get two extra services courtesy of shortcodes:

- [bandcamp] for audio on Bandcamp
- [8tracks] for audio on 8tracks

Once again, the shortcode syntax varies subtly for each service, so you need to get the exact details at *http://support.wordpress.com/shortcodes*. Figure 10-22 shows a site that uses SoundCloud.

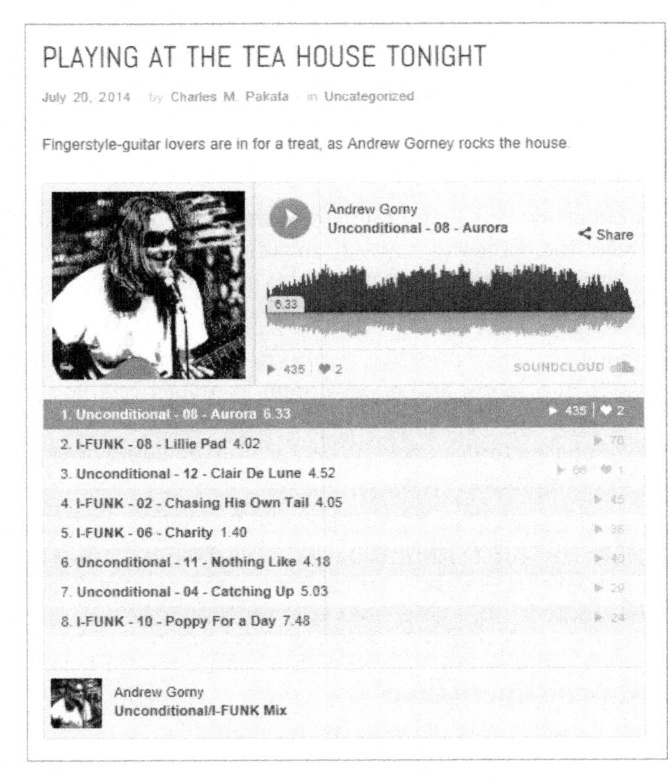

FIGURE 10-22

SoundCloud is more refined than just about any other plug-in-powered music player. It includes the artist's profile picture, a list of tracks, and a waveform of the song currently playing.

SoundCloud offers a sweet deal: no charge for the first 120 minutes of audio you upload, and a polished music player that makes almost any music look good. If you need more storage, you have to pay a yearly fee. (Currently, that's $55 a year for 240 minutes, or $135 per year for unlimited uploads.) If you plan to sell your music, a service like Bandcamp may make more sense—it gives you unlimited room to store audio but takes a percentage of your sales, if anyone buys your tracks.

To sign up with SoundCloud, start at *http://soundcloud.com*, click Sign Up, and follow the instructions. Once you upload some audio files, you can start embedding them in your WordPress posts. SoundCloud gives you the option of a single-track music player, or you can assemble a group of tracks into a playlist (as in Figure 10-22).

To embed your SoundCloud content in a WordPress post, browse to the song or playlist you want to use, and then copy the URL out of the address bar. Here's the URL that creates the music player in Figure 10-22:

```
https://soundcloud.com/andrewgorny/sets/ag-com-splash
```

If you want to adjust the size of the SoundCloud player, use the [embed] shortcode with the height and width attributes.

Podcasting

So far, you've seen how to let viewers play individual audio tracks or a playlist with a bunch of music on it. *Podcasting* is a similar, but slightly different, way to present audio. It gives readers the choice of listening to audio files the normal way (in their browsers by clicking the Play button) or downloading the audio files so they can put them on a mobile device.

The central idea with podcasting is that you prepare content that busy people will listen to on the go. Usually, the content is long—30 minutes to an hour is common for podcasts. If your audio file is only a couple of minutes long, it's not worth a visitor's trouble to download it and transfer it to a mobile device.

Podcast creators also tend to organize podcasts in groups—for example, they make each audio file an episode in a series, and release them at regular intervals (say, weekly). Good examples of podcasts include a web talk show with commentary and interviews, a motivational lecture, a spoken chapter from an audio book, or a 45-minute techno mix for a workout session.

NOTE The word *podcasting* is a mash-up of *pod* and *broadcast*—*pod* because this form of audio file distribution first gained popularity with the iPod music player, and *broadcasting* because a podcast creator provides easily accessible, regularly released audio "shows," a concept that's a bit like television broadcasting.

CREATING PODCAST-FRIENDLY AUDIO

You don't need any special technique to upload a podcast audio file. You can simply create a post and add an ordinary link to the file. If you want to get a bit fancier, you can use the audio player feature described on page 360. That way, visitors can play the audio in their browsers if they haven't caught the podcast bug.

You should save podcast audio as MP3 files, because a range of mobile devices can play back that format. You can also create podcast *video* files, but that process is a bit more complicated. You first need to make sure the video is in MP4 format, then you have to upload it to a host, and finally you need to link to it from your post.

NOTE If you want to use a video file for podcasting *and* embed it so guests can play it directly inside their browsers, you need the help of a high-caliber podcasting plug-in, as explained in the box on page 368.

GETTING YOUR PODCAST FEED

Although podcast audio is the same as normal audio, there's a slight difference in the way you *present* podcasts. For readers to find your podcasts quickly and download new episodes easily, you need a way to separate these audio files from the rest of your site.

To do that, you create a dedicated category for posts that contain podcasts. You can give this category a name like "Podcasts" or "Lectures" or "Audio Book." Then, when you create a new post that has an audio file in it and you want to include that audio as part of your podcast, assign the post your podcast-specific category (Figure 10-23). Depending on the structure of your site (and the way you let viewers browse it), you may decide to set two categories—one to identify the type of post (say, "Sports"), and one to flag the post as a podcast ("Podcasts").

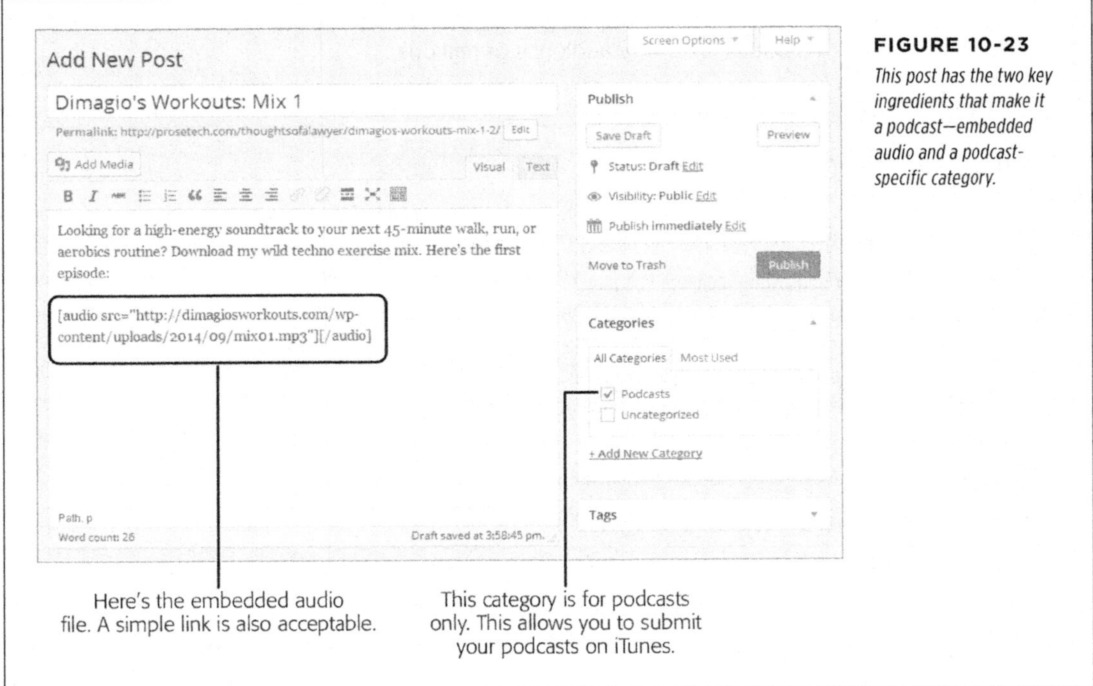

FIGURE 10-23

This post has the two key ingredients that make it a podcast—embedded audio and a podcast-specific category.

You group audio files into a single podcast category so you can generate a *feed* for that category. As you'll learn on page 433, a feed is a sort of index to your content. In the case of podcasting, your feed tells other programs and websites where to get the podcast files on your site. It also lets you notify visitors when you publish a new file—say, if they subscribe to your podcast in iTunes.

NOTE iTunes is one of the favorite tools for podcast-lovers. If your site offers podcasts and you'd like to use them to attract new visitors (and why wouldn't you?), you need to submit some podcast information to iTunes.

You can get the feed for a category using a URL with this syntax:

```
http://[Site]/category/[CategoryName]/feed
```

So if you have a site named *http://dimagiosworkouts.com*, you can get a feed for the Podcasts category like this:

```
http://dimagiosworkouts.com/category/podcasts/feed
```

This is a valuable link—it's the piece of information you need to supply to iTunes to register your podcast.

To register with iTunes, start by reviewing Apple's instructions at *http://tinyurl.com/podcastspecs*. First, read the "Testing Your Feed" section, which explains how to make sure your feed includes the podcast files you expect, and that the feed works. Then, follow up with the instructions in the "Submitting Your Podcast to the iTunes Store" section to learn how to officially tell iTunes about your feed, and make it visible to a podcast-hungry audience of millions.

PLUG-IN POWER

Better Podcasting with a Plug-In

Podcasting with WordPress is easy. All you need is the right type of audio file (MP3) and a post category just for podcasts.

However, if you're a power podcaster—meaning you plan to invest serious effort in making podcasting a part of your web presence—it's worth considering a plug-in that can make your life easier. The most popular podcasting plug-in for self-hosted WordPress sites is Blubrry PowerPress (*http://tinyurl.com/wp-podcast*).

Among PowerPress's most useful features is its tight integration with iTunes. PowerPress can optimize your feeds for iTunes, submit your feed to iTunes, and even help you manage your iTunes cover art. PowerPress is also invaluable if you want to forge into the world of video podcasting, because it lets you embed your video content in your page, using a JavaScript-based video player. (That way, visitors have the choice of downloading your podcast for a mobile device, as usual, or playing it right in their browser, as they would with a YouTube video.) PowerPress also offers statistics that help you gauge the popularity of your podcasts and an optional paid hosting plan for audio and video files.

CHAPTER

11

Collaborating with Multiple Authors

When you first create a WordPress site, it's a solo affair. You choose your site's theme, write every post and page, and put every widget in place. Your readers can add comments, but you're in charge of starting every conversation.

You might like this arrangement (and if so, that's fine), but WordPress also makes it possible for you to have friends, colleagues, family members, and even complete strangers contribute to your site. You can, for example, create a site where several people post content, or you could be more selective, letting some people write content and others review and edit it. You can also implement an approval system to check the work of contributors before it goes live, and you can even create an entirely private site that only the people you approve can view.

In this chapter, you'll learn how to enable all these features by registering new people—not new *visitors,* but new WordPress *users* who have special privileges on your site. You'll also consider WordPress's more ambitious multisite feature that's open to self-hosters only. With a multisite network, you can let other people create their own sites on *your* web server. For example, big companies can use the multisite feature to give each employee a personal blog. Essentially, the multisite feature lets a whole family of WordPress sites exist side by side, on the same domain.

Adding People to Your Site

A new WordPress website starts with only one member: you. You assume the role of administrator, which means you can do anything from write a post to vaporize the entire site. Eventually, you may decide to make room for company. Usually, you make that decision because you want to work with co-authors, who will write posts for your site.

Before you add someone to your site, though, you need to decide what privileges that person will have. WordPress recognizes five roles, listed here in order of most to least powerful:

- **Administrator.** Administrators can do absolutely everything. For example, if you add a friend as an administrator to your site, he can remove you, delete all your posts, and switch your site to a Hawaiian beach theme. WordPress strongly recommends that every site have just one administrator, to prevent power struggles.
- **Editor.** Editors have full control over all posts and pages. They can create their own posts, and they can edit or delete any post, even ones they didn't create. Editors can also manage post categories and tags, upload files, and moderate comments. They can't change site settings, tweak the site's layout and theme, or manage users.
- **Author.** Authors have control over their own posts *only.* They can create new ones and upload pictures, and they can edit or delete their posts anytime. Everyone else's content is off limits.
- **Contributor.** Contributors are a more limited form of author. They can create draft posts, but they can't actually publish them. Instead, contributors submit their work for review, and an editor or administrator approves and publishes it. Sadly, contributors can't upload pictures, even for their own posts.
- **Follower or Subscriber.** These people can read posts and add comments. WordPress.com calls them followers, while WordPress.org calls them subscribers. If you run a WordPress.com site, it automatically notifies your followers about newly posted content (perhaps by email, depending on their personal preferences). If you run a self-hosted site, your subscribers won't get any notifications, but they can opt in to an email subscription service (page 425).

Now that you know what roles WordPress recognizes, you're ready to start creating new user accounts. There's one wrinkle, however. The steps you take for a self-hosted site are significantly different from the ones for a WordPress.com site. If you're a self-hoster, continue reading. If you're a WordPress.com fan, skip ahead to "Inviting People to Join a WordPress.com Site" on page 375.

NOTE In WordPress lingo, all of these different types of people—administrators, editors, authors, contributors, and so on—are *users*. Technically, a user is any person who has an account on your site. This account identifies the person and determines what he's allowed to do. Everyone else is an ordinary, anonymous visitor.

FREQUENTLY ASKED QUESTION

The Role of a Subscriber

Why would I add subscribers? Can't everyone read my posts and make comments?

Ordinarily, there are no limits to who can read posts and write comments. In that way, subscribers are no different from regular, unregistered guests. Yes, subscribers may get email notifications about your content (if your site is hosted on WordPress.com, or if you added the right plug-in to a WordPress.org site). But they certainly won't get any extra privileges.

However, the situation changes in these special cases:

- If you create a private site (page 397), every reader needs a subscriber account. Without one, they won't be able to see anything on your site.
- If you restrict comments with the "Users must be registered and logged in to comment" setting on a self-hosted site, and you don't allow Facebook or Twitter logins (page 270), only subscribers can leave comments. This is a pretty severe restriction, and few sites use it.
- If you add a social plug-in like BuddyPress (*http://buddypress.org*), you want to give accounts to as many people as possible in the hope that they exploit the plug-in's enhanced features, like sharing content with friends and chatting in discussion groups. That'll make your site feel more like a community.

Adding New People to a Self-Hosted Site

Using the dashboard, you can register new users, one at a time. You supply a few key details (like a user name, password, and email address), and let your users take it from there.

Here's what to do:

1. **Choose Users→Add New.**

   The Add New User page opens (Figure 11-1).

2. **Choose a good user name for the person you're inviting.**

   The best approach is to use a consistent system you can apply to everyone you add. For example, you might choose to combine a person's first and last name, separated by an underscore (like *sam_picheski*).

3. **Type in the person's email address.**

   WordPress uses that address to send the person important notifications, including password resets.

4. **Optionally, specify the person's first name, last name, and website.**

   These are three descriptive details that become part of the person's profile.

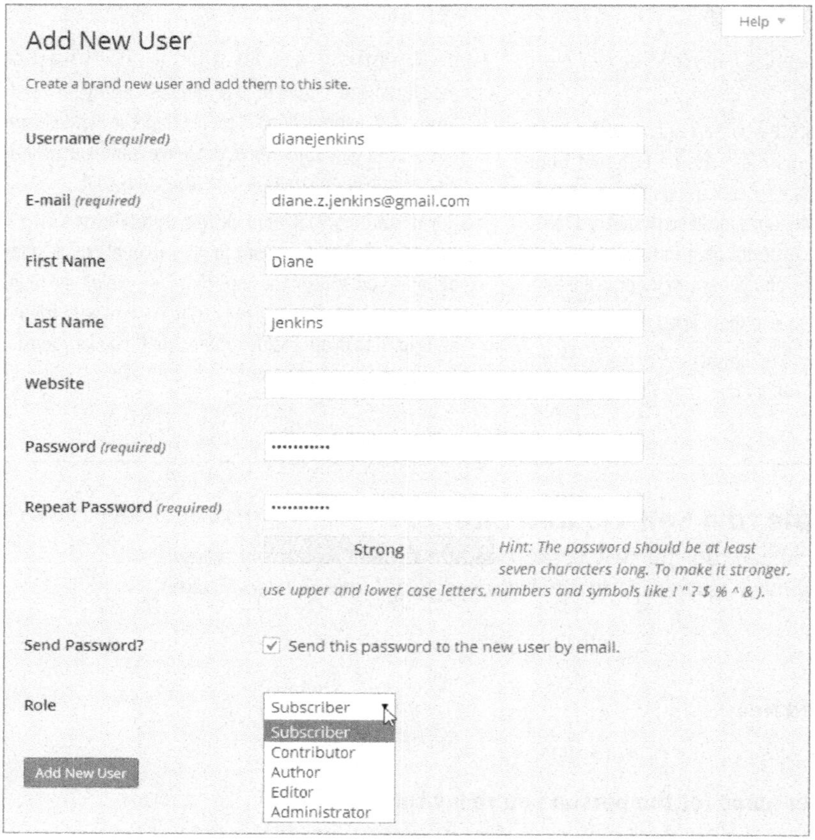

FIGURE 11-1

There's nothing mysterious about the Add New User page. Here, the site's administrator has typed in the sign-up information for a person with the user name dianejenkins and is specifying her site privileges using the Role drop-down list.

NOTE The emails WordPress sends often end up in an email account's junk folder, because they contain links. You may need to tell new users to check their junk mail to find the messages with their WordPress credentials.

5. **Type in a strong password. (See the box on page 27 for tips.)**

   When you create a new account, you *must* supply a password—WordPress doesn't let people pick their passwords the first time they log in. However, if you check "Send this password to the new user by email," WordPress emails the person her user name and password, along with a link to your site's login page (Figure 11-2). (And even if you don't ask, WordPress sends you, the administrator, an email with a record of the new user's name and email address.)

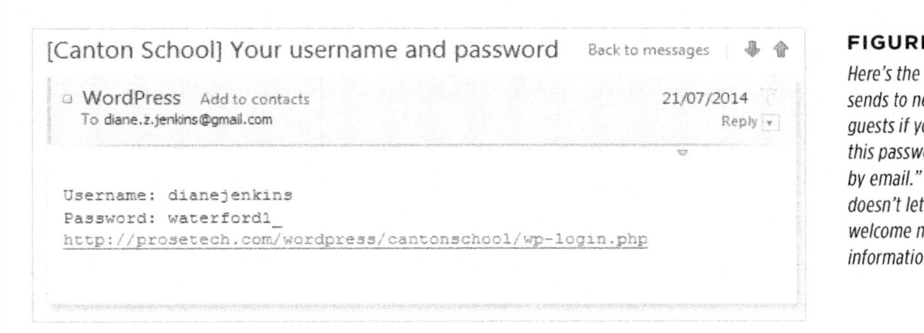

FIGURE 11-2

Here's the message WordPress sends to newly registered guests if you select "Send this password to the new user by email." Sadly, WordPress doesn't let you add a custom welcome message or any extra information.

TIP If a frustrated user arrives at your site but doesn't know his password, he can click "Lost your password?" on the login page. WordPress emails him a link that lets him pick a new password.

6. **Pick a role from the drop-down list.**

   You can use any of the roles described on page 370.

7. **Click Add New User.**

   WordPress creates the account, sends a notification email (if you chose the "Send this password..." option), and takes you to the Users→All Users section of the dashboard. There, you can review a list of everyone you ever added to your site. Point to a user name, and you see two straightforward links—use Edit to change the person's account info and Delete to remove the account.

UP TO SPEED

Helping Your Peeps Log In

To log into your site, users need to request the *login* page. That means that if your site is at *http://cantonschool.org*, they need to visit *http://cantonschool.org/login*. Alternatively, people can go straight to the dashboard by requesting the *wp-admin* page (as in *http://cantonschool.org/wp-admin*). In that case, WordPress asks them to log in before they can continue.

If you have a lot of users who haven't used WordPress before, you may need to help them find the login or dashboard page. Here are two good options:

- You can create your own welcome email message that contains a link to the login page, and send it to everyone. Use your favorite email program or get the Email Users plug-in (*http://tinyurl.com/emailusers*), which lets you send a mass email to all your users at once. This plug-in is a big help if you don't have their email addresses handy.
- You can add a link that goes to your login page. Put that link in the main site menu, or add the link to a sidebar using a Text widget (page 166) or a Custom Menu widget (page 228). Make sure you give your link some descriptive text that clearly explains why the person needs to log in, like "Log in to write your own posts" or "Log in as a contributor."

You might want to add one other detail when you add a new user: changing the name WordPress displays when that person contributes content.

When your site has a single author (you), there's no reason to attach the author's name to every post. But once you have multiple people contributing to your site, it's important to distinguish one author's work from another's. The standard year themes (like Twenty Twelve) handle this gracefully: As soon as your site publishes posts from more than one person, it modifies the text it adds to every post to include author information, like this:

> This entry was posted in Uncategorized by mpm_site_admin. Bookmark the permalink.

Ordinarily, WordPress identifies a post author by his user name, which often makes for a lousy byline. Fortunately, you can choose something more meaningful and readable (both for you and your visitors). Here's how:

1. **Choose Users→All Users.**

   WordPress opens the Users page and lists everyone your site recognizes.

2. **Point to the user name of the person whose info you want to change, and then click Edit.**

   The person's profile page opens, where you see all her settings. You can tweak her personal preferences, like the dashboard's color scheme and proofreading settings, but you probably won't worry about these details—instead, you'll let invited people configure their own profiles. But the person's nickname affects the readability of the site for all your visitors, so it's worth getting it right.

3. **Choose an option from the "Display name publicly as" list.**

   For example, you can replace the WordPress user name from the previous example (*dianejenkins*) with the first name only (Diane), the last name (Jenkins), or a combination of the two (Diane Jenkins).

   If you don't see an option you like, type the name you want into the Nickname box, exactly as you want it to appear (for example, "Di Jenkins," "Miss J," or "Super Shorty"). WordPress adds the new nickname to the entries in the "Display name publicly as" list. To use it in place of her registered name, choose it.

4. **Click Update Profile.**

   Your change is official.

NOTE You can change an author's name anytime. The change affects all the posts the person has written—the next time you view a post, you see the new name in the byline. This is one of the benefits of dynamic websites like the ones you create with WordPress—they're intelligent enough to keep everything up to date.

Inviting People to Join a WordPress.com Site

Before you can register someone as a user on your WordPress.com site, that person must have a WordPress.com account. Some people may already have one (they might, for example, have their own site or they may be following someone else's blog). Non-WordPressers need to sign up, and they need to do it themselves—you can't create a WordPress.com account for someone else.

Instead, your job is to *invite* people to become users. For example, imagine you invite two friends, Cathy and Sanjeev. Cathy already has a WordPress.com account, which means that all she needs to do is accept your invitation. WordPress then authorizes her to read, edit, or manage your site (depending on the role you grant her). On the other hand, Sanjeev doesn't have a WordPress.com account, so WordPress asks him to create one. Once he does, Sanjeev can accept your invitation and become a contributor, just like Cathy.

You can invite one person or several at a time. The only rule is that if you create an invitation for several people, all those people must have the same role. That means you can invite a batch of followers all at once, or a group of contributors, but not a mix of the two.

To create an invitation, follow these steps:

1. **Choose Users→Invite New in the dashboard.**
2. **Enter a list of email addresses, one for each person you want to invite, separated by commas (Figure 11-3).**

   If you invite someone who already has a WordPress.com account, you can supply his WordPress.com user name instead of his email address (either way, the invitation reads the same).
3. **Choose a role from the Role drop-down list.**

   You can specify any of the roles described on page 370.

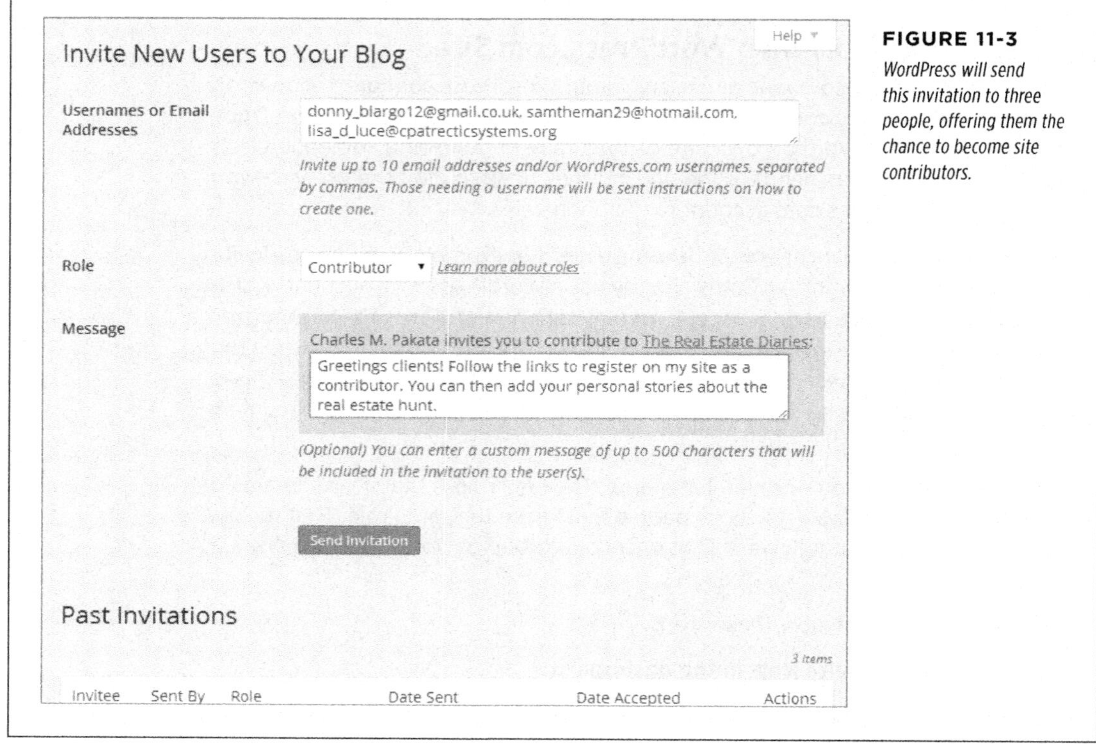

FIGURE 11-3

WordPress will send this invitation to three people, offering them the chance to become site contributors.

4. **In the Message box, type a short invitation.**

   For example, if you're inviting contributors, you might write "Come share your stories on my blog." This note becomes part of the welcome message WordPress sends to each person on your list (Figure 11-4).

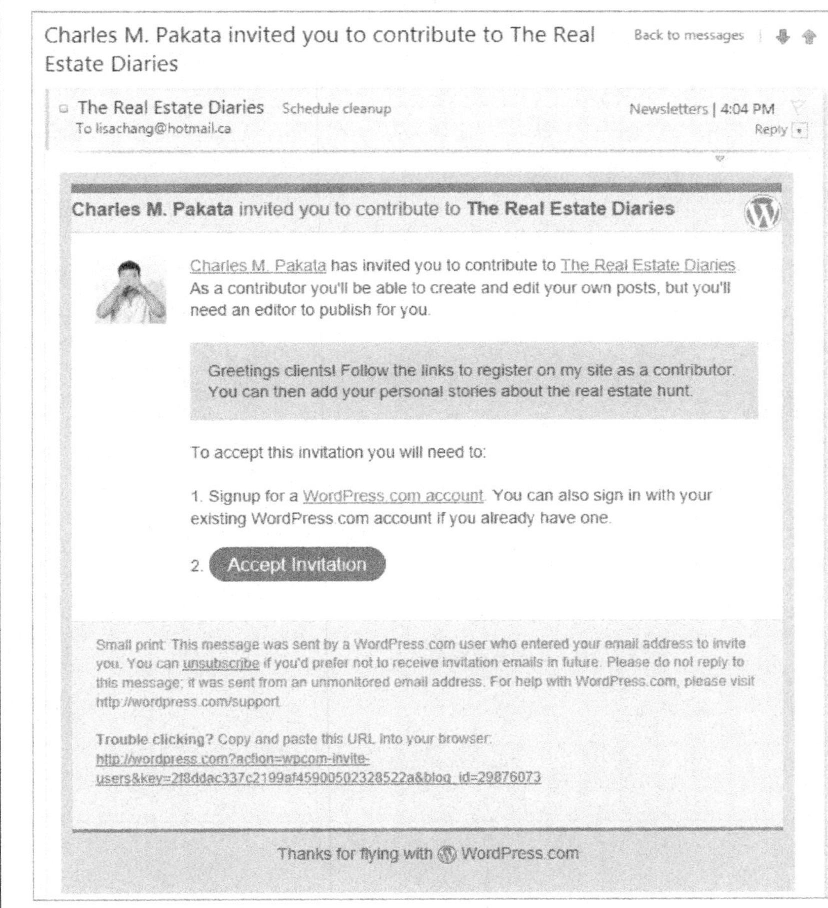

FIGURE 11-4

Here, site owner Charles Pakata invites Lisa Chang to contribute to his WordPress site, "The Real Estate Diaries." If Chang clicks Accept Invitation, WordPress prompts her to sign in with her WordPress.com account (or to create an account if she doesn't have one). She can then accept the invitation and become a contributor.

5. **Click Send Invitation.**

   WordPress sends the invitation into cyberspace.

   Below your message, on the same "Invite New Users" page, WordPress keeps track of whom you invited and how they responded (Figure 11-5). It keeps the records until you delete them (more about that in a moment).

   If you think a previously invited person missed your email, you can ask WordPress to send it again by clicking Resend. If you want to revoke an invitation that hasn't been accepted, click Delete. Now, if that person clicks the activation link in the invitation message, WordPress displays an error message.

Once someone accepts your invitation, you may choose to remove the record of the invitation (click Delete) so you can focus on the people who haven't responded. Deleting an invitation for a registered user has no effect on that person—he remains registered on your site. (If you decide that you *do* want to take down an existing user, you need to go to the Users→All Users section of the dashboard and click Remove next to the persona non grata.)

NOTE The Users→All Users page shows all the administrators, editors, authors, and contributors you've signed up. It doesn't include mere followers, because they have no special powers on your site.

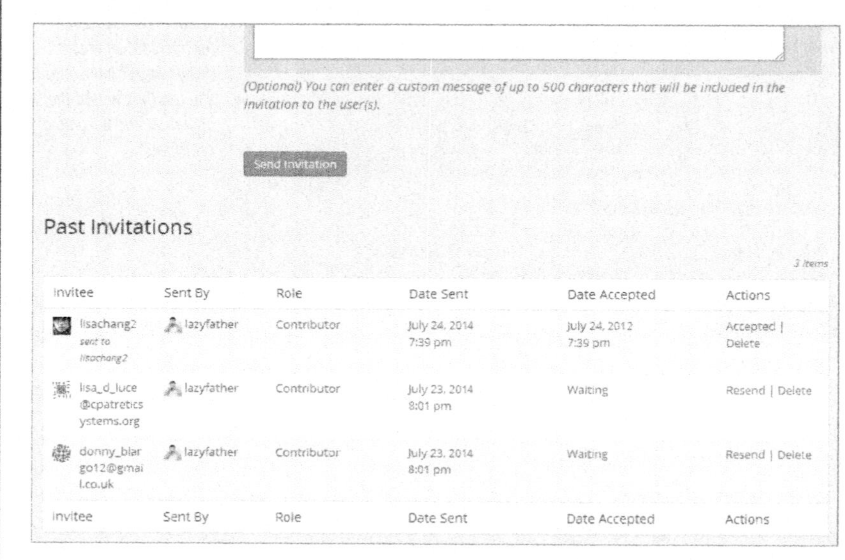

FIGURE 11-5

Lazyfather invited three people to join his site. One has accepted, while the other two have yet to respond.

Working with Authors

The most common reason to add new users to your WordPress site is to get more content from more people. After all, new and interesting content is the lifeblood of any site, and by recruiting others to help you write it, you increase the odds that your site will grow and flourish.

As you already learned, all but one type of WordPress user (followers for WordPress.com sites, subscribers for self-hosted sites) can write posts. Whether you're an administrator, editor, author, or contributor, the first step is the same: To write a post, you have to log in to the dashboard.

WordPress tailors the dashboard to the person's role, so that each person sees only the menu commands he can use. For example, if you log in as a contributor, you see the stripped-down dashboard in Figure 11-6.

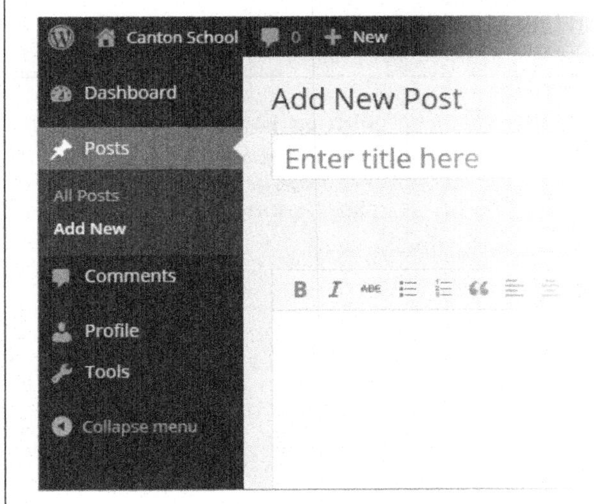

FIGURE 11-6

Different people see different versions of the WordPress dashboard. In this example, a contributor has logged into the Canton School site. This dashboard has commands for creating posts, reading comments (but not moderating them), and changing the contributor's profile. It doesn't offer commands for changing the site's theme, its widgets, or its settings.

If you run a site on WordPress.com, every type of user can log in and see the dashboard, except followers. Why leave out followers? On WordPress.com, a person's profile isn't tied to your site—it's actually part of that person's WordPress.com account. For that reason, there's no need for followers to use your site's dashboard to change their profiles.

If you run a self-hosted site, every type of user can log in to the dashboard, although subscribers get just one option—the Profile command that lets them change their preferences and personal information.

Either way, the only type of user who can see the full, unrestricted version of the dashboard is an administrator—and, ideally, that's just you.

The Post Approval Process for Contributors

Administrators, editors, and authors can add posts and pages to your site in the usual way. When they finish writing, they simply click Publish to make their content go live.

As you know, contributors have more limited powers. They can create posts but not publish them, which gives you a broad safety net—there's no chance that bad content can get on your site, because you get to review it first. When contributors create posts, they have two options: They can save the post as a draft so they can return to it and edit it later, or they can submit it for review (Figure 11-7).

When a contributor submits a post this way, WordPress assigns it a special status, called *pending*. A pending post won't appear on your site until an editor or administrator approves it. Here's how you do that:

1. **In the dashboard, choose Posts→All Posts.**
2. **Click the Pending link (Figure 11-8).**

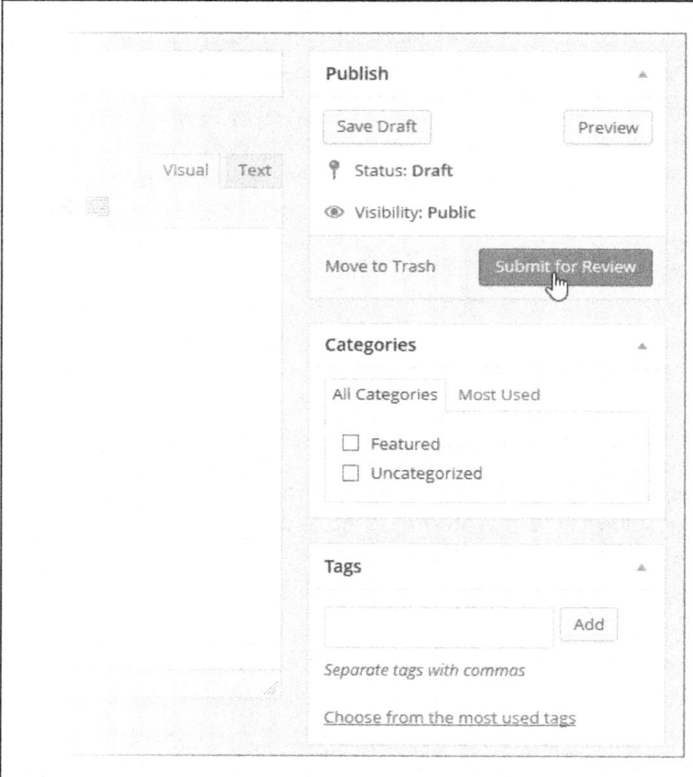

FIGURE 11-7

When a contributor logs in to your site, WordPress changes the familiar Publish button to a "Submit for Review" button.

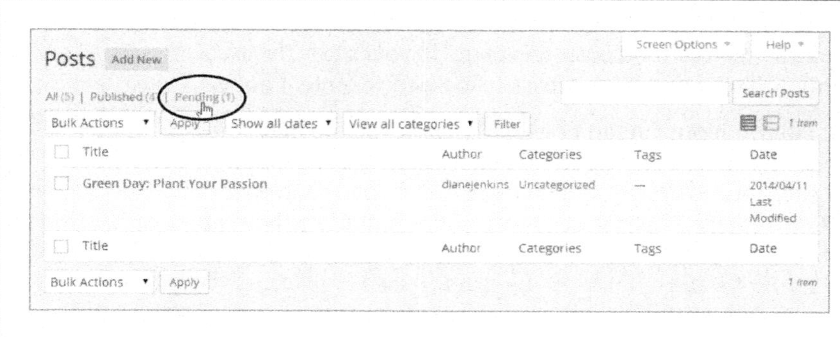

FIGURE 11-8

When a contributor submits a post for review, it becomes a pending post.

3. **If you see a pending post you want to review, click its title.**

   WordPress opens the post in the Edit Post window. Make any changes you want, from minor corrections to adding completely new content.

4. **If the post is ready for prime time, click Publish.**

   This is the same way you publish your own posts. In this case, however, the newly published post will have the original author's byline, even if you edited the post.

   If you make changes to a post but you're not quite ready to publish it, click "Save as Pending" to store the edited version. You might do this to add questions or comments to the author's work, for example. You can wrap your comments in square brackets [like this]. Then the post author can make changes and re-submit the post.

NOTE Don't be confused by the way WordPress uses the term "author." Even though WordPress has a specific type of user called *author,* WordPress experts often use the same term to refer to anyone who writes a post on a WordPress site. Thus, administrators, authors, editors, and contributors can all act as post authors.

PLUG-IN POWER

Better Workflow for Reviewing Posts

WordPress gives you the basic procedures you need to get multiple contributors working together on the same site, but the process has a few rough edges.

The problem is the *workflow*—the way a task passes from one person to another. Right now, it's up to editors or administrators to go looking for pending posts. WordPress makes no effort to notify you that there's content waiting for review. Similarly, if an administrator edits a post but decides it needs more work, there's no easy way to let the contributor know that you need a rewrite. And when you *do* publish a pending post, WordPress once again fails to notify the original author.

WordPress's creators are aware of these gaps, and they may fix them in future versions of the program. But because the contributor feature is a bit of a specialized tool, those fixes are low on the list of WordPress priorities.

However, if you run a self-hosted site and want to implement a better system, there's a plug-in that can change everything. It's called Edit Flow (*http://tinyurl.com/editflow*) and it adds the structure you need to manage a multistage review process, including:

- **Custom status notices.** Instead of designating a post as Pending or Published, you can give it a status that reflects its stage in your organization's workflow. For example, if you run a news site, you might want posts to go from "Pitched" to "Assigned" to "Pending Review" to "Published." Edit Flow can help manage that sequence.
- **Editorial comments.** Edit Flow lets people attach brief notes to a post as it whizzes back and forth between them (as in "I love your post, but can you expand on paragraph 3?")
- **Email notifications.** Edit Flow can send notifications at key points in the review process—when authors submit new posts for review, when an editor publishes a post, when an editor places a comment on a post asking for changes, and so on. On a bustling site, these emails keep the post review process running quickly and efficiently.
- **Calendar.** If you want to make long-term content plans to ensure that there's always something new on your site, the Edit Flow calendar can help you plan authors' contributions.

Although Edit Flow is stuffed full of features, they're arranged in a logical way, and you can find helpful information at *http://editflow.org*. If you need to coordinate the publishing efforts of a small or midsized group of people, don't be afraid to give it a whirl.

Post Locking

As you already know, authors and contributors are limited to editing their own work. But editors and administrators have more sweeping powers; they can dip into any page or post and make changes.

This setup creates the possibility of conflicts. An editor could start editing a post that a contributor is still writing. Or two editors could attempt to revise the same work at the same time. WordPress doesn't have any post collaboration features—instead, only one person at a time can revise a post and save changes. To prevent one person's edits from wiping out another person's work, WordPress uses a simple *post locking* system.

Here's an example of how it works. If Diane starts editing a post, WordPress takes note. Every 15 seconds, it sends a message from Diane's browser to the server, which essentially says, "I'm still working!" (This message is part of an internal system called the Heartbeat API.) If Diane stops editing—say, she saves her work and navigates to another page, or she just closes the browser window without a second thought—the messages stop and WordPress realizes (within 15 seconds or so) that Diane has stopped working.

When you look at the posts on the All Posts page, WordPress shows you which ones are currently being edited (Figure 11-9).

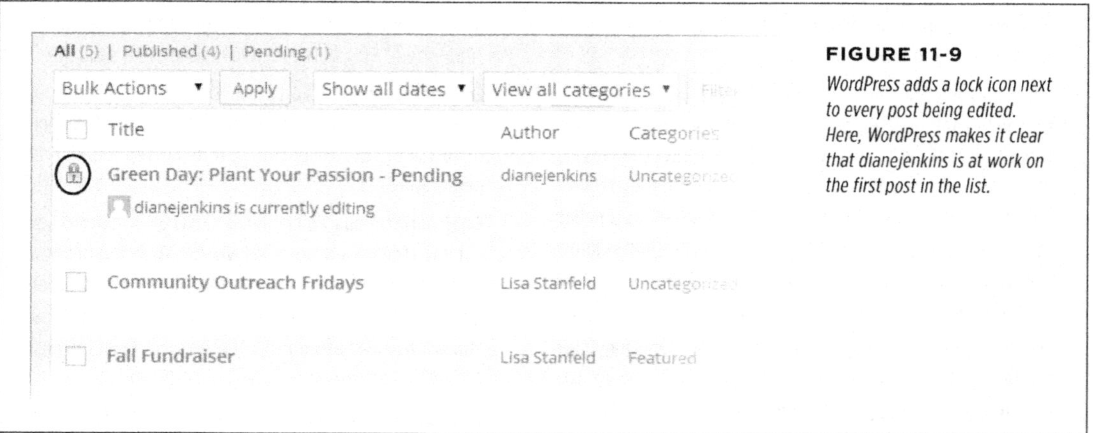

FIGURE 11-9

WordPress adds a lock icon next to every post being edited. Here, WordPress makes it clear that dianejenkins is at work on the first post in the list.

Life gets more interesting when someone else joins the editing party. For example, consider what happens if Lisa attempts to edit the post Diane is working on. WordPress notices the conflict the moment Lisa picks up the post, and shows a warning message (Figure 11-10, top). Now it's up to Lisa to decide whether she wants to wait for Diane to finish (by clicking "Go back") or push her out of the way and take over (by clicking "Take over"; see Figure 11-10, bottom).

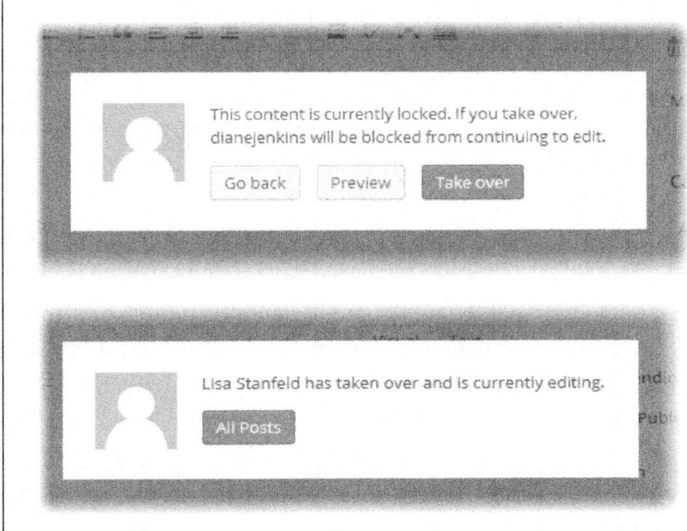

FIGURE 11-10

Top: Lisa tried to edit a post that Diane is editing. Now she has a choice.

Bottom: If Lisa clicks "Take over," WordPress boots Diane out of the editing window with this message.

NOTE When it comes to taking over a post, everyone is created equal. For example, if Lisa wants to take over the post that Diane is editing, it doesn't matter if Diane is an administrator or a lowly contributor. Nor does it matter who created the post. As long as Lisa is allowed to edit the post, she'll be able to wrest control from anyone who's currently working on it.

Diane has no chance to stop Lisa's post takeover. Once it happens, her editing session ends. All she can do is click "All Posts" to return to the post list. However, once Diane is back at the post list, nothing stops her from editing the same post *again*. If she does, she'll see the same warning message that Lisa saw, informing her that someone else is working on the post. If she forges ahead, Lisa will be kicked out of her editing session.

Of course, the point of the post locking system isn't for editors and authors to become locked in a series of dueling edits. Instead, it's for times when someone still has a post open but probably isn't editing it anymore. For example, if Diane starts revising a post but walks away from her computer for lunch, Lisa can still get some work done by assuming control of Diane's work in progress.

Revision Tracking

WordPress has another tool that can help you manage successive edits. It's called *revision tracking*, and it saves old versions of every post. You can step through a post's edit history to see who changed a post, when the edit took place, and exactly what that person changed.

NOTE Revision tracking is particularly useful on sites that have multiple authors. (And it's a life-saver when an overeager author overwrites another person's work.) However, revision tracking works just as well on single-author sites, where it lets you review your own edits.

You don't need to turn on revision tracking—it's always at work. Every time someone saves a post as a draft, publishes it, or updates it, WordPress takes a snapshot of the post's content and adds it to the revision history. WordPress may also take a snapshot of a post-in-progress as you edit it, but it won't keep more than one copy of your post in this state. After all, you wouldn't want to clutter your revision list with thousands of in-progress autosaves.

To see the edit history of a post, find the post in the All Posts page, and then click Edit. WordPress displays the revision history in two places (Figure 11-11):

- **The Publish box.** Look here to find the number of revisions WordPress stored. Click Browse to review these snapshots in the Compare Revisions page.
- **The Revisions box.** Check here to see a list of snapshots, from most recent to oldest. To inspect a revision, click the timestamp next to it.

NOTE If you don't see the Revisions box, click Screen Options in the top-right corner of the page, and then add a checkmark next to the Revisions option.

FREQUENTLY ASKED QUESTION

Co-Authoring Posts

What if several people edit the same post? Can they all be credited as authors?

Revision tracking is neat, but your readers don't see any of that information. All they see is the name of the post author—the person who initially created the post. Even when someone else edits a post, it remains the property of the initial author. An editor or administrator can edit a post and attribute it to someone else, but you can't credit two people as authors of the same post—unless you run a self-hosted site and you're willing to fiddle with your theme, as explained next.

To create true co-authored posts, you need to take two steps. First, you need to add the Co-Authors Plus plug-in (*http://tinyurl.com/co-authors-plus*), which lets you designate multiple authors for any post or page. Second—and this is the hard part—you have to get your posts and pages to actually display the names of the authors who worked on them. To make that possible, you need to edit your theme, as the Co-Authors Plus plug-in explains (see *http://tinyurl.com/ccr7896*).

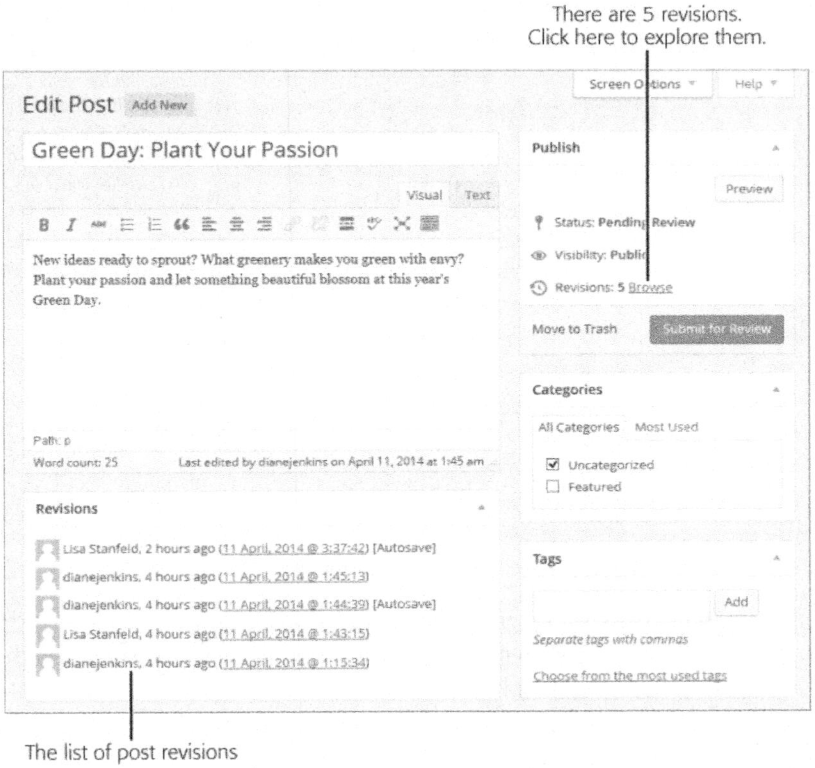

There are 5 revisions. Click here to explore them.

The list of post revisions

FIGURE 11-11

This post has been edited five times. In the Revisions box, WordPress tells you when each revision was made, and who made it.

The easiest way to study the changes made to a post is to click the Browse link, which appears in the Publish box next to the Revisions count. WordPress takes you to the Compare Revisions page (Figure 11-12). Initially, it compares the differences between the current version of a post (shown in green on the right) and the previously saved version (shown in red on the left).

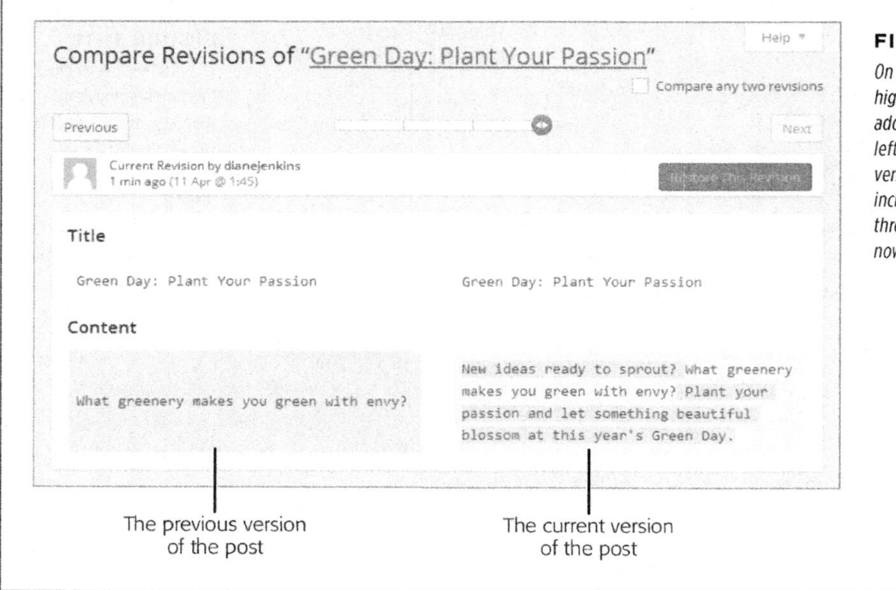

FIGURE 11-12

On the right, WordPress highlights the newly added bits of text. On the left, you see the previous version of the post, which included just one of the three sentences it holds now.

Once at the Compare Revisions page, you can dig deeper into the post's edit history. First, grab hold of the circle that sits in the small slider near the top of the page. To see an older snapshot, drag the circle to the left. For example, if you drag the circle one notch left, WordPress compares the previous version of the post (which it shows on the right) to the version it saved just before that (which it shows on the left). Keep dragging and you'll go further and further back in time (Figure 11-13).

Alternatively, you can use the buttons on either side of the slider button. Click Previous to go one step backward in time and Next to go one step forward.

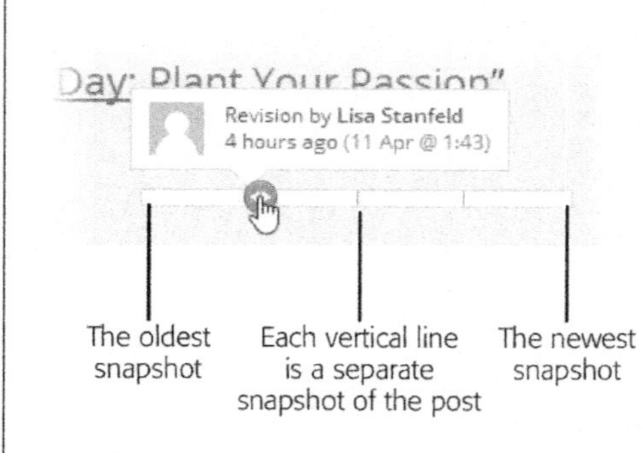

FIGURE 11-13

Every vertical line indicates a version of your post. Here, you positioned the circle over the second-oldest revision.

To revert to an older version of a post, drag the slider back until the version you want appears on the right, in green. Then, click Restore This Revision, which appears just above the snapshot's content.

When you drag the circle, WordPress compares two successive versions of a post (the one you pick, and the one just before that). But WordPress also allows curious administrators to perform an in-depth comparison that puts *any* two versions of a post under the microscope. For example, you could compare the oldest version of a post with the newest.

To do that, turn on the "Compare any two revisions" checkbox in the top-right corner of the page. Two circles appear in the slider, representing the two posts you want to compare. Drag the two circles to the two snapshots you want to examine, and WordPress compares their content underneath.

Revision tracking has one drawback. Keeping extra versions of all your posts takes space. If you host your site on WordPress.com, this isn't a problem, because your revision history tops out at 25 snapshots per post. After this point, WordPress tosses out the oldest snapshot every time it takes a new one. But on a self-hosted site, there's no limit. If you're an obsessive sort who revises the same post over and over, your revision history can balloon into hundreds of snapshots per post. Even if you have room for all these revisions (which you almost certainly do), it's never a good idea to waste space in your WordPress database. An unnecessarily big database makes backups slower and can even slow down the overall performance of your pages.

Unfortunately, there's no way to delete old revisions using the dashboard. Instead, you need a plug-in to clear out the bloat. Numerous plug-ins can do the job, but WP-Optimize (*http://tinyurl.com/wp-opti*) is a popular, versatile choice. It clears several types of old data out of your database, including old post revisions, old drafts, and unapproved comments.

Alternatively, you can tell WordPress to save fewer snapshots. For example, you could set WordPress to store a maximum of five revisions for each post. You can do that with a plug-in (try the straightforward Revision Control, at *http://tinyurl.com/rev-control*), or you can edit the *wp-config.php* configuration file using the process described on page 570.

If you decide to edit the *wp-config.php* file, you need to add a line like this to the end of the file in your website folder:

```
define('WP_POST_REVISIONS', 5);.
```

This tells WordPress to store a maximum of five revisions per post. However, you can replace the 5 with whatever number you want. Or you can tell WordPress to never store *any* revisions by substituting this line of code:

```
define('WP_POST_REVISIONS', false );
```

Now you'll never have to worry about database bloat from old revisions, but you'll also lose the safety net that lets you recover content if you accidentally erase or mangle it.

Browsing an Author's Posts

Once you've added a few authors to your site and figured out a way for them to work without stepping on each other's toes, it's worth thinking about what your multi-authored site looks like to visitors. How can they browse the work of specific authors, or find out more about the writers they like best?

The first issue—reading the work of a specific author—is the easiest to resolve. Just as you can view all the posts in a particular category or all the posts that have the same tag, so you can browse all the posts by a specific author. The easiest way to do that is to click the author's name, which appears just before or after the post content, depending on the theme (Figure 11-14).

NOTE The name WordPress uses to sign posts is the author's *display name*, which might be the person's WordPress user name (the standard setting), her full first and last name, or a nickname. Users can configure their display names by editing their profile settings (Users→My Profile).

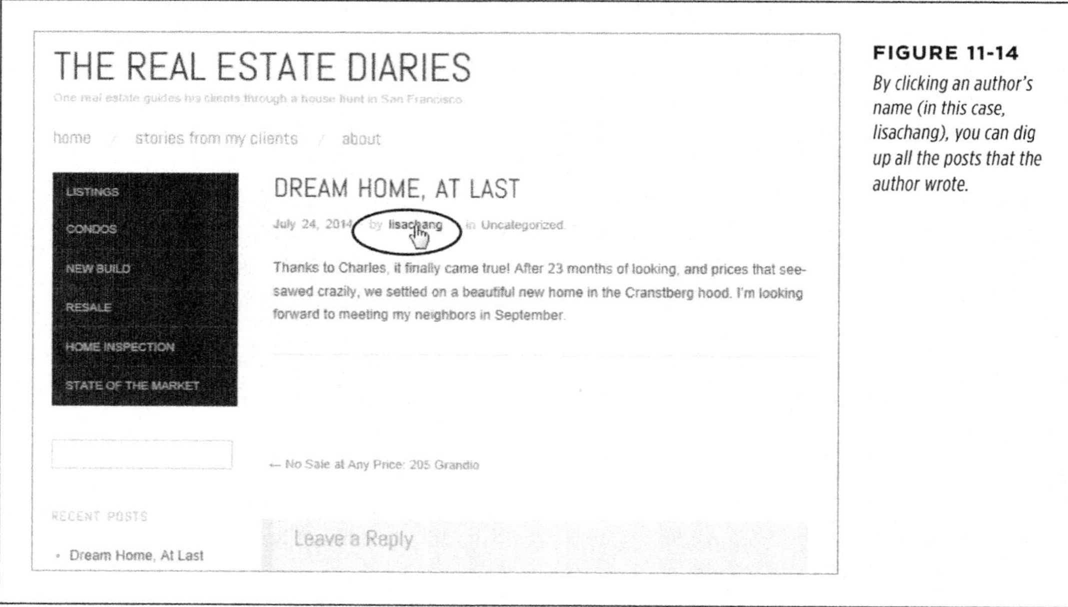

FIGURE 11-14

By clicking an author's name (in this case, lisachang), you can dig up all the posts that the author wrote.

WordPress uses special web addresses to make it easy to browse posts by author. For example, if you click *lisachang*, WordPress adds */author/lisachang* to the end of the site address, like this:

```
http://therealestatediaries.com/author/lisachang
```

This is essentially the same way that category web addresses work (page 123).

Now that you know how to get the posts for a specific author, you can make it easier for visitors to get them as well. For example, you could create a menu that has a link for each author, and then display that menu in the main navigation area of your site (Figure 11-15), or in a sidebar, with the help of the Custom Menu widget (page 228).

FIGURE 11-15

This menu includes a link to each author's posts, making it easy for readers to browse content by author.

PLUG-IN POWER

More Ways to Browse Authors

The custom menu approach gives you a great way to create author post links. But if you're building a self-hosted site, you may want to check out one of the many author-browsing plug-ins, which give you more display options and may save a bit of effort.

The Authors Widget (*http://tinyurl.com/authorswidget*) is a basic but effective example. It offers two display options. The first is a list that's not much different from what you get with the Custom Menu widget, just slightly more convenient, and it gives you the option to show the post count next to each author's name. The second display setting is an author *cloud* that works like the Tag Cloud widget (page 165), creating a jumbled mass of author links, with the most prolific authors' names the biggest.

The Author Avatars List plug-in (*http://tinyurl.com/authoravatars*) is one of many author-browsing widgets that use avatars, the tiny headshots that you can pair up with any email account (page 263). As with the more pedestrian author list, you can click an author headshot to start browsing the author's posts.

Adding Author Information

Ordinarily, WordPress keeps author information to a minimum. Even though it stores a few key details in each user's profile—including a basic "Biographical info" box—none of these details show up in a post. All your readers see is the author's name.

In some cases, you might prefer to showcase your author. For example, you might want to add a more detailed byline or include a brief bio that highlights the author's achievements. The low-tech solution is to add this information to the bottom of the post (consider setting it in *italics* to make it stand apart from the rest of the content). But if you run a self-hosted site, this is one more challenge you can tackle with the right plug-in.

The WordPress plug-in repository is overflowing with author info widgets and bio boxes. One decent starting point is the WP About Author plug-in (*http://tinyurl.com/wp-about-author*), which automatically adds an author box to the bottom of every post. It also adds several new text boxes to every user's profile, where authors can enter links to sites where they have public pages (like Facebook, Twitter, and Pinterest). The author's bio will then include these links (Figure 11-16).

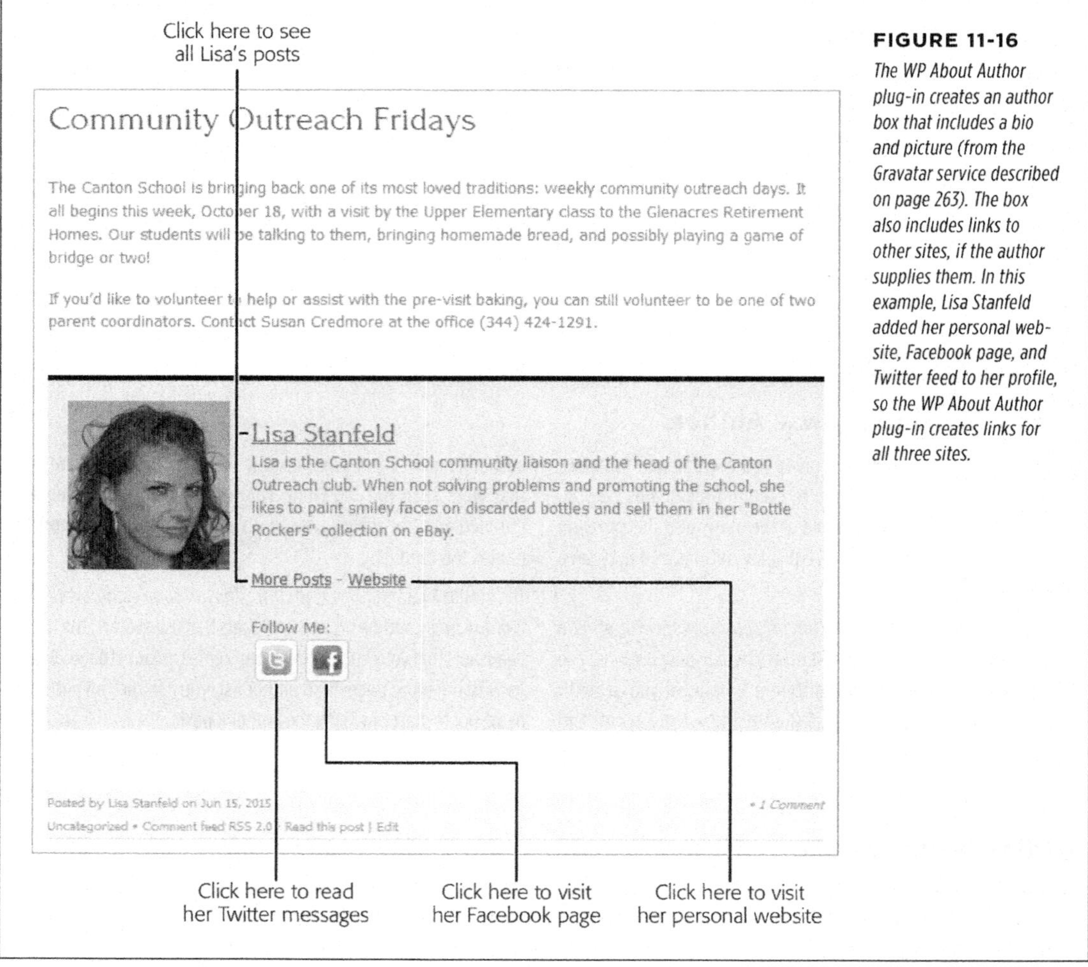

Click here to see all Lisa's posts
Community Outreach Fridays
The Canton School is bringing back one of its most loved traditions: weekly community outreach days. It all begins this week, October 18, with a visit by the Upper Elementary class to the Glenacres Retirement Homes. Our students will be talking to them, bringing homemade bread, and possibly playing a game of bridge or two!
If you'd like to volunteer to help or assist with the pre-visit baking, you can still volunteer to be one of two parent coordinators. Contact Susan Credmore at the office (344) 424-1291.
Lisa Stanfeld
Lisa is the Canton School community liaison and the head of the Canton Outreach club. When not solving problems and promoting the school, she likes to paint smiley faces on discarded bottles and sell them in her "Bottle Rockers" collection on eBay.
More Posts - Website
Follow Me:
Posted by Lisa Stanfeld on Jun 15, 2015
• 1 Comment
Uncategorized • Comment feed RSS 2.0 | Read this post | Edit
Click here to read her Twitter messages
Click here to visit her Facebook page
Click here to visit her personal website

FIGURE 11-16

The WP About Author plug-in creates an author box that includes a bio and picture (from the Gravatar service described on page 263). The box also includes links to other sites, if the author supplies them. In this example, Lisa Stanfeld added her personal website, Facebook page, and Twitter feed to her profile, so the WP About Author plug-in creates links for all three sites.

Another good author footer plug-in is the Fancier Author Box by ThematoSoup (*http://tinyurl.com/authorbox*). It uses a slightly smaller version of the author picture, fewer links, and a neato two-tab view that lets you see the author's recent posts without leaving the current page (Figure 11-17).

Bio
Latest Posts
Lisa Stanfeld
Lisa is the Canton School community liaison and the head of the Canton Outreach club. When not solving problems and promoting the school, she likes to paint smiley faces on discarded bottles and sell them in her "Bottle Rockers" collection on eBay.
Bio
Latest Posts
Latest posts by Lisa Stanfeld (see all)
Community Outreach Fridays - June 15, 2015
Fall Fundraiser - June 14, 2015
School Year Starts! - June 14, 2015

FIGURE 11-17

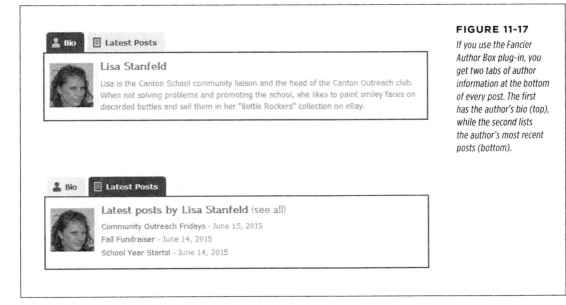

If you use the Fancier Author Box plug-in, you get two tabs of author information at the bottom of every post. The first has the author's bio (top), while the second lists the author's most recent posts (bottom).

Alternatively, you can use one of several plug-ins that puts author information into a widget. That way, you can take the author details out of a post and tuck them into a sidebar. One such plug-in is Author Spotlight (*http://tinyurl.com/authorspot*). Of course, this idea works only if your theme includes a sidebar in its single-post view. Most themes do, but the older Twenty Eleven theme limits its sidebar to the main post list, so author box widgets aren't much use.

Finally, some themes include a ready-made author information page that you can drop into your site. Twenty Fourteen is an example—it includes a contributor page that shows information for every author (Figure 11-18).

CANTON SCHOOL STAFF

Lisa Stanfeld

Lisa is the Canton School community liaison and the head of the Canton Outreach club. When not solving problems and promoting the school, she likes to paint smiley faces on discarded bottles and sell them in her "Bottle Rockers" collection on eBay.

4 ARTICLES

Diane Jenkins

Diane Jenkins wears many hats at Canton School. She's the librarian, cafeteria director, and wellness coach. She also tends to the beautiful community gardens at the front of the school.

1 ARTICLE

Peter Bradley

1 ARTICLE

FIGURE 11-18

As long as you have at least one published post, the Twenty Fourteen theme adds you to the contributor page, complete with a brief bio, a picture, and a post-browsing button.

Here's how to create a contributor page if your site uses Twenty Fourteen:

1. **In the dashboard, choose Pages→Add New.**

   Type in a title for your contributor page. The example in Figure 11-18 uses the title "Canton School Staff."

   Don't bother typing in any page content, because none of it will appear in the contributor page.

2. **In the Page Attributes box, change the Template setting to Contributor Page.**

   WordPress infuses the Contributor Page template with the magic code you need. It prepares a list of all your site's authors and builds a page that describes them.

3. **Optionally, alter the permalink for your page (page 119).**

   For example, you might want to use a short, meaningful address like *http://cantonschool.org/staff.*

   If you don't see the permalink (and the Edit button) under the page title, click in the empty content box underneath. That makes WordPress save a draft of your page, which forces it to create the permalink.

4. **Click Publish to add the contributor page to your site.**

   The contributor page uses a few key details for each author. If you run a self-hosted site, it's up to you (and your authors) to make sure this information is available, or you'll end up with a distinctly drab contributor page.

   Here's what each author needs:

   - **A proper display name.** You specify that using the "Display name publicly as" setting (page 374).
   - **A descriptive biography.** You enter this in the Biographical Info box when you edit a user's profile (page 374). In Figure 11-18, Peter Bradley lacks a biography.
   - **A Gravatar picture.** If you want a cute head-and-shoulders shot to appear next to your author details, you need the help of WordPress's Gravatar service, which attaches a personal picture to any email address. Page 263 explains how to set it up.

Removing Authors (and Other Users)

As your site evolves, the group of people you work with may change. You already know how to *add* users, but at some point you may decide to *remove* one. To do that, you first need to view your site's user list by choosing Users→All Users.

If your site is on WordPress.com, the list includes all the administrators, editors, authors, and contributors registered on your site (it doesn't include followers). To remove someone, point to the person's user name and then click Remove. That person's WordPress.com account remains intact, but she no longer has privileges on your site. If you remove a person who's published posts on your site, the posts will remain (although you can delete them by going to the Posts→All Posts list).

If you run a self-hosted site, the user list includes everyone who can publish on your site. Unlike a WordPress.com site, you don't merely remove authors, you *delete* them by clicking the Delete link. Deleting someone's account is a fairly drastic step, because it completely wipes the traces of that person off your site. WordPress will ask you what to do with any posts that belong to the newly deleted author (Figure 11-19). You can either delete her posts or assign them to another person.

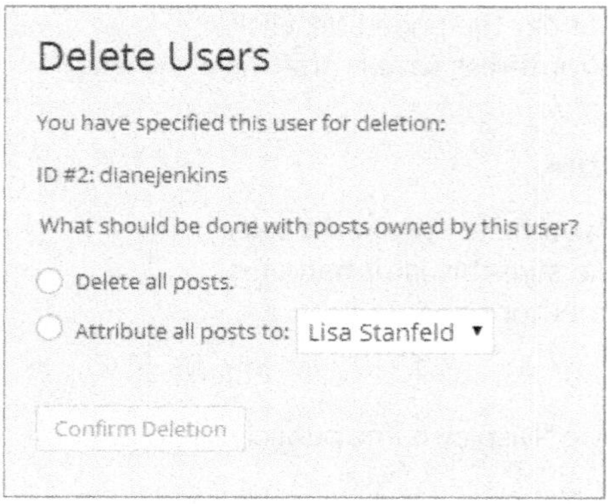

Delete Users

You have specified this user for deletion:

ID #2: dianejenkins

What should be done with posts owned by this user?

○ Delete all posts.

○ Attribute all posts to: Lisa Stanfeld ▾

Confirm Deletion

FIGURE 11-19

When you delete an author from a self-hosted site, WordPress asks you what to do with her posts. (If you have a last-minute change of heart, click somewhere else in the dashboard, and WordPress abandons the delete operation.)

If you don't want to take such a drastic step, you can *demote* a user, so that he remains on your site but has fewer privileges. For example, you could change a contributor to an ordinary subscriber. That way, his existing posts will remain on your site, but he won't be able to create any new ones. And if, sometime in the future, you decide to reenlist this person's help, you can simply change his status from subscriber back to contributor.

To change a role, find the person in the user list and click Edit. Then pick a new role from the Role list and click Update User.

Building a Private Community

So far, you've used WordPress's user registration features to open up your site to new contributors. Ironically, those same features are also an effective way to close the door to strangers. For example, you can prevent unregistered guests from reading certain posts, or even stop them from seeing any content at all.

Before you build a private site, however, make sure you have enough interested members. Transforming an ordinary site into a members-only hideout is a sure way to scare off 99.9 percent of your visitors. However, a private site makes sense if you already have a locked-in group of members. Your site might be the online home for a group of related people in the real world—for example, a team of researchers planning a new product, or a local self-help group for cancer survivors. But if you hope that people will stumble across your site and ask to sign up, you're in for some long and lonely nights.

NOTE The goals of a private site are very different from the goals of the average public site. A public site aims to attract new faces, gain buzz, and grow ever more popular. A private site is less ambitious—it allows certain types of discussions or collaboration in a quiet space.

Hiding and Locking Posts

You don't need to make your site entirely private; WordPress gives you two ways to protect individual posts, so the wrong people can't read them.

The first technique is *password protection.* The idea is simple—when you create a post, you pick a password that potential readers need to know. When someone tries to read the post, WordPress refuses to display it until the reader supplies the right password (Figure 11-20).

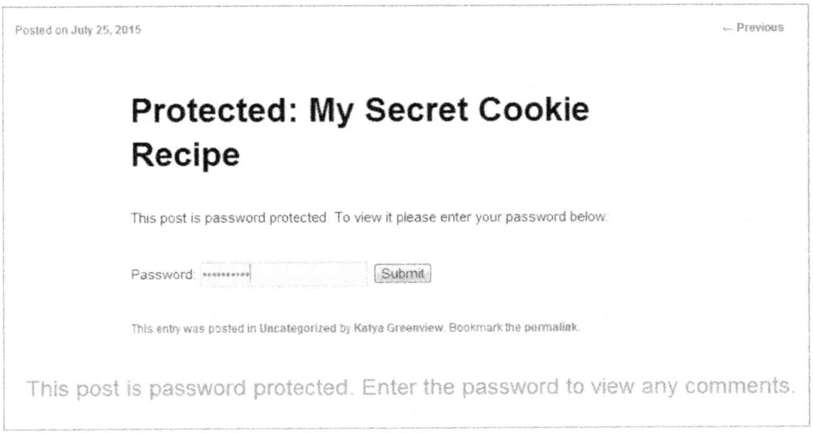

Posted on July 25, 2015 ← Previous

Protected: My Secret Cookie Recipe

This post is password protected. To view it please enter your password below:

Password: •••••••••• Submit

This entry was posted in Uncategorized by Katya Greenview. Bookmark the permalink.

This post is password protected. Enter the password to view any comments.

FIGURE 11-20

WordPress adds the text "Protected" to the title of every password-protected post. To read the post, you need to type in the correct password.

The nice part about password protection is that it's straightforward: You either know the password or you don't, and the password is all you need—protected posts don't require that a reader be registered with the site. Of course, administrators and editors can edit any post, so password protection doesn't affect them.

NOTE Use password-protected posts sparingly. If your site includes a mix of public and password-protected posts, frustrated readers are likely to give up on you altogether. Password-protected posts make sense if your site isn't really on the Web, but hosted on an organization's internal network (a.k.a. an intranet).

WordPress's second post-protection technique is *private posts,* which are hidden from everyone except logged-in administrators and editors. When other people visit the site, WordPress scrubs every trace of your private posts. They won't appear in the post list, show up in searches, or appear when you browse by category, tag, date, or author.

To see your options, click the Edit link next to a post's Visibility setting (see Figure 11-21).

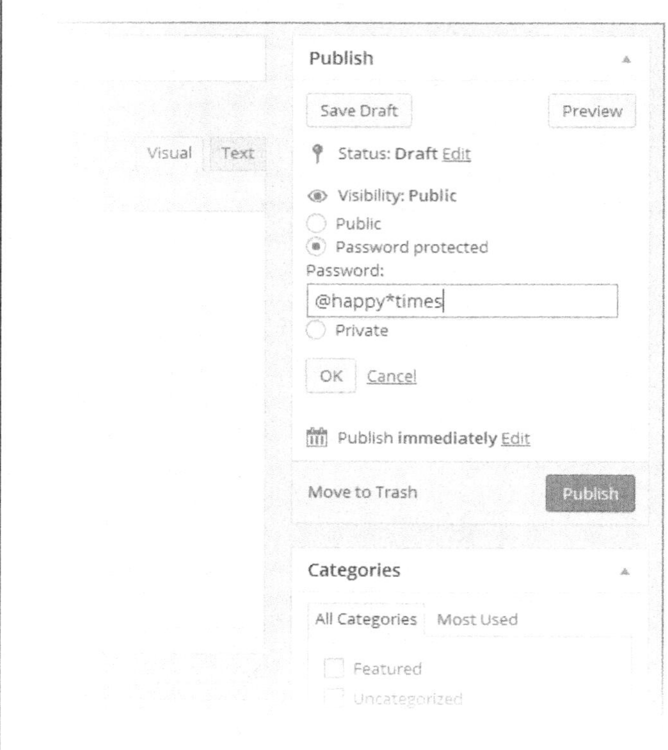

FIGURE 11-21

You can choose from three Visibility options for posts: Public (the standard), Password protected (the post's title is visible to everyone, but only people with the right password can read the content), or Private (the title, post, and comments are hidden from everyone except editors and administrators). Once you choose, click OK.

You can also add a password to a private post or make it private using the familiar Publish box, which appears in the Add New Post and the Edit Post pages.

PLUG-IN POWER

Creating More Specific Privacy Rules

The problem with private posts is that they're *too* private. You need to be an editor or administrator to view them, and that may be more power than you want to give other people.

If you're developing a self-hosted site, a good plug-in can provide a solution. One is Page Security by Contexture (*http://tinyurl.com/page-security-c*). It lets you create groups of users and then give them permission to read specific posts or pages. For example, you could create a group called Managers, add several people to that group, and then give the entire group permission to read your "Tax Evasion Secrets" post.

Be careful about going too far with the Page Security plug-in, however. If you need to set security rules for dozens of pages, WordPress might not be the right tool for the job—you might be better off with a content management system like SharePoint or Alfresco. And although Page Security does a good job of grafting on some basic security features, things can get messy, and there's no guarantee that the complex security rules you set up now will continue to work in future versions of WordPress.

Creating a Private Site

A completely private site is one that forces visitors to log in to view *anything*. If they don't sign in, they can't read a single post or page.

You can turn a WordPress.com site into a private site by flipping a single setting. Choose Settings→Privacy, turn on the "I would like my site to be private, visible only to users I choose" checkbox, and then click Save Changes. Now visitors will encounter the WordPress login page, no matter what they try to read (Figure 11-22).

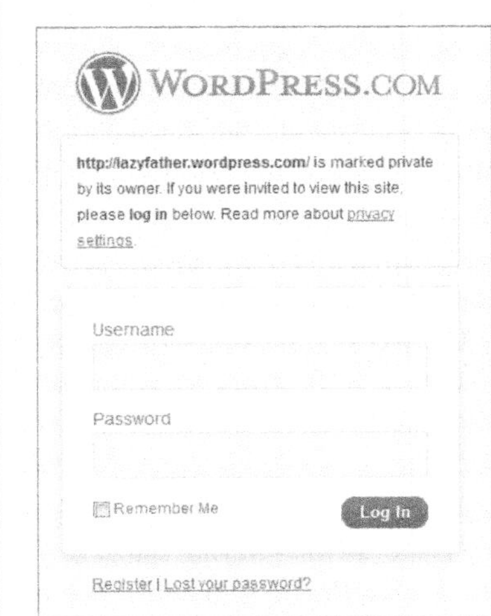

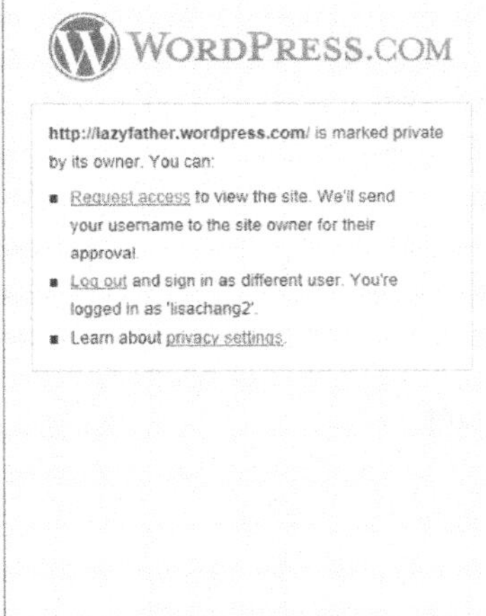

FIGURE 11-22

Left: WordPress asks visitors who try to view a private site to log in.

Right: This is what a visitor sees if he's logged in to WordPress.com, but not registered on your private site. Clicking "Request access" sends an email to the site owner, who decides whether or not to add the hopeful new guest.

Oddly enough, self-hosted sites lack the private site feature that WordPress.com offers. However, several simple plug-ins can fill the gap. One is Page Restrict (*http://tinyurl.com/page-restrict*), which lets you prevent people from accessing specific pages—or your entire site—until they log in. Page Restrict also lets you pick a suitable message that explains the issue to anonymous visitors, such as "This content is private. To view it, you must log in."

NOTE You've reached the end of the line for WordPress.com sites in this chapter. The following sections cover a few more plug-ins and features that self-hosters can use. So if you run a WordPress.com site, you may as well skip ahead to the next chapter).

Letting People Register Themselves on a Self-Hosted Site

If WordPress hosts your site, WordPress.com is in charge of registering your users. But if you run a self-hosted site, you're in control, and that gives you a unique ability. If you're feeling a bit daring, you can open the floodgates to your site and let your readers register themselves.

This strategy might seem a bit dangerous—and if you don't think it through, it is. Giving random web visitors extra powers on your site is an extreme step for even the most trusting person. However, there are several scenarios where self-registration makes a lot of sense. Here are the most common:

- You're creating a private blog and you want to prohibit anonymous contributors, but you don't want to make your restrictions onerous—you simply want to deter spammers and other riffraff. Often, the process of signing up is enough to keep out these troublemakers. And if you let readers sign themselves up, you save yourself the task of doing so, and save visitors the need to wait for your approval.
- You're creating a site that welcomes community contributors. You're ready to let anyone sign up as a contributor, but you want to approve their content before it gets published (page 379). Be aware, however, that this is no small task—reviewing other people's content and sniffing out spam makes comment moderation seem like a day at the spa.
- You've restricted comments to people who have registered and logged in to the site (page 272), but you're willing to let people comment if they go through the trouble of creating an account. Sometimes, site owners take this step to lock out spammers, and typically it works well, although it also drives away legitimate commenters who can't be bothered signing up. In most cases, it's better to allow Facebook and Twitter authentication (page 270), and to use Akismet to fight spam (page 275).
- Your WordPress site isn't really on the Web; it's on the internal network of a business or organization. Thus, you can assume that the people who reach your site are relatively trustworthy. (Of course, you still shouldn't grant them any privileges more powerful than a contributor account without your personal review.)

Flipping on the self-registration feature takes just a few seconds. In the dashboard, choose Settings→General. Add a checkmark next to "Anyone can register," choose a role in the New User Default Role box below, and then click Save Changes.

WARNING You should set the role for new users to subscriber or contributor—subscriber to welcome new readers to a private blog, and contributor to let potential authors sign themselves up. Never allow new people to sign themselves up as authors or editors, unless you want spammers to paste their ads all over your site.

When you turn on self-registration, WordPress adds an extra link to the login page (Figure 11-23).

If you allow self-registration on a public website, you'll eventually have spammers creating accounts. Usually, the offender is an automated computer program called a *spambot*. It searches the Web for WordPress sites and attempts to sign up on every one it finds, in the hope that the site will grant the spambot author or editor permissions. If a site is unwise enough to do so, the spambot immediately gets to work spewing spam into new posts. As long as you limit new users to the role of contributor or (powerless) subscriber, the spambot won't be able to do anything.

(To make sure your site is clean, periodically review your user list and delete bad accounts.)

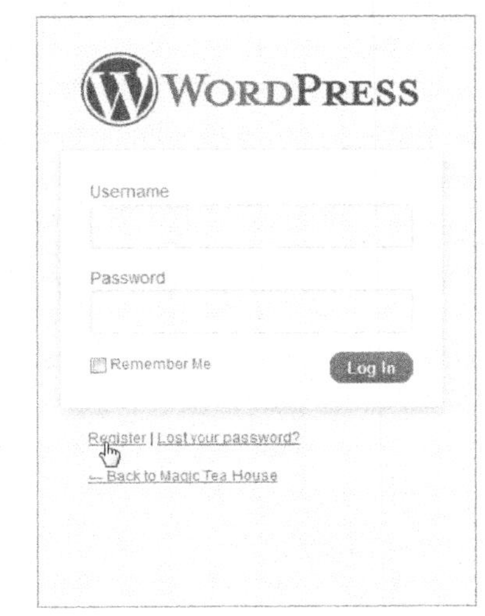

FIGURE 11-23

This blog lets people register themselves. They simply click the Register link (left), enter an email address and password (right), and then wait for an activation link to arrive by email.

Creating a Network of Sites

So far, you've learned how to transform your site from a lonely one-man-band to a collaborative workspace full of authors, editors, and contributors. This transformation keeps you in control of your site but allows new recruits so you can expand your content, extend your reach, and attract new visitors.

Now you'll take a step in a different direction. Instead of looking at adding multiple people to a crowded site, you'll see how to create multiple WordPress *sites* that coexist on the same web server. Think of it as a way to empower your users to do even more. Now, each author gets a separate site, complete with its own web address, dashboard, theme, and reverse-chronological list of posts. Your web server hosts all these sites alongside your own, much like children living in their parent's home.

For example, say you create a WordPress multisite network at *http://EvilCompanyOfDoom.com*. An employee named Gareth Keenan might create a site at *http://EvilCompanyOfDoom.com/garethkeenan*. Similarly, another employee might add a site at *http://EvilCompanyOfDoom.com/dawntinsley*. Of course, you don't need to create sites based on individual people—you can just as easily create sites that represent departments, teams, clubs, or any other group of people who need to blog together.

NOTE The multisite feature works well if you have a community of people who need to work independently, keep their content separate from everyone else's, and have complete control over the way their content is organized and presented. For example, the Canton School site might use the multisite feature to give each teacher her own site. Teachers could then use their sites to post assignments and answer student questions. The multisite feature isn't very useful if you want people to team up on the same project, share ideas, or blog together—in all these cases, a single site with multiple users makes more sense.

The multisite feature is particularly convenient when it comes to administration. When you build a network of sites, you become its *network administrator*—a special sort of administrator with sweeping powers over all the sites in the network. Using these powers, you can choose what themes your users can install and what plug-ins they use. And when a new version of WordPress comes out, you can update all the sites in a single step.

UP TO SPEED

Multisites in Action

To really understand the multisite feature, it helps to check out some websites that already use it. Here are some examples:

- **Reuters Blogs** (*http://blogs.reuters.com*). The multisite feature is a great way to handle columnists in a news site. On Reuters, each columnist gets a separate blog that uses the same distinctive theme. But because each site is separate, columnists can create their own categories and tags, and moderate their own comments.
- **Harvard Law School** (*http://blogs.law.harvard.edu*). Harvard Law offers a free WordPress site to anyone in the Harvard University community. They can even sign themselves up and create a site immediately, as long as they have an email address that ends with *harvard.edu*.
- **Adobe Blogs** (*http://blogs.adobe.com*). Here, different teams of Adobe employees blog about their projects. This example is particularly interesting because it combines the multisite *and* multiuser features. For example, if you check out just one site, the Adobe Digital Media Blog (*http://blogs.adobe.com/digitalmedia*), you find a number of Adobe experts weighing in.
- **Best Buy Stores** (*http://stores.bestbuy.com*). The omnipresent electronics store isn't known for website innovation, but it makes good use of WordPress, giving each store its own WordPress site. For example, visit *http://stores.bestbuy.com/577* to see the latest news for the Best Buy in Fairless Hills, Pennsylvania.
- **WordPress.com**. The largest and most impressive example of a WordPress multisite network is WordPress.com, the free blogging hub for several hundred thousand people. If the multisite feature works for a network this popular and this big, it's a safe bet that it will serve the needs of your community, too.

Before going any further, be aware of one thing: Building a network of sites is significantly more complex than adding people to an existing one. Expect to spend more time feeling your way around and relearning how to configure sites and users. Furthermore, be careful with the plug-ins you use, because some won't work in a multisite network.

By the end of this chapter, you'll know how to set up a network of sites, add sites, and perform the basic configuration that holds it all together. However, there are significant aspects of the multisite feature that are outside the scope of this book, like using it with subdomains (see the following Note).

NOTE There are two ways to create addresses for the sites in a network. You can give each site its own subfolder (as in *http://OrilliaBaseballTeams.com/madcats*), or you can give each site its own subdomain (as in *http://madcats.OrilliaBaseballTeams.com*). The latter is the way WordPress.com works. It's slightly more complicated, because it requires some additional settings on your web host. In this chapter, you'll stick to the subfolder approach.

Creating a New Multisite Network from Scratch

The easiest way to create a multisite network is to create a new WordPress site from scratch, using an autoinstaller that supports the multisite feature. For example, if you use Softaculous, the installation process is almost exactly the same as the one you used in Chapter 3 (page 55). The difference is that somewhere in your autoinstaller, you need to find a setting named something like "Enable Multisite" and switch it on (Figure 11-24).

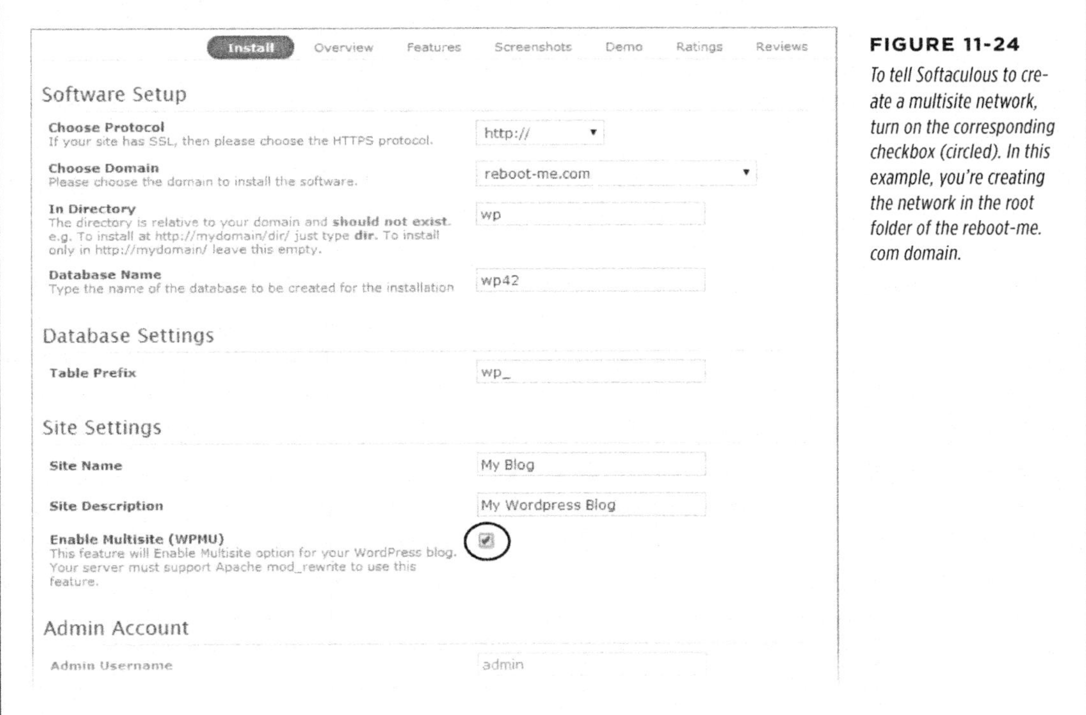

FIGURE 11-24

To tell Softaculous to create a multisite network, turn on the corresponding checkbox (circled). In this example, you're creating the network in the root folder of the reboot-me.com domain.

Once you install your site, you can go straight to the dashboard and look around. Skip ahead to the section "Your Multisite Network: A First Look" on the following page.

If you don't have an autoinstaller that supports the multisite feature, you'll need to install a normal WordPress site first and then go through the somewhat awkward conversion process outlined in the next section.

Converting an Existing Site to a Multisite Network

Converting an existing WordPress site into a multisite network is trickier than creating a new network from scratch. If you use subfolders (rather than subdomains) in your network, the conversion process will break any links within posts (see the Note near the bottom of this page to learn why). For that reason, it's best to convert a newly created WordPress site, rather than one you've been using (and that other people have been reading) for some time.

But if you know how to use an FTP program and you're undaunted by the challenge, it *is* possible to transition from an ordinary site to a multisite network. WordPress has the full and rather technical step-by-step instructions at *http://tinyurl.com/2835suo*. The process involves modifying two files in your site—*wp-config.php* and *.htaccess*—and changing a few related settings in the dashboard. But because you can't directly edit the files on your site, you need to download them to your computer (that's where the FTP program comes in), make your changes in a text editor, and then upload the new, modified files. If you've never fiddled with a WordPress installation before, it's a bit tedious.

WARNING Make sure you really want a multisite network before you forge ahead, because there's no easy way to change a multisite network back to a single site after you make the jump.

Your Multisite Network: A First Look

When you create a multisite network, WordPress starts you out with a single home site in the root of the installation folder. For example, if you install a multisite network at *http://prosetech.com*, the first site is at *http://prosetech.com*. This is exactly the same as when you create a standalone site. When you create *additional* sites, however, WordPress places them in subfolders. So if you add a site named teamseven, WordPress creates it at *http://prosetech.com/teamseven*. (You might think that it makes more sense to write TeamSeven rather than teamseven, but to WordPress it's all the same. No matter what capitalization you use, WordPress shows the site name in lowercase letters when you manage it in the dashboard.)

NOTE If you're using subfolders (not subdomains) to arrange your multisite network, you'll find one quirk in WordPress's naming system. When you view a post or page on your home site, WordPress adds */blog* to the address. For example, WordPress puts a post that would ordinarily be found at *http://prosetech.com/2014/06/peanut-butter-prices-spike* at *http://prosetech.com/blog/2014/06/peanut-butter-prices-spike*. This slightly awkward system makes sure that WordPress can't confuse your home site blog with another site in the network, because it doesn't allow any other site to use the name *blog*.

When you finish creating your multisite network, you find yourself at the dashboard of your home site. But if you attempt to augment your site's features, you'll find a new restriction. Even though you can activate an existing plug-in or theme, WordPress won't let you install new ones. On a fresh WordPress install, you'll probably get just a single theme (Twenty Fourteen) and two basic plug-ins (the essential Akismet spam-catcher, and the pointless Hello Dolly example).

If you haven't already guessed, your home site has these new and slightly unwelcome limitations because it's now part of your multisite network. These rules can be frustrating, but they have sound logic behind them. First, the theme limitations guarantee that your sites share a consistent look. Second, the theme and plug-in restrictions act as safeguards that prevent inexperienced users from uploading spam-filled extensions, which could compromise your entire network.

That said, you'll probably want to tweak these restrictions to make them better suit your site. For example, you may want the sites on your network to use a different standard theme, or you may want to allow site creators to choose from a small group of approved themes. You might also have trusted plug-ins that you want to run on everyone's site. You'll learn how to make these changes shortly. But first, you need to understand how to add new sites to your network.

Adding a Site to Your Network

To add a site, you need to enter network administration mode. This is a step that only you, the network administrator, can take. Other administrators on your network will be able to manage their own sites, but they won't be able to change the network settings—or even look at them.

NOTE In WordPress parlance, a *network administrator* (also known as a *super admin*) is the person who manages a multisite network and has full power over all the sites inside. A *site administrator* oversees a single site—the site you create for him.

To start managing the network, point to the My Sites menu, which sits to the right of the navigation bar (that's the black bar that stretches across the top of the page). Then click Network Admin (Figure 11-25).

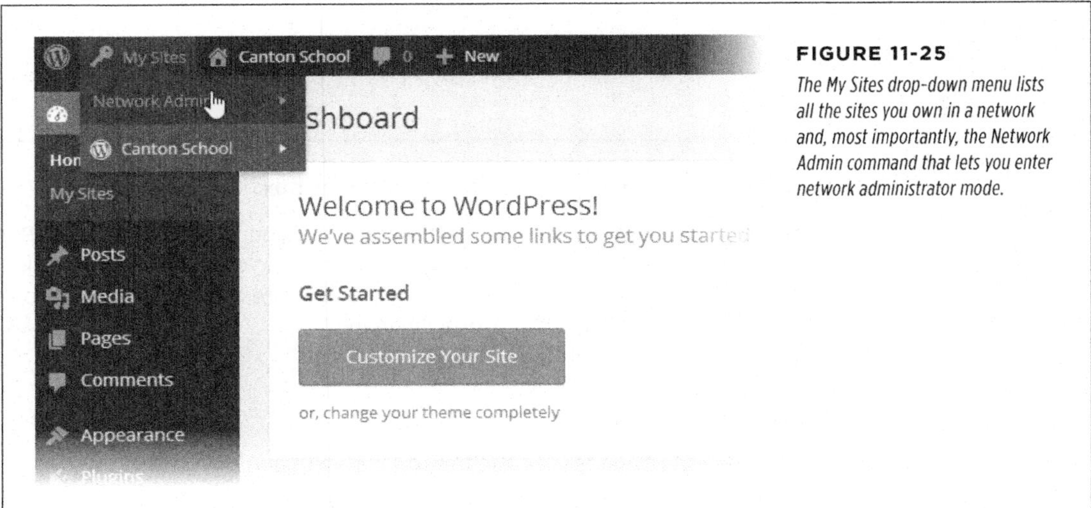

FIGURE 11-25

The My Sites drop-down menu lists all the sites you own in a network and, most importantly, the Network Admin command that lets you enter network administrator mode.

In network administration mode, the dashboard changes. Because you're no longer managing a specific site, the Posts, Pages, Comments, Links, and Media menus all disappear. In their place is a smaller set of commands for managing sites, users, themes, plug-ins, network settings, and updates.

TIP You can go straight to the network administration page by adding */wp-admin/network* to the end of your home site address, as in *http://prosetech.com/wp-admin/network*.

Once in network administration mode, you can create a new site:

1. **Choose Sites→Add New from the dashboard.**

   The Add New Site page opens (Figure 11-26).

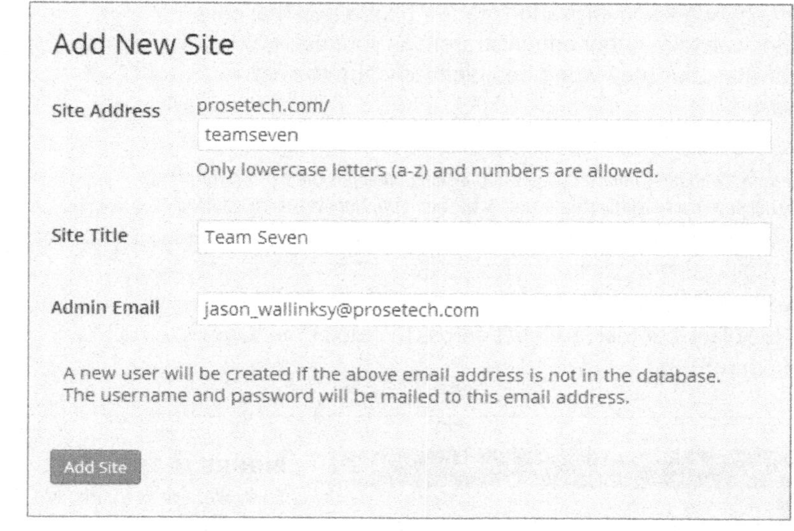

FIGURE 11-26

WordPress knows that a network administrator may need to create dozens of sites. To keep your life simple, it asks for just three pieces of information: the site address, the site title, and the email address of the person who will become the site's administrator. Here, WordPress will create the new site at http://prosetech.com/teamseven.

2. **Type the site's folder name in the Site Address box.**

   WordPress adds the folder name to the address of your multisite network. For example, if you use the folder name drjanespears and your multisite network is at *http://StMarciMarguerettaDoctors.org*, the new site has the address *http://StMarciMarguerettaDoctors.org/drjanespears*.

3. **Give the site a title.**

   The site administrator can change this later.

4. **Supply the email address of the person who will own the site.**

   That person will become the site's administrator.

Adding people to a multiuser network is different from adding people to a standalone site in one important respect: You don't need to pick the password for new users. WordPress knows you're busy, and it generates a random password and emails it to the new administrator.

5. **Click Add Site.**

   WordPress creates the site and adds two links to the top of the Add New Site page: Visit Dashboard (which takes you to the new site's dashboard) and Edit Site (which lets you change the site's settings). The dashboard is in its familiar place—just add */wp-admin* to the end of the site address to go straight to its front door.

   Ideally, you won't need to visit the new site's dashboard, because the newly christened administrator will take it from there.

TIP If, sometime later, you need to delete a site, modify it, or assign it to a new administrator, start at the list of sites in the Sites→Add Sites section of the network administration dashboard.

GEM IN THE ROUGH

Letting People Create Their Own Sites

Ordinarily, it's up to you to create every site in a multisite network. WordPress helps you out by automatically creating an account for the new administrator, so you can create a site in one step instead of two. But if you have dozens or even hundreds of users who want sites, manually creating each one is tedious. WordPress gives you another option—you can choose to let people create their own sites.

This isn't quite as crazy as it sounds. As long as you don't let people create their own accounts, WordPress allows only registered users to start site-building. If you're crafty, you can use a WordPress plug-in like Add Multiple Users (*http://tinyurl.com/add-multiple*) to create accounts automatically, based on a list of email addresses in a text file or spreadsheet. Then you can let people build the sites they need on their own. (There's no restriction on the number of sites, so if someone can create one, she can also create 12. If you notice a power-drunk author creating too many sites, you need to step in, delete some, and send the miscreant a stern email.)

To allow people to create their own sites, choose Settings→Network Settings in the network administration dashboard. Then, next to "Allow new registrations," choose "Logged in users may register new sites." Make sure "Send the network admin an email notification every time someone registers a site or user account" is also turned on so WordPress notifies you about newly created sites. Finally, click Save Changes at the bottom of the page.

New users might not realize that they're allowed to create sites. WordPress won't tell them unless they ask for the sign-up page, by requesting *wp-signup.php* in the root site (as in *http://prosetech.com/wp-signup.php*). Figure 11-27 shows the page.

Understanding How Users Work in a Multisite Network

You can create as many sites as you want in a multisite network. In each site, you can add as many users as you need.

Sometimes, the same person needs to work on more than one site. For example, one person might need to contribute to different blogs maintained by different people. Or an administrator who manages one site in a network might also want to contribute to another.

To understand how to deal with this, you need to realize that a multisite network maintains a master list of all the users who belong to *any* site in the network. Each of those people has subscriber privileges on every site. (As you learned on page 370, subscribers are the lowest class of WordPress user—they can't do anything more than read posts and write comments.)

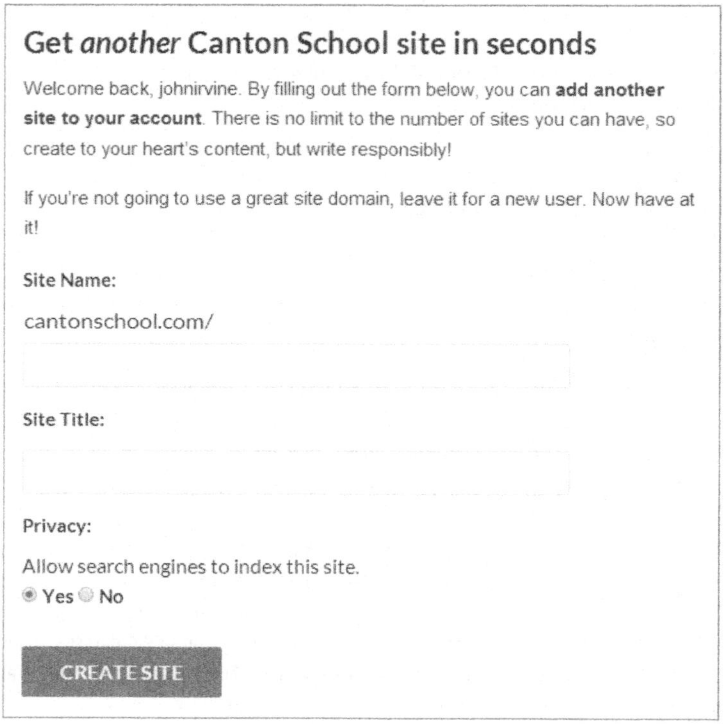

Get *another* Canton School site in seconds

Welcome back, johnirvine. By filling out the form below, you can **add another site to your account**. There is no limit to the number of sites you can have, so create to your heart's content, but write responsibly!

If you're not going to use a great site domain, leave it for a new user. Now have at it!

Site Name:

cantonschool.com/

Site Title:

Privacy:

Allow search engines to index this site.

Yes No

CREATE SITE

FIGURE 11-27

To create a new site, a logged-in user needs to supply the site folder name and the site's title on the sign-up page, and then click the big Create Site button. The sign-up text shown here is WordPress boilerplate. Once you learn how to edit a theme (Chapter 13), you'll be able to customize this text.

In addition, you can give people special privileges for specific sites. For example, you might make someone an administrator on one blog and an author on another. In this case, there's still just one record for that user, but now it's registered with two different sets of capabilities on two different sites.

NOTE Happily, WordPress makes people log in only once. When visitors move from one site to another in the same network, WordPress remembers who they are and determines what privileges they should have on each site.

If you choose Users→Add New on the network administration dashboard, you can add people to the master list (Figure 11-28, top). But WordPress won't give new users any special privileges for any site.

Life is different for ordinary site administrators. Consider what happens if an administrator named Suzy logs into her dashboard. When she chooses Users→Add New, she's not given the option to create an account for someone else. Instead, she can invite an existing user to take on a more powerful role on *her* site (Figure 11-28, bottom).

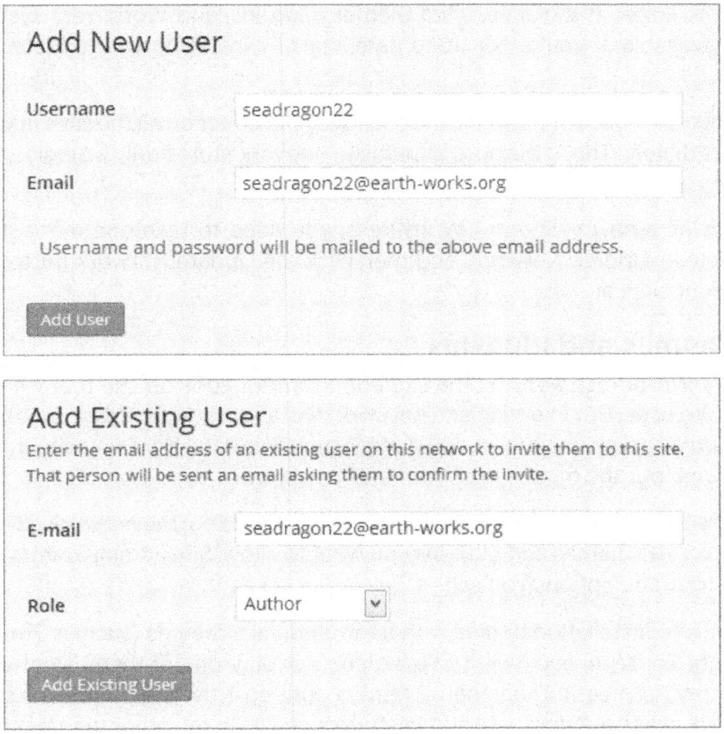

Add New User
Username seadragon22
Email seadragon22@earth-works.org
Username and password will be mailed to the above email address.
Add User

Add Existing User
Enter the email address of an existing user on this network to invite them to this site.
That person will be sent an email asking them to confirm the invite.
E-mail seadragon22@earth-works.org
Role Author
Add Existing User

FIGURE 11-28

Ordinarily, only network administrators can create new accounts (top) while site administrators can register existing users on their sites, and assign them the appropriate WordPress role (bottom).

One potential problem with the user registration system is that it can create a lot of extra work. For example, if a site administrator needs to add someone new, he needs to ask you, the network administrator, to create the account first. To circumvent this restriction, go to Settings→Network Settings, choose "Allow site administrators to add new users to their site," and then click Save Changes. Now site administrators can add new people to the master list.

Another problem occurs if one person contributes to several sites. In that case, someone needs to visit each dashboard and invite the user separately to each site. If you're not the sort of person who likes to spend all weekend tweaking WordPress settings, you may want to enlist the help of a plug-in like Multisite User Management (*http://tinyurl.com/multisite-um*). It lets you set a *default role* for each site in a multisite network. Then, when you create a new user, she's automatically registered on each site with the default role you chose.

Rolling Out Updates

One advantage of a multisite network is that it streamlines certain management tasks. For example, you can update WordPress on all the sites in your network in a single operation from the network administration page.

To get started, choose Updates→Available Updates from the network administration dashboard. You'll see, at a glance, what themes, plug-ins, and WordPress system updates are available. If you're not up to date, start by installing your updates on this page.

When you update themes or plug-ins, the changes take effect on all the sites in your network immediately. That's because a multisite network stores only a single copy of each theme and each plug-in.

When you install a new version of WordPress, you need to take one more step. Choose Updates→Update Network, and then click the Update Network button to upgrade all your sites at once.

Adding Themes and Plug-Ins

In an ordinary WordPress website, the site administrator controls the themes and plug-ins the site uses. But in a multisite network, this approach would be too risky, because a single malicious plug-in could steal sensitive data from any site in the network, or wipe out the database of your entire network.

Instead, multisite networks use a more disciplined system. You, the network administrator, can pick the themes and plug-ins you want to allow. Site administrators can then choose from the options you set.

A typical multisite installation begins with a few standard themes (such as Twenty Twelve, Twenty Thirteen, and Twenty Fourteen), but only one of them is network enabled (Twenty Fourteen). That means Twenty Fourteen is the only theme the sites in your network can use. In fact, site administrators can't see the other themes at all.

To add a new theme and make it accessible to the sites in your network, follow these steps:

1. **Choose Themes→Add New, and search for the themes you want.**

   If you need a refresher, page 138 has the full story on theme searches.

   To activate a standard year theme already on your network (but not enabled), such as Twenty Thirteen, jump straight to step 3.

2. **When you find a suitable theme, click Install Now.**

   This downloads the theme to your multisite network but doesn't actually make it available to any sites.

3. **Click Network Enable.**

   The Network Enable link takes the place of the Activate link you see when you install a theme on an ordinary, standalone WordPress website. You can click Network Enable immediately after you install a theme, or you can view all your themes (Figure 11-29) and then click Network Enable next to the ones you want.

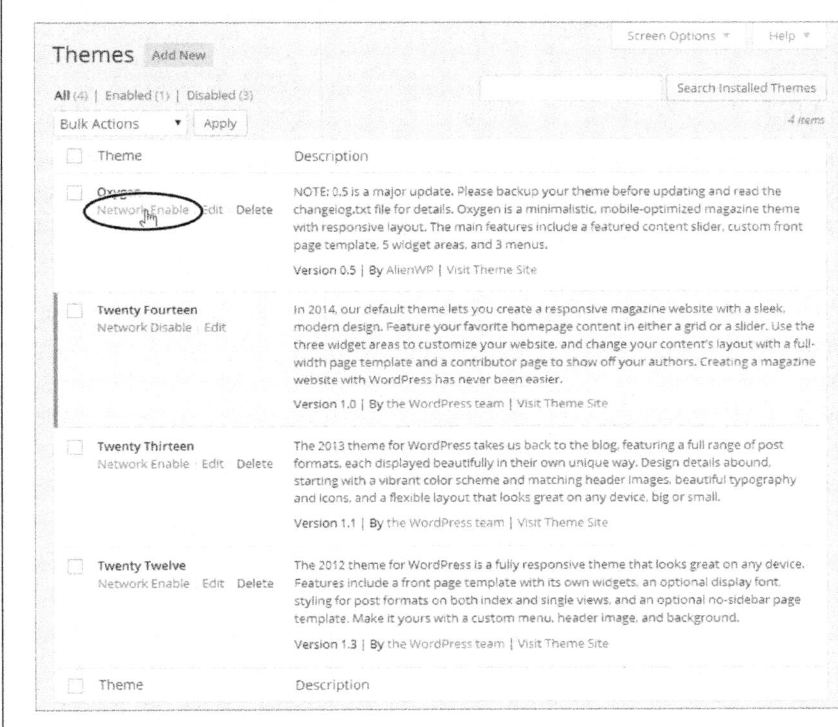

FIGURE 11-29

When you click Network Enable below a theme title, WordPress makes that theme available to all the sites in your network.

You can also enable a theme for some sites but not others, although it's awkward. First, make sure your theme isn't network-activated. Then choose Sites→All Sites and click the Edit link under the site where you want to apply the theme. When the Edit Site page appears, click the Themes tab. In the list of disabled themes, click Enable next to the ones you want to add.

The process for installing plug-ins is similar but subtly different. First, choose Plugins→Add New and then search for the plug-in you want. When you find it, click Install Now. Now you have a choice:

- **Make the plug-in optional (don't do anything).** Once you install a plug-in, WordPress makes it available to every site administrator in your network. Each administrator can log in, visit the Plugins section of the dashboard, and choose what plug-ins to activate.

- **Activate the plug-in for every site.** To do this, click the Network Activate link. When you network activate a plug-in, that plug-in automatically runs on every site in your network. However, site administrators won't see the plug-in the Plugins section of the dashboard, and they won't be able to deactivate it. That's your job (click Network Deactivate to switch off a network activated plug-in).

Not all plug-ins work properly when network-activated, so it's worth contacting the plug-in maker to ask, or testing a new plug-in the first time you network activate it.

GEM IN THE ROUGH

Setting a Storage Limit

Themes and plug-ins aren't the only restrictions that come into play on a multisite network. You can also set storage limits to restrict how many pictures, documents, and other files people can upload to their sites. These settings prevent space hoggers from swallowing gigabytes of hosting room, leaving your web server starved for space.

Ordinarily, your network has no site restrictions. To put one into effect, choose Settings→Network Settings on the network administration dashboard. Scroll down to the "Site upload space" heading and switch on "Limit total size of files uploaded." That caps the amount of space for posts, pages, pictures, and uploaded files on a site to 100 MB. However, you can type in whatever maximum you want. You can also change the "Max upload file size" to set the maximum size of an individual file (usually 1.5 MB).

Site administrators can use a dashboard to keep an eye on the size of their sites. Choose Dashboard→Home, and look at the "At a Glance" box. At the bottom, you find the key details: the maximum size allotment, the current size of the site, and the percentage of space used so far.

CHAPTER

12

Attracting a Crowd

Now that you know how to build a fantastic WordPress site, you need to show it off to the world. That means you need to spend some serious time *promoting* your site.

Web promotion can be grueling work, and many WordPressers would rather avoid the subject altogether. Not only does it take a significant amount of effort, but the benefits aren't always clear, and you often need to pursue a promotional strategy without knowing how well it'll work. The best approach is to make web promotion as easy and natural as possible. That means weaving it into your daily routine and integrating it into the way your website works. It also means using honest promotional strategies rather than search engine ploys and other trickery. Follow the guidelines here, and you'll still have plenty of time to pursue your real job—publishing fabulous content.

In this chapter, you'll learn a common-sense approach to web promotion. You begin with the best type of advertising a site can have, word-of-mouth recommendations. That doesn't mean waiting for your site to crop up in casual conversation. Instead, it involves learning how to help your readers rate, "Like," and tweet your content through social media services such as Facebook and Twitter.

Next, you'll help existing readers bond with your site. You'll notify them when you publish new posts and alert them when their comments receive a reply. Done right, these steps build long-term relationships with your fans and increase the number of repeat visitors.

After that, you'll consider a few basics of SEO (search engine optimization). You'll learn how to use plug-ins to make your site more Google-friendly, so web searchers can stumble across your site while hunting for content. Finally, you'll take a look at web statistics so you can assess how well your promotional strategies are working.

Encouraging Your Readers to Share

There's a gaping chasm of difference between commercial promotion and personal recommendations. If you can get your readers to share your posts and recommend your site to friends, you'll accomplish far more than the average ad campaign.

Usually, sharing means enlisting the help of Facebook and Twitter, two social sites that are all about exchanging information, from gossipy chitchat to breaking news. With the right WordPress settings and widgets, you can make it easy for your visitors to recommend your site to their friends and followers.

NOTE Most of the features in this chapter require WordPress.com or the Jetpack plug-in for self-hosted sites. So if you're building a WordPress.org site, now is a good time to get Jetpack up and running, if you haven't already; page 297 explains how.

UP TO SPEED

Facebook and Twitter: A Refresher

Without doubt, Facebook and Twitter are the kingpins of the social Web. It's unlikely that either service needs an introduction, but if you've spent the last several years asleep in a cave, here's what you need to know:

- **Facebook** (*www.facebook.com*) is a social hub where you keep up with your friends and report the goings-on in your life (usually by uploading pictures and writing short, semi-public posts). Facebook is also a great place for musicians, artists, local businesses, and big companies. They can interact with customers and fans through a *Facebook Page*, a special promotional tool you'll consider on page 420.
- **Twitter** (*http://twitter.com*) is a service for sending micro-sized messages out to the world, for anyone who wants to read them (by signing up to become your "follower"). For example, the people following your messages might include friends, colleagues, or rabid fans.

The two sites are complementary—some people favor one over the other, while many use both. The important detail for a website builder like yourself is this: Out of all the people visiting your site, a significant portion will have a Facebook or Twitter account. So far, your website has ignored this fact. But WordPress helps you put social media to good use with features like enhanced comments (page 270), sharing (page 412), and publicity (page 427).

How Sharing Buttons Work

Sharing is often an impulsive act. You stumble across a site, it catches your easily distracted mind for a few seconds, and you pass the word out to a few choice friends. You're more likely to share a site if the process is quick and easy—for example, if the site provides a handy link that does the bulk of the job for you. If a guest has to fire up her email program or log in to another site (like Facebook or Twitter), she might just defer the task for another time—and then forget about it altogether.

The best way to make sharing easy, quick, and convenient is to add buttons that reduce the task to a couple of mouse clicks (Figure 12-1). That way, your readers can share your site before they move on to their next distraction.

FIGURE 12-1

This site has three sharing buttons, which appear after the post and just before the comments section. Readers can share a link to this post by email, Twitter, or Facebook.

Email sharing is great for guests who may not use social media. Best of all, it works even if your visitor doesn't have an email program handy, because WordPress sends the message on your guest's behalf.

To share a post by email, a visitor starts by clicking the Email link. A box drops down so he can type in the recipient's email address, his name, and his email address. Once he fills in those details and clicks Send Email, WordPress delivers a short message that looks something like this:

> Jason Minegra (*jackerspan4evs@gmail.com*) thinks you may be interested in the following post:
>
> The Felon I Didn't Represent
>
> *http://thoughtsofalawyer.net/the-felon-i-didnt-represent/*

Facebook sharing is another good option, simply because of Facebook's mind-boggling popularity. When a guest clicks the Facebook button, WordPress takes her to the Facebook site, where she can share the link and post an excerpt on her timeline (Figure 12-2).

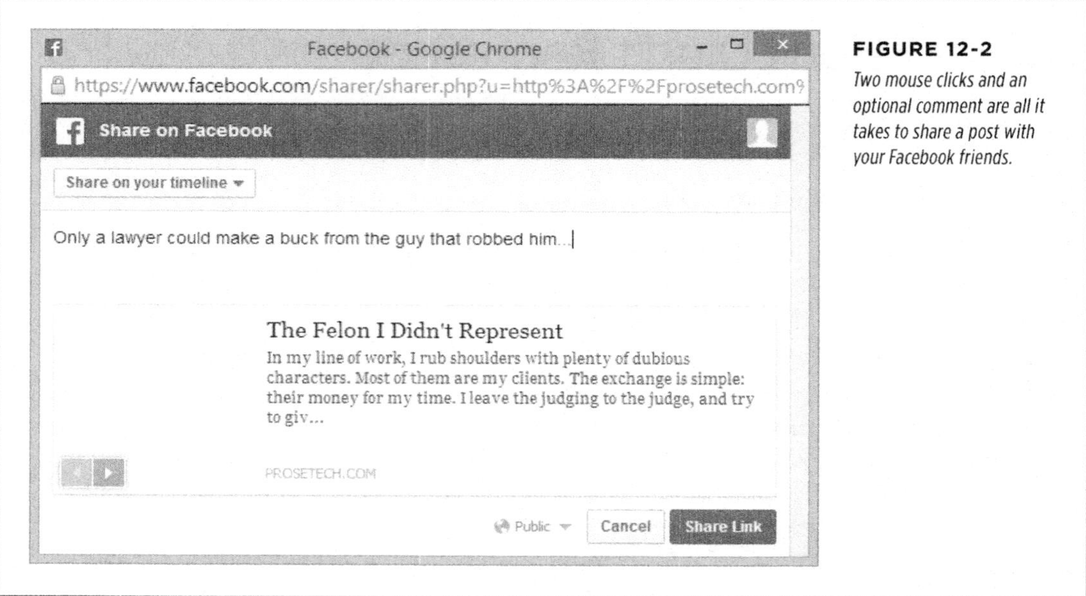

FIGURE 12-2

Two mouse clicks and an optional comment are all it takes to share a post with your Facebook friends.

Twitter sharing is a great way to get the word out into the ever-chattering Twitter-verse. Serious Twitter fans are always looking for small tidbits of interesting material, and your Tweet button will be a hard temptation for them to resist. When a guest clicks it, WordPress pops up a new browser window, asking the tweeter to log in to Twitter and offering to send the link to his followers.

Adding Sharing Buttons

To add sharing buttons to posts or pages, your site needs to run on WordPress.com or use a plug-in. In this chapter, you'll stick to the familiar Jetpack plug-in, which adds the same sharing buttons as WordPress.com. To get started, choose Settings→Sharing to go to the Sharing Settings page. There, you choose the buttons you want to add to your site and decide where they appear.

WordPress divides the Sharing Settings page into several sections. In the Available Services area, it displays a long list of sharing buttons. To add one to your site, drag it to the Enabled Services section of a post or page (Figure 12-3).

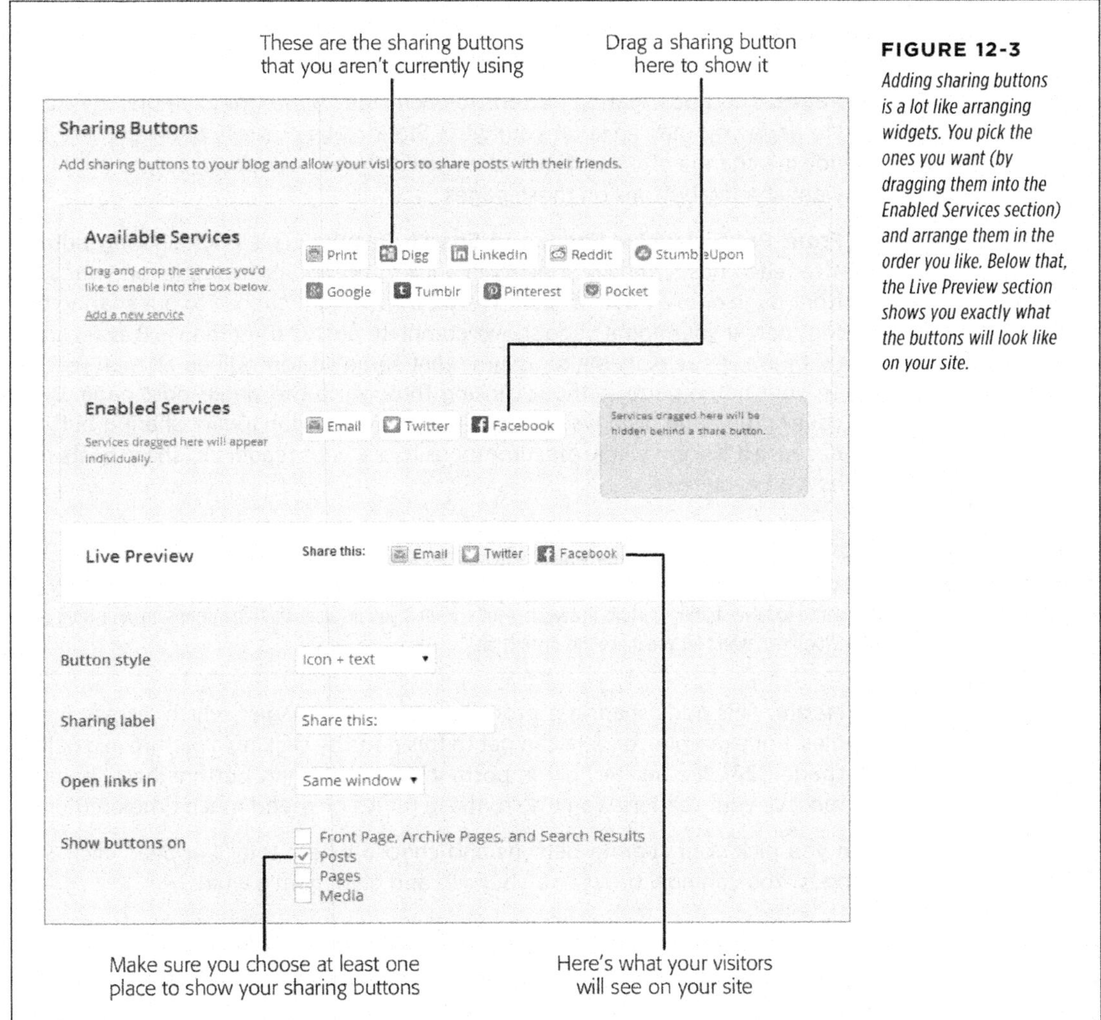

FIGURE 12-3

Adding sharing buttons is a lot like arranging widgets. You pick the ones you want (by dragging them into the Enabled Services section) and arrange them in the order you like. Below that, the Live Preview section shows you exactly what the buttons will look like on your site.

TIP Email, Facebook, and Twitter aren't your only sharing options, but they're three of the best. Another good choice is the Print button, which gives people an easy way to print out your post and take it to their friends on foot. But the best advice for sharing buttons is to use just a few of the most useful ones (ideally, cap it at four or five). Too many buttons can overwhelm your readers and make you look needy.

Once you pick your sharing buttons, you need to tell WordPress where to display them—on your home page, on posts, and so on. You do that by turning on the checkboxes next to the places listed under "Show sharing buttons on." Here are your options:

- **Posts.** This adds the sharing buttons to single-post pages—the ones with your post content and comments section. You definitely want sharing buttons here.
- **Pages.** This adds sharing buttons to each static page (for example, the About Me page you may have on your site). Static pages usually show content that doesn't change often and isn't as newsworthy as your posts, so you might not want sharing buttons on these pages.
- **Front Page, Archive Page, and Search Results.** This adds sharing buttons after each post, when it appears in a list of posts—for example, on your site's front page or in a page of search results. You might choose to put sharing buttons here if your home page shows complete posts rather than just excerpts. In that case, it's reasonable to assume that some visitors will do all their reading on your home page, without clicking through to the single-post page. But if your home page displays excerpts, you definitely don't want sharing buttons, because it'll seem wildly presumptuous to ask your readers to share posts they haven't even read.

NOTE It's unfortunate that WordPress combines the Front Page, Archive Page, and Search Results options into a single setting. When you perform a search, you never see more than an excerpt of a post, so it doesn't make sense to have sharing buttons in search results, even if you do want sharing buttons on your front page. Sadly, WordPress won't let you make this distinction.

- **Media.** This adds sharing buttons to attachment pages, which display media files. For example, readers can get to this page by clicking a picture in a gallery (page 322). It's not terribly important to add sharing buttons here, because most of your readers won't go to these pages or spend much time on them.

Once you pick your sharing buttons and choose where they'll appear, click Save Changes. You can now browse to your site and give them a whirl.

More Ways to Customize Your Sharing Buttons

WordPress gives you a surprising degree of control over your sharing buttons. Under the Live Preview section, you'll find several options:

- **Button style.** Ordinarily, this is set to "Icon + text." Choose "Text only" to remove the tiny pictures from your sharing buttons, or use "Icon only" if you want tiny picture buttons with no text (which makes the buttons more difficult for people to understand but does save space). The "Official buttons" option is a bit weirder—it uses the style conventions of the appropriate service (in other words, the Facebook button has the visual styling set by Facebook, the Twitter button has the look designed by Twitter, and so on). The drawback is that you end up with a mishmash of subtly different fonts, colors, and spacing in your sharing buttons (see Figure 12-4).

- **Sharing label.** This is the text that appears just before your sharing buttons. The standard is "Share this:" but if you want to write "Spread the word!" no one's going to stop you.
- **Open links in.** Some sharing buttons take your readers to another site. For example, the standard Facebook button takes guests to Facebook and asks for a comment (Figure 12-2). Ordinarily, this means your visitor leaves your site. But if you choose "New window" for the "Open links in" option (Figure 12-3), the browser opens a new window when a visitor clicks a sharing button.

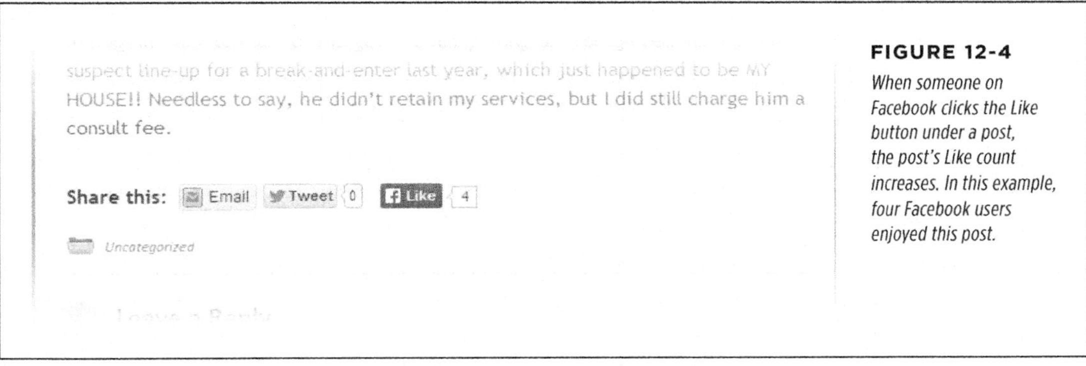

FIGURE 12-4

When someone on Facebook clicks the Like button under a post, the post's Like count increases. In this example, four Facebook users enjoyed this post.

If you have a self-hosted site, you'll see the option "Disable CSS and JS." If you select this, it's up to you to supply the styles and JavaScript code that makes the sharing buttons work (so don't). It's intended for hardcore webheads who need to customize everything.

FREQUENTLY ASKED QUESTION

Selectively Hiding Sharing Buttons

I don't want all my posts and pages to be the same. Can I show sharing buttons on some but not all posts and pages?

Yes.

To understand how, you need to understand that WordPress displays sharing buttons only if your site meets two criteria. First, in the "Show sharing buttons on" section, you must turn on the Posts checkbox. Second, when you create or edit a post, you need to check "Show sharing buttons on this post." WordPress automatically adds the checkmark for every new post, but you can change that.

Consider an example. Imagine you have a site with 36 posts and you want to allow sharing on all but three. First make sure you have the Posts checkbox at Settings→Sharing turned on. Then, turn off the "Show sharing buttons on this post" checkbox for the three posts that *shouldn't* have sharing buttons.

The same technique works for pages, except that WordPress pays attention to the Pages checkbox rather than the Posts checkbox on the Settings→Sharing page.

If you host your site on WordPress.com, you see an additional option that lets you turn WordPress.com "Likes" on or off. You'll learn more about that feature on page 421.

There's one quirk in the way the Facebook button functions. Ordinarily, clicking the Facebook button shares a post by inviting you to publicize it on your timeline. But when you switch on the "Official buttons" option, the Facebook button becomes a Like button, which simply collects your vote of approval and counts the number of Likes the page has (Figure 12-4).

NOTE "Liking" isn't quite the same thing as sharing. For example, if Victor Gonzales shares a post (using the standard Facebook button), he gets the chance to add a comment on his Facebook timeline. If he "Likes" a post (using the Like button), Facebook makes a note of the action but doesn't ask Victor to supply a comment. In both cases, Victor's friends will see a link to the post in their News Feeds, along with an excerpt.

The Sharing Settings page has one more nifty feature you haven't used: a pop-up panel you can add to a post that reveals additional sharing buttons. If you feel compelled to stuff your page with a large number of sharing buttons, you can hide some of the less important ones in this panel. That way, they'll be tucked out of sight until a visitor clicks the "+ Share" button, which WordPress adds automatically (Figure 12-5).

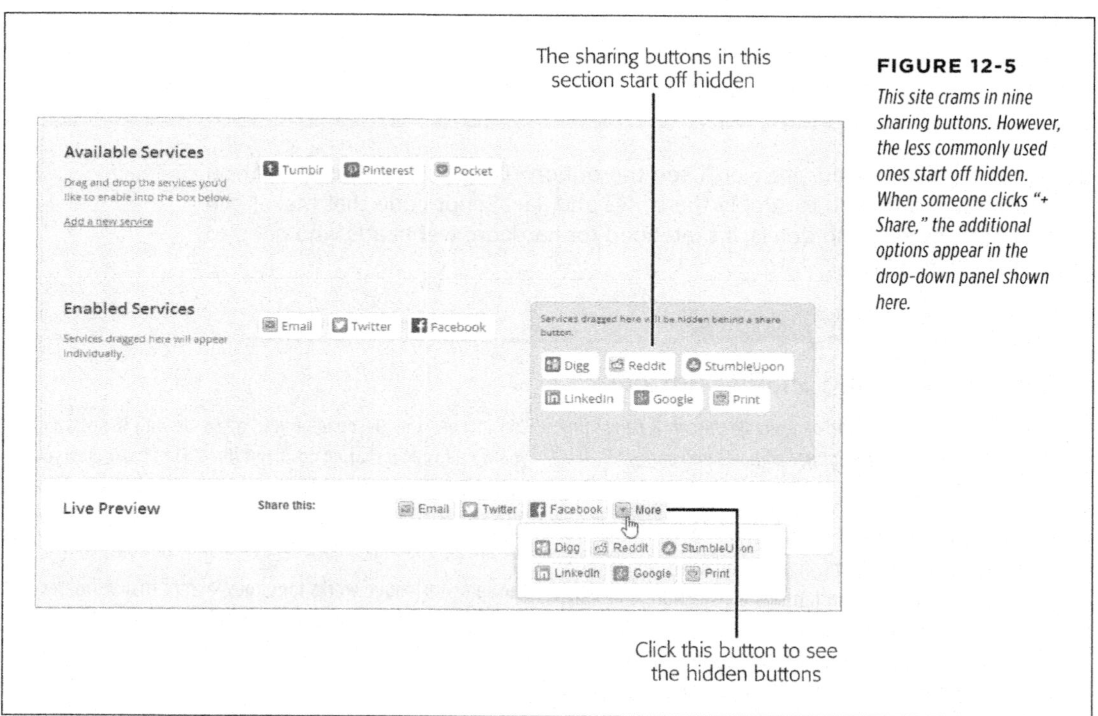

FIGURE 12-5

This site crams in nine sharing buttons. However, the less commonly used ones start off hidden. When someone clicks "+ Share," the additional options appear in the drop-down panel shown here.

Letting People Like Your Site

As you've seen, visitors can use the Facebook button to share and "Like" your posts. But you might prefer to let Facebookers show their appreciation for your site as a whole, using the sort of Like box shown in Figure 12-6.

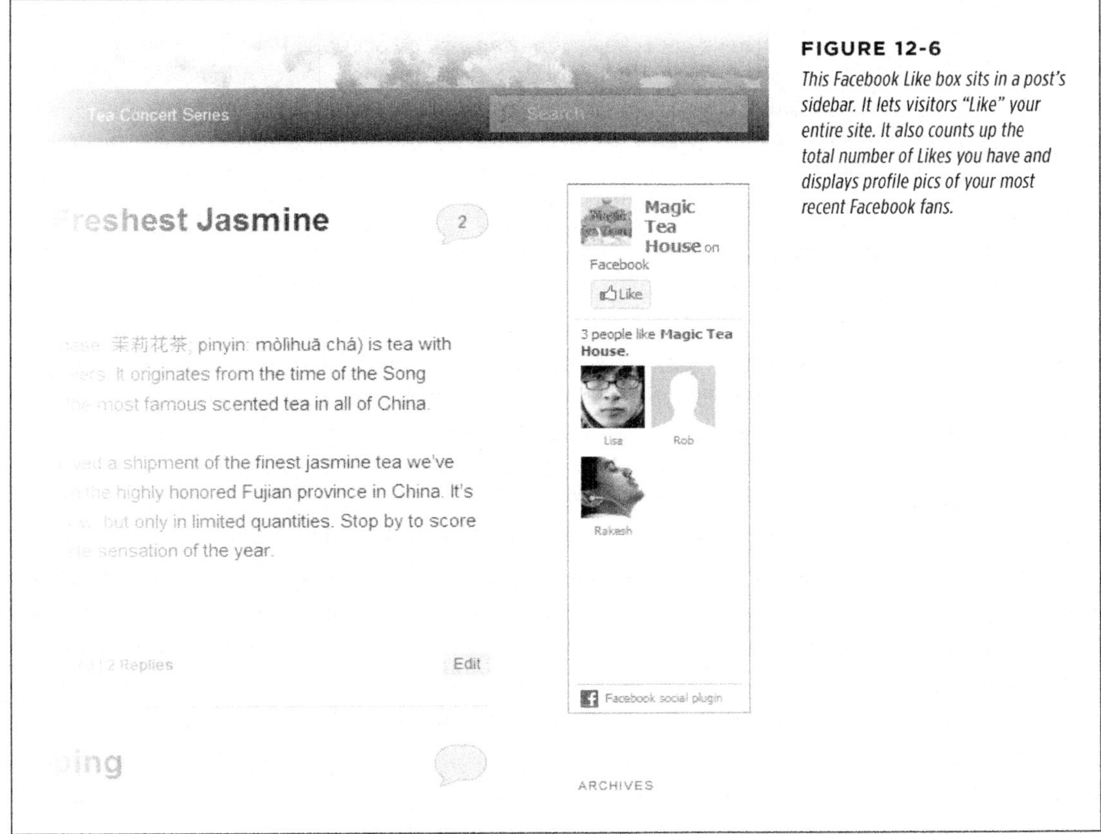

FIGURE 12-6

This Facebook Like box sits in a post's sidebar. It lets visitors "Like" your entire site. It also counts up the total number of Likes you have and displays profile pics of your most recent Facebook fans.

There are two good reasons to create a site-wide Like box:

- It advertises your *whole* site on Facebook, not just one post. As a result, it's more likely to get people interested in your content.
- It centralizes voting in one place. If your site doesn't attract huge amounts of traffic, your posts may accumulate only a few Likes. But if you include a single Like button for your entire site, your Like count will probably reach a larger, more respectable-looking number.

There's one extra hassle with the Like button: To let people "Like" your site, you need to create a *Facebook Page* for it.

A Facebook Page is a public meeting spot you create on Facebook. You use it to promote something—say, a company, a cause, a product, a television show, or a band. You might already have a Facebook Page to promote your business or yourself (for example, musicians, comedians, and journalists often do). Any Facebook member can create one.

A Facebook Page is similar to a personal Facebook profile, but it's better suited to promotion. That's because anyone can visit a Facebook Page and read its content, even if they aren't Facebook friends with the page owner, or don't even have a Facebook account. Those who do have accounts can do the usual Facebook things—click Like to follow the page, post on the page's timeline, and join in any of its discussions. Generally, a personal Facebook profile is better suited to keeping up with friends or networking with business contacts, while a Facebook Page offers a better way to promote yourself, your business, or your cause to masses of people you don't know. If you don't have a Facebook Page and you aren't sure how to create one, see the box on page 421.

Once you create a Facebook Page, it's easy to add a Facebook Like box to your site. Once again, your site needs to run on WordPress.com, or you need the Jetpack plug-in. If it meets either of these requirements, follow these steps:

1. **Choose Appearance→Widgets.**

   The familiar Widgets page opens.

2. **Drag the Facebook Like box into one of the widget areas.**

   Ideally, you should add the widget to your home page (with its list of posts), *and* to your single-post pages. Some themes (like Twenty Eleven) don't include a sidebar on the single-post page. That means you need to put the Like box somewhere else, such as in the footer area.

3. **Type in the Facebook Page web address.**

   The easiest way to do that is to visit your page through Facebook and then copy the address from your browser's address bar.

4. **Optionally, configure the other settings for the Facebook Like box.**

   Like any widget, you can give the Facebook Like box a title, but that's really not necessary. You can also set its width, change its color scheme, and choose whether you want to display your fans' faces (as in Figure 12-6), the latest posts from your page's news stream, or the latest posts from its timeline. If you opt out of all these options, you get a very compact box that includes a Like button, the number of Likes you've received, and a tiny thumbnail of the profile picture from your Facebook Page.

5. **Click Save.**

   This adds the Like box widget to your page.

UP TO SPEED

Creating a Facebook Page

To create a Facebook Page, go to *www.facebook.com/pages/create.php*. You start by clicking the button that best represents the type of page you want—for example, you can create one for a local business, a big company, a band, a product, a public figure, or a cause. Depending on the button you click, Facebook asks you for more information, like your name and address. Once you fill that in, you click Get Started.

You now need to either sign in to your Facebook account or create a new one. It's easy—all you need is an email address, a password, and a birth date.

When you finish signing in or registering, Facebook asks for a few final ingredients (Figure 12-7):

- **A description.** This is a few sentences that describe you or your business. It shows up on your Facebook Page, so make sure your description is fun and engaging.
- **A link to another site.** This part is optional, but it makes sense to supply a link to your WordPress site here.
- **A profile picture for your page.** You can upload it from your computer or grab it off your WordPress site, if you have a link. Facebook pictures are square-shaped, so don't try to use your WordPress site header picture.

Click Save Info, and Facebook creates your page. Make note of its web address, which appears in your browser's address bar—you need to copy it into the Facebook Like box widget to set up the link in WordPress.

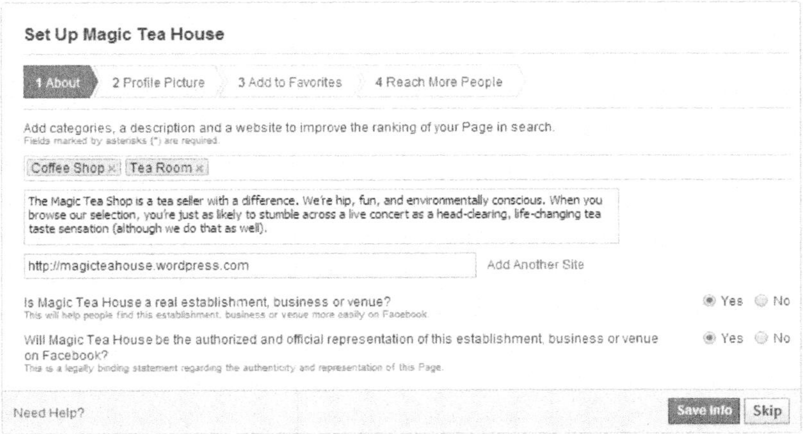
Set Up Magic Tea House
1 About
2 Profile Picture
3 Add to Favorites
4 Reach More People
Add categories, a description and a website to improve the ranking of your Page in search.
Fields marked by asterisks (*) are required.
Coffee Shop
Tea Room
The Magic Tea Shop is a tea seller with a difference. We're hip, fun, and environmentally conscious. When you browse our selection, you're just as likely to stumble across a live concert as a head-clearing, life-changing tea taste sensation (although we do that as well).
http://magicteahouse.wordpress.com
Add Another Site
Is Magic Tea House a real establishment, business or venue?
This will help people find this establishment, business or venue more easily on Facebook.
Yes
No
Will Magic Tea House be the authorized and official representation of this establishment, business or venue on Facebook?
This is a legally binding statement regarding the authenticity and representation of this Page.
Yes
No
Need Help?
Save Info
Skip

FIGURE 12-7

This is the description for the Magic Tea House's Facebook Page.

Using WordPress.com Ratings

WordPress.com offers another rating system you can use. It's called WordPress.com Likes.

Ordinarily, WordPress turns WordPress.com Likes on, and a Like button appears in every post, just after the sharing buttons. It works just like the Facebook Like button, but only registered WordPress.com members can use it. (WordPress asks everyone else to sign up when they click it.)

WordPress.com tracks all the posts a person likes, just as it tracks the sites he follows (page 40). WordPress visitors can review their favorite pages in their account—to do that, they visit *http://wordpress.com*, log in, click the Reader tab, and then choose Posts I Like (on the right).

TIP If you don't want to use WordPress.com Likes, you can turn them off site-wide at Settings→Sharing. You can also switch them off when you create or edit an individual post, by unchecking "Show likes on this post" in the Likes and Shares box.

WordPress.com Likes are a good way to engage the very active community of WordPress.com bloggers. Some people get quite fanatical about them. They also work with two nifty widgets:

- **Top Posts & Pages.** This widget shows the hottest pages on your site, based on either the number of times guests have viewed them or the number of times visitors have liked them. It's a great way to highlight popular content. But don't confuse the Top Posts & Pages widget with the similarly named Top Rated widget. The latter is for Polldaddy ratings, an alternative ranking system described in the box on page 423.
- **Posts I Like.** This widget shows the posts on any WordPress.com site that *you* like. Similarly, if someone uses this widget on her WordPress.com site and then "Likes" one of your pages, a link shows up on her site, inviting readers to check out your content. That makes it a great way to lure new readers.

GEM IN THE ROUGH

Yet Another Ratings System

If you use WordPress.com, you can be forgiven for getting confused by the panoply of rating options available. You already know how to integrate Facebook sharing and WordPress.com Likes. In addition to those options, you can use the Polldaddy rating system on WordPress.com sites. (Self-hosters can get a plug-in that offers the same features at *http://tinyurl.com/wp-polls*. However, it's a bit finicky, and it forces you to sign up for a free Polldaddy account.)

Initially, WordPress has Polldaddy ratings turned off. To add them to posts, pages, or comments, go to the Ratings→All Ratings section of the dashboard. There you can position the ratings section above or below your content. When you apply the ratings to posts and pages, readers can rate a post from one star (very poor) to five stars (excellent). When you add the rating system to comments, visitors choose from simple thumbs-up and thumbs-down buttons. Self-hosters who use the Polldaddy widget get a rating system called Top Rated; it lets guests link to your top posts, pages, or comments, depending on the options you pick.

It doesn't really make sense to use both WordPress.com Likes and Polldaddy ratings. There's only so much feedback you can request before your readers get tapped out. Both systems have advantages. WordPress.com Likes requires guests to sign in but provide extra features—namely, it lets people log in to the WordPress.com home page and see all the posts they've "Liked." But Polldaddy ratings are more inclusive, because they let everyone participate, no login required. They also include a reporting feature that lets web authors review their most popular posts (to see it, choose Feedback→Ratings). You may need to play with both systems before you decide which one better suits your site.

Finally, it's worth noting that even if you choose WordPress.com Likes for your posts, you might still decide to use Polldaddy to let readers rate comments (page 259), because you can't add WordPress.com Likes to the comments section.

Keeping Readers in the Loop

The best sites are *sticky*—they don't just attract new visitors; they encourage repeat visits.

To make a site sticky, you need to build a relationship between your site and your readers. You want to make sure that even when your readers leave, they can't forget about your site, because they're still linked to its ongoing conversation. One way to do that is to notify readers about posts that might interest them. Another strategy is to tell readers when someone replies to one of their comments. Both techniques use email messages to lure visitors back to your site.

If your site is on WordPress.com or you installed Jetpack on a self-hosted site, you automatically get a convenient opt-in system for email notifications. It starts with two checkboxes that appear in the "Leave a Reply" section (Figure 12-8).

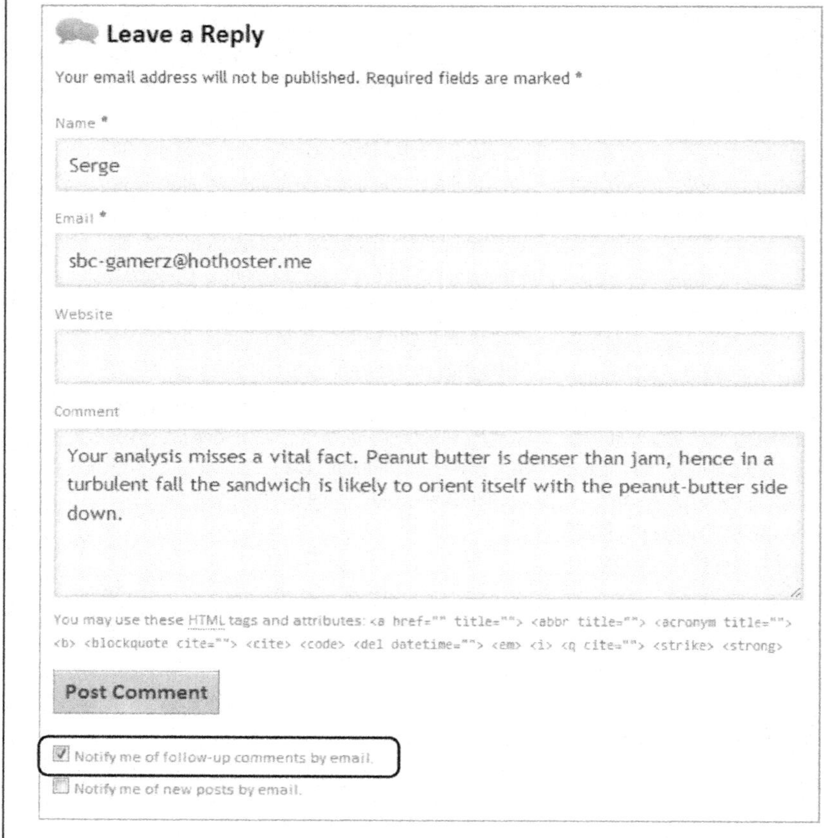

FIGURE 12-8

After Serge enters his email address and writes his comment, he can sign up for WordPress notifications. WordPress lets him know when someone replies to his comments (so he can remain part of the conversation), or when you publish a new post (if he really loves your content).

You can hide the post notification and comment options. Go to Settings→Discussion and then uncheck "Show a 'follow comments' option in the comment form" and "Show a 'follow blog' option in the comment form." But there's really no reason to do that, unless you use a plug-in that adds similar options somewhere else on your site.

UP TO SPEED

Taking Care of Your Peeps

Even on sites with thousands of comments, most readers keep quiet. Whether that's due to laziness, indifference, or the fear of being ignored, the average reader won't leave a comment. So when someone does speak up, you need to do your best to keep him in the discussion.

One way to do that is with the comment-tracking option you just read about (see Figure 12-8). You can also reward commenters and stoke the conversation several more ways:

- **Comment on your commenter's sites.** You already know that, every once in a while, you need to step into a discussion with your own comment. Visitors like to see you involved because it shows you read their opinions just as they read yours. However, if you see a particularly good comment, you can take this interaction a little further. Follow the commenter's website link. If the commenter has a blog, stick around, read a bit, and add a comment to one of *his* posts. Comments are a two-way street, and the more you participate with others, the more likely it is that a reader will keep coming back.
- **Thank commenters.** Not every time—maybe just once. If you notice a new commenter with some useful feedback, add a follow-up comment that thanks her for her input. If you want to get fancier, you can use a plug-in like Thank Me Later (*http://tinyurl.com/wp-thank*) to send an email message to first-time commenters, telling them you appreciate the feedback. (But be warned, you need to tweak this plug-in carefully to make sure you don't send out too many emails and annoy both your commenters and your web hosting company.)
- **Ask for comments.** Sometimes, non-commenters just need a little push. To encourage them to step up, end your post with a leading question, like "What do you think? Was this decision fair?" or an invitation, like "Let us know your best dating disaster story."

Signing Up Subscribers

Although it makes sense to put the comment notification checkbox in the comments area of your posts, that spot isn't a good place for the checkbox that lets readers subscribe to your posts. Ideally, you'll put a prominent subscription option after every one of your posts *and* on your home page.

There's another problem with the standard post notification checkbox. To sign up for notifications, a reader needs to leave a comment. Not only is this requirement a bit confusing (readers might not realize they need to write a comment, tick the site-subscription checkbox, and *then* click Post Comment), it's also unnecessarily limiting.

Fortunately, WordPress offers a better option, with a subscription widget that can sign up new followers any time. If you use WordPress.com, the widget is called Follow Blog. If you use Jetpack, it's called Blog Subscriptions. They're virtually identical, the only difference being that the WordPress.com version recognizes WordPress.com users and lets you address them with a customized message.

NOTE WordPress.com site owners get one other feature: They can adjust the frequency of their outgoing emails so readers get notified only once a day at most, or just once a week.

To use the subscription widget, choose Appearance→Themes, and then drag the plug-in onto one of your site's widget areas. You can then customize several bits of information, including the widget title, the text that invites readers to sign up, and the text on the Subscribe button (Figure 12-9). (For best results, keep the text in the widget brief.)

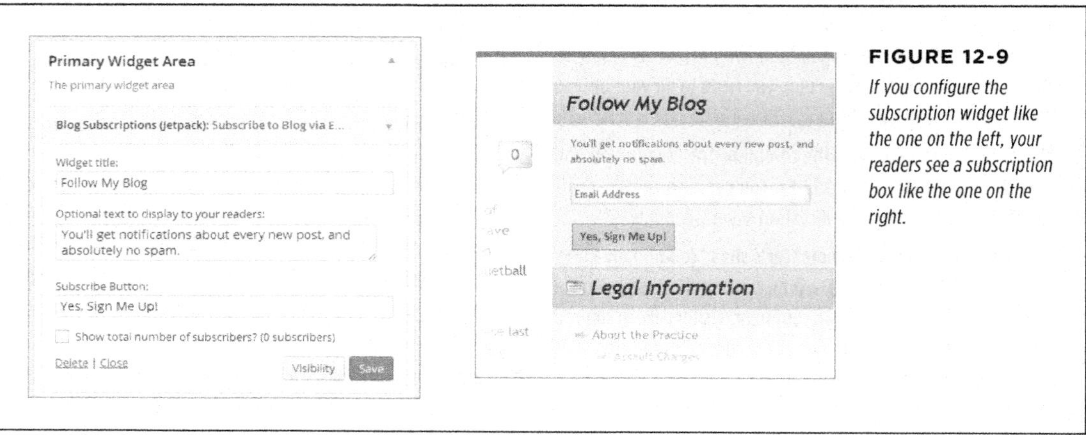

FIGURE 12-9

If you configure the subscription widget like the one on the left, your readers see a subscription box like the one on the right.

You can also choose to show the total number of subscribers, in which case the subscription box adds a line like "Join 4 other followers."

TIP It's a good idea to include the subscription widget in two places: your home page sidebar and the footer area of each post, with a message like "Liked this article? Subscribe to get lots more."

Emailing Subscribers

Occasionally, you might want to reach out to your followers and send them an email that doesn't correspond to a post. For example, you might offer a special promotion or solicit feedback on a website change. If you decide to take this step, tread carefully—if you harass readers with frequent or unwanted emails, they'll feel like they're being spammed.

If you decide to go ahead and email your followers, you first need to get their email addresses. Here's how:

- If you use WordPress.com, visit the WordPress.com home page (*http://wordpress.com*), log in, and choose the Stats tab. Scroll down to the "Totals, Followers & Shares" box. Under the heading "Followers," WordPress counts up the total number of people subscribing to posts and comments. Click the Blog link to get their email addresses.

- If you use Jetpack on a self-hosted site, choose Jetpack→Site Stats and scroll down to the Subscription box. You see the total number of people subscribed to your blog (and those who are registered to receive replies to a particular comment). Click the Blog link next to the number to see the full list of email addresses.

PLUG-IN POWER

Even Better Email Subscription Services

Jetpack gives self-hosters a solid, straightforward subscription package. The WordPress.com servers handle all the user tracking and emailing, making your life easy. But Jetpack doesn't include any settings that let you customize the way it handles subscriptions. More advanced email and newsletter plug-ins (some of which will cost you a bit of cash) offer more features.

One example is the popular Subscribe2 plug-in (*http://tinyurl.com/wp-sub2*). It adds the following useful features:

- **Digests.** Instead of sending readers an email after you publish every new post, Subscribe2 lets you send a single email, periodically, that announces several new posts at once. Subscribe2 calls this message a *digest*. For example, you might choose to send subscribers a weekly digest summarizing the past seven days' posts.
- **Excluded categories and post types.** Perhaps you don't want to send notifications for every new post. Subscribe2 lets you exclude certain categories or post types (like asides and quotes) from notification emails.
- **User-managed subscriptions.** If you're willing to let readers sign up as subscribers on your site (page 370), they can manage their own subscriptions. For example, they can subscribe to just the post categories that interest them, and pick the most convenient digest option.

Publicizing Your Posts on Social Media

As you've seen, one good way to get the word out about your site is to get your readers talking and sharing on social media sites. But you don't need to wait for them to do the work for you—if you have a Facebook or Twitter account, you can use it yourself to announce new content.

This technique is often called *publicizing*, and it's not quite the same as the social sharing you learned about earlier. Sharing is when a visitor introduces new people to your content. Publicizing is when *you* tell readers about new content. The difference is that the people you tell probably already know about your site. Your goal is to get them interested enough to come back.

Publicizing is an increasingly important way to reach your readers. Twitter fanatics may pay more attention to tweets than they do to email messages. Facebook fans who won't bother to sign up for an email subscription might not mind liking your Facebook Page and getting notifications from you in their News Feeds. For these reasons, many WordPressers choose to publicize their posts.

WordPress.com sites get a built-in Publicize feature, and self-hosters can use the Jetpack plug-in. Either way, you need to connect your site to the social media account (or accounts) you want to use. To do that, choose Settings→Sharing and then click Connect next to the appropriate social media icon (Figure 12-10).

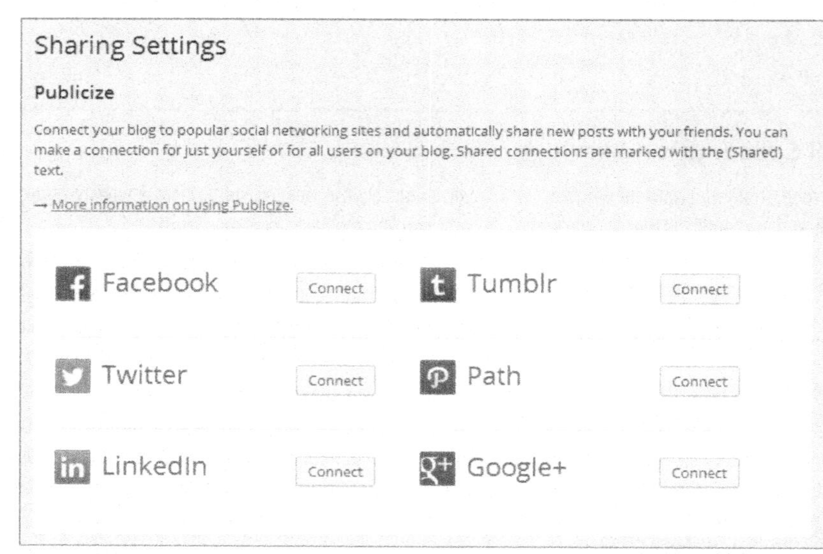

FIGURE 12-10

The WordPress.com Publicize feature lets you post to services like Facebook, Twitter, LinkedIn, Tumblr, and Yahoo Updates. Once you pick a service, you need to log in to your social media account to complete the connection.

The Publicize feature springs into action every time you publish a new post. However, WordPress lets you control the process using the Publish box.

Once you write a post, look in the Publish box. Next to the word "Publicize," you see a list of the services you can use to publicize your post. Click the Edit link, and more options appear (Figure 12-11). You can choose to tout your post on only some services, or none at all. You can also edit the message that WordPress sends out to announce the new post. Ordinarily, WordPress uses the post title for the message, but you can substitute more descriptive text.

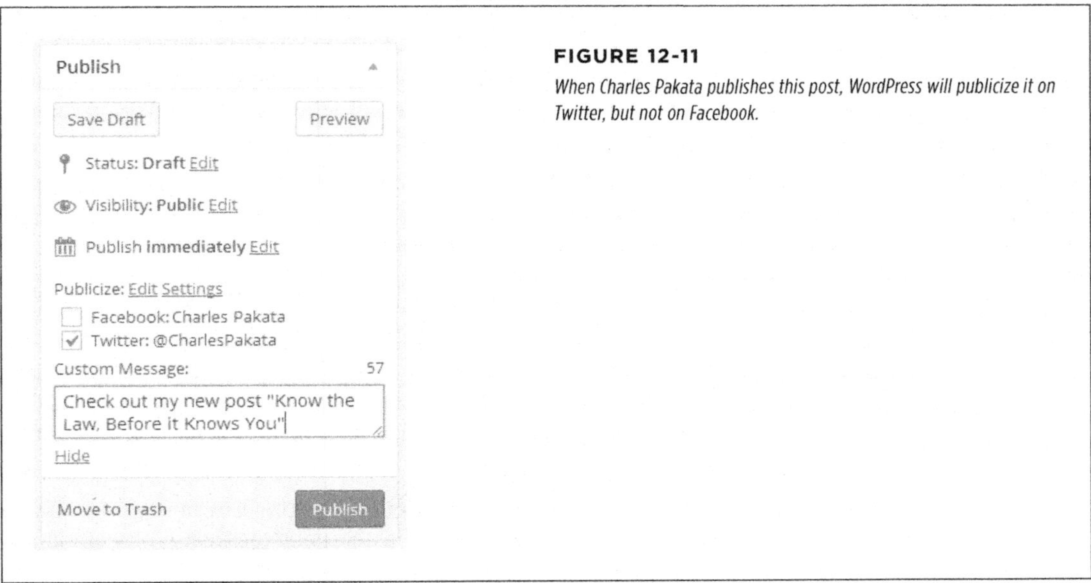

FIGURE 12-11

When Charles Pakata publishes this post, WordPress will publicize it on Twitter, but not on Facebook.

If Charles Pakata publicizes the post in Figure 12-11 to Twitter, his followers will see the tweet shown in Figure 12-12.

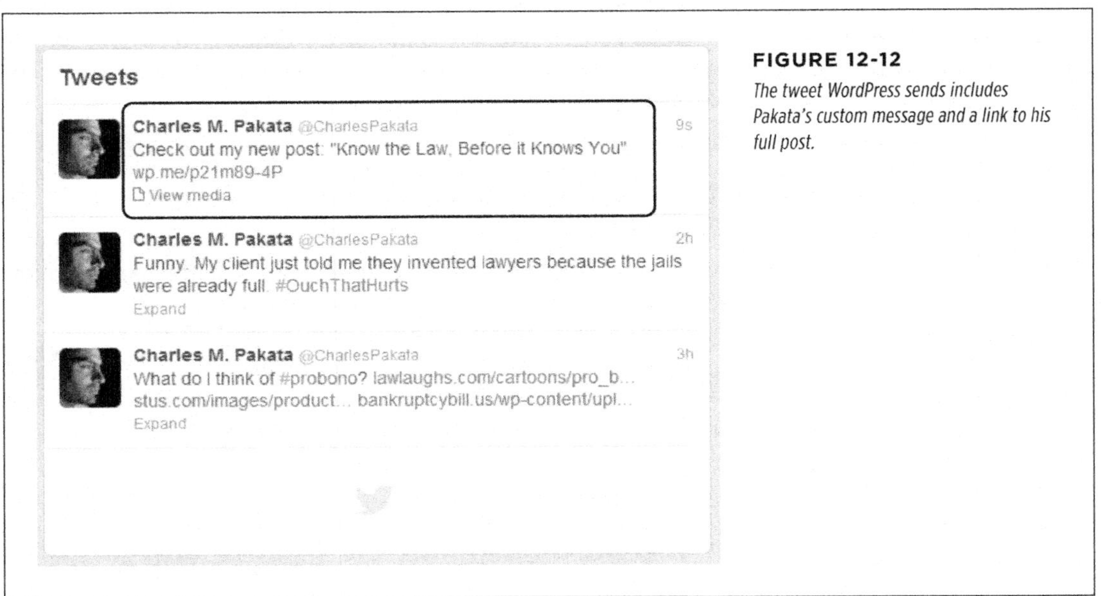

FIGURE 12-12

The tweet WordPress sends includes Pakata's custom message and a link to his full post.

Sharing Your Tweets on Your Site

You already learned how to encourage people to tweet about your site, but the integration between WordPress and Twitter runs deeper than that. If you're a Twitter-holic, WordPress has a nifty way to integrate *your* Twitter feed into your own site.

Before you dive into this feature, it's worth taking a moment to ask why you'd use it and how it fits into your site's promotional plans. There are several good reasons to use it:

- **To offer extra content.** If you're an avid Twitterer, you can stuff your feed with news, tiny tips, and micro observations related to your site. Those details might be interesting to your readers even if they aren't worth a full post.
- **To make your site feel alive.** Having a Twitter feed can make your site seem more current and dynamic—provided that you tweet regularly.
- **To attract new followers.** If you display your Twitter feed on your site, there's a chance that some of your readers will decide to follow your feed. If they do, you'll have another way to reach them. This is particularly useful if you use Twitter to announce your blog posts using WordPress's Publicize feature (page 427).

To display a Twitter feed on your site, you need the Twitter Timeline widget. WordPress.com sites automatically offer it, but self-hosters need the trusty Jetpack plug-in.

To use the Twitter Timeline widget, you follow an unusual two-part setup process. First, you head to the official Twitter website, where you create a customized widget that has the exact look you want. Then, you go to your trusty WordPress dashboard and link your site to the widget you just built. (This system is made more confusing by the fact that Twitter and WordPress use the word *widget* for two slightly different things. You already know that a WordPress widget is a chunk of intelligent content that you insert into your site. A Twitter widget is a customized view of a Twitter feed that you can show on any site.)

Here's a walkthrough of the process:

1. **Go to the Twitter site (*http://twitter.com*) and log in with your email address and password.**

   Now you're on the Twitter home page, where you see recent tweets from the people you follow.

2. **In the top-right corner of the page, click the gear icon ("Settings and help") and then choose Settings.**

   The settings page lets you configure a great number of details about how Twitter works.

3. **In the panel on the left, click Widgets.**

   You see a list of all the Twitter widgets you've created. (Chances are, that will be exactly none.)

4. **To create your first widget, click Create New.**

   Twitter takes you to the widget-creation page shown in Figure 12-13.

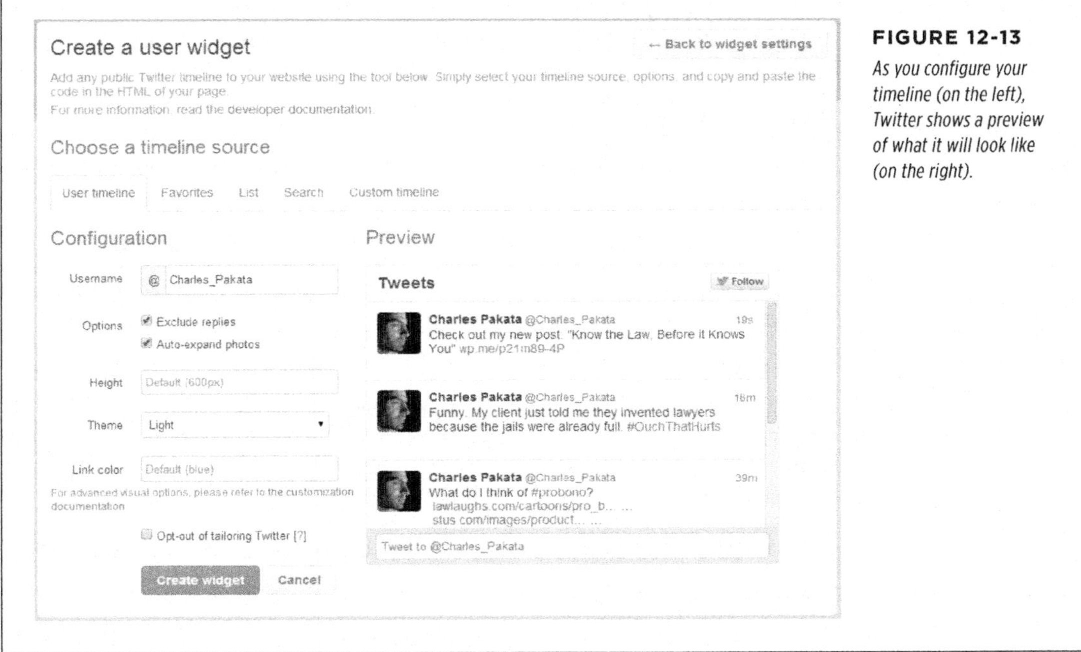

FIGURE 12-13

As you configure your timeline (on the left), Twitter shows a preview of what it will look like (on the right).

5. **Configure your widget.**

   You don't need to change anything if you don't want to. Twitter automatically creates a timeline that shows just your tweets. However, here are some details you might want to change:

   - **Exclude replies** hides a tweet if it's just a reply to someone else's tweet (which readers can find confusing because they're out of context).
   - **Auto-expand photos** displays the pictures you link to in your tweets right in your timeline (no extra click required).
   - **Height** sets the vertical size of the timeline, and therefore determines how many tweets readers can see at once. Choose a height that fits nicely into your sidebar alongside your post content and leave room for any other widgets you need. Don't worry about the width of the timeline, because you set that when you add the Twitter Timeline widget to your site.
   - **Theme** lets you change the color scheme from light (the standard) to dark. The dark option blends in better on dark backgrounds, like the black background featured in the Twenty Fourteen theme.

Alternatively, you can create a different type of Twitter timeline by picking a different tab (just under "Choose a timeline source." Ordinarily, Twitter assumes you want the "User timeline" option, which shows all your tweets. Alternatively, you can show favorite tweets, tweets from a list you created, tweets that match a search keyword (for example, tweets about you or your business), or tweets from a custom timeline you created. Twitter provides plenty of information about these more exotic choices.

6. **When you finish, click Create Widget.**

   You can always return to Twitter and modify the widget later (or create a new one).

7. **Now copy the widget ID, which you can find in the web address.**

   Take a look at the address that appears when you view or edit your widget. It will look something like this:

   ```
   https://twitter.com/settings/widgets/456104541360881667/edit?focus_textarea=1
   ```

   The only important detail is the long numeric code that follows the */widget/* text. That's the widget ID, which WordPress needs in order to show your widget. In the example above, the ID is 456104541360881667. Select it and copy it to the clipboard by pressing Ctrl+C (Command+C on a Mac)

8. **Return to the WordPress dashboard and choose Appearance→Widgets.**

   The familiar Widgets page appears.

9. **Drag the Twitter Timeline widget into a widget area, and then configure it.**

   To properly configure the Twitter Timeline widget, you need to supply the widget ID you copied in step 7 (put it in the Widget ID box). You should also set a value for the width that's narrow enough so that the widget fits in the available space.

10. **Click Save to finalize your changes.**

    Figure 12-14 shows the final result.

NOTE WordPress.com truly loves Twitter. Although the Twitter widget may be the only tool you need, WordPress.com sites can get additional Twitter integration by using two shortcodes (page 323) that put Twitter content inside a post. The [tweet] shortcode lets you show a single tweet, and customize its appearance (learn about it at *http://tinyurl.com/cwfa77u*). The [twitter-follow] shortcode lets you add a Follow button anywhere you need it (*http://tinyurl.com/cn29khu*). Jetpack doesn't offer these features, so self-hosters will need to choose from one of the many available Twitter plug-ins to get the same feature.

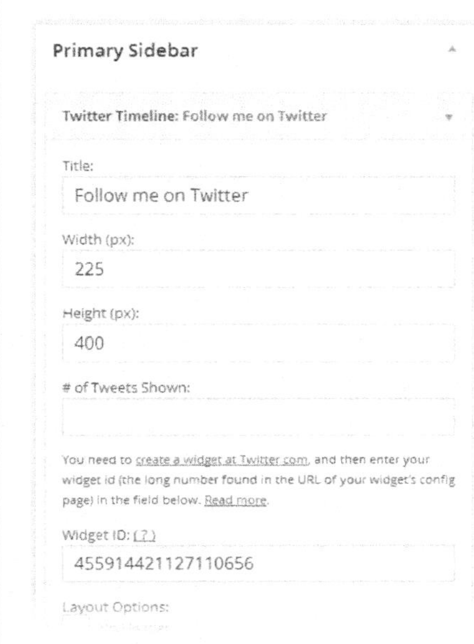

FIGURE 12-14

If you configure the Twitter widget like the one on the left, your readers will see a Twitter feed like the one on the right. In the feed, each tweet becomes a link that, if clicked, takes readers to Twitter to read the whole conversation.

Managing Your Site's Feed

A *feed* is a computer-generated document that lists your recent posts, and the content they contain, in a computer-friendly format. Feeds are a cool and slightly geeky tool that people use to keep up with their favorite sites. The essential idea is that a site—say, a WordPress blog—provides a feed of recent posts. People who read that blog can use another program—a browser or a feed reader—to *subscribe* to the feed.

Here's the neat part. Once you subscribe to a feed, your browser or feed reader automatically checks the sites you signed up with for new content. That saves you from visiting the same site 47 times a day, or digging through an endless stream of spammy notification messages in your email inbox. Best of all, one feed-reading program tracks as many sites as you want.

NOTE Feeds have been around a long time—they're far older than social networking sites like Twitter. The advantage to them is that the feed-reading program does all the work—you don't need to check sites for new posts, read your emails, or click a link in a tweet. However, feeds today are a niche feature. The average person doesn't use them (or even know they exist), but plenty of computer geeks can't live without them.

All WordPress sites automatically support feeds. In fact, you can take a look at the feed *your* site sends out by adding */feed* to the end of your website address. So if you have a WordPress site at *http://lazyfather.wordpress.com*, you can see its feed by requesting *http://lazyfather.wordpress.com/feed.*

NOTE On a self-hosted site, the */feed* syntax works only if you use post titles in your permalinks, which you definitely should (page 116). Otherwise, you'll need to replace */feed* with the more convoluted code */?feed=rss2.*

Depending on the browser you use, you might see the raw feed document when you request it, or you might see a lightly formatted feed (Figure 12-15).

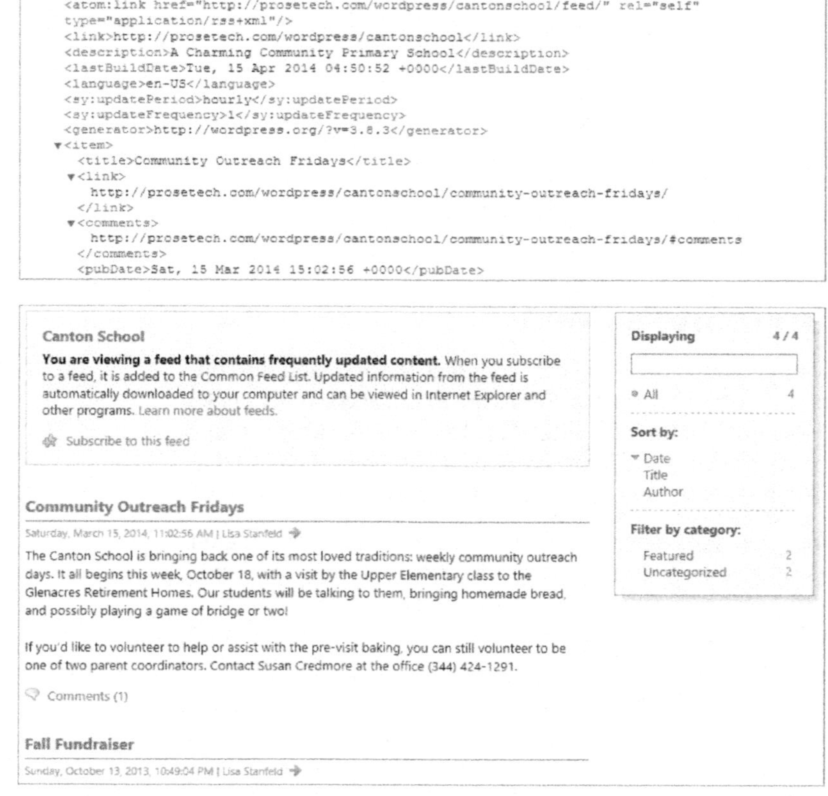

FIGURE 12-15

Top: Behind the scenes, a feed is a long and technical-looking document written in a computer language called XML. Here's a very small portion of it.

Bottom: When you view a feed in Internet Explorer, it automatically creates a page like this, based on the information in the feed.

Most browsers provide some sort of feed-reading feature. For example, Internet Explorer keeps a list of the feeds you bookmark in the Feeds tab of the Favorites panel. Point to one of these links, and it automatically tells you how many new posts have been published since your last visit. Firefox has a slightly different feature—subscribe to a feed and it adds a *live bookmark* that automatically collects every new post behind the scenes. Google Chrome works similar magic with a tiny icon in the search box that, when you click it, pops open a list of new posts (however, you have to install a small browser extension to activate it; find it at *http://tinyurl.com/28q8dth*). Safari is the lone holdout, with no built-in feed reader.

To make reviewing feeds truly convenient, you can use a specialized feed-reading program (or a feed-reading app, if you want to check feeds on a smartphone or tablet). Good options include FeedDemon (*www.feeddemon.com*, Figure 12-16) for Windows and NetNewsWire (*http://netnewswireapp.com*) for Mac addicts. Tablet lovers can use feed-reading apps like Flipboard (*http://flipboard.com*) and feedly (*www.feedly.com*) to stay current. All these programs let you read posts right inside your feed reader, without making a separate trip to the website that publishes the feed.

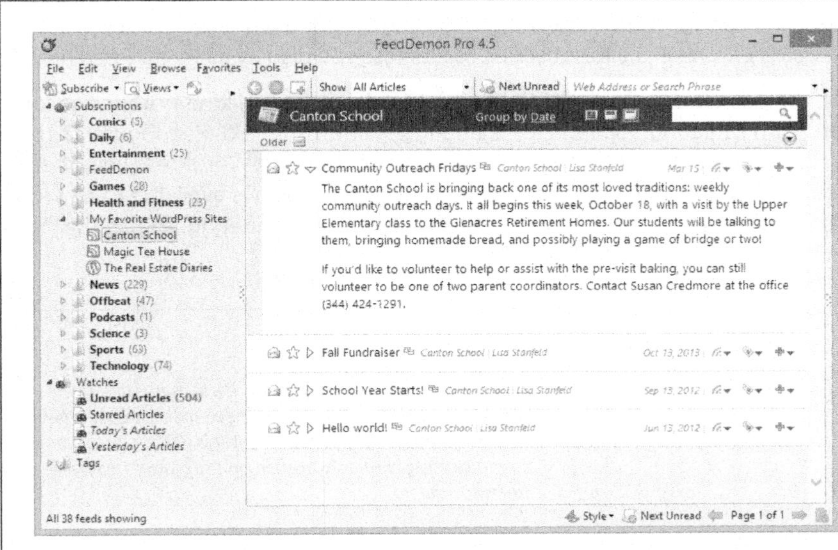

FIGURE 12-16

In a feed-reading program, you see all the new posts for all the sites you follow. With FeedDemon, it's like checking your inbox for new email.

Getting Customized Feeds

Adding */feed* to the end of a site address gets you the standard feed, the one with all the site's posts. But you can filter a feed if you tweak the web address slightly.

For example, you can get a feed that provides all the posts in a specific category, like this:

```
http://www.magicteahouse.net/category/green-tea/feed
```

Or all the posts with a certain tag:

```
http://www.magicteahouse.net/tag/promotions/feed
```

Or all the posts by a specific author:

```
http://www.magicteahouse.net/author/katya_g/feed
```

But the most interesting type of feed just might be the one that grabs the comments from a post (on crystal jasmine tea in this example):

```
http://www.magicteahouse.net/crystal-jasmine-named-tea-of-the-year/feed
```

Or the comments from your entire site:

```
http://www.magicteahouse.net/comments/feed
```

Try plugging all these variations into a feed reader to see what posts show up. Or check out the WordPress feed documentation at *http://tinyurl.com/64lmdo* to learn about a few more exotic feed filters, such as the ones that exclude a specific category or tag, and those that return all the posts that match a search keyword.

Using a Feed Widget

Here's a universal truth of the web publishing world: Even if your site supports a feed, visitors aren't likely to subscribe to it unless you display a big, fat Feed button.

Some themes automatically include one. Usually, it looks like an orange-colored square with radiating semi-circles that suggest transmission (see Figure 12-17). If your theme doesn't offer a Feed button—and the standard WordPress year themes don't—you can add one using the RSS Links widget, which is available to all WordPress.com sites and included with Jetpack. (If you're wondering, RSS is the name of the standard that feeds must follow.)

FIGURE 12-17

When you add a Feed button to your site, it tells readers they can easily keep up with your posts. Clicking the button launches your feed document, although this isn't much help unless you click that button in a feed-supporting browser, or copy the link to a genuine feed reader, like FeedDemon.

When you add the RSS Links widget, you need to choose whether to include a link for the posts feed, the comments feed, or both. If you want a more specialized feed, like one for a specific category, you need to create the link yourself and put it in the Text widget (page 166).

You also need to choose the format for the feed button (text only, image only, or image and text). If you use an image, you need to specify its size and color. Once you finalize these details, you'll be rewarded with a button like the medium-sized text-and-image link shown in Figure 12-17.

NOTE Don't confuse the RSS Links widget with the similarly named but completely different RSS widget. The RSS Links widget provides links to your feeds. The RSS widget looks at someone *else's* feed, finds the most recent entries, and displays links for them on your site. In other words, the RSS Links widget tells visitors that your website provides feeds. The RSS widget lets you display links on your site that lead to someone else's content.

Search Engine Optimization

As you've seen, you have an exhaustive range of options for getting the word out about your site. You can share your posts, publicize them, use email notifications, and tweet the heck out of everything. All these techniques share something in common—each one is a type of *social networking,* where you use connections to people you already know to reach out just a bit further.

There's another way to get people to your site, but it's more difficult and less fun. You can try to attract complete strangers when they run a web search for content related to your site. To perform this trick, you need to understand *search engine optimization* (SEO), which is the sometimes cryptic art of getting web search engines like Google to notice you.

The goal is to make your site appear in a highly ranked position for certain searches. For example, if your WordPress site covers dog breeding, you'd like web searchers to find your site when they type *dog breeding* into Google. The challenge is that for any given search, your site competes with millions of others that share the same search keywords. If Google prefers those sites, your site will be pushed farther down in the search results, until even the most enthusiastic searcher won't spot you. And if searchers can't find you on Google, you lose a valuable way to attract fresh faces to your site.

Next, you'll learn a bit more about how search engines like Google work, and you'll consider how you can help your site rise up the rankings of a web search.

NOTE In the following sections, you spend a fair bit of time learning about Google. Although Google isn't the only search engine on the block, it's far and away the most popular, with a staggering 80 percent (or more) of worldwide web-search traffic. For that reason, it makes sense to consider Google first, even though most of the search engine optimization techniques you'll see in this chapter apply to all the major search engines, including Bing, Yahoo, and even Baidu, the kingpin of web search in China.

PageRank: Scoring Your Site

To help your site get noticed, you need to understand how Google runs a web search.

Imagine you type *dog breeding* into the Google search page. First, Google peers into its gargantuan catalog of sites, looking for pages that use those keywords. Google prefers pages that include the keywords "dog breeding" more than once, and pages that put them in important places (like headings and page titles). Of course, Google is also on the lookout for sites that try to game the system, so a page that's filled with keyword lists and repetitive text is likely to get ignored at best, and blacklisted at worst.

Even with these requirements, a typical Google search turns up hundreds of thousands (or even millions) of matching pages. To decide how it should order these pages in its search results, Google uses a top-secret formula called *PageRank*. PageRank determines the value of your site by the community of websites that link to it. Although the full PageRank recipe is incredibly convoluted (and entirely secret), its basic workings are well known:

- The more sites that link to you, the better.
- A link from a better, more popular site (a site with a high PageRank) is more valuable than a link from a less popular site.
- A link from a more selective site is better than a link from a less selective site. That's because the more outgoing links a site has, the less each link is worth. So if someone links to your site and just a handful of others, that link is valuable. If someone links to your site and *hundreds* of other sites, the link's value is diluted.

FINDING YOUR PAGERANK

Because of the power of PageRank scores, it's no surprise that web authors want to know how their pages are doing. But Google won't give out the real PageRank of a web page, even to its owner.

That said, Google does allow website owners to see a *simplified* version of their PageRank score, which gives you a general idea of your site's performance. The simplified PageRank is based on the real thing, but Google updates it just twice a year, and it provides only a value from 1 to 10. (All things being equal, a website rated 10 will turn up much higher in search results than a page ranked 1.)

There are two ways to find your website's simplified PageRank. If you use the Google Chrome browser, you can add a handy browser plug-in to do the job (get it at *http://tinyurl.com/pr-extension*). Another approach is to use an unofficial PageRank-checking website, like *www.prchecker.info* (Figure 12-18).

The simplified PageRank score isn't always accurate. If you submit a site that's very new, or hasn't yet established itself on the Web (in other words, few people are visiting it and no one's linking to it), you may not get a PageRank value at all.

TIP Don't worry too much about your exact PageRank. Instead, use it as a tool to gauge how your website improves or declines over time. For example, if your home page scored a PageRank of 4 last year but a 6 this year, your promotion is clearly on the right path.

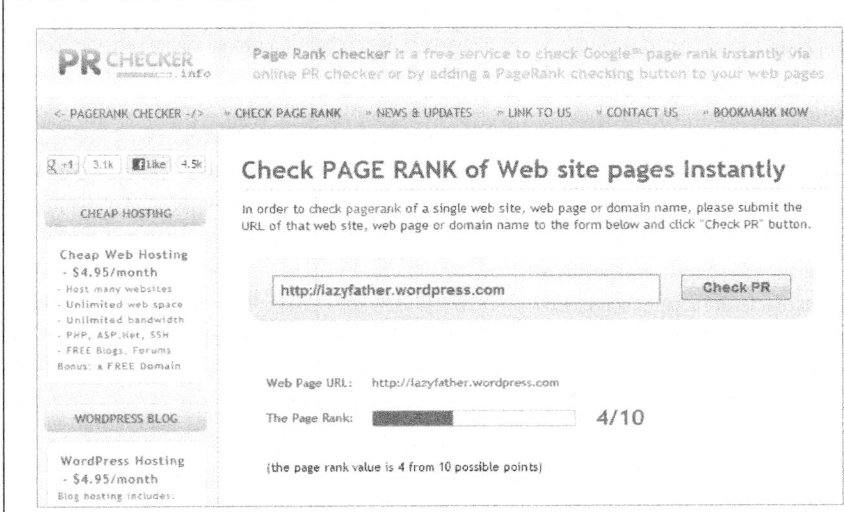

FIGURE 12-18

To see the PageRank for your home page, type in your site's address and then click Check PR. Here, http://lazyfather.wordpress.com *scores a middle-of-the-road 4 out of 10.*

Making Your Site Google-Friendly

You can't trick Google into loving your site, and there's no secret technique to vault your site to the top of the search page rankings. However, you can give your site the best possible odds by following some good habits. These practices help search engines find their way around your posts, understand your content, and recognize that you're a real site with good content, not a sneaky spammer trying to cheat the system.

UP TO SPEED

Getting More Links

The cornerstone of search-engine ranking is links—the more people connect to you, the greater your web prestige and the more trustworthy your site seems to Google. Here are some tips any WordPresser can use to build up her links:

- **Look for sites that are receptive to your content.** To get more links, you need to reach out and interact with other websites. Offer to guest-blog on a like-minded site, join a community group, or sign up with free website directories that include your type of business. Or, if your site has a broader reach, search for your topic in Google Blogsearch (*http://blogsearch.google.com*) to find similar sites.
- **Keep sharing.** The social sharing techniques you learned about in the first part of this chapter are doubly important for PageRank. Although tweets and Likes aren't as powerful as website links, Google still counts them in your favor when respected people talk about your content on social media sites.
- **Add off-site links (that point to you).** You don't need to wait for other people to notice your content. It's perfectly acceptable to post a good comment on someone else's blog, with a link that references something you wrote. Or post in a forum, making sure your signature includes your name *and* a link to your site. The trick is to find sites and forums that share the same interests as your site. For example, if you're an artisanal cheese maker in Chicago, it makes sense to chat with people running organic food cooperatives. But be careful. There's a thin line between spreading the word about your fantastic content and spamming other people. So don't post on a forum or someone else's site unless you can say something truly insightful or genuinely helpful. If you're not sure whether to post, ask yourself this question: "If this were my site, would I appreciate this comment?"
- **Research your competitors' links.** If you find out where other people are getting their links from, you may be able to get links from the same sites. Google has a nifty feature that can help, called *link*. To try it out, go to the Google search page and type in a full website address, with *link:* in front of it. Google will then find other pages that lead to the web address you asked about. For example, searching for *link:www.magicteahouse.net* shows you all the sites that link to the home page on *www.magicteahouse.net*.

Here are some guidelines to SEO that don't require special plug-ins or custom coding:

- **Choose the right permalink style.** Every WordPress post and page gets its own permalink. If you create a self-hosted site, your permalinks should include the post title, because the search engine pays special attention to the words in your web address. (Page 117 explains how to change your permalink.) If WordPress.com hosts your site, you already have the right permalink style.
- **Edit your permalinks.** When you first create a post, you have the chance to edit its permalink. At this point, you can improve it by removing unimportant words (like "a", "and," and "the"). Or, if you use a cute, jokey title for your post, you can replace it in the permalink with something more topical that includes the keywords you expect web searchers to use. For example, if you write a post about your favorite cookware titled "Out of the Frying Pan and Into the Fire," you ordinarily get a permalink like this: *http://triplegoldcookwarereview.com/out-of-the-frying-pan-and-into-the-fire*. If you remove some words, you can shorten it to *http://triplegoldcookwarereview.com/out-of-frying-pan-into-fire*.

And if you substitute a more descriptive title, you might choose *http://triple-goldcookwarereview.com/calphalon-fry-pan-review*.

- **Use tags.** Google pays close attention to the tags you assign to a post. If they match a web searcher's keywords, your post has a better chance of showing up in search results. When choosing tags, pick just a few, and make sure they clearly describe your topic and correspond to terms someone might search for (say, "artisanal cheese," "organic," and "local food"). Some search-obsessed bloggers scour Google statistics to find the best keywords to use in attracting web searchers, and use those as their tags in new posts. However, that's too much work for all but the most fanatical SEO addicts.
- **Optimize your images.** Google and other search engines let people search for pictures. When someone searches for an image, Google attempts to match the search keywords with the words that appear near the picture on a web page, and with the alternate text that describes the picture. That means people are more likely to find your pictures if you supply all the details the Insert Media window asks for, including a title, alternate text, a caption, and a description (page 182). Remember to use descriptive, searchable keywords when you do.

GEM IN THE ROUGH

Hiding from Search Engines

You don't *have* to let search engines find you. If you want to keep a low profile, choose Settings→Privacy, and then turn on the radio button beside "Ask search engines not to index this site." That way, your website won't appear in most search engine listings.

People will still be able to find you if they click a link that leads to your site, or if they know your site address. For that reason, you shouldn't rely on this trick to conceal yourself if you're doing something dubious or risky—say, planning a bank robbery or cursing your employer. In cases where you need utmost privacy, you can use WordPress's private site feature (page 397), or just keep yourself off the Web.

Boosting SEO with a Plug-In

If you run a self-hosted site, you can make it even more attractive to Google and other search engines by using an SEO plug-in. But be warned, most SEO plug-ins are an extreme case of overkill for the casual WordPress site-builder. Prepare to be swamped by pages of options and search settings.

If you search WordPress's plug-in repository for "SEO," you discover quite a few popular plug-ins. One of the best is WordPress SEO by Yoast (*http://tinyurl.com/seo-yoast*). Its creator is WordPress über-guru Joost de Valk, who also blogs some useful (but somewhat technical) SEO articles at *http://yoast.com/cat/seo*.

Once you install and activate WordPress SEO, you see a new SEO menu in your dashboard, packed with a dizzying array of options. You can ignore most of them, unless you want to change the way the plug-in works. The following sections explain two useful features you can tap into right away.

CREATING AN XML SITEMAP

After installing the SEO plug-in, your site gets one immediate benefit: an *XML sitemap*. This is a document that tells Google where your content resides on your site. It ensures that all your posts get indexed, even if your home page doesn't link to them. Although you don't need to give your XML sitemap another thought, you can take a look at it by choosing SEO→XML Sitemaps and then clicking the XML Sitemap button. Needless to say, WordPress SEO updates your sitemap every time you publish a new post or page.

NOTE The XML sitemap feature works only if you use descriptive permalinks that include post names (as explained on page 116). If you use the stock ID-based permalinks, the plug-in won't create an XML sitemap.

TWEAKING TITLES AND DESCRIPTIONS

The WordPress SEO plug-in also gives you control over two important details: the title and description (known to web nerds as the *meta description*) of each post or page. These details are useful—even to SEO newbies—because Google displays them when it lists a page from your site in its search results. Figure 12-19 shows an example.

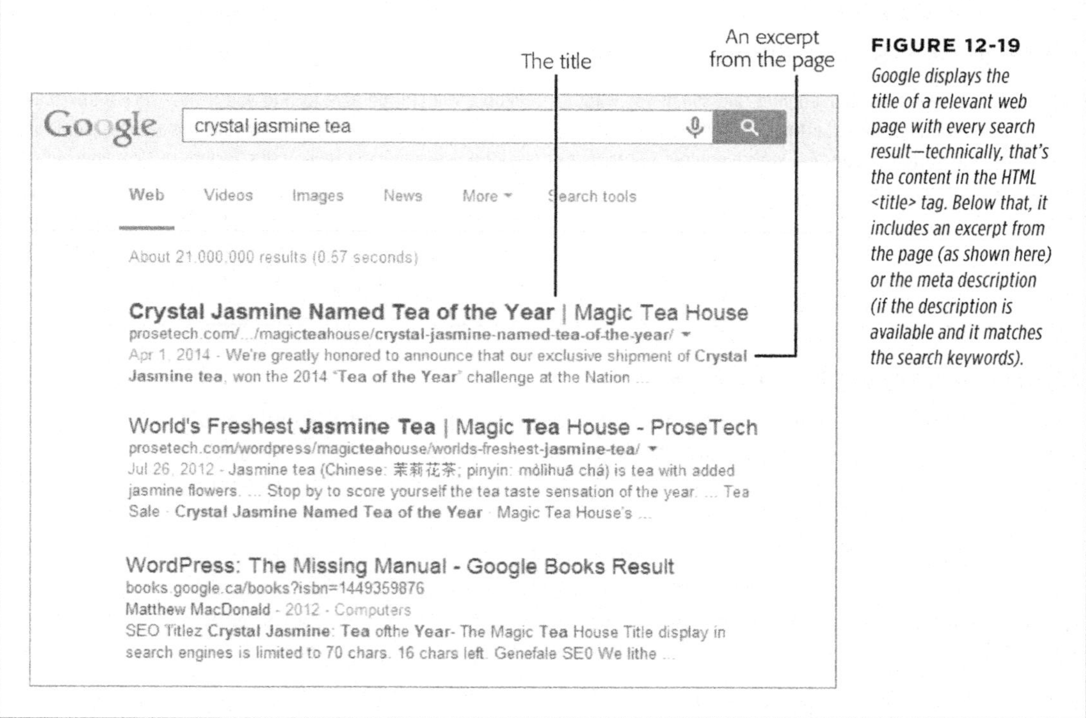

FIGURE 12-19

Google displays the title of a relevant web page with every search result—technically, that's the content in the HTML <title> tag. Below that, it includes an excerpt from the page (as shown here) or the meta description (if the description is available and it matches the search keywords).

The title and description are also important because Google gives more weight to keywords in those places than keywords in your content. In other words, if someone searches for "dog breeding" and you have those words in your title, you can beat an equally ranked page that doesn't.

Ordinarily, the WordPress SEO plug-in creates a good title for a post, based on a title-generating formula in the SEO→Titles & Metas section. This formula puts your post name first, followed by your site name, like this for the "crystal jasmine" post:

```
Crystal Jasmine Named Tea of the Year - Magic Tea House
```

However, you can customize the title before you publish the post using the WordPress SEO by Yoast box, which appears on the Add New Post page (Figure 12-20). For example, it's a good idea to shorten overly long post titles, and to replace cutesy titles with ones that clearly describe your content. You can also use the WordPress SEO box to type in a meta description.

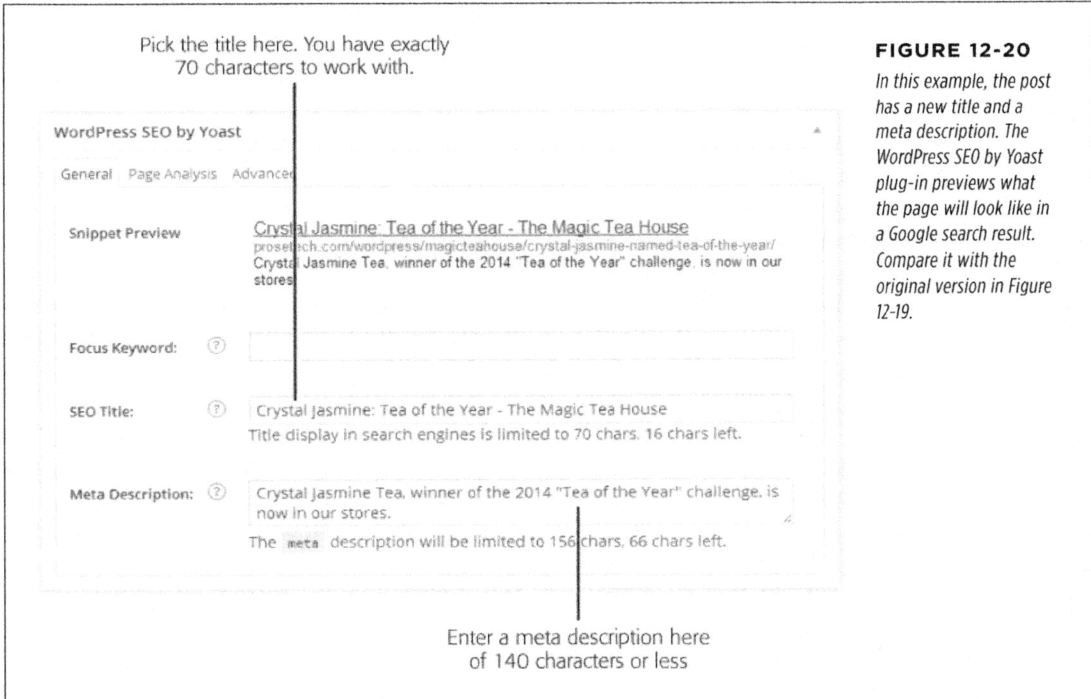

FIGURE 12-20

In this example, the post has a new title and a meta description. The WordPress SEO by Yoast plug-in previews what the page will look like in a Google search result. Compare it with the original version in Figure 12-19.

The WordPress SEO by Yoast box also lets you run a pretend Google search so you can see how your newly chosen title and description work. To do that, type the search keyword you want to test in the Focus Keyword box. Figure 12-21 shows an example.

TIP For even more ways to optimize your site for search engines using the WordPress SEO by Yoast plug-in, check out the detailed tutorial at *http://tinyurl.com/seo-yoast2*.

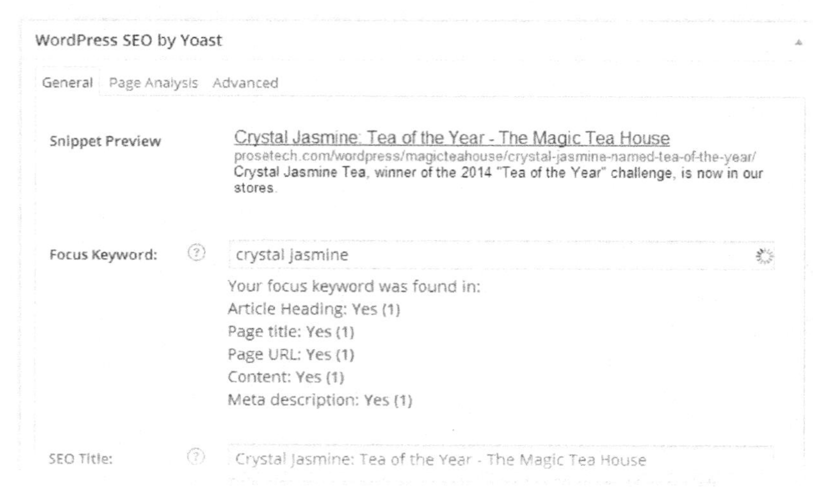

FIGURE 12-21

Because you included the keywords "crystal jasmine" in the heading of your post, the title of your page, the permalink, the actual post content, and your meta description for the page, you increase the odds that a visitor searching for these words will find your page. Of course, all these efforts are for naught if you haven't written a decent post.

WordPress Site Statistics

Once you have some solid promotion tactics in place, you need to evaluate how well they perform. There's no point in pursuing a failed strategy for months, when you should be investing more effort in a technique that actually *works*. The best way to assess your site's performance, and see how it changes over time, is to collect *website statistics*.

There are a number of popular statistics packages that work with WordPress, and a range of plug-ins that automatically add tracking code to your site. In this section, you'll focus on WordPress's own statistics-collection service, which it offers to all WordPress.com sites and which is available to self-hosted sites through the Jetpack plug-in.

Viewing Your Statistics

The best place to view your site statistics is on the WordPress.com home page. Go to *http://wordpress.com*, log in, and click the Stats tab. If you have more than one site, you need to pick from the drop-down list in the top-right corner (Figure 12-22).

NOTE Jetpack users can see the same statistics by choosing Jetpack→Site Stats in the dashboard. However, WordPress encourages everyone to view statistics on the WordPress.com home page, and it may remove the statistics link from the dashboard in the future.

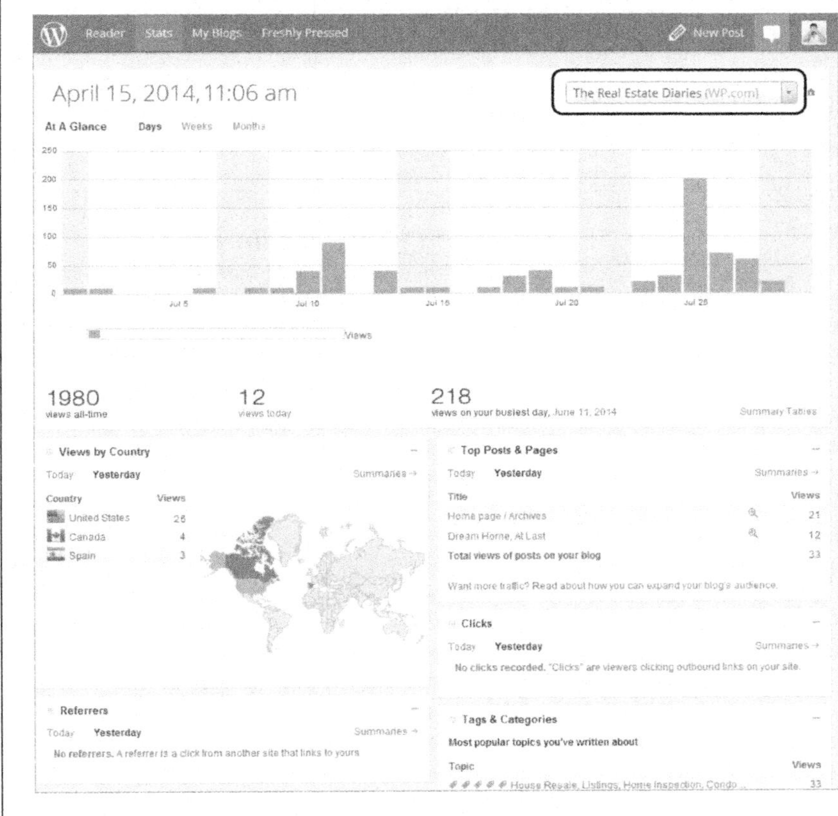

FIGURE 12-22

There's a lot of information jockeying for your attention on the Stats tab. Here are the details for The Real Estate Diaries site.

The obvious question is now that you have all this raw data, what can you do with it? Ideally, you'll use site statistics to focus on your strengths, improve your site, and keep your visitors happy. You should resist the temptation to use it as a source of endlessly fascinating trivia. If you spend the afternoon counting how many visitors hit your site from Bulgaria, you're wasting time that could be better spent writing brilliant content.

The following sections present four basic strategies that can help you find useful information in your statistics, and use that insight to improve your site without wasting hours of your time.

Strategy 1. Find Out What Your Readers Like

If you know what you're doing right, you can do a lot more of it. For example, if you write a blog with scathing political commentary, and your readers flock to any article that mentions gun control, you might want to continue exploring the issue in future posts. (Or, to put it less charitably, you might decide to milk the topic for all the pageviews you can get before your readers get bored.)

To make decisions like that, you need to know what content gets the most attention. A Facebook Like button (page 419), a WordPress.com Like button (page 421), or Polldaddy ratings (page 423) may help you spot popular posts, but a more thorough way to measure success is to look at your traffic. On the Stats page, focus on the Top Posts & Pages box, which shows you the most read posts and pages over the past couple of days (Figure 12-23).

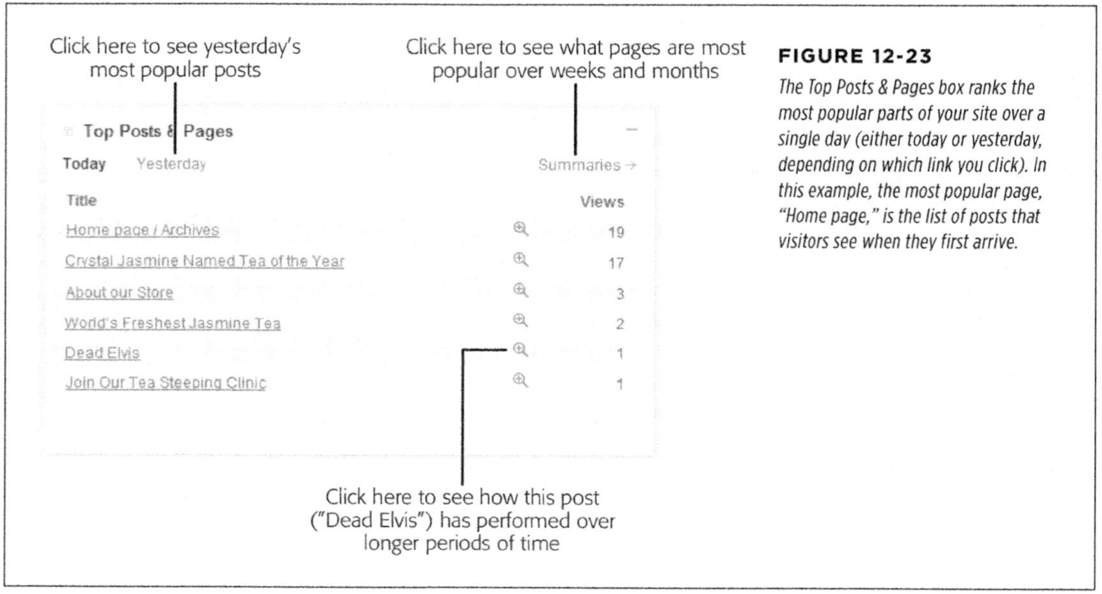

FIGURE 12-23

The Top Posts & Pages box ranks the most popular parts of your site over a single day (either today or yesterday, depending on which link you click). In this example, the most popular page, "Home page," is the list of posts that visitors see when they first arrive.

The Top Posts & Pages box gives you a snapshot of the current activity on your site, but to make real conclusions about what content stirs your readers' hearts, you need to take a long-term perspective. To do that, click the Summaries link. Now WordPress lets you compare your top pages over the past week, month, quarter, year, or all time. Just keep in mind that bigger timeframes are often biased toward older articles, because they've been around the longest.

If you analyze a site on WordPress.com, you can also check out the Tags & Categories section. It shows you the categories and tags that draw the most interest. You can form two conclusions from this box: Popular categories may reflect content your readers want to keep reading, and popular tags may indicate keywords that align with popular search terms (see Strategy 3 on page 448).

Strategy 2. Who's Giving You the Love?

There are three ways a visitor can arrive at your site:

- By typing your address into his browser (or by using a bookmark, which is the same thing).
- By following a link from another site that points to you.
- By performing a search and following a link in the search results page.

The first type of visitor already knows about you. There's not much you can do to improve on that.

The second and third types of visitor are more difficult to predict. You need to track them so you can optimize your web promotion strategies. In this section, you focus on the second type of guest. These people arrive at your site from another website, otherwise known as a *referrer.*

If you followed the link-building strategies laid out on page 440, the social sharing tips from page 414, and the publicizing techniques described on page 427, you've created many different routes that a reader can take to get to your site. But which are heavily traveled and which are overgrown and abandoned? To find out, you need to check the Referrers box, which ranks the sites where people come from, in order of most to least popular (Figure 12-24).

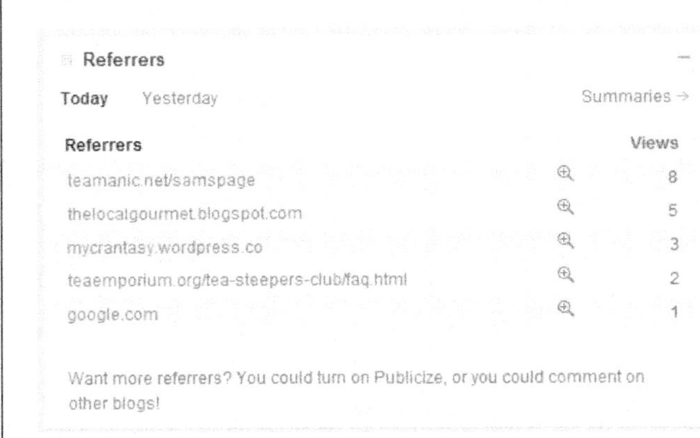

FIGURE 12-24

Use the Referrers box to see where your visitors come from. It shows you the referring sites from a single day. You can click a specific referrer to get more information, or you can click Summaries to examine your top referrers over longer periods of time.

Once you know your top referrers, you can adjust your promotional strategies. For example, you may want to stop spending time and effort promoting your site in places that don't generate traffic. Similarly, you might want to spend more effort cultivating your top referrers to ensure you keep a steady stream of visitors coming to your site.

Strategy 3. Play Well with Search Engines

In any given minute, Google handles well over a million search queries. If you're lucky, a tiny slice of those searchers will end up at your site.

Webmasters pay special attention to visitors who arrive through search engines. Usually, these are new people who haven't read your content before, which makes them exactly the sort of people you need to attract. But it's not enough to know that visitors arrive through a search engine. You need to understand what *brought* them to your site, and to understand that, you need to know what they were searching for.

The Search Engine Terms box can help you find out (Figure 12-25). It lists the top queries that led visitors to your site for a single day (or, if you click Summaries, over a longer period of time).

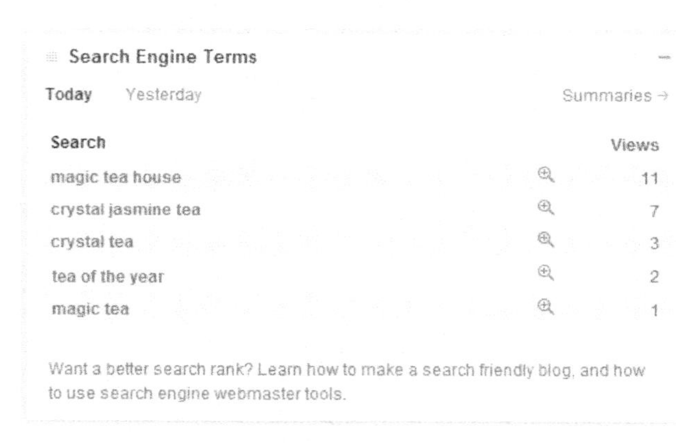

FIGURE 12-25

Here are the keywords that led searchers to the Magic Tea House. Notice that you may not see the common, short keywords that you expect (like "tea," by itself). That's because the more general a keyword is, the more sites there are competing for that keyword, and the less likely it is that a searcher will spot your site.

If you use SEO to find what you think are the best keywords for tags, titles, and descriptions (see, for example, page 443), the Search Engine Terms box helps you determine if your efforts are paying off. And even if you don't, it gives you insight into hot topics that attract new readers—and which you might want to focus on in the future.

Strategy 4. Meet Your Top Commenters

If WordPress.com hosts your site, you can tap one more set of useful statistics. Take a look in the Comments box to see which of your visitors left the greatest number of comments and which posts stirred the most conversation (Figure 12-26).

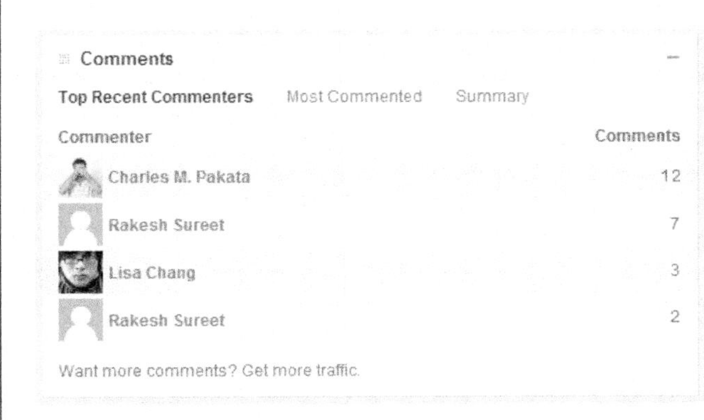

FIGURE 12-26

Comments are the lifeblood of a WordPress site. A site with a thriving Comments section is more likely to attract new visitors and to keep existing ones. By examining the Comments box, you can see who deserves the most credit for keeping your conversations alive.

The most interesting information is the top commenters. These people are particularly valuable, because their input can start discussions and keep the conversation going.

Once you identify your top commenters in the past week or month, you can try to strengthen your (and therefore your site's) relationship with them. Make an extra effort to reply to their comments and questions, and consider making a visit to their blog, and commenting on their posts. If they stick around, you might even offer them the chance to write a guest post for your site, or to become a contributor.

PART

4

From Blog to Website

CHAPTER

13

Editing Themes: The Key to Customizing Your Site

As you've traveled through this book, you've taken a look at every significant feature that WordPress offers and used those capabilities to build a variety of sites. However, you've always played by the rules, picking themes from the theme gallery, installing plug-ins from the plug-in directory, and sticking to the safety of the WordPress dashboard. But there's a whole other world of possibilities for those who can color outside the lines.

The key to unlocking more flexibility and building a truly unique WordPress site is to create your own theme. As you know, a theme is a mash-up of HTML markup, formatting rules, and PHP code. Ordinarily, WordPress hides these details from you—the people who create the themes and plug-ins your site uses handle all this, while you focus on writing fab content and adjusting settings in the dashboard. But if you decide to cut loose and become a theme customizer (or even a theme *creator*), you step into a different world. Be forewarned: This world can seem dizzyingly complex. But you don't need to understand every detail. Instead, you simply need to find the parts of a theme you want to change, and work on those.

In this chapter, you'll start your journey by taking a close look at how themes work, and you'll learn how to make small alterations that can have big effects. First, you'll try modifying styles. Then, you'll crack open a theme's template files to change the code inside. All this is preparation for the next chapter, where you'll build a new theme for a completely customized website.

The Goal: More Flexible Blogs and Sites

Before you begin fiddling with themes, you need to have a clear idea of *why* you'd want to do so. In other words, what do you hope to gain by changing a theme that you can't get by using a good, preexisting theme with just the right combination of WordPress settings and plug-ins?

There are several good answers:

- To get something *exactly* the way you want it
- To make your site unique
- To create a site that doesn't look "bloggy" (see the next section)

Custom themes are the key to unlocking WordPress and to building any sort of website you can imagine. Your task might not be easy, but custom themes make it *possible*.

NOTE Often, WordPressers first delve into a theme to make a tiny alteration. But they rarely stop there. The ability to transform a site, often by changing just a single style rule or modifying a single line of code, is addictive. If you catch the bug, you'll want to customize every theme you touch, and you won't be able to rest until you get exactly what you want for your site.

WordPress Sites That Aren't Blogs

One reason to customize a theme is to create a site that looks and feels less like a blog (see the box on page 456). Most WordPress sites have some characteristics that make them feel more bloggish and less like the sort of complex, traditional websites that rule the world of business and ecommerce. For example, WordPress sites usually display dated posts in reverse-chronological order. But what if you want to build a product showcase where the posts are actually product profiles, and you don't want those profiles to include any date information at all?

Another limitation is the fact that WordPress treats all posts the same way. But what if you want to create an e-magazine with a custom-made home page for each news category you cover (Sports, Current Affairs, Lifestyle, and so on)? You can't make those kinds of changes unless you're willing to step away from WordPress's blog origins and customize your theme. Do that, and you can build a WordPress site that behaves like almost any other type of site you see on the Web.

But before you get there, you need to learn a bit more about the way WordPress themes work—and lucky for you, that's the point of this chapter. Figure 13-1 shows the final goal—a completely customized website, which you'll learn to build in Chapter 14.

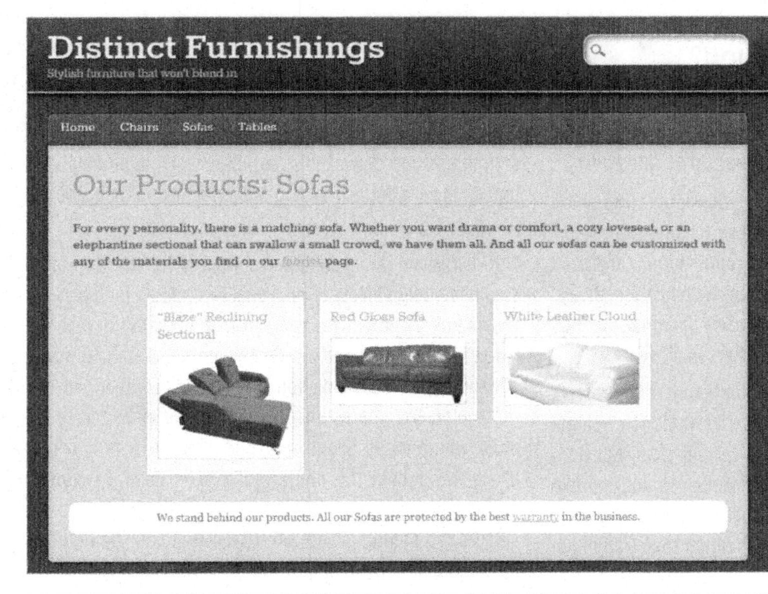

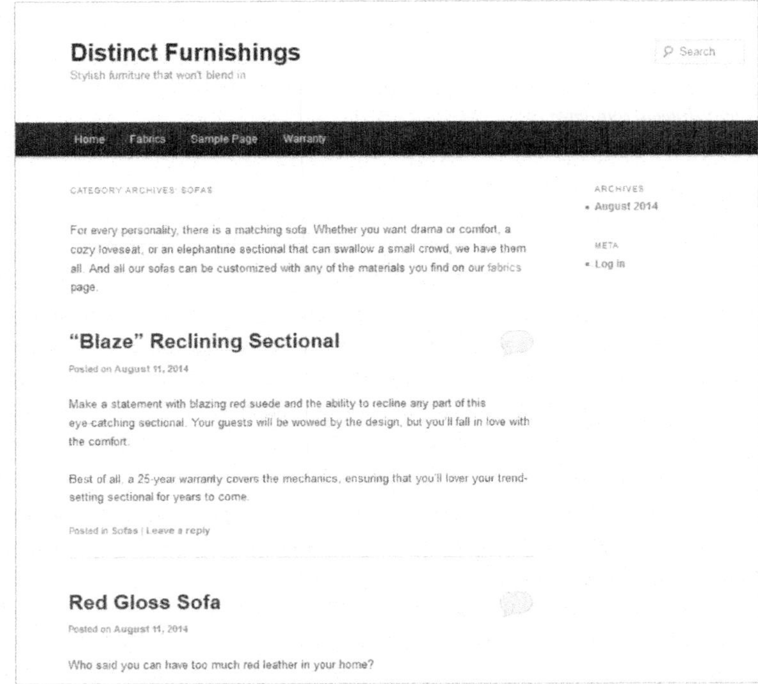

FIGURE 13-1

Top: Not many clues tell you that WordPress's blogging engine powers this ecommerce store.

Bottom: Here's the same site, without a custom theme. It still functions (more or less), but it feels like a blog.

UP TO SPEED

When Is a Blog Not a Blog?

Originally, WordPress was designed to be the world's best tool for building a blog. To most people, the word "blog" (short for *web log*) meant a personal journal made up of dated posts.

No sooner were blogs created than the definition of what a blog could do started to expand. Bloggers began creating more topical blogs—ones that provided political commentary, chronicled cooking exploits, or deconstructed popular television shows. For the most part, blogs were still intensely personal, but they were no longer restricted to people's personal lives.

Since then, the definition of *blog* has continued its aggressive expansion. Today, blogs aren't necessarily written by a single person in the first-person voice. They include sites that were never described as blogs before—for example, magazine-like news sites and picture-focused photoblogs or portfolio sites. Businesses often create "bloggy" sites rather than traditional websites, especially if they want to build social buzz or emphasize news and events. (For example, that hot restaurant setting up shop down the street might feel, legitimately so, that a blog is a better way to get people talking than a boring brochure site.)

This discussion raises an important question: When do blogs stop being blogs? Most often, you'll recognize a blog because it contains dated entries you can read (usually) in reverse-chronological order, and browse by category or tag. However, depending on the theme you pick and the content you use, these blog-like characteristics can be deemphasized to the point where many people won't consider your blog a blog at all. Throughout this book, you've seen several examples of "blogs" that stretch the definition of the word this way, such as the Canton School site (page 192) and the Pernatch Restaurant site (page 229).

NOTE If you're curious to get more ideas for non-bloggish sites that WordPress can create, visit the gallery of examples at *http://tinyurl.com/9dvpn3y*.

Getting Ready

Before you can move from WordPress-the-blogging-platform to WordPress-the-site-design-tool, you need to satisfy a few conditions.

First, you need to have a self-hosted WordPress site. WordPress.com doesn't give you the ability to edit themes, although it does provide a few carefully limited theme-customization features, which are outlined in the box on page 457. Handy as these are, they don't measure up to the power and flexibility of self-hosted sites, where you can customize absolutely *anything*—as long as you're prepared to do a little detective work to figure out what you need to change.

Second, you need to be ready to crack open the template files that run the WordPress show. To understand what's inside, you should be familiar with the basics of HTML markup—comfortable enough to find your way through the tangle of angle brackets and elements that live in every web page. It also helps to know some CSS (that's the Cascading Style Sheets standard that formats every modern web page). If you don't, you'll still be able to feel your way around with the introduction you'll get in this chapter, but be prepared for a steep learning curve.

If your web skills aren't quite up to snuff, here are some good resources that can help perk them up:

- If you've never edited a web page before, or you need to brush up on your HTML skills, consider *Creating a Website: The Missing Manual* (O'Reilly) which covers HTML and CSS standards (and plenty more). Or you can read a barebones HTML tutorial at *http://tinyurl.com/4mwq8.*
- To learn about CSS only, consider *CSS3: The Missing Manual* (O'Reilly). Or you can try an online CSS tutorial at *http://tinyurl.com/mlqk7.*

NOTE You don't need to understand *everything* about HTML and CSS to change a WordPress theme. You can often Google your way to the style rule or PHP code you need to implement a feature you want. You can then copy and paste that code into the right theme file, without worrying about any other details.

UP TO SPEED

What About WordPress.com?

Self-hosted sites give you free rein to customize your theme, using all the techniques you'll study in this chapter and the next. However, people with WordPress.com sites aren't completely left out. If you buy the Custom Design upgrade (or you have a Premium account, as described on page 359), WordPress.com gives you a set of useful but more modest theme-editing features.

To see these features, choose Appearance→Custom Design in the dashboard menu. It's worth noting that you can *preview* the features, even if you haven't bought the Custom Design upgrade. While you won't be able to make any changes to your site, you will be able to take a look at the options WordPress.com offers and get a sense of how much control you have over your site's appearance.

If you plan to make straightforward changes to your site's color scheme or fonts, the Custom Design upgrade shines. That's because it lets you point and click your way through recommended color palettes and popular web fonts, making these types of adjustments utterly painless. But if you want to adjust other details, like the size of the sidebar or the placement of the header, you need to write your own style rules. Click CSS on the Custom Design page to get started (Figure 13-2).

With the help of the Custom Design upgrade, you can make most of the style tweaks discussed in the first part of this chapter (starting on page 474). However, you definitely won't be able to edit template files, change the PHP code, or build a complex, custom site like the one demonstrated in Chapter 14.

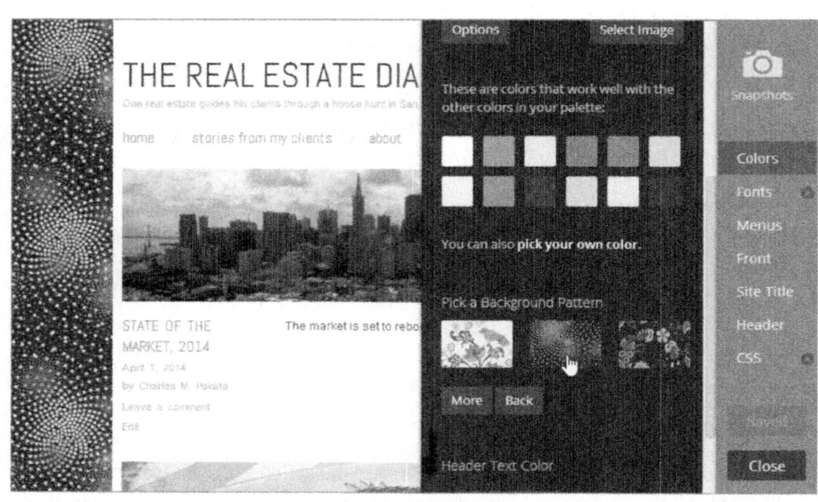

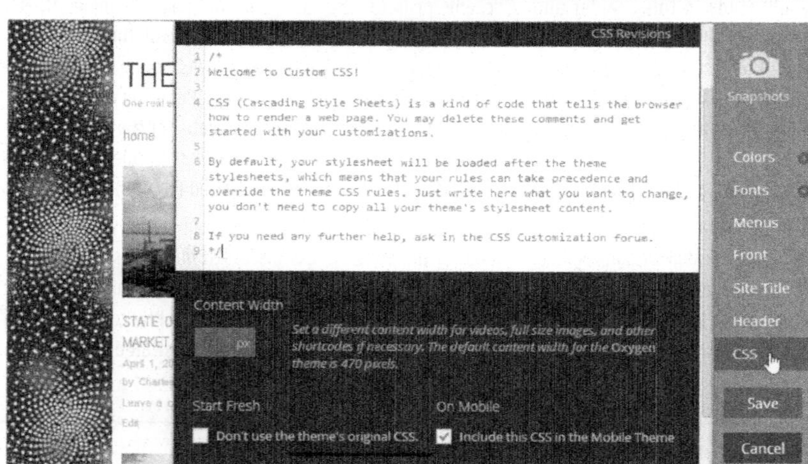

FIGURE 13-2

Top: WordPress.com's Custom Design upgrade lets you easily change your site's colors and fonts and apply a new background (like the multicolored star field shown here).

Bottom: Choose CSS in the righthand menu and you can make more drastic changes, but you need to know how to write a good CSS style rule and what site element to target. You'll learn to do that starting on page 479.

Taking Control of Your Theme

Before you can create a brilliantly customized WordPress theme, you need to know a bit more about how themes work behind the scenes.

When you first met themes in Chapter 5, you discovered that every theme consists of a combination of files. These files work together to create all the pages on your WordPress site, and they fall into three basic categories:

- **Style sheets.** These files contain style rules that format different parts of your site, such as headlines, sidebar headings, and links. They use the much-loved CSS standard, which will be familiar to anyone who's dabbled in web design.
- **Templates.** These files contain a mix of ordinary HTML and PHP code. Each template is responsible for a different part of your site—for example, there's a template for the list of recent posts, the page header, the footer, the single-post view, and so on.
- **Resources.** These are other files that your theme's templates might use, often to add a bit of pizzazz. Examples include image files, like the one Greyzed used to create its dirty stone background (page 136), and JavaScript code, like the stuff the Brightpage theme used to run its featured image slideshow (page 192).

At a bare minimum, every theme needs two files: a single style sheet named *style.css*, which sets the colors, layout, and fonts for your entire site, and a template named *index.php*, which creates the list of posts on your home page. Most themes have a few more style sheets and many more templates, but you'll get to that in a moment.

How WordPress Stores Themes

On your WordPress site, the *wp-content/themes* folder holds all your themes. For example, if your website address is *http://magicteahouse.net*, the Twenty Twelve theme will be in the following folder:

```
http://magicteahouse.net/wp-content/themes/twentytwelve
```

Each theme you install gets its own subfolder. So if you install seven themes on your website, you'll see seven subfolders in the *wp-content/themes* folder, even though you use only one theme at a time.

All of a theme's style sheets and template files reside inside the theme's folder (Figure 13-3). Most themes also have subfolders. For example, they might tuck JavaScript files into a subfolder named *js* and image files into a subfolder named *images*. You don't need to worry about these details as long as you remember that themes are a package of files and subfolders you need to keep together in order for your site to function properly.

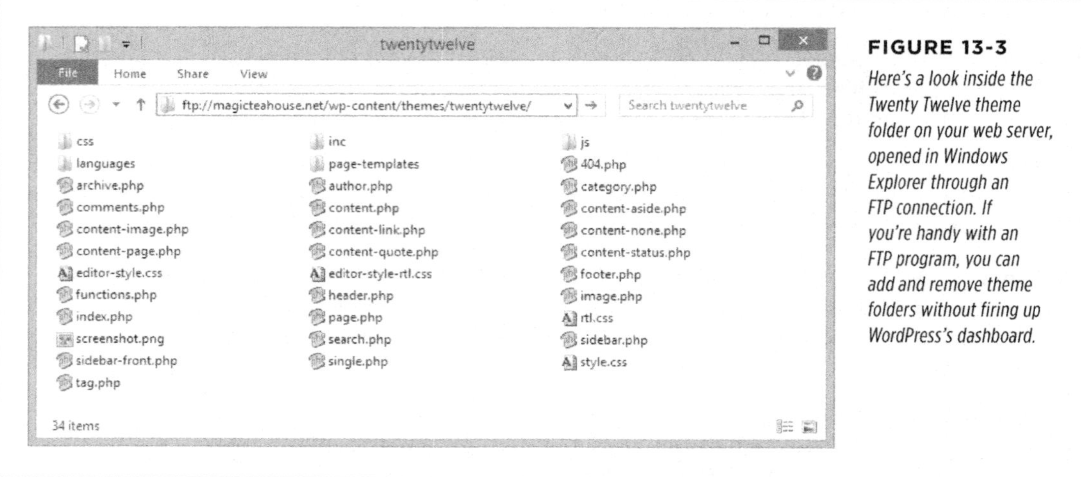

FIGURE 13-3

Here's a look inside the Twenty Twelve theme folder on your web server, opened in Windows Explorer through an FTP connection. If you're handy with an FTP program, you can add and remove theme folders without firing up WordPress's dashboard.

Style.css: How a Theme Identifies Itself

The *style.css* file is the starting point for every theme. In most themes, it's a huge file packed with formatting instructions. For example, the Twenty Twelve theme's *style.css* file weighs in with nearly *2,000* lines of formatting magic.

The *style.css* file defines a few essential pieces of information about the style itself, using a *theme header* at the beginning of the file. Here's a slightly shortened version of the header that starts the Twenty Twelve *style.css* file. Each distinct bit of information is highlighted in bold:

```
/*
Theme Name: Twenty Twelve
Theme URI: http://wordpress.org/themes/twentytwelve
Author: the WordPress team
Author URI: http://wordpress.org/
Description: The 2012 theme for WordPress is a fully responsive theme ...
Version: 1.3
License: GNU General Public License v2 or later
License URI: http://www.gnu.org/licenses/gpl-2.0.html
Tags: light, gray, white, one-column, two-columns, right-sidebar, fluid-lay-
out,
...

*/
```

WordPress brackets the header with two special character sequences: It starts with /* and ends with */, the CSS comment markers. As a result, browsers don't pay any attention to the header. But WordPress checks it and extracts the key details. It uses this information for the theme description you see in the Add Themes page (page 141). It also tracks the version number and checks the theme URL for new versions. (Although it says "URI" in the theme file, a URI is the same as a URL when you deal with content on the Web, as in the case of themes.)

If your theme lacks these details, WordPress won't recognize that it's a theme. It won't show it in the Appearance→Themes section of the dashboard, and it won't let you activate it on your site.

NOTE Many themes include style sheets beyond *style.css*. However, these style sheets add extra features or handle special cases—for example, they provide alternate color schemes, deal with old browsers, handle languages that write text from right to left, and format the content in the editing box on the Add New Post page so that it provides the most realistic preview possible.

The Theme Editor

To edit a theme, choose Appearance→Editor in the dashboard. This takes you to the Edit Themes page, with your theme's main style sheet, *styles.css*, open (Figure 13-4).

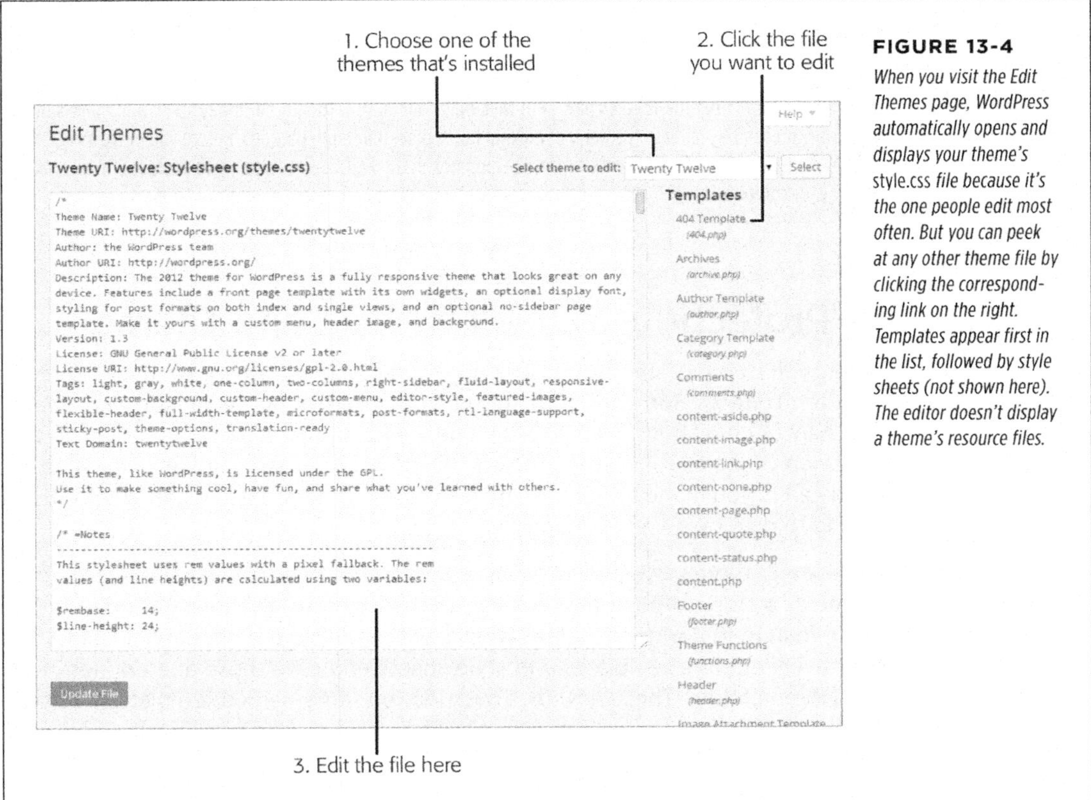

FIGURE 13-4

When you visit the Edit Themes page, WordPress automatically opens and displays your theme's style.css *file because it's the one people edit most often. But you can peek at any other theme file by clicking the corresponding link on the right. Templates appear first in the list, followed by style sheets (not shown here). The editor doesn't display a theme's resource files.*

WordPress splits the Edit Themes page into two parts. On the left is a giant text box where you edit your theme, one file at a time. On the right is a sidebar that lists all the files in your theme.

Once you finish editing a file in your theme, click Update File to save your changes. You can then choose a different file to edit.

If you want to make extensive changes to a theme, you might not want to do all the work in the cramped environment of the dashboard. You might prefer to download your theme files and edit them offline, using a more powerful program. Some web editing programs, like Dreamweaver, even have built-in theme-editing features for WordPress.

One way to do this is to pick the file you want to edit, copy its content, and paste it into a text editor (like Notepad on Windows PCs or TextEdit on Macs). Then, after you make your changes, copy the edited content back into the editing box on the Edit Themes page. But if you're going to edit multiple files, it's easier to download the whole theme folder. To do that, browse to your website with an FTP program (as shown in Figure 13-3) and then drag the theme folder to your computer's desktop. When you finish making changes, delete the original folder from your website and then upload the updated folder from your desktop computer to your site.

WARNING The theme editor can be an unforgiving tool. WordPress does not store past versions of your theme files, so once you save an edit, there's no way to restore your site to its previous state. (You can reapply the original theme from the Themes page, but that wipes out all your theme-editing changes.) To make sure you don't run into trouble, get into the habit of making basic, bare-minimum backups. Before you make a big change to a theme file, copy all the content from the editing box in the Edit Themes page, and paste it into a blank text file on your computer.

Protecting Yourself with a Child Theme

Before you start mucking around with one of your themes, you should think about the long-term effects. Someday, probably not long from today, the person who created the theme you're editing will release a new and improved version that you'll want to use on your site. Here's the problem: If you install a theme update, you wipe out all the edits you made to your theme files. Editing themes is enough work without having to do it over and over again.

Fortunately, there's a solution. You can create a *child theme*, which takes the current theme as a starting point and lets you slap your customizations on top of it. You don't change the original theme (known as the *parent theme*) at all. Instead, you selectively edit the templates and style sheets and save those altered files in the child theme folder. These new files override the same-named templates and style sheets in the parent theme, so you get the features you want in your site. And when you update the *parent* theme at some future date, your customizations stay in place, because WordPress stores the child theme as a separate group of files.

When you customize a theme, you should *always* start by creating a child theme. It's the safest approach, and the only way to guarantee that your work will survive future changes.

However, if you want to create a completely *new* theme (rather than customize an existing one), you need a different approach. You might still use an existing theme as a starting point for your work, but there's no need to create a child theme. Your changes will be so significant that future updates and fixes won't be relevant to your tricked-out theme.

All the examples in this chapter use child themes. Creating a complete theme on your own is a significant undertaking for even the best propeller heads among us, although you'll get an introduction to the practice in Chapter 14.

Creating a Child Theme

To create a child theme, start by adding a new theme folder in the *wp-content/themes* section of your website. Name the folder whatever you want. However, unlike a normal theme folder, you don't need to fill this folder with files. All you need to do is put a new *style.css* file inside the folder—one that links itself to the parent theme via the theme header.

If this sounds like a slightly intimidating challenge, don't worry. Rather than go through the hassle of creating the folder for your child theme and creating the *style.css* file with the right header, you can use a tiny plug-in, called One-Click Child Theme (*http://tinyurl.com/child-theme*), to help you out. Here's what to do:

1. **Install and activate the One-Click Child Theme plug-in.**

   Choose Plugins→Add New, and search for it by name.

TIP WordPress has several similar plug-ins that can help you create child themes. To see them all (and possibly choose a different one), search the plug-in repository for "child theme."

2. **Activate the theme you want to customize.**

   The One-Click Child Theme plug-in assumes you want to create a child theme for the currently active theme on your site. If that's not the case, go to Appearance→Themes and activate the right theme before you continue.

3. **Choose Appearance→Child Theme.**

   This is a new menu command, courtesy of the One-Click Child Theme plug-in. It opens the Create a Child Theme page (Figure 13-5).

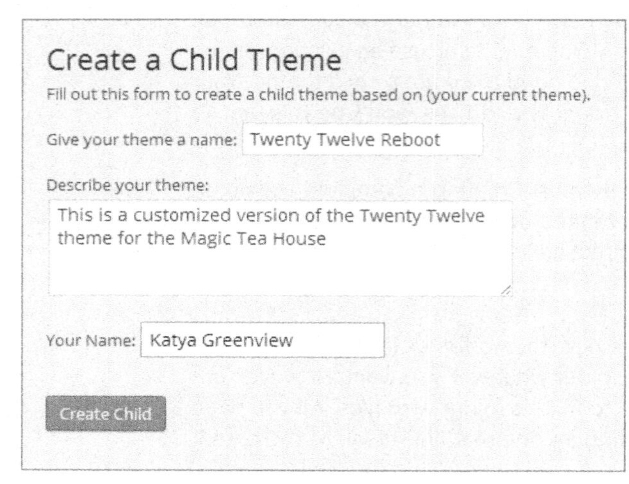

FIGURE 13-5

You need to provide only a few pieces of information to create a child theme. Here, you're about to create a child theme named "Twenty Twelve Reboot."

NOTE To follow along with the examples in this chapter, use the Twenty Twelve theme. It's a good starting point for theme-customization practice because it's clean, straightforward, and adaptable. If you decide to start with a different theme, all the concepts described in this chapter still apply, but the exact class names and formatting details will vary.

4. **Supply a name for the theme, a brief description, and your name.**

   The One-Click Child Theme plug-in puts these details in the header of the *style.css* file. It uses your name as the theme's author.

5. **Click Create Child.**

   The One-Click Child Theme plug-in creates the child theme folder on your web server and creates a new *style.css* file inside it. It then activates the child theme on your site.

   In this example, the theme is named Twenty Twelve Reboot, so the newly created folder will be named *twenty-twelve-reboot.*

6. **To verify that your child theme is working, choose Appearance→Themes.**

   You'll see your new child theme at the top of the page (Figure 13-6).

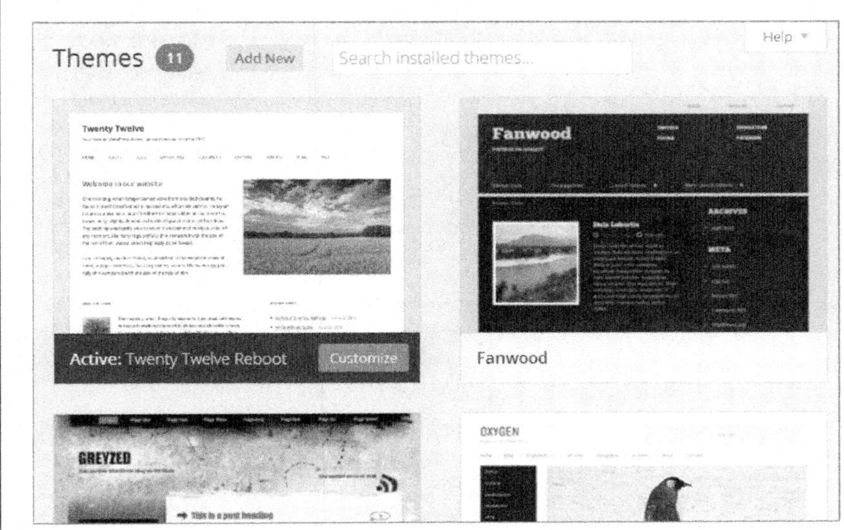

FIGURE 13-6

Right now, the Twenty Twelve Reboot child theme is identical to its parent theme, Twenty Twelve. The One-Click Child Theme Plug-In even gives it the same thumbnail picture.

7. **Optionally, deactivate the One-Click Child Theme plug-in.**

   Unless you plan to create another new child theme, you don't need to keep One-Click Child Theme active. Head to the plug-in page (click Plugins) and use the Deactivate link to switch it off.

How Child Themes Work

If you check out the newly created folder for your child theme, you'll find that it holds just three files. The first is the all-important *style.css*. The second is a supplementary style sheet for right-to-left languages, named *rtl.css*. The third is an image named *screenshot.png* that WordPress copied from the parent theme; it uses that image as the thumbnail on the Themes page (Figure 13-6).

To start editing your child theme, choose Appearance→Editor. Start with the *style.css* file (Figure 13-7), as you do when you edit a normal theme.

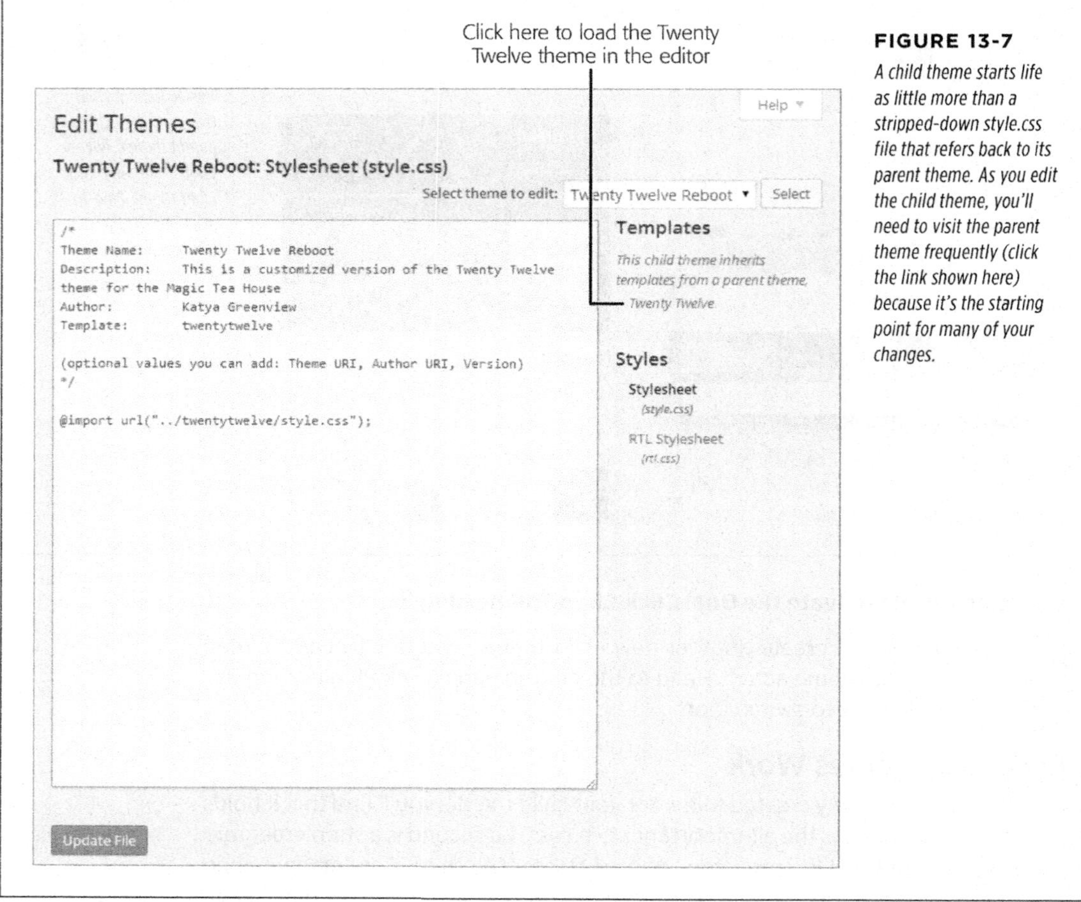

FIGURE 13-7

A child theme starts life as little more than a stripped-down style.css file that refers back to its parent theme. As you edit the child theme, you'll need to visit the parent theme frequently (click the link shown here) because it's the starting point for many of your changes.

The key to a child theme is its *style.css* style sheet. Unlike the *style.css* file in the parent theme, *style.css* in the child theme contains just a few lines of text. Here's the complete *style.css* file in the Twenty Twelve Reboot theme:

```
/*
Theme Name: Twenty Twelve Reboot
Description: This is a customized version of the Twenty Twelve Theme for the
Magic Tea House.
Author: Katya Greenview
Template: twentytwelve
*/

@import url("../twentytwelve/style.css");
```

You've already seen the first three details (theme name, description, and author). However, the template setting is new—it points to the parent theme's folder. When WordPress sees this setting, it knows to look in a folder named *twentytwelve* (in the themes section of your site). When it does, it finds the files for the familiar Twenty Twelve theme.

Unlike the original version of the *style.css* file in the Twenty Twelve theme, the child theme contains just a single line after the header. This line grabs all the styles from the Twenty Twelve theme and applies them to the child theme:

```
@import url("../twentytwelve/style.css");
```

If you're foolish enough to delete this line, your site will lose all the styles from the parent theme. (You can try it out; just remember to add the `@import` statement back when you finish.) Suddenly, all your text will switch to the generic Times New Roman font, your nicely formatted headings will disappear, and the layout of your headers, footers, and sidebar will get scrambled together in a mess.

TIP Child themes are a great way to customize your site permanently, but they're also a handy tool for *temporarily* changing your formatting. For example, if you're running the Magic Tea House site, you might decide to hold a special winter promotion. During this promotion, you plan to make sweeping changes to your site's color scheme. If you use a child theme to redecorate, you can quickly go back to your original theme when the promotion ends—just choose Appearance→Themes and activate the parent theme.

GEM IN THE ROUGH

Adding Styles with Jetpack: Another Approach

A child theme is the tried-and-true method for safely customizing a theme, but if you use Jetpack—the handy plug-in that aims to give self-hosters the features of WordPress.com—you have another option.

Recent versions of Jetpack include a CSS-editing feature that acts like the Custom Design upgrade in WordPress.com. Its chief advantage is that it lets you add to your site's style rules without modifying your theme's style sheet, so there's no need to create a child theme. But this simplicity comes at a price: It limits your power and flexibility. Although this feature is good enough for the style refinements you'll see in the next section, it doesn't let you safely edit templates—a key feature you'll tap in the latter half of this chapter and in Chapter 14.

To use Jetpack's CSS editing feature, choose Appearance→Edit CSS. You'll see an editing box that looks strikingly similar to the one you use when editing a style sheet in a child theme. As with a child theme, the style rules you add here override those in your original theme. Unlike a child theme, you won't see the @import statement, because Jetpack automatically merges the original styles with your customizations.

When you add custom styles with Jetpack, your styles aren't stored in a file; they're stored in your site's database. This can cause a few quirks—for example, you lose the styles you edited if you disable Jetpack (remember to copy your custom styles from the editor and paste them into a text file first). And every time you switch themes, Jetpack wipes the slate clean and deletes your custom styles. However, Jetpack also includes a handy revision tracker that works just like the post revision system (page 338), and "remembers" your 25 most recent theme revisions. If you make a big editing mistake, or if you switch themes and want to get your old work back, click the revision you want in the CSS Revisions box.

Overall, Jetpack is a worthy tool for minor theme changes if you already use the plug-in. But if you're more ambitious and you might be editing a template or two in the future, a child theme is the only way to go.

Editing the Styles in Your Theme

There are a number of reasons you might crack open your theme's styles and make changes:

- **Unique-ify your theme.** You might change your theme to make sure your site doesn't have the same look as other sites that share that theme. After all, there are only so many themes, and if you pick a good one, it's a safe bet that you're following in the footsteps of thousands of other webmasters.
- **Branding.** Perhaps you need your theme to match the official corporate colors of your business. Or you might want it to more closely resemble another website, run by the same business, that doesn't use WordPress.
- **Highlight certain design elements.** By changing a theme, you can emphasize details that are important to you. For example, you may want to use a style that makes author comments stand out (page 496).

To make changes to any theme, you follow two steps. First, you create a child theme (page 462), and then you add one or more style rules to the *style.css* file in that theme. These rules selectively override the original theme, letting you change whatever you don't like. Some of the details you alter include colors, fonts, spacing, and borders. You can also hide design elements you don't want to see.

However, making these changes isn't quite as easy as it sounds. To cook up the right style rule, you need to know a bit more about the CSS standard and the styles your theme uses. Every theme is slightly different, but most include a gargantuan *style.css* file stuffed full of formatting instructions. Finding the exact detail you want to override may take some digging. In the next section, you'll take your first look at the sort of instructions the *style.css* file contains.

NOTE If you're already well versed in the CSS standard, you can skip the next section and continue on to the one after that, "Changing the Twenty Twelve Theme," on page 474.

Taking a Look at the Style Rules in Your Theme

Reading the average *style.css* file is not for the faint of heart. As explained earlier, the typical theme includes hundreds or thousands of formatting instructions. Understanding any one of them isn't too difficult, but finding the exact one you want can be a challenge.

FREQUENTLY ASKED QUESTION

Find Your Style Sheet in WordPress.com

I bought the Custom Design upgrade so I can add my own styles, but where can I find the rules from the original style sheet?

To create your own styles, you need to understand the styles that are already at work on your site. Unfortunately, WordPress.com hides your theme's style sheet, even after you buy the Custom Design upgrade. Why? In the past, when this style sheet was more visible, WordPress.com users kept making the same mistake: They'd copy the whole thing into the CSS editor and then make their changes. (Of course *you* know better, and you'll only put *changed* styles into the CSS editor.)

So how do you find your site's style sheet, so you can study it and figure out what you want to change? It's a bit tricky, but here's how to dig it up:

1. Click Appearance→Custom Design. Then click CSS. This takes you to the CSS editor where you enter your custom styles.
2. Click CSS Revisions, just above the post editor. This shows the CSS editor with your customized CSS file, as before, but now with more options.
3. In the Publish box, next to the Mode option, click Edit. You'll see two options that control how WordPress.com uses your styles.
4. Look at the "Replace theme's CSS" option, but don't turn it on. (In fact, there's almost never a good reason to use this setting.) Instead, notice how part of the option—the words "theme's CSS"—is a link. Click that link, and you see the full style sheet for your theme, nicely formatted so you can read it in your browser.

DECODING A BASIC STYLE RULE

The first step to understanding CSS styles is to take a look at a few rules and get familiar with their syntax.

Every style sheet is a long list of rules, and every rule follows the same format, which looks like this:

```
selector {
  property: value;
  property: value;
}
```

Here's what each part means:

- **The selector** identifies the type of content you want to format. A browser hunts down all the elements on a web page that match that selector. There are many ways to write a selector, but one of the simplest (shown next) is to identify the elements you want to format by their element name. For example, you could write a selector that picks out all the level-1 headings on a page.
- **The property** identifies the type of formatting you want to apply. Here's where you choose whether you want to change colors, fonts, alignment, or something else. You can have as many property settings as you want in a rule—the example above has two.
- **The value** sets a value for the property. For example, if your property is *color,* the value could be light blue or queasy green.

Now here's a sample rule, of the sort you'll find in a theme like Twenty Twelve:

```
body {
  background: #fff;
  line-height: 1;
}
```

This tells a browser to find the web page's <body> element, which wraps all the content on the page. The browser applies two formatting instructions to the element. First, it changes the background color. (You'll be excused for not knowing that *#fff* is an HTML color code that means white.) Second, it sets the line spacing to a normal value of 1. (A higher value would add more space between each line of text.)

You need several skills to decode a style rule like this. First, you need to know the basics of HTML, so you can understand what the <body> element is and what it does in a web page. Second, you need to know what style properties are available for you to tweak. Style rules let you change color, typeface, borders, size, positioning, and alignment. To understand the sample rule shown above, you need to know that CSS defines a background property that lets you change the color behind an element. Third, you need to know what values are appropriate for a property—for example, you set a page's background color using an HTML color code. (In the case of colors, you can pick the color you want and get its HTML color code from a color-picking site like *www.colorpicker.com*.)

TIP You can get style sheet help from a book like *CSS3: The Missing Manual* (O'Reilly). Or, if all you need is an overview of the style properties you can change and their acceptable values, check out the style sheet reference at *http://tinyurl.com/bz5tcp*.

MULTIPLE RULES AND MEDIA QUERIES

Sometimes, a style sheet contains multiple rules for the same element. In such a situation, the browser combines all the property settings into one super-rule. For example, you can break the style sheet rule you just saw into two pieces, like this:

```
body {
  background: #e6e6e6;
}

body {
  line-height: 1;
}
```

In this case, the effect is the same. Big style sheets may use this approach to break down complex rules and better organize them.

Some style sheets include *media queries*—one or more blocks of conditional rules that spring into action when certain browser conditions are met. You can recognize a media query by the fact that it starts with the code `@media`. Here's an example:

```
@media screen and (min-width: 960px) {

  /* Conditional styles go in here.

}
```

This translates into the following instruction: "If this page is currently being displayed on a screen (not sent to a printer or some other device), and the width of the page is at least 960 pixels, then run the following styles." Older themes don't use media queries, but mobile-aware themes rely on this technique to change your layout for different devices, like smartphones (page 168).

All the WordPress year themes, from Twenty Twelve on, use media queries. In fact, if you dig through the Twenty Twelve style sheet, you'll find no fewer than *three* style rules that target the <body> element—two that are always in effect, and one that conditionally changes the background color from white to gray:

```
@media screen and (min-width: 960px) {

  body {
    background-color: #e6e6e6;
  }

}
```

If you wonder why Twenty Twelve uses this color-changing trick, visit a site that uses the theme and shrink your browser window. In a wide window, the conditional rule applies a gray outline around the content (which always appears on a white background). But if you shrink the window, that gray edge disappears.

CLASS AND ID SELECTORS

The style sheet rules above target the <body> element. This type of rule is called an *element rule*, because it applies to a specific element on a page. For example, if you write a rule that formats <h1> headings, every first-level heading on the page gets the same formatting.

CSS supports other types of selectors, and WordPress themes use them heavily. One of the most popular is the *class selector*, which starts with a period, like this:

```
.entry-header {
  margin-bottom: 24px;
}
```

This rule formats any element that has a class named *entry-header* applied to it. If you look at the HTML markup for one of your posts, you'll find an element tagged with the entry-header class, like this:

```
<header class="entry-header">
  <h1 class="entry-title">Magic Tea House's Grand New Opening</h1>
```

```
    <div class="comments-link">
      <a href="http://magicteahouse.net/grand-new-opening/#respond"
       title="Comment on Magic Tea House's Grand New Opening">
        <span class="leave-reply">Leave a reply</span>
      </a>
    </div>
  </header>
```

Here, the theme uses the entry-header class to wrap the header section of each post, which includes the post title and the "Leave a reply" comments link.

It's important to realize that the word "entry-header" doesn't mean anything special to WordPress or to a browser. It's simply a naming convention the Twenty Twelve theme uses (as do many other themes).

NOTE Sometimes, you'll see a CSS rule that combines element selectors and class selectors. So the selector *h1.entry-title* refers to any level-1 heading that uses the entry-title class.

There's one more selector that's similar to class selectors, called an *ID selector*. It starts with a # character. Here's an example that uses an ID named colophon:

```
#colophon {
}
```

NOTE In Twenty Twelve, a *colophon* is the footer at the very bottom of each page of your site. Ordinarily, it contains the text "Proudly powered by WordPress."

Here's the snippet of HTML that gets its formatting from this rule:

```
<footer id="colophon" role="contentinfo">
  <div class="site-info">
    <a href="http://wordpress.org/"
     title="Semantic Personal Publishing Platform">
     Proudly powered by WordPress</a>
  </div>
</footer>
```

The difference between class selectors and ID selectors is that a class selector can format a number of elements (provided they all have the same class applied to them), while an ID selector targets just a single HTML element (because two elements can't have the same ID). A WordPress page will have only one colophon, so it makes sense to use an ID selector for it, even though a class selector would work just as well.

NOTE Some style sheets use ID selectors heavily, while others do all their work with class selectors. It's really a matter of preference. You simply need to follow the convention your theme uses.

This is where things can get a bit head-spinny. Understanding the syntax of CSS is one thing, but editing the styles in a theme means knowing which class and ID names that theme uses, and what elements are associated with those names. You'll get some pointers on page 479.

COMBINING SELECTORS

You can *combine* selectors to create even more powerful formatting rules, so long as you separate them with a comma. WordPress then applies the style rule to any element that matches any *one* of the selectors.

Here's an example that changes the alignment of three HTML elements—the <caption> element used with figures and the <th> and <td> elements used with tables.

```
caption, th, td {
    text-align: left;
}
```

You can also create more complex rules that match elements *inside* other elements. This is called a *contextual selector*, and you build one by combining two ordinary selectors, separated by a space. Here's an example:

```
.comment-content h1 {
  ...
}
```

This selector matches every <h1> element inside the element with the class name *comment-content*. It formats the heading of every comment, while ignoring the <h1> elements that appear elsewhere on the page.

WordPress loves contextual selectors—in fact, most of the Twenty Twelve theme's style rules use contextual selectors. If you haven't seen them before, they may take some time to decipher. Just remember that a browser works on the selectors one at a time. It starts by finding an element that matches the first selector, and then it looks inside that element to match the second selector (and if the rule includes another selector, the browser searches inside *that* element, too).

Here's another example to practice your CSS-decoding skills:

```
.entry-header .entry-title {
  font-size: 20px;
  line-height: 1.2;
}
```

Got it? This selector looks for an element with the class name *.entry-title* inside an element with the class name *.entry-header*. The end result is a rule that targets the title in the post header. The creators of the Twenty Twelve theme could have written a simplified rule that applies to the entry-title class, no matter where it appears, but they chose to be more specific.

Sometimes there are good reasons for being more specific and writing contextual selectors. For example, the creators of Twenty Twelve might want to show the post title in different places, without using the same formatting. In other cases, theme designers use a contextual selector to indicate the relationship of classes and the structure of the site. (For example, the *.entry-header .entry-title* rule tells you that this theme puts entry titles inside an entry header.) To you, it shouldn't matter. In most cases, when you want to modify your theme's CSS, you find the style rule that controls the detail you want to change and you copy the selector *exactly*.

UP TO SPEED

Pixels and Rems: Two Ways to Measure the Same Thing

The style sheet rules you see in this chapter are slightly simplified from the versions you'll find in the Twenty Twelve theme. Oddly enough, Twenty Twelve sets dimensions *twice*, using two different units of measure. First, it uses pixels, and then it sets the same amount of margin space using a curious unit called *rems:*

```
font-size: 20px;
font-size: 1.25rem;
```

Browsers that understand rems pay attention to the second line. Browsers that don't (old versions of Internet Explorer) use the first line. Either way, the result is equivalent and the element looks the same in the page.

Of course, this practice raises two clear questions: What's the difference between a pixel and a rem, and why would you prefer one over the other? The short answer is that it's a historical quirk fuelled by browser behaviors of the past. Today, the choice between pixels and rems is really a matter of personal preference. But if you want to know the nitty-gritty, keep reading.

The most obvious difference between the two units of measure is that the scale is different. A single rem adds up to 14 pixels, which is the type size of normal text. So if you set a width of 300 pixels, you'd use 21.43 rems to match. Beyond that, the situation gets murky. In the recent past, rems were special because they were a *relative* unit of measurement. Web pages that used them could scale themselves to suit a browser's text size setting, satisfying visually impaired people and fitting into the small screens of mobile devices. By comparison, pixels were bad, because they trapped pages in fixed layouts that couldn't adapt to different situations. Today, these problems are resolved, and browsers can scale pages that use pixel sizes in much the same way they scale pages that use rems. In fact, the year themes that came after Twenty Twelve, like Twenty Fourteen, have switched back to using pixels only.

Changing the Twenty Twelve Theme

The Twenty Twelve theme is filled with styles, and you can override any of them. For example, say you decide that you don't want the standard menu bar to appear on your site. The menu isn't a widget; it's a built-in part of the Twenty Twelve theme. But here's where your child theme and CSS knowledge pay off, because you can hide the menu by using the right style rule.

To do that, choose Appearance→Editor to start editing the *style.css* file in your child theme (Figure 13-8). Then add this rule:

```
.main-navigation {
  display: none;
}
```

This works because the *.main-navigation* class is attached to a <nav> element that holds the menu for your site. The *display: none* instruction tells browsers to collapse this element, and its contents, into nothingness.

NOTE When you add a style rule to a child theme, it *overrides* any conflicting rule in the parent theme, but it allows style settings that don't conflict. For example, if you change the *color* of your post title in the child theme, that won't affect the *font* the parent theme applies to the title.

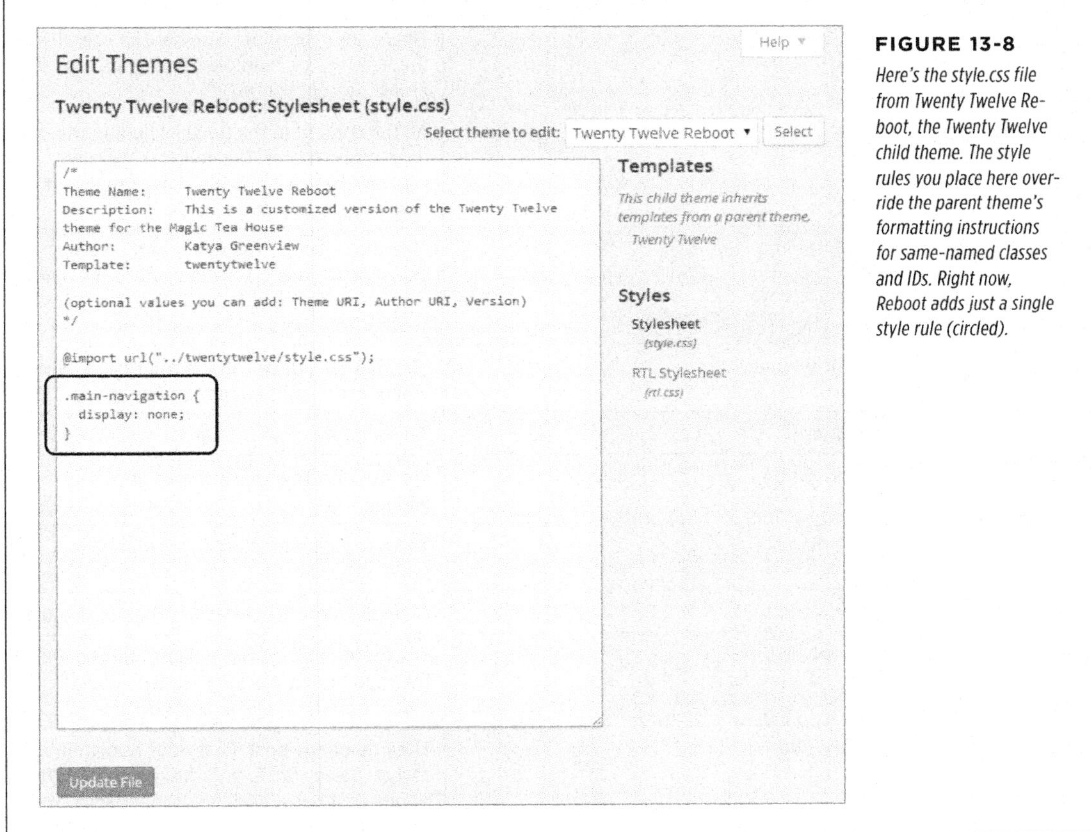

FIGURE 13-8

Here's the style.css file from Twenty Twelve Reboot, the Twenty Twelve child theme. The style rules you place here override the parent theme's formatting instructions for same-named classes and IDs. Right now, Reboot adds just a single style rule (circled).

If you're comfortable with CSS (or you're using one of the CSS resources mentioned on page 457), you'll have no trouble understanding the *display* property. However, you might have more trouble finding the ID and class names of the elements you want to change. Table 13-1 provides a cheat sheet to some of the key elements in the Twenty Twelve theme.

TABLE 13-1 *Class Names in the Twenty Twelve Theme*

STYLE SELECTOR	CORRESPONDS TO...
.site-header	The header section at the top of every page; it includes the site title, site description, navigation menu, and header image.
.site-header img	Just the header image. Use this class to change the header's size or position.
.site-title	The site title in the header (for example, "Magic Tea House").
.site-description	The byline that appears under the site title in the header (for example, "Tea Emporium and Small Concert Venue").
.site	All the content in the page, including the header and footer. The style for this class sets the maximum width of the site layout (currently, that's 960 pixels).
.widget-area	The right sidebar that holds all the widgets. The style for this class allocates 26 percent of the available width to the sidebar, and the content area gets the remaining space.
.front-widgets	The bottom sidebar on the front page, when you use the Front Page template (page 235).
.widget	Any widget in a widget area.
.widget-title	The optional title that appears above a widget.
.nav-menu	The navigation menu at the top of each page.
.nav-menu li	An individual entry in the navigation menu.
.colophon	The footer area on every page, starting with the solid horizontal line that separates the footer from the main content area.
.entry-title	The title of any post. Post titles appear in several places (including the home page, the single-post page, and the search page). You probably don't want to format titles all the same way, so you need to combine a class name with another selector, as shown in the next three examples.
.blog .entry-title	The title of any post in the main list of posts.
.single .entry-title	The title of any post on a single-post page.
.template-front-page .entry-title	The title of any post on a showcase page.

STYLE SELECTOR	CORRESPONDS TO...
.entry-content	The content in the post. As with the entry-title class, this applies to the post content no matter where it appears, unless you combine this selector with another one.
.entry-meta	The information about the post, which appears before it (for example, "Posted on January 14, 2014" and after it ("This entry was posted in News by Katya Greenview on March 16, 2014.")
.comments-area	The comments area after a post.
.comment-meta	The byline for a comment, such as "Salah on April 26, 2014 at 11:00 pm said:"
.comment-content	The comment text, after the byline.
.commentlist li.bypostauthor	A comment left by you (the author of the post).
.commentlist li.byuser	A comment left by someone other than you.
.logged-in	A class added if the current visitor is logged in as a website user (page 370). For example, you can use the selector *.logged-in body* to change the formatting of the <body> element for people you know.

Although Table 13-1 is tailored to the Twenty Twelve theme, many other WordPress themes follow a similar structure. The standard year themes (such as Twenty Thirteen and Twenty Fourteen) are particularly consistent. And WordPress itself is responsible for adding class names like *.blog, .single,* and *.logged-in* to the <body> element to flag key details about the current state of a page. However, other themes are free to change many of these details in ways both subtle and maddening. For most class names, there are no guarantees, so every theme customization task must begin with a process of exploration.

Once you get the right class or ID name, you can target the exact visual ingredient you want to alter. For example, to change the font, color, and size of the text in a blog post in a single-post page, you can add a style rule like this:

```
.entry-content {
  font-family: "Times New Roman";
  color: red;
  font-size: 21px;
}
```

Type it into the editor (Appearance→Editor), hit Update File, and refresh the website to see the change (Figure 13-9).

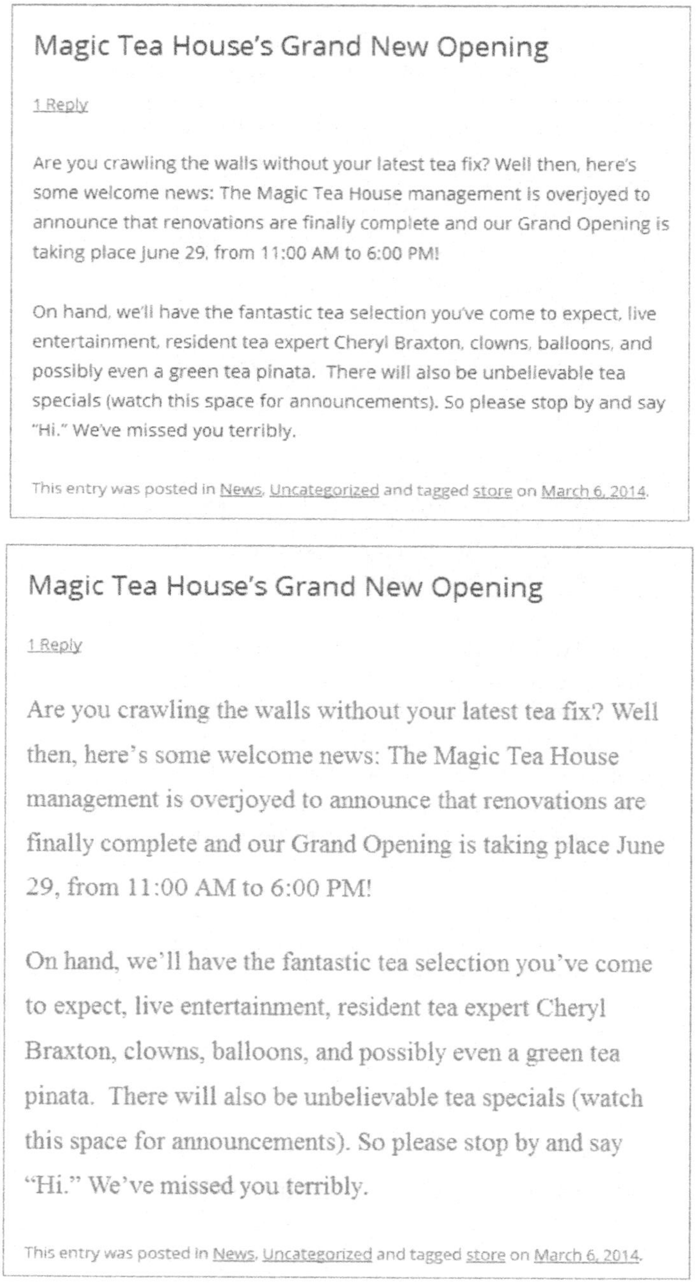

Magic Tea House's Grand New Opening

1 Reply

Are you crawling the walls without your latest tea fix? Well then, here's some welcome news: The Magic Tea House management is overjoyed to announce that renovations are finally complete and our Grand Opening is taking place June 29, from 11:00 AM to 6:00 PM!

On hand, we'll have the fantastic tea selection you've come to expect, live entertainment, resident tea expert Cheryl Braxton, clowns, balloons, and possibly even a green tea pinata. There will also be unbelievable tea specials (watch this space for announcements). So please stop by and say "Hi." We've missed you terribly.

This entry was posted in News, Uncategorized and tagged store on March 6, 2014.

Magic Tea House's Grand New Opening

1 Reply

Are you crawling the walls without your latest tea fix? Well then, here's some welcome news: The Magic Tea House management is overjoyed to announce that renovations are finally complete and our Grand Opening is taking place June 29, from 11:00 AM to 6:00 PM!

On hand, we'll have the fantastic tea selection you've come to expect, live entertainment, resident tea expert Cheryl Braxton, clowns, balloons, and possibly even a green tea pinata. There will also be unbelievable tea specials (watch this space for announcements). So please stop by and say "Hi." We've missed you terribly.

This entry was posted in News, Uncategorized and tagged store on March 6, 2014.

FIGURE 13-9

Top: The ordinary face of Twenty Twelve.

Bottom: This revamped post, with its large red-lettered text, doesn't exactly look better, but it does look different.

It's a simple recipe: Find the class name or ID name for the element you want change, add some style properties, and your page gets an instant makeover.

Here's another example that makes your comments ridiculously obvious, with a yellow background, bold text, and a gray border:

```
.commentlist li.bypostauthor {
  background-color: LightYellow;
  font-weight: bold;
  border: 1px solid gray;
}
```

In this case, it isn't enough to just use the *.bypostauthor* selector on its own. That's because the *style.css* file in the original Twenty Twelve theme uses a more specific version of *.bypostauthor*. CSS won't allow a more general selector (like *.bypostauthor*) to override a more specific one (like *.commentlist li.bypostauthor*) if their properties conflict. For that reason, you need to use the longer selector *.commentlist li.bypostauthor* in your child theme if you want the theme to apply your new rule.

Puzzling Out the Styles in a Theme

Half the battle in editing *style.css* is figuring out how to write your selector. Often, you won't know the class or ID name of the page element you want to change, so you need to do a bit of detective work.

The best starting point is to scour the HTML that WordPress creates for your page. You can do this in any browser by visiting the page, right-clicking it, and choosing a command with a name like "View Source." This shows you the complete HTML markup, and you need to search for the piece of content you want to change. To get started, hit Ctrl+F (Command+F on Macs), and type in a bit of the text that's near the part of the page you want to change. For example, to change the comments section, you might search for "Leave a Reply" to jump to the heading that starts off the section. Many browsers make this process easier with a feature for homing in on the HTML in a specific part of a page (Figure 13-10).

Once you find the right place—roughly—the real hunt begins. Look at the elements just before your content, and check the *class* and *id* attributes for names you recognize, or that seem obvious. Pay special attention to the <div> element, which HTML pages use to group blocks of content, like sidebars, posts, menus, headers, and footers. You'll often find one <div> nested inside another, which lets the theme apply a layered tapestry of style settings (which is great for flexibility, but not so good when you're trying to understand exactly what rule is responsible for a specific formatting detail).

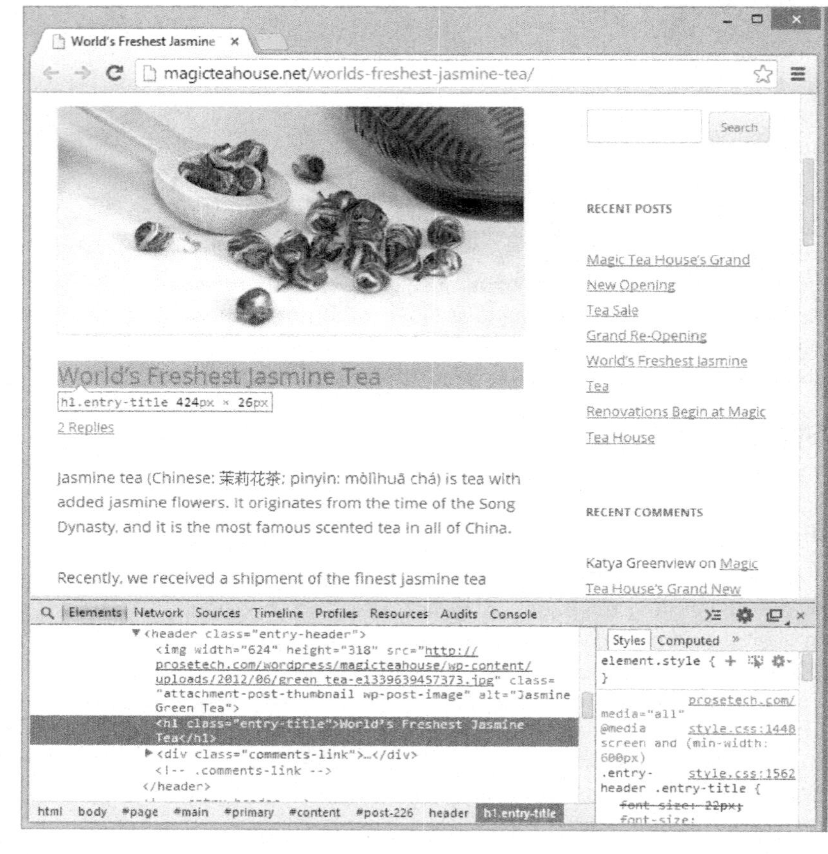

FIGURE 13-10

In the Firefox and Google Chrome browsers, there's an easy way to find the class name of an element without searching through all the HTML on a page. Just right-click the part of the page you want to examine and choose "Inspect element." A panel opens with the corresponding bit of HTML markup selected. That quickly tells you that the post title is an <h1> element with the class name entry-title (but you already knew that). In Internet Explorer, you need to first press F12 to open the Developer Tools panel. Then choose Find→"Select element by click" at the top of the panel and click the part of the page you want to examine.

TIP WordPress.com has a few helpful videos that show how to pinpoint individual elements in a web page, using different web browsers. You can watch these micro-overviews at *http://tinyurl.com/css-inspection.*

Once you have a potential class or ID name, it's time to experiment. Pop open the theme editor and add a new style rule that targets the section you identified. Do something obvious first, like changing the background color with the *background-color* property. That way, you can check your site and immediately determine if you found the right element.

Using Fancy Fonts

One of the most common reasons to edit the styles in a template is to change an element's font. In fact, it's often the case that all you need to do to turn a popular theme into something uniquely yours is to change some of the typefaces.

Originally, HTML pages were limited to a set of *web-safe fonts*. These are the typefaces every web surfer has seen, including stalwarts like Times New Roman, Arial, and Verdana. But web design has taken great strides forward in recent years with a CSS feature called *embedded fonts*. Essentially, embedded fonts let you use almost any typeface you want on your web pages—you just need to upload the font to your web server in the right format.

The embedded fonts feature has a few quirks. First, it doesn't work with older browsers, so you need to make sure your pages look respectable even if your visitor's browser can't load the embedded fonts. Second, although every modern browser supports embedded fonts, they don't all understand the same font files. For that reason, web designers often have to upload several copies of the fonts they want to use, each one in a different format. And, third, the CSS rule you write to use embedded fonts is a bit convoluted, which can make for a few unnecessary headaches.

Happily, you can sidestep all these problems by using a web font service like Google Web Fonts. There, you can pick from a huge gallery of attractive typefaces. When you find a font you want, Google spits out the CSS style rule for you. Best of all, Google *hosts* the font files on its high-powered web servers, in all the required formats, so you don't need to upload anything to your site.

TIP If you want to learn everything there is to know about web fonts, including how to host them on your website, write the CSS rules yourself, and web-ify your own fonts, check out *HTML5: The Missing Manual* (O'Reilly), which has a section all about embedded fonts.

To use a Google font on a WordPress site, follow these steps:

1. **Go to *www.google.com/fonts*.**

   Google displays a long list of fonts (Figure 13-11). At the time of this writing, there were well over 500 typefaces to choose from.

2. **When you see a font you like, click the "Pop out" button to take a closer look.**

   Google opens a font preview page that shows the font at different sizes.

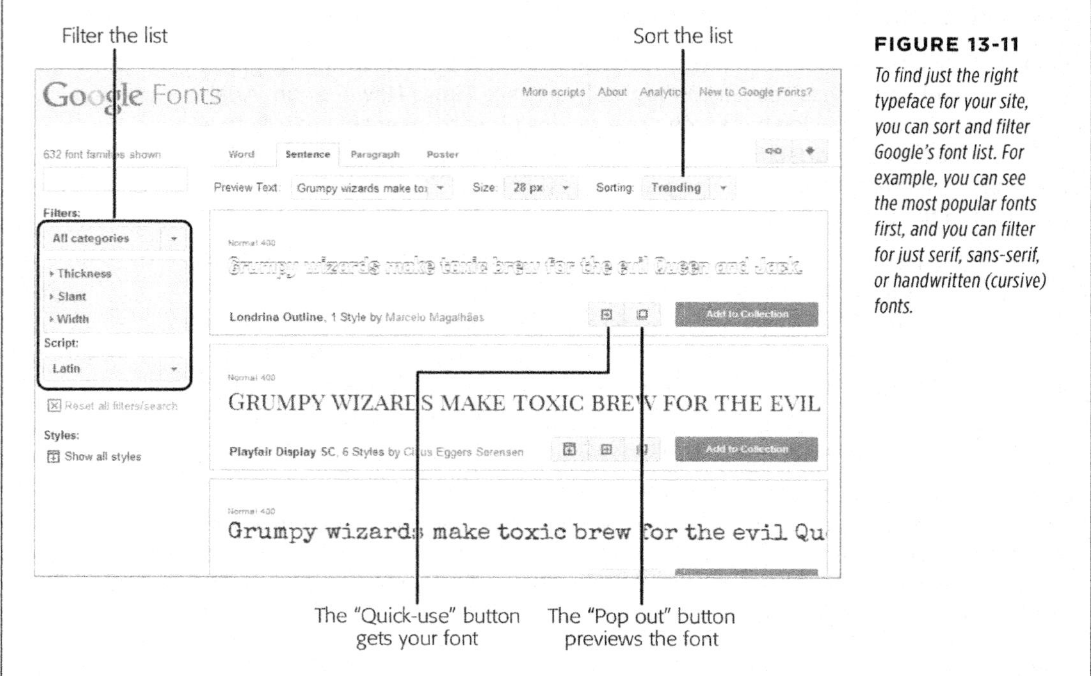

FIGURE 13-11

To find just the right typeface for your site, you can sort and filter Google's font list. For example, you can see the most popular fonts first, and you can filter for just serif, sans-serif, or handwritten (cursive) fonts.

3. **If you like the font, click the "Quick use" button.**

   Google shows you a page with information on how to use the font. It consists of a style sheet link (which you must add to your web page) and an example of a style sheet rule that uses the font.

TIP Google also lets you choose your favorite fonts from its site and put them in a personalized collection. If you do, Google gives you a few added features, like the ability to download a copy of the font to install on your computer for print work. Google also remembers the fonts you store in your collection when you return to the Google Web Fonts site.

4. **Scroll down the page until you find the blue set of tabs with the caption "Add this code your website" (Figure 13-12). Click the @import tab.**

   Google has created a ready-made style sheet for every font on its site. To use the font, you need to link that style sheet to your web page, or import Google's style sheet into *your* style sheet (that's the *style.css* file in the child theme). With WordPress, the second approach is easier.

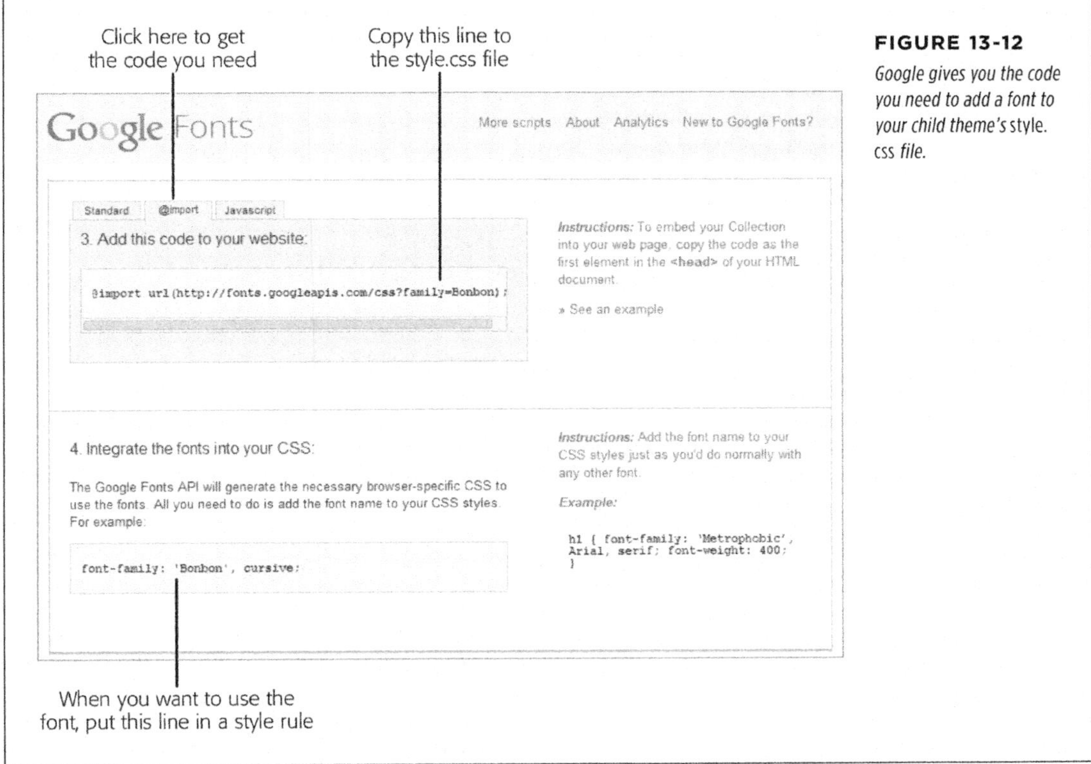

FIGURE 13-12

Google gives you the code you need to add a font to your child theme's style.css *file.*

5. **Copy the @import line and then paste it into your *style.css* file.**

   Put it right after the @import line for the standard Twenty Twelve styles.

TIP If you use several embedded fonts, you can add more than one @import command. However, there's a slightly more efficient approach—if you create a font collection, Google gives you a single @import line that grants you use of all the fonts you picked.

6. **Create a style that uses the font.**

   Once you import the Google style sheet, you can use your new font, by name, wherever you want. Just set the *font-family* property, as you would with a normal web-safe font. But remember to add a true web-safe font name after it as a fallback, in case you're dealing with an old-school browser that can't display embedded fonts or can't download the font file.

Here's a complete *style.css* file that uses this technique. The newly added parts are highlighted in bold.

```
/*
Theme Name: Twenty Twelve Reboot
Description: This is a customized version of the Twenty Twelve Theme for the
Magic Tea House.
Author: Katya Greenview
Template: twentytwelve

*/
@import url("../twentytwelve/style.css");
@import url(http://fonts.googleapis.com/css?family=Bonbon);

.entry-header .entry-title {
  font-family: 'Bonbon', 'Times New Roman';
  font-size: 30px;
}
```

Figure 13-13 shows this font in action in a post.

Magic Tea House's Grand New Opening

1 Reply

Are you crawling the walls without your latest tea fix? Well then, here's some welcome news: The Magic Tea House management is overjoyed to announce that renovations are finally complete and our Grand Opening is taking place June 29, from 11:00 AM to 6:00 PM!

On hand, we'll have the fantastic tea selection you've come to expect, live entertainment, resident tea expert Cheryl Braxton, clowns, balloons, and possibly even a green tea pinata. There will also be unbelievable tea specials (watch this space for announcements). So please stop by and say "Hi." We've missed you terribly.

This entry was posted in News, Uncategorized and tagged store on March 6, 2014.

FIGURE 13-13

The Bonbon font is perhaps not the best for this site, but it's impossible to deny that it makes for eye-catching post titles.

Editing the Code in Your Theme

When you want to customize the appearance of a theme, the first place you should look is the *style.css* file. But if you need to make more dramatic changes—for example, revamp the layout, change the information in the post list, or add new widget areas—you have to go further. Your next step is to consider the theme's *template files.*

A typical theme uses anywhere from a dozen to 50 templates. If you crack one open, you see a combination of HTML markup and PHP code. The PHP code is the magic ingredient—it triggers the specific WordPress actions that pull your content out of the database. Before WordPress sends a page to a visitor, it runs all the PHP code inside it.

Writing this code is a task that's well beyond the average WordPress website owner. But that's not a problem, because you don't need to write the code yourself, even if you're building a completely new theme. Instead, you take a ready-made page template that contains all the basic code and *edit* that file to your liking. Here are two ways you can do that:

- **Change the HTML markup.** Maybe you don't need to change the code in the template file at all. You might just need to modify the HTML that wraps around it. After all, it's the HTML (in conjunction with the style sheet) that determines how your content looks and where it appears.
- **Modify the PHP code.** You start with a template full of working code. Often, you can carefully modify this code, using the WordPress documentation, to change the way it works. For example, imagine you want the list of posts on the home page to show fewer posts, include just post titles or images instead of content, or show posts from a specific category. You can do all this by adjusting the code that's already in the home page template.

Of course, the more thoroughly you want to edit the PHP, the more you need to learn. Eventually, you might pick up enough skills to be an accomplished PHP tweaker.

UP TO SPEED

Learning PHP

The actual syntax of the PHP language is beyond the scope of this book. If you want to develop ninja programming skills, there are plenty of great resources for learning PHP, whether you have a programming background or are just starting out. Don't rush off just yet, however, because while learning PHP will definitely help you customize a WordPress theme, it may not help you as much as you expect.

Learning to customize a WordPress template is partially about learning PHP (because it helps to understand basic language details like loops, conditional logic, and functions). But it's *mostly* about learning to use WordPress's functions in PHP code (see the Note on page 493 for more about WordPress functions). For that reason, you'll probably get more practical value out of studying WordPress functions than learning the entire language, unless you plan to someday write dynamic web pages of your own.

To get started with WordPress functions, check out the function reference at *http://tinyurl.com/func-ref.* To learn more about PHP, start with the absolute basics with the tutorial at *http://tinyurl.com/ctzya55.*

Introducing the Template Files

Every theme uses a slightly different assortment of templates. The WordPress staple Twenty Twelve uses a fairly typical set of about 30 templates.

You can recognize a template by the fact that its filename ends with *.php*. Although template files hold a mix of HTML and PHP, the *.php* extension tells WordPress that there's code inside that the WordPress engine needs to run before it sends the final page to a browser.

Even though a template is just a mix of HTML and PHP, understanding where it fits into your site can be a bit of a challenge. That's because every page WordPress stitches together uses several template files.

For example, imagine you click through to a single post. WordPress has a template, called *single.php,* that creates the page on the fly. However, *single.php* needs help from a host of other templates. First, it inserts the contents of the *header.php* template, which sits at the top of every page in a WordPress site. The *header.php* file takes care of basics, like linking to the style sheet, registering some scripts, and showing the header section, complete with the top-level menu. (Some themes farm out the menu-creation work to yet another template file, but Twenty Twelve doesn't go that far.)

Next, the *single.php* file adds the Previous and Next navigation links to the post, and then calls out to another template to display the actual post. If it's a regular post, it uses *content.php,* but the Twenty Twelve theme has a number of specialized alternatives for different post formats. For example, an "aside" post (page 203) uses the *content-aside.php* template, a "status" post uses *content-status.php,* and so on.

Finally, the *single.php* template ends by calling three more templates into action. The *comments.php* template creates the comments section, the *sidebar.php* template adds the widgets on the right, and the *footer.php* template ends the page.

If you're going cross-eyed trying to follow this template assortment, Figure 13-14 shows how it all breaks down.

At first glance, this system seems just a bit bonkers. How better to complicate life than to split the code for a single page into a handful of template files that need to work together? But in typical WordPress fashion, the design is actually pretty brilliant. It means that a theme designer can create a single template file that governs a repeating site element—like a header—and use it everywhere, without needing to worry about duplicating effort or being inconsistent.

When you edit theme styles, your first challenge is finding the right style rule to change. When you edit *templates,* the first challenge is finding the right template file to modify. Table 13-2 can help you get started. It describes the fundamental templates that almost every theme, including Twenty Twelve, uses.

FIGURE 13-14

When you view a single post, the single.php template is in charge. It calls for help from several other templates.

Keep in mind, however, that themes commonly add extra templates to create the formats for different types of posts and pages, and to handle special formatting (for example, to create different layouts that move the sidebar around). You may also decide to add extra templates of your own (for example, to change the way your site presents specific categories or authors, a technique you'll see in Chapter 14).

TABLE 13-2 *Essential WordPress templates*

TEMPLATE FILE	DESCRIPTION
index.php	This is a theme's main template, and the only one that's absolutely required. WordPress uses it if there's no other, more specific template to use. Most themes use *index.php* to display a list of posts on the home page.
header.php	Displays the banner that appears across the top of every page. Often, *header.php* includes a navigation menu.
footer.php	Displays the footer that stretches across the bottom of every page.
sidebar.php	Shows the sidebar widget area. Twenty Twelve also has a more specialized *sidebar-front.php* template that creates the footer area for pages that use the Front Page template.
single.php	Displays a single post.
page.php	Shows a static page. Themes often have additional page templates that let you create different "flavors" of pages (page 233). For example, Twenty Twelve adds a *full-width.php* template that creates a page that doesn't include a sidebar and a *front-page.php* template that includes a two-column widget area in the footer.
content.php	Displays the content of a post or page. Some themes create many different content templates, for different types of posts and pages. Twenty Twelve, for instance, has eight content templates. An ordinary post uses *content.php*, a page uses *content-page.php*, and special post formats (page 202) use a corresponding template (for example, asides use *content-aside.php*).
comments.php	Displays the comments section after a post or page.
image.php	Shows the attachment page for images—what you see when you click a picture in a post, if you've set the Link To setting (page 336) to Attachment Page.
archive.php	Lists posts when you browse by author, category, tag, or date. Or you can use one of the four more specific templates listed next.
category.php	Lists posts when you browse a category. You can also create templates that target specific categories, like *category-tea.php* for a category with "tea" as its simplified name (page 123).

TEMPLATE FILE	DESCRIPTION
tag.php	Lists posts when you browse by tag. You can also create templates that target specific tags, like *tag-promotion.php*.
author.php	Lists posts when you browse by author. You can also create templates that target specific authors, like *author-grabinksy.php*.
search.php	Lists posts after you execute a search.
404.php	Displays an error message when the requested post or page can't be found.

A Basic Editing Example

By this point, you've digested a fair bit of WordPress theory. It's time to capitalize on that by editing a template file.

You'll begin with an example that seems simple enough. You want to remove the "Proudly powered by WordPress" message that appears at the bottom of every page on your site, just under the footer widgets (Figure 13-15). (It's not that you're embarrassed by WordPress. You just can't help but notice that none of the other big-gun WordPress sites have this message slapped on their pages. Sometimes, being professional means being discreet.)

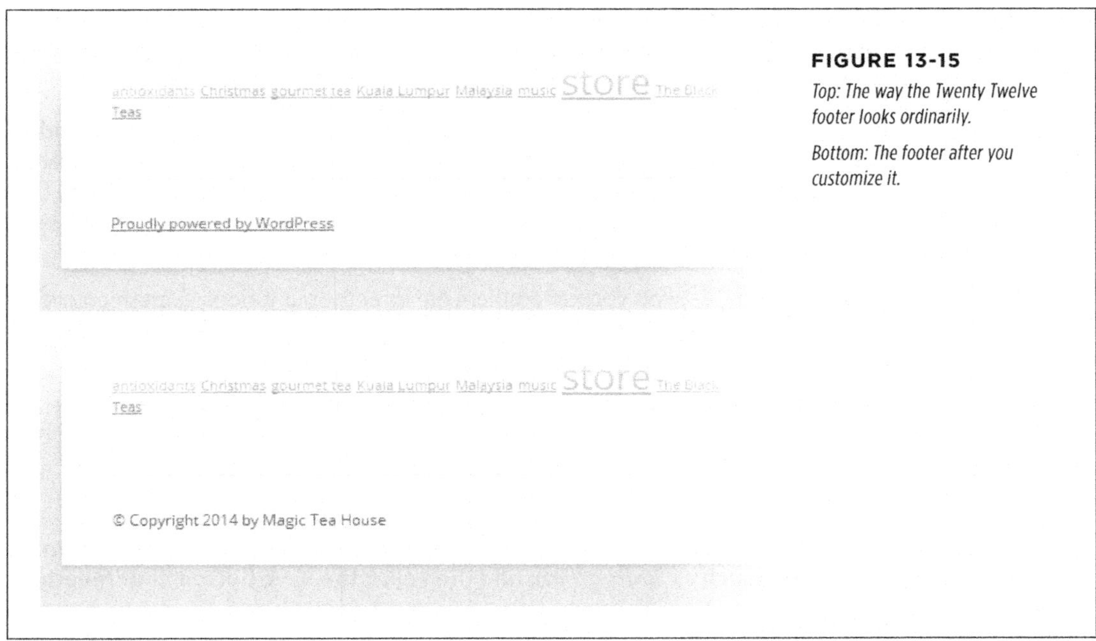

FIGURE 13-15

Top: The way the Twenty Twelve footer looks ordinarily.

Bottom: The footer after you customize it.

STEP 1. FIND THE TEMPLATE FILE

Start by examining the list of templates in Table 13-2. In this case, the *footer.php* file is the obvious candidate. It creates the entire footer section, widgets and all, for every page.

STEP 2. CREATE A COPY OF THE TEMPLATE FILE

Once again, you need to start with a child theme (page 462). If you don't, you can still customize the footer, but your hard-won changes will vaporize the moment you install a theme update.

Here's where things get a bit more awkward. As you know, WordPress templates are really a collection of many template files. To change a template, you need to figure out the changes you want to make to your pages, and then find the template file responsible for that part of the page (*single.php, comment.php,* and so on). Then you add a new version of that template file to the child theme. That new template will override the one in the parent theme.

You do this by copying the template file you want to edit from the parent theme to your child theme and then making your changes. In this example, that means you need to copy the *footer.php* file in the *twentytwelve* folder and paste it into the *twenty-twelve-reboot* folder.

Unfortunately, the dashboard doesn't have any tools to help you copy a template. The quickest and most straightforward solution is to use an FTP tool. First, copy the file (say, *footer.php*) from the parent theme folder (*twentytwelve*) to your computer. Second, copy that file from your computer to the child theme folder (*twenty-twelve-reboot*). Job done. You can now choose Appearance→Editor and start modifying the newly copied template.

If you don't feel comfortable doing that, it's plug-in time. This time, the solution is the Orbisius Child Theme Creator (*http://tinyurl.com/orb-theme*), which creates child themes and helps you create and copy templates. Install it, activate it, and then choose Appearance→Orbisius Theme Editor. You see a two-part page that lets you view and edit two themes side by side (Figure 13-16).

Orbisius doesn't let you copy a template file directly, but it does something almost as good: It lets you create a new blank template file in your child theme, and then copy the content of the parent's template into that new file. Here's how:

1. **In the Theme #1 box, pick your child theme, if it isn't already selected.**
2. **Underneath the editing box on the left, click New File.**

   A few more options drop into view.

3. **In the New File text box, type the exact name of the template you want to create (such as *footer.php*), and then click the Save button underneath.**

   This creates a new template file in your child theme and loads it up in the editing box on the left. However, there's nothing in the file yet.

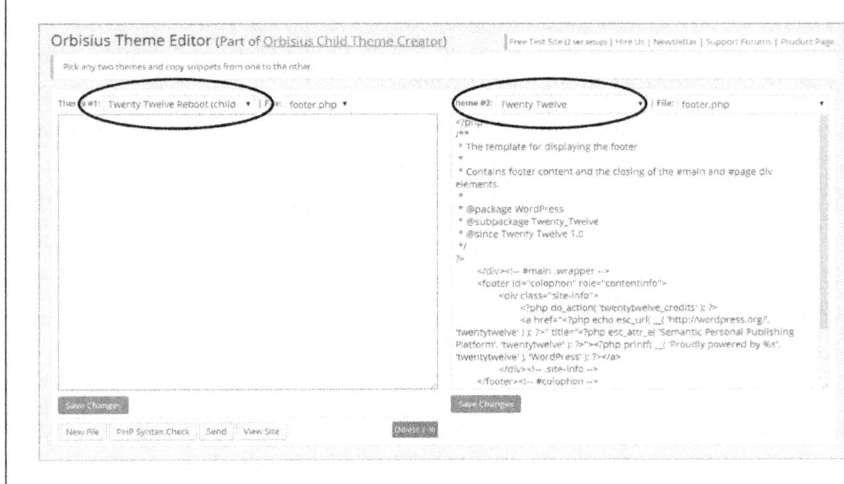

FIGURE 13-16

Using the Orbisius Theme Editor plug-in, you can compare any two themes by picking from the Theme #1 and Theme #2 lists. However, it makes the most sense to load up your current child theme on the left (which Orbisius does automatically) and choose the parent theme on the right.

4. **In the Theme #2 box, pick your parent theme. Then, in the adjacent File box, pick the name of the template you want to copy.**

   In this case, that's *footer.php*. When you pick a file, you see the content of the template in the editing box underneath.

5. **Copy the template markup from the old template file (on the right) to the new template file (on the left).**

   To do this, select the full text of the markup in the original template file on the right (in this case, that's *footer.php*). Click at the very beginning of the file and then press Ctrl+A (Command+A on a Mac) to select all the content. Then press Ctrl+C (Command+C on a Mac) to copy the content. Lastly, click in the blank editing box on the left, and then press Ctrl+V (Command+V on a Mac) to paste it in.

6. **Click Save Changes underneath the editing box on the left.**

   Now the new template in your child theme has the same content as the original template in the parent theme. This is the best starting point for your changes.

   From this point on, it makes no difference whether you edit the new template file in the Orbisius page or in the Edit Themes page (which you open by choosing Appearance→Editor).

NOTE The child theme's version of a template completely overrides the parent theme's copy of the template. In this example, that means WordPress ignores the original version of the *footer.php* file, which is in the original theme folder (*twentytwelve*). You can refer to it anytime to check the code or copy important bits, but WordPress won't run the code anymore.

STEP 3. EXAMINE THE TEMPLATE FILE

Footer.php is one of WordPress's simpler template files. But even simple templates have a fair bit of boilerplate to wade through.

In this section, you'll look at the entire contents of *footer.php*. You don't always need to take this step, but it's good practice when you're just starting out and trying to make sense of WordPress's template system.

If you've written web pages before, you probably know that programming code, like JavaScript, needs to be carefully separated from the HTML on the page. The same is true for PHP, although it has its own special syntax. Every time a block of PHP code appears, it starts with this:

```
<?php
```

Similarly, the following character sequence marks the end of a block of PHP code:

```
?>
```

You can see this system at work at the very beginning of every template file, where there's a block of PHP that has no real code at all, just a long comment. The comment lists some basic information about the template. Here's what you see in *footer.php:*

```
<?php
/**
 * The template for displaying the footer.
 *
 * Contains footer content and the closing of the #main and #page div ele-
ments.
 *
 * @package WordPress
 * @subpackage Twenty_Twelve
 * @since Twenty Twelve 1.0
 */
?>
```

The next line is a puzzling bit of HTML that looks like this:

```
</div><!-- #main .wrapper -->
```

Even seasoned HTML veterans will be a bit thrown off here. The </div> tag closes a <div> element. But you haven't seen an opening <div> tag, so this code snippet seems a bit strange.

It makes more sense when you remember the way WordPress stitches together a page, as shown in Figure 13-14. The <div> element *was* opened, but it happened when WordPress processed an earlier template file (*header.php*). The HTML comment in the line above (`<!--#main .wrapper -->`) is WordPress's way of reminding you that the </div> in that line is the closing element for a <div> that has the ID *main* and the class *.wrapper*. In other words, it's the closing element for the <div> that holds the main content of the page.

The next line of HTML is easier to interpret. It identifies the beginning of the footer content. This section has the ID *colophon,* which you might remember from Table 13-1.

```
<footer id="colophon" role="contentinfo">
```

The next line starts a new <div> element and gives it the ID *site-info.* The creators of the Twenty Twelve theme chose that name because this is the section of the page that indicates some basic information about how the site was created (in other words, "Proudly powered by WordPress").

```
<div id="site-info">
```

The next bit is another block of PHP code, but it's compressed into a single line:

```
<?php do_action( 'twentytwelve_credits' ); ?>
```

The `do_action()` function is a WordPress feature found throughout its template files. It's a notification mechanism—it signals when something is about to happen (for example, that the page credits are about to be shown). Hardcore WordPress developers can write instructions that react to one of these notifications, but the `do_action()` function is no help in your mission to change the footer.

NOTE A *function* is a block of programming code stored somewhere other than the page it appears on. WordPress is full of useful functions, and `do_action()` is one of many. To browse the full catalog of functions and find out what they do, visit *http://tinyurl.com/func-ref.*

The section that appears after the `do_action()` function is the part of the footer template you've been looking for. It's a link that displays the "Proudly powered" message:

```
<a href=
 "<?php echo esc_url( __( 'http://wordpress.org/', 'twentytwelve' ) ); ?>"
 title= "<?php esc_attr_e( 'Semantic Personal Publishing Platform',
 'twentytwelve'); ?>" rel="generator">
  <?php printf( __( 'Proudly powered by %s', 'twentytwelve' ),
  'WordPress'); ?>
</a>
```

The markup looks a bit complicated, because there are three PHP code statements embedded inside the <a> element. The first one generates the actual link address, the second one generates the title, and the third one generates the text inside the <a> element. You don't need to understand exactly how these statements work to realize that this is the part you want to change. But first, scan through the rest of the footer template to make sure you understand what's going on.

It's pretty straightforward. First, *footer.php* closes the <div> and <footer> elements. Then it closes another <div> that represents the entire page.

```
    </div><!-- .site-info -->
  </footer><!-- #colophon -->
</div><!-- #page -->
```

Next, the footer template triggers WordPress's `wp_footer()` function.

```
<?php wp_footer(); ?>
```

This is a bit of WordPress infrastructure. Many plug-ins wait for this call and then do something important. Removing this line can cause those plug-ins to break, so it's best to leave it in, even though it isn't doing anything right now.

Finally, the template closes the <body> and <html> elements, proving that you have really and truly reached the end of the page. WordPress won't call any more templates into action, or add any more content after this point.

```
</body>
</html>
```

STEP 4. MAKE YOUR CHANGE

Now you've found the culprit—the piece of the WordPress template you want to change. In this example, it's a single <a> element.

You could delete the <a> element completely, or you can replace it with some text of your own, like this:

```
&copy; Copyright 2014 Magic Tea House
```

The `©` is a *character entity,* an HTML code that inserts a special character—in this case, a copyright symbol.

If you consider yourself a bit of a PHP whiz, you can get fancier in your footer. For example, instead of sticking in the current year for the copyright notice, you could ask PHP to *do that for you.*

First, you need to explicitly tell WordPress that you need PHP's help. You do that by adding the `<?php` and `?>` character sequences. You'll put your code inside.

```
&copy; Copyright <?php [ Your code goes here. ] ?> by Magic Tea House
```

Next, you need a PHP command. In this case, it's the trusty `echo` command, which means (in PHP language) "take the result of the next statement, and spit it out onto the page."

```
&copy; Copyright <?php echo ?> by Magic Tea House
```

But what exactly do you want to spit out? That's the current date, which you can fetch with the help of a function built into the PHP language, called `date()`. Unsurprisingly, the `date()` function displays the current date. But by supplying the capital letter *Y*, you tell the `date()` function that you're interested only in getting the current year.

```
&copy; Copyright <?php echo date('Y'); ?> by Magic Tea House
```

Like every line of PHP code, you indicate the end of a statement by adding a semicolon at the end (;)

This completes the example, and drives home a clear point: Even the most straightforward theme-editing tasks require a bit of slogging.

TIP Since the changes you need to make to the *footer.php* template are relatively small in this example, it's easy enough to do all your editing in the dashboard. For more significant changes, you may want to copy the theme file to a text editor on your computer, work with it there, and then copy it back to the Edit Themes page when you finish. And if you decide to edit a theme on your computer, it's worth considering a text editor that has a few more frills. For example, Windows users can grab the free Notepad++ program (*http://notepad-plus-plus.org*), which uses color-coded text to distinguish the different ingredients in PHP code.

FREQUENTLY ASKED QUESTION

Updating a Child Theme

What happens when I update a theme that uses customized templates?

Child templates don't work in exactly the same as child styles. Child styles extend style rules already put in place by the parent theme. Even if the parent gets a new, updated *style.css* file, the child styles remain, and WordPress applies them on top of the parent styles.

But page templates don't extend parent templates, they *replace* them. As soon as you add *footer.php* to your child theme, WordPress starts ignoring the *footer.php* in the original theme. That means that if you update the parent theme and change the original *footer.php* file, no one really notices.

This is probably the safest way to handle theme updates, because there really isn't a way that WordPress could combine two versions of a template. However, it means that if you plan to customize all the templates in a theme, you probably shouldn't create a child theme. Instead, you may as well build a completely separate theme of your own.

Delving into the Loop

WordPress experts talk in hushed tones about "the loop," which is the heart of WordPress. Its job is to fetch content from your website's database, one piece at a time, until it reaches the post limit (that's the "Blog pages show at most" option in the Settings→Reading section of the dashboard).

The loop appears in many templates. WordPress uses it to create the main list of posts on the home page (*index.php*), the list of results after a search (*search.php*), and the list of articles you see when you browse by category, tag, author, or date (*category.php, tag.php, author.php,* and *date.php,* or *archive.php* when one of the former is missing). The loop even appears on Twenty Twelve's showcase page (*showcase.php*), twice—first to grab the featured posts that it puts up top, and again to grab the recent posts that it shows underneath. (Showcase pages are explained on page 236.)

In the following example, you'll take a look at the loop in the *index.php* file and change the way it works by adding a new feature: the ability to highlight recent posts (Figure 13-17).

STEP 1. PREPARE THE TEMPLATE FILE

Your first task is to prepare your template. You can copy the *index.php* file into your child theme folder using an FTP program, or you can use the Orbisius Child Theme Creator plug-in to copy it for you.

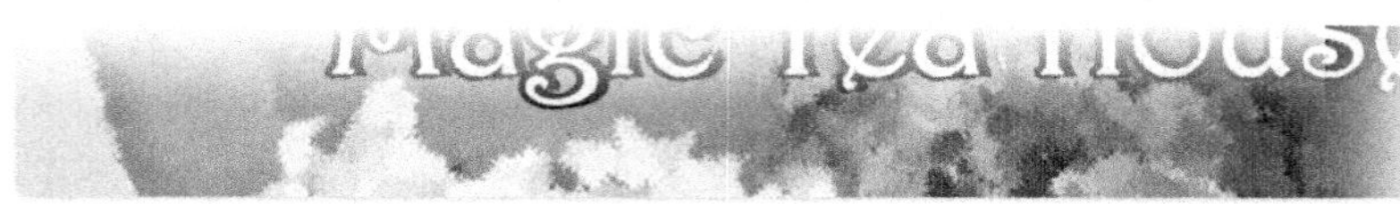

Tea Sale
Leave a reply
For a limited time, our Oriental Gold and Jade Express teas are offered at a staggering 60% off! Come by our store and enjoy these enchanting exotics while we still have them.
This entry was posted in Uncategorized on April 8, 2014. Edit
Crystal Jasmine Named Tea of the Year
Leave a reply
We're greatly honored to announce that our exclusive shipment of Crystal Jasmine tea, won the 2014 "Tea of the Year" challenge at the Nation Tea Drinkers Colloquium in Seattle. We're talking to our suppliers now to see if we can bring back a similarly exquisite vintage in the 2015 season.
This entry was posted in Uncategorized on April 1, 2014. Edit
Magic Tea House's Grand New Opening
1 Reply
RECENT POSTS
Tea Sale
RECENT COMMENTS
ARCHIVES
April 2014
March 2014
February 2014
September 2013
August 2013
July 2013
June 2012
May 2012

FIGURE 13-17 *This page gives the "Tea Sale" post, which was published today, preferential treatment—it gets a bigger headline, a border, and a yellow background. Tomorrow, the post will revert to its normal look.*

STEP 2. EXAMINE THE TEMPLATE FILE

The next step is to dig through *index.php* to get a handle on what's going on and what area you need to change. Overall, *index.php* has this structure:

```
<?php get_header(); ?>

<div id="primary">
  <div id="content" role="main">

    [ The stuff for displaying posts goes here. ]
```

```
  </div><!-- #content -->
</div><!-- #primary -->

<?php get_sidebar(); ?>
<?php get_footer(); ?>
```

This boils the template down to its essentials. As you can see, the template calls other templates to create the page's header, sidebar, and footer. In the middle of this action are two <div> elements, and inside them is the heart of the *index.php* template and the loop. This is the part you'll focus on.

The first ingredient here, inside the <div> elements, is a block of *conditional logic*—code that tests a condition, and takes different actions depending on whether that condition is true or false. Essentially, the template here uses PHP to ask a question: Are there any posts?

Here's how the template structures the conditional logic:

```
<?php if ( have_posts() ) : ?>

  [ If there are posts, you end up here. ]

<?php else : ?>

  [ If there are no posts, this section shows the "sorry" message.]

<?php endif; ?>
```

The `have_posts()` function gets the answer to the question, "Are there any posts?" If there are, the condition is true, and the first section springs into action. That's the part you're interested in. (If there aren't any posts, the condition is false, and you can let the template handle it in the usual fashion, by showing an apologetic message.)

So what takes place inside the first section, which runs as long as your site has at least one post? The code starts by adding a navigation link, if necessary. This is the link that appears before the post list and lets visitors step forward to newer posts. (If your guest is already viewing the most recent post, this link doesn't show up.) Then the code triggers the loop (shown here in bold), and ends by inserting another navigation link—the one that lets readers step back to see older posts.

```
<?php twentytwelve_content_nav( 'nav-above' ); ?>

<?php while ( have_posts() ) : the_post(); ?>
  <?php get_template_part( 'content', get_post_format() ); ?>
<?php endwhile; ?>

<?php twentytwelve_content_nav( 'nav-below' ); ?>
```

The actual loop comes down to just three lines. The `while` and `endwhile` commands delineate the start and end of the loop. As long as you have posts, the loop keeps running. Every time it runs, it grabs a post, using the WordPress function `the_post()`, and feeds it to the single line of code inside. This code is less exciting—it simply farms out the work of displaying the post to one of the content templates you learned about earlier, using the `get_template_part()` function.

Although the code doesn't seem that exciting right now, there's a lot you can do if you wedge yourself inside the loop, between the `while` and `endwhile` lines. Currently, there's just a single line of code there, but you can expand it to suit your needs. For example, before the code calls `get_template_part()` to display a post, you can run some extra code that does something more clever, like change the post's formatting based on one of the post details. Examples include making the post look different based on its category, author, or publication date. The latter is what this example does.

STEP 3. ADD NEW CODE

The final step is to add the code that checks the post's date and decides whether or not to highlight it. Here it is, inside the loop you saw earlier. The new code is boldfaced:

```
<?php while ( have_posts() ) : the_post(); ?>
  <?php
    $postdate = get_the_date('Y-m-d');
    $currentdate =
      date('Y-m-d',mktime(0,0,0,date('m'),date('d'),date('Y')));

    if ($postdate == $currentdate) {
      echo '<div class="newpost">';
    } else {
      echo '<div>';
    }
  ?>

  <?php get_template_part( 'content', get_post_format() ); ?>
  </div>
<?php endwhile; ?>
```

To understand what's taking place, you need to examine the code one line at a time. First, it uses a WordPress function named `get_the_date()`, which returns the date the current post was published.

```
$postdate = get_the_time('Y-m-d');
```

WordPress takes the result from `get_the_date()` and puts it into a variable (a storage slot in memory) named `$postdate`. That way, the code can use the date stored there at a later time, when the function compares dates.

NOTE It doesn't matter what you call your variables, as long as you're consistent. (So you can't call the variable `$postdate` in one place and `$date_of_post` in another, because you'll end up creating two separate variables.) However, your variable names must start with the dollar sign ($), which has the side effect of making them easily recognizable.

The next line of code creates a second variable, named `$currentdate`. It stores the current date, as retrieved by the PHP `date()` function, which you saw earlier (page 494). Only now the date is returned in a slightly different format, so it matches up with the publication date format WordPress uses with posts.

```
$currentdate = date('Y-m-d');
```

The moment of drama occurs next. An `if` statement compares the two variables (in this case, the two dates) to see if the current date matches the publication date (in other words, to see if the post was published today). If the answer is yes, then the code adds a new <div> element, with the class name *newpost*.

```
if ($postdate == $currentdate) {
   echo '<div class="newpost">';
```

If the answer is no, then the code adds a <div> that doesn't use any class name.

```
} else {
 echo '<div>';
 }
?>
```

Either way, the code tacks on the closing </div> element at the end of this block of content, after it inserts the post content into the page.

```
<?php get_template_part( 'content', get_post_format() ); ?>
</div>
```

NOTE This code may seem slightly magical, because it relies on a tight combination of PHP commands and WordPress functions that you haven't seen before. Obviously, you wouldn't be able to cook up this sort of code on your own. However, you *will* be able to grab this sort of code from one of the many WordPress recipe sites (page 503), and insert it into your templates when you need it. And the more you do that, the easier it'll be to recognize the code you want to change, and the more comfortable you'll be adjusting that code to solve a problem.

STEP 4. ADD A NEW STYLE

Right now, the revised template doesn't have much of an effect. All it does is add a <div> element around the post content. However, this <div> gives you a new way to apply a customized style. You do that by creating a style rule for the *newpost* class.

Here are the style rules that create the effect shown in Figure 13-17. The first rule adds the border, spacing, and background color around the post. The second rule targets the link in the heading, which holds the post title, and gives it large red text.

```
.newpost {
  padding: 8px;
  border: 2px solid darkgray;
  border-radius: 10px;
  background-color: lightyellow;
  margin-bottom: 50px;
}

.newpost h1 a {
  font-size: 2.5em;
  color: red;
}
```

This two-part approach—using the PHP code to add a style, and then defining the style—is a common technique in theme customization. It gives you the most flexibility, because you can change the formatting anytime, without editing the template and wading through the PHP again.

Extending WordPress with Functions.php

Some WordPress themes contain one PHP file that isn't a template, named *functions.php*. Experienced theme designers place important parts of their code here, and then call that code from their template files when they need it. WordPress gurus also use the *functions.php* file to add other features, like new shortcodes and widgets, so they don't need to create a complete plug-in.

All these tasks are advanced operations, best kept to WordPress gurus. However, even people with no PHP experience can use the *functions.php* file to unlock extra WordPress features. Usually, you do that by copying a few lines of code you read about online (or in a book), and pasting them into the *functions.php* file in the theme editor.

For example, in Chapter 10, you used WordPress's auto-embed feature to turn certain types of website addresses into embedded objects, like Flickr slideshows and YouTube videos. Normally, WordPress turns off this handy feature in widget areas, like the sidebar. But those in the know can enable shortcodes and embeds in widget areas with just a couple of lines in the *functions.php* file. Figure 13-18 shows the result.

The *functions.php* file works a bit differently from the template files you've learned about so far. The key quirk is that the *functions.php* file in your child theme *extends* the *functions.php* file in your parent theme; it doesn't replace it. For that reason, you can't simply copy the *functions.php* file from your parent theme to your child theme. You need to create a new, empty text file on your computer, change its name to *functions.php,* and then upload that new *functions.php* file to your child theme folder.

If you use the Orbisius Child Theme Creator plug-in, your job is easy. Follow the process described on page 490 to create a new, blank *functions.php* file, but don't copy any content to that file.

April 2014
March 2014
February 2014
September 2013
August 2013
July 2013
June 2012
May 2012

VIDEO BOX

An auto-embed in a widget:

FIGURE 13-18

This sidebar holds a miniature YouTube video, courtesy of the Text widget and the auto-embed feature.

WARNING If you accidentally copy the *functions.php* file from your parent theme to your child theme, your site will stop working. That's because *functions.php* is full of important routines that Twenty Twelve uses, and having two copies of this code is enough to blow WordPress's mind. The only fix (if you disregard this warning and put the full *functions.php* file in your child theme folder) is to log in to your site with an FTP program and delete the copied *functions.php* file.

Once you add the blank *functions.php* file to your site, you can edit it in the Edit Theme page, as you can any other theme file. To enable widget-embedding, as shown in Figure 13-18, you need to add these lines:

```
<?php
  add_filter( 'widget_text', array( $wp_embed, 'run_shortcode' ), 8);
  add_filter( 'widget_text', array( $wp_embed, 'autoembed'), 8 );
?>
```

Now you can put an auto-embed URL in a Text widget, just as you can in a post (Figure 13-19).

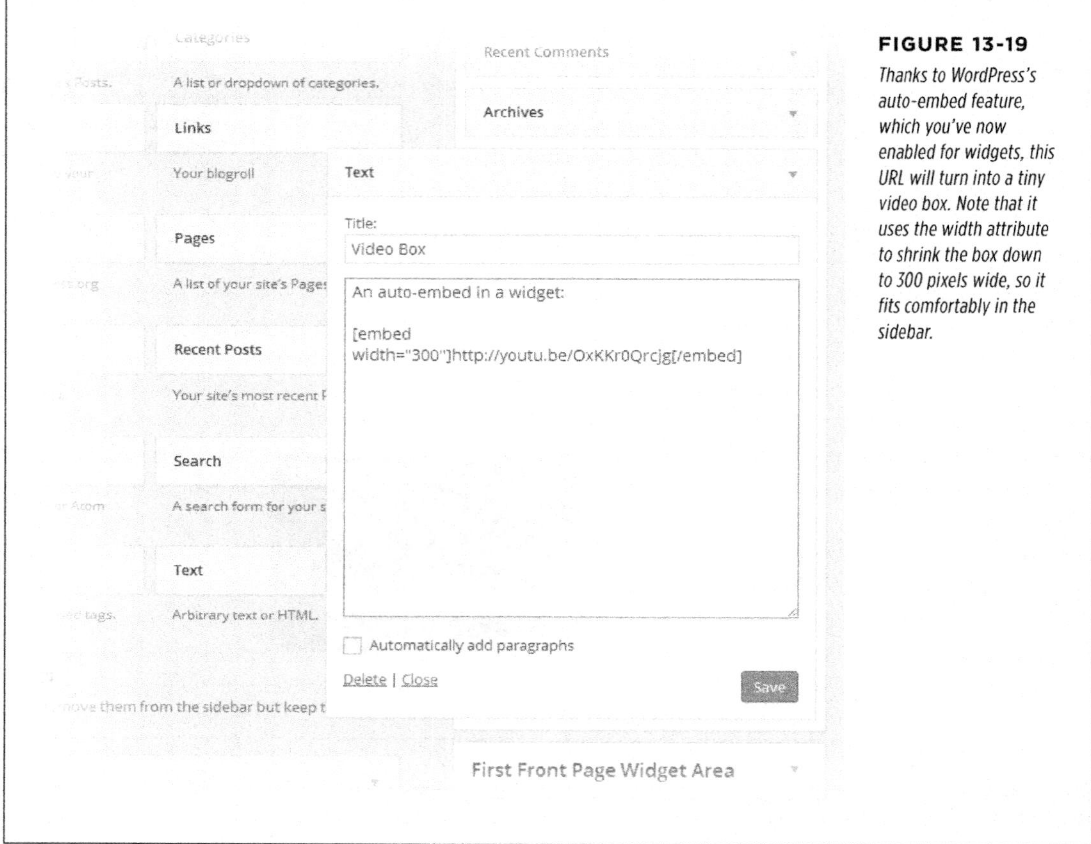

FIGURE 13-19

Thanks to WordPress's auto-embed feature, which you've now enabled for widgets, this URL will turn into a tiny video box. Note that it uses the width attribute to shrink the box down to 300 pixels wide, so it fits comfortably in the sidebar.

POWER USERS' CLINIC

Learning More About Theme Customization

This chapter offers a glimpse of the styles, templates, and PHP code that underpins WordPress. Even if you don't understand how it all works (and most people don't), you still know enough to start making template changes. You may need trial-and-error experimentation to get the result you want, and you may need to search for other people's hacks and tricks to help you out (Google is your friend). But as long as you're not afraid to open a template file, look inside, and make changes, you have the potential to change anything.

In the next chapter, you'll methodically explore a complete end-to-end site example. In the meantime, it's worth pointing out some resources you can use to develop your theme-tweaking skills:

- **Template recipes.** You can practice a grab bag of simple theme tricks at *http://tinyurl.com/templatetrix*. They're divided into short, practical chunks. The more you try out, the more comfortable you'll become navigating the tangled maze of templates that constitute a theme.
- **Blogs by WordPress pros.** Lorelle van Fossen (*http://lorelle.wordpress.com*) has acres of practical content about customizing WordPress sites, including many adventures in theme customization.
- **Smashing Magazine.** If you're looking to get more serious, Smashing Magazine (*http://wp.smashingmagazine.com*) has hardcore articles about every aspect of WordPress site development. They often go far beyond ordinary features and deep into theme customization.
- **Theme frameworks.** Theme frameworks extend the core WordPress code with new features. The cost is extra complexity, although you won't need to fiddle with low-level details and PHP code anymore. Popular examples include Thematic (*http://tinyurl.com/themat*), which is free, and Genesis (*http://tinyurl.com/gen-theme*), which isn't.

CHAPTER

14

Building an Advanced WordPress Site

In the previous chapter, you learned how to stretch WordPress's capabilities by editing your theme files. You saw how a few small changes, like adding a style rule or changing a section of PHP code, let you customize details that would ordinarily be out of reach.

Tinkering with your WordPress theme is a great way to make a number of small but genuinely useful tweaks to your site. But once you start poking around the inner workings of a theme, you open the door to a more ambitious endeavor: reworking the entire theme to create a completely customized site.

In this chapter, you'll learn how to modify a theme by creating a showcase site for the furniture company Distinct Furnishings. You'll see how to create a browsable product catalog, with custom post types and custom category pages. You'll even get a taste of ecommerce with a simple, yet functional, shopping cart powered by PayPal.

NOTE The theme customizing you'll do in this chapter is just a first step in a long journey, but it's a valuable one even if you choose not to design your own theme from scratch. That's because the more you know about the inner workings of WordPress, the better you can evaluate themes you might want to use, and the more successful you'll be if you decide to customize a theme.

Planning Your Site

The first step to building an advanced, customized site is to get out a notepad and start planning. Before you set fingers to keyboard, you should ask (and answer) a few questions:

- What type of content will your site feature?
- How will your content be arranged, and how will visitors browse your site?
- Will your content use posts or pages or both?
- Do you need to create separate types of posts for different content?

It's important to think about these questions early on, because you need to consider how you want visitors to interact with your site. And that, in turn, determines the kind of changes you need to make to your theme. In the case of Distinct Furnishings, for example, the site's job is to display information about the different pieces of furniture the company sells. Visitors will arrive at the site and browse through the items that interest them. Essentially, the Distinct Furnishings site is a *product catalog,* which is a common type of advanced WordPress site.

Picking a Theme

Every WordPress theme has similar underpinnings, but no two themes are quite the same. If you start out editing a theme that isn't well suited to your site, you'll create extra work for yourself. So before you commit to a theme, make sure you've got the best, most workable one for your needs.

There are many ways to pick a good theme for customization:

- Some WordPressers pick one they understand (like Twenty Twelve) and use that in all their customization projects.
- Some web designers pick a theme that's as close as possible to the final result they want. This means they have much less customization to do, but it also forces them to spend time learning the subtly different workings of a new template.
- Some WordPress pros use a heavily stripped-down theme, which provides very little beyond the core WordPress code. This way, they don't need to worry about removing built-in features and embellishments they don't want, but it also means they need to supply the majority of the markup and styles that format the site, which takes time and requires some serious web design skills.
- Some WordPressers favor theme frameworks, which are simple, foundational themes designed for other developers to extend. The drawback is choice and complexity: There are many theme frameworks to choose from, and they all have their own subtly different structure. (To learn more, read what WordPress has to say at *http://tinyurl.com/theme-f.*)

The Distinct Furnishings site follows the second approach. It uses the PinBlack theme (*http://tinyurl.com/pinblack*), which already has most of the right layout and formatting in place (Figure 14-1).

Before you go any further, you need to decide whether you want to work on a child theme (page 462) or the original theme files. As you learned in Chapter 13, child themes are always the right choice when you make cosmetic changes to a theme you love. They're also a good idea if you plan to make targeted changes to specific aspects of a theme, while leaving the rest of it alone. But if you plan to make extensive changes that will require you to modify most of the template files in a theme, a child theme doesn't make as much sense. Since you'll override almost all the functionality in the original template, there's little reason to use a child theme that retains its relationship with its parent.

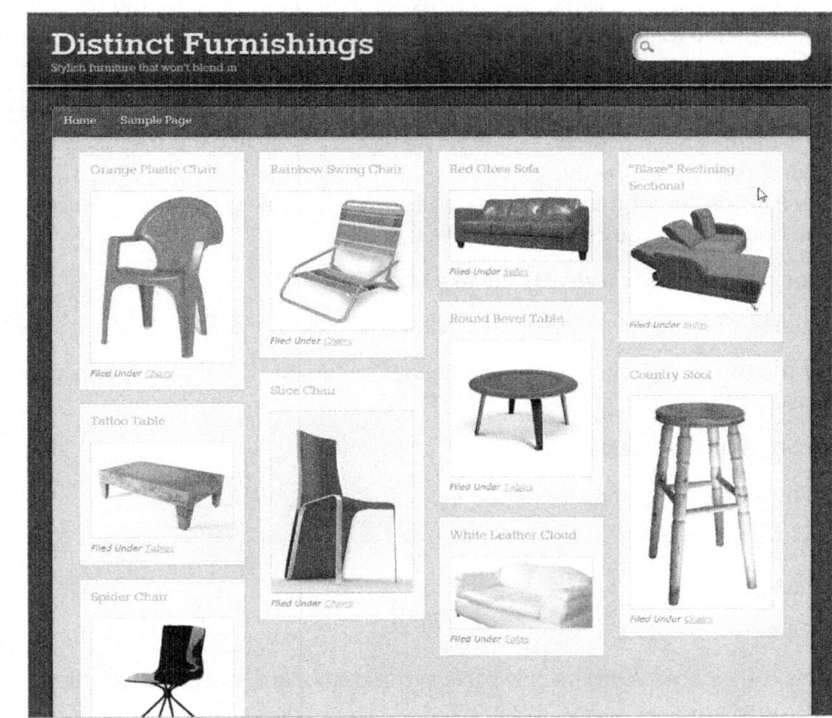

FIGURE 14-1

PinBlack is a portfolio theme that arranges posts in a grid of packed-together tiles. Each one includes the title of the post (that's the product name in this case), its featured image, and its category ("Filed Under"). This makes PinBlack an almost perfect theme for browsing products, except that it orders the posts based on their publication date.

Once again, there's no clear-cut answer for all situations. It depends on how complex a theme you start with, and how heavily you plan on customizing it.

- If you decide to create a child theme that *extends* an original theme, follow the instructions on page 463.
- If you decide to create a completely new theme that *replaces* the original theme, continue reading the next section. This is the approach the Distinct Furnishings example follows with the PinBlack theme.

Creating a Custom Copy of a Theme

In theory, you can edit any theme in the dashboard without taking any special steps. But doing so is risky. Eventually, the creator of the original theme will distribute an update, and it's all too easy to accidentally install the update and wipe out all your carefully crafted customizations.

To protect yourself, create a copy of the theme that WordPress won't ever try to update. Here's how:

1. **Download the theme files to your computer.**

   You can do this two ways. One is to use an FTP program and drag the appropriate theme folder (say, *pinblack*) from your site's */wp-content/themes* folder to your computer.

   The other option is to visit the WordPress themes directory at *http://wordpress.org/themes*. Search for the theme you're using, view it, and then click Download. WordPress stores the theme files in a ZIP file. Double-click the ZIP filename to peek inside, find the theme folder, and copy that folder to your computer (say, the desktop) so you can edit the files it contains.

2. **Open the theme's *style.css* file in a text editor.**

   Usually, that means Notepad on a Windows computer and TextEdit on a Mac.

   At the top of the file, you see the header comment with its basic information about the theme.

3. **Change the theme name.**

   For example, where it says this:

   ```
   Theme Name: PinBlack
   ```

   Change it to:

   ```
   Theme Name: PinBlack_Custom
   ```

   This is the name WordPress will use in the dashboard for the copied theme.

NOTE PinBlack_Custom is a good theme name, because it clearly communicates that this is a customized version of the original PinBlack theme. PinBlack2 would be a bad choice, because the person who created PinBlack might use that name to denote a significant revamp of the original theme.

4. **Remove the theme URL.**

   That's the line that starts with "Theme URI." Find it and delete it. This severs the link between your theme and the original one, ensuring that any theme update won't overwrite your customized files.

5. **Rename the theme folder to match the theme name.**

   For example, if you used the name PinBlack_Custom, you might rename the theme folder *pinblackcustom*. It doesn't really matter what name you use, as long as you change the folder name from the original (*pinblack*) in some way.

6. **Upload the new theme to your site.**

   You can do this two ways, too. The most direct is with an FTP program, where you drag the new theme folder (say, *pinblackcustom*) from your computer to your site's */wp-content/themes* area.

   The other option is to ZIP up your theme folder, and then upload it using the dashboard. Once you create the ZIP file, choose Appearance→Themes, click the Install Themes tab, and then click Upload. Select your ZIP file (click Browse or Choose File—the button's name depends on your browser), and then send it off to your site (click Install Now).

   Either way, once you upload the custom version of your theme, you can start using it.

7. **Choose Appearance→Themes, point to your theme, and then click Activate.**

   Figure 14-2 shows the PinBlack_Custom theme being activated.

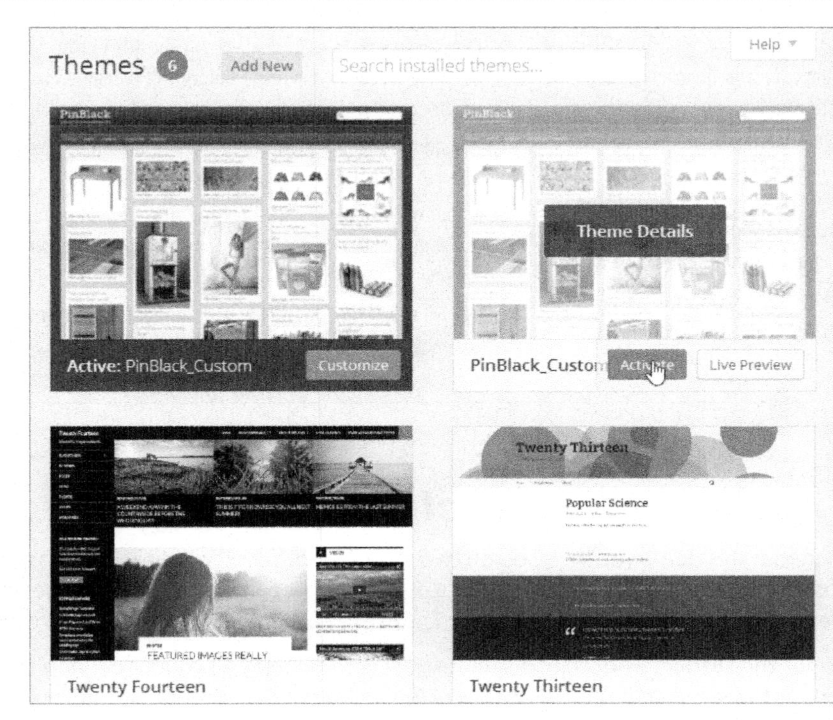

FIGURE 14-2

The only difference between a copy of a theme and a child theme is the information in the header of each one's style.css file. In a child theme, the style header includes a reference that links the child theme to the parent theme. But a theme copy is completely self-sufficient; it has its own version of every template, style sheet, and resource file, and no link to the original theme.

GEM IN THE ROUGH

Avoid Confusion with a Test Site

It may take some time to transform your new site from a few good ideas into a final, polished product. This raises a risk—while you're hard at work, your half-finished, slightly broken site will be on the Web, visible to potential visitors and slightly embarrassing.

If you're creating a brand-new site where none existed before, this might not be an issue. Because no one knows about your site, there won't be many people stopping by (and anyone who stumbles across your work by chance won't expect much). But if you're replacing an old, traditional-style website with a new WordPress site, you'll want to avoid the potential risk of a work in progress.

One way to do this is to create your website in a subfolder on your web server, and then transfer it to the real location once you finish it. For example, say you own the domain *super-chic.com*. You could create your new website in a subfolder (page 51), like *super-chic.com/v1*. Then, when your site is ready to go, you change the configuration of your root site (*super-chic.com*) so that it actually uses the files from *super-chic.com/v1*.

WordPress has the instructions to make this sort of changeover at *http://tinyurl.com/89wochm*, but here's a slightly compressed overview:

1. Go to the Settings→General section of the dashboard in your test site, and change the "Site Address (URL)" setting to the root of your website. For example, you would replace *http://super-chic.com/v1* with *http://super-chic.com*. (But don't change the "WordPress Address (URL)" setting.)
2. Using an FTP program, copy the *index.php* and *.htaccess* files from the test site folder (in this example, that's *v1*) to your computer.
3. Edit the *index.php* file (the copy you downloaded to your computer) using a text editor. Find the command that says `require('./wp-blog-header.php')` and insert your folder name before the filename, like this: `require('./v1/wp-blog-header.php')`.
4. Upload the modified *index.php* file and the untouched *.htaccess* file to the root folder of your website.
5. If your website's root folder has any other default pages that it might show instead of *index.php* (like *index.htm*), rename or remove them now.

That's it—your test site is now live. Don't forget to delete any posts or pages you created for testing purposes.

Adding New Types of Posts

Throughout this book, you've relied on two basic WordPress ingredients: posts and pages. But WordPress has a semi-secret superpower: It can manage other types of content, provided you define them first. These are called *custom post types*.

Consider the Distinct Furnishings site. Its goal is to present a product catalog that describes the items that it offers for sale. You *could* put each furniture item into an ordinary post, but that approach could get messy, especially if you want your site to feature ordinary news-style postings as well as product postings.

A better system is to create a custom post type called *product* that's tailored to the furniture items you want to show. Using this post type, you can create a separate *product post* for each piece of furniture in the catalog.

Product posts (or any type of custom post) are a lot like ordinary posts, except that they come with extra features. For example, you can choose to put your product posts in a separate section of your website, organize them in a different way, and attach different bits of information to them. Custom post types are also a linchpin of professional ecommerce plug-ins and themes, as you'll learn at the end of this chapter.

NOTE Custom post types are the gateway between an ordinary blog and a true *content-management system* (CMS)—in other words, they let you create a site that can display any type of content you create.

Here's the catch: Creating a custom post type is a bit of work. Not only do you need to define a custom post type (using code or a plug-in), you also need to alter your theme to use it. In fact, without these changes, your custom post type won't appear on your site at all.

In the following sections, you'll consider two ways to create a custom post type for products. First, you'll consider the raw code approach, which requires nothing more than the WordPress dashboard and a bit of bravery. Then, you'll pick up a plug-in that can do the same job more efficiently.

Defining a Custom Post Type in Code

To create a custom post type, you begin by choosing a name for it. This name should be short, with all lowercase letters and no fancy characters. (Hyphens are technically allowed, but can cause various annoyances, so avoid them.) Examples of good post type names include *review, recipe, book, employee, exhibit, article,* and so on. Distinct Furnishings uses a custom post type named *product*.

Someday in the future, WordPress may offer a dashboard menu for creating custom post types, but today it asks you to do the work the hard way, by running a snippet of code. You add this code to your theme's *functions.php* file—the all-purpose theme extender you use to unlock new features (page 500).

To edit *functions.php*, choose Appearance→Editor in the dashboard, and then click the "Theme Functions (functions.php)" link on the right. Scroll down past all the code that's already there. You can add your code at the end.

TIP If you're working with a child theme, you won't already have a *functions.php* file, but you can make one (page 490). Once you create a new, blank *functions.php* file, write <?php on the first line to begin a block of PHP code. Then add the code that registers your custom post type underneath.

The easiest way to register a custom post type is to copy a ready-made block of code and change the details to suit your post type. Here's an example that you can paste straight into the *functions.php* file on your site, provided you edit the details in bold:

```
function create_product_post_type() {
  $labels = array(
    'name'             => 'Products',
```

```
        'singular_name'  => 'Product'
      );
      $args = array(
        'labels'      => $labels,
        'public'      => true,
        'supports'    => array( 'title', 'editor', 'thumbnail', 'excerpt' ),
        'taxonomies' => array( 'category' ) );
      register_post_type( 'product', $args );
    }

    add_action( 'init', 'create_product_post_type' );
```

TIP Many parts of this chapter introduce useful snippets of code that you can adapt for your own site. Rather than type this code in by hand, you can download these excerpts from the Missing CD page for this book (*http://www.oreilly.com/pub/missingmanuals/wpmm2e*). You can then modify them and paste them into your own template files. And if you want to browse the example site from this chapter, visit *http://prosetech.com/wordpress.*

This code has two pieces. First, it includes a custom function named `create_product_post_type()`, which defines the custom post type. Then, it uses the `add_action()` function to tell WordPress to run the `create_product_post_type()`function when it initializes the theme. This makes sure that your site starts out with your custom post type, ready to go.

NOTE The name you use for your custom-type-creating function is unimportant, as long as you're clear, consistent, and you don't use the name of an existing function. The name `create_product_post_type()` makes sense in this example, because it registers a new custom post type named *product.* If you created a custom post type for movie reviews, for example, you might choose to name the function `create_review_post_type()`, but this detail doesn't change the way the code works.

Inside the `create_product_post_type()` function is the meat of the code: the instructions that determine the key details for your new post type. When registering a custom post type, you have the chance to specify an avalanche of settings, including many minor details. The current example includes just the essentials:

- **Name and singular name.** These are the descriptive titles that appear in the dashboard, as you'll see on page 516. Choose names that match your post type. In the Distinct Furnishings example, the custom post type is *product,* so it makes sense to use the singular name Product and the plural name Products. (But it's not always as straightforward as adding an "s." For example, if you have a custom product type called *story,* you'd want to use the titles "Story" and "Stories.")
- **Public.** If a post type is public, it appears in the dashboard, allowing you to manage all the posts of that type. In the case of Distinct Furnishings, that means you can log in to the dashboard and create new products or edit existing ones, as you'll see shortly. Private post types are hidden from view and managed with

code. (For example, plug-ins sometimes use private post types for their own information-storing purposes.)

- **Supports.** A custom post type can use some or all of the features of ordinary posts and pages. You get the features you want by including them in a list. In this example, *products* support featured images and excerpts, but not revision-tracking or comments. For the list of features from which you can choose, go to *http://tinyurl.com/reg-cpt*.
- **Taxonomies.** As you learned earlier in this book, a taxonomy is a way of organizing posts. In this example, the new product post type uses the standard category organization system, as do posts. The product post type doesn't elect to use tags—although it could, if you replaced `('category')` with `('category', 'post_tag')`. But the most powerful (and complex) approach is to create *your own* taxonomy. You'll dip your feet into those waters on page 542.

Finally, the `register_post_type()` function is the part that works the magic, creating the custom post type according to the recipe you provide. When registering a custom post type, you need to provide the all-lowercase name you picked, which is the key bit of information that identifies your type.

Once you add this code to the *functions.php* file, it's time to see if you successfully created the post type. Click the Update File button to store your changes, and then refresh your browser. Assuming all is well, your new post type will appear in the dashboard menu (Figure 14-3).

UP TO SPEED

Creating a Custom Post Type That Suits Your Site

The Distinct Furnishings example uses a custom post type named *product* because each post represents a piece of furniture. However, you could just as easily create a custom post type to represent something else, like movie reviews, how-to articles, celebrity biographies, employee resumés, recipes, or any other kind of content (so long as it's made up of text and pictures). For example, here's how you might alter the code you just saw to define a custom post type for restaurant reviews:

```
function create_review_post_type() {
  $labels = array(
   'name'              => 'Reviews',
   'singular_name'     => 'Review'
  );
  $args = array(
   'labels'     => $labels,
   'public'     => true,
   'supports'   => array( 'title', 'editor',
        'thumbnail', 'excerpt'),
    'taxonomies' => array( 'category' )
   );
   register_post_type( 'review', $args );
}

add_action( 'init',
   'create_review_post_type' );
```

There are many more details you can configure in your custom post type. For example, you can tweak the text that appears in various places in the dashboard when you add or edit posts that use your custom post type. For more information, refer to the function reference at *http://tinyurl.com/reg-cpt*, or try out a custom post type plug-in, which lays out all the possible options (page 518).

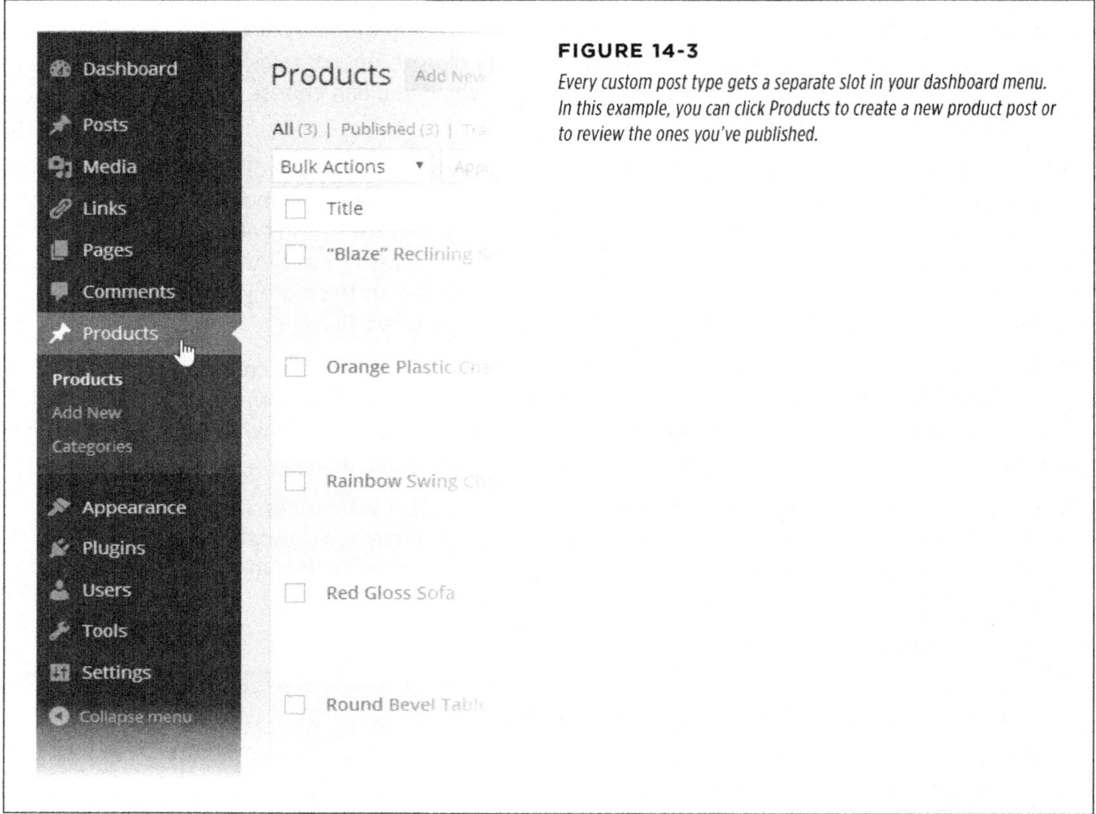

FIGURE 14-3

Every custom post type gets a separate slot in your dashboard menu. In this example, you can click Products to create a new product post or to review the ones you've published.

There's one more task to carry out before you continue. Because of a quirk in the way WordPress handles permalinks, you need to force it to refresh its permalink settings when you create a custom post type. If you don't, WordPress may fail to show posts that use your custom post type. To fix this problem, follow these steps:

1. **Choose Settings→Permalinks in the dashboard.**
2. **Make sure you're using one of the pretty permalink settings, such as "Post name" (page 117).**
3. **Click Save Changes, even if you haven't changed anything.**

Now you're ready to start adding content to your site.

Creating Sample Content

Now that you have a custom post type, you're ready to put it to use by creating some sample posts. Adding a post that uses a custom post type is the same as adding an ordinary post, but instead of choosing Posts→Add New, you choose Products→Add New (Figure 14-4).

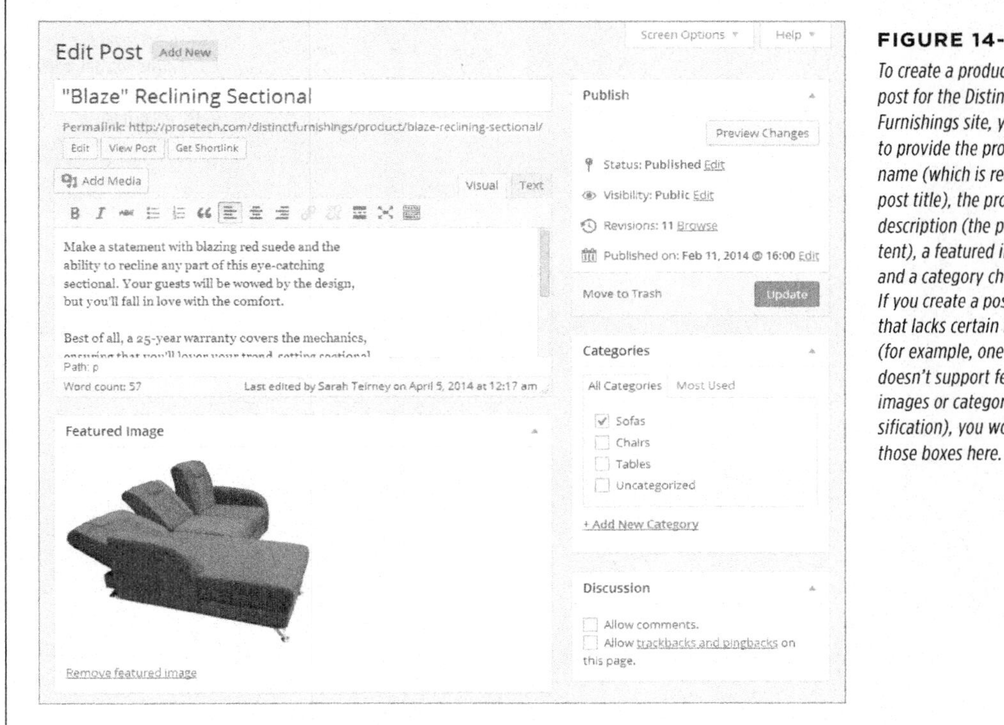

FIGURE 14-4

To create a product post for the Distinct Furnishings site, you need to provide the product name (which is really the post title), the product description (the post content), a featured image, and a category choice. If you create a post type that lacks certain features (for example, one that doesn't support featured images or category classification), you won't see those boxes here.

Just like an ordinary post, your new product post gets its own page and permalink. And just like an ordinary post, you click Preview to take a look at the work in progress and Publish to add it to your site. When you finish, choose Products→Products to look at a list of all the products you added (Figure 14-5).

NOTE Keen eyes will notice that the permalink for a custom post type includes the name of the custom post type. For example, if you create a product named Country Stool, WordPress gives it a permalink like *http://distinctfurnishings.net/***product***/country-stool*.

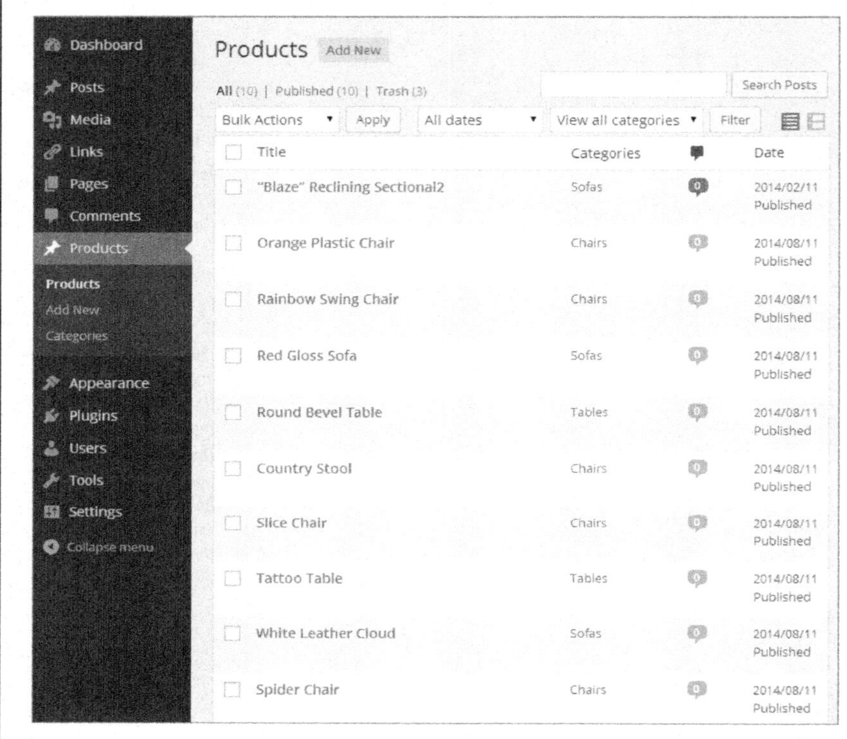

FIGURE 14-5

Here's a fully stocked product catalog for Distinct Furnishings. Although it looks like the list of posts you get when you choose Posts→All Posts, it's actually a completely separate list.

Making Your Custom Post Type Appear on Your Site

So far, life with custom post types is good. In the Distinct Furnishings site, you can easily review your products and add new ones. But dig a little deeper, and you'll find a glaring problem. Although you can visit each product post using its permalink (for example, *http://distinctfurnishings.net/product/red-gloss-sofa* to take a look at the Red Gloss Sofa), your products won't appear in any of WordPress's *archive pages*. These include the pages that display a list of posts by author, category, tag, or date, and the home page that shows the reverse-chronological listing of all your posts.

In other words, if you hit up the home page, you'll find it empty. And if you visit a category page like *http://distinctfurnishings.net/sofas*, you won't see the products you put in the Sofas category.

FREQUENTLY ASKED QUESTION

Editing Custom Post Types

I created a custom post type and added some posts that use it. Now I want to change the custom post type. Is that safe?

You can return to your *functions.php* file and edit your custom post type any time, without causing a problem. For example, you can change the labels that appear in the dashboard, the features that your custom post type supports, and the taxonomies it uses.

You might, for instance, create a custom post type for products that doesn't support categories, then add some product posts, and then decide that you actually *do* want to use categories. No problem—just change the code in *functions.php*. When you go back and edit one of your product posts, the category-picking box will magically appear.

If you want to remove a custom post type, you can delete the block of code that creates it in *functions.php*. However, you should delete the posts that *use* your custom post type first. Otherwise, those posts will continue to live, zombie-like, even though you can't see or manage them in the dashboard.

There's one detail that you should probably never change once you create a custom post type: its lowercase name. This is the detail you supply as the first argument you pass to the `register_post_type()` function. If you change the name, WordPress assumes you removed the old custom post type and you're adding a new one. As a result, any posts that use the old custom post type will disappear from the dashboard, which obviously isn't what you want.

There are two ways to fix this. The most versatile approach (and the one preferred by WordPress experts), is to create your own archive pages that use custom queries to pull out the product posts you want, in the order you want them. You'll learn how to do that later in this chapter (starting on page 519). But in the meantime, you can use a simpler solution: Tell WordPress to always include your custom post type in all its archive pages. You do that by revisiting the *functions.php* file and adding one more block of ready-to-roll code:

```
function add_product_to_archives( $wp_query ) {
    $types_array = array( 'post', 'product' );
    if( is_archive() && empty( $query->query_vars['suppress_filters'] ) ) {
        set_query_var( 'post_type', $types_array );
    }
}

add_action('pre_get_posts', 'add_product_to_archives');
```

This code tells WordPress to include product posts in all its archive pages. (If you created a different custom post type, substitute its name instead of *product* in the code above.)

Now if you visit the Distinct Furnishings home page, you'll see a list of all its products, just like the one shown in Figure 14-1. (Of course, the arrangement of these products needs a bit of work to look good, but that's a task you'll tackle on page 527.)

Defining a Custom Post Type with a Plug-In

Creating a custom post type with code really isn't that bad. As long as you have the right code in hand, it's a simple case of copy, paste, and edit. However, even WordPress gurus get tired of writing code—and exasperated by the way minor typos can cause big-time headaches.

The problem gets worse if you get more ambitious and decide to add custom taxonomies to your site. As described in the box on page 542, custom taxonomies let you attach extra bits of information to your custom post types. For example, Distinct Furnishings might use custom taxonomies to add color, style, and price information to its products. The problem is that every custom taxonomy needs to be registered in code, much like every post type, and that adds up to a tedious afternoon.

For all these reasons, most WordPress developers use some sort of plug-in to create custom post types. Two of the best and most popular are Custom Post Type UI (*http://tinyurl.com/cust-pt-ui*) and Types (*http://wordpress.org/plugins/types*). Both work the same way: They add tools to the dashboard that let you define new posts types and new taxonomies, no coding required.

For example, if you install and activate the Custom Post Type UI, you can follow these steps to create a custom post type:

1. **Choose CPT UI→Add New in the dashboard menu.**

   This brings you to a management page where you can create a new custom post type (using the boxes on the left) or a new taxonomy (on the right).

2. **Fill in three key details: the name of your custom type, the plural and singular labels, and an optional description (Figure 14-6).**

3. **Click Advanced Options.**

   You'll see a whack of extra settings (all of which are explained, somewhat tersely, in the function reference at *http://tinyurl.com/reg-cpt*).

4. **In the Supports section, select the features you want with your custom post type.**

   To duplicate the code-only example you saw earlier, you need to tick the Title, Editor, Featured Image, and Excerpt checkboxes.

5. **In the Built-in Taxonomies section, add a checkmark next to Categories if you want your custom post type to use categories.**

   You can also switch on the Tags checkbox to use tags with your custom post type.

6. **Click Create Custom Post Type.**

   The Custom Post Type UI plug-in creates the code that builds your custom post type. You'll see it in the dashboard menu, exactly as if you added the necessary code to the *functions.php* file.

To modify your new custom post type, you need to use the plug-in. Choose CPT UI→Manage Post Types to see all the post types you created, and to edit or delete any of them.

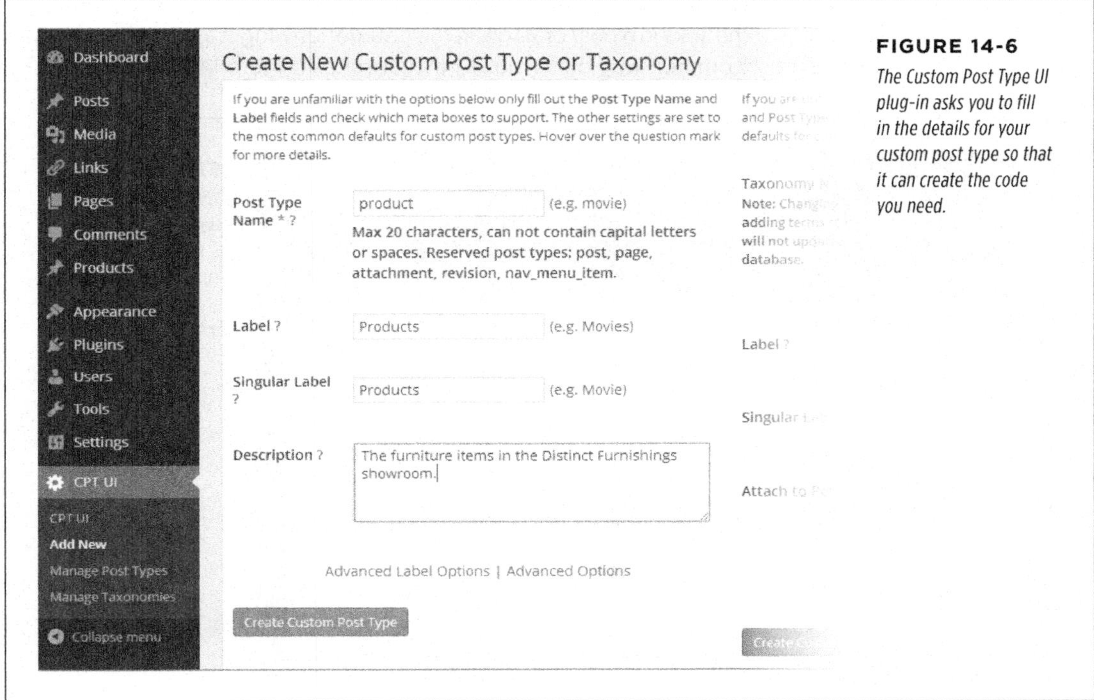

FIGURE 14-6

The Custom Post Type UI plug-in asks you to fill in the details for your custom post type so that it can create the code you need.

Creating Custom Category Pages

Now that you've picked a theme, created a custom post type, and added a bit of sample content, you're ready to start reengineering your site. Your goal is to remove the "bloggish" details that don't really fit, and make your site feel like a fine-tuned custom creation.

The first challenge is to give your visitors a decent way to browse Distinct Furnishing's products. Right now, WordPress sorts the products the same way that it sorts posts—in reverse-chronological order, based on the date you published the post. While that makes sense for a blog, a news website, and many other types of sites, it isn't terribly useful in a product catalog. Visitors who arrive at Distinct Furnishings probably won't want to see every item crowded into a somewhat disordered single page of tiles (Figure 14-1). Instead, they'll want to focus on the *type* of furniture they need—like a sofa, chair, or table.

This is clearly a job for the WordPress category system. As you already know, you can browse posts by category by putting the category name in the web address, like this:

```
http://distinctfurnishings.net/sofas
```

Of course, you won't expect your visitors to type this address on their own. Instead, you'll supply the links in a post or page, in the Categories widget, or in a menu. Menus are the most common way that visitors navigate sites (Figure 14-7).

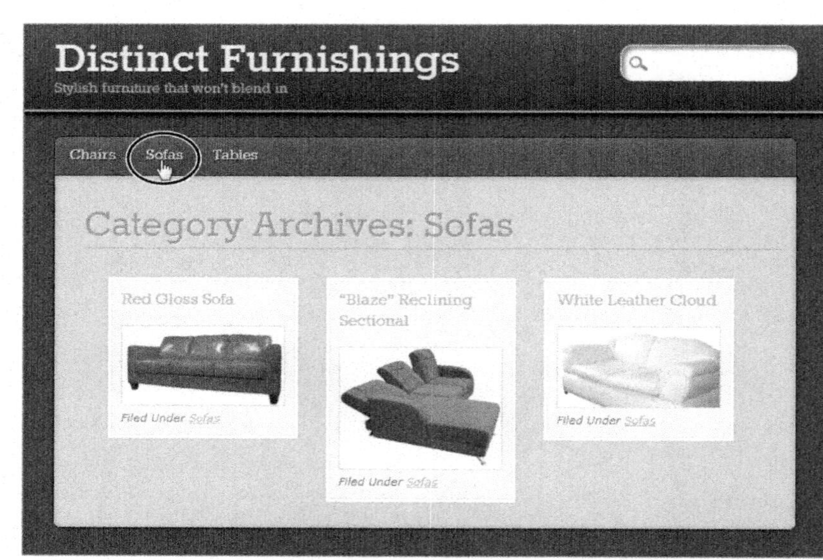

FIGURE 14-7

The easiest way to organize a product catalog is to create links that let your visitors focus on one category of product at a time.

The menu approach is probably the best browsing experience you can create without editing your theme. However, it's not perfect. It has several shortcomings:

- You can't display different categories of products in different ways. For example, you might want the sofa-browsing page to look different from the tables-browsing page.
- You can't display additional information about a category.
- You can't control the order of products *within* a category—WordPress still puts them in reverse-chronological order by publication date.

However, you *can* control all these options by customizing the category page template (also known as a *category archive page*), which creates the page shown in Figure 14-7. For example, when you visit a web address like *http://distinctfurnishings.net/sofas*, the category page grabs the products in the Sofas category and displays them.

The stock category page does a decent enough job, but you can do better by editing your theme. Figure 14-8 shows a revamped version of the category page that adds a number of refinements. In the following sections, you'll learn how to make these improvements.

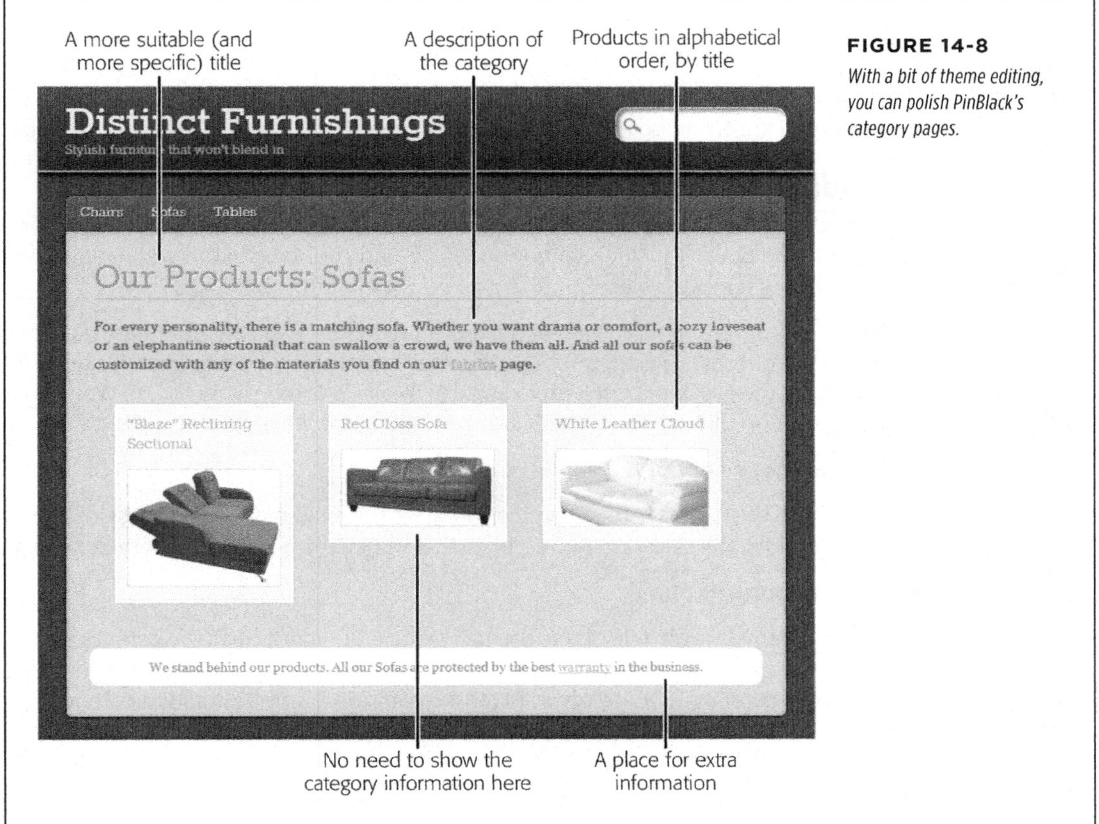

FIGURE 14-8

With a bit of theme editing, you can polish PinBlack's category pages.

Adding a Category Description

The first and easiest change you can make to the category page template is adding a category description. Many themes, including PinBlack, automatically display the category description on the category page. You don't even need to edit your theme.

When you first create a category, it doesn't have a description, but you can easily add one to the category record. Start by choosing Posts→Categories to see a list of all your categories, and then click the Edit link under the category you want to edit. Then type the category description in the Description box.

TIP Although the Description box doesn't give you the editing conveniences you get when editing a post or a page, you can still type in any HTML you want. For example you can insert <img> elements that show pictures, <a> elements that create links, and formatted <div> elements that use classes from the *style.css* file.

Here's the description for the Sofas category shown in Figure 14-8:

```
For every personality, there's a matching sofa. Whether you want drama
or comfort, a cozy loveseat, or an elephantine sectional that can swallow
a small crowd, we have them all. And all our sofas can be customized
with any of the materials you find on our
<a href="http://distinctfurnishings.net/fabrics">fabrics</a> page.
```

When you finish editing the category description, click Update to save your changes.

Finding the Right Template File

To add more information to the category page, or to change any other detail (or if your theme doesn't include category descriptions to begin with), you need to edit the theme's template files. But first, you have to find the right files.

When WordPress assembles a page, it prefers to use a specific template (say, one designed for browsing categories) rather than a more general one (one designed for browsing any group of posts, for example). To pick a category template, WordPress goes through this list, from top to bottom, and stops when it finds a match:

1. **category-slug.php**

   This is the template for a specific category. For example, if you browse the Sofas category, the slug-specific template that WordPress uses is *category-sofas.php*.

2. **category-ID.php**

   This template also displays category pages, but it specifies the category using the category ID. For example, if the Sofas category has an ID of 4, the template file is *category-4.php*. You can get the category ID by editing the category record and looking carefully at the web address in your browser. But instead of going to that trouble, use the category-*slug* naming system instead—it's easier to understand and has the same effect as the older category-*ID* approach.

3. **category.php**

   This is the standard template for category pages that don't have specialized formatting. If you haven't customized your theme, this is probably the template doing the work displaying category pages.

4. **archive.php**

   This is a more general template that lets you browse by category, tag, author, or date when you don't have a more specific template doing the work.

5. **index.php**

   This is your home page, and the final fallback if every other template file is missing.

Almost no theme uses either of the first two types of template (*category-slug.php* and *category-ID.php*) out of the box. That's because these templates are for you, the website creator, so you can add category-specific formatting wherever you need it, to suit the types of posts you want to put on your site.

Most themes include a *category.php* page, but a few don't, relying on *archive.php* instead. In such a case, the *archive.php* template may include complex instructions that display different text or formatting depending on whether your visitor browses by category, tag, author, or date.

PinBlack includes the *category.php* file, so this is the one you want to edit. Choose Appearance→Editor and click the "Category Template (category.php)" link to get started. Inside, you find several dozen pages of interwoven HTML markup and PHP code. The overall pattern will be familiar from the previous chapter (page 486). First, a `get_header()` instruction starts the page and inserts the header, then the loop displays all your posts, and finally a `get_footer()`instruction adds the footer and ends the document.

TIP Before you edit these templates, it's a good idea to make a backup copy of each. The easiest way to do that is to launch an FTP program and drag the templates to your computer to download them. A backup is important because you might decide later that you need to display some posts in a more typical single-post page. If so, you'll have a copy of the unedited template ready to roll. Keeping a backup is also a good idea in case you get carried away with your template surgery and accidentally lobotomize your page.

Changing a Category Page's Title

Once you crack open the category template, there's nothing you can't change. The first target is the title of the page. Most themes use something generic, if they use a title at all.

The PinBlack theme shows a heading with text like this: "Category Archives: Sofas" (Figure 14-7). To quickly home in on this part of the template, press Ctrl+F (Command+F on a Mac) and type in "category archive." That takes you to a part of the template that looks like this:

```
<h1 class="archive-title">
<?php
    printf( __( 'Category Archives: %s', 'pinblack' ), '<span>' .
      single_cat_title( '', false ) . '</span>' );
?>
</h1>
```

It may take a second to puzzle out this markup, because it relies on some hardworking PHP code. The `printf()` function inserts some formatted text into the current page. Here's where things get a bit tricky. The `printf()` function actually stitches together several pieces of text, using single quotation marks to demarcate each piece of text and periods to link the pieces together. The result is a bit of HTML that looks like this, which the template spits out onto the page (Figure 14-7):

```
Category Archives: <span>Sofas</span>
```

The words "Category Archives" sound a bit jargony—imagine you're browsing a list of bestsellers on Amazon.com and see "Category Archives: Bestsellers" at the top of the page instead of the more recognizable "Recent Bestsellers."

To replace this heading with the more suitable text shown in Figure 14-8, make this simple edit:

```
<h1 class="archive-title">
<?php
    printf( __( 'Our Products: %s', 'pinblack' ), '<span>' .
      single_cat_title( '', false ) . '</span>' );
?>
</h1>
```

As always when you edit a template, click Update to save your changes and then take a look at your site to see the change.

Adding Extra Information

One of the most common ways to soup up a category page is to add extra bits of useful information. You know how to add a category description (page 113), which the category page includes automatically. But when you edit the template, you can add content elsewhere on the page. One example is the white, rounded box at the bottom of Figure 14-8, which provides a reassuring message about the furniture warranty, and a link to the relevant page.

To add this sort of detail, you need to find the right spot in the template and insert your own HTML. For example, to place something at the end of a page, you need to scroll down until you're nearly at the end of the template, where you find a line like this:

```
</div> <!-- end #content -->
```

This is the closing </div> tag, which ends the content section of the page. After this line, the template adds the final footer.

To add more content, you need to add a section before the closing </div> tag. Here's the markup that creates the white box in the Distinct Furnishings example:

```
<div id="WarrantyBox">
    We stand behind our products. All our
    <?php single_cat_title(); ?> are protected by the best
    <a href="http://distinctfurnishings.net/warranty">warranty</a>
    in the business.
</div>
    </div> <!-- end #content -->
```

Notice that the new content doesn't include the word "Sofas." That's because you want the template to work for *all* your categories, so you use the `single_cat_title()` function to grab the name of the current category. The category page uses the same trick to add the category name to the title of the category page, as you saw earlier.

NOTE This code assumes there's a page with warranty information at *http://distinctfurnishings.net/warranty*. You can create this page the usual way, using the Pages→Add New command.

There's another important detail in this example—the box applies custom formatting using the technique you saw in Chapter 13. First, you make sure your new content has a unique ID (if it occurs just once on the page) or a unique class name (if it occurs multiple times). In the Distinct Furnishings example, the new section has the ID *WarrantyBox*. But the exact ID name doesn't matter, as long as you add a corresponding style rule in the *style.css* file (page 460).

Here's the style rule that makes the warranty box look pretty by setting the colors, spacing, and border:

```
#WarrantyBox {
    color: #708090;
    background: white;
    margin: 25px;
    padding: 10px;
    text-align: center;
    border-radius: 10px;
}
```

TIP As you start adding new rules to your *style.css* file, make sure you keep them all in one place, either at the beginning or the end of the file. That way you won't mix up the new and old rules, and forget what formatting you added and what formatting is part of the original theme.

Reordering Posts

By now, you're well aware of WordPress's fascination with fresh content. Whenever you have a list of posts, WordPress puts the newest ones first, leaving the older entries to languish at the end. This makes sense for a series of news bulletins, but it's less helpful for a product catalog. To fix the problem, you need to tweak the loop in the category page. (The loop is the crucial bit of code that creates the list of posts in a WordPress site. You first considered it on page 495, where you learned to highlight new posts. Now you'll modify it to put posts in a different order.)

The first step is to find out where the loop begins. In most well-designed themes—including Twenty Eleven and PinBlack—a comment clearly signals its start. It looks like this:

```
<?php /* Start the Loop */ ?>
```

To change the order of posts, you need to act here, before the loop pulls any posts out of the database. The easiest way to do that is with a handy WordPress function called `query_posts()`, which changes the query that an archive page uses to get its posts. (A *query* is a database operation that fetches a group of records that meet the criteria you specify.)

Before you look at the solution for reordering posts, it helps to consider the simplest operation query_posts()can perform. It looks like this:

```
<?php
    $posts = query_posts( $query_string );
?>

<?php /* Start the Loop */ ?>
```

This code takes the query that WordPress wants to run, which is stored in the $query_string variable, hands it to the query_posts() function, and stuffs the result (the group of matching posts) into the $posts variable. That creates the plain-vanilla version of the category page, with all the posts you normally get, in the order you expect.

To get a different result, you need to stick some extra text onto the end of the query command in the $query_string variable. For example, to sort posts by their titles in alphabetical order, you modify $query_string like this:

```
<?php
    $posts = query_posts( $query_string . '&orderby=title&order=asc' );
?>

<?php /* Start the Loop */ ?>
```

Here, it helps to understand the SQL language that databases love, because that's what $query_string uses. But even if you're not a database god, you can decipher the query command above. The *&orderby=title* portion tells WordPress "and by the way, sort the posts by title." The *&order=asc* portion adds "and when you do that sort, use ascending alphabetical order, just like a dictionary does." Together, these two instructions override the reverse-chronological order that WordPress would otherwise apply.

This is just one way to edit the loop that creates a post list. You'll see a similar but slightly different example later in this chapter. In the meantime, you can explore the query_post() function in more detail in WordPress's function reference at *http://tinyurl.com/yhjtze5.*

Removing Post Footers

The final detail to adjust on your catalog page is the footer that appears under every product tile. It displays the category information (for example, "Filed Under Sofas"). Because you put every product in Distinct Furnishings into a single category, and because all the posts on a category page share the same category, this information doesn't help anyone.

To remove it, look for and delete this markup:

```
<footer>
  <p class="cat"><?php _e("Filed Under", 'pinblack'); ?>
  <?php the_category(', '); ?>
```

```
    </p>
  </footer> <!-- end article footer -->
```

GEM IN THE ROUGH

Different Category Pages for Different Categories

In some situations, you might decide to have significantly different content on your category pages, depending on the category. In that case, you need to create more than one copy of your category template, using names like *category-sofas.php*, *category-tables.php*, and *category-chairs.php*. This approach obviously requires more work, so don't go down this road unless it clearly benefits your site.

One type of site that frequently needs category-specific pages is a news site structured like an online magazine. In a site like that, it's often important to emphasize the difference between topics, and to give each category a distinct, compelling identity. For example, if you create an online magazine that includes posts in the categories Politics, Sports, and Lifestyle, you may want to give each category a slightly different style. And if you have multiple contributors, you may want give each columnist his own author page, by augmenting the *authors.php* template with author-specific templates like *author-rami.php*, *author-grabinsky.php*, and so on.

In a product catalog site like Distinct Furnishings, category-specific formatting is less useful. That's because the goal of the site is to help visitors browse the product selection as quickly as possible, so they can find the items that interest them. And to do that, it helps to minimize the differences between categories and keep your formatting and layout consistent.

Building a Better Home Page

The Distinct Furnishings site now has a first-rate browsing system, which lets potential customers hunt through the product catalog one category at a time. However, new visitors still arrive at the standard home page, which features every product in one big jumble.

The easiest way to fix this is to add a static page and set it as the home page for the site. This new home page can provide a welcome message and invite visitors to dig into the content by offering a navigation menu. If this solution suits your needs, follow the instructions on page 218. You don't need to customize a template, or look at any PHP code.

But the home page also presents an opportunity to do more. Instead of using a plain page, you can add links that take visitors straight to specific products. You could type in an <a> element with the exact web address for each one, but that's not flexible, and it forces you to make frequent page edits to keep your home page current. A more ambitious approach is to use some clever PHP to create links that appear on your home page *automatically*.

Figure 14-9 shows this technique in action. Here, the home page includes a welcome message and links to every product category, sorted by title.

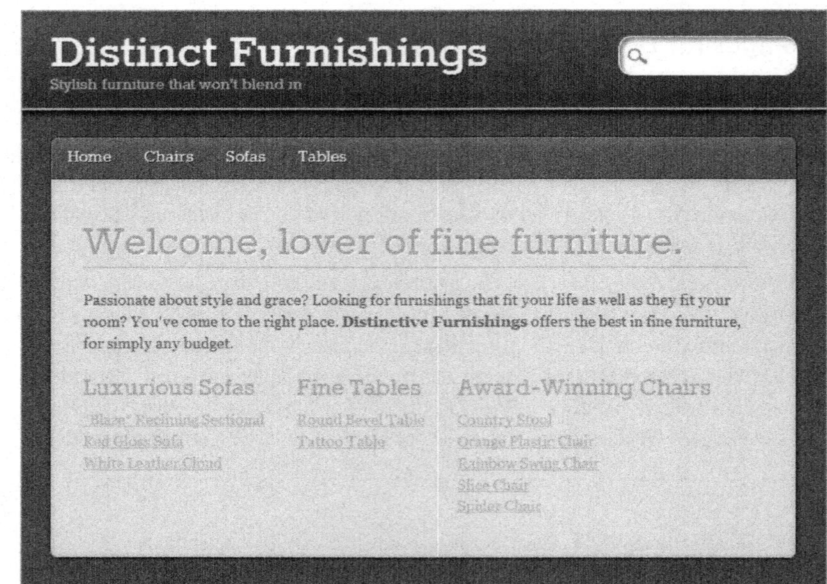

FIGURE 14-9

The links in this custom home page give readers a bird's-eye view of the products Distinct Furnishings offers. Because the content is brief and well-organized, the links don't become overwhelming.

Creating a page like this is easier than it appears. It's a technique worth learning even if you don't want the exact result shown in Figure 14-9, because you can easily adapt it to display other product links—for example, for featured products, new products, or products on sale (see the box on page 535).

The following sections show you how to create a custom home page like this one.

Cleaning Out the Template

The first step in creating this sort of custom home page is to find the template you want and prepare it for editing. In virtually all modern themes, the *index.php* template is the one you want. It creates a home page with the standard list of posts. (The only exception is if your theme has a *home.php* file—if it does, edit that template instead.) To get started, choose Appearance→Editor and then pick "Main Index Template (index.php)."

In many ways, the *index.php* template is like the *category.php* template you considered in the first part of this chapter. The heart of both is a loop that extracts and displays posts. The most significant difference is that *category.php* uses a narrower query that includes the posts in just a single category.

You could keep the standard loop in the *index.php* template and simply change the way it displays each post. You've seen examples that use this technique to highlight new posts (page 495) and change the post order (page 525). But Figure 14-9 makes a more radical change—it grabs several separate post lists, by category, and then displays them. The easiest way to make this happen is to remove the existing loop entirely and add all new code. In most themes, that means deleting everything inside the content <div>.

In the PinBlack theme, deleting the loop leaves you with this exceedingly simple skeleton:

```
<?php get_header(); ?>

  <div id="content" class="clearfix">

  </div> <!-- end #content -->

<?php get_footer(); ?>
```

All this template does is add a header and footer to a page. In between is a great big empty section where you can slot in your own content.

NOTE Remember, the header template (*header.php*) isn't just a header—it has the HTML markup that begins each page, which includes the title, style sheet links, background, and menu. Similarly, the footer template (*footer.php*) includes the HTML that ends every page. So even in a simple stripped-down template like the one shown above, your site ends up with a fully formatted home page, albeit one that doesn't have any content in it.

Adding Text

Now that you've removed everything you don't need from the home page, you can start adding the content you *do* want to the *index.php* template. First, start with the plain text and HTML. Wrap it in a <div> so you can apply style sheet formatting. In the Distinct Furnishings page, the main section is in a <div> that has the ID *WelcomePageMain*. Inside is a heading and a single paragraph of text:

```
<?php get_header(); ?>

  <div id="content" class="clearfix">

    <div id="WelcomePageMain">
      <h1 class="archive-title">Welcome, lover of fine furniture.</h1>
      <p>Passionate about style and grace? Looking for furnishings that
fit your life as well as they fit your room? You've come to the right place.
<b>Distinct Furnishings</b> offers the best in fine furniture, for simply
any budget.</p>
    </div>

  </div> <!-- end #content -->

<?php get_footer(); ?>
```

The specific ID you use isn't important, as long as it doesn't clash with the names in your theme's *style.css* file, and as long as you create a matching rule in your style sheet. In the Distinct Furnishings example, the style sheet rule adds some margin space around the main content area, so it isn't smushed up against the edges:

```
#WelcomePageMain {
   margin: 30px;
}
```

You can also use existing styles where appropriate—in this example, the <h1> heading uses the ready-made *archive-title* class, the same one that formats the title in the category page. (Keen eyes may have noticed this detail when editing the category page on page 523.) Every theme uses different class names, and if you can't find the class name that adds the formatting you want, you need to create a new style rule and add the formatting on your own.

Creating the Links

The next step is more interesting. Immediately after the introductory text on Distinct Furnishing's home page, you want to create three sections, each with a heading and a list of links. You can decide exactly how you structure this markup—and if you're an HTML whiz, you may already have a plan. The Distinct Furnishings example places each column of links in a separate <div> element, as explained in the box below.

UP TO SPEED

The Multiple-Column Effect

There are several ways to create the multicolumn layout shown in Figure 14-9. Possible approaches include using the <table> element or putting each column in a separate <div>, which is what the Distinct Furnishings example does.

The trick to the <div> approach is to use a CSS feature called *floating layout*. This technique is commonly used with images, because it lets you put a picture on one side of a page while the rest of the content (the text) flows around it. The same technique lets you create multiple columns, by floating each column to the left side of your page. That way, the first column goes hard up against the left side of the page, the second column goes right up against the right edge of the first column, the third column goes up against the second column, and so on. If the browser runs out of width, it bumps the next column farther down the page, starting again on the left side.

To put this effect into practice, you need a style rule that sets the *float* property. Here's an example that uses the class name *FloatingColumn:*

```
.FloatingColumn {
    float: left;
    margin-right: 30px;
    margin-bottom: 30px;
}
```

You can then create a <div> for each column, and use the same style rule for each one:

```
<div class="FloatingColumn">
   ...
</div>
```

This is a standard technique in the stylesheet world, and it works in WordPress as well as it does in any other website. If you want to polish your CSS skills, consider a good book like *CSS3: The Missing Manual* (O'Reilly).

Here's how the first column starts:

```
<div class="FloatingColumn">
  <h2>Luxurious Sofas</h2>
```

Next, you add the links that belong in this category. The best way to do that is through the miraculously useful WordPress function called get_posts().

UP TO SPEED

Comparing get_posts() and query_posts()

The get_posts() function is similar to the query_posts() function you learned about on page 525. The difference is where and when you use them.

The get_posts() function lets you grab a bunch of posts (and all their information) whenever you need it. Database nerds call such an operation *querying*. You can use get_posts() anytime, in any template. However, the get_posts() function takes more work than the query_posts() function. That's because get_posts() requires that you write the code that examines each post, pulls out the information you want, and displays it on the page.

The query_posts() function does a similar job, but it's designed to work with the loop code already in your archive page. That means you can use query_posts() to change the query that an archive page uses, while keeping everything else the same. If this approach works (as it did with the category page example on page 526), it's less work.

In the Distinct Furnishings home page, you removed the original loop, and you need to execute several queries to get several separate lists of results (one for each category). For both of these reasons, you need to accept the extra work and use the get_posts() function.

If you've never written a computer program before (and we assume you haven't), using get_posts() is a sizeable task. Not only do you need to create the database query that gets your posts, but you also need to write the code that looks at each post and extracts the information you want displayed on the home page. Fortunately, you don't need to do this from scratch. You can start with one of the chunks of code from WordPress's function reference for get_posts() at *http://tinyurl.com/23km6q5*. There, you'll see code that displays post titles, displays posts in random order, and gets the posts that belong to a specific category. You can copy one of these examples into the *index.php* page to try it out. Or start with this very basic code:

```
<?php
  global $post;
  $args = array( [ Your search and sort criteria go here. ] );
  $myposts = get_posts( $args );
  foreach( $myposts as $post ) :
    setup_postdata($post); ?>

    [ This is where you display the post data you want. ]

<?php endforeach; ?>
```

This is an all-purpose function that handles any post-querying task. All you need to do is replace the two square-bracketed sections with the right details. (If you want to use this code in your own templates, you can get it as a text file on the Missing CD page at *http://www.oreilly.com/pub/missingmanuals/wpmm2e.*)

The first detail you need to supply is the $args variable. It holds all the criteria and settings that WordPress uses to query the database. There are plenty of options you can stuff into $args, and WordPress has the full list at *http://tinyurl.com/yhjtze5*. But in this example, the $args variable has just three settings. Taken together, they tell WordPress to get the product posts from a specific category and sort them by post title (that's the product name) in ascending alphabetical order:

```
$args = array( 'post_type' => 'product', 'category' => 4,
 'orderby' => 'title', 'order' => 'asc' );
```

This query grabs the posts in the Luxurious Sofas category, because that category has the ID of 4.

TIP To find the ID for your categories, go to the Posts→Categories section and edit the category. Then examine your browser's address bar for the *tag_ID* code:

```
http://distinctfurnishings.net/wp-admin/edit-tags.php?action=edit&taxonomy=cat
egory&tag_ID=4&post_type=post
```

In this example, the category ID is 4.

The next detail you need to supply is the HTML markup you want to add to the page. WordPress copies your content to the page multiple times, once for each post it finds. This is more or less the same way the standard loop works.

In your HTML markup, you use WordPress's oddly named "the_" functions to get information about each post. For example, to get the post title, you use the_title(), like so:

```
foreach( $myposts as $post ) :
  setup_postdata($post); ?>

  <?php the_title(); ?>
  <br />

<?php endforeach; ?>
```

This inserts a list of post titles into the page. After each title, the <br /> element adds a new line. The result is something like this:

"Blaze" Reclining Sectional
Red Gloss Sofa
White Leather Cloud

The example in Figure 14-9 is a bit more practical. It creates a link (an <a> element) for each post. The post title becomes the link's label. The target of the link is the post web address. To get the title of the post, you use the function the_title(), which you just saw. To get the post address, you use the function the_permalink(). Here's how the code fits into the markup:

```
<a href="<?php the_permalink(); ?>"><?php the_title(); ?></a>
</br>
```

UP TO SPEED

Extracting Information from a Post

The Distinct Furnishings example uses two well-worn WordPress functions to get information about each post: the_title() and the_permalink(). But WordPress has many more useful functions that let you extract even more information from a post. You can determine the post's ID, publication date, publication time, category, and tag using the functions the_ID(), the_date(), the_time(), the_category(), and the_tags().

There are also some WordPress information-extracting functions that, for historical reasons, start with "get_the_" instead of "the_". These include get_the_title(), get_the_excerpt(), get_the_post_thumbnail(), get_the_author(), and get_the_content(). All these functions are terrifically useful in different loop-customization scenarios. For example, the PinBlack theme's tile-based display relies on get_the_post_thumbnail() to grab the featured image for every post. It then inserts that image into a fluid, style-based layout.

Some of the "get_the" functions also work in other places in a template file, outside the loop. For example, you can use get_the_title() to retrieve the title of any post, as long as you provide the post ID. (Page 550 has an example that uses this technique.)

WordPress describes all these information-gathering functions on its function reference page at *http://tinyurl.com/func-ref.* Because the functions aren't always consistent, you should always start by reading the function reference before you use a new function.

Just to make sure you haven't lost your place, here's the complete markup that creates the list of products in the Luxurious Sofas category. The customized details are in bold.

```
<div class="FloatingColumn">
  <h2>Luxurious Sofas</h2>
  <?php
    global $post;
    $args = array('post_type' => 'product', 'category' => 4,
     'orderby' => 'title', 'order' => 'asc' );
    $myposts = get_posts( $args );
    foreach( $myposts as $post ) :
      setup_postdata($post); ?>
    <a href="<?php the_permalink(); ?>"><?php the_title(); ?></a>
    <br />
  <?php endforeach; ?>
</div>
```

To create the other two columns (Fine Tables and Award-Winning Chairs), copy the section shown above (once for each column), and adjust the heading and the category ID accordingly.

Here's the result:

```
<div class="FloatingColumn">
  <h2>Fine Tables</h2>
  <?php
    global $post;
    $args = array('post_type' => 'product', 'category' => 5,
     'orderby' => 'title', 'order' => 'asc' );
    $myposts = get_posts( $args );
    foreach( $myposts as $post ) :
      setup_postdata($post); ?>
    <a href="<?php the_permalink(); ?>"><?php the_title(); ?></a>
    <br />
  <?php endforeach; ?>
</div>

<div class="FloatingColumn">
  <h2>Award-Winning Chairs</h2>
  <?php
   global $post;
   $args = array('post_type' => 'product', 'category' => 3,
    'orderby' => 'title', 'order' => 'asc' );
   $myposts = get_posts( $args );
   foreach( $myposts as $post ) :
     setup_postdata($post); ?>
   <a href="<?php the_permalink(); ?>"><?php the_title(); ?></a>
   <br />
  <?php endforeach; ?>
</div>
```

The result is a page that looks up posts from three different categories and combines them into a compact, perfectly organized set of links.

Making a Smarter Product Page

The changes you've made so far have transformed the Distinct Furnishings site into a sleek, browsable product catalog, with no trace of its WordPress blog roots—at least, not until you click a product. Once you do, you see the standard post-viewing page that includes plenty of unnecessary information, like the author name and publication date, and a sidebar of mostly useless widgets (Figure 14-10).

GEM IN THE ROUGH

Highlighting Products on Sale

In the current example, the Distinct Furnishings site uses three loops and offers a link to every product in its catalog. This works well in a site that has a few dozen products, but it's not practical in one that has hundreds.

Of course, there's no need to fetch posts from every category. Instead, you can highlight just *some* of your posts. Using this technique, you can create even more interesting home pages, such as ones that highlight recently added products, clearance products, or new promotions. The only challenge is writing a query that gets the posts you want.

The easiest approach is to create an *additional* category and apply it to the items you want to highlight. For example, you could create a category named Featured. Then, if you have a loveseat that warrants special attention, you assign it two categories: Sofas and Featured. Because it's in the Sofas category, visitors will find it when they click Sofas in the navigation menu. And because it's in the Featured category, your home page can retrieve it with a category-specific query and display it prominently. (Just remember not to add the Featured category to your menu, because having the same set of products appear in more than one place can confuse visitors.)

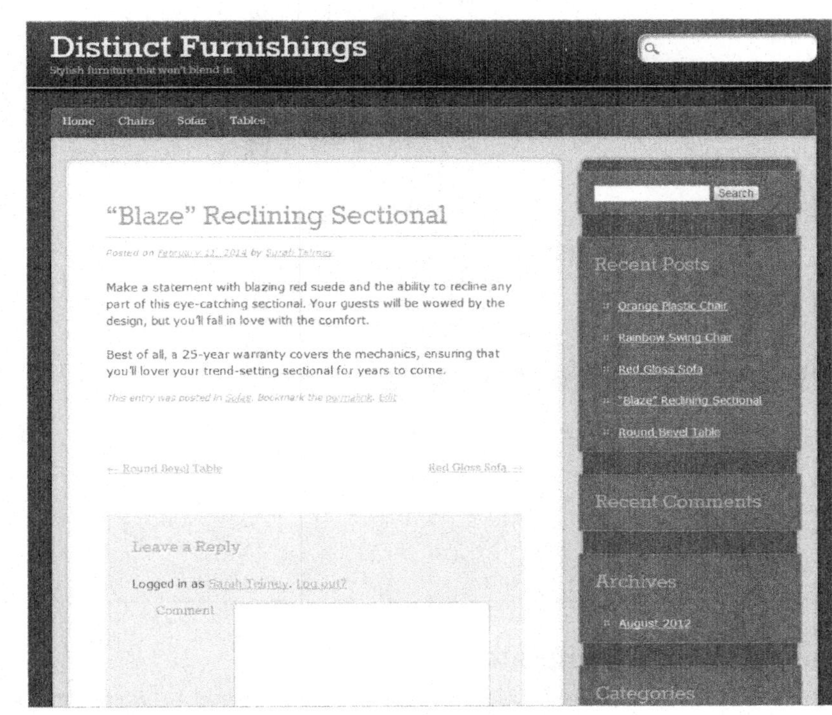

FIGURE 14-10

On close inspection, the product pages on the Distinct Furnishings site still look a lot like blog posts.

Fortunately, it isn't hard to change the product posts. Once again, the task involves editing a template, but with significantly less work this time. You don't need to tamper with loop code or change your query. In fact, most of the work involves removing post details that don't apply to your product listings.

Figure 14-11 shows the goal: a cleaned-up post that showcases the current product.

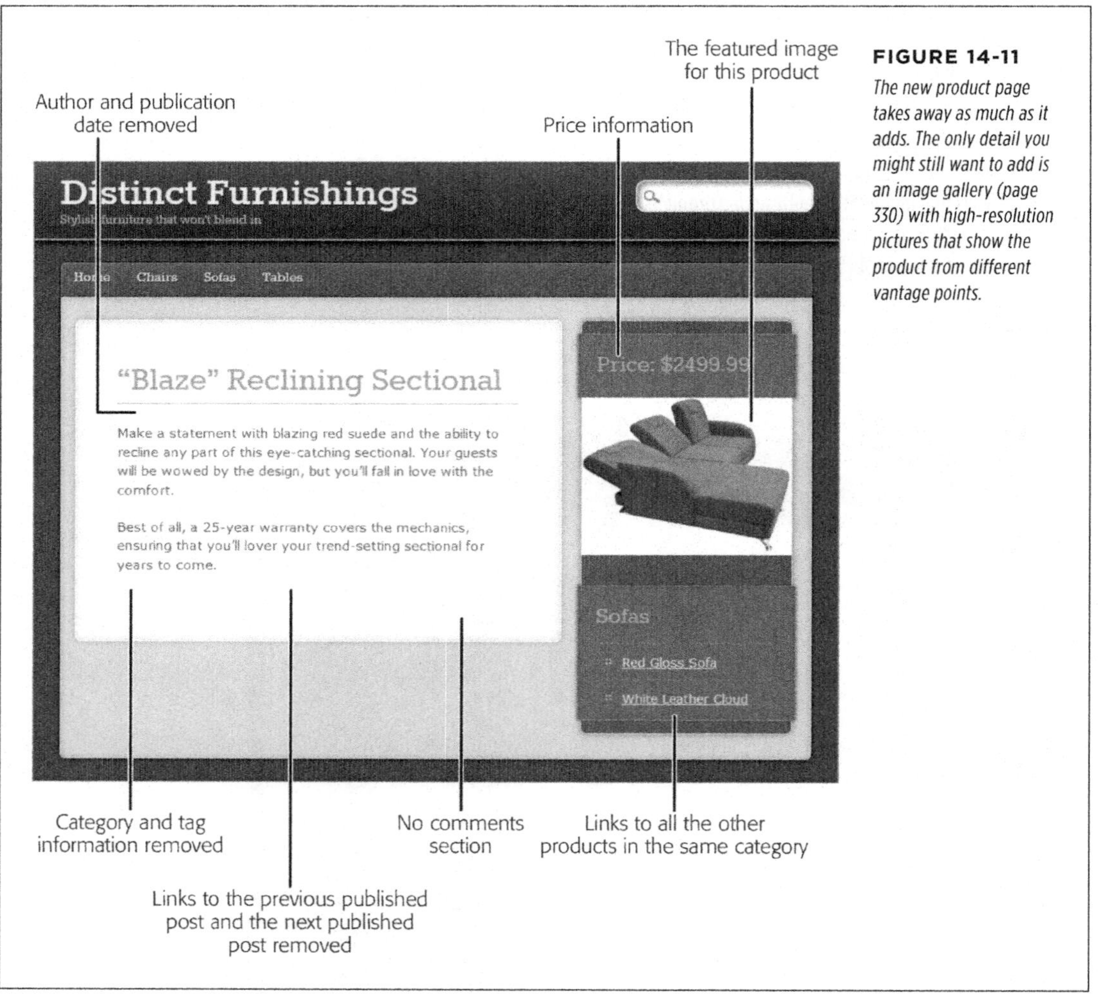

FIGURE 14-11

The new product page takes away as much as it adds. The only detail you might still want to add is an image gallery (page 330) with high-resolution pictures that show the product from different vantage points.

Cleaning Out the Templates

To change the way WordPress displays your posts, you need to work with two template files. As you may remember from Chapter 13, *single.php* creates the single-post view for every post and page. However, it gets help from another template, depending on the type of content it's displaying. In the case of an ordinary post, *single.php* asks *content-single.php* to do the real work of showing the post content (page 486 explains the process).

Although you could do all your work by editing these two files, that's not the best approach. That's because changing *single.php* and *content-single.php* changes the appearance of *all* your posts, including product posts and regular posts (and any other custom post types you choose to create). A better solution is to create new versions of *single.php* and *content-single.php* that are tailored for displaying products.

WordPress makes this job surprisingly easy. In fact, when it displays a post that uses a custom post type, it checks the theme to see if there's a specialized template that can help out. It does this by looking for a file that has a name in this form:

```
single-[type].php
```

For example, when you view a product in the Distinct Furnishings site, WordPress looks for a template named *single-product.php*. Unless you created this file, it won't exist, and WordPress will fall back on the standard *single.php* template. But now that you understand how WordPress selects the single-post template, you can create new, more specialized templates.

CREATING SINGLE-PRODUCT.PHP

The easiest way to get started is to create a copy of *single.php*, and name that copy *single-product.php*. You can do that using an FTP program—just copy *single.php* to your computer, rename it, and then upload it back to the theme directory.

Once you create *single-product.php*, you can edit it. As usual, you can choose Appearance→Editor and do all your editing in the dashboard.

Your first task is to remove the navigation links that let readers step from one post to another. They don't make sense when you profile products, because the links are based on the publication date, which is an arbitrary order for furniture items.

The navigation links appear inside the loop, just before the comment section. In the PinBlack theme, you need to find and remove this line:

```
<?php pinblack_content_nav( 'nav-below' ); ?>
```

Your second task is to modify the line just above that one, which loads the content template:

```
<?php get_template_part( 'content', 'single' ); ?>
```

When WordPress processes this instruction, it injects the content and runs the code from the *content-single.php* template. But that's a problem, because you need a type-specific version of the content template—one that WordPress will use for product posts *only*.

Although WordPress does look for a type-specific version of your single-post template (like *single-product.php*), it won't look for a type-specific version of the *content* template. Instead, it's up to you to change the `get_template_part()` function to tell WordPress what template to use.

Here's an example:

```
<?php get_template_part( 'content', 'single-product' ); ?>
```

This tells WordPress to load up a template named *content-single-product.php,* and use that for the post content.

If you've gotten lost in the morass of templates, here's a quick review of what happens on the Distinct Furnishings site:

- When WordPress displays an ordinary post, it uses the *single.php* template, which, in turn, tells WordPress to use the *content-single.php* to show the post content.
- When WordPress displays a product post, it finds the *single-product.php* template, which tells WordPress to use the *content-single-product.php* to show the post content.

CREATING CONTENT-SINGLE-PRODUCT.PHP

It's up to you to create the *content-single-product.php* file. The best starting point is to make a copy of *content-single.php,* and change its name to *content-single-product.php.*

Now you're ready to edit *content-single-product.php.* Here, you want to remove two sections. First, find the section just under the post title, which displays the publication author and date. It looks like this:

```
<div class="entry-meta">
  <?php pinblack_posted_on(); ?>
</div>
```

Remove it completely.

Next, find the section that adds the category and tag information after the post content. The PinBlack theme wraps this section in a massive <footer> element. You can delete the whole thing, from the opening <footer> tag to the closing one (</footer>).

NOTE Now that you've gone through the heavy lifting—creating a custom post type and giving it its own pair of templates—you're ready to enjoy the rewards. Your site now has the flexibility to separate different types of content and deal with it in different ways. For example, if you add a news post, you'll get the familiar date, author information, and previous and next links. Add a product, and none of these unnecessary details will appear. In the rest of this chapter, you'll see how to add even more product-specific details to your product pages, like prices and shopping cart buttons.

Custom Fields: Adding Extra Pieces of Information to a Post

As you probably know, WordPress stores the information for every post in a separate record in a database on your website. That record includes obvious details like the post title and post content, along with a slew of extra info about the author, the publication date, the last modified date, the excerpt, and so on. (Database geeks can get the full, behind-the-scenes details at *http://tinyurl.com/3a88qt*.)

The product posts don't include price information, and why would they? Price is one of many additional possible details that apply only to certain sites in certain scenarios. Of course, you're free to put the price information in the post content, but that's a bit sloppy. There's no way to make sure that every post puts its price in the same place and formats it the same way. There's also no guarantee that every post includes a price, and there's no easy way to extract it if you need it (for example, if you want to create a query that pulls out posts in a certain price range).

You're probably prepared to live with this limitation, but WordPress has a surprisingly flexible feature that can help. It's called *custom fields*, and it lets you bolt extra pieces of information onto any post.

Here's how:

1. **Start editing one of your product posts.**

   The quickest approach is to choose Posts→All Posts, and then click the Edit link under the first post in the list.

2. **Click the Screen Options button in the top-right corner of the Edit Post page, and then turn on the checkmark next to Custom Fields.**

   If you haven't used any custom fields on your site, the Custom Fields box is tucked away out of site (Figure 14-12). But once you change the screen options, it appears under the editor box that holds the post content.

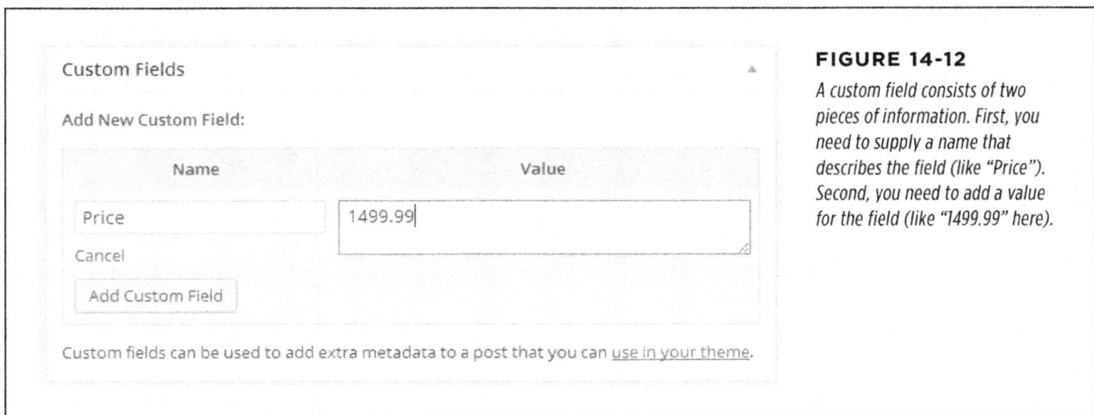

FIGURE 14-12

A custom field consists of two pieces of information. First, you need to supply a name that describes the field (like "Price"). Second, you need to add a value for the field (like "1499.99" here).

3. **In the Custom Fields box, fill in a name for your custom field.**

   In the Distinct Furnishings example, that name is *Price*.

   If you see the word "—Select—" in the Name box, your theme already has one or more custom fields that it uses for its own purposes. To add a new field, you must first click the "Enter new" link. That clears the text box so you can type in a name.

4. **Type in a value for your custom field.**

   The value applies to this particular post. For example, if you add a custom field named Price, the custom field value is the price of the current product (say, *1499.99*). Enter the number only—don't include a currency symbol, a "thousands" comma, or any additional text.

5. **Click Add Custom Field.**

6. **Click Update to save the changed version of your post.**

   You're done. WordPress creates a new custom field for your posts and attaches the value you supplied to the current post.

   Next you need to set the price for every other product. You already created the custom field you need, but you need to supply the correct value for each product.

7. **Choose Posts→All Posts to see your list of posts, and then click Edit under the post you want to change.**

8. **In the Custom Fields section, select "Price" from the Name box (Figure 14-13).**

FIGURE 14-13

Once you add a custom field, WordPress makes it available to every other post. All you need to do is select it and fill in suitable values.

NOTE You may find entries that you didn't create in the custom field list. That's because a WordPress theme, plug-in, or feature has added it. (For example, if you add a video file to a post, your site gets a new *enclosure* custom field.) These fields aren't meant for your use, and you can safely ignore them.

9. **Type in the appropriate price in the Value box, and then click Add Custom Field.**
10. **Click Update to save the post.**
11. **If you have posts left to edit, return to step 7.**

    Continue editing posts until you assign a price to each one.

Creating a custom field doesn't change what your posts look like. In fact, WordPress carries on exactly as it did before, displaying the post content and ignoring the extra information. To change this state of affairs, you need to extract the information from your custom field and show it in the right place.

The most straightforward way to do so is to edit the *content-single-product.php* template, fetch the price information, and show it somewhere on the page. To do this, you use the `get_post_meta()` function, like so:

```
<?php echo get_post_meta( get_the_ID(), 'Price', true ); ?>
```

The `echo` command takes the price information that the `get_post_meta()` function provides and copies it into the page.

The revised post page in Distinct Furnishings (Figure 14-11) uses this approach. It styles the price using the <div> element, like this:

```
<div class="Price">
  Price: $
  <?php echo get_post_meta( get_the_ID(), 'Price', true ); ?>
</div>
```

The only step left is to add a style rule for the Price class in the *style.css* file. This lets you apply the formatting you need to your custom field.

POWER USERS' CLINIC

Classifying Your Posts with Custom Taxonomies

Custom fields let you attach additional information to any post, which is ridiculously useful. However, WordPress has another post-extending trick that's more specialized but also more powerful. It's called *custom taxonomies,* and it lets you create a completely new classification system for your posts.

To understand custom taxonomies, it helps to remember the two staples of post organization: categories and tags. These are examples of taxonomies—ways to organize posts. But with a *custom* taxonomy, you set up other ways to group posts.

For example, the Distinct Furnishings site might add a taxonomy called Color. You could then create a list of color choices, including Black, White, Red, and so on. When you create a product post, you would pick one of these colors, and visitors could browse products by color (to check out all the red furniture, for example). Other possible taxonomies Distinct Furnishings might use include Size (Full, Luxurious, Apartment-Sized) and Material (Fabric, Leather, and so on). As with custom fields, custom taxonomies let you add extra information. The difference is that custom taxonomies are *browsable.*

For a small or medium-sized product catalog, custom taxonomies add extra work with no obvious benefit. But if you have a gargantuan catalog, they can give visitors more flexible ways to look around and find what they want.

Unlike custom fields, the WordPress dashboard won't help you add a custom taxonomy. To do that, you need to run some code (which is ugly) or use a plug-in (which is much nicer). There are many plug-ins that can help you out, including the two custom-post-type creators described earlier: Custom Post Type UI (*http://tinyurl.com/cust-pt-ui*) and Types (*http://wordpress.org/plugins/types*). Of course, you also need to extend the single-post template to show the information from your custom taxonomy.

For a more detailed overview of custom taxonomies, with examples, you can read a tutorial on the subject at *http://tinyurl.com/8slqbkn.*

Adding eCommerce

A product catalog is a great way to advertise your wares to the world. But some sites go further by giving visitors the ability to *buy* products.

eCommerce isn't suited for every site. For example, a furniture store like Distinct Furnishings might prefer to let salespeople handle all the selling in person. If your business has items that are difficult to ship, available to local buyers only, or one of a kind (for example, individual items in an antique warehouse), you might make a sensible decision to pass on any type of ecommerce.

Of course, there are even more sites that *will* want to take advantage of ecommerce. Some will need to ship items (for example, a shop that sells handcrafted jewelry), while others will be able to deliver the goods right away (like an indie band that lets purchasers download high-quality audio tracks). And although ecommerce features aren't a part of the WordPress software, they're available through a wide range of plug-ins. In the rest of this chapter, you'll consider one that lets you integrate a PayPal shopping cart into your site.

PLUG-IN POWER

The Many Ways to Make Money

Shopping carts are only one way that your site can start making bank. Here are three more money-earning methods, along with the plug-ins that will help you implement them.

- **Donations.** Begging for coin is awkward, but it may work. If your site offers genuinely useful advice, you can ask for tips with something like this: "Like what you read? Buy me a coffee!" If you're writing in support of a charitable cause or if your writing entails danger or significant sacrifice, you can ask for support, as in "Donate today to support independent journalism." Whatever the case, the easiest approach is to set up a PayPal account and add the PayPal Donations plug-in (*http://tinyurl.com/paypal-d*) to your site.
- **Advertising.** If you get masses of traffic reading the posts on your site, you might be able to accumulate some click-through money with the right advertising program. One popular choice is Google AdSense (*www.google.com/adsense*), which automatically shows ads that match the content on your site and pays you every time someone clicks one of them.
- **Subscription services.** This is probably one of the hardest ways to make money, because potential customers need to be completely convinced of the value of your content before they sign up to read it. Subscription services are also quite complex because you need to register every reader. But if your site offers one-of-a-kind information that has real value to other people, it's an option worth exploring. The powerful subscription plug-in s2Member (*http://tinyurl.com/s2member*) can help you get started.

Signing Up with PayPal

PayPal strikes a simple but compelling deal: You tell it the name and price of your product, and it gives you a shopping cart that you can drop into your website, with little (if any) customization.

When a customer buys one of your products, PayPal handles the checkout process and then notifies you by email. At this point, you need to deliver the goods (for example, by shipping them out or sending them electronically). Shortly after the transaction, the money appears in your PayPal account. You can then transfer it to a bank account or use it to buy stuff on other PayPal-equipped websites.

You might already have a PayPal account, but odds are it's a personal one—suitable for buying other people's goods but not much else. Before you can set up a PayPal shopping cart, you need a premier or business account (see the box on the next page).

NOTE All PayPal accounts are free to set up. PayPal makes its money on the commission it takes when you make a sale, as detailed below.

UP TO SPEED

The Three Types of PayPal Account

The first decision you need to make when you sign up with PayPal is the kind of account that's right for you. PayPal gives you three options:

- **Personal account.** This type of account lets you use PayPal to buy items on sites like eBay. You can also *accept* money transfers from other PayPal members without having to pay any fees. However, there's a significant catch—personal accounts can't accept credit card payments, so they won't work on an ecommerce site.
- **Premier account.** This type of account gives you an easy way to run a small business. You can still make payments to others, and you can accept any type of payment that PayPal accepts, including both credit and debit cards. However, PayPal charges you for every payment you receive, an amount that varies by sales volume but ranges from 1.9 percent to 2.9 percent of the payment's total value (with a minimum fee of 30 cents). That means that on a $25 sale, PayPal takes about $1 off the top. If you accept payments in another currency, you surrender an extra 2.5 percent. To get the full scoop on fees and to see the most current rates, refer to *www.paypal.com/fees.*
- **Business account.** This type of account has the same features and fees as a premier account, with two key differences: First, it lets you do business under your business name (instead of your personal name). And second, it supports multiple users. For that reason, a business account is the best choice if you have a large business with employees who need to access your PayPal account to help manage your site and its finances.

If you already have a personal PayPal account, you can upgrade to a premier or business account quickly by visiting *www.paypal.com/upgrade*. If you don't have an account, you need to sign up for one by following these steps:

1. **Head to the PayPal website (*www.paypal.com*) and click the Sign Up link.**

   PayPal's Sign Up page opens.

2. **Choose your country and language.**

3. **Choose the type of account you want to create (Personal, Premier, or Business), and then click Get Started in the corresponding box.**

   PayPal takes you to a new page to fill in your account information.

4. **Enter your email address, choose a password, and then fill in your personal details.**

   PayPal wants your name, address, and phone number.

   Make sure you create a complex password—you don't want a malicious hacker guessing it and using your PayPal account to go on an electronic buying binge.

   If you create a business account, you have two pages of information to fill out. The extra information includes the type of business you run, the business name, and the business address.

5. **Finally, click "Agree and Create Account" to complete the process.**

   PayPal sends you an email confirmation immediately. Once you click the link in the message, it activates your account, and you can create your first PayPal shopping cart.

Installing a Shopping Cart Plug-In

PayPal has a shopping cart feature that lets you put a cart on *any* website. If you're building a traditional site, you need to use the PayPal site to create a form, which you can then cut and paste into a web page. But if you're building a WordPress website, the job gets significantly easier, because you can install a plug-in that does all the form-generating work for you.

There's no shortage of PayPal-powered shopping cart plug-ins. Overall, they fall into two categories:

- **Simple PayPal shopping carts.** These no-nonsense plug-ins give you the quickest way to add a no-frills PayPal shopping cart to your site. One popular example is the WordPress Simple PayPal Shopping Cart (*http://tinyurl.com/paypal-c*). This is the type of plug-in you'll consider in this chapter.
- **Advanced ecommerce frameworks.** The best examples are the wildly popular plug-ins WooCommerce (*http://tinyurl.com/woo-com*) and WP ecommerce (*http://tinyurl.com/wp-ecom*). Both let you build a customized shopping cart and checkout page, using the payment gateway that you choose (such as PayPal or Google Checkout). And both define a custom post type for products, which is packed with useful product details. Serious sellers with lots of products almost always go this route.

In this section, you'll use the WordPress Simple PayPal Shopping Cart plug-in. To get started, choose Plugins→Add New, and search for "simple paypal." When you find the plug-in, install and activate it.

To configure the plug-in, choose Settings→WP Shopping Cart. At a minimum, you need to enter your PayPal email address at the top of the Settings form. The other details are optional; they let you customize the text in the shopping cart pages, the default currency, shipping costs, the threshold for free shipping, and the web address the customer goes to after making a purchase, among other details.

Adding the Shopping Cart

PayPal doesn't care about the details of your products. All it needs to know is the name of your product and its price. With these two pieces of information, you can create an "Add to Cart" button, and PayPal takes it from there.

The WordPress Simple PayPal Shopping Cart plug-in adds a shortcode (page 323) that makes it easy to create an "Add to Cart" button. The shortcode looks like this:

```
[wp_cart:ProductName:price:Price:end]
```

So if you want to sell the Blaze Reclining Sectional for $2,499.99, you need to edit the post for the Blaze Reclining Sectional and add the shortcode to the end of the post, after your content. Here's what the shortcode should look like:

```
[wp_cart:Blaze Reclining Sectional:price:2499.99:end]
```

Now, when you view this product, the shortcode turns into an "Add to Cart" button (Figure 14-14).

"Blaze" Reclining Sectional

Make a statement with blazing red suede and the ability to recline any part of this eye-catching sectional. Your guests will be wowed by the design, but you'll fall in love with the comfort.

Best of all, a 25-year warranty covers the mechanics, ensuring that you'll lover your trend-setting sectional for years to come.

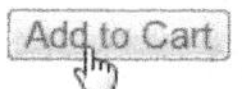

FIGURE 14-14

Although you can't tell by looking at it, you customized this button so that one click adds the Blaze Reclining Sectional sofa to a PayPal shopping cart.

You can click the "Add to Cart" button, but you won't know what's going into your shopping cart (and you won't be able to complete your purchase). To properly test the button, you need a way to display the contents of the cart. The WordPress Simple PayPal Shopping Cart plug-in gives you two options: adding another shortcode to your product posts, or using a widget.

Using the shortcode approach, you can create a shopping cart that appears at the bottom of the post. To try this out, begin by editing a product post (say, the Blaze Reclining Sectional). Scroll to the bottom, after the shortcode that creates the "Add to Cart" button, and add this shortcode:

```
[show_wp_shopping_cart]
```

Now update the product post and take a look. The first time you view the product, you'll see the "Add to Cart" button, same as before. But once you click it, the shopping cart becomes visible underneath (Figure 14-15). Click "Check out with PayPal," fill in some credit card details, and voilà!—your first ecommerce sale.

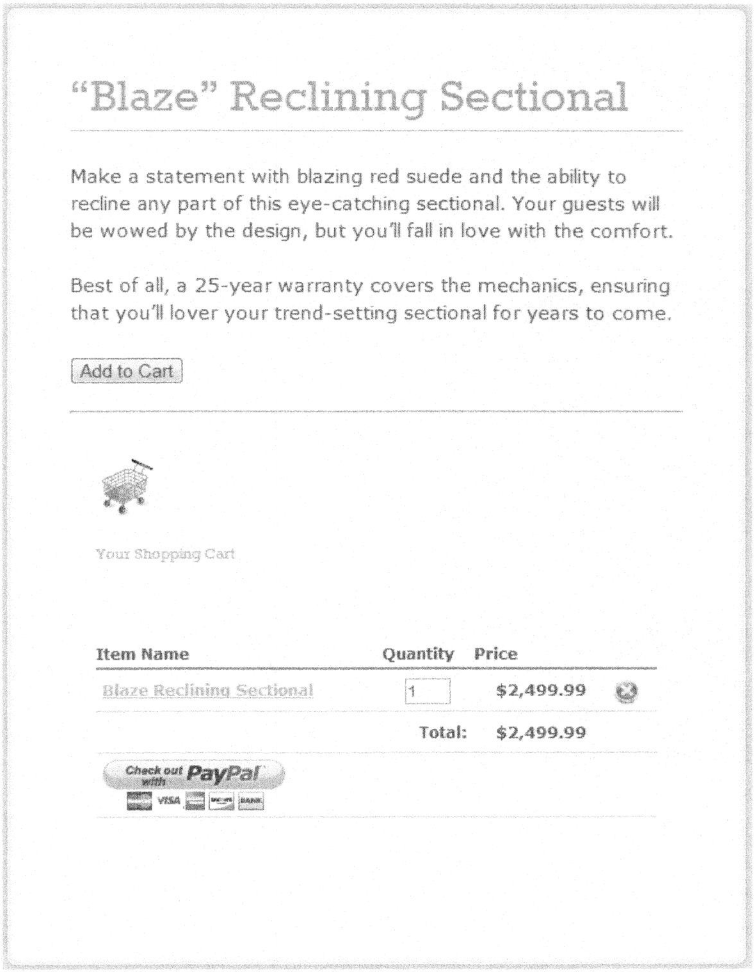

"Blaze" Reclining Sectional

Make a statement with blazing red suede and the ability to recline any part of this eye-catching sectional. Your guests will be wowed by the design, but you'll fall in love with the comfort.

Best of all, a 25-year warranty covers the mechanics, ensuring that you'll lover your trend-setting sectional for years to come.

Add to Cart

Your Shopping Cart

Item Name	Quantity	Price
Blaze Reclining Sectional	1	$2,499.99
	Total:	$2,499.99

Check out with PayPal

FIGURE 14-15

If your visitor's shopping cart is empty, WordPress doesn't display it on the page. But once your guest clicks "Add to Cart," he'll see something like this.

The only problem with the shopping cart shortcode is that you need to add it to *every* product post. That's understandable in the case of the "Add to Cart" shortcode, because every product has a different price. But it's needless extra work for the shopping cart.

There are two solutions that can save you the effort. One is to add the shopping cart shortcode to a template file (as explained in the next section). A simpler approach is to use the handy shopping cart widget described next.

To use the shopping card widget, choose Appearance→Widgets. Then, drag the WP PayPal Shopping Cart widget to the right place in your template. (Common choices include a sidebar or a footer.) Figure 14-16 shows the shopping cart in a sidebar.

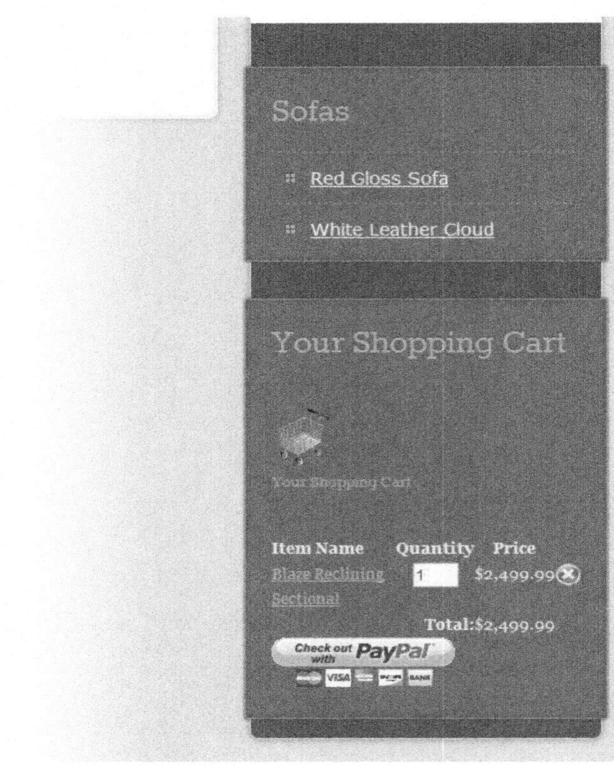

FIGURE 14-16

The sidebar is a great place to put your shopping cart (as long as it fits). That way, it remains visible but doesn't look like part of a post.

TIP To tweak the formatting around the shopping cart (for example, to change its margins, background color, or border), write a style rule that targets the *shopping_cart* class.

The shopping cart follows your visitors around your site. They can visit several product pages and add several items to their carts before checking out. When a visitor clicks "Check out with PayPal," the PayPal service takes over, asking for a shipping address and credit card information. At the end of the checkout process, you get an email that confirms the purchase.

TIP Make sure your customers leave with a good feeling. After someone places an order, take her to a thank-you page. All you need to do is create this page (like any other WordPress page), and then type the page's web address into the "Return URL" box in the Settings→WP Shopping Cart page.

Putting the Shopping Cart in Your Template

The Distinct Furnishings shopping cart does its job. Visitors can choose items, place simple orders, and—most importantly—send money your way. However, you can improve the way the shopping cart fits in with your site.

Right now, the Simple PayPal Shopping Cart plug-in forces you to do some serious extra work, especially if you have a large catalog of products. After all, you need to edit *every* product post to add an "Add to Cart" button and, optionally, to add the shopping cart. You also need to enter the price for each product *twice:* once as a custom field, so it appears on the page (page 539), and once in the shortcode for the "Add to Cart" button. This is a hazardous approach because, later on, it's all too easy to change a price in one place without updating the other. Make a minor mistake, and you can end up with products that are listed at one price but sell at their old price, creating a discount program you definitely didn't anticipate.

Happily, there's a solution. You can take details like the shopping cart and the "Add to Cart" button and add them to the product post template (*single-product.php*)—the same file you customized on page 537. This technique saves time and avoids the problem of inconsistent prices.

However, this approach isn't as convenient as you might expect. Based on the template-editing experience you picked up in this chapter, you probably assume that the solution is to edit the *single-product.php* template file and put the handy Simple PayPal Shopping Cart shortcodes there. But that presents a problem. Most of the time, WordPress ignores shortcodes that appear in template files. That means you'll end up with useless bits of text in your site (like "[show_wp_shopping_cart]") instead of the shopping cart features you really want.

Sometimes, there are workarounds. For example, you can try WordPress's `do_shortcode()` function, which searches for the code attached to a shortcode and attempts to execute it. But `do_shortcode()` is slow, and it doesn't always work, depending on the plug-in. A better option is to find the actual plug-in function that does the work and use *it.*

To do that, you could look through the complete plug-in code (browse it at Plugins→Editor), but that's a hit-or-miss effort that requires a ninja-level understanding of WordPress code. A better choice is to check your plug-in's documentation or support forum. If you trawl the forum for the Simple PayPal Shopping Cart (*http://tinyurl.com/spp-forum*), you'll dig up two plug-in-provided functions that can help.

First, you can use `print_wp_shopping_cart()` to display the shopping cart wherever you want it:

```
<?php
  echo print_wp_shopping_cart();
?>
```

Here, the trusty `echo` command grabs the cart and inserts it into the page.

Second, you can use `print_wp_cart_button_for_product()` to create an "Add to Cart" button. This option is slightly more involved, because you need to supply two key product details: the product name and price. You can grab the product name from the post title, and you can get the price from the custom field. Here's the code that does the job:

```
<?php
  $productname = get_the_title();
  $price = get_post_meta( get_the_ID(), 'Price', true );

  echo print_wp_cart_button_for_product($productname, $price);
?>
```

Add both of these code snippets to the right place in the *single-product.php* template file, and you end up with a streamlined shopping cart that appears exactly where you want it, and an "Add to Cart" button that works for every item.

POWER USERS' CLINIC

Professional eCommerce Frameworks

If your goal is to build a professional ecommerce storefront, you'll need all the hardcore features described in this chapter, including custom post types, custom templates, custom fields, and custom taxonomies. However, you don't need to do all the work yourself. There are a dizzying number of ecommerce plug-ins that can extend an ordinary WordPress site with the bells, whistles, and low-level plumbing you need to sell large volumes of products. Many of these work with a ready-made theme so that you don't need to fiddle with templates.

You've already heard about the two most popular ecommerce plug-ins (WooCommerce and WP eCommerce), but you can find plenty more at *http://wordpress.org/plugins*, including Cart66, iThemes Exchange, TheCartPress, Jigoshop, and DukaPress. All are free, but you usually need to pay to get all the premium features you really need. You'll also be in for a steep learning curve, because even though you'll avoid some of the grunt work you saw in this chapter, you'll spend just as much time learning to customize the plug-ins' panoply of options and settings to suit your needs. For a good overview of the issues that face any WordPress site owner who wants to add ecommerce, you can read a free ebook on the subject at *http://tinyurl.com/wpe-ebook*. To get started with the leading WooCommerce plug-in, you can visit its voluminous documentation center at *http://tinyurl.com/woo-doc*.

PART

5

Appendixes

APPENDIX A:

Migrating from WordPress.com

APPENDIX B:

Securing a Self-Hosted Site

APPENDIX C:

Useful Websites

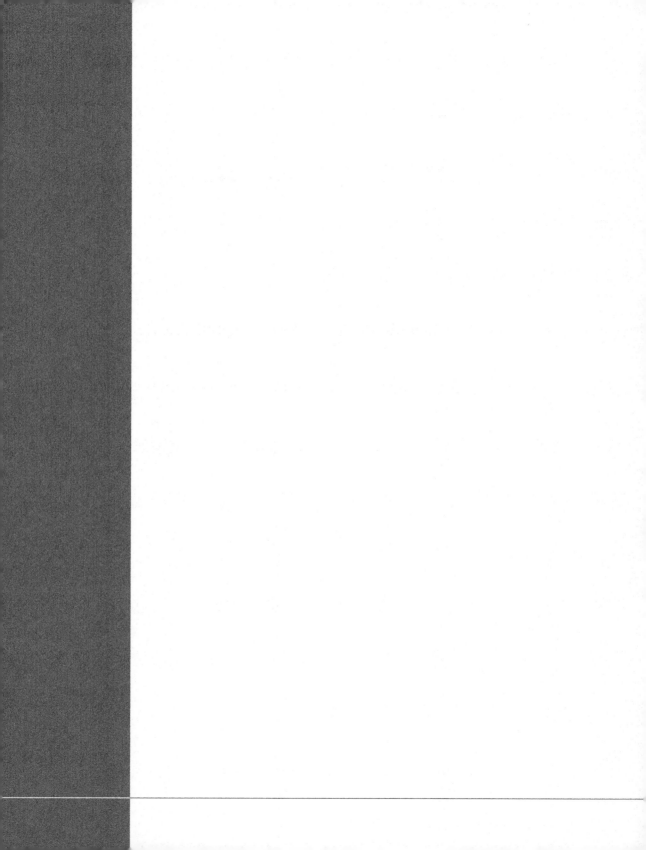

APPENDIX

A

Migrating from WordPress.com

WordPress.com is a great place to start your WordPress venture, and many fans stay there forever. But there are several reasons to strike out on your own and set up a self-hosted WordPress site. Most commonly, it's because you want to customize your site beyond what WordPress.com allows.

Here are the two features that can compel otherwise happy WordPress.com users to move on:

- **Themes.** WordPress.com site owners can choose from a collection of barely 200 themes, while self-hosters get to pick from well over 1,000 themes in the WordPress theme repository (and still more if you're willing to trawl the Web). More important, self-hosters can *modify* themes without restriction, which lets you do everything from swapping in your favorite Google font for headlines (page 481) to redesigning the site so that it works like a product catalog (Chapter 14).
- **Plug-ins.** You can't add plug-ins to a WordPress.com site. You're limited to a very small set of preinstalled plug-ins, chosen by Automattic. But on a self-hosted site, you have your choice of thousands of plug-ins that can extend your site with useful features, like better search optimization (page 441), new tools for multiauthor collaboration (page 381), and money-making options like ads and donation buttons (page 543).

Making the jump from WordPress.com to a self-hosted site can be awkward, but it's nothing you can't handle. Happily, WordPress has an import/export tool that does most of the work. In this appendix, you'll learn how to make the shift and deal with some of the inevitable hiccups.

Before You Begin

Before you do anything, it helps to have an overview of the migration process. You need to complete several steps, in this order:

1. **Sign up for a new site with a web host (for a monthly or annual fee).**

   This is also the point where you register a custom domain name (like *www.supernovatattooparlor.com*) if you don't already own one. If you bought a domain name through WordPress.com, don't worry—you can have it point to your new site when you finish the transfer process, as explained on page 561.

2. **Install a fresh copy of WordPress on your new site.**

   Unfortunately, you can't move a complete WordPress site as is. You need to start with a basic blank shell of a site and then load it up with the data from your old site.

3. **Export the data from your old site.**

   You download this data to your computer as a single, compact file.

4. **Import the data into your new site.**

   In this step, you add the downloaded content from step 3 to the empty WordPress site on your web host.

5. **Configure and clean up your new site.**

   This is the part where you fiddle with your theme and install Jetpack, all in an attempt to make your new site function as much as possible like the old one.

6. **Reroute your web visitors from the old WordPress.com site to your new self-hosted site.**

   This is optional, but you don't want visitors going to an out-of-date copy of your site, missing your new posts. Ideally, visitors will be seamlessly redirected to your new site, without needing to click a link or type in a new web address.

The first two steps are covered in Chapter 3. Make sure you complete them before you continue any further in this appendix, because there's no use trying to transfer a WordPress.com site if you don't have a self-hosted site ready and waiting to receive it. The rest of this appendix covers everything else you need to do, beginning with step 3 above.

Transferring Your Data

Assuming you signed up with a web host and installed WordPress on your new site, the next step is to copy all the information from your WordPress.com site. That includes the posts and pages you wrote, the menus you created, and all the comments your readers submitted.

Transferring this data takes two steps. First, you download it from your WordPress.com site to your computer. Then, you upload it from your computer to your new site.

GEM IN THE ROUGH

Guided Transfers

If this transition sounds like altogether too much work—or the thought of configuring anything to do with web hosting is enough to wake you, screaming, in the middle of the night—there's an easier option. You can pay WordPress.com to perform a *guided transfer*, in which a nerd-for-hire at Automattic sets up your domain, transfers your site, and configures a few plug-ins that make the site run more like a standard WordPress.com site.

Unfortunately, there are two significant caveats: You need to cough up a one-time fee of $129, and you need to use one of WordPress's recommended web hosts. To learn more, read up at *http://tinyurl.com/guidedtransfer*. To sign up, visit the Store section of the dashboard for your site, find the Guided Transfer box, and then click Buy Now.

Exporting Your Data from WordPress.com

Here's how to get information out of your original WordPress.com site:

1. **Log in to your WordPress.com site's dashboard and choose Tools→Export.**

   The Export page opens, which gives you the option to export your data (described here) or to opt for the guided transfer process (described in the box above).

2. **Click Export.**

   Now WordPress.com asks what data you want to extract (Figure A-1).

3. **Choose "All content."**

   If you want to create a significantly different site from your current one, you may want to bring over just some data; if so, choose one of the other options. Usually, though, you want to export everything.

4. **Click Download Export File.**

   Depending on your web browser, you may be asked for a filename, or it may automatically save the exported file in your Downloads folder. The file will have a name like this:

   ```
   therealestatediaries.wordpress.2015-01-17.xml
   ```

   The first part is the name of your WordPress.com site (*therealestatediaries*), the second part is the date you performed the export (January 17, 2015), and the final part is the file extension that indicates it's an XML file, which is a format computers often use to store structured data.

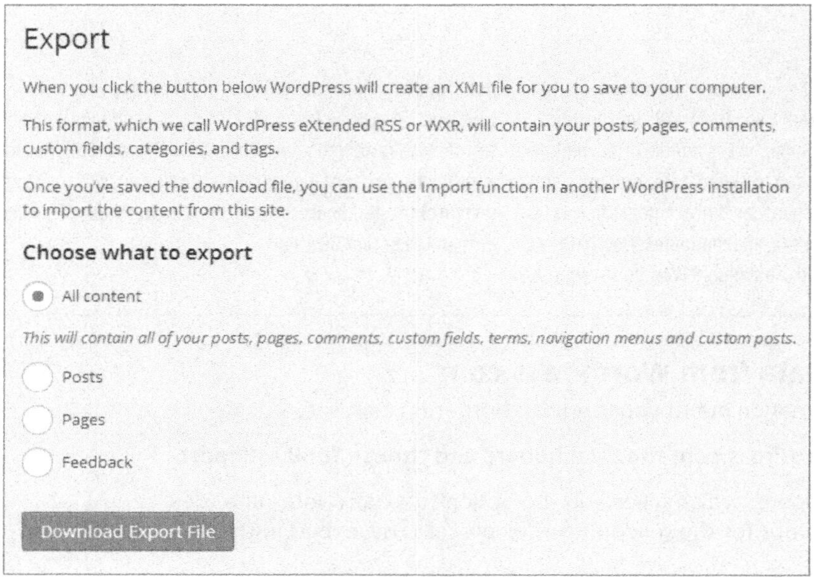

Export

When you click the button below WordPress will create an XML file for you to save to your computer.

This format, which we call WordPress eXtended RSS or WXR, will contain your posts, pages, comments, custom fields, categories, and tags.

Once you've saved the download file, you can use the Import function in another WordPress installation to import the content from this site.

Choose what to export

All content

This will contain all of your posts, pages, comments, custom fields, terms, navigation menus and custom posts.

Posts

Pages

Feedback

Download Export File

FIGURE A-1

WordPress.com's "All content" option exports every exportable piece of site data: posts, pages, and comments.

FREQUENTLY ASKED QUESTION

Where Are the Pictures?

My site uses plenty of pictures, but they aren't in the export file. Where are they?

WordPress doesn't attempt to put pictures and other post attachments in the export file. If it did, the export file could easily balloon to a gargantuan size. Instead, WordPress adds a *link* for each picture that belongs to an exported post or page. When you import your WordPress.com site to your new self-hosted site, the import tool processes these links, fetching the associated file from your old site and copying it to your new one. Problem solved!

Importing Your Data into a Self-Hosted Site

Although the exported file doesn't look like much, it holds the nucleus of your site—the raw text of every post you've ever written. To add it to your new site, you need an import operation, as described in the following steps:

1. **Log in to the dashboard of your new site, and choose Tools→Import.**

   WordPress lists the sites from which it can import data, including Blogger, LiveJournal, Movable Type, Tumblr, and several more.

2. **Click the WordPress link to import the data you exported from your WordPress.com site.**

   The "Install importer" window opens (Figure A-2).

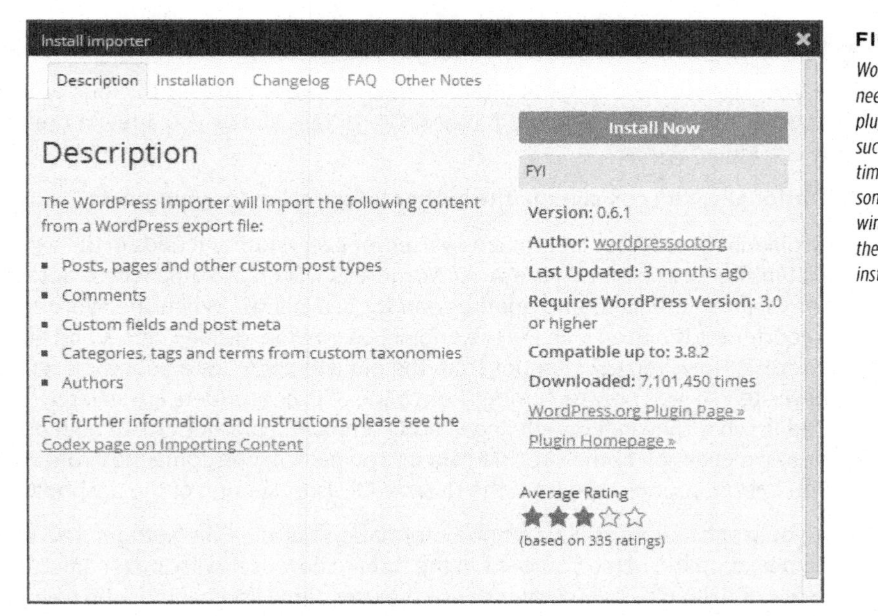

FIGURE A-2

WordPress self-hosters need to install the Importer plug-in before they can suck in any data. The first time you try to import something, you see this window, which describes the plug-in and lets you install it.

3. **Click Install Now.**

   WordPress installs the plug-in in a fraction of second.

4. **Click the "Activate Plugin & Run Importer" link to start the import process.**

   The Import WordPress window appears (Figure A-3).

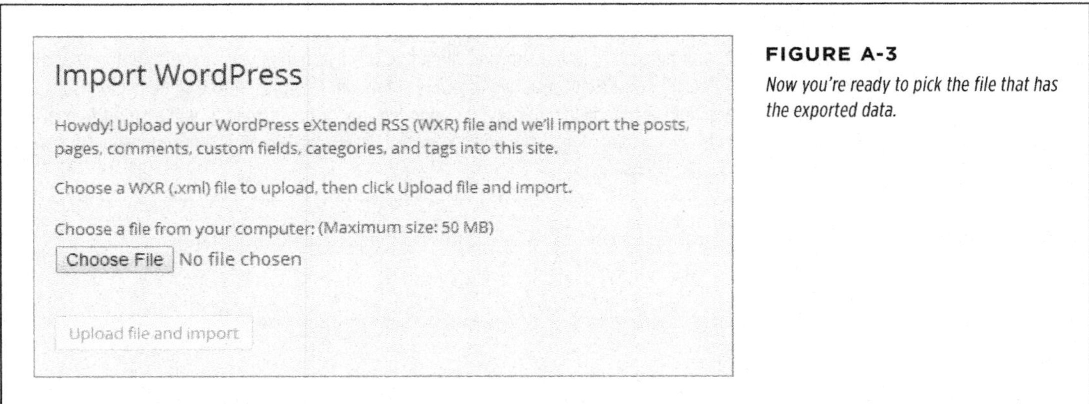

FIGURE A-3

Now you're ready to pick the file that has the exported data.

5. **Click Browse or Choose File (the exact name of the button depends on your browser). When the file selection window opens, browse to the exported XML file and select it.**

   That's the file you created in the previous section, like *therealestatediaries.wordpress.2015-01-17.xml.*

6. **Click "Upload file and import."**

   If your export file is large, it'll take a while for your browser to transfer it to your WordPress site. When it finishes, WordPress shows you a few more options (Figure A-4).

7. **Optionally, you can change the author information for your posts.**

   Ordinarily, WordPress creates a new user for every author it finds in the export file. In the example in Figure A-4, WordPress will create a new user account for Charles M. Pakata and another one for lisachang2. When the WordPress importer adds a user, it keeps the original user name, display name, and email address. However, each author from the old site becomes a *subscriber* in the new site. (As you may remember from page 370, subscribers are severely limited in what they can do—they can add comments, but not create new posts or make changes to the site). Of course, you can change someone's role after you import your old site from the Users→All Users section of the dashboard.

   If you want to import your author information but give the authors new user names, type the name you want in the "create new user with login name" text box. For example, if you prefer to use the user name lisachang on the new site for the user formerly known as lisachang2, now is the time to make that change.

   In some cases, you might want to assign imported posts to an author who already exists on your site. In this case, choose the author's name from the "assign posts to an existing user" list. It doesn't matter whether the author has the same user name on both your old and new sites; you still need to pick that name from the list to link up your imported posts.

NOTE If you have the same user account on your new site and your old site, but you don't bother to pick the author from the "assign posts" list, you'll run into a strange problem. Say, for example, that you're importing the user lisachang2 (and her posts) into a site that already has a lisachang2 user account. Unfortunately, the WordPress importer doesn't know that these two accounts are meant to represent the same person, so it won't create a new user account for lisachang2, nor will it assign her any posts. Instead, it will assign the posts that belong to lisachang2 to the currently logged-in person who is running the WordPress importer tool (that's you), which probably isn't what you want.

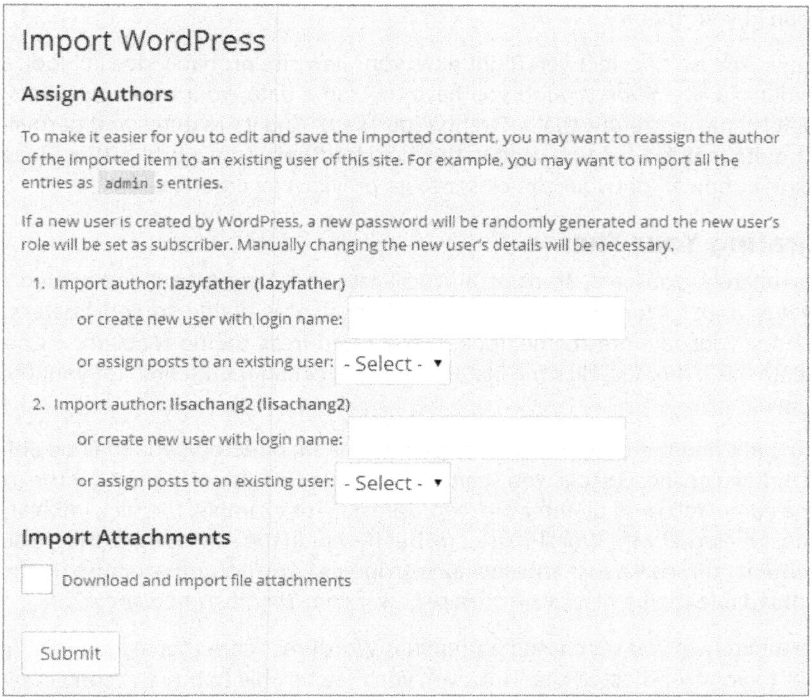

Import WordPress

Assign Authors

To make it easier for you to edit and save the imported content, you may want to reassign the author of the imported item to an existing user of this site. For example, you may want to import all the entries as `admin` s entries.

If a new user is created by WordPress, a new password will be randomly generated and the new user's role will be set as subscriber. Manually changing the new user's details will be necessary.

1. Import author: **lazyfather (lazyfather)**
   or create new user with login name:
   or assign posts to an existing user: - Select -
2. Import author: **lisachang2 (lisachang2)**
   or create new user with login name:
   or assign posts to an existing user: - Select -

Import Attachments

Download and import file attachments

Submit

FIGURE A-4

In this example, the imported posts have two authors. You can choose to transfer this author information to your new site or assign the posts to different authors.

TIP If you're the only author on your site, you should assign all the posts you import to your administrator account on the new WordPress site—that's the account you use to log in to the dashboard and write new posts.

8. **Check the box next to "Download and import file attachments."**

   This way, the WordPress importer copies all your old pictures and other media files from your old site to the new one. However, the copy process doesn't include videos—if you've got any, WordPress.com's VideoPress hosts them, and you need the Jetpack plug-in to display them on your new site (page 297).

9. **Click Submit.**

   WordPress gets to work updating your site. If it needs to transfer a large number of pictures, it may take a bit of time before it finishes.

Cleaning Up Your New Site

Congratulations, your website is now under new management! As a self-hosted WordPress site owner, you're in complete control of every setting, plug-in, and line of code in your theme.

However, life isn't perfect yet. Right now, your new site probably doesn't look a lot like your old site. Even though you have the same data, your new site sports the default theme (currently, that's Twenty Fourteen). And its features and permalinks don't quite match what you used in the old WordPress.com world, either. Read on to find out how to get your site closer to its previous incarnation.

Migrating Your Theme

Unfortunately, you can't transfer a WordPress.com theme to a self-hosted site. However, most WordPress.com themes are also available to self-hosters. To check for your favorite theme, look in the WordPress theme repository. Choose Appearance→Themes, click the Install Themes tab, and then search for your theme by name.

If you can't find the theme in the WordPress theme directory, you may be able to hunt it down online. Go to a web search engine like Google and search for the exact theme name, followed by the word "wordpress." For example, the slick Imbalance2 theme is included with WordPress.com, but it's not in the self-hosters' theme directory. But if you search for "imbalance2 wordpress," you'll stumble across the freely downloadable theme files at *http://wpshower.com/themes/imbalance-2*.

Unfortunately, if you purchased a premium WordPress.com theme, you can't port it over to your self-hosted site. However, you may be able to buy a second copy for your new site (usually for the same price). To look into this option, follow these steps:

1. **Go to the WordPress.com theme gallery at *http://theme.wordpress.com.***

2. **Search for your theme, and then click it to see a page with more theme information.**

3. **Scroll down until you see the "Stats & Info" section at the bottom of the right-hand sidebar.**

4. **Look for a "More themes by" link, and then click it.**

   This takes you to a page with information about the theme creator. Look for a link to the theme creator's site, and click that.

5. **Finally, browse through the theme creator's site.**

   Hopefully, you'll find a self-hosted version of the theme you want, which you can buy and download. You can then add the theme to your site by visiting the Add Themes page and clicking the Upload Theme button (page 141).

If you're unlucky, you might not be able to find a version of your theme for your self-hosted site. In that case, you need to start over by choosing a new theme and customizing it to get the look you want. Chapter 5 has plenty of information that can help you find a good theme.

Even if you do find the theme you want, you may need to redo some of the basic customization you did before, when your site was running on WordPress.com. For example, you probably need to resubmit your site header (choose Appearance→Header) and add the widgets you want to the appropriate widget areas (Appearance→Widgets). And even though WordPress transfers your old menus, you need to reattach them to the right part of your theme (Appearance→Menus).

Missing WordPress.com Features

Although self-hosted sites and WordPress.com sites have most of the same features, they're not identical. The chief culprit is WordPress.com's built-in plug-ins, which provide features like slideshows, Facebook comments, web statistics, and sharing buttons. Throughout this book, we note what plug-ins you need to duplicate WordPress.com features. The best way to fill most of the gaps at once is to install the Jetpack plug-in. In fact, Automattic created Jetpack to help level the playing field between WordPress.com sites and self-hosted sites. You can learn more about it on page 297.

Permalinks

Every new self-hosted WordPress site starts out using ID-based permalinks. That means that when you click through to a specific post, you get sent to a page with a web address like this:

```
http://therealestatediaries.net/?p=299
```

By contrast, WordPress.com uses a permalink style that avoids IDs, instead combining the date and the post names to create links. They look like this:

```
http://therealestatediaries.wordpress.com/2014/07/30/know-the-law-before-it-
knows-you
```

As a result, when you transfer posts to your new site, they won't have the same permalinks. You can easily fix this inconsistency. Choose Settings→Permalinks and pick a new permalink style. Page 117 describes the options for self-hosted sites, but if you choose "Day and name," you get the same web addresses that WordPress.com uses. Click Save Changes to make your selection permanent, and all your posts will automatically use the style you picked.

Redirecting Your Website Address

The last thing you want is to have two copies of your site on the Web. Not only will this thoroughly confuse visitors, but it'll also baffle search engines. You need a single identity and a single web address for your site.

The exact steps you follow depend on your original website address—that's the one you used with WordPress.com. If you bought a custom domain name when you originally signed up with WordPress.com, read the next section ("Keeping

Your Custom Domain"). If your old site used a *.wordpress.com* address, jump to the second section ("Moving from .wordpress.com").

KEEPING YOUR CUSTOM DOMAIN

If you followed the good advice in Chapter 2 and bought a custom domain name when you first signed up with WordPress.com, the transfer process is easy. You can keep the same domain for your new site.

If you bought the custom name through a domain registrar, you already know what to do—log in to your account and point your domain to the new site (see page 45).

If you bought the custom name through WordPress.com, you have two choices:

- Transfer your domain from WordPress.com to your new web host.
- Keep it registered with WordPress.com but point it to your new site.

Both options have the same effect. The only difference is who charges you the yearly domain registration fee (either your web host or Automattic, the people who run WordPress.com). You might choose to transfer your domain if your web host charges you less, or if it offers a free domain with your website package.

No matter which option you choose, you need to configure your WordPress.com domain. To do that, log in to your old WordPress.com site and go to the Store→Domains section of the dashboard. Then follow the instructions at *http://tinyurl.com/8ese4cp.*

MOVING FROM .WORDPRESS.COM

If your original site uses a *.wordpress.com* domain, you need to redirect guests to your new domain. Your best bet is to buy the Site Redirect upgrade, which costs $13 per year. To get it, log into your old WordPress.com site, visit the Store section, find the Site Upgrade box, and then click Buy Now. Tell WordPress.com about your new site, and it handles the redirection automatically, serving out a special sort of notice called an HTTP 301 code, which clearly tells search engines that you've moved to a new home (so they can update your listing).

In a year or so, when your readers (and the search engines of the world) have gotten used to your new address, you can cancel the upgrade and delete your WordPress.com site using the Tools→Delete Blog command in the dashboard.

NOTE Instead of buying the Site Redirect upgrade, you *could* try to redirect traffic on your own. The basic technique is to change the home page on your old site to a static page that has a message explaining that you moved your site, along with a link to your new home. But this technique is fraught with problems, because readers may enter your site through bookmarks and miss your message, and search engines will continue funneling people to the wrong site (because it will have a higher ranking than your new site). So don't do this unless your site has virtually no readers or search engine traffic to worry about.

APPENDIX

B

Securing a Self-Hosted Site

As you know, WordPress is one of the world's most popular site-building tools. Thanks to its popularity, it attracts plenty of attention—and not all of it is good.

The uncomfortable truth is that the Internet is swarming with nefarious people who would love to get their hands on your site. The good news is that these enemies aren't the sort of computer super-geniuses you see in movies, using semi-magical powers to hack into government sites faster than you can make a slice of toast. Instead, they're the sort of riffraff you find loitering in the bushes near an empty house, or lurking around parked cars in an alleyway. They're looking for low-hanging fruit—easy crimes of opportunity that become possible when someone leaves a door unlocked, forgets to close a window, or just plain stops paying attention. In the WordPress world, slip-ups like these occur when you forget to install a plug-in update, say, or fail to conceal your password. These attackers aren't out to steal your stuff—usually, they just want to pull your site into their spam network by planting garish ads, dummy links, and other sorts of garbage.

Fortunately, you don't need to make your WordPress site bulletproof; you just need to close the gaps and avoid the mistakes that allow 99 percent of the attacks. Do that, and hackers will move on from your site and find other places to cause trouble.

In this brief appendix, you'll learn the five best security practices you can use to harden your site. Implement these techniques, and you're sure to sleep soundly.

NOTE Don't underestimate the threat of a WordPress attack. Even though your site may not be large enough to attract a hacker's personal attention, hackers run automated tools that can launch attacks against thousands of WordPress sites at a time.

1. Crash-Proof Your Site with Backups

If you take only one piece of advice from this appendix, it should be this: Back up your site regularly. It won't prevent an attack, but it will let you recover from almost any catastrophe.

To keep your site safe, you need to create a proper backup schedule. You can't just make an occasional backup whenever the thought crosses your mind. The ideal frequency depends on how often you add new content, the cost of recreating lost content, and the size of your site. A weekly backup is good—it ensures that you'll never lose more than seven days' worth of work. For frequently updated sites, a daily backup is better, because it limits your losses to a day or two.

You also need to think about how many old backups you save. Your goal is to keep enough to make sure you have a good copy of your site even if you don't notice an attack immediately after it occurs. For example, if a hacker sneaks into your site and adds some subtle spam, you might not notice it for a couple of weeks. If you use a rolling backup strategy that keeps site snapshots from the last seven days, you'll be left with a week's worth of spam-compromised backups, and no good copy of your site. One way to avoid this problem is to combine a frequent, automated rolling backup (for example, 10 daily backups) with a less-frequent manual backup (every month or so).

Finally, you should think about where you *store* your backups. Usually, you put them in a private area on your website. But for the absolute best protection, you should download the occasional backup to your computer, so you have something to fall back on if a severe attack scrambles your entire hosting account.

If you installed your WordPress site with Softaculous, you've got easy access to the excellent backup feature described on page 60. If not, you can get a WordPress plug-in to do the same job, as described on page 313.

2. Change Your Posting Account

When you install a new WordPress site, you start with a single account. This is an all-purpose administrator account that can do everything from writing posts to switching themes and installing plug-ins. This is exactly the sort of access a hacker would like to have, and every time you log into your site, you increase the chance that someone might steal your login details—whether that's by snooping through network traffic or looking over your shoulder. And once hackers have those credentials, they can take complete control of your site, and even lock *you* out.

A safer strategy is to do all your posting using a more limited user account. That way, if a shady character gets your password, she can write posts (which you can easily delete after the fact), but she won't be able to wreak real damage (like poisoning your plug-ins with malware). The only disadvantage to this approach is that you need to juggle two login credentials. Most of the time, you'll use the more limited account to work with content. But if you want to reconfigure your site, you need to switch to the administrator account.

Putting this approach into practice is easy, provided that you rely on the user management skills you picked up in Chapter 11. Here's what to do:

1. **In the dashboard, choose Users→Add New.**

   Fill in the key details for your new account.

   At a minimum, you need a user name, email address, and password. You can use the same email address as your administrator account, but you must choose a distinct user name (and you should definitely pick a different password). If you need some good password advice, see page 27.

2. **In the Role list, choose Editor.**

   An editor can do all the daily tasks necessary for a WordPress site. Editors have full control over every page and post, and they can moderate comments. However, they can't change themes, plug-ins, and configuration of the site. This gives your site a wide margin of safety.

   Alternatively, you can use the author role. The disadvantage is that you need to log in with different credentials to create pages or moderate comments. Page 370 details the different roles for a WordPress site.

3. **Click Add New User.**

   This creates the user account. You can now log out of the dashboard and log back in as an editor.

Ideally, you should also make sure WordPress doesn't display your user name as a byline, where a hacker's screen scraping tool might grab it. (And besides, user names look ugly in posts.) To change how your name appears on the site, log in, visit Users→Your Profile, and choose a different name in the "Display name publicly as" setting. If you don't see the exact name you want, type it into the Nickname box. WordPress automatically copies your nickname into the "Display name publicly as" list, where you can then select it.

NOTE One last thing: Your admin account should never be named "admin"; that's just too obvious. You already learned to avoid this rookie mistake when you installed your site, but if you failed to heed this good advice, you can fix the problem after the fact. Just create a new user that has the administrator role, log in under those new credentials, and then delete the original admin account.

3. Be Cautious When Extending Your Site

One of the great advantages of WordPress is its extensibility, which lets you change your site's style and bolt on new features with themes and plug-ins. However, every theme and plug-in contains bits of PHP code that attackers can exploit. Most won't bother (they'd rather use attacks that target every WordPress site, rather than hunt for sites with specific plug-ins). But some hackers are more devious. They create themes and plug-ins that *contain* spamware, and then attempt to get you to install them. If you do, there's no need for a spammer to hack your site, because you just invited him in.

To steer clear of this danger, you need to stick to the official repositories for your plug-ins and themes. For example, you probably won't go wrong on the official WordPress site, with its thousands of themes (*http://wordpress.org/themes*) and tens of thousands of plug-ins (*http://wordpress.org/plugins*). Most of the themes and plug-in links in this book are taken from WordPress repositories, although there are a few from other highly trustworthy sources. However, if you venture further afield, be careful. If you Google "free WordPress themes," you're almost certain to stumble across seemingly innocent offerings that have malware embedded in their code. So if you find an interesting theme or plug-in but have even a faint doubt about its provenance, stay safe and don't install it.

Even respectable extensions from honest developers can have unexpected security vulnerabilities. Remember, all themes and plug-ins contain PHP code, which means there's always a possible security flaw lurking in your files that's waiting to be exploited. The more plug-ins and themes you have, the greater the risk you run. To keep the odds in your favor, use a small set of plug-ins—only ones that have proved to be truly valuable to your site. Always update your themes and plug-ins in the Dashboard→Updates page to make sure you're protected should hackers discover a new security exploit. And remember to delete themes and plug-ins you don't intend to use. As long as they're installed on your site, an attacker can exploit them, even if you haven't made them active.

NOTE Several years ago, a number of WordPress site-builders ran into trouble thanks to an error in an image resizing script (called TimThumb), which turned up in a few dozen themes. Many site owners had one of the affected themes, and some assumed they were safe because the themes were inactive. But that wasn't the case—the attackers were still able to use the inactive theme files to launch attacks and take over sites. The only defense was to upgrade or delete the flawed themes.

4. Prevent Password-Guessing Attacks

When you created your site, you learned about the dangers of bad passwords (page 27). But even the best passwords are just a combination of a letters, numbers, and a few other characters, which means they can all be guessed—eventually. To help with the guesswork, hackers use automated tools that attempt to log in to WordPress sites thousands of times a minute. Often, these tools use a long list of words and names, into which they substitute numbers and special characters.

Although password-guessing hacks aren't the most common type of attack, they're surprisingly easy to defend against. The Limit Login Attempts plug-in (*http://tinyurl.com/limit-login-a*) is the perfect tool. It notices suspicious activity—repeated failed login attempts—and temporarily locks up your account. This frustrates attackers and ties up their automated password-guessing tools, making it virtually impossible for them to gain access to your site by brute force.

To use the Limit Login Attempts plug-in, just install and activate it. You don't need to perform any further customization. However, if you choose Settings→Limit Login Attempts, you can control how the lockout feature works (Figure B-1)

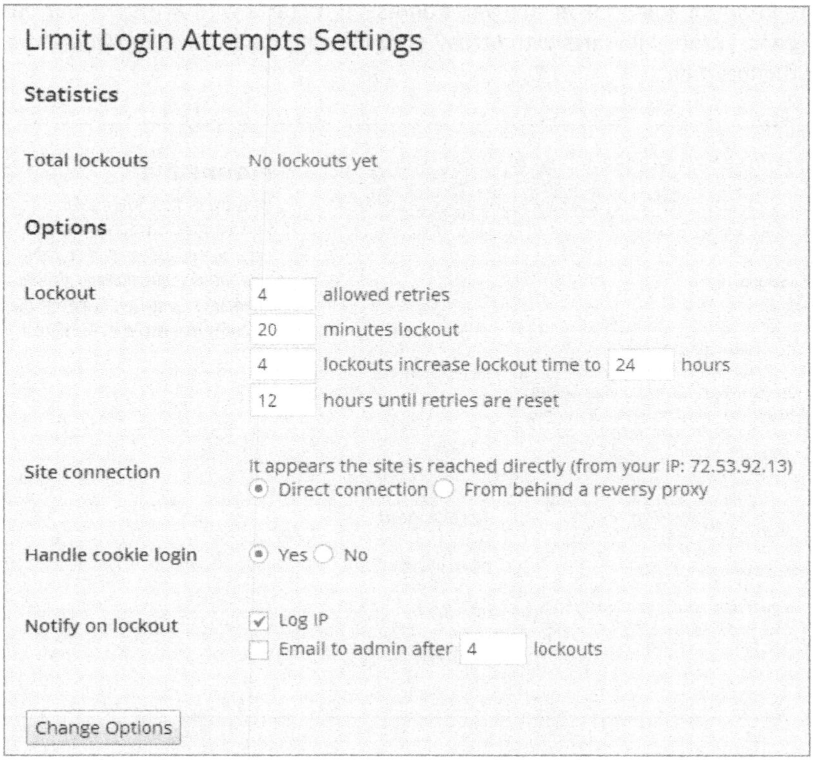

FIGURE B-1

The Limit Login Attempts plug-in lets you set how many consecutive failed logins you allow before the lockout applies (four is typical), how long the lockout should last (20 minutes to start), and whether the plug-in should notify you (by email) about the attempted incursion.

TIP An alternate choice is the excellent (and very popular) Wordfence plug-in (*http://tinyurl.com/w-fence*). It provides a comprehensive suite of security features, including a configurable login lockout that works like Limit Login Attempts. Although it's overkill for most small sites, Wordfence boasts some truly impressive features, including the ability to scan your WordPress files looking for malware, and real-time monitoring that checks your site for signs of an attack.

5. Hide Passwords with SSL

SSL (Secure Sockets Layer) is an Internet standard that *encrypts* information before it's sent to a website. For example, when you make a purchase at Amazon, SSL encrypts your credit card details. The recipient of your message (Amazon) has no trouble decoding your secret message (the credit card number) and processing your payment. If Internet eavesdroppers intercept your message, they'll find just a chunk of impenetrably scrambled data.

Wherever there's ecommerce, and whenever you need to log in to a secure site (from Facebook to Gmail), SSL is at work. Browsers let you know when you're visiting a secure site by displaying a tiny padlock in the address bar (Figure B-2), but if you're in doubt, just look at the web address. If it starts with *https://*, your data is being encrypted; if it starts with *http://*, your information is travelling free and clear over the Internet.

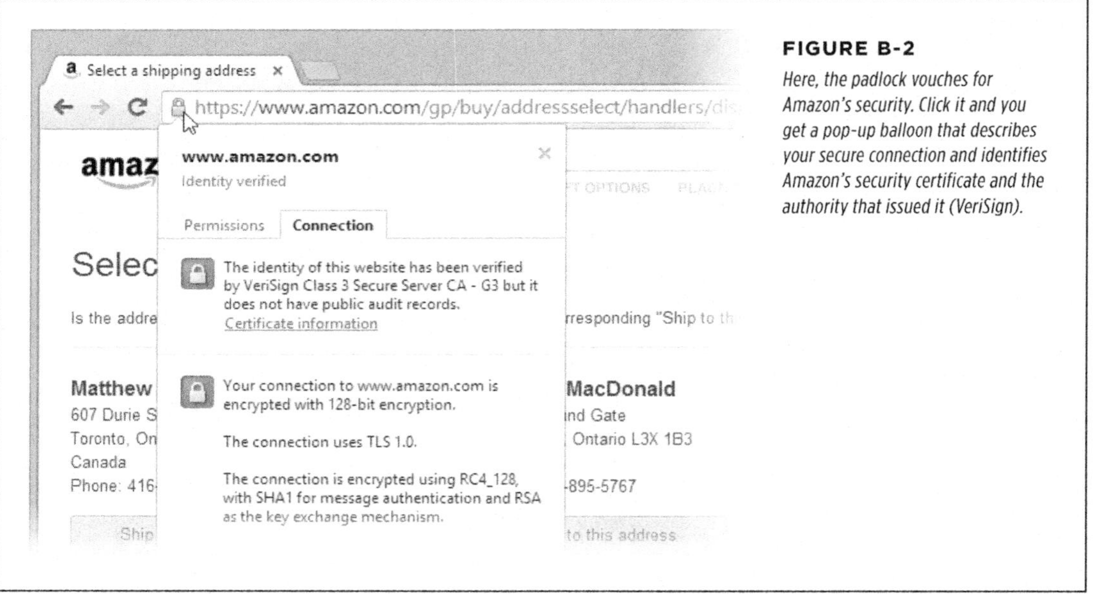

FIGURE B-2

Here, the padlock vouches for Amazon's security. Click it and you get a pop-up balloon that describes your secure connection and identifies Amazon's security certificate and the authority that issued it (VeriSign).

When you're not using SSL, hackers have the opportunity to steal your data. All they need to do is watch the traffic as it flows over one of the network devices between your computer and the website you're talking to. (If you're curious to learn more, the detailed walkthrough at *http://tinyurl.com/steal-pass* explains how a password can get stolen from an unsuspecting WordPress administrator.)

It comes as a great surprise to many WordPress fans to learn that a newly installed self-hosted WordPress site doesn't use SSL. As a result, every time you log into the dashboard, your user name and password are exposed. A potential thief doesn't need any special coding skills to steal your credentials, just good timing.

Although this vulnerability is disappointing, it's not WordPress's fault. In order to participate in an SSL-encrypted conversation, a website, like your newly launched WordPress site, needs to be able to prove its identity. And a site can do that only with a *digital certificate*—an electronic document from a trusted third party (known as a *certificate authority*) that vouches for the site's identity.

For example, Amazon can accept your securely encrypted credit card details only because another organization has certified the Amazon site's authenticity. Its digital certificate verifies that the *www.amazon.com* domain name truly belongs to Amazon. In other words, if you see a web address starting with *https://www.amazon.com* in your browser, you can be confident that you have a secure connection to the Amazon site, not another web server that's attempting to impersonate it. If you want to have a secure conversation with your website, it needs a similar certificate. Think of the digital certificate as a license to use SSL.

UP TO SPEED

How Does a Certificate Authority Decide to Trust a Website?

Obviously, there are massive numbers of websites with certificates, and in most cases the certificate authority doesn't know much about them beyond their business name and address. And in recent years, certificate authorities have begun issuing cheaper certificates that simply guarantee that the certificate holder owns a certain domain. They don't attempt to prove that there is a real person or business operating under that name.

However, the clever part about certificates is that they're *revocable*. If it turns out that a business is defrauding people, misrepresenting itself, or engaged in spamware or illegal activity, the certificate authority can cancel the certificate immediately, rendering it useless. It's much the same as a driver's license—although the license itself can't guarantee safe driving, a serious enough offense will lead to a suspended license.

The easiest way to get a certificate is to purchase it through your web hosting company. Typically, the cheapest type of certificate (called "domain-verified only") requires an annual fee that falls between $50 and $150 per year, depending on your web host. To buy a certificate, contact your web host and file a certificate request.

Once your host certifies your site, you can log in to the dashboard with a secure connection—just modify your web address so that it starts with *https://*. You should see the comforting padlock icon in your browser's address bar.

Even after you get a certificate, your site will still let people log in with normal, unencrypted connections. If they do, their passwords are just as vulnerable as they were before. To protect your site, you should *force* everyone (including yourself) to use SSL. In other words, you should tell WordPress to always demand an encrypted SSL connection for the dashboard. To do that, you need to change your site's *wp-config.php* file.

You can do that two ways. Lazy administrators can use the WordPress HTTPS plug-in (*http://tinyurl.com/wp-https*). But if you're comfortable using a text editor and an FTP program, you can make the change by hand:

1. **Using an FTP program, download the *wp-config.php* file.**

   You find it in the root folder of your WordPress site.

2. **Open the file you just downloaded in a text editor, and edit it.**

   Look for this comment:

   ```
   /* That's all, stop editing! Happy blogging. */
   ```

   Immediately before that comment, add this line (Figure B-3):

   ```
   define('FORCE_SSL_ADMIN', true);
   ```

   This tells WordPress that someone can manage your site only if she uses an SSL connection.

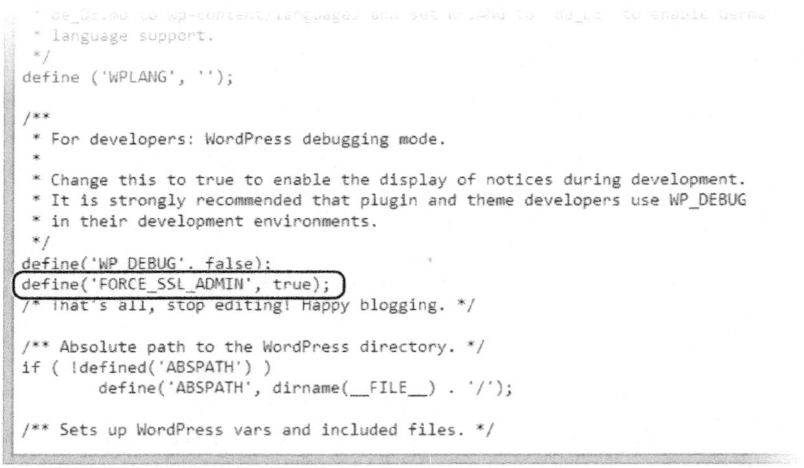

```
 * language support.
 */
define ('WPLANG', '');

/**
 * For developers: WordPress debugging mode.
 *
 * Change this to true to enable the display of notices during development.
 * It is strongly recommended that plugin and theme developers use WP_DEBUG
 * in their development environments.
 */
define('WP_DEBUG', false);
define('FORCE_SSL_ADMIN', true);
/* That's all, stop editing! Happy blogging. */

/** Absolute path to the WordPress directory. */
if ( !defined('ABSPATH') )
	define('ABSPATH', dirname(__FILE__) . '/');

/** Sets up WordPress vars and included files. */
```

FIGURE B-3

Here's the single line you need to add to your wp-config.php file to enforce an SSL connection, assuming your site has a digital certificate. Although some content appears after the "stop editing" comment, your SSL code should not.

NOTE Don't be intimidated if your site's version of the *wp-config.php* file doesn't look as tidy as the one in Figure B-3. The line breaks are optional, and some web hosts strip them out automatically, creating a more cluttered (but equally functional) configuration file. Just ignore the mess and add the SSL line above the "stop editing" comment.

3. **Save your changes, and upload the new version of *wp-config.php* back to its original place.**

   Your FTP program will ask if you want to overwrite the old copy, which you do.

Now if you attempt to log in using an unsecured *http://* connection, WordPress redirects you to the same page using the proper *https://* encrypted connection. This means there's no longer a way for passwords to slip out into the open during the login process.

APPENDIX

C

Useful Websites

Throughout this book, you learned about a number of great websites where you can get valuable information or download WordPress plug-ins. Odds are you'll want to revisit some of those sites. To save you the effort of leafing through hundreds of pages to find the link you want, this appendix provides the links, grouped by chapter.

If just the thought of typing in these links gives you carpal tunnel syndrome, you can use the online version of this appendix, located on the *WordPress: The Missing Manual, Second Edition* Missing CD page at *http://www.oreilly.com/pub/missing-manuals/wpmm2e*. That way, once you find a site you want to visit, you're just a click away.

Chapter Links

The following tables list the links found in each chapter. Each table lists the links in the same order they appear in the text.

INTRODUCTION

DESCRIPTION	URL
WordPress usage statistics	*http://tinyurl.com/3438rb6*
Missing CD page for this book	*http://www.oreilly.com/pub/missingmanuals/wpmm2e*
Try-out site for this book	*http://prosetech.com/wordpress*
Register this book	*www.oreilly.com/register*

DESCRIPTION	URL
The Missing Manuals feedback page	*www.missingmanuals.com/feedback*
Submit errata for this book	*http://tinyurl.com/7mujhnx*

CHAPTER 1 *The WordPress Landscape*

DESCRIPTION	URL
Paul Krugman's blog	*http://krugman.blogs.nytimes.com*
Technorati	*http://technorati.com/blogs/top100* (top 100 blogs) *http://bit.ly/1fSbmAT* (Digital Influencer's report)
FAIL Blog	*http://failblog.org*
Damn You Autocorrect!	*http://damnyouautocorrect.com*
How to plan your blog	*http://learn.wordpress.com/get-focused*
The Sartorialist blog	*www.thesartorialist.com*
The Internet Encyclopedia of Philosophy	*www.iep.utm.edu*
Wappalyzer	*http://wappalyzer.com*
WordPress-powered Ford site	*http://social.ford.com*
Examples of self-hosted WordPress sites	*http://wordpress.org/showcase*
WordPress.com WordAds	*http://wordpress.com/apply-for-wordads*
WordPress.com upgrades	*http://support.wordpress.com/upgrades*
WordPress.com popular subjects	*http://wordpress.com/tags*
WordPress.com complaints	*http://wordpress.com/complaints*
WordPress support forums	*http://wordpress.org/support* (self-hosted sites) *http://forums.wordpress.com* (WordPress.com sites)
WordPress.com VIP hosting	*http://vip.wordpress.com*
WP Engine	*http://wpengine.com*
Synthesis	*http://websynthesis.com*

CHAPTER 2 *Signing Up with WordPress.com*

DESCRIPTION	URL
WordPress.com sign-up page	*http://wordpress.com/signup*
Worst passwords	*http://onforb.es/v2rdOb*
Forward email from a custom domain	*http://support.wordpress.com/email-forwarding*

DESCRIPTION	URL
Examples of self-hosted WordPress sites	*http://wordpress.org/showcase*
Use external email with a custom domain	*http://tinyurl.com/ext-email*

CHAPTER 3 *Installing WordPress on Your Web Host*

DESCRIPTION	URL
Web Hosting Talk forum	*http://bit.ly/vQ7tkH*
WordPress-recommended hosts	*http://wordpress.org/hosting*
WordPress software (to download)	*http://wordpress.org/download*
List of WordPress releases	*http://wordpress.org/news/category/releases*

CHAPTER 4 *Creating Posts*

DESCRIPTION	URL
Wayback Machine	*http://web.archive.org*
URL shortening services	*http://bit.ly* *http://tinyurl.com* *http://tiny.cc*
WordPress mobile apps	*http://wordpress.org/mobile*

CHAPTER 5 *Choosing and Polishing Your WordPress Theme*

DESCRIPTION	URL
Stock.xchng	*www.sxc.hu*
WordPress reference for `wp_tag_cloud()`	*http://tinyurl.com/wptagcloud*
WPtouch (plug-in)	*http://tinyurl.com/wptouch*

CHAPTER 6 *Jazzing Up Your Posts*

DESCRIPTION	URL
WordPress reference for smilies	*http://tinyurl.com/using-smilies*
WordPress plug-ins	*http://wordpress.org/plugins*
TinyMCE (plug-in)	*http://tinyurl.com/tinyeditor*
Windows Live Writer (desktop post editor for Windows)	*http://tinyurl.com/win-essentials*
Mars Edit (desktop post editor for Mac OS)	*www.red-sweater.com/marsedit*
List of desktop post editors	*http://tinyurl.com/blog-client*

DESCRIPTION	URL
WordPress themes	*http://wordpress.org/themes* (self-hosted sites) *http://theme.wordpress.com* (WordPress.com sites)
WordPress reference for `wp_link_pages()`	*http://tinyurl.com/wplinkpages*
Excerpt Editor (plug-in)	*http://tinyurl.com/csudedx*
WordPress reference for `the_excerpt()`	*http://tinyurl.com/the-excerpt*

CHAPTER 8 *Comments: Letting Your Readers Talk Back*

DESCRIPTION	URL
WP Content Filter (plug-in)	*http://tinyurl.com/wpcontentfilter*
Better WordPress Recent Comments (plug-in)	*http://tinyurl.com/wprecentcomments*
Polldaddy (plug-in)	*http://tinyurl.com/wp-polls*
Gravatar	*http://gravatar.com*
Anti-spam (plug-in)	*http://tinyurl.com/wp-anti-spam*
Antispam Bee (plug-in)	*http://antispambee.com*
AVH First Defense Against Spam (plug-in)	*http://tinyurl.com/avhspam*
Akismet	*http://akismet.com/wordpress*
Growmap Anti Spambot (plug-in)	*http://tinyurl.com/growmapspam*
Captcha (plug-in)	*http://tinyurl.com/wp-captcha*
Anti-Captcha (plug-in)	*http://tinyurl.com/wp-anticaptcha*
WP-Optimize (plug-in)	*http://tinyurl.com/wp-opti*
Batch delete comments with phpMyAdmin	*http://tinyurl.com/deletepen2*

CHAPTER 9 *Getting New Features with Plug-Ins*

DESCRIPTION	URL
How to write a plug-in	*http://tinyurl.com/write-plugin*
WordPress plug-ins	*http://wordpress.org/plugins*
Smashing Magazine	*http://wp.smashingmagazine.com*
WPMU DEV	*http://premium.wpmudev.org*
CodeCanyon	*http://codecanyon.net*
WordPress plug-in directory	*http://wordpress.org/plugins*
Jetpack	*http://jetpack.me*

DESCRIPTION	URL
LaTeX tutorial	*http://tinyurl.com/latexmath*
LaTeX equation generator	*http://tinyurl.com/latexequation*
WordPress documentation for LaTeX	*http://support.wordpress.com/latex*
WPtouch (plug-in)	*http://tinyurl.com/wptouch* *http://tinyurl.com/wptouchpro* (Pro version)
VaultPress	*http://vaultpress.com* *http://vaultpress.com/jetpack* (sign-up page)
BackupBuddy (plug-in)	*http://ithemes.com/purchase/backupbuddy*
Dropbox	*www.dropbox.com*
Google Drive	*http://drive.google.com*
Amazon S3	*http://aws.amazon.com/s3*
WP-DB-Backup (plug-in)	*http://tinyurl.com/wp-db-backup*
WP-DBManager (plug-in)	*http://tinyurl.com/wp-dbmanager*
BackWPup (plug-in)	*http://tinyurl.com/backwpup*
Online Backup for WordPress (plug-in)	*http://tinyurl.com/wponlineb*
Gmail	*http://mail.google.com*
WP Super Cache (plug-in)	*http://tinyurl.com/wpsupercache*
BuddyPress (plug-in)	*http://buddypress.org*

CHAPTER 10 *Adding Picture Galleries, Video, and Music*

DESCRIPTION	URL
Flickr	*www.flickr.com*
WordPress embeds	*http://codex.wordpress.org/Embeds*
WordPress.com shortcodes	*http://support.wordpress.com/shortcodes*
TED Talks videos	*www.ted.com*
Regenerate Thumbnails (plug-in)	*http://tinyurl.com/rthumb*
Photonic (plug-in)	*http://tinyurl.com/wp-photonic*
YouTube	*www.youtube.com*
How to remove YouTube's length limit	*http://tinyurl.com/long-vids*
Miro Video Converter	*www.mirovideoconverter.com*
The MediaElement.js library	*http://mediaelementjs.com*
Vimeo	*http://vimeo.com*

DESCRIPTION	URL
VideoPress	*http://videopress.com* *http://tinyurl.com/vidpress* (plug-in)
SoundCloud	*http://soundcloud.com*
How to submit podcasts to iTunes	*http://tinyurl.com/podcastspecs*
Blubrry PowerPress (plug-in)	*http://tinyurl.com/wp-podcast*

CHAPTER 11 *Collaborating with Multiple Authors*

DESCRIPTION	URL
BuddyPress (plug-in)	*http://buddypress.org*
Email Users (plug-in)	*http://tinyurl.com/emailusers*
Blogs you own or write for on WordPress.com	*http://wordpress.com/my-blogs*
Edit Flow (plug-in)	*http://tinyurl.com/editflow* *http://editflow.org* (documentation)
Co-Authors Plus (plug-in)	*http://tinyurl.com/co-authors-plus* *http://tinyurl.com/ccr7896* (theme changes)
WP-Optimize (plug-in)	*http://tinyurl.com/wp-opti*
Revision Control (plug-in)	*http://tinyurl.com/rev-control*
Authors Widget (plug-in)	*http://tinyurl.com/authorswidget*
Author Avatars List (plug-in)	*http://tinyurl.com/authoravatars*
WP About Author (plug-in)	*http://tinyurl.com/wp-about-author*
Fancier Author Box (plug-in)	*http://tinyurl.com/authorbox*
Author Spotlight (plug-in)	*http://tinyurl.com/authorspot*
Page Security (plug-in)	*http://tinyurl.com/page-security-c*
Page Restrict (plug-in)	*http://tinyurl.com/page-restrict*
Examples of multisite networks	*http://blogs.reuters.com* *http://blogs.law.harvard.edu* *http://blogs.adobe.com* *http://stores.bestbuy.com* *http://wordpress.com*
How to convert a site to a multisite network	*http://tinyurl.com/2835suo*
Add Multiple Users (plug-in)	*http://tinyurl.com/add-multiple*
Multisite User Management (plug-in)	*http://tinyurl.com/multisite-um*

CHAPTER 12 *Attracting a Crowd*

DESCRIPTION	URL
Facebook	*www.facebook.com*
Twitter	*http://twitter.com*
Create a Facebook Page	*www.facebook.com/pages/create.php*
Polldaddy (plug-in)	*http://tinyurl.com/wp-polls*
Thank Me Later (plug-in)	*http://tinyurl.com/wp-thank*
Subscribe2 (plug-in)	*http://tinyurl.com/wp-sub2*
How to use the [tweet] shortcode	*http://tinyurl.com/cwfa77u*
How to use the [twitter-follow] shortcode	*http://tinyurl.com/cn29khu*
Chrome extension for feeds	*http://tinyurl.com/28q8dth*
FeedDemon	*www.feeddemon.com*
NetNewsWire	*http://netnewswireapp.com*
Flipboard	*http://flipboard.com*
feedly	*www.feedly.com*
WordPress feed reference	*http://tinyurl.com/64lmdo*
PageRank for Chrome	*http://tinyurl.com/pr-extension*
Check PageRank online	*www.prchecker.info*
Google Blogsearch	*http://blogsearch.google.com*
WordPress SEO by Yoast	*http://tinyurl.com/seo-yoast* (plug-in) *http://tinyurl.com/seo-yoast2* (tutorial)
SEO articles by Yoast	*http://yoast.com/cat/seo*

CHAPTER 13 *Editing Themes: The Key to Customizing Your Site*

DESCRIPTION	URL
Gallery of non-blog WordPress sites	*http://tinyurl.com/9dvpn3y*
HTML tutorial	*http://tinyurl.com/4mwq8*
CSS tutorial	*http://tinyurl.com/mlqk7*
One-Click Child Theme (plug-in)	*http://tinyurl.com/child-theme*
HTML color codes	*www.colorpicker.com*
CSS property reference	*http://tinyurl.com/bz5tcp*
How to examine elements and CSS with a browser	*http://tinyurl.com/css-inspection*
Google Web Fonts	*www.google.com/fonts*

DESCRIPTION	URL
WordPress function reference	*http://tinyurl.com/func-ref*
Basic PHP tutorial	*http://tinyurl.com/ctzya55*
Orbisius Child Theme Creator (plug-in)	*http://tinyurl.com/orb-theme*
Notepad++	*http://notepad-plus-plus.org*
Template customization recipes	*http://tinyurl.com/templatetrix*
Blog with WordPress tips	*http://lorelle.wordpress.com*
Smashing Magazine	*http://wp.smashingmagazine.com*
Thematic	*http://tinyurl.com/themat*
Genesis	*http://tinyurl.com/gen-theme*

CHAPTER 14 *Building an Advanced WordPress Site*

DESCRIPTION	URL
Understanding theme frameworks	*http://tinyurl.com/theme-f*
PinBlack theme	*http://tinyurl.com/pinblack*
WordPress theme directory	*http://wordpress.org/themes*
How to create a test site	*http://tinyurl.com/89wochm*
Registering custom post types	*http://tinyurl.com/reg-cpt*
Custom Post Type UI (plug-in)	*http://tinyurl.com/cust-pt-ui*
Types (plug-in)	*http://wordpress.org/plugins/types*
WordPress reference for `query_posts()`	*http://tinyurl.com/yhjtze5*
WordPress reference for `get_posts()`	*http://tinyurl.com/23km6q5*
WordPress function reference	*http://tinyurl.com/func-ref*
WordPress database reference	*http://tinyurl.com/3a88qt*
Article about custom taxonomies	*http://tinyurl.com/8slqbkn*
PayPal Donations (plug-in)	*http://tinyurl.com/paypal-d*
Google AdSense	*www.google.com/adsense*
s2Member (plug-in)	*http://tinyurl.com/s2member*
PayPal	*www.paypal.com* *www.paypal.com/fees* (fee information) *www.paypal.com/upgrade* (upgrade your account)
WordPress Simple PayPal Shopping Cart (plug-in)	*http://tinyurl.com/paypal-c* *http://tinyurl.com/spp-forum* (support forum)

DESCRIPTION	URL
WP eCommerce (plug-in)	*http://tinyurl.com/wp-ecom*
WooCommerce	*http://tinyurl.com/woo-com* (plug-in) *http://tinyurl.com/woo-doc* (documentation)
Free *WordPress & eCommerce* ebook	*http://tinyurl.com/wpe-ebook*

APPENDIX A *Migrating from WordPress.com*

DESCRIPTION	URL
How to buy a guided transfer	*http://tinyurl.com/guidedtransfer*
WordPress.com theme gallery	*http://theme.wordpress.com*
How to manage your custom WordPress.com domain	*http://tinyurl.com/8ese4cp*

APPENDIX B *Securing a Self-Hosted Site*

DESCRIPTION	URL
Limit Login Attempts (plug-in)	*http://tinyurl.com/limit-login-a*
Wordfence (plug-in)	*http://tinyurl.com/w-fence*
How attackers steal WordPress passwords	*http://tinyurl.com/steal-pass*
WordPress HTTPS SSL (plug-in)	*http://tinyurl.com/wp-https*

Index

A

B

C

D

E

H

I

J

K

L

M

X

Y

WordPress

THE MISSING CD

There's no
CD with this book;
you just saved $5.00.

Instead, every single Web address, practice file, and piece of downloadable software mentioned in this book is available at *missingmanuals.com* (click the Missing CD icon). There you'll find a tidy list of links, organized by chapter.

CPSIA information can be obtained at www.ICGtesting.com
Printed in the USA
BVOW09s1224270315

393557BV00005B/5/P

9 781449 341909